Social Cognition

From Brains to Culture

Susan T. Fiske

Princeton University

Shelley E. Taylor

University of California, Los Angeles

McGraw-Hill
Higher Education

Boston   Burr Ridge, IL   Dubuque, IA   New York   San Francisco   St. Louis
Bangkok   Bogotá   Caracas   Kuala Lumpur   Lisbon   London   Madrid   Mexico City
Milan   Montreal   New Delhi   Santiago   Seoul   Singapore   Sydney   Taipei   Toronto

McGraw-Hill
Higher Education

Published by McGraw-Hill, an imprint of The McGraw-Hill Companies, Inc., 1221 Avenue of the Americas, New York, NY 10020. Copyright © 2008. All rights reserved. No part of this publication may be reproduced or distributed in any form or by any means, or stored in a database or retrieval system, without the prior written consent of The McGraw-Hill Companies, Inc., including, but not limited to, in any network or other electronic storage or transmission, or broadcast for distance learning.

This book is printed on acid-free paper.

1 2 3 4 5 6 7 8 9 0 CCW/CCW 0 9 8 7

ISBN: 978-0-07-340552-0
MHID: 0-07-340552-3

Editor in Chief: *Mike Ryan*
Publisher: *Beth Mejia*
Sponsoring Editor: *Michael J. Sugarman*
Editorial Coordinator: *Jillian Allison*
Marketing Manager: *James R. Headley*
Associate Production Editor: *Alison Meier*
Design Manager: *Margarite Reynolds*
Illustrator: *Dartmouth Publishing, Inc.*
Production Supervisor: *Dennis Fitzgerald*
Composition: *10/12 Palatino by Laserwords*
Printing: 45# *New Era Matte Plus, Courier*

Cover: Kaz Chiba/Getty Images

Library of Congress Cataloging-in-Publication Data
Fiske, Susan T.
    Social cognition : from brains to culture / Susan T. Fiske and Shelley E. Taylor.—1st ed.
        p. cm.
    Includes bibliographical references and index.
    ISBN-13: 978-0-07-340552-0 (alk. paper)
    ISBN-10: 0-07-340552-3 (alk. paper)
    1. Social perception. 2. Cognitive neuroscience. I. Taylor, Shelley E. II. Title.
BF323.S63F55 2007
302'.12—dc22
                                                                2007018062

The Internet addresses listed in the text were accurate at the time of publication. The inclusion of a website does not indicate an endorsement by the authors or McGraw-Hill, and McGraw-Hill does not guarantee the accuracy of the information presented at these sites.

www.mhhe.com

To Doug, Geoff, Lydia, and Vanessa
and
To Mervyn, Sara, and Charlie

Contents

Preface

Since the publication of our first text on social cognition, a lot has changed for us personally (children come and gone, new jobs, new houses) and professionally (both of us are doing a lot more neuroscience and culture than we would have predicted). For our first text, we were dictating or writing long-hand on lined pads, with secretaries who typed our day's writing and chided us on our less productive days. We used physical mail to exchange drafts. And we chose the color of the first edition's cover based on airline ticket carbons, its design enlivened by some decidedly 1980s woodcut portraits of hipsters.

That text had its day, defining the birth of social cognition in its modern form. Social psychology was emerging from a crisis, which was partly resolved in the excitement of the fresh ideas and methods newly available from cognitive psychology. Skeptics predicted social cognition to be a short-lived fad. Social psychologists faulted it for not being social enough, and cognitive psychologists faulted it for not being cognitive enough. But the intrepid investigators remained enthused about the cutting-edge insights into social attention, memory, inference, and schemas, as applied to topics from self to health to prejudice to primaries. At first, we debated the inclusion of classic areas such as attribution, self, and attitudes in a book on current social cognition. We ultimately aimed for inclusion, showing the relevance of social cognitive approaches to both classic and newer issues. This joint relevance remains true today.

Our second book demonstrated the robust health of social cognition, which proved not to be a mere fad, an interlude, or an era. Social cognition is here to stay and, indeed, has permeated all corners of social psychology. The second cover took a longer view, featuring a more subdued, classic green and reaching back to Renoir. The painting is crowded with people, and so was our bibliography; the book was encyclopedic in its coverage, reflecting the explosion of research in the intervening seven years.

This new text—nearly 24 years after our first—takes an even longer view, still starting with the founding ideas but fast-forwarding to the present. This text reflects the latest in social neuroscience, which for some skeptics is not social enough and for others is not neuroscientific enough. (Sound familiar?) But we cheerfully predict the thriving of this new field, social cognitive affective neuroscience, building substantially on the social cognition that was controversial in its own early days.

What's more, the current text reflects much more research on culture, an increasingly salient topic in social cognition as globalization takes hold in our field as well as in our lives. Social cognition originally helped pull the field out of its doldrums, but the other factor has always been a lively concern for the human condition—health, intergroup relations, politics, inequality, and more. We hope this book makes clear the contributions of this exciting field.

Acknowledgments

This book has benefited from the help of many colleagues, who read one or more chapter drafts: David DeSteno—Northeastern University; Daniel Gilbert—Harvard University; Kerry Kawakami—York University; Bernadette Park—University of Colorado; Emily Pronin—Princeton University; Ann Marie Russell—Princeton University; Charles Stangor—University of Maryland; Alexander Todorov—Princeton University. In addition, the spring 2006 Interpersonal Perception class (Princeton's Psych 313) provided feedback, as did assistant-in-instruction Lasana Harris. Thanks to all of them. We would like to thank secretary Vera Sohl and research assistants Tamar Kozanian and Loren Post, who helped us organize, worked diligently on the references, and provided feedback, though they were spared the long-hand on paper pads of the first book.

Our McGraw-Hill editor, Michael Sugarman, stayed with us from recruitment through publication, testimony to his friendly tenacity. His firm and helpful oversight also motivated us to finish this book faster than the previous two manuscripts, which tended to outlast their respective editors.

Finally, we thank our families, both immediate and far-flung, who supported us.

STF, Princeton

SET, Los Angeles

About the Authors

SUSAN T. FISKE is Eugene Higgins Professor of Psychology, Princeton University (PhD, Harvard University; honorary doctorate, Université Catholique de Louvain-la-Neuve, Belgium). She has authored two previous books titled *Social Cognition* (1984, 1991, both with Taylor) on how people make sense of each other. She has written around 200 articles and chapters and edited about a dozen books and journal special issues. Notably, she edits the *Annual Review of Psychology* (with Schacter and Sternberg) and the *Handbook of Social Psychology* (with Gilbert and Lindzey). She authored the first edition of an upper-level text, *Social Beings: A Core Motives Approach to Social Psychology* (2004).

Currently, her research investigates emotional prejudices (pity, contempt, envy, and pride) at cultural, societal, interpersonal, and neural levels. This work identifies fundamental dimensions of social cognition. Her expert testimony in discrimination cases was cited by the U.S. Supreme Court in a 1989 landmark decision on gender bias. In 1998 she also testified before President Clinton's Race Initiative Advisory Board, and in 2001–2003, she co-authored a National Academy of Sciences report on Methods for Measuring Discrimination. In 2004 she published a *Science* article explaining how ordinary people can torture enemy prisoners through processes of prejudice and social influence.

She won the American Psychological Association's Early Career Award for Distinguished Contributions to Psychology in the Public Interest for antidiscrimination testimony and the Society for the Psychological Study of Social Issues' Allport Intergroup Relations Award for ambivalent sexism theory (with Glick), as well as Harvard's Graduate Centennial Medal. With Shelley Taylor, she won the Thomas M. Ostrom Award for Outstanding Lifetime Contributions to Theory and Research in Social Cognition. She was elected president of the American Psychological Society, president of the Society of Personality and Social Psychology, president of the Foundation for the Advancement of Brain and Behavioral Sciences, and a fellow of the American Academy of Arts and Sciences.

Her expert witness work has familiarized her with discrimination in settings from shipyards and assembly lines to international investment firms, and she has served on diversity committees in several nonprofit settings. She grew up in a stable, racially integrated community and still wonders why the rest of the world does not work that way.

SHELLEY E. TAYLOR is Distinguished Professor of Psychology at the University of California, Los Angeles, where she has been since 1979. She earned her PhD from Yale University in 1972, pursuing interests in attribution theory. She joined the faculty at Harvard and began a program of research in social cognition, examining the impact of salient stimuli on attributions, memory, and interpersonal perceptions. In this context, she and her colleague, Susan Fiske, identified the implications of the salience phenomenon for minority group members, noting that "solos," or those in minority positions, such as women or Blacks in work organizations, may be subject to disproportionate scrutiny, exaggerated inferences, and pernicious stereotypes as a result of their highly visible status. Since 1979, Taylor's work has focused on social cognition under threat, and in 1980 she initiated a program of health psychology research to identify the cognitive factors that may promote or impede recovery from threatening events such as cancer, AIDS, heart disease, and other stressful events. In this context, she helped to develop the Health Psychology Program at UCLA.

Currently, Taylor's work focuses on the role of positive illusions and other psychosocial resources (such as social support) for maintaining well-being. Her other books, *Health Psychology, Positive Illusions,* and *The Tending Instinct,* develop these and related themes. Using a combination of experiments and field studies, her work integrates psychological perspectives with neuroscience methodologies, including neuroendocrine functioning, psychoneuroimmunology, fMRI methodology, and genetics. Her work combines the pursuit of theoretical issues in the context of important social issues and thereby seeks to contribute to both theory and research in social psychology, as well as point in the direction of applications that help people manage stressful events.

Taylor received both the Early Career Award and the Distinguished Scientific Contribution Award from the American Psychological Association. She is the inaugural recipient of the Clifton Strengths Prize and has received other awards for her work, including the Donald Campbell Award for Distinguished Scientific Contributions to the Field of Social Psychology and the Thomas M. Ostrom Award for Outstanding Lifetime Contributions to Theory and Research in Social Cognition. She is a fellow of the American Academy of Arts and Sciences and the National Academy of Science's Institute of Medicine. She has served as president of the Western Psychological Association and president of the Society of Personality and Social Psychology.

Introduction

This is not a self-help book, but it will help you navigate your social world. This is not a do-good book, but it will help you make a difference in the world. This is not fiction, but it tells some good stories. Social cognition captures a remarkable range of phenomena useful to individuals and to the human condition.

Consider a common experience of mistaken social cognition. Try telling someone at a party that you are a psychologist or even that you are simply studying psychology. It does no good to say you do research and do not read minds. The inevitable reaction is either that the person draws back in horror of being analyzed on the spot or that the person leans over to disclose all sorts of intimate secrets. One psychologist we know avoids these situations by claiming to be a computer programmer. We have hit upon a different strategy, which is to say calmly, "I study how people make first impressions on strangers." This comment promptly stops that conversation.

Suppose, however, that the conversation did not end right there. Suppose the person began to talk about what makes people tick, about impressions of various friends, relatives, and strangers at the party. That is the kind of raw data with which this book is concerned. Social cognition is the study of how people make sense of other people and themselves. It focuses on how ordinary people think and feel about people—and on how they think they think and feel about people.

People's understanding of the social world can be studied by *asking* them how they make sense of others (Heider, 1958). This is the route of *phenomenology:* to describe systematically how ordinary people say they experience their world. If people are right, researchers can use these insights to build formal theories by pulling together patterns across many people's intuitions. Even if people are wrong, researchers can study people's commonsense theories in and of themselves to learn how people think. Social cognition researchers are also concerned with commonsense theory, or *naive psychology*, for its own sake. That is, people's everyday theories about each other are themselves interesting to study. Thus, if the person at the party has some ideas about how people form impressions of each other, the person's informal ideas are interesting in their own right.

Research on social cognition also goes beyond naive psychology. The study of social cognition entails a fine-grained analysis of how people think about themselves and others, and it leans heavily on the theory and methods of cognitive psychology. One of the hallmarks of social cognition is the influence of detailed models from cognitive psychology. These models are important because they

2

precisely describe mechanisms of learning and thinking that apply in a wide variety of areas, including social perception. Because these models are general and because cognitive processes presumably influence social behavior heavily, it makes sense to adapt cognitive theory to social settings.

Both the naive psychology viewpoint and the cognitive viewpoint are important themes in social cognition research. These two viewpoints characterize the double appeal of social cognition. The entertaining part of studying how people think about others is its appeal to your intuitions; it resembles what is fun and absorbing about sitting around with a friend after midnight, speculating about human nature. The fine-grained part forces you to be accurate and precise; its appeal resembles that of a favorite intricate puzzle. Whether your taste runs to crosswords, math games, jigsaw puzzles, or mystery novels, there is considerable pleasure in getting all the pieces to fit.

APPROACHES TO STUDYING THE SOCIAL THINKER

Two broad intellectual approaches to the study of social cognition—elemental and holistic—can be traced to psychology's origins in philosophy. Knowing something of social cognition's intellectual history will give perspective to researchers' current efforts. The *elemental approach* is characterized by breaking scientific problems down into pieces and analyzing the pieces separately and in detail before combining them. The *holistic approach* is characterized by analyzing the pieces in the context of other pieces and focusing on the entire configuration of relationships among them. This distinction will become clearer as the two approaches are described.

The Elemental Origins of Social Cognition Research

Until the beginning of the 20th century, psychology was a branch of philosophy, and philosophers provided some basic principles of mind that still carry weight today (Boring, 1950). In the elemental tradition of the British philosophers, the mind is likened to chemistry, in which ideas are the elements. Any concept, whether concrete such as "salt" or abstract such as "shame," is a basic element, and any element can be associated with any other element. The bonds between concepts create mental chemistry (Locke, 1690/1979).

In the elemental view, ideas first come from our sensations and perceptions. Then they are associated by contiguity in space and time (Hume, 1739/1978). That is, if salt is next to pepper on the table, the two can become a unit through contiguity. Repetition is the key to moving from simple contiguity to a mental compound (Hartley, 1749/1966). If salt and pepper are on the table together every day of your life, when you think of salt you will automatically think of pepper. Salt and pepper becomes a mental compound. Similarly, if the concept "professor" often comes up (on television, for example) at the same time as the concept "absentminded," they are likely to be associated simply as a function of repeated pairings. People consciously use the principles of repetition and contiguity in daily life too; think of the last time you attempted to memorize the seven contiguous digits of a phone number by repeating them until they became a unit. Frequency of repetition is a major factor that determines the strength of an association (Mill, 1869, 1843/1974).[1]

Psychology began to emerge as a discipline separate from philosophy in the early 20th century, and at that time the notions of mental chemistry were first put to empirical test. The first laboratory psychologists, such as Wilhelm Wundt and Hermann Ebbinghaus, trained themselves and their graduate students to observe their own thought processes: to introspect on how they committed ideas to memory and on how they retrieved ideas from memory (Ebbinghaus, 1885/1964; Wundt, 1897). Their method was to analyze experience into its elements to determine how they connect, and to determine the laws that govern those associations. These themes, which began with the British philosophers, continue to form the basis of modern experimental psychology. In a later section of this chapter and in Chapter 4, we will see how the elemental approach is currently represented within the study of social cognition.

The Holistic Origins of Social Cognition Research

In reaction to the elemental approach, the German philosopher Immanuel Kant (1781/1969) argued for an emphasis on tackling the whole mind at once. In his view of the mind, mental phenomena are inherently subjective. That is, the mind actively constructs a reality that goes beyond the original thing in and of itself. A bunch of grapes is perceived as a unit, but that perception is a construction of the mind. Perceiving a "bowl of grapes" differs from perceiving each individual grape separately. Similarly, if someone cuts off some grapes and the remaining ones topple out of the bowl, the two movements are perceived as linked in a cause-effect relationship. Again, that perception is furnished by the mind; it is not inherent in the stimulus. The intellect organizes the world, creating perceptual order from the properties of the surrounding field.

Gestalt psychology drew on these initial holistic insights (Koffka, 1935; Kohler, 1938/1976). In contrast to analysis into elements, psychologists who use Gestalt methods first describe the phenomenon of interest, the immediate experience of perception, without analysis. This method, already introduced as phenomenology, focuses on systematically describing people's experience of perceiving and thinking. It later became one of the major foundations of social cognition research: the reliance on asking people how they make sense of the world.

Although both the elemental and holistic groups drew on introspections, Gestalt psychologists focused on people's experience of dynamic wholes, and elementalists focused on the expert's ability to break the whole into pieces. As an illustration of the difference between Gestalt and elemental approaches, think of a song in your mind. A song can be perceived as a series of individual notes (elemental) or as a melody that emerges from the relationships among the notes (Gestalt). The emergent structure is lost by analyzing it into its sensory elements, in the Gestalt view. Gestalt psychologists saw the mental chemistry metaphor of the elementalists as misguided because a chemical compound has properties not predictable from its isolated elements. Similarly, the perceptual whole has

---

[1]Other principles of association were proposed at various times and then dropped in favor of repeated contiguity. These included similarity and causality as creating associations, and vividness as strengthening associations (Boring, 1950).

properties not discernible from the isolated parts. For example, the note middle C can seem high in the context of many lower notes or low in the context of many higher notes, but it would not stand out at all in the context of other notes close to it. Similarly, an average-height basketball player stands out in the subway but not on the team. Many arriving college students who had topped their high school classes discover that they no longer stand out as intellectual stars in college. Again, the individual acquires meaning in the immediate context. Psychological meaning goes beyond raw sensory parts to include the organization people impose on the whole. The importance of Gestalt stimulus configurations guided two researchers whose work directly informs social cognition research and theory: Solomon Asch and Kurt Lewin.

Asch's Configural Model

In his pioneering work, Asch (1946) examined how people combine the components of another person's personality and come up with an integrated overall impression. In so doing, he set the stage for much of person perception research (E. E. Jones, 1990; D. J. Schneider, Hastorf, & Ellsworth, 1979). In his analysis of how people form impressions of others, Asch theorized that we experience another person as a psychological unit, that we fit the person's various qualities into a single unifying theme. Asch originally made this point in an impressive series of 12 studies (Asch, 1946). The participants' task was to form an impression of someone described by one or another list of personality traits. One group, for example, was told about someone who was "intelligent, skillful, industrious, cold, determined, practical, and cautious." (Form an impression of this person before reading on.) Another group was told about someone who was "intelligent, skillful, industrious, warm, determined, practical, and cautious." The simple manipulation of the traits warm and cold created large differences in people's descriptions of the target person. For example, the cold, intelligent person was seen as calculating, and the warm, intelligent person was seen as wise.

Asch proposed two models to account for these results: the configural model and the algebraic model. The configural model hypothesizes that people form a unified overall impression of other people, and that the unifying forces work on individual elements to bring them in line with the overall impression. Thus the pressure toward unity may change the meaning of the individual elements to fit better in context. An intelligent con artist is sly; an intelligent child is clever; an intelligent grandmother is wise. In addition to meaning change, people use a variety of strategies to organize and unify the components of an impression; they not only change the meaning of ambiguous terms, but they also resolve apparently discrepant terms with considerable ingenuity. All of this mental activity results, according to the configural model, in an impression made up of traits and their relationships, just as a *schema* later would be defined as consisting of attributes and their relationships.

The alternative, the algebraic model, directly contrasts with the configural model and, by extension, with the subsequent schema models. The algebraic model takes each individual trait, evaluates it in isolation from the others, and combines the evaluations into a summary evaluation. It is as if, upon meeting someone new, you were simply to combine together all the person's pros (e.g., intelligence) and cons (e.g., coldness) to form your impression. The algebraic model of information averaging boasts an impressive program of research

(N. H. Anderson, 1981), as does a related algebraic model of combining beliefs to form an overall attitude (Fishbein & Ajzen, 1975).

The configural and algebraic models represent, respectively, the holistic and elemental approaches to social cognition described here. As such, they represent two fundamentally different ideas about how people form impressions of others. These two competing approaches originally proposed by Asch were thoroughly researched and, as you might imagine, hotly debated for a number of years (see Fiske & Taylor, 1991, for references). However, from a theoretical perspective, the contest was essentially a draw because both models were flexible enough to account for each other's data and neither was stated in a strictly falsifiable form. This led to a consensus on the "futility of the adversarial approach" (Ostrom, 1977) and pleas for more theory development. Neither approach any longer focuses on "disproving" the other side. Indeed, many of the dual-process theories described in Chapter 2 in effect resolve this old debate by noting that both models are right but that people follow each under different informational and motivational circumstances that, not surprisingly, mimic the respective research paradigms of the two approaches.

Lewin's Person-Situation Field Theory

Kurt Lewin (1951) imported Gestalt ideas to social psychology and ultimately to social cognition research (Boring, 1950; Bronfenbrenner, 1977; Deutsch, 1968). Like other Gestalt psychologists, Lewin focused on the person's subjective perceptions, not on "objective" analysis. He emphasized the influence of the social environment *as perceived by the individual*, which he called the psychological field. A full understanding of a person's psychological field cannot result from an "objective" description by others of what surrounds the person because the crucial factor is the person's own interpretation. This is not to say that the person can necessarily verbalize his or her perceived environment, but that the person's own reports typically provide better clues than do the researcher's intuitions. For instance, a researcher may objectively report that Barb complimented Ann on her appearance. The researcher may even have strong hunches about why Barb did it. But Ann's reaction will depend on her own perception of Barb's intent: ingratiation, envy, reassurance, or friendliness. A prime way to find that out is to ask Ann to describe what happened in her own terms. Just as in Gestalt psychology generally, Lewin emphasized the individual's phenomenology, the individual's construction of the situation.

Another theme imported from Gestalt psychology to social psychology was Lewin's insistence on describing the total situation, not its isolated elements. A person exists within a psychological field that is a configuration of forces. One must understand all the psychological forces operating on the person in any given situation in order to predict anything. For example, some forces might motivate an individual to study (e.g., an upcoming exam, the sight of one's roommate studying), but other forces might motivate the individual to spend the evening another way (e.g., a group of friends suggesting a movie). No one force predicts action, but the dynamic equilibrium among them, the ever-changing balance of forces, does predict action.

The total psychological field (and hence behavior) is determined by two pairs of factors. The first pair consists of the *person in the situation*. Neither alone is sufficient to predict behavior. The person contributes needs, beliefs, perceptual abilities, and more. These act on the environment to constitute the psychological field. Thus, to know that a particular person is motivated to study does not predict whether or how much he or she will study. But a motivated person in a library is extremely likely to study a lot. Ever since Lewin, social psychologists have seen both the person and the situation as essential to predicting behavior. The study of social cognition focuses on perceiving, thinking, and remembering as a function of who and where a person is.

The second pair of psychological field factors that determines behavior is *cognition and motivation*. Both are joint functions of person and situation and jointly predict behavior. Cognition provides the perceiver's interpretation of the world; without clear cognitions, behavior is not predictable. If a person has incomplete or confused cognitions about a new setting, behavior will be unstable. For example, if you do not have the foggiest idea about what an upcoming exam in music composition will be like, you may behave erratically and unpredictably; you may try several study strategies, none of them very systematically. Cognitions help determine *what* a person will do, which direction behavior will take. If a musician friend explains what composition exams typically contain, your cognitions and your studying will settle down along the lines laid out. But this assumes that you actually do study. The second feature of the psychological field is motivation; its strength predicts whether the behavior will occur at all and, if it does, how much of it will occur. Knowing what to do does not mean you will do it; cognition alone is not enough. Motivation provides the motor for behavior.

To summarize, Lewin focuses his analysis on psychological reality as perceived by the individual; on confronting a whole configuration of forces, not single elements; on the person and the situation; and on cognition and motivation. These major themes, which date back through Gestalt psychology to Kant, are theoretical points that still survive in modern approaches to social cognition as well as in psychology as a whole.

Conclusion

We have characterized the historical origins of social cognition as a contrast between the elemental and the holistic viewpoints. The elemental approach aims to build up from the bottom, combining smaller pieces into larger ones until the whole puzzle is assembled. The piecemeal nature of this approach contrasts sharply with the holistic nature of the Gestalt alternative. To describe a person's active construction of reality, in the holistic view, it is necessary to tackle the entire configuration as seen by the perceiver. The tension between the elemental and configural or holistic approaches will surface again, in a different form, in Chapter 2. We will see that they can be integrated as two complementary processes.

THE EBB AND FLOW OF COGNITION IN PSYCHOLOGY

Psychologists have not always agreed that it is important to get inside the mind. The study of cognition has received both good and bad reviews over time. To prevent an overly myopic view of the importance of cognition, let's take a brief look at its place in experimental and social psychology. Early psychologists, whether elemental or holistic, relied heavily on introspection as a central tool for understanding human thought. As you will see, however, introspection developed a bad reputation, and with it cognition fell into disrepute. Experimental psychology rejected cognition for many years, but social psychology did not. The next two sections present the contrasting histories of cognition in the two subfields, experimental and social psychology.

Cognition in Experimental Psychology

Wundt's work at the dawn of empirical psychology relied heavily on trained introspection.[2] The use of introspection was linked to the fact that Wundt's goal was emphatically cognitive: people's experience was the subject matter of interest. Wundt and others gathered data about mental events and constructed theories to account for those data. However, introspection was ultimately abandoned as a methodology in experimental psychology because it did not conform to the principles appropriate to scientific investigation. By usual scientific standards, one's data should be publicly reproducible. Other scientists ought to be able to examine the data, replicate them following the same procedures, and analyze the data to see if they confirm the theory. In early experimental psychology, theories were required to account for introspections (i.e., self-observations), and therein lay the problem. If the criteria for a theory's success depended on private experience, the evidence could not be produced in public. The research could not be checked by others. The most absurd version of the problem would be this: If my theory accounts for my introspections and your theory accounts for yours, how do we decide who is right?

When introspection was abandoned because of problems such as this, the study of cognition was also neglected. There was a shift away from studying internal (cognitive) processes and toward external, publicly observable events. The ultimate development of this approach was American behaviorist psychology in the early decades of the 20th century. Behaviorists held that only overt, measurable acts are sufficiently valid objects for empirical scrutiny. One of the founders of this approach was Edward L. Thorndike. B. F. Skinner and others further developed Thorndike's work. For example, Thorndike's (1940) theory of instrumental learning held no place for cognition. According to the theory, behavior has certain rewarding and punishing effects, which cause the organism to repeat or avoid the behavior later. In short, "the effect becomes a cause." Both effect and cause are observable, and cognition is thought to be irrelevant (Skinner, 1963). One behaviorist even called the idea of cognition a superstition (Watson, 1930).

Behaviorists argued that specifying an observable stimulus (S) and response (R) for every part of one's theory is the strict scientific discipline necessary to the advancement of psychology, including social psychology (Berger & Lambert, 1968). For example, a behaviorist might approach the topic of racial and ethnic discrimination by noting that some children are punished for playing with

---

[2]Wundt also took measures that did not rely on people's own reports of their internal processes; for example, he also emphasized the measurements of reaction time, which is the time between stimulus and response. If you ask us how old we are, we can respond instantly. If you ask either of us how old the other author is, we have to calculate it, and that takes longer. Thus from reaction time one could infer more or less intervening thought. Such measures supplemented introspective data.

children of certain other ethnic groups and rewarded for playing with children of the family's own ethnic group. A simplified model of this would include "the other ethnic group" as the stimulus and "not playing together" as the response. A behaviorist would not consider the possible role of stereotyping (cognition). In experimental psychology generally, one net effect of behaviorism was that ideas about cognition fell into disrepute for about half a century and behaviorist theories dominated.

Several events caused experimental psychologists to take a fresh interest in cognition during the 1960s (J. R. Anderson, 1980; Holyoak & Gordon, 1984). First, linguists criticized the failure of the stimulus-response framework's attempts to account for language (cf. Chomsky, 1959, criticizing Skinner, 1957). It became clear that the complex, symbolic, and uniquely human phenomenon of language would not easily yield to behaviorist approaches.

Second, a new approach called *information processing* arose out of work on how people acquire knowledge and skills (Broadbent, 1958). Information processing refers to the idea that mental operations can be broken down into sequential stages. If you ask one of us when her niece was born, she thinks back to personal circumstances surrounding the event and recalls that it was August 1979. An information processing theory might represent those cognitive operations as follows:

$$\text{understand the question's meaning} \longrightarrow \text{search for information on that topic} \longrightarrow \text{verify answer} \longrightarrow \text{state answer}$$

The point of an information processing theory is to try to specify the steps intervening *between* stimulus (question) and response (answer). From this point of view, the important feature is the sequential processing of information. Information processing approaches entail the effort to specify cognitive processes, which behaviorists would not do.

New scientific tools have developed that allow cognitive psychologists to trace the nonobservable processes presumed to intervene between stimulus and response. The most important of these tools is the computer, which has become a methodological tool as well as a theoretical metaphor. It serves as a tool in that cognitive scientists use computers to simulate human cognitive processes; they write complex programs that play chess, learn geometry, and summarize the news (J. R. Anderson, 1976; Newell & Simon, 1972; Schank & Abelson, 1977). Social cognition researchers have developed computer simulations of how people form impressions and memories of each other (Hastie, 1988a; Linville, Fischer, & Salovey, 1989; E. R. Smith, 1988) and influence each other (Latané & Bourgeois, 2001). The computer has also been a metaphor in providing a framework and a jargon for characterizing mental processes; cognitive psychologists talked about input-output operations, or memory storage and retrieval, with respect to human cognition. More important, much of that early cognitive theory built on the idea that human cognition resembles computer information processing in important ways.

With the advent of cognitive neuroscience, the metaphors and models are changing. Cognitive psychologists are focusing more on modeling processes that are plausible with regard to increasingly understood brain systems, neural networks, their timing, and even single-cell responses. The current challenges include modeling how clusters of individually dumb neurons can make us do such exquisitely intelligent things. Some of the models draw on insights from individually simple organisms, such as ants, that collectively accomplish optimal choices, such as finding nests safe from predators (Mallon, Pratt, & Franks, 2001). Another example is the coordination of flocks of birds that individually have, well, birdbrains, but collectively move together across thousand of miles, alighting, flying, and taking off in unison, in effect making group decisions (Couzin, Krause, Franks, & Levin, 2005). Simple biological collectives may provide metaphors, models, and methods for understanding neural systems.

To summarize, experimental psychology began with introspection as a legitimate method for gaining insight into thinking and with cognition as a legitimate focus for theory. Behaviorists virtually eliminated such techniques and concerns for decades, and cognition fell into disrepute. During the 1970s, cognitive psychology reemerged as a scientifically legitimate pursuit (J. R. Anderson, 1990; Neisser, 1967; D. A. Norman, 1976). More recently, during and after the 1990s Decade of the Brain, cognitive neuroscience has profoundly altered the landscape, for example, highlighting the interplay between human cognition and emotion (Phelps, 2006), the diffuse neural systems involved in language production and comprehension (Gernsbacher & Kaschak, 2003), the neural bases of cognitive control including inconsistency monitoring (Miller & Cohen, 2001), the distinct neural bases for distinct types of category learning (Ashby & Maddox, 2005), and the neural evidence for long-standing concepts such as episodic memory for past experiences, supported by both the neuropsychology of brain damage and neuroimaging studies of memory (Tulving, 2002). It might seem that the neural emphases are remote from social cognition, threatening to tear psychology apart. Fortunately, human neuroscience has the potential to glue psychology back together because the brain is not divided up the way psychology departments are. We are simultaneously social, affective, cognitive actors in the world.

Cognition in Social Psychology

In contrast to experimental psychology, social psychology has consistently leaned on cognitive concepts, even when most psychology was behaviorist. Social psychology has always been cognitive in at least three ways. First, since Lewin, social psychologists have decided that social behavior is more usefully understood as a function of people's perceptions of their world rather than as a function of objective descriptions of their stimulus environment (Manis, 1977; Zajonc, 1980a). For example, an objective reward such as money or praise that people perceive as a bribe or as flattery will influence them differently than a reward they perceive as without manipulative intent. Their reaction is predicted by their perception, not simply by the giver's actions.

Other people can influence a person's actions without even being present, which is the ultimate reliance on perceptions to the exclusion of objective stimuli. Thus someone may react to a proffered bribe or to flattery by imagining the reactions of others (e.g., "What would my mother say?" or "What will my friends think?"). Of course, such thoughts are the person's own fantasies, having perhaps tenuous connection to objective reality. Thus the causes of social behavior are doubly cognitive; our perceptions of others actually present and our imagination of their presence both predict behavior (cf. G. W. Allport, 1954).[3]

Social psychologists view not only causes but also the end result of social perception and interaction in heavily cognitive terms, and this is a second way in which social psychology has always been cognitive. Thought often comes before feeling and behaving as the main reaction that social researchers measure. A person may worry about a bribe (thought), hate the idea (feeling), and reject it (behavior), but social psychologists often mainly ask: "What do you think about it?" Even when they focus on behavior and feelings, their questions are often, "What do you intend to do?" and "How would you label your feeling?" These arguably are not behavior and feelings but cognitions about them. Thus social psychological causes are largely cognitive, and the results are largely cognitive.

A third way in which social psychology has always been cognitive is that the person in between the presumed cause and the result is viewed as a *thinking organism;* this view contrasts with regarding the person as an emotional organism or a mindless automaton (Manis, 1977). Many social psychological theories paint a portrait of the typical person as reasoning (perhaps badly) before acting. In attempting to deal with complex human problems, as social psychology always has, complex mental processes seem essential. How else can one account for stereotyping and prejudice, propaganda and persuasion, altruism and aggression, and more? It is hard to imagine how a narrowly behaviorist theory would even begin. A strict stimulus-response (S-R) theory does not include the thinking organism that seems essential to account for such problems. In several senses, then, social psychology contrasts with strict S-R theories in its reliance on S-O-R theories that include stimulus, organism, and response. Consequently, the thinker, who comes in between stimulus and response, has always been paramount in social psychology.

The social thinker has taken many guises in recent decades of research (S. E. Taylor, 1998). These guises describe the various roles of cognition in social psychology. Besides the varied roles of cognition, motivation has played different roles in the view of the social thinker. Keeping in mind these two components, cognition and motivation, we can identify five general views of the thinker in social psychology: consistency seeker, naive scientist, cognitive miser, motivated tactician, and activated actor (Table 1.1).

The first view emerged from the massive quantities of work on attitude change after World War II. In the late 1950s several theories were proposed, all sharing some crucial basic assumptions. The consistency theories, as they were called, viewed people as *consistency seekers* motivated by perceived discrepancies among their cognitions (e.g., Festinger, 1957; Heider, 1958; see Abelson et al., 1968, for an overview). Dissonance theory is the best-known example: If David has publicly announced he is on a diet and knows that he has just eaten a hot fudge sundae, he must do some thinking to bring those two cognitions into line. (Changing the subjective definition of "diet" would be a start.)

Chapter 9 deals more thoroughly with consistency theories, but for the moment two points are crucial. First, these theories relied on perceived inconsistency, which places cognitive activity in a central role. For example, if would-be

---

[3]One might well ask, what is the logical alternative to this approach? Who does research on reactions to the objective as opposed to the cognized world? The answer is behaviorists, as described, and some perceptual theorists (Gibson, 1966; see Chapter 3).

TABLE 1.1. Models of the Social Thinker in Social Cognition Research

Model of the Social Thinker	Era	Main Role of Motivation	Main Role for Cognition	Theoretical Example (Relevant Chapter)
Consistency seeker	1950–1960s	Drive to reduce discomfort from cognitive discrepancy	Cognitions about behavior, beliefs	Dissonance theory of attitudes (Ch. 9)
Naive scientist	1970s	Prediction and control, qualifies rationality	Primary, rational analysis	Covariation model of attribution (Ch. 6)
Cognitive miser	1980s	Rapid, adequate understanding	Shortcuts conserve limited capacity	Heuristic decision making (Ch. 7)
Motivated tactician	1990s	Thinking is for doing in social context	Interaction goals organize cognitive strategies	Dual-process models (Ch. 2), especially stereotyping (Ch. 11)
Activated actor	2000s	Social surviving and thriving	Automatic affect and behavior	Implicit associations (Ch. 3–4, Ch. 12–15)

dieters can convince themselves that one splurge will not matter, eating a sundae is not inconsistent for them. Objective inconsistency is not important. Subjective inconsistency among various cognitions or among feelings and cognitions is central to these theories. Actual inconsistency that is not perceived as such does not yield psychological inconsistency.

Second, once inconsistency is perceived, the person is presumed to feel uncomfortable (a negative drive state) and to be motivated to reduce the inconsistency. Reducing the aversive drive state is a pleasant relief, rewarding in itself. This sort of motivational model is called a drive reduction model. Less formally, the sundae-consuming dieter will not be free from anxiety until he manufactures some excuse. Hence, consistency theories posit that people change their attitudes and beliefs for motivational reasons because of unmet needs for consistency. In sum, motivation and cognition both are central to the consistency theories.

Ironically, as they proliferated, consistency theories ceased to dominate the field, partly because the variants on a theme became indistinguishable. Moreover, it was difficult to predict what a person would perceive as inconsistent and to what degree, and which route to resolving inconsistency a person would take. Finally, people do, in fact, tolerate a fair amount of inconsistency, so the motivation to avoid it as an overriding principle was called into doubt (cf. Kiesler, Collins, & Miller, 1969).

Research in social cognition began in the early 1970s, and with it new models of the thinker emerged. Cognition and motivation played rather different roles in these new models compared to the roles they played in the consistency seeker model. In the new models, motivation is secondary in importance to cognition. These views are central to social cognition research, and they will be covered in more detail throughout the book. At present, however, a brief look is useful.

The first model within the framework of social cognition research is the *naive scientist,* a model of how people uncover the causes of behavior. Attribution theories concern how people explain their own and other people's behavior; they came to the forefront of research in the early 1970s (see Chapter 6). Attribution theories describe people's causal analyses of or attributions about the social world. For example, an attribution can address whether someone's behavior seems to be caused by the external situation or by the person's internal disposition. If you want to know why your acquaintance Bruce snapped at you one morning, it would be important to decide whether there were mitigating circumstances (e.g., his girlfriend left him; you just backed into his car) or whether he has an irritable disposition (he always behaves this way to everyone).

Attribution theorists at first assumed that people are fairly rational—like scientists—distinguishing among various potential causes. In part, this was a purposeful theoretical strategy designed to push a rational view of people as far as possible to discover its shortcomings. The theories started with the working hypothesis that, given enough time, people will gather all the relevant data and arrive at the most logical conclusion. In this view, you would think about your friend's behavior in a variety of settings and carefully weigh the evidence for a situational or a dispositional cause of his behavior. Thus the role of cognition in the naive scientist model is as an outcome of fairly rational analysis.

If you are wrong about why Bruce was irritable, the early theories would have viewed your error as an emotion-based departure from the normal process or as a simple error in available information. For example, if you attribute Bruce's unpleasant behavior to his irritable disposition, it may be because you are motivated to avoid the idea that he is angry at you. Viewed from this perspective, errors arise mainly as interference from nonrational motivations. In the early attribution theories, motivation enters mainly as a potential qualification on the usual process.

Recall that in consistency theories, in contrast, motivation drives the whole system. The role of motivation in consistency theories is quite central; it acts as an aversive drive state that persists until inconsistencies are resolved. Attribution theorists traditionally have not viewed unresolved attributions as causing an aversive drive state. Motivations for predicting and controlling one's social world presumably set attributions in motion; in that sense, motivation does help to catalyze the attribution process, just as it catalyzes the entire consistency seeking process. Nevertheless, motivation is far more explicit in consistency theories than in attribution theories.

Unfortunately, people are not always such careful naive scientists. The cognitive system is limited in capacity, so people take shortcuts. The limitations of the cognitive system can be illustrated by such trivial problems as trying to keep a credit card number, an area code, and a telephone number in your head as you dial, or by more serious problems such as working poorly when you are distracted. The impact of cognitive limitations shows up in social inferences too. To illustrate, in deciding why Bruce was irritable, you may seize on the easiest explanation rather than the most accurate one. Rather than asking Bruce what is disturbing him, you may simply label him as unpleasant, without giving it much thought. Quite often, people simply are not very thorough.

Hence, the third general view of the thinker is the *cognitive miser* model (S. E. Taylor, 1981b). The idea is that people are limited in their capacity to process information, so they take shortcuts whenever they can (see Chapters 7–8). People adopt strategies that simplify complex problems; the strategies may not be correct or produce correct answers, but they emphasize efficiency. The capacity-limited thinker searches for rapid, adequate solutions rather than for slow, accurate solutions. Consequently, in this view, errors and biases stem from inherent features of the cognitive system, not necessarily from motivations. Indeed, the cognitive miser model is silent on the issue of motivations or feelings of any sort except rapid, adequate understanding (which is fairly cognitive rather than motivational in flavor). The role of cognition was central to the cognitive miser view, and the role of motivation vanished almost entirely, with isolated exceptions.

As the cognitive miser viewpoint matured, the importance of motivations and emotions again became evident. Having developed considerable sophistication about people's cognitive processes, researchers began to appreciate anew the interesting and important influences of motivation on cognition (see Chapter 2). In addition, affect has been a continued source of fascination, as Chapters 13–14 indicate. With growing emphasis on motivated social cognition (Showers & Cantor, 1985; Tetlock, 1990), researchers returned to old problems with new perspectives gained from studying social cognition. Social interaction became more important. People's thinking is for doing, to paraphrase William James (1890/1983), and their social thinking is for their social doing (S. T. Fiske, 1992, 1993). The 1990s view of the social perceiver might best be termed the *motivated tactician*, a fully engaged thinker with multiple cognitive strategies available, who (consciously or unconsciously) chooses among them based on goals, motives, and needs. Sometimes the motivated tactician chooses wisely, in the interests of adaptability and accuracy, and sometimes the motivated tactician chooses defensively, in the interests of speed or self-esteem. Thus views of the social thinker came full cycle back to appreciating the importance of motivation, but with increased sophistication about cognitive structure and process.

As the 21st century gets well under way, views of the social perceiver are shifting slightly yet again, building on all that came before. The motivated tactitian is nowhere near as deliberate as the goals viewpoint seemed to imply. Currently, with a heavy emphasis on unconscious associations, cued in the barest fraction of a second, people are viewed as *activated actors*. That is, social environments rapidly cue perceivers' social concepts, without awareness, and almost inevitably cue associated cognitions, evaluations, affect, motivation, and behavior (e.g., Dijksterhuis & Bargh, 2001; Fazio & Olson, 2003; Greenwald et al., 2002; Macrae & Bodenhausen, 2000). This latest look emphasizes rapid reactions, variously viewed as implicit, spontaneous, or automatic indicators of responses unconstrained by perceiver volition (see Chapters 3–4 and 10–13). These interpretations remain controversial, but one thing is clear: People's motives affect surprisingly unconscious responses. Using ever-faster and more precise methods for presenting stimuli at speeds outside awareness and neuroscience measures of neural responses from the earliest moments of perception, we are rapidly learning just how much occurs in the first moments of social perception. At the same time, social cognition is not simply returning to the cognitive miser view (i.e., fast but not very good). The current view combines the cognitive economy view with a view that incorporates motivation and affect at every stage, even the preconscious ones. The farther upstream we go, the more we realize that cognition, affect, and behavioral readiness are inseparable.

In summary, social psychology has always been cognitive in the broad sense of positing important steps that intervene between observable stimulus and observable response. One early, major set of theories viewed people as consistency seekers, and motivation played a central role in driving the whole system. With the rise of social cognition research, new views emerged. In one major wave of research, psychologists view people as naive scientists. These psychologists regard motivation mainly as a source of error. In another recent view, psychologists see people as cognitive misers and locate errors in the inherent limitations of the cognitive system, saying almost nothing about motivation. More recently, motivational influences on cognition have reemerged in a revitalized view of the social thinker as a motivated tactician. Finally, researchers are currently realizing the limited degree of conscious choice in engaging automatic and controlled processes. With an emphasis on the functioning social thinker-feeler-actor, current work views people as activated actors, influenced by their social environments at even earlier stages than previously understood.

WHAT IS SOCIAL COGNITION?

The study of social cognition does not rely on any one theory. The field concerns how people make sense of other people and themselves. All social cognition research shares some basic features: unabashed mentalism, orientation toward process, cross-fertilization between cognitive and social psychologies, and at least some concern with real-world social issues (for other reviews, see Augustinos & Walker, 1995; Bless, Fiedler, & Strack, 2004; Kunda, 1999; Macrae & Bodenhausen, 2000; Moskowitz, 2005; and cf. Hastie & Carlston, 1980; Ostrom, 1984; S. E. Taylor, 1981b, on these points).

Mentalism

The first of these assumptions, an unabashed commitment to mentalism (cognition), has just been discussed at some length. *Mentalism* is the belief in the importance of mental representations and processes. The cognitive elements people naturally use to make sense of other people constitute the "what" of social cognition. Mental representations are cognitive structures that both represent one's general knowledge about a given concept or stimulus domain and one's memory for specific experiences. For example, your general knowledge about a new friend may be organized into a view of him as independent but not a loner, friendly but not saccharine, and athletic but not a star. A concept (e.g., this person) includes both relevant attributes (e.g., independent, friendly, athletic) and the relationships among the attributes (e.g., what his independence has to do with his friendliness). General knowledge about ourselves and others provides us with the expectations that enable us to function in the world; as noted, thinking is (mostly) for doing. People also have specific memories for unique events. Both types of representation appear in Chapter 4 on mental representation. People also have mental representations of self (Chapter 5), attitude objects (Chapter 9), and outgroups (Chapter 10), among other significant social cognitions.

Cognitive Processes in Social Settings

The second basic assumption in research on social cognition concerns cognitive process; that is, how cognitive elements form, operate, and change over time. A process orientation follows from the fundamental commitment to cognition: concern with cognitive elements that intervene between observable stimulus and observable response requires an explanation of *how* one gets from S to R. Recall that behaviorists explicitly avoided discussion of internal processes because they were concerned with predicting a publicly observable response from a publicly observable stimulus. In that sense, they were response or outcome oriented rather than process oriented.

But outcome orientations arose elsewhere too. The early methodology of research on consistency theories, for example, was more outcome oriented than process oriented. Although the researchers originally theorized and made assumptions about process, they focused empirically on predicting outcomes from stimuli. For example, inconsistency was manipulated (stimulus) and the resulting attitude change measured (outcome). Later psychologists conducting consistency research did attempt to measure the intervening processes, but the initial thrust of the research methods was outcome oriented. One of the recent shifts in attitude research and in social psychology generally has been away from outcome-oriented approaches and toward examinations of process.

In social cognition research, theories are now available to describe and tools are available to measure various implicit but hitherto unexamined assumptions about process. Social cognition research attempts to measure the stages of social information processing. That is, when a person confronts a social stimulus, several steps occur before he or she makes a response. Social cognition, and now social neuroscience, analyzes these processes from the earliest moments.

Cross-Fertilization

So far we have described two themes in social cognition research and in this book: a commitment to cognition or mentalism and a commitment to process analysis. The third theme, cross-fertilization between cognitive and social psychology, addresses another feature of social cognition research. Although social psychology has always been cognitive, it has not always had purely cognitive neighbors from whom it can borrow new approaches. Borrowing relatively fine-grained cognitive and cognitive neuroscience theory and methods has proved fruitful for social psychological research. Not only do researchers specify the steps in a presumed process model, but researchers attempt to measure the steps in some detail. For example, the first new wave social cognition research relied heavily on measuring milliseconds of reaction time. The most recent social cognitive neuroscience relies on detailed brain imaging techniques. Borrowing measures from other areas of psychology enriches social psychology's home-grown methods, as we will see. Various traditional and newer experimental methods enable researchers to support differing aspects of process models: for example, attention, memory, and inference.

Real-World Social Issues

The fourth theme of social cognition research is application to the real world. Social psychologists have a long tradition of addressing important contemporary issues. Early research provided insights into crowd behavior, propaganda, anti-Semitism, military morale, and other social issues. In keeping with this tradition, research in social cognition informs us about important issues. It applies the often heavily cognitive theory and method to real-world social problems. Throughout this book, we illustrate the ways social cognition can guide work in areas such as psychotherapy, health care, the legal system, stereotyping, advertising, political campaigns, strangers helping strangers, and romantic involvements. All these applications illustrate the flexibility of social cognition research and demonstrate how some otherwise highly technical or abstract ideas generalize outside the laboratory.

Social cognition applications to real-world issues define some boundary conditions for cognitive processes. That is, the research reveals phenomena that do not lend themselves to a purely cognitive analysis; other factors must be considered in many interpersonal settings of consequence. For example, how does cognition trade off accuracy and efficiency? How does social information processing operate in situations of intense personal involvement? How do social cognitions translate into voting behavior? How does the neuroscience of social cognition relate to the social problems of people with autism?

This book addresses the four major themes of social cognition research: unabashed mentalism in the study of cognitive representations of people, a commitment to fine-grained analyses of cognitive process, cross-fertilization between cognitive and social theory and methods, and a commitment to real-world social issues.

PEOPLE ARE NOT THINGS

As we review research on social cognition, the analogy between the perception of things and the perception of people becomes increasingly clear. The argument is made repeatedly: Principles that describe how people think in general also describe how people think about people. Many theories of social cognition have developed in ways that undeniably build on fundamental cognitive principles. Nevertheless, in borrowing such principles we discover fundamental differences when applying them to cognition about people. After all, cognitive psychology is relatively more concerned with processing information about inanimate objects and abstract concepts, whereas social psychology is more concerned with processing information about people and social experience.

At this point you already may be saying, "Wait, you can't tell me that the way I think about mental arithmetic or about my coffee cup has anything to do with the way I think about my friends." The wisdom or folly of applying the principles of object perception to the perception of people has been debated for some time (Heider, 1958; Higgins, Kuiper, & Olson, 1981; Krauss, 1981; Schneider, Hastorf, & Ellsworth, 1979; Tagiuri & Petrullo, 1958). Some of the important differences between people and things as targets of perception include the following:

- People intentionally influence the environment; they attempt to control it for their own purposes. Objects, of course, are not intentional causal agents.
- People perceive back; as you are busy forming impressions of them, they are doing the same to you. Social cognition is mutual cognition.

- Social cognition implicates the self because the target is judging you, because the target may provide you with information about yourself, and because the target is more similar to you than any object could be.
- A social stimulus may change upon being the target of cognition. People worry about how they come across and may adjust their appearance or behavior accordingly; coffee cups obviously do not.
- People's traits are nonobservable attributes that are vital to thinking about them. An object's nonobservable attributes are somewhat less crucial. Both a person and a cup can be fragile, but that inferred characteristic is both less important and more directly seen in the cup.
- People change over time and circumstance more than objects typically do. This can make cognitions rapidly obsolete or unreliable.
- The accuracy of one's cognitions about people is harder to check than the accuracy of one's cognitions about objects. Even psychologists have a hard time agreeing on whether a given person is extraverted, sensitive, or honest, but most ordinary people easily could test whether a given cup is heat resistant, fragile, or leaky.
- People are unavoidably complex. One cannot study cognitions about people without making numerous choices to simplify. The researcher has to simplify in object cognition too, but fewer distortions may result. One cannot simplify a social stimulus without eliminating much of the inherent richness of the target.
- Because people are so complex, and because they have traits and intents hidden from view, and because they affect us in ways objects do not, social cognition automatically involves social explanation. It is more important for an ordinary person to explain why a person is fragile than to explain why a cup is.

For these reasons, social cognitive psychology will never be a literal translation of cognitive psychology. It profits from theories and methods adapted to new uses, but the social world provides perspectives and challenges that are dramatic, if not unique, features of thinking about other people and oneself.

BRAINS MATTER

The Decade of the Brain in the 1990s acknowledged the exciting and crucial roles of neural systems in a variety of human processes, including social ones. Social psychophysiology was not new, of course (e.g., Cacioppo & Berntson, 1992; Shapiro & Crider, 1969). The current palpable excitement among researchers and the public stems partly from the invention and popularity of functional magnetic resonance imaging (fMRI) techniques, which yield images of the brain at work. These techniques allow researchers to place a person into an MRI magnet, provide the person some stimuli, and observe blood flow to distinct areas of the brain, providing clues as to their possible functions in different tasks. The fMRI techniques are developing increasingly precise indicators of spatial location in the brain. These are complemented by older techniques, such as electroencephalograms (EEG) and facial electromyography (EMG), as well as new techniques being developed as we write. EEG provides only approximate spatial locations (noninvasive electrodes are distributed over the surface of the skull) but extremely precise temporal information. The facial EMG (electrodes at crucial locations on the face) can detect micromovements of facial muscles not yet visible to observers but potentially indicative of facial expressions.

Added to these techniques are measures of cardiovascular activity and palmer sweat, which measure various forms of arousal. Assessments of cardiovascular activity provide information about physiological arousal. Social neuroscientists who are especially interested in stress processes also often assess hypothalamic pituitary adrenal (HPA) functioning, especially changes in cortisol in response to threat or stressful tasks. Elevations in cortisol or disruptions in its diurnal rhythm have been tied to stressful events and to psychosocial states. For example, social threat predicts elevated cortisol responses to stressful tasks (Dickerson & Kemeny, 2004), and psychosocial resources such as a strong sense of self have been tied to lower cortisol responses to stress (Creswell et al., 2005). Social neuroscientists make use of a broad array of immune measures as well, including those that assess numbers of different types of immune cells and those that assess immunological functioning. The immune system is responsive to stress and other threats (Dickerson, Kemeny, Aziz, Kim, & Fahey, 2004); assessing immunologic functioning in conjunction with resources, such as optimism or a sense of personal control, can help identify those aspects of social cognition that protect against stress and psychological distress (Reed, Kemeny, Taylor, & Visscher, 1999; Segerstrom, Taylor, Kemeny, & Fahey, 1998). Taken together, these measures open new doors into the life of the social mind.

For social cognition researchers, the possibilities also allow dissociating distinct social cognitive processes on the basis of distinct neuroscientific responses. Relevant to our assertion that "people are not things," recent studies demonstrate distinct neural systems activating in social perception compared to object perception. In one early study (Castelli, Happé, Frith, & Frith, 2000), people watched a large red triangle and a small blue triangle under one of three labels for the animation: interaction with feelings and thoughts, random movement, or simple interaction. Independently, the animated movements also on different trials resembled scripts involving either mental inferences (e.g., persuading, bluffing), simple goals (e.g., chasing, dancing), or straightforward physical movement (e.g., floating, bouncing off walls). When the movements involved attributing a (quasi-human) mental state to the triangles, distinct activation patterns emerged, among them, medial prefrontal cortex (mPFC), superior temporal sulcus (STS or temporoparietal junction), and fusiform gyrus (FFA).[4] This study is exciting because it was one of the first to show something special about perceiving an entity as having intentions and personality, dubbed a "theory of mind" effect. Note how this study fits our earlier distinctions between people and things.

A related study (Mitchell, Heatherton, & Macrae, 2002) supports this distinction, also at the neural systems level. Undergraduates saw a series of adjective-noun pairs and had to decide if the adjective "could ever be true of" the noun. The nouns named people (e.g., David, Emily) or objects (e.g., shirt, mango),

---

[4]The Castelli et al. study also showed activation to temporal poles and the extrastriate cortex (occipital gyrus). The Mitchell et al. study described next activated the intraparietal sulcus. We focus on the other areas for simplicity here.

and the adjectives included typical person descriptors (e.g., assertive, nervous) and relevant object descriptors (e.g., patched, seedless). Neural activity differed when people made these semantic judgments about people and objects. Brain activity associated with people included some of the same areas previously seen by Castelli et al. (2000) and others for social cognitive responses: medial prefrontal cortex (mPFC), superior temporal sulcus (STS), and fusiform gyrus (FFA).

These areas of the brain (mPFC and STS) appear frequently throughout this book when people are generally engaged in social cognition (mPFC) or judgments of intent and trajectory (STS). The mPFC in particular appears to have a unique role in social cognition across many studies (Amodio & Frith, 2006). What's more, the FFA particularly responds to faces or other objects in one's domains of expertise, such as birds for a birdwatcher and cars for a car expert (Farah, 1994; Gauthier, Skudlarski, Gore, & Anderson, 2000). The main point, made by the Mitchell et al. (2002) study, as in the prior one, is the dissociation (separation) between the social and the nonsocial neural activation patterns. Moreover, in these two studies and others (e.g., Mitchell, Macrae, & Banaji, 2005), some of the same areas are implicated in social cognition. One exciting possibility is that these areas link to reward systems in the brain, accounting for the attraction people have to social interaction and belonging (S. T. Fiske, 2004; Baumeister & Leary, 1995).

What is also exciting about these findings is the provocative possibility that social cognition could be the default, resting state (Iacoboni, et al., 2004). In many social neuroscience studies, the characteristically social "activations" often emerge as relatively little change from a supposedly neutral baseline (e.g., staring at the fixation point between trials). In contrast, object judgments often create *de*activations from the baseline. This study suggested that the neutral condition may not be neutral at all, but instead people spontaneously engaging in social cognition (What's that experimenter doing now? I hope she knows what she's doing. Will my friends wait for me for lunch? Why didn't my roommate wake me up as promised?). Suppose for the moment that much of people's random thinking concerns other people, engaging relatively active social systems in the brain. When the experimenter makes people do mental arithmetic or other nonsocial tasks, the social cognition processes shut down, so these "socially implicated" areas shut down. In contrast, when people look at social stimuli, their activation in these areas does not change much from baseline because they were already thinking about other people. This is essentially Iacoboni et al.'s (2004) argument. They compared people watching film clips of two people interacting compared with a single person engaged in everyday activities or a resting baseline. They found activations even relative to baseline in the dorsal part of the mPFC, as well as in the STS and FFA. And similarly, in the Mitchell et al. study, for example, the socially relevant regions were generally marked by relatively little change from baseline brain activity for person judgments along with significant deactivations for object judgments. Other studies that intensify social thinking above social daydreaming do find activations above baseline (Harris, Todorov, & Fiske, 2005).

As the evidence accumulates for the unique neural status of thinking about other people's dispositions and states, researchers are learning much about what makes social cognition special. Some of the more intriguing recent findings using these neural criteria suggest that people can think about dogs as people (Mitchell, Banaji, & Macrae, 2005) more easily than they can think about drug addicts and the homeless as people (Harris & Fiske, 2006). That is, people's default response to an outgroup that elicits disgust (as evidenced by typical ratings of homeless and addicted people) activates neural patterns typical of disgust (e.g., insula) but not neural patterns typical of social cognition to ingroups and even other outgroups (e.g., mPFC). On the other hand, people readily attribute psychological states (anthropomorphize) to dogs (Mitchell, Banaji, & Macrae, 2005), at least as indexed by mPFC and "yes" responses to trait terms ("curious") as potentially applicable to a dog. While interpreting the activation of the vast mPFC is rapidly developing, it clearly is implicated in cognition that is emphatically social.

In discussing the importance of the social brain, we should clarify its context. People sometimes mistakenly pit biological explanations against cultural explanations, rehashing the nature–nurture debate. Although individual researchers tend to be drawn to distinct levels of analysis, brains and cultures are not competing explanations for the same phenomena.

First, our brains are predisposed to pick up our cultures as they socialize us. For example, as just hinted, social thinking activates particular neural configurations. Moreover, social exclusion recruits neural systems linked to the experience of physical pain (Eisenberger, Lieberman, & Williams, 2003). That is, people who are ostracized—even from a simple video game with strangers—activate the anterior cingulate cortex (ACC), and this activation is dampened by activation of the right ventral prefrontal cortex (rvPFC). These patterns also occur for physical pain. Adding to the evidence for this parallel, people's baseline sensitivity to physical pain predicts their sensitivity to social pain, and experiencing social pain sensitizes people to physical pain (Eisenberger, Jarcho, Lieberman, & Naliboff, 2006). As we increasingly understand the neural correlates of social life, we will see how sensitive our brains are to social cues.

Second, cultural information is stored in our brains. As Chapter 4 indicates, mental representations of social information are complex and distinctly characterized by features that differ from nonsocial representations.

Third, people's brains change physically depending on their cultural experience. For example, taxi drivers have larger posterior hippocampus areas (associated with spatial memory storage) the longer they drive, as a function of their learning street locations (Maguire et al., 2000). As these examples indicate, our brains dwell in particular cultural experiences, and both matter to social cognition.

CULTURES MATTER

Exciting new cultural comparisons have been forcing social cognition researchers to reexamine the entire basis of our field. Many of the basic assumptions about how people think about other people turn out to be culturally bounded, challenging long-held assumptions. Many of these comparisons to date contrast American or Canadian with Japanese, Chinese, or Korean undergraduates. Even with these limited comparisons, some provocative findings are emerging. For example, cultures vary in thinking about causality more analytically (Westerners) or holistically (East Asians), as Chapter 6 will show (Nisbett, Peng, Choi, & Norenzayan, 2001). This affects, for example, how people decide whether people or social circumstances are responsible for actions taken, which has implications for law, morality, social roles, and more.

As another example, configurations of beliefs differ across cultures (Leung & Bond, 2004). Cultures with general beliefs in social cynicism assume that power displays elicit compliance, and accordingly, people endorse such influence strategies (Fu et al., 2004). The same goes for variations in beliefs about religiosity, reward for effort, and fate control; that is, people endorse influence strategies that fit their culture's expectations about what makes people tick. Given globalization of business, education, and politics, social cognitive insights into cultural variation are crucial for people to understand each other's assumptions about interaction.

One of the most striking social cognitive differences in cultures compares the self as more independent and autonomous (Westerners) or more interdependent and harmonious (East Asians) (e.g., Markus & Kitayama, 1991; see Chapter 5). The implications of this distinction range from self-definition, to self-esteem, to life tasks, to the roles of others—all critical to social cognition.

All of these cultural patterns relate to each other, as we will see. While the contrasts are real, so are the similarities and so are the places between the extremes. At their best, cultural comparisons create interesting complexity, not stereotypes or caricatures. As social cognition research outgrows its original Western (North American and European) boundaries and simultaneously reaches into the brain, it extends its cultural reach as well.

Summary

The study of social cognition concerns how people make sense of other people and themselves. It focuses on people's everyday understanding both as the phenomenon of interest and as a basis for theory about people's everyday understanding. Thus it concerns both how people think about the social world and how they think they think about the social world. It also draws heavily on fine-grained analyses provided by cognitive theory and method.

Two general approaches to social cognition date back to early modern philosophy. The elemental approach begins with ideas as elements that become linked into increasingly complex compounds. People form associations between ideas by the ideas' repeated contiguity in space or time. Early psychologists used introspective analysis as a method to break down their memory processes into those basic elements.

Gestalt psychologists adopted a holistic approach. They focused on the mind's active construction of reality rather than on objective descriptions of the stimulus field. They also focused on the person's experience of dynamic wholes rather than elements. Lewin and Asch imported such ideas to social psychology. Asch focused on Gestalt impressions. Lewin emphasized that the perceived environment—that is, the psychological field—predicts behavior and that one must consider the entire dynamic equilibrium of forces acting on an individual. The psychological field is the joint product of person and situation, and of motivation and cognition.

Cognition has not always been prominent in experimental psychology. When introspection proved to be a weak basis for an empirical science, cognition fell into disfavor with psychologists. Behaviorists dominated psychology for decades, insisting on an observable stimulus, an observable response, and no intervening cognitions. Later, behaviorist approaches seemed inadequate to explain language; at the same time, information processing theories and computer-aided theory and technology paved the way for the reemergence of cognition in experimental psychology.

In social psychology, however, cognition has always been a respectable idea. The causes of social interaction predominantly lie in the perceived world, and the results of social interaction are thoughts as well as feelings and behavior. In addition, social psychologists have always been cognitive in their view of the thinker who reacts to the perceived stimulus and generates a substantially cognitive response. They have viewed the social thinker at some times as a consistency seeker, motivated to reduce perceived discrepancies; at other times, they have seen the social thinker as a naive scientist who makes every effort to ferret out the truth, with motivation contributing mainly error. Subsequently, social psychologists regarded the social thinker as a cognitive miser who attempts to increase or maintain the efficiency of a capacity-limited cognitive apparatus, and they had little to say about motivation. This viewpoint was followed by a view of the social perceiver as a motivated tactician, which gained acceptance as researchers documented the flexibility of the social perceiver. Currently, with emphasis shifting to ever-faster, more immediate responses, as well as their effects on overt behavior, researchers tend to emphasize social perceivers as activated actors, heavily influenced by social environments.

Social cognition, as an area of study, emphasizes unabashed mentalism, social settings, cross-fertilization, and real-world social issues. Social cognition departs from the general principles of cognition in some ways: compared to objects, people are more likely to be causal agents, to perceive as well as being perceived, and to involve intimately the observer's self. People are difficult targets of cognition; because they adjust themselves upon being perceived, many of their important attributes (e.g., traits) must be inferred, and the accuracy of observations is difficult to determine. People frequently change and are unavoidably complex as targets of cognition. Hence those who study social cognition must adapt the ideas of cognitive psychology to suit the specific features of cognitions about people.

Some of the most exciting recent developments include work on social cognitive affective neuroscience, adding to insights about the special status of emphatically social cognition at the neural level, with particular systems implicated in uniquely social cognitive processes. Complementing that work are insights from cultural psychology, examining variations in the way humans solve the challenge of making sense of each other in a variety of settings.

PART ONE

Basic Concepts in Social Cognition

CHAPTER 2

Dual Modes in Social Cognition

AUTOMATIC PROCESSES ◆ CONTROLLED PROCESSES ◆ MOTIVATIONS INFLUENCE WHICH MODES OPERATE ◆ MODELS OF BOTH AUTOMATIC AND CONTROLLED PROCESSES

First impressions really do count. People judge each other within a fraction of a second, for better or worse. Luckily, under some circumstances people are capable of going beyond those split-second impressions. The relatively automatic first impressions nevertheless anchor subsequent thinking, so they are difficult to undo. Conventional wisdom is correct in this instance—that first impressions matter—but common sense doesn't know the half of just how automatic impressions can be, nor does common sense reveal much about exactly how the deliberate processes operate when they do kick in.

This chapter addresses these two modes of social cognition, a theme that appears and reappears throughout the book. The dual-mode approach has become so established that one edited volume collected thirty-some chapters on this framework (Chaiken & Trope, 1999) and one social psychology handbook devoted a full chapter to it (Wegner & Bargh, 1998). The mind contains a variety of processes, and these models aim to explain the diversity of people's thoughts, feelings, and behaviors toward each other, most models assuming more than one core process (Gilbert, 1999).

The motivated tactician, described in Chapter 1, refers to people's tendency to rely on relatively automatic processes or alternatively on more effortful ones, depending on the situational and motivational demands. The term *tactician* implies that people choose modes in the thick of the action, in the midst of dealing with other people, thinking harder or less hard as they deem necessary. More recent work notes that people typically do not consciously choose between automatic and controlled processes, and that automatic processes influence both motivations that trigger social cognition and behavior that results from it.

In this chapter we begin by illustrating and explaining automatic processes, then describe controlled ones. Next, we examine the motivations that move people from one mode to the other. We then explore some examples of two-mode models, anticipating their appearance in subsequent chapters. Finally, we close with some counterpoints to the prevailing two-mode view.

AUTOMATIC PROCESSES

Automatic processes come in all varieties. Everyday examples include times when people seem not to be thinking; early research dubbed this "mindless-ness" (Langer, Blank, & Chanowitz, 1978). Table 2.1 shows the progression from most automatic toward controlled processes. We begin our discussion with the most pure form of automaticity, which is unintentional, uncontrollable, efficient, autonomous, and outside awareness (Bargh, 1997).

TABLE 2.1. Varieties of Automatic and Controlled Processes

Mode	Definition
Full Automaticity	*Unintentional, uncontrollable, efficient, autonomous responses outside awareness*
Subliminal priming, or preconscious	Prime registers on senses, but no awareness of it or its effect on responses; depends on context
Conscious priming, or postconscious	Conscious perception of prime, but no awareness of its effects on responses; depends on context
Individual differences in chronic accessibility	Can be preconscious or postconscious, habitual processing by particular categories or concepts, as if chronically primed; depends on person (role, personality, culture, practice—a process called proceduralization)
Goal-dependent automaticity	Intentional control starts process, but without subsequent awareness, need to monitor completion, or intending all specific outcomes
	Unintended effects of goal-dependent automaticity include failures of thought suppression and unwanted rumination
Intent	Requires having options, especially obvious when making the hard choice, and paying attention to the intended response
Conscious will	Experienced when a thought precedes, fits, and explains a subsequent action
Consciousness	Defined variously as reportable thoughts; thoughts consistent with behavior; epiphenomenon irrelevant to ongoing mental processes; executive directing mental processes; necessary condition for intent; constructed from accessible concepts; involved in learning and troubleshooting; stimulus field composed of thoughts, emotional experiences, and body sensations that can compete successfully with the external world
Full Control	*Intentional responses within conscious awareness*

Subliminal Priming

Consider the following study (Bargh, Chen, & Burrows, 1996): Undergraduate participants in a psychology experiment saw 4 to 20 circles on a series of screens for 3 seconds each time and had to judge whether they were odd or even in number. After 130 tiresome trials, the computer suddenly beeped and displayed an error message indicating that none of the data had been saved and that the experiment would have to restart. Needless to say, participants reacted. Without their prior knowledge (although with their subsequent consent), their faces were videotaped as the computer and experimenter conveyed the bad news. Also unknown to the participants, just prior to each set of circles, they had seen a black-and-white photo of an African American or European American man, displayed at subliminal speeds (13–26 milliseconds). Participants were non-African American, and their facial expressions were reliably more hostile when they had been exposed to a series of Black faces than when they had been exposed to White faces. Hostile emotions were primed, especially ready to appear under provocation.

Subliminal priming of emotion appears reliable. Other studies have shown related effects of rapidly presented smiling and frowning faces on later liking for Chinese ideographs, which were otherwise neutral and without meaning to the research participants (e.g., Murphy, Monahan, & Zajonc, 1995). A host of other studies similarly show how affect can be conveyed by verbal concepts that are primed by being flashed below awareness. For example, priming hostility-related words affects impressions of others (one of the earliest demonstrations being Bargh and Pietromonaco, 1982).

The neural mechanisms of immediate emotional priming likely include the amygdala, an interior almond-shaped pair of brain regions implicated in detecting emotionally significant stimuli (Phelps, 2005). Faces with fearful expressions elicit amygdala responses even when presented subliminally, below conscious thresholds (Whalen et al., 1998). Emotionally arousing words presented rapidly are easier to detect than more neutral words, and the amygdala again is key because patients with amygdala lesions show a diminished ability to detect these same words (A. K. Anderson & Phelps, 2001). The amygdala may be more oriented to automatically detecting negative cues, whereas the basal ganglia may be more focused on automatic processes related to rewards (Lieberman, Gaunt, Gilbert, & Trope, 2002). Besides the amygdala and basal ganglia, the more reflex-like, relative automatic forms of social cognition implicate (a) the lateral temporal cortex (posterior superior temporal sulcus, pSTS, and temporal pole, TP), (b) the ventromedial prefrontal cortex (vmPFC), and (c) the dorsal anterior cingulate (dACC). Figure 2.1 shows the locations of these areas, for those inclined toward brain imaging. For those not so inclined, the point is that relatively automatic social cognitive-affective processes dissociate from relatively controlled ones in the neural areas typically activated (Lieberman, in 2007).

Subliminal priming is not limited to emotionally significant cues; emotionally neutral concepts also can be primed below awareness (for a review, see Dijksterhuis, Aarts, & Smith, 2005). Conceptual priming that is not primarily affective is likely to invoke brain systems particularly involved in pattern matching, categorizing, and identifying processes that implicate the inferior-temporal

A   B

X-System (Automaticity)   C-System (Control)

Ventromedial PFC (VPFC) [BA11]   Lateral PFC (LPFC)
Basal Ganglia (BG)   Medial Temporal Lobe (MTL)
Amygdala (A)   Medial Parietal Cortex (MPAC)
Lateral Temporal Cortex (LTC)   Lateral Parietal Cortex (LPAC)
Posterior Superior Temporal Sulcus (pSTS) Rostral ACC (rACC)
Temporal Pole (TP)   Medial PFC (MPFC) [BA10]
Dorsal Anterior Cingulate (dACC)   Dorsomedial PFC (DMPFC) [BA8/9]

FIGURE 2.1. Hypothesized neural correlates of the C-system supporting reflective social cognition (analogous to controlled processing) and the X-system supporting reflexive social cognition (analogous to automatic processing) displayed on a canonical brain rendering from (*a*) lateral and (*b*) medial views.

Source: Adapted from "Social cognitive neuroscience: A review of core processess" by M. D. Lieberman, p. 262. Reprinted, with permission, from the Annual Review of Psychology, Volume 58, © 2007, by Annual Reviews, www.annualreviews.org

cortex, the lower, outside region, just above one's ears, on the surface of the brain (Lieberman et al., 2002). Categorical pattern matching of a prime influences perceptions of related subsequent stimuli, especially ambiguous ones; the neural accounts are consistent with the cognitive activation data.

In addition to priming emotions and neutral cognitions, subliminal priming can affect behavior (see Ferguson & Bargh, 2004, for a recent review). In the Bargh, Chen, and Burrows (1996) study that opened this section, after participants' subliminal exposure to different race faces and subsequent provocation, the experimenter privately rated the participant's behavior on irritability, hostility, anger, and uncooperativeness, based on their interaction. Non-Black participants primed with Black faces behaved in reliably more hostile ways when provoked.

Subliminal priming studies are not easy to run; they require that the prime be displayed precisely and reliably for exceedingly brief times, and often that the prime be masked immediately afterward by perceptually related but conceptually neutral stimuli. For example, a subliminally primed word might be immediately followed by a scrambled letter-string of the same length; a subliminally primed face might be immediately masked by a random pattern of color-matched clusters covering the same visual area. A *subliminal* prime has to pass the objective standard of registering on the senses but not exceed the subjective standard of registering on awareness. The delicate threshold between perceptual but not conscious impact depends on the prime, participant, current goals, context, and technical features of the presentation screen (Dijksterhuis et al., 2005). Each factor can change a prime's tendency to be activated above or below perception, and, if so, above or below consciousness. All this means that it is not so easy as one might think for advertisers to convey subliminal messages, although in theory they could do it (Cooper & Cooper, 2002).

So far, the illustrative experiments all exemplify the most *subliminal, preconscious form* of automatic processing, in which people are not aware of the priming cue, nor of its effects on their reaction to a relevant stimulus. Although this is the most dramatic form of automatic response, fully automatic processes are likely to be rare. This kind of empirical demonstration is most useful to make the theoretical point that even unconsciously activated concepts prime related concepts, which then shape the interpretation of subsequent stimuli, still outside awareness. This form fits the most stringent definition of *pure automaticity*, which, as noted earlier, is unintentional, uncontrollable, efficient, autonomous, and outside awareness (Bargh, 1997).

Conscious Priming

Less dramatic but probably more impactful on a daily basis, *postconscious automaticity* entails conscious perception of the prime but no awareness of its effects on subsequent reactions (see Table 2.1). In one study, participants first imagined a day in the life of a typical professor, listing activities and lifestyle. Then they played Trivial Pursuit, the knowledge quiz game. Primed participants actually outscored other participants who had skipped that task (Dijksterhuis & van Knippenberg, 1998). Although the mechanism remains unclear, they may have been prompted to try harder, use better strategies, or trust their hunches. Priming a soccer hooligan or the trait of stupidity was not helpful to the knowledge test, but priming the trait of intelligence was. As another example, students unscrambled word lists to make sentences that primed the category "elderly" (and thus, slowness); they walked to the elevator more slowly after the experiment (Bargh, Chen, & Burrows 1996). In still another study in that series, students covertly but consciously primed with the trait "rudeness" were faster to interrupt another person.

Many of these priming studies replicate with either postconscious or preconscious priming, as in the Bargh, Chen, and Burrows (1996) series. As another example, students primed either consciously or preconsciously with words related to the elderly then expressed more conservative attitudes; others primed with the skinhead category expressed more prejudiced attitudes (Kawakami, Dovidio, & Dijksterhuis, 2003). Both pre- and postconscious effects operate similarly, in part because people are unacquainted with priming effects, so even conscious primes—if subtle and covert—do not typically prompt efforts to counteract them.

Chronic Accessibility

Somewhere between preconscious and postconscious automaticity are individual differences in chronically accessible concepts. People may or may not be aware that they habitually code other people in terms of, say, their friendliness, intelligence, or independence (Higgins, King, & Maven, 1982). Nevertheless, particular trait dimensions tend to capture different people's attention and repeatedly surface in their descriptions and impressions of others. One can measure this simply by counting the frequency of traits used to describe a series of familiar others. The chronically used traits ease people's impression formation processes along familiar, well-established grooves, for better or worse, but certainly more efficiently than would be the case without these habitual sources of influence.

How do people develop certain favorite trait dimensions? Certain traits might be family favorites ("this is my smart one; this is my nice one") or cultural favorites (Americans tend to focus on honesty and friendliness) or reflect survival skills (in certain neighborhoods, for example, aggressiveness) or job requirements (probation officers judging trustworthiness). If a person (e.g., a probation officer) over time judges hundreds of instances of behavior as honest or dishonest, some of those repeated inferences (e.g., shoplifting is dishonest) will show "specific" practice effects, becoming faster and easier to invoke over time. The development of automaticity occurs through practice, a process termed *proceduralization*. Becoming a procedure can happen relatively quickly, within a few dozen trials, and can last over at least a day's delay.

Procedural processes constitute one theoretical account of some priming effects (E. R. Smith & Branscombe, 1987, 1988; E. R. Smith, Branscombe, & Bormann, 1988). People may start with the effortful use of general rules that are independent of the particular setting (behavior reflects a trait), but with practice they can make automatic inferences about certain frequently encountered stimuli (E. R. Smith, 1984). Proceduralization involves two kinds of practice effects. With practice, any judgment of honesty, regardless of the particular behavior, will also speed up, showing a trait-specific practice effect. A second kind of practice effect speeds judgments of traits even in general (E. R. Smith, 1990; E. R. Smith et al., 1988). That is, proceduralization requires repeated execution of the same process, for example, making trait inferences; it can entail judging identical content such as judging only honesty (E. R. Smith & Lerner, 1986). But it can also entail more general processes, such as rapidly judging any trait. With consistent practice, both kinds of judgments (specific and general) become proceduralized so that exposure to an appropriate stimulus (e.g., either honesty or any trait) automatically speeds the inference. In Chapter 4, we discuss different memory systems that may account for these two effects (E. R. Smith, 1984), but the point here is that practice can automate the judgment process.

Procedural (automatic) judgments speed up people's responses, but how much does that matter to social interactions? It does matter because a well-practiced judgment will preempt an equally reasonable but less-practiced judgment (E. R. Smith, 1990). For example, if a teacher is used to judging intelligence, a person who is intelligent but unsociable would be viewed positively, primarily in terms of the intelligence; in contrast, a sales supervisor might emphasize the unsociability over the intelligence and make a negative judgment. The speed-up of proceduralized judgments may also have implications for stereotyping: People are members of several social categories; well-practiced reliance on, say, race might cause perceivers to emphasize that dimension over others, such as age, gender, social class, or individual traits (Zárate & Smith, 1990). Another way in which the proceduralization of judgment may matter is in accounting for the speed and unconscious quality of some affective responses (Branscombe, 1988).

Conclusion

So far, we have seen various kinds of automated responses that differ in degree. Various kinds of encoding may occur in an automated fashion, below consciousness, in subliminal or preconscious perception. Postconscious processes are cued by a conscious prime and can proceed rapidly, without effort, intent, or awareness. Practice seems to be the crucial element in developing automatic responses, as research on proceduralized processes suggests.

Certain types of judgments seem especially likely to be automated: Trait inferences seem to be necessary first steps in encoding information about others (see Chapter 6). This makes sense in that trait inferences allow people to predict what others will do in future encounters. Moreover, much of the time, people's behavior probably does reflect what they will do again later, at least in the situations in which we habitually encounter them. Other types of encoding are likely to be automatic as well, although there is less accumulated evidence on these points: Self-relevant knowledge is likely to be encoded automatically (see Chapter 5). Certain people (e.g., the depressed) automatically encode certain content (e.g., negative traits) about themselves (Bargh & Tota, 1988). For people in general, stimuli related to threat would be likely candidates for automatic encoding; for example, an angry face in a crowd of happy faces stands out (more than vice versa), suggesting a preattentive search for threatening cues (Hansen & Hansen, 1988a), and negative cues may carry particular weight preconsciously (Erdley & D'Agostino, 1988). Stimuli relevant to our current needs and goals may be encoded automatically (Bruner, 1957). Finally, stimuli likely to be relevant to our interests are noticed, so that people especially notice others their own age, and males especially notice attractive females (M. Rodin, 1987), a process that may represent automatic encoding. Research on all kinds of automaticity, especially automatic behavior, led us to coin the term *activated actors* in Chapter 1. Much social reaction is relatively automatic.

Why might so many of people's social cognitive responses be automatic? The main reason, of course, is sheer efficiency. To the extent that people are much of the time cognitive misers, they simply have to take well-worn shortcuts because they cannot always deal with other people in all their complexity. Apart from sheer processing capacity, people can recruit similar previous decisions that worked well enough in the past in order to predict decent outcomes of similar decisions in the future. Finally, unconscious thought can manage more complex information more rapidly, leading to more coherent and clear choices (Dijksterhuis, 2004).

Automatic activation of mental representations subliminally (preconsciously) and supraliminally (consciously) have similar effects. Both can influence evaluations and emotions, associated cognitions and strategies, and behavior. The main difference is that activation above awareness can invoke controlled strategies, if one is aware that the prime might affect responses. That takes us to our next topic.

CONTROLLED PROCESSES

Just as automaticity comes in degrees, so does control. A *controlled* process is any process in which the perceiver's conscious intent substantially determines how the process operates. Along the range between relatively automatic processes of the last section and relatively controlled processes of this section lie goal-driven automatic processes. They could have appeared at the end of the previous section because they occupy the boundary between the two extremes (see Table 2.1).

Goal-Driven Automatic Processes

As befits its location at the boundary, goal-dependent automaticity is automatic according to some of the criteria, such as lack of awareness of the process itself, not needing to monitor the process to completion, and lack of intending all the specific outcomes. For example, on a bleary Saturday morning, more than one distracted parent operating on autopilot has been known to feed the cereal to the dog and the kibbles to the kids (A. P. Fiske, Haslam, & Fiske, 1991). In this example, two goal-dependent automatic processes interfere with each other. A simpler example would be someone at a party asking about your research, whereupon you launch into a standardized automatic account more suited to your thesis committee than to a prospective romantic interest.

However, by definition, goal-dependent automaticity also varies by the perceiver's goals, so it is partially responsive to intentional control. Goal-dependent automaticity thus is not entirely automatic in that it requires intentional processing and depends on the task undertaken. Conscious intent launches preconscious automaticity.

One example is habits, behaviors that one repeats frequently. When relevant goals are activated, thoughts about habitual behaviors are cued along with the relevant behavior itself. When bike riders think about getting to the other side of town, bike-related thoughts are accessible (Aarts & Dijksterhuis, 2000). This is not the case for people who do not habitually ride their bikes. The goal–habit linkage likely drives more of our actions than we like to admit.

Other examples of goal-dependent automaticity are illustrated by what happens at a party when one approaches some people and avoids others. Attending the party presupposes the goal to socialize, and various relatively automatic processes support this goal: spontaneous trait inferences based on exposure to behavioral information (see Chapter 6) or facial cues (see Chapter 3). For example, people form first impressions at a party, deciding rapidly and superficially who looks entertaining and who looks boring. This process has both automatic and controlled components. Because spontaneous trait inferences occur more under certain goals (socializing) than others (distraction while memorizing a phone number), it is goal dependent and therefore not fully automatic. However, once launched, such trait inferences (who looks entertaining or boring) do seem to occur unintentionally and without much awareness, so they are automatic once the appropriate goal triggers the process.

Many social cognitive processes qualify as goal-driven automaticity. Forming impressions depends on one's goals, as a later section details, but the process itself otherwise can occur without much awareness or effort. Remembering someone's attributes likewise depends on one's goals, but otherwise occurs automatically (Chapter 4). Noticing relationships or covariation between social events (Chapter 7) may be another example. A variety of other goal-directed processes with substantial automatic components—such as typing, driving, or perhaps rehashing the same old issues in a relationship—also illustrate this category.

Goal-Inconsistent Automaticity

Sometimes people's goals trigger automatic thoughts consistent with their conscious preferences, but people can't always think what they want, even if they try (Wenzlaff & Wegner, 2000). Try to spend the next 60 seconds *not* thinking about a white bear but noting the instances when you fail. (If you try it, you'll find it's harder than you think.) A pair of studies (Wegner, Schneider, Carter, & White, 1987) asked participants to think aloud for 5 minutes while suppressing thoughts of a white bear; however, they were asked to ring a bell whenever they did think about a white bear. They were unable to suppress white-bear thoughts. Moreover, when asked afterward to think about white bears, they showed a rebound effect, thinking about white bears quite a lot; most important, they thought about white bears even more than did people who had been explicitly thinking about them all along. Both parts of this phenomenon are familiar to dieters, unrequited lovers, and procrastinators. (The dieter in particular knows all too well the potential for a postdiet binge of food thoughts and compensatory eating.) The only way out, as successful dieters and practiced meditators know, is to find a substitute thought. Participants who thought about a red Volkswagen as a distracter were no more successful in suppressing white-bear thoughts, but they showed no rebound afterward, suggesting that the suppression had not created the same kind of mental logjam as it had without the distracting thought.

The process is ironic (Wegner, 1994): Because one has the goal to suppress a specific thought, one sets up an automatic detection-monitoring system, which keeps the forbidden thought active, making it come to mind more easily. This kind of goal-dependent automaticity shows how goals can prime automatic processes that defeat the very goals they were intended to serve. For example, people who care about suppressing their stereotypes can do so when they are self-focused (attending to their internal standards), but this spontaneous suppression of stereotypes nevertheless produces a rebound effect in which the associations return with a vengeance (Macrae, Bodenhausen, & Milne, 1998).

Future neuroscience may identify the neural correlates of this goal-driven automatic inconsistency. The anterior cingulate cortex, which monitors a variety of disruptions (Botvinick, Cohen, & Carter, 2004), also monitors attempts to suppress unwanted thoughts (Wyland, Kelley, Macrae, Gordon, & Heatherton, 2003). This may be the neural indicator of the ironic process, showing how deeply embedded it is in fundamental systems of goal maintenance.

The difficulty of thought suppression is implicated in the inability of depressed people to avoid negative thoughts, although they can suppress positive thoughts just as well as control subjects can (Wenzlaff, Wegner, & Roper, 1988). As you will see in Chapter 5, depression makes negative thoughts more accessible. For example, depressed people perseverate on (i.e., persist in ruminating about) failures longer than do nondepressed people (Carver, La Voie, Kuhl, & Ganellen, 1988). Providing depressed people with positive distracter thoughts seems to be helpful in the suppression of negative material (Wenzlaff et al., 1988).

When not successfully repressed, a single intrusive thought may lead the way to brooding and rumination; that is, unwanted thinking about a particular object for a long time. Repetitive, counterproductive thinking may stem both from cognitive associations cued by goal-directed thinking, as already noted, and from the motivation to remember uncompleted tasks (Zeigarnik, 1927). Rumination is said to entail several stages, which can be illustrated by the problem of attempting not to dwell on an unrequited attraction: (a) initially intensified repetition of the interrupted behavior (despite rebuffs, one persists in attempts to contact the loved person), (b) problem solving at lower and lower levels (one tries to calculate details of the person's schedule and habits to maximize successful contact), (c) end-state thinking (one fantasizes about the desired outcome of being together), (d) trying to abandon the goal (one attempts to give up on the person), (e) channelized thinking (even after resolving to give up, one may persist in thinking along well-worn associative pathways that all lead to thoughts of the other), and (f) depression from continued powerlessness (if one cannot escape from the preoccupation, one must mourn the lost ideal) (Martin & Tesser, 1989). A demonstration of the interrupted-goal aspect of rumination was obtained in one study that asked newly arrived college women how much they thought about some close person they had left behind; ruminations were positively related to the number of shared activities that were interrupted by being apart from the person (Millar, Tesser, & Millar, 1988).

Although some of the most interesting research on goal-directed automaticity has emphasized people's failures, much of the time goals can aid the performance of habitual behavior. As creatures of habit, this result may be less surprising but still important because adaptive forms of automaticity run our days.

Intent

Having moved through preconscious, postconscious, chronic, and goal-dependent automaticity, as well as unintended consequences of automaticity, we land on intent, a crucial feature of control. When is it fair to say that we fully intend a particular train of thought? This matters because people are often held legally and morally responsible for intended consequences. Cognitive explanations are important for a range of social problems, such as prejudice, aggression, biased judgments, and the like. For example, consider prejudice (detailed in Chapters 11–12). If people's prejudice is not strictly intentional, then perhaps they are not responsible for its consequences. Similarly, aggression in self-defense or the heat of jealous passion is viewed as less bad than premeditated aggression, which is defined by intent.

How do laypeople, psychologists, and the law define intent? People may be said to intend their train of thought and resulting interpretation if they perceive themselves as *having options* to think about it in other ways (S. T. Fiske, 1989). Hence, if on reflection one understood that another interpretation were possible, then the way one does think may be considered intentional. For example, if one interprets a family member's "I hate you!" as a murder threat, reasonable people might claim one had options to think in other ways. Similarly, if one categorizes an African American in a three-piece suit as a potential mugger, reasonable people might note that one had options to make other interpretations.

When one does have options, a particular choice is likely to be easier, and others are likely to be harder. That is, if one's accustomed way of thinking is the easy way, then *making the hard choice* is likely to be seen as especially intentional, by ordinary observers, psychologists, and even legal experts. Thus a clinically paranoid person who resists interpreting family hostility as a threat will be viewed as overcoming a predisposition to respond in the easier way, and this harder response will be viewed as especially controlled and intended. Similarly, if one overcomes a societal stereotype of a young street tough as necessarily a mugger, observers will judge this as an act of will more so than if one goes along with the prevailing stereotypes. Rejecting the default, making the harder choice, is seen as especially intentional. However, if one has the capability of thinking either way, then both the hard and easy choice are intentional by the first criterion.

Finally, people implement their intended way of thinking by *paying attention*. Hence if a person wanted to interpret an intimate's hostility as a provocation to violence and attended to details of revenge, observers would interpret this as intentional. Similarly, to overcome a habitual stereotype applied to another person, paying attention to nonstereotypic attributes is the most effective route (S. T. Fiske & Neuberg, 1990). Intentional thought is characterized by having options, most obviously by making the hard choice, and enacted by paying attention to implementing the intent.

From intent, society takes a short step to responsibility. For example, completely unintentional discrimination is not illegal, and accidentally killing someone (manslaughter) is viewed less negatively than killing someone on purpose (murder). Regardless, one is not held socially responsible for one's thoughts, only for one's actions. The intent problem matters especially when analyzing the thoughts that provoked a particular action, but this analysis presumes, as society often does, that people have free will.

Conscious Will

Some social psychologists question the extent of free will. Is the automaticity of social cognition the "cognitive monster" that cannot be stopped (Bargh, 1999)? Perhaps situations automatically cue certain motives, which Bargh (1997) calls "auto-motives." In this view, situations determine behavior fairly directly. Situations trigger goals, and goals trigger actions—all automatically and outside consciousness. Bargh provocatively aligns himself with Skinnerian stimulus-response behaviorism, which was overthrown by the cognitive revolution in the middle of the 20th century. Social cognition comes full circle in the activated actor metaphor of the social (non)thinker.

In a related vein, Wegner argues that conscious will is an illusion created by people thinking about an action before performing it (Wegner, 2003; Wegner & Wheately, 1999). If the thought precedes the action, fits the action, and explains the action, people infer that the thought caused it. People often think about an action before performing it, so they infer that the thought caused the action. But what if something else (e.g., the situation) cued the thought, and the action was independent?

To test this, experimenters first had to create the thought that allegedly caused the result. They subliminally primed the desired endpoint for a moving square on a grid displayed on a computer screen (Aarts, Custers, & Wegner, 2005). Both the participant and the computer controlled squares moving in opposite directions through the grid. When the participant pressed a key, both squares started moving, and when the participant stopped, the endpoint of one square was revealed, without making it clear whether it was the computer's square or the participant's own square. Participants rated whether they felt they had caused that outcome (i.e., whether it was their square or the computer's). Prior subliminal priming of the endpoint biased participants' beliefs that they had caused it, though it did not actually affect how they performed the action (i.e., the timing of their key-press). The participants were more likely to experience agency (personal authorship of the outcome) when they were subliminally primed beforehand to think of the effect. People can think erroneously that their actions caused outcomes that they demonstrably did not control.

In the extreme, people even think they can control other people's outcomes and behavior. In one experiment (Pronin, Wegner, McCarthy, & Rodriguez, 2006), people had the illusion that they had magically caused someone else's outcomes. Some participants were first induced to harbor evil thoughts about a confederate who was obnoxious (compared to neutral), and then participants role-played a "witch doctor" by sticking pins into a "voodoo doll" allegedly representing the other person. When the victim indeed reported feeling a slight headache, participants indicated that they felt causally responsible. Similar effects occurred for spectators who silently rooted for a peer shooting basketballs into a hoop when the shooter subsequently succeeded. They felt that their silent wishes had helped the person to succeed.

These demonstrations make the crucial point that in addition to not controlling our thoughts we do not control our own (or other people's) actions as much as we think we do. Is this a reversion to behaviorism? Do situations entirely control behavior, and people's intentions merely correlate as irrelevant epiphenomena? Recent work draws on cognitive concepts that were forbidden to behaviorists, but social psychology need not pit the conscious person against the deterministic situation (Mischel, 1997). Both are important, but the automaticity of everyday life and the illusion of conscious control remind us that many processes do not operate through conscious intent.

Consciousness

If our conscious control does not serve to influence our actions as much as we might think and prefer, what does pass through our minds and why? What occupies our minds? What do we think about? What is in consciousness and why? Social psychologists have not concentrated on consciousness, which has traditionally been the topic of philosophers, psychoanalysts, and (recently) cognitive scientists. Accordingly, we will not attempt a comprehensive review but merely note some interesting points that potentially inform social cognition research and that increasingly matter as more social cognition researchers tackle these issues.

William James (1890/1983) described consciousness eloquently as the stream of thought:

> Consciousness, then, does not appear to itself chopped up in bits. Such words as "chain" or "train" do not describe it as fitly as it presents itself in the first instance. It is nothing jointed; it flows. A "river" or a "stream" are the metaphors by which it is most naturally described. (p. 233)

Consciousness was not only a stream to James, it was a stream "teeming with objects and relations" (p. 219) private and perpetually separate from the nearby streams belonging to other people.

Consciousness subsequently received a bad name from introspectionist experiments (recall from Chapter 1 that specially trained investigators reflected on their own mental processes in an effort to uncover basic processes such as memory retrieval). However, given the inherent inability to reproduce such introspective data publicly, and given the rise of antimentalistic behaviorism, consciousness went into hiding. With early work in cognitive psychology, it crept back in as "attention," then interpreted as what was being held in current awareness (see Chapter 3). Subsequently, some cognitive psychologists narrowly defined consciousness as either (a) simply being aware of (able to talk about) something or, alternatively, (b) being aware of something only in the sense that it reflects one's behavior even though one might not be able to report on it (Bower, 1990). In the first case, one might report feeling hungry and thinking about food; in the second case, one might find oneself snacking without conscious awareness of feeling hungry or intending to eat.

Consciousness has been viewed more broadly by various cognitive psychologists (Mandler & Nakamura, 1987). However, these views are not well integrated with each other because they usually represent particular attempts to solve theoretical problems using the concept of consciousness. One view represents consciousness as an epiphenomenon irrelevant to ongoing mental processes. As noted, it is reminiscent of behaviorist views, although distinct because, at least as used in the research just described, both the research methods and the presumed processes draw heavily on cognitive mechanisms.

Another idea is that consciousness is an executive that directs mental structures. When memory contents are activated sufficiently above a threshold, they are conscious, coming into short-term or working memory (see Chapters 3 and 4; D. A. Norman & Shallice, 1986; Shallice, 1972, 1978). At that point, the mental representations can be utilized under conscious control. As an executive, consciousness can inhibit and therefore control automatic associations, so it makes them responsive to one's current intents (Posner & Rothbart, 1989). A parallel social cognition account similarly labels consciousness simply as an "Executor" (Wyer & Srull, 1986).

Another perspective views consciousness as a necessary condition for human understanding and intent, as noted earlier. Consciousness as a possible condition for intent comes into discussions of how people assign blame (K. G. Shaver, 1985) and intent (S. T. Fiske, 1989; Uleman, 1989). That is, one cannot discuss what people intend to do unless one assumes that they are conscious of at least some aspects of their intent.

Finally, a novel and provocative viewpoint represents consciousness as a constructed device. Consciousness as a construction requires a bit of explanation, for it would seem less obvious than the other views. In this view, consciousness is a state that makes sense of currently activated unconscious contents using a number of applicable concepts. Consciousness is constructed from the accessible concepts. It operates within the constraints of a limited-capacity system and for the purpose of furthering the needs and goals of the moment (Mandler & Nakamura, 1987; Marcel, 1983a, 1983b).

Consciousness is involved in learning, as one often proceeds from the conscious to the automatic and unconscious (as in learning to drive a car). In learning, consciousness allows the formation of new associations in which previously separate things come together into awareness. Should an otherwise overlearned and automatic sequence later fail, consciousness again is implicated in troubleshooting. And consciousness is necessary for choice, which compares two alternatives held in awareness at the same time. In this view, constructive consciousness serves a variety of important functions in ongoing goal-directed behavior. Cognitive psychologists generally have been concerned with such functions of consciousness.

Contents of Consciousness

Closer to home, social-personality psychologists have focused on the contents of consciousness just for its own sake. They describe ongoing consciousness as the stimulus field composed of thoughts, emotional experiences, and body sensations (i.e., daydreaming) that can compete successfully with the external world (Singer, 1978, 1984). Such internal landscapes (Csikszentmihalyi, 1978; Csikszentmihalyi & Larson, 1984) are often made up of unfinished business or current concerns (Klinger, 1978; Klinger, Barta, & Maxeiner, 1980; see also Srull & Wyer, 1986). These include any unmet goals, whether trivial low-level projects (getting to the gym), problems in significant relationships (Will my true love marry me?), or value dilemmas (Should I cooperate in my friend's tax evasion?). One study sampled college students' thoughts, finding them mostly specific, detailed, visual, unfanciful, controllable, and related to the immediate situation; only about a fifth of the reported thoughts were strange and distorted (Klinger, 1978).

Kinds of Thought

Ongoing thought may be stimulus dependent or stimulus independent (Antrobus, Singer, Goldstein, & Fortgang, 1970; Klinger, 1978; Singer, 1966). That is, we sometimes think *stimulus-dependent thoughts* about environmental cues. However, even when we are highly motivated to attend to the environment, we are constantly experiencing *stimulus-independent thoughts* (that is, our mind wanders a lot). In some research demonstrating this principle, the investigators motivated subjects by paying them for correctly monitoring external signals, penalizing them for errors, and forcing them to maintain rapid responding; even then, distracting thoughts occurred 55% of the time (Antrobus et al., 1970; Antrobus, Fein, Goldstein, & Singer, 1989). However, the nature of the task at the time probably influences the relative amounts of stimulus-dependent and stimulus-independent thought.

Relation to the outside world is not the only way to carve up the contents of consciousness. A separate set of dimensions differentiates between operant and respondent thought processes (Klinger, 1977a, 1977b, 1978). As its name implies, *operant thought* is instrumental and problem solving in nature; it is volitional, it monitors progress toward a goal, and one tries to protect it against external and internal distractions. *Respondent thought* is neither volitional nor effortful but receptive; it constitutes all the ordinary distractions of unbidden images (Horowitz, 1970) or preemptory thoughts (Klein, 1967) that seem to arise of their own accord. Most daily thought is operant, with respondent components, according to one study (Klinger, 1978). That is, while you are reading this book, your thought is operant; when you stop to think about how you will choose a term paper topic, that thought also is operant. But when you daydream about the party last night, that is respondent thought. Doubtless, people's tasks and their stage of implementation influence the proportion of operant thoughts (e.g., Heckhausen & Gollwitzer, 1987). There are also individual differences in task (operant) focus (e.g., Jolly & Reardon, 1985).

Although it might seem that these two dimensions of thought—stimulus dependent versus stimulus independent, operant versus respondent—are completely redundant, they are not. A person may have operant (goal-directed) thoughts that depend on external stimuli or thoughts that are stimulus independent and wholly internal (as when one concentrates on making a decision). Similarly, one may have respondent (spontaneous) thoughts that do or do not depend on external stimuli (funny how the computer keyboard can suddenly demand cleaning just when one is trying write the first sentence of a paper).[1]

Sampling People's Thoughts

How often have we wished to read another person's thoughts? Indeed, strangers often think newly introduced psychologists or psychology students can read (or at least analyze) people's minds. Fortunately or unfortunately, psychologists have only indirect access to people's inner worlds. Some thought-sampling studies have examined people's inner worlds while they are attempting to concentrate on a perceptual task (Antrobus et al., 1970); others have attached people to electronic pagers that beep at random moments during the day, prompting participants to write down their thoughts just before the signal (Klinger, 1978). Experience-sampling methods that allow researchers to query participants about their current states at random moments have explored conscious experiences regarding cooperative learning, parenthood, mood, well-being, loneliness, and everyday psychotic perceptions (respectively: Delle Fave & Massimini, 2004; Peterson & Miller, 2004; Oishi, Diener, Napa Scollon, & Biswas-Diener, 2004; Updegraff, Gable, & Taylor, 2004; Hawkley, Burleson, Berntson, & Cacioppo, 2003; Verdoux, Husky, Tournier, Sorbara, & Swendsen, 2003).

Other techniques of thought sampling ask subjects to think aloud as they are receiving information about other people (Erber & Fiske, 1984; S. T. Fiske, Neuberg, Beattie, & Milberg, 1987; Ruscher & Fiske, 1990). As participants read verbal materials describing someone, they talk into a tape recorder, providing their spontaneous and relatively unfiltered reactions, which enables researchers to observe the encoding process in detail. Although a number of methodological cautions are in order, the technique has proved useful in social cognition (S. T. Fiske & Ruscher, 1989; S. E. Taylor & Fiske, 1981). For example, one can trace the gradual development of suspicion about another person's ulterior motives and the evolving negative impressions (Marchand & Vonk, 2005).

A related series of studies has attempted the challenge of examining people's thoughts during ongoing social interaction. In these studies of naturalistic social

---

[1]Other dimensions too numerous to cover here distinguish among conscious thoughts: well-integrated or degenerative, probable or fanciful, self-involving or observation oriented, vivid or pallid, primarily verbal or sensory, and involving particular senses (J. L. Singer, 1984; see also Klinger, 1978).

cognition (Ickes, Robertson, Tooke, & Teng, 1986; Ickes & Tooke, 1988; Ickes, Tooke, Stinson, Baker, & Bissonnette, 1988), strangers are unobtrusively videotaped as they pass the time awaiting the experimenter's return. After being informed that they have been recorded on a candid camera and giving permission for use of the tapes, participants separately replay the tape, stopping it each time they recall having a particular thought or feeling. This research examines such dimensions of the interaction partners' thoughts and feelings as their object (self, partner, others, environment), their valence (positive or negative), and their perspective (own or other's). It finds, for example, that people's positive thoughts about their partners are related to their involvement in the interaction (as measured by both their verbal and nonverbal behavior). Moreover, in same-sex dyads, male strangers show greater convergence in their thought/feeling content than do female strangers, perhaps because they operate within a more narrow range of interactional involvement and thus have to monitor their interaction more closely. That is, in Anglo American culture, male strangers carefully regulate the degree of intimacy they display, and this results in their thinking and feeling similarly because their options are relatively limited. In contrast, the interactional involvement of female strangers is less constrained, but their thought/feeling content shows more convergence in taking each other's perspective and in focusing on third parties (Ickes et al., 1988). This paradigm can explore empathic accuracy by comparing what people think their partners are experiencing and what the partners actually experience. In married couples, empathic accuracy helps emotional intimacy except when one person's thoughts are relationship threatening, in which case empathic accuracy naturally reduces the perceiver's felt closeness (Simpson, Oriña, & Ickes, 2003).

A related paradigm also samples people's thoughts within relatively realistic social settings. Participants role-play participation in one part of an audiotaped interpersonal encounter; that is, the tape portrays half the interaction and the participant mentally supplies the remainder. Alternatively, the tape depicts an overheard conversation in which two people discuss a third party, and the participant then role-plays the third party as the self. At predetermined points the tape is stopped, and participants articulate their thoughts. People report more irrational thoughts (i.e., rigid absolute demands) in stressful, evaluative social situations, and this is especially true for people who are socially anxious (Davison, Feldman, & Osborn, 1984; Davison, Robins, & Johnson, 1983; Davison & Zighelboim, 1987; Kashima & Davison, 1989). The inventiveness of these various paradigms illustrates the challenge of obtaining people's thoughts online, during social interactions.

Conclusions About Consciousness

Studies that attempt to access people's thoughts must do so with their cooperation and, more important, within their ability to comply. As you will see (Chapter 8), there is some controversy about people's ability to access their own thought processes. People often cannot report accurately on what affects their behavior (Nisbett & Wilson, 1977), suggesting that they have imperfect access to at least some of their own thought processes. Nevertheless, within certain limits people can report usefully on the content of their thoughts under certain conditions: if they do so simultaneously with their thoughts, if the relevant thoughts are already in verbal form, and if they are asked to report content and not process (Ericsson & Simon, 1980; S. T. Fiske & Ruscher, 1989; S. E. Taylor & Fiske, 1981).

Cognition and social cognition researchers are thinking about consciousness in ways that go beyond the teeming stream of William James. Consciousness may be considered an executive, a necessary condition for intent, or a construction inferred from material activated unconsciously. It tends to be occupied by unfinished business, but it may be more or less instrumental and more or less dependent on external stimuli. Studies sampling thought during interaction are currently inventing a number of techniques to cope with this particular challenge. However, all studies of consciousness must be wary of the introspective-access problem.

MOTIVATIONS INFLUENCE WHICH MODES OPERATE

If the primary modes of social cognition are automatic and unconscious thoughts versus controlled and conscious thoughts, with gradations between them, it matters how people move between modes. As the motivated tactician metaphor implies, people's tactics (the modes they use) depend on their motives. In social cognition, a variety of motives have mattered over the past decades. They go by various names, but the following five terms capture the most frequent motives (Fiske, 2004): belonging, understanding, controlling, enhancing self, and trusting ingroup. As a mnemonic device, consider them a buc(k)et of motives (Table 2.2).

Belonging

Social cognition is importantly *social,* as noted in Chapter 1. Social cognition preoccupies people because our social survival depends on it. People do not do well unless they are motivated to get along with at least a few other people. The age-adjusted mortality risk of social isolation is comparable to cigarette smoking; both cardiovascular and immune responses are damaged by isolation (House, Landis, & Umberson, 1988). People respond poorly to being ostracized, feeling bad, reporting less control, and losing a sense of belonging (Williams, Cheung, & Choi, 2000). The neural signature of social pain mimics the neural signature of physical pain in that both activate the anterior cingulate cortex (Eisenberger et al., 2003), which more generally responds to disruptions and inconsistencies

TABLE 2.2. Motivations That Influence Modes of Social Cognition

Motive	Goal
Belonging	Being accepted by other people, one's group
Understanding	Socially shared cognition; belief that one's views correspond to those of one's group
Controlling	Influencing one's own outcomes that depend on other people
Enhancing self	Viewing self positively or at least sympathetically
Trusting ingroup	Viewing people, at least in one's own group, positively

(Botvinick et al., 2004). Clearly, the need to belong is central to people's health and well-being (Baumeister & Leary, 1995; Leary, 1990).

Not surprisingly then, people's social cognition is shaped by their motives to be accepted by other people. This is most evident in the belonging-related motives of socially shared understanding and social control (covered next), but belonging by itself also changes how and what people think. First, the focus of people's thoughts is importantly social. As noted in discussing consciousness, people spend a lot of time thinking about current concerns in relationships, and as Chapter 1 noted, people's resting state may be social thought.

People's need to belong can motivate relatively automatic modes of impression formation designed to ease the social interaction; people automatically categorize stimuli as related to "us" and "them," for instance (Perdue, Dovidio, Gurtman, & Tyler, 1990). More generally, people readily see themselves as part of a group (e.g., Tajfel, 1981; Turner, 1985), automatically attuned to its beliefs, norms, and roles. This feeling of belonging affects people's interpretation of social stimuli. In a classic study, students from Princeton and Dartmouth watched a football game between their schools and rated the number of infractions; school membership biased how many infractions students saw for their own versus the other team (Hastorf & Cantril, 1954). Belonging probably operated fairly automatically in this case. Belonging is also illustrated by the fact that people conform to the majority in relatively automatic ways (Wood, 2000).

The overall need to belong provides an orienting framework for studying social cognition in that belonging underlies more specific cognitive motives, including social understanding and social control.

Understanding

The social motive that most obviously drives social cognition is understanding, the need for socially shared cognition. People think about other people in order to interact with them; one of the founders of American psychology, William James, noted that "my thinking is first and last and always for my doing" (1890/1983, p. 960), and much of people's thinking and doing is social (S. T. Fiske, 1992, 1993). Socially shared understanding is the need to believe that one's views correspond to those of one's group (Turner, 1991, ch. 10). Understanding is the dominant motive driving most social cognition.

Automaticity often serves socially shared understanding well enough, as we have seen. However, people are sometimes socially motivated to be especially accurate or accountable to others (e.g., respectively, Fiske & Neuberg, 1990; Tetlock, 1992). Sometimes, also, people's level of information falls below acceptable levels (Kelley, 1972a), and this leads them to gather information. Sometimes, too, people arrive in a new place (e.g., the first week of college) or a new culture (due to travel or immigration), and they cannot assume their perceptions fit the general outlook (Guinote, 2001). When the necessity of socially shared understanding is uppermost, people switch to relatively deliberate processes, seeking and using a lot of information until their judgments become automated again. Socially shared understanding seeks to make the world more predictable, and when this need falls short, people deliberately engage in information seeking and analysis until understanding is restored.

Controlling

In social relationships people are interdependent; that is, their outcomes depend on each other (Thibaut & Kelley, 1959). When another person controls significant desired resources, people attend carefully to that person in an attempt to influence the contingencies between actions (what they do) and outcomes (what they get) (S. T. Fiske & Neuberg, 1990). Being outcome dependent often shifts people to more controlled, deliberate processes in an effort to feel in control. Control needs also appear in nonsocial circumstances, such as when one receives arbitrary feedback on one's performance from a machine, and this impaired sense of control carries over to social circumstances in which people seek additional information about other people (Pittman, 1998). In general, heightened control needs make people deliberately seek additional information to avoid error and feel effective. Threatened control can increase the apparent costs of being wrong, so people switch to deliberate modes as flexible motivated tacticians.

Control threats do sometimes occur in circumstances of scarce resources (time pressure, mental fatigue), in which case pressures for a decision, any decision, will increase. Pressures for urgency (quick decisions) and permanence (lasting decisions) come from a variety of situational factors (Kruglanski & Webster, 1996) and individual differences (Neuberg & Newsom, 1993). All of these processes probably operate automatically to a greater degree than the information-seeking processes cued by a special need to feel accurate. Note that most of the preceding remarks about thoughtful processing concern threatened control in which the motive becomes most evident. In circumstances of satisfied control, decisive thinking is the norm.

This motive for controlling and the previous one for understanding overlap somewhat but differ in that people want to predict (understand) even when they cannot influence (control) because it aids in adjustment even if they can only anticipate but not change an outcome. Both understanding and controlling motives appear relatively cognitive and information oriented. The next two motives are more affective and feelings oriented but also are traceable to the core social motive of belonging.

Enhancing Self

People's tendency to see themselves in a positive light is well documented, particularly in American and European settings (Chapter 5). Both automatic and controlled processes operate here, but people's immediate, automatic first reactions favor positive self-esteem. For example, people's relatively automatic reactions favor positive feedback (Swann, Hixon, Stein-Seroussi, & Gilbert, 1990). On subsequent reflection (more controlled), however, people prefer feedback that fits their self view, even if it is negative.

More generally, much social cognition automatically orients toward viewing the self positively. In particular, people have enhanced senses of self: overly optimistic for the future, exaggerated sense of personal control, and more positive self-concept than is perhaps realistic. Nevertheless, these illusions are adaptive, benefiting both mental and physical health (Taylor, Kemeny, Reed, Bower, & Gruenewald, 2000; Taylor, Lerner, Sherman, Sage, & McDowell, 2003a, 2003b). Moderately high self views encourage people to participate in social life, so (within reasonable bounds) self-enhancement helps people to adapt to their groups. Thus the self-enhancement motive shapes social cognition (see Chapter 5).

Trusting Ingroup

Social cognition more generally operates under a clear and persistent positivity bias for most social stimuli, all else being equal (Matlin & Stang, 1978; Rothbart & Park, 1986; Sears, 1983). That is, people essentially expect good things from other people (not just themselves). For example, people routinely use only the top half of rating scales, only rarely rating other people below the numerical midpoint. Thus the psychological midpoint is positive for both expectations and reactions, and negativity stands out (S. T. Fiske, 1980). When negative events do occur, people mobilize rapidly (and automatically), seeking to minimize the damage (often a more controlled response) and returning to a positive baseline (S. E. Taylor, 1991). Negativity jumps out incredibly early, within milliseconds (Ito, Larsen, Smith, & Cacioppo, 1998), precisely because it stands out against a relatively positive baseline (Skowronski & Carlston, 1989).

You may doubt this motive because trust shows individual differences, as do all these social motives. People's intention to trust others and people's receipt of trusting behavior both correlate with the neuroactive hormone oxytocin (Zak, Kurzban, & Matzner, 2005). Oxytocin, particularly active in women, is implicated in caretaking and befriending, especially under threat (S. E. Taylor, 2006). Trusting ingroup others links to the pervasive positivity bias observed throughout social cognition. This baseline positivity extends mainly to people's own group members; in this sense, people trust ingroup others to do and be good.

Conclusion

Social cognition is animated by a variety of social motives traceable to belonging, including understanding, controlling, enhancing self, and trusting others. This framework fits the history of motivations in psychology (S. T. Fiske, in press) as well as current work in social psychology generally (S. T. Fiske, 2004) and social cognition in particular (S. T. Fiske, 2002). Although this framework originates with one of the authors (and other frameworks are possible), it does serve to highlight some of the motives that determine when and how people operate in more automatic or more controlled modes.

The distinction between relatively automatic and controlled processes is well established as a social cognitive principle. The motivated tactician metaphor captures the flexible use of different modes. What are the directions for future research? Social neuroscience, at one end of the spectrum, surely will matter increasingly. The social neuroscience of automaticity and control is in its infancy (Lieberman, 2007). Earlier, we noted areas implicated in automatic processing (see Figure 2.1): Controlled processing of the kinds just described implicate large portions of the prefrontal cortex toward the front (lateral PFC, medial PFC) and upper back (lateral and medial parietal cortex). The point here is that the spectrum is reflected in neural patterns just now emerging; we note this social neuroscience in later chapters where specifically relevant as it is likely one wave of the future. At the other end of the spectrum, cultural variations in the core motives and their effects on social cognition also will matter increasingly.

MODELS OF BOTH AUTOMATIC
AND CONTROLLED PROCESSES

Throughout social cognition in all its varieties, people make sense of themselves and each other in more and less thoughtful ways, depending on the circumstances. *When* they do *what*—that is, the circumstances that guide more automatic or more controlled processing—concerns dozens of theories in social cognition (Chaiken & Trope, 1999). We sample some here, from person perception to attribution, to attitudes, and more.

Examples in Person Perception

Some models focus on when people perceive other people in more and less automatic ways. One way of conceptualizing people's use of automatic expectancies versus more deliberate attention to individuals is to view the two modes as branching off into different strategies as the situation demands. According to this "dual-process" perspective (M. B. Brewer, 1988; M. M. Brewer & Harasty Feinstein, 1999), people initially identify a person automatically, and they stop there if the person is not relevant to their goals. Identifying the gas station attendant as a youngish man in the right uniform illustrates this relatively automatic process.

If the person is relevant, and if the perceiver is sufficiently involved, people personalize the other using individually tailored concepts in a memory network. If not sufficiently involved, perceivers first categorize using images (holistic, nonverbal patterns) that fit the perceived person, unless the category fit is poor. In that case, they individuate, using subtypes (more specific categories such as local versus highway attendant) or exemplars (familiar examples such as the guy at one's neighborhood station). Chapter 4 details these distinct forms of mental representation, but the point here is that one way to view dual-mode models is as a series of choice points and branching processes that channel people into various relatively automatic and controlled forms of thinking about others.

An alternative viewpoint views impression formation not as a series of branches into distinct types of processing but as an evolving continuum. In this view, people engage in a continuum of processes ranging from the most automatic, category-based processes (relying, for example, on age, sex, race) to the most deliberate, piecemeal impression formation processes (relying on the available data about each individual). Along this "continuum of impression formation," one can specify both information configurations and motivations that move people from one end of the continuum to another (e.g., S. T. Fiske et al., 1987; for reviews, see S. T. Fiske & Neuberg, 1990; S. T. Fiske, Lin, & Neuberg, 1999).

People start at the automatic end and may (or may not) proceed in stages along the continuum. In this view, they initially categorize each other automatically on the basis of noticeable physical cues and verbal labels. For example, the person approaching on the sidewalk is a White, college-aged woman. People automatically use these initial categories, especially when that is all they have. If sufficiently motivated to attend to the other person, people attempt to confirm these initial categories in a slightly more deliberate fashion. On closer inspection, her face confirms her apparent age. Category confirmation is generally successful if the data fit well enough.

If category confirmation fails (e.g., the data contradict the category, as when the woman has a moustache), people recategorize. They generate new, better-fitting categories ("she" is a feminine "he"), subcategories (she is wearing stage makeup and a tie), exemplars (like your cousin, she has facial hair that shows in daylight), or self-reference (well, maybe you yourself are androgynous). Finally, when it is not easy to recategorize, people proceed piecemeal, attribute by attribute, through the data. As you sit across from her on the subway, you try to figure her out by covert but closer inspection. As the continuum model indicates, people are not fools. We often rely on automatic processes when they are good enough, but we also know when to quit and move to more controlled processes.

There are some important differences between dual-process and continuum models approaches. For example, the dual-process model proposes distinct types of cognitive representations (images, categories, exemplars) in distinct branches of impression formation. In contrast, the continuum model posits stable kinds of information across its evolving stages, with the prior stage carrying over to the subsequent one. In addition, the dual-process model posits specific rules for passing along each processing branch, whereas the continuum model proposes constant rules; namely, that ease of categorization depends on information and motivation. There are other differences (Bodenhausen, Macrae, & Sherman, 1999; M. B. Brewer, 1988; S. T. Fiske, 1988), but both approaches integrate relatively automatic and relatively controlled processes within plausible unified frameworks.

Given current knowledge, moving between automatic and controlled impression formation could be cued by relatively automatic neural systems that respond to external features, cuing emotional vigilance (e.g., amygdala, basal ganglia), familiar others (the lateral temporal cortex's temporal pole, TP), and biological movement (the lateral temporal cortex's superior temporal sulcus, STS). Discrepancies register on the anterior cingulate cortex (ACC), thereby engaging more controlled processing about the other as a human being with mental states (medial prefrontal cortex, mPFC) and intentions (Amodio & Frith, 2006; Botvinick et al., 2004; Lieberman, 2007). As social neuroscience research develops, these patterns will doubtless clarify with new data.

Examples in Attribution

People engage in a variety of more and less automatic forms of causal reasoning (see Chapter 6). For example, suppose people observe a person chewing her fingernails, speaking hesitantly, and avoiding eye contact; they might decide this is a nervous person, or they might decide that the person is describing the most embarrassing moment of a lifetime on national television. In one integration model (Trope, 1986; Trope & Gaunt, 1999), people first identify behavior, aided by context (nail-biting could indicate nerves or frustration, but on national TV it's probably nerves). Because much behavior is ambiguous, identification is a necessary first step. Next people explain the nervous behavior, now subtracting the situation (everyone's nervous on national television) and the person's disposition (maybe not such an anxious type). The first process, identification, is relatively automatic and effortless, whereas the second, explanation, is more deliberate and controlled.

A related model splits the first process into categorization of behavior and its characterization in dispositional terms, both automatic, followed by a controlled correction for situational factors if the perceiver has the capacity and the motivation (Gilbert, 1991; Gilbert, Pelham, & Krull, 1988). The relative automaticity and control in these processes are illustrated by studies in which participants have to remember a phone number for the experimenter (a subtle imposition of cognitive load) while simultaneously making a causal attribution about another person. Cognitive load does not interfere with the initial, relatively automatic dispositional inference (categorization and characterization), but it does interfere with the subsequent controlled correction for situational pressures.

A third model contrasts spontaneous trait inferences, guided by concepts that come easily to mind, linked to the person, whether appropriate or not, with more intentional, goal-driven processes (Uleman, 1999; Winter & Uleman, 1984). Again, these models have important differences (Gilbert, 1998), but all three contrast relatively automatic and controlled causal attributions for behavior. We will return to them in a closer examination of causal attributions in Chapter 6.

Examples in Attitudes

Some of the best-known two-mode models occur in the realm of attitudes—people's evaluations of objects in their world. The elaboration likelihood model (Petty & Cacioppo, 1981; Petty & Wegener, 1999) describes two routes to persuasion: peripheral (more automatic and superficial) and central (more deliberate and controlled). Low-effort processes use peripheral cues, such as noting that the message has a lot of arguments or comes from an ingroup source (so it must be right), and people perhaps read this message only superficially. In a high-effort process people carefully scrutinize all the arguments and elaborate on them; that is, they add some kind of personal reaction, pro or con. Most variables can serve as both peripheral cues or information for more central processing, depending on circumstances.

In a related vein, the heuristic-systematic model (Chaiken, 1980; Chen & Chaiken, 1999) contrasts the systematic mode (relatively analytic and comprehensive) with the heuristic mode (previously stored rules of thumb). The two modes can operate in parallel, adding to each other's impact, although the heuristic one is likely to be faster. Perceivers stop when their confidence is sufficient for present purposes, so the balance of the two modes' influence depends on when people make a decision.

Not only persuasion processes but also processes linking attitudes to behavior can come in more spontaneous, rapid ways (Fazio, Powell, & Herr, 1983; Fazio & Towles-Schwen, 1999) or in more deliberate, cost-benefit ways (Ajzen & Fishbein, 1980; Ajzen & Sexton, 1999). These models are detailed in Chapters 10 and 15, but for now we focus on their integration of relatively automatic and controlled modes in the processing of persuasive communications.

Other Areas: Self, Prejudice, Inference

In the domain of thinking about the self (Chapter 5), people sometimes react rapidly, on the basis of self-schemas (automatic self-concepts), and at other times review self-relevant evidence more carefully (Markus, 1977). And we saw earlier that people sometimes react immediately and positively to positive feedback but may react more deliberately to its consistency (Swann et al., 1990).

In thinking about outsiders, too, people swing between two extremes: relatively automatic, culturally conditioned prejudices and more controlled, personally endorsed viewpoints (Chapters 11–12; Devine, 1989; Devine & Monteith, 1999; Dovidio & Gaertner, 1986; Greenwald et al., 2002).

Indeed, in every kind of inference a kind of System 1 intuition versus System 2 reasoning contrast may be drawn (Epstein, 1990a; Kahneman, 2003; Smith & DeCoster, 2000). The intuitive side is holistic, rapid, effortless, parallel, affective, associative, crude, and slow-learning. The rational reasoning side is analytic, slow, effortful, serial, neutral, logical, differentiated, and flexible. The intuitive, associative mode relies on the slow-learning but rapidly responding form of memory, which concentrates on consistencies; whereas the rational, fast-binding, rule-based system acquires detailed new memories quickly, focusing on novel and inconsistent cues for subsequent consideration in deliberate processes. The two-system contrast suggests that each is suited to distinct forms of learning and reacting (see Table 2.3 for a summary). This powerful theme drives much social cognition work as psychological scientists of every stripe document the ways people make sense of their social worlds.

The Dissent: Single-Mode Alternatives

Lest you think this understanding of social cognition represents an uncontested dual-mode supremacy, some alternatives do appear. A unimode model builds on a lay epistemic theory of ordinary knowledge (Kruglanski, 1980; Kruglanski, Thompson, & Spiegel, 1999). This proposes that people's subjective understanding

TABLE 2.3. Characteristics of Automatic Versus Controlled Processing

Automatic	Controlled
intuitive	rational
categorical	individuated
holistic	analytic
rapid	slow
effortless	effortful
parallel	serial
affective	neutral
associative	logical
crude	differentiated
reflexive	reflective
slow-learning	fast-learning
rigid	flexible
consistency	novelty

essentially tests their everyday hypotheses. Because all types of lay hypothesis-testing processes draw on evidence, capability, and motivation, in this view various processes are more similar than different. All these processes theoretically follow "if-then" rules of relevance according to the unimode approach. Regardless of whether the evidence presented under the "if" condition is simple or complex, certain reactions follow from it, assuming the evidence is relevant. That is, the overarching if-then structure is similar regardless of domain (if fatigued, drink coffee; if in love, get married). Capability and motivation operate in a similar manner, in this view, regardless of mode.

Another single-mode alternative argues that impression formation processes all operate in parallel, blending many attributes that are simultaneously activated (Kunda, 1999; Kunda & Thagard, 1996). It treats all types of information as equivalent, not privileging certain types of information (e.g., race, gender) over others (e.g., personality traits). In this view, a person's race, gender, and age are weighted equivalently to the person's personality, abilities, and preferences. This blending operates by combining and resolving every cue simultaneously, in parallel. Impressions develop from all sources of information at once, combining them into a coherent impression immediately and continuously constrained to be internally consistent. This model differs from dual-process models primarily in cases of unmotivated processing in which most such models assume superficial use of information, relying on only a few cues. In motivated processing, both this model and the dual-process models assume people will use more information.

These single-mode models provide an important counterpoint, but as often occurs in debates, they tend to caricature the opposition. Indeed, all dual-mode theorists take pains to point out that their processes represent endpoints of a continuum and that most processes take place somewhere in between.

Summary

This chapter previews one of the main themes in social cognition over the past 25 years, in particular, but anticipated even earlier: People's thought processes can operate in relatively automatic or relatively controlled manners, or at locations between the two. The most automatic processes occur without effort, awareness, control, intent, or capacity use. Subliminal, preconscious processing of social cues (faces, concepts) affects cognitive associations, affective reactions, and behavior. Conscious priming of (exposure to) concepts can trigger unconscious, automatic processes. Some cues may be chronically accessible to some people, but situations also prime particular concepts and even motives.

People control some types of automatic processing by deliberately instigating a goal, which then triggers automatic processes. Habits serve as one example. People also consciously attend to certain actions, plan for them, and execute them. However, people do tend to overestimate the extent to which their thoughts control their actions, or even the extent to which they can control their thoughts. Consciousness serves multiple functions, both internally and externally driven, often taken up by unfinished business and social concerns.

A variety of motivations determines whether people engage in more or less automatic and controlled processes. Each motive can push toward either automaticity or control, depending on circumstances. Belonging with other people powerfully motivates people to go along with others and look to others. Socially shared understanding motivates much of social cognition, both relying on consensus and seeking information in the service of prediction. Controlling the contingencies between what one does and what happens to oneself is important to well-being. On the affective side, people enhance the self and optimistically trust ingroup others. The interplay of these motives and available information determines when people rely on well-worn, relatively automatic processes and when on more deliberate, controlled processes.

Examples of dual-processing models appear in person perception, attribution, attitudes, self, inference, and prejudice, to name a few. They are countered by single-mode alternatives that argue for similar processes, regardless of information and motivation. Social cognition researchers continue to debate these points, as you shall see.

Attention and Encoding

A friend of ours was sitting on a bench in a crowded shopping mall when he heard running footsteps behind him. Turning, he saw two Black men being pursued by a White security guard. The first runner was past him in a flash, but he leapt up in time to tackle the second runner, overpowering him. From the ground, the panting Black man angrily announced that he was the store owner. Meanwhile, the thief had escaped. Our friend, who is White and devotes his life to helping the oppressed, was mortified.

For our purposes, this case of mistaken identity illustrates the sometimes tragic consequences of instantaneous social encoding based on interpretations. People rapidly take in other people as stimuli and react to them, so encoding determines much of social interaction as people react immediately in the course of their daily encounters. But what do we notice in the first place?

As artist Frank Stella put it, "what you see is what you see." Attention and encoding are the first steps in mental representation. Before any internal information management can occur, the stimuli outside the person have to be represented in the mind. The name for this general process is *encoding*. Encoding transforms a perceived external stimulus into an internal representation. The encoding process involves considerable cognitive work, which nevertheless can be accomplished with relatively little effort. The instant a stimulus registers on the senses, the process of interpretation begins. Immediately, some details are lost, others altered, and still others may be misperceived. Inferences are stored in memory along with the raw data and may become indistinguishable from them.

Encoding breaks down into several stages useful to social cognition (e.g., Bargh, 1984; Burnstein & Schul, 1982). Most theorists agree that we perform some kind of unconscious, "preattentive analysis" of environmental stimuli, combining features into the objects and events we notice consciously. Once noticed, a stimulus may come into conscious "focal attention" to be identified and categorized. As "comprehension" occurs, the stimulus is given semantic meaning. Finally, "elaborative reasoning" links the particular stimulus to other knowledge, allowing for complex inferences.

Attention is an integral part of encoding because attention often focuses on what is currently being encoded. If you are thinking about something external, it is at least temporarily represented in your mind. However, attention is not limited to the encoding of external stimuli; whatever occupies consciousness is defined as the focus of attention, as noted in Chapter 2.

Attention can also be occupied by information retrieved from memory. If you are thinking about something you remember, that memory is the focus of your attention. Attention is also occupied by the current contents of the mind (see Chapter 4 discussion of active, working, and short-term memory). People attend to the internal or external stimuli that are in conscious focal awareness.

Whether attention is directed outward toward encoding external objects or inward toward memory, attention is usually seen as having two components: direction (selectivity) and intensity (effort). When you read this book, you are presumably focusing on it rather than on the radio, the conversation in the hall, the itch on your leg, or your love life. Even given your selective focus on this book, you can allocate more or less intense mental effort to it. Attention is the amount of selective cognitive work you do (Kahneman, 1973; Norman, 1976; Posner, 1982).

When people are encoding external stimuli, they do not attend evenly to all aspects of their environment. They watch some things closely and ignore others altogether. Attention affects what enters thought and memory, but conscious attention is not necessary for encoding into memory. Cognitive psychologists distinguished between early and late selective attention (Broadbent, 1958, 1982; Deutsch & Deutsch, 1963); that is, the amount of rudimentary perceptual processing that occurs outside of focused attention. Cognitive neuroscience indicates that even unattended stimuli register on the brain (Kanwisher & Wojciulik, 2000), suggesting that selection for conscious attention occurs later. Moreover, with regard to social cognition, the brain is exquisitely attuned to emphatically social stimuli—namely, faces.

This chapter examines what captures attention in social settings because that affects everything that follows in social interactions. We examine *salience*, the extent to which particular stimuli stand out relative to others in their environment, and *vividness*, which constitutes the inherent attention-getting features of a stimulus regardless of environment. In Chapter 2, we introduced accessibility, which describes how people's attention is primed for categories (or particular interpretations of stimuli) that fit what they have thought about recently or frequently. In this chapter we examine how that most social of stimuli, the face, affects attention.

SALIENCE: A PROPERTY OF STIMULI IN CONTEXT

What captures our attention? Salience, the seemingly trivial factor of attracting attention, although logically irrelevant to most social judgment, can have important effects. Think back to the last time you were the only one of your "kind" in a room full of other people. The striking experience of being a salient social stimulus is the same. One *feels* conspicuous, that all eyes have a single target, and that one's every move is overinterpreted. As a result, one may feel anxious and concerned about how the interaction is going (Ickes, 1984). Moreover, the mere belief that one is a solo can impair one's ability to take in and remember what people say (Lord & Saenz, 1985; Lord, Saenz, & Godfrey, 1987; Saenz & Lord, 1989) and impair one's performance (Sekaquaptewa & Thompson, 2003). Being a solo more generally depletes a person's ability to self-regulate effectively; symptoms include talking too much, disclosing too much or too little, or being arrogant (Vohs, Baumeister, & Ciarocco, 2005). Research on salience supports the uncomfortable experience of the solo as being a center of attention, as looming larger than life, and as the recipient of extreme reactions (S. E. Taylor, 1981a).

Antecedents of Social Salience

The causes of social salience all depend on the immediate or larger context (McArthur, 1981; S. E. Taylor & Fiske, 1978). Solo status results from immediate perceptual and social novelty: having a novel gender, race, and other visual distinction, such as the only red shirt in a room full of blue ones (e.g., Crocker & McGraw, 1984; Heilman, 1980; Higgins & King, 1981, Study 1; McArthur & Post, 1977; Nesdale, Dharmalingam, & Kerr, 1987; Spangler, Gordon, & Pipkin, 1978).

Another form of salience draws on perceptual features of the stimulus that make it figural in the immediate context. Gestalt psychology predicts that stimuli will be salient if they are bright, complex, changing, moving, or otherwise stand out from their drab background (McArthur & Post, 1977), and they do attract longer gazes (McArthur & Ginsberg, 1981). People also notice the addition of a person to a group more than the removal of the person; addition is more salient than subtraction. Most of us fail to recognize that our absence from the gathering will not be as salient as our presence (Savitsky, Gilovich, Berger, & Medvec, 2003).

In the larger social context, people attend to expectancy-inconsistent information. People are salient if they contradict prior knowledge about them as individuals, as social category members, or as people in general (E. E. Jones & McGillis, 1976). Physically disabled people attract attention in part because they are novel compared to people in general (Langer, Taylor, Fiske, & Chanowitz, 1976).

The latter principle of salience, based on expectations about people in general, has been extended in two ways (S. T. Fiske, 1980). First, extreme social stimuli—being unusual—are more salient than moderate stimuli. For example, people stare at extremely positive social stimuli, such as movie stars, and at extremely negative stimuli, such as traffic accidents. Second, most people expect mildly positive inputs: people are optimistic about life outcomes (Parducci, 1968) and rate other individuals positively (Nilsson & Ekehammar, 1987; Sears, 1983; Sears & Whitney, 1973). Hence, negative social stimuli are more salient than positive ones because they are relatively unexpected.[1] Negative events capture preattentive processing (Pratto & John, 1991). What's more, negative events demand immediate coping in order for the individual to return to normal (S. E. Taylor, 1991).

---

[1]There are some exceptions as well as other explanations for the typically higher weight of negative information in impressions of likability; see Skowronski and Carlston, 1989, for a review.

Salience also depends partly on perceiver goals. People attend to significant others, those on whom their outcomes depend. If two people are talking and one is your new boss, a prospective date, or a new teammate, you will watch that person more closely (Berscheid, Graziano, Monson, & Dermer, 1976; Erber & Fiske, 1984; Neuberg & Fiske, 1987; Ruscher & Fiske, 1990; S. E. Taylor, 1975).

Salience can hinge on mere physical position, such as seating position in a group; the person directly opposite you should be especially salient because that person dominates your visual field (S. E. Taylor & Fiske, 1975). People expect that those who sit in the professor's line of sight—in the middle of many people—will be leaders (Raghubir & Valenzuela, 2006). Thus, to have maximum impact on a meeting, sit at the head or foot of a long table, or sit in the middle, especially the front, of class; to fade into the background, sit on the sidelines.

In a videotape, increasing or decreasing a person's time on camera has similar effects (Eisen & McArthur, 1979; Storms & Nisbett, 1970), even in a videotaped confession (Lassiter, 2002). Sheer visual exposure even holds for political issues: The amount of time an issue is aired on the evening news affects how much weight people give it in subsequent decisions (Iyengar & Kinder, 1987).

A person can be salient relative to an immediate context, relative to the perceiver's prior knowledge or expectations, or relative to other attentional tasks (Table 3.1). Note that the key word common to all these ways of creating salience is *relative:* stimulus novelty occurs relative to an immediate or broader context, a stimulus is figural relative to other stimuli present, and perceiver perspective is created relative to context. The common element in all these forms of salience is that a stimulus is distinctive in relation to other factors in the perceiver's context.

Consequences of Social Salience

Regardless of the way salience is created, its effects are robust and wide ranging (McArthur, 1981; S. E. Taylor & Fiske, 1978). As suggested by the experience of the solo, salience makes a stimulus larger than life in various judgments.

TABLE 3.1. The Causes of Social Salience

A person can be salient relative to the perceiver's

Immediate context

   By being novel (solo person of that race, sex, hair color, shirt color)

   By being figural (bright, complex, moving)

Prior knowledge or expectations

   By being unusual for that person (e.g., behaving in unexpected ways)

   By being unusual for that person's social category (e.g., behaving in out-of-role ways)

   By being unusual for people in general (e.g., behaving negatively or extremely)

Other attentional tasks

   By being goal relevant (e.g., being a boss, a date)

   By dominating the visual field (e.g., sitting at the head of the table, being on camera more than others)

   By the perceiver being instructed to observe the person

Prominence shows up most in perceptions of causality. Salient people are seen as especially influential in a given group.

This principle extends to causal analyses of the person's own behavior. Perceptually salient behavior is seen as particularly indicative of the person's underlying disposition and as less under the control of the situation. In both cases, causal attributions follow the focus of attention. Videotaped confessions focused on the suspect make the behavior seem more voluntary and, consequently, the person seems more guilty (Lassiter, 2002).[2]

Salience also exaggerates evaluations in whichever direction they initially tend. If a person is unpleasant, being a solo will cause disproportionate condemnation; similarly, a pleasant solo is exaggeratedly praised (S. E. Taylor, Fiske, Close, Anderson, & Ruderman, 1977). Evaluations can be nudged in one direction or another by prior expectations as well. For example, if a defendant in criminal proceedings is viewed negatively, salience should cause the person to be evaluated especially negatively. On the other hand, if the same person is viewed as a person (a more positive expectation), salience causes an especially positive evaluation (Eisen & McArthur, 1979; cf. McArthur & Solomon, 1978). Salience cuts both ways in evaluations.

If salient stimuli elicit attention, perceived prominence, and extreme evaluations, it would stand to reason that they also should enhance memory. Unfortunately, the data are strikingly uneven. Within social cognition research on salience, the main measure of memory has been people's free recall: Sometimes recall is enhanced and sometimes not (McArthur, 1981; S. E. Taylor & Fiske, 1978).

Although salience does not reliably enhance the quantity of recall, it does increase the organization and consistency of impressions in several ways. The more attention one pays to another person, the more coherent the impression becomes. Attention structures impressions, emphasizing features that fit and adjusting those that do not. For example, the solo student at a faculty meeting is likely to be seen as typical of the student category and as presenting the "students' perspective," whether or not the person truly represents most peers (S. E. Taylor, 1981a). The effects of salience on stereotyping mean that salience combines with prior knowledge to produce polarized evaluations (cf. Nesdale et al., 1987). Consequently, a solo man is perceived to be prominent and therefore a good leader, but a solo woman in an all-male group is perceived to be an intruder and is caused to feel like one (Crocker & McGraw, 1984). Attention (mere thought) brings into line the evaluative components of an impression, which then becomes more extreme, at least under certain conditions (Chaiken & Yates, 1985; Millar & Tesser, 1986b; Tesser, 1978).

We have seen that salience and attention have a variety of effects on judgments. Attention exaggerates evaluations and causal prominence in whatever direction they initially tend. Attention sometimes increases recall and can encourage stereotypic interpretations. How robust and important are these

---

[2]Because people generally see other people as causal agents (Heider, 1958; E. E. Jones & Nisbett, 1972; L. Ross, 1977), attention normally exaggerates this tendency (S. T. Fiske, Kenny, & Taylor, 1982). However, if a person's passivity is emphasized, attention can exaggerate perceptions of susceptibility to influence as well (Strack, Erber, & Wicklund, 1982). Salience exaggerates causal judgments in the direction implied by prior knowledge.

effects of temporary salience on important social judgments? Efforts to increase importance and to enrich stimulus materials, in fact, enhance salience effects (Eisen & McArthur, 1979; McArthur, 1981; McArthur & Solomon, 1978; Strack, Erber, & Wicklund, 1982; S. E. Taylor, Crocker, Fiske, Sprinzen, & Winkler, 1979), and comparable salience effects occur in real-world organizations (Kanter, 1977; Wolman & Frank, 1975) and even television shows (Raghubir & Valenzuela, 2006).

If salience effects have such impact on significant decisions, it becomes especially important to know how controllable salience effects are. Despite early speculations that salience effects might be automatic (S. E. Taylor & Fiske, 1978), they apparently do not qualify as fully automatic because people sometimes can control them. That is, salience effects can be qualified by some forms of involvement, such as self-interest (Borgida & Howard-Pitney, 1983), although not simply by making the task more important (S. E. Taylor et al., 1979). And salience effects may be qualified by some instructions, such as expecting to "describe each member of the stimulus group" (Oakes & Turner, 1986), which would enhance a person-by-person accuracy goal.

A Closer Look at Salience: What Mediates Its Effects?

Given the range of perceptions and behaviors guided by the seemingly trivial factor of what catches the eye (or ear), why should attention have such pervasive effects on social judgment? Psychologists have proposed several processes to connect differential attention and differential judgments; some of these candidates for mediation (i.e., connection) have been debunked and some supported. Sheer quantity of recall and channel-specific recall do not seem to account for the effects of salience on attributions (quantity: S. T. Fiske, Kenny, & Taylor, 1982, S. E. Taylor & Fiske, 1975; but see Harvey, Yarkin, Lightner, & Town, 1980; E. R. Smith & Miller, 1979; channel-specific: S. T. Fiske et al., 1982; McArthur & Ginsberg, 1981; Robinson & McArthur, 1982; S. E. Taylor et al., 1979, Study 1). The ease or accessibility of recall is one plausible mediator (Pryor & Kriss, 1977; Rholes & Pryor, 1982; see also Higgins & King, 1981). In addition, causally relevant recall, especially memory for dominant behavior and appearance, seems to be enhanced by attention and, in turn, leads to exaggerated attributions. Accordingly, the judgment is in effect being made at encoding, on the basis of information that is doubly salient—salient because the person is salient and salient because the dominant behavior itself is salient (S. T. Fiske et al., 1982).

Conclusion

Salience makes a stimulus stand out relative to other stimuli in that context. Salient stimuli may be novel, figural, expectancy-consistent, extreme, negative, rare, physically prominent, or long in duration. Salience exaggerates attention, perceived prominence, evaluations, and the coherence but not the sheer amount of memory. Salience effects show goal-dependent automaticity in that they typically occur outside awareness but can moderate according to perceiver goals. Salience effects may be mediated by causally relevant recall or its accessibility.

VIVIDNESS: AN INHERENT PROPERTY OF STIMULI

Salience has well-established effects, so its cousin, vividness, would seem obvious. However, whereas salience is determined by the relation of an object to its context, vividness is inherent in a stimulus itself. For example, a plane crash is more salient during peacetime than in the context of wartime carnage. Further, by this logic, a plane crash would be inherently more vivid than a normal flight; a detailed description of a particular accident would be more vivid than the statistics about it; and an accident in your local airport would be more vivid than an accident elsewhere. A stimulus is defined as vivid to the extent that it is "(a) emotionally interesting, (b) concrete and imagery-provoking, and (c) proximate in a sensory, temporal or spatial way" (Nisbett & Ross, 1980, p. 45). Do vivid stimuli have effects similar to those of salient stimuli? Although theory and common sense would suggest that vivid stimuli are especially impactful, research suggests that they are not.

The Case for Vividness Effects

Vividness effects seem commonplace in daily life. Consider two versions of the same sponsor-a-child advertisement, one with a poignant photo and case study, the other with dry statistics. In both cases your conscience gives the same counsel, but the first ad seems more likely to attract your attention initially, to change your attitudes, and to elicit the desired behavior. All this is obvious, and as the idea person in an ad agency, you could have thought up the vivid ad yourself.

Psychological theorists have postulated precisely such vividness effects on several conceptual grounds. Vivid information is predicted to be more persuasive than pallid information of equal or greater validity, first, because vivid information should come to mind more easily (Nisbett & Ross, 1980; Tversky & Kahneman, 1973). Second, vivid information by definition easily provokes internal visual representations, which are especially memorable. Third, vivid information seems to have more emotional impact on the perceiver, which would enhance its impact on judgments. In short, the impact of vivid information on human judgment, especially persuasion, would seem to be self-evident.

Unfortunately, scant empirical evidence supports vividness effects (S. E. Taylor & Thompson, 1982). According to the research, messages that are written in concrete and colorful language are no more likely to change attitudes than are abstract and dry messages. Research shows that messages accompanied by photographs usually have no greater appeal. Similarly, videotaped messages only sometimes have enhanced impact. And finally, direct experience, which would seem the ultimate in vividness, does not necessarily change attitudes more effectively than does secondhand contact.[3] In sum, vividness does not work well empirically, although intuitively it seems as if it should.

The major exception to this pattern of negative results is that individual case histories persuade more effectively than do group statistics. The heartrending story carries more impact than worldwide hunger statistics. For example,

---

[3]Saying that direct experience may not change attitudes is not the same as denying that direct experience may affect the *acquisition* of attitudes or the impact of attitudes on *behavior;* it clearly does both (see Chapters 10 and 15).

an individually identified wrongdoer elicits more anger and therefore more punishment than an otherwise similar but unidentifiable wrongdoer (Small & Lowenstein, 2005). However, this result may not speak to the vividness effect, in part because it concerns identifiability, not vividness per se.

What's more, other vividness research—which manipulates concrete (versus dull) language, photographs (versus none), and videotapes (versus transcripts)—holds most other information constant. However, holding information constant is more problematic when contrasting case history and statistical information. They differ in far too many ways to assume that it is only differences in vividness that cause any differences in their persuasive impact. For example, a case history communicates one particular scenario by which the existing facts could occur: a starving child might survive by selling firewood. Statistics communicate a different sort of information, such as life expectancy averaged over many instances. Hence, information nonequivalency is confounded with (not separable from) vividness. Together with the failure to find effects from other types of vividness, this problem suggests that the information difference and not vividness per se accounts for the fact that case histories are persuasive (S. E. Taylor & Thompson, 1982).[4]

Why Does the Vividness Effect Seem So Plausible?

Apparently, little evidence supports the vividness effect. So what would lead people to the intuitive conclusion that there is a vividness effect? Vividness may have some effects on us that are mistaken for persuasion. For example, we believe that interesting, attention-getting messages are persuasive for other people in general, but we do not rate vivid messages as more personally convincing (R. L. Collins, Taylor, Wood, & Thompson, 1988). People also recall vivid information more easily than pallid information (Lynn, Shavitt, & Ostrom, 1985), but memorability does not explain the persuasion occasionally obtained in vividness studies (Shedler & Manis, 1986; Sherer & Rogers, 1984). Moreover, vivid information may make us more confident in our opinions without changing the actual judgment (N. K. Clark & Rutter, 1985).

Finally, vivid information is entertaining, arousing, and emotional, as in the visual embellishments of rock music videos (Zillmann & Mundorf, 1987). The independence of persuasiveness and entertainment was put well by one of Carl Sagan's colleagues in describing Sagan's "gift for vividness": "Carl is very often right and always interesting. That is in contrast to most academics, who are always right and not very interesting" ("A Gift for Vividness," 1980, p. 68). Vivid communications are frequently perceived as more graphic, more vivid, or more interesting than nonvivid communication in precisely those studies that go on to find no effect on judgments. Thus the entertainment value of vividness does seem to be functionally distinct from its persuasive impact (S. E. Taylor & Wood,

[4]One lingering possibility suggests that vivid information would have its greatest impact after a delay. By this logic, all information is relatively easy to recall immediately after receiving it. After a delay, however, the pallid information's relative weakness allows it to fade, leaving vivid information intact. Although one study has found evidence for this hypothesis (Reyes, Thompson, & Bower, 1980), several others have not, and one (P. Wright & Rip, 1981) found the opposite.

1983). People can mistakenly infer that their attitudes have changed when they have only been entertained or emotionally aroused (R. L. Collins et al., 1988).

Future Directions for Vividness Research

Assuming for a moment that our real-world intuitions are correct and that a vividness effect does exist, it then follows that the attempts to examine it experimentally have been flawed in some important way, or that it does occur, but only under special circumstances that most experiments have so far failed to duplicate. Several principles define the boundaries of the vividness effect (S. E. Taylor & Thompson, 1982). First, many attempts to operationalize vividness confuse vivid messages with vivid presentations. If the message context is too vivid, the gimmicks may draw people's attention away from the message itself (Eagly & Himmelfarb, 1978; Isen & Noonberg, 1979). Recent evidence suggests that vividness that fits the message—as opposed to being incongruent—does enhance processing and persuasion, whereas incongruent, gimmicky vividness undermines it (S. M. Smith & Shaffer, 2000).

Second, some empirical evidence shows that pallid written material conveys more information but that vivid video or live material helps to catch people's attention if they are relatively uninvolved (Chaiken & Eagly, 1976). Video ads do capture people's attention, but they also prompt people to deal mostly with superficial information, such as whether the speaker is good-looking (Chaiken & Eagly, 1983). Vivid information may work on the attentional stage, especially for uninvolved recipients.

If recipients of a message are already highly involved, vividness is not needed to capture attention. Their attention is already captured. What they need are cogent arguments and time to think about them. Written materials allow involved recipients the time to consider the message arguments in detail, which is crucial to persuading such individuals (Petty & Cacioppo, 1979; see also Chapter 10). In this view, vivid ads serve mainly to alert people who are uninvolved, if the vivid material is relevant, but written information persuades people who are involved.

Finally, people differ in their chronic reliance on vivid imagery (Pham, Meyvis, & Zhou, 2001). For vivid imagers, this can exaggerate or attenuate the effects of vividness because they rely less on the information in front of them and rely more on less obvious cues taking off from there.

Conclusion

Vividness is an inherent property of a stimulus. Although vividness effects seem plausible according to both theory and common sense, they appear mostly in contrasting case histories and statistics, which typically confound other kinds of information with the sheer vividness of the presentation. People may be emotionally aroused or entertained by vividness, which is one reason the effects seem plausible. But vivid presentations if irrelevant and gimmicky can actually interfere with persuasion. Future research could focus on relevance, stages of processing, involvement, and individual differences in imagery vividness.

ACCESSIBILITY: A PROPERTY OF CATEGORIES IN OUR HEADS

So far we have discussed contextual salience and inherently vivid stimuli. A third predictor of attention is accessibility of categories, which depends mainly on priming. As noted in the discussion of automaticity in Chapter 2, priming describes the effects of prior context on the interpretation of new information. We also saw that priming can influence cognition, affect, and behavior. This chapter focuses on the cognitive mechanism of priming—namely, accessibility—and how it determines attention, encoding, and, ultimately, mental representation. Accessibility concerns the fact that recently and frequently activated ideas come to mind more easily than ideas that have not been activated. Many years ago, Jerome Bruner (1957, 1958) pointed out that much social information is inherently ambiguous, so social perception is heavily influenced by the *accessibility* of relevant categories: those easily activated given the perceiver's current goals, needs, and expectations.[5] Priming occurs when knowledge is activated (becomes accessible) and is applicable to currently attended stimuli.

Situational Accessibility Effects

Every charity has a newsletter, or so it seems. Why? Presumably, those who run the charity want to stay on your mind. Being constantly reminded of pollution, disease, violence, or the local arts council creates a context for interpreting events. In effect, the newsletter primes the issue, keeping it accessible in your mind and presumably when you interpret the urgency of various charitable causes.

Accessibility also applies for interpreting people. Exposing people to positive or negative trait terms (e.g., adventurous versus reckless) causes people soon afterward to interpret ambiguous behavior (e.g., shooting rapids in a canoe) as correspondingly positive or negative because of the meaning that had been primed (e.g., Bargh, Bond, Lombardi, & Tota, 1986; Higgins, Rholes, & Jones, 1977; Srull & Wyer, 1979; for a review, see Higgins, 1996).

Accessibility effects are strongest, as in this example, when relevant meanings as well as positive or negative valences are primed. That is, the ambiguous behavior is more likely to be seen as reckless when *relevant* negative concepts, compared to irrelevant ones, have been primed. Moreover, experimenters construct the priming and stimulus contexts such that participants do not consciously connect the two. In priming studies, participants must not think that the primed interpretation comes to mind because it was previously provided to them (i.e., accessible due to the primed construct); instead, participants must think the primed construct comes to mind because of the stimulus itself. Because they do not consciously link prime and stimulus, primed participants cannot be merely responding because of what they think the experimenters want

---

[5]The terms *accessibility* and *availability* have been used in two contradictory ways. We use *accessibility* to mean ease of recall and *availability* to denote whether the information has been stored at all (Higgins & Bargh, 1987, footnote 1; Tulving & Pearlstone, 1966). Note, however, that this is inconsistent with the Tversky-Kahneman usage of availability to mean ease of bringing information to mind (see Chapter 7). In this chapter, accessibility refers to the readiness with which stored knowledge can be used.

them to do (i.e., due to experimental "demand"). The apparent independence of the prime and the stimulus also means that participants have no particularly rational reason to be using the prime in their interpretation of the stimulus. As we saw when first introducing the concept, priming can operate automatically, without one's conscious awareness of the initial prime (Bargh et al., 1986; Bargh & Pietromonaco, 1982).

Accessibility is not limited to trait concepts. Other socially significant concepts can be primed. For example, several studies suggest that racial categories can be primed in an apparently spontaneous fashion (Devine, 1989; Dovidio, Evans, & Tyler, 1986; Gaertner & McLaughlin, 1983); when White participants see words related to African Americans, even presented below the threshold for conscious recognition, they subsequently respond faster to stereotype-related words and evaluate an ambiguous (race unspecified) person as more hostile, consistent with the idea that their racial categories have been primed. On a more overt level, overhearing an ethnic slur can exaggerate White people's negative evaluations of a poor performance by a Black person (Greenberg & Pyszczynski, 1985), perhaps through priming. Police officers and probation officers subliminally primed with Black, race-related words then interpreted a hypothetical adolescent, race unspecified, as having a worse personality, more culpability, expected recidivism, and harsher punishment (Graham & Lowery, 2004).

Similarly, other studies hint that various gender-role stereotypes are subject to priming. For example, men who had just viewed a pornographic film went on to respond more stereotypically to a woman they encountered in an apparently unrelated context: their behavior was judged to be more sexually motivated, and later they initially remembered mainly her physical features rather than the interview. But these results held only for gender-schematic men for whom gender role is likely to be especially accessible (McKenzie-Mohr & Zanna, 1990). Relatedly, women primed with family terms remember more accurately and judge more confidently the goals of a wife/mother target person compared to a career woman target or compared to neutrally primed participants (Trzebinski & Richards, 1986; cf. Trzebinski, 1985). And rock music videos that are gender-role stereotypic seem to prime stereotypic interpretations of men's and women's interactions (Hansen & Hansen, 1988b).

A variety of other stimulus interpretations also result from accessibility: person categories, as a function of unconscious affective primes (Niedenthal & Cantor, 1986); reported anxiety, as a function of unconscious threatening and violent primes (Robles, Smith, Carver, & Wellens, 1987); arousal and reported mood, as a function of self-discrepancies from standards (Higgins, Bond, Klein, & Strauman, 1986; Strauman & Higgins, 1987); good–bad judgments of affectively loaded words, as a function of unconscious evaluatively polarized primes (Greenwald, Klinger, & Liu, 1989); perceptions of whether an ambiguous adult–child interaction is a kidnapping, as a function of prior exposure to a missing child poster (K. James, 1986); reported life satisfaction, as a function of relevant prior questions (Strack, Martin, & Schwarz, 1988); judged desirability of national policies, again as a function of relevant prior questions (Tourangeau, Rasinski, Bradburn, & D'Andrade, 1989); and aggressive content in stories, as a function of heat (Rule, Taylor, & Dobbs, 1987). All kinds of responses, from temporary states to initial judgments to seemingly well-established opinions, change with accessibility due to situational primes.

Priming subsequently has long-term as well as short-term consequences. The initial priming of a stimulus can affect its ratings as much as a week later when it is no longer in that context (Higgins & King, 1981; Higgins et al., 1977; Sinclair, Mark, & Shotland, 1987; Srull & Wyer, 1980). This is an important point: A transitory and perhaps arbitrary juxtaposition of prime and stimulus can affect the way that stimulus is encoded permanently. If a stimulus potentially can be encoded as fitting one of several alternative categories, short-term priming may determine which category applies in the long run.

Moreover, accessibility affects important social behavior. Chapter 2 described studies priming race-hostility and elderly-slowness (Bargh, Chen, & Burrows, 1996), as well as professor-intelligence and transportation-biking (Aarts & Dijksterhuis, 2000). Earlier examples include participants primed by moderately hostile categories of then-famous people (rock singer Alice Cooper, Indiana coach Bobby Knight) in one context. Participants next rated an ambiguous partner as more hostile and behaved in a more hostile, competitive manner toward their partner, in line with the categories that had been primed (Herr, 1986). In another study, participants encountered competition-related words at a level below the threshold for conscious recognition; primed participants then played more competitively if they were relatively competitive people. In effect, the primes activated their competitive personalities (Neuberg, 1988). Moreover, one classic set of research can be further interpreted as consistent with the effects of priming on aggression. When people are angry at someone, the impulse to harm the person is more likely to be carried to action in the presence of aggressive cues. A gun lying on a nearby table provokes aggressive behavior even by other means (Berkowitz, 1974), and priming can explain this.

Accessibility can also affect problem solving and creativity. In one study, participants attempted to solve the following problem: Given a candle, a book of matches, and a box of tacks, how can the candle be attached to the wall so it burns properly and does not drip wax on the floor? Some participants, who had been primed to think of containers as separate from their contents (e.g., tray *and* tomatoes versus tray *of* tomatoes), were able to solve the problem quickly. The configuration (container and contents as separable entities) primed related configurations and facilitated problem solving (Higgins & Chaires, 1980). The solution to the problem, incidentally, is to empty the box of tacks, treating it as a box *and* tacks, and to tack up the box as a platform for the candle.[6]

Assimilation and Contrast

Most of the priming research shows stimuli being assimilated to accessible categories. For example, when participants are primed with positive or negative traits, they often interpret relevant ambiguous behavior in ways that assimilate it to the category, as we have just seen. However, contrast effects have sometimes emerged. That is, when people are blatantly primed with a trait (e.g., foolhardiness), they may instead contrast their judgment of the ambiguous target, judging the fact that Donald wants to sail across the Atlantic in a sailboat as not especially foolhardy and even adventurous. If the prime is blatant enough, people may avoid using it, rating the person in the opposite or contrasting direction. Certain conditions seem to undermine the usual assimilation effects and instead encourage contrast.

[6]This particular study is now interpreted as an instance of "procedural" priming (Higgins, 1989a).

Contrast occurs particularly when consciousness of the priming task is likely to be higher than usual (Martin, 1986). *Consciousness of the prime* is potentially important, for conscious priming appears to be more flexible than unconscious priming. When people are aware of a blatant prime and its potential link to a stimulus, they may resist its all-too-obvious influence or simply see it as too extreme compared to the ambiguous stimulus. In at least some circumstances, only unconscious perception of the prime leads to assimilation of the stimulus to the accessible category; conscious perception of the prime instead can either contrast or assimilate the stimulus to the accessible category (Lombardi, Higgins, & Bargh, 1987; L. S. Newman & Uleman, 1990). Conscious resources allow people to assimilate extreme similarity, but contrast moderate similarity, and ignore utterly different comparisons. Under cognitive load, conscious priming lumps together both extreme and moderate similarity, contrasting only dissimilarity (Stapel & Marx, 2006).

Assimilation and contrast also depend on features of the stimuli involved. As implied by the previous example, degree of *overlap* between the prime and the stimulus is clearly important; similar primes, which tend to increase overlap, are most likely to show assimilation in either conscious or unconscious priming. Contrast effects are obtained when the stimuli do not overlap much with the primed category, as when extreme primes are used (Herr, 1986; Herr, Sherman, & Fazio, 1983).

Stimulus *ambiguity* also matters because an ambiguous stimulus easily assimilates to a prime. Unambiguous stimuli may result in contrast effects (Herr et al., 1983). Presumably, with an unambiguous stimulus, the complete lack of fit between prime and stimulus becomes especially obvious, and perceivers overcompensate, contrasting the two.

Finally, the perceiver's *goal* matters, even with unconscious priming. Failing to see an expected stimulus can cause contrast even at the unconscious level (Stapel & Koomen, 2006). Self-protective motivations matter (Spencer, Fein, Wolfe, Fong, & Dunn, 1998).

These and other factors come together in a selective accessibility model of assimilation and contrast (Mussweiler, 2003). Because the model addresses conscious comparisons rather than automatic ones, it assumes accessibility is more flexible (controllable) and specific to the judgment at hand (rather than general semantic priming). Nevertheless, the model does hinge on accessibility, and it pulls together several useful principles relevant to when assimilation and contrast most likely occur, perhaps extending to both conscious and unconscious accessibility. If similarity testing is the accessible strategy, then people search for similarity, and assimilation results; if difference testing is accessible, then people search for differences, and contrast results. Similarity testing occurs most often; people tend to focus on similarities because they spontaneously make an overall, holistic comparison of a target to the baseline standard. For example, in comparing pineapples and avocadoes, one first decides whether they belong to the same category (fruit), and then assimilates, but if they seem to belong to different categories (sweet versus savory), one contrasts them. In thinking about someone who is neat and tidy, one assimilates to a person of one's own gender and contrasts to someone of the other gender; the mechanism here is accessibility of the standard (Mussweiler & Bodenhausen, 2002). Thus the principles of overlap, ambiguity, and goals that apply to unconscious priming also apply to

FIGURE 3.1. Priming as a function of timing

conscious comparisons to the extent that both depend on accessibility of similarities versus differences.

Priming at Encoding

Priming operates primarily through accessibility at encoding. Researchers suggest several reasons for this role of encoding. First, priming effects decrease with wider gaps between a prime and a stimulus. The wider gap presumably interferes with encoding the stimulus in terms of the prime (Srull & Wyer, 1979, 1980). When the prime and stimulus do occur in close temporal proximity, the effect depends on the stimulus being encoded together with the prime (Figure 3.1).

A second argument for the importance of encoding in priming comes from research that delays just the rating. Priming effects increase with wider temporal gaps between the already-primed stimulus and rating. As the effect increases with time, details of the original stimulus are lost, and the primed representation becomes relatively more important.

The third argument for encoding is simpler: Presenting primes *after* the stimulus has little or no effect, whereas presenting primes before the stimulus, which allows it to affect encoding, does show effects. This further supports the conclusion that encoding a stimulus in the context of a prime is more important than retrieving it in the context of the prime (Srull & Wyer, 1980).

Finally, prime-relevant information appears to elicit differential attention (S. J. Sherman, Mackie, & Driscoll, 1988). That is, participants do not rate primed dimensions as more important in decision making, but they do recall them better, suggesting that the primed dimension may elicit attention.

Chronic Accessibility

Accessibility can occur because of categories recently primed or categories frequently primed (e.g., Bargh & Pietromonaco, 1982; Bargh et al., 1986; Higgins et al., 1977, 1982; Srull & Wyer, 1989; Wyer & Srull, 1986). Various models have been proposed to account for these effects, and experiments clarify the models' differences by setting recency and frequency in competition against each other (Higgins, 1989a), as work on chronically primed concepts shows.

Persistent differences in what is primed by one's typical situation may lead to individual differences in what is chronically accessible for different people. As noted in Chapter 2, well-practiced judgments become automatic or *procedural-ized*. We all know people who seem to perceive everyone in terms of how smart they are, how trustworthy, or how good-looking. People for whom a particular personality dimension is an easily and typically accessible construct are more likely to remember and describe others in those terms (Higgins & King, 1981). For example, Higgins, King, and Mavin (1982) identified people's most typically accessible personality dimensions by recording the first and most frequent dimensions that arose in their descriptions of themselves and their friends (e.g., intelligent, funny, nice). The dimensions that people spontaneously mention are presumably the ones that come to mind most easily when the environment provides cues that can be interpreted in that way. Dimensions that are frequently accessed or permanently primed may become central aspects of one's personality, and one develops *chronicity* on that dimension.

Moreover, given that chronicity theoretically results from a history of frequent exposure to a category, it should operate as does sheer frequency in situational priming, at least in any particular setting. Comparing the principles of frequency and recency, frequently primed constructs have the advantage in the long run, although recently primed constructs predominate in the short term (Higgins, Bargh, & Lombardi, 1985). Parallel results are obtained for individual differences in chronicity and for recent priming; that is, recently primed categories predominate in the short term, but like frequently primed categories, chronically primed categories also predominate after a delay (Bargh, Lombardi, & Higgins, 1988).

Chronically accessible categories are used efficiently, allowing one to encode relevant information in less time than would someone who is nonchronic on that dimension (Bargh & Thein, 1985). Moreover, chronically accessible categories seem to be used without one's intention (Bargh et al., 1986; Higgins et al., 1982) and even outside one's control (Bargh & Pratto, 1986). As we saw, these characteristics of chronicity qualify it as truly automatic (Bargh, 1984, 1988).

The automatic application of chronically accessible constructs to new information has significant social consequences. For example, the automatic, chronic processing of negative social categories regarding oneself—but not others in general—appears to be an important component of depression (Bargh & Tota, 1988). In a meta-analysis, negative self-focus strongly relates to negative affect across both correlational studies and experimental studies that manipulate self-focus and valence of thoughts; positive self-focus reduces negative affect. These results held for depression, not just temporary bad moods; depression was especially related to private self-focus (negativity regarding one's own goals, thoughts, and feelings), whereas anxiety was related to public self-focus (negativity in the impression one makes on others) (Mor & Winquist, 2002). The good news is that these effects are not solely a function of individual differences in chronic accessibility; given that they also differ as a function of context, they potentially can change.

Individual differences in other forms of chronicity also matter interpersonally. For example, gender accessibility exaggerates gender-stereotypic encoding biases (Stangor, 1988). That is, after seeing a series of male- and female-stereotypic behavior performed by men and women equally, gender-accessible participants were especially likely (a) to report stereotype-consistent behaviors (e.g., women doing feminine things) and (b) to mix up the women with each other and the men with each other. Chronic gender-accessibility influences responses to female politicians' ads, especially when they are positive or uninformative (compared to negative ads) (Chang & Hitchon, 2004). Chronicity may also explain a positive side effect of stereotyping. People accustomed to being stereotyped (e.g., African Americans) sometimes show more tolerance for another potentially stereotyped person, presumably because they can see the similarity of their shared experiences, at least if their own victimization is also primed (Galanis & Jones, 1986); chronicity for stereotyping may help explain this phenomenon.

Conclusion

In this section on accessibility's role in attention and encoding, we have seen that accessibility is the mechanism by which priming operates. Situational priming affects the accessibility of a wide range of stimuli: traits, social categories, valence (positivity-negativity), procedures, and behaviors. Accessibility usually causes assimilation of the stimulus to the prime, but it can also cause contrast, depending on consciousness of the prime, stimulus and prime overlap, stimulus ambiguity, and perceiver goals. Accessibility is primarily an encoding effect, influencing interpretations of stimuli as they are noticed and stored. Chronic accessibility affects encoding in similar ways to contextual accessibility; both affect important social behaviors.

DIRECT PERCEPTION: NOT JUST IN OUR HEADS

This chapter opened with an example of a social perceiver unfortunately misperceiving who was chasing whom in a series of three runners. One might argue that the example reflects the automatic activation of stereotypic categorization processes (interpreting the trio as a White police officer chasing two Black suspects), and one might marvel at the complexity of the inferential processes that occurred in the split second before the perceiver responded in such a misguided fashion. Alternatively, one might argue that, for that perceiver, the particular stimulus configuration effectively furnished his response. From this perspective, the perception was direct, from seeing and hearing straight to the intrinsic behavioral possibilities.

Inspired by J. J. Gibson's (1966, 1979) work in object perception, several theorists have suggested that much of the important activity in social understanding occurs immediately during perception (Baron, 1980; Kassin & Baron, 1986; Lowe & Kassin, 1980; McArthur, 1980; McArthur & Baron, 1983; Neisser, 1976, 1980; Weary, Swanson, Harvey, & Yarkin, 1980; Zebrowitz, 1990). This view rejects perception as the result of complex inferential activity, however automated. In particular, the ecological approach emphasizes external stimulus information and the organization inherent in it rather than the organization constructed or imposed by the perceiver (Zebrowitz, 1990). Organization is "inherent in a stimulus" for a particular perceiver, based on that person's history of perceptual experiences. A particular stimulus *affords* or offers particular behaviors to a perceiver, and the perceiver is reciprocally *attuned* or sensitive to particular stimulus properties. The Gibsonian approach is called *ecological perception* because it emphasizes perceivers interacting with their environments and embedded in their own characteristic niche. Perception is analyzed as adaptive for perceivers; "perceiving is for doing," in this view, so perception will typically be accurate if perceivers are given sufficient information and context.

An Ecological Example of Causal Perception

The Gibsonian perspective suggests, for example, that social interpretations result from segmenting the perceptual field, and that inferences and memory are irrelevant (McArthur, 1980). To illustrate, assume you overhear your neighbors quarreling. She screams at him, and he murmurs in reply; this sequence alternates for some minutes. In relating the incident to your roommate, you describe the woman as causing the argument because each segment of the interaction begins with her salient vocal behavior. Each of her loud comments marks a new perceptual unit that finishes with his soft reply. She shouts, he murmurs. Since responsibility requires temporal precedence, starting each unit with her then irresistibly blames her for the argument (Figure 3.2).

Now replay the fight but assume that you can see what is going on as well as hear it. (Assume further that they both do not turn on you for spying, however scientifically disinterested you might be.) The fight actually commences with him walking into the room and gesturing violently at her. She replies and retreats. He threatens her again, speaking in ominously low tones, and she backs off, arguing defensively. He threatens, and she retreats. The segments now commence each time with his physical gestures and her retreats. His physical gestures are perceptually big relative to her little retreats, in much the same way her shouts were loud compared to his soft murmurs. The units now begin with him: he makes big physical threats, and she makes little movements of retreat. Now the man would be described as causing the argument. Note that this

FIGURE 3.2. Perceptual segmentation of behavioral sequences resulting in different causal judgments

First segmentation of neighbors' quarrel

She	He		She	He		She	He	
shouts ➔ murmurs			shouts ➔ murmurs			shouts ➔ murmurs		
LOUD ➔ soft			LOUD ➔ soft			LOUD ➔ soft		

Second segmentation of neighbors' quarrel

He	She		He	She		He	She	
threatens ➔ retreats			threatens ➔ retreats			threatens ➔ retreats		
BIG ➔ small			BIG ➔ small			BIG ➔ small		

Note: Each vertical rule represents a breakpoint between two perceptual units.

perceptual analysis of responsibility de-emphasizes cognitive activity. The blame judgments are implicit in perception from the outset (McArthur, 1980).

With respect to interpretations, the Gibsonian view would argue that they result from perceptual organization, such as temporal sequence, or the contrast of large to small stimuli, as in our example of the neighbors' fight; the Gibsonian view suggests that inferred blame occurs automatically during the perception of an event, an idea with which others agree (R. C. Sherman & Titus, 1982; E. R. Smith & Miller, 1979).

Perceptual Units

The direct perception analysis is all the more interesting because considerable evidence indicates that inherent perceptual units have important effects on social judgments. This has been shown by researchers who measure perceptual segmentation directly (for a review, see Newtson, Hairfield, Bloomingdale, & Cutino, 1987; for a critique, see Ebbesen, 1980). The technique for measuring perceptual segments or units involves subjects watching a film and pushing a button to indicate the end of each given segment and the beginning of a new one; the button push is taken to indicate what is called a breakpoint between segments. Segments are defined in whatever way seems natural to the individual (Newtson & Enquist, 1976; Newtson, Enquist, & Bois, 1977). The unitizing method (as it is called) is reliable and valid and surprisingly comfortable for participants. People largely agree on the perceptual units in a given scene. For example, if the neighbors' quarrel were shown in a silent film, people would generally agree on the breakpoints.

Unitizing research suggests that the breakpoints between perceptual units have special properties. The breakpoint moments of a film, when shown as a series of stills in isolation from the rest of the film, nonetheless coherently convey the story. Nonbreakpoints (at equivalent intervals) do not adequately summarize the story. Recognition memory for breakpoints is also superior to recognition for nonbreakpoints (see Newtson, 1976). The implication is that behavior is segmented at points of maximal information (Newtson, 1980; but for dissent, see C. E. Cohen & Ebbesen, 1979). Breakpoints occur at peaks of behavioral complexity when many body parts are changing at once (Newtson et al., 1977). That is, one can perceive the core of an action when it is most distinctively changing, so that is seen as a breakpoint. If action slows down to a pause or stops, that is not typically a breakpoint. Moreover, the rise and fall of action complexity follow a wave pattern: when two people are interacting, their actions jointly create a coordinated wave pattern (Newtson et al., 1987). This suggests that basic perceptual-motor configurations could function independently of complex cognitive processes.

People can use fine-grained units or grosser units, depending on instructions to do so or other goals. For example, people use finer units when their goal is observing nonverbal behavior (Strenta & Kleck, 1984), remembering task behavior (C. E. Cohen & Ebbesen, 1979), and observing individuals within an aggregate of people (Wilder, 1986). People also use finer units when they encounter an unexpected action (Newtson, 1973; Wilder, 1978a, 1986) or a person about whom they have no prior information (Graziano, Moore, & Collins, 1988). Finer levels of perception are associated with measures indicating more information gained:

more confident and differentiated trait inferences, more dispositional attributions (Deaux & Major, 1977; Newtson, 1973; Wilder, 1978a), and better memory for the person observed (Lassiter, 1988; Lassiter, Stone, & Rogers, 1988). Finer unitizing even seems to be associated with greater liking of an otherwise neutral person, perhaps because of an increased sense of familiarity independent of one's improved memory for the finely unitized other (Lassiter, 1988; Lassiter & Stone, 1984). The unitizing research as a whole addresses basic perceptual processes in ongoing interaction, suggesting how information is gained over time and made immediately useful to action.

A Note on Implications for Social Cognition Research

Researchers who support the direct perception or ecological view argue that it directly contradicts the idea that inferences depend on complex cognitive processes. According to this view, cognitive constructs (such as observational goals or category-based expectations) enter into the inference process only to the degree that such factors influence the initial perception of an event as it is directly observed (Enquist, Newtson, & LaCross, 1979; Massad, Hubbard, & Newtson, 1979). Although there is some evidence to the contrary (Vinokur & Ajzen, 1982), the Gibsonian view is a helpful counterpoint to the standard explanations of complex cognitive processes as the only basis for social judgments.

The Gibsonian perspective is a useful antidote to some biases in mainstream research on encoding. Ecological perception recognizes the intrinsic richness of stimulus information and insists that stimuli be ecologically valid: namely, that they occur in multiple sensory modes, that they change and not be utterly static, that they be presented in configuration instead of isolation, and that they be extended in time instead of brief. The Gibsonians' frequent use of naturalistic filmed stimuli illustrates this set of concerns. The ecological approach also emphasizes the adaptive functions of perception, in particular the link between perception and action. Hence, as we will see, it examines why people would develop the perception that baby-faced people need nurturance and protection (namely, that most baby-faced people are in fact babies, whom it is useful for adults to perceive as vulnerable). Moreover, the ecological approach explicitly acknowledges the relationship between the environment and the particular perceiver's goals, capabilities, and history. Although the social cognition literature does this as well, the Gibsonian view emphasizes the environment as full of action possibilities (affordances). Finally, it points to the relevance of cross-cultural, animal, and developmental research for comparative purposes.

In closing, it is probably not useful to pit the ecological approach directly against the cognitive approaches for several reasons. First, each approach is itself a meta-theory, which is not intrinsically falsifiable. At the broadest levels, each can always account for the other's data in perceptual or cognitive terms, respectively. Second, in practice it is difficult to distinguish between perception and cognition. On one hand, perception entails taking in stimulus features in order to respond to the environment, and on the other hand, cognition can entail immediate automatic inferential activity. Whether one labels such processes "cognitive," or sometimes "perceptual" and sometimes "cognitive," depending on their rapidity or accessibility to awareness, is a matter of theoretical preference, and the distinction begins to evaporate. Third, the relative impact of perceptual and cognitive activity in any one experiment depends on the relative strengths with which each is manipulated, so any empirical "advantage" of one over the other would be a function of the particular experiment's operationalization of the perceptual process or the cognitive process, not reflecting the intrinsic relative power of the two types of process. Finally, some would argue that stimulus variation (what a particular stimulus intrinsically affords) is the mark of the ecological approach, but perceiver variation (cognitive structures that perceivers bring with them) marks the cognitive approach. If so, one is stuck comparing apples and oranges, phenomena on altogether different scales. That is, one can assess how much the stimulus contributes and how much the perceiver contributes, but they cannot be directly compared because they come from separate populations (the population of all social perceivers or all possible stimuli).

In short, the two approaches are complementary, each with its own strengths (R. M. Baron, 1988). The ecological perception approach focuses on what people learn from particular stimulus configurations. The work on causal perception and unitizing the behavior stream (as well as work, to be discussed, on trait inferences from physical cues) illustrate important patterns of social stimuli that perceivers use for adaptive functioning. Social cognition focuses more on the cognitive structures and routines that people use to interpret, elaborate, and construct their memory and judgments. This type of ecological perception attunes the perceiver to what actions the context affords.

FACES: THE FOCUS OF SOCIAL ATTENTION

So far we have seen that people's social attention follows people who are salient in context, vivid case histories instead of abstract statistics, dimensions that have been recently or frequently activated in the past, and action-relevant features of the social environment. All of these attentional phenomena apply to perceptions of objects as well as people, though they have been studied more thoroughly in social than nonsocial cognition. An even more dramatically social driver of attention is another person's face. Faces are intrinsically the focus of attention in any social interaction. We examine how faces direct people's attention elsewhere, some neuroscience of face perception, and the rapid inference of traits from faces.

Gaze: A Cue From Other People

People are acutely attuned to other people's gaze direction. Consider how quickly you notice that someone is staring at you, even out of your peripheral vision. This makes sense, of course: the other person's gaze communicates attention and perhaps intention, so survival dictates being alert to other people's gaze.

Faces with directed (looking at you) as opposed to averted gaze compel attention: people more rapidly categorize them by gender and link them to stereotypic information (Macrae, Hood, Milne, Rowe, & Mason, 2002). Both adults and children more easily recall them (Hood, Macrae, Cole-Davies, & Dias, 2003; Mason, Hood, & Macrae, 2004). Gaze appears primarily as an encoding phenomenon (Hood et al., 2003). All else being equal, people find direct gaze both likable and attractive (Mason, Tatkow, & Macrae, 2005). "Here's looking at you, kid" can be a compliment, as early film actor Humphrey Bogart knew, but "Whaddaya lookin' at?" can be a response to unwanted and especially provocative attention.

People not only notice people who are looking at them, but people also use another person's averted gaze to guide their own attention. When someone looks away at something else, most people find it hard to resist following the other person's gaze to see what is so interesting. We not only look where other people are looking but also where animals are looking and where arrows point. However, this reflexive shift in our attention is most efficient (rapid) when we take our cues from eyes (Quadflieg, Mason, & Macrae, 2004), consistent with the idea that the eyes are the window, if not to the soul, to intent. Gaze detection implicates neural systems, including the superior temporal sulcus (Hoffman & Haxby, 2000), often implicated in tracking biological movement.

Face Perception

Cognitive neuroscience argues that face perception, a highly developed visual skill, implicates a number of neural systems, some for identifying fixed features of faces, and some for changeable facial expressions (Haxby, Hoffman, & Gobbini, 2000). A face-responsive region, sometimes called the fusiform face area, recognizes invariant features of faces (Kanwisher, McDermott, & Chun, 1997; Kanwisher & Wojciuluk, 2000). A different face-responsive region in the superior temporal sulcus responds to changeable aspects of faces (gaze, noted earlier; expression; and movement). And knowledge about the person constitutes a third set of processes (Bruce & Young, 1986). Face perception is distributed both over the brain and over the time course of perception (Haxby, Gobbini, & Montgomery, 2004). Although some argue that people's responsivity to faces merely reflects practice effects or expertise, much evidence supports the face as a domain of unique neural sensitivity (McKone, Kanwisher, & Duchaine, 2007). The use of all this work by social judgment researchers is just beginning.

Facial recognition appears to be a global, configural, holistic process that perceptually integrates across the whole rather than a local, feature-oriented process. Indeed, the feature-oriented processing of a face (separate focus on eyes, nose, mouth, chin, etc.) undermines recognition. Verbally describing a bank robber ironically interferes with recognizing him on a later line-up (Schooler & Engstler-Schooler, 1990), apparently because this "verbal overshadowing" invokes a local, feature-by-feature processing orientation (Tanaka & Farah, 1993). A direct manipulation of global versus local (feature) processing orientation respectively enhances or impairs subsequent recognition (Macrae & Lewis, 2002).

Faces are processed globally when people are distinguishing among unique individuals. When people are merely categorizing individuals, treating individuals as more interchangeable, they use single salient cues (e.g., hair) to determine, for example, gender, race, age, and the like. Right hemispheric specialization in global, configural processing facilitates identification and individuation; left hemispheric feature-based processing facilitates categorization (Mason & Macrae, 2004). Similarly, the right hemisphere specializes in individual, person-based learning, whereas the left focuses on group-based learning (Sanders, McClure, & Zárate, 2004). In general, the right hemisphere often participates in basic perceptual, episodic encoding, and the left in conceptual, abstract processes (Zárate, Sanders, & Garza, 2000) such as categorizing.

According to face-selective neural activations, people identify a face as a face in 100 msec (a tenth of a second) and recognize familiar faces in 170 msec (Liu, Harris, & Kanwisher, 2002). Other data suggest 170 msec for distinguishing faces from nonfaces, then at 250 msec distinguishing own-racial-group members from outgroup members, with differential evaluation kicking in at 520 msec (Ito, Thompson, & Cacioppo, 2004). Still other data suggest racial differentiation as early as 100 msec and gender differentiation as early as 150 msec (Ito & Urland, 2003). As more data accumulate, both the parameters of these kinds of social cognition and the circumstances that speed and slow these processes will be clarified.

In general, categorical information is easier to extract from faces than is individual identity information. When faces are blurry, inverted, or merely glimpsed, people can still readily extract categorical knowledge (Cloutier, Mason, & Macrae, 2005), and they do this unintentionally (Macrae, Quinn, Mason, & Quadflieg, 2005). When people examine faces, they sometimes extract individuating trait information and link it directly to the face. The face-traits links appear in work from both an ecological perception viewpoint and a spontaneous perception viewpoint, as we shall see now.

Baby Faces as Ecological Phenomena

In addition to the social perception work mentioned earlier, research from an ecological perspective examines how people make specific inferences about personality on the basis of physical features and other features intrinsic to the social stimulus configuration. Such appearance-based perceptions are fundamental factors in social perception. For example, old-time gangster movies often featured a ruthless criminal with a name like "Babyface" Norton. What made such figures especially sinister was the contrast between their cherubic features and their villainous behavior. Why do we expect people with baby-faced features to have equally innocent personalities? A series of studies in ecological perception indicates that baby-faced adults are perceived to have more childlike qualities than mature-faced adults; across cultures, people with large eyes, big foreheads, and short features (e.g., snub noses, small chins) are seen as less strong, dominant, and intellectually astute, and as more naive, honest, kind, and warm, regardless of perceived age and attractiveness (Berry & McArthur, 1985; McArthur & Apatow, 1983-84; McArthur & Berry, 1987; see Berry & McArthur, 1986, for a review). Baby-faced adults are less likely to be judged guilty of intentional criminal behavior (hence, the baby-faced gangster is disconcerting), but they are more likely to be judged guilty of crimes involving negligence (Berry & Zebrowitz-McArthur, 1988). Cross culturally, people with childlike voices are also perceived as weaker, less competent, and warmer (Montepare & Zebrowitz-McArthur, 1987). And people with more youthful gaits are perceived to be happier and more powerful, regardless of perceived age and gender (Montepare & Zebrowitz-McArthur, 1988).

The ecological approach argues that these perceptions result from the normal covariation between babylike features and actual age, such that most babyish humans *are* more weak, submissive, intellectually undeveloped, naive, and innocent precisely because they are very likely to be actual babies. Such perceptions based on babylike features are normally adaptive for species' survival because it is important for adults to nurture and protect the young. Adults are therefore likely to perceive childlike features as needing or affording the behavioral opportunity of caretaking, which fits with perceiving a babylike person as weak. To a properly attuned organism, such perceptions are biologically and socially useful. Consequently, it is not surprising that children as young as 2½ can use baby-face cues to judge age (Montepare & McArthur, 1986).

Spontaneous Trait Inferences From Faces

The attention-grabbing power of faces appears in an early study showing that angry faces "pop-out" of an array of faces, no matter how many other faces are in the crowd, and more so than other incongruent faces (Chapter 2; Hansen & Hansen, 1988a). And angry outgroup faces are especially well encoded (Ackerman et al., 2006). Of course, angry faces are particularly salient given the impact of negative information noted earlier (S. T. Fiske, 1980; Pratto & John, 1991). Even subliminally presented angry or fearful faces activate the brain's early-warning system of the amygdala (Morris, Ohman, & Dolan, 1998; Whalen et al., 1998). But people go beyond immediately reading expressions to immediate inferences of personality traits, perhaps building on the same systems that read facial expression (from an angry expression to a hostile personality). Faces otherwise judged as untrustworthy also activate the amygdala, even when people's alleged task is judging the age of the faces (Winston, Strange, O'Doherty, & Dolan, 2002).

People make spontaneous trait inferences from people's behavior, and they "bind" (link) them directly to the person's face in memory (Carlston & Skowronksi, 1994; Carlston, Skowronksi, & Sparks, 1995; Todorov & Uleman, 2002, 2004) even under rapid presentation and high cognitive load (Todorov & Uleman, 2003). Trait inferences from merely a minimal interaction also bind to the person's face (Todorov, Gobbini, Evans, & Haxby, 2007), even when people are not focused on inferring personality. Moreover, the inferences and activated brain regions are specific (e.g., disgusting faces lead to different inferences and activation of different brain regions than aggressive faces). Similarly, people show different neural responses to trustworthy and untrustworthy faces (Winston et al., 2002) or attractive and unattractive faces (Aharon et al., 2001). Even 100 msec exposures are enough time for people to make trait inferences from faces (Willis & Todorov, 2006) that agree with the judgments of people who have no time constraints.

What is true of strangers is even more true for a person's evaluation of close others. Personally familiar faces activate a distributed network of brain regions—precuneus, superior temporal sulcus, and medial prefrontal cortex— that go beyond the mere memory for the face (Gobbini, Leibenluft, Santiago, & Haxby, 2004).

People's immediate trait inferences from faces can have important consequences: seeing candidates for the Senate for even a second enabled people to make competence judgments that predicted nearly 70% of the elections (Todorov, Mandisodza, Goren, & Hall, 2005). At the other extreme, Black faces that are stereotypically Black are more likely to activate associations of criminality in people's immediate inferences (Eberhardt, Goff, Purdie, & Davies, 2004). Blacks and even Whites with Afro-typic features receive longer criminal sentences (Blair, Judd, & Chapleau, 2004; Eberhardt, Davies, Purdie-Vanghns, & Johnson, 2006). Faces can be a matter of life and death.

Summary

We now have some answers to what captures our attention. We especially notice what is salient: novel or perceptually figural in context, people or behaviors that are unusual or unexpected, extreme and sometimes negative behavior, and stimuli relevant to our current goals. All such salience subsequently influences our reactions to other people. Our attention may also be captured by vivid stimuli, and often we are entertained, but vivid stimuli do not influence our reactions much except when they are vivid case histories. Our attention also orients us to situationally or personally primed categories. Recently, frequently, and chronically encountered categories are more accessible for use, and they profoundly influence the encoding of stimuli. They are applied to relevant, moderate, ambiguous stimuli, guiding their interpretation and subsequent representation in our heads. Our attention also orients to ecologically relevant features of our social context; that is, features that afford action. Finally, people reflexively orient to people's faces, especially those who are orienting to them. We also look in the direction others gaze when they are looking away. And we immediately infer people's personalities from their faces. In short, we have learned a lot about social attention, which determines what gets encoded into memory, the topic for the next chapter.

Representation in Memory

This chapter covers social and nonsocial models of memory and closes with mental representations—the social categories and individual exemplars that we keep in mind. Several models of memory are introduced. First we outline each cognitive model, and then we describe the social cognitive models derived from it. In this area more than any other, social cognition researchers have adapted general cognitive models to develop models specific to social cognition, in particular, memory for people. We discuss associative networks, procedural memory, connectionist (parallel) models, embodied memory, and memory structures such as categories and exemplars.

ASSOCIATIVE NETWORKS: ORGANIZING MEMORY

Suppose you are standing at a busy intersection waiting for the light to change. Across the street, you see a young man knock down an elderly woman, grab her purse, and run away. By the time you can get across the street, he is long gone, so you turn your attention to the woman. Just as you have discovered that she is angry but unhurt, a police officer arrives and takes down your description of what happened. How is this event stored in your memory, and why does its mental representation matter? Several models of memory account for this phenomenon. In this section we detail the most common and well-developed type of memory model, the associative network approach. This model underlies most social cognitive studies, especially the earliest ones. Later sections address advances beyond this initial approach.

The Basic Cognitive Model of Associative Networks

The most important general principle of this approach is that the more links or associations from other concepts to any given concept in memory, the easier it is to remember that concept because many alternative routes can locate it in memory. The following sections elaborate this point in detail because social cognition research grew out of this approach. Table 4.1 summarizes some of these key features in the first column.

TABLE 4.1. **Key Features of Cognitive Memory Models and Related Social Cognitive Memory Models**

Associative Memory (declarative memory for content)	Procedural Memory (automatic memory for practiced cognitive processes)	Parallel Distributed Processing (connectionist models)	Embodied Memory (perceptual symbol systems)
Long-Term Memory (LTM) Storage (can include *intermediate, recent* memory and *remote, longer-term* memory)			Includes top-down expectations (frames)
(can include *episodic* memory for specific events and *semantic* memory for facts, word meaning, and general encyclopedic knowledge)	(includes all kinds of information)	(includes all kinds of information)	Includes bottom-up, sensory information, introspection, and proprioception
Propositions in a node–link structure	If-then (condition-action) productions	Patterns of connections	Simulators that organize related perceptual symbols
Labeled links (not used in social models)		Inhibitory and facilitative connections	
Process: spreading activation	Process: matching, selection, and execution	Process: adjusting connection strengths	Process: simulates online, in presence of object, and offline, in absence of object
Alternative retrieval routes			
Degree of activation determines retrieval	Current goals and stimuli determine selection and use of procedures	Input patterns and connection weights jointly determine retrieval	Focuses on perception for action
Implicates hippocampus immediately, cortical consolidation in longer term	Productions implicate basal ganglia loop; goals implicate dorsolateral prefrontal cortex		

Short-Term or Working Memory

Most activated portion of LTM but also attended stimuli, may be consolidated for storage in LTM

Implicates ventrolateral prefrontal cortex

Fast, easy learning requires STM capacity

Automatic or controlled execution

Widely available use

Flexible

Slow learning, requires practice

Fast, automatic execution

Specific, focused use

Durable

Person Memory Models

Hastie: person memory-1

Srull & Wyer: person memory, and judgment

Marques & Hamilton: twofold retrieval and associative processing model

Carlston: associated systems theory

Social Procedural Models

E. R. Smith: proceduralization

Lewicki: implicit recognition

Social Connectionist Models

Kunda & Thagard: parallel constraint satisfaction model

Van Overwalle: connectionist models

Kashima: tensor-product model

Read: Gestalt connectionism

Vallacher & Nowak: dynamical systems

Smith & DeCoster: social connectionism

Embodied Social Cognition

Niedenthal et al.: embodied social cognition and emotion

Feldman Barrett: embodied experience of emotion

E. R. Smith & Semin: socially situated cognition

The exact format of the representation is called a memory code. A variety of possible codes are discussed later, but the best known in early cognitive psychology was a *proposition* (J. R. Anderson, 1976; Rumelhart, Lindsay, & Norman, 1972; Wickelgren, 1981). For example, "The woman stands on the corner" is one proposition; others are "The woman is elderly," "The man knocks down the woman," and so forth. Each proposition consists of nodes and links: each node being an idea (noun, verb, adjective) and each link being the relation between ideas.

One critical feature of these models of human memory is that they are *associative;* that is, most refer to associations between nodes (the woman) linked to other nodes (elderly). The associative feature of a propositional code has implications for important interpersonal events. Suppose you are called in to give eyewitness testimony on the mugging case (Figure 4.1). The organization of long-term memory into an associative node–link structure means that you will recall related facts together. That is, if you begin by thinking about the woman herself, it may be easier to recall her attributes (e.g., elderly, standing on the corner) than to recall the man's attributes (e.g., young). Moreover, the links are *labeled.* If asked who (agent) mugged whom (object), you would have the proper relationships stored in memory. (This particular labeling feature has not been adopted in social cognition.)

An important feature of propositional memory models is that the links are strengthened each time they are *activated.* That is, recall starts at one point (e.g., the woman), and activation spreads along links between the nodes (Collins & Loftus, 1975). Recalling that the woman was elderly, for example, activates both nodes in memory ("elderly" and "woman"), strengthening the link between them. The practical implication of joint activation is that frequent rehearsal (that is, mental repetition) of your testimony makes it more memorable than unrehearsed facts. The lawyer preparing you to be a witness is likely to know that frequent reviews of the testimony ahead of time will strengthen its coherence and avoid awkward surprises, such as your remembering new events on the witness stand.

In addition to strengthening links among ideas by activating them together, the more separate linkages to any given idea, the more likely it is to be recalled. More links create more *alternative retrieval routes* and enhanced memory. Thus, a smart lawyer will help you to form many alternative memory routes to any given fact to minimize last-minute forgetfulness.

Long-Term Versus Short-Term Memory

A critical feature of many network memory models is the distinction between long-term memory and short-term (or working) memory. In this view, *long-term memory* consists of the vast store of information one can potentially bring to mind. *Short-term memory* refers to the information that one is considering at any given moment, which is why it is also called "working memory." In many memory models, the activated portion of long-term memory represents short-term memory or consciousness. That is, the long-term memory nodes that are currently most active make up the contents of focal attention.

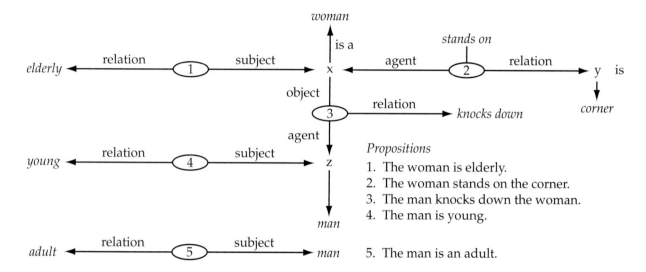

FIGURE 4.1. Propositional network model for knowledge that "The elderly woman standing on the corner is knocked down by the young man." (After J. R. Anderson, 1980a.) Each separate proposition is indicated by an ellipse. For example, the first proposition ("The woman is elderly") is represented by the nodes and links on the upper left of the figure. The numbered ellipses indicate the other propositions. Starting at ellipse 1, anything connected by arrows moving *away* from the ellipse is part of that particular proposition. For example, "elderly" and "woman" both are connected to the ellipse by arrows from it and to them. But "stands on" is not part of the first proposition; accordingly, the link from the ellipse labeled "1" to "stands on" is interrupted by an arrow pointing the wrong way. The other notation that needs explaining is the use of x, y, and z. They indicate that x is one particular woman, who is also elderly. If the proposition were "Woman are elderly" (i.e., the entire category of women is elderly), the x would be replaced by the word "woman" in the figure. For example, the proposition "The man is an adult" (true of all men) would be denoted differently than "This particular man is young" (see propositions 4 and 5 in the figure). For present purposes, the notation illustrates the precision with which details of meaning can be represented in a propositional network.

The contents of short-term memory can be consolidated for storage in long-term memory.

In associative models, memory retrieval consists of activating the appropriate nodes in long-term memory, which brings them to consciousness if activation is above a certain threshold. Because the most active nodes can change rapidly, the conscious part of long-term memory (that is, what you are thinking about right now) is considered short-term. Things move in and out of consciousness, or short-term memory, as they become activated and fade from being activated. The limited capacity for activation means that short-term memory is quite limited in scope. In other words, few things can be held in mind simultaneously.

The consequences of the rather severe limits on short-term memory can be illustrated by a lawyer's questioning of a witness on the stand. A witness will be unable to keep lots of details in mind at once, so the person may contradict earlier testimony that is out of current consciousness. Short-term memory is normally assumed to hold about seven items of information (classically, 7 ± 2; G. A. Miller, 1956). An "item" of information could be as small as a single letter or digit, or it could be a "chunk" of letters (i.e., a word on the mugger's sweatshirt) or a chunk of digits (i.e., the time on your watch). In practical terms, short-term memory limits mean that people can keep only a few things in mind at once.

In contrast to the limits of short-term memory, the capacity of the overall network of long-term memory storage seems, practically speaking, to be limitless. A lawyer who urges a witness to struggle to remember crucial details may be banking on this: The information might all be there; it is only a question of finding it. For long-term memory, the issue is not capacity (or how much one knows) but retrieval (whether one can find it). Skilled performance depends in part on having efficient cues to relevant material in long-term memory (Ericsson & Kintsch, 1995). Many models of social memory are concerned primarily with how retrieval is influenced by the organization of long-term memory, by the links among items, and by accessibility.

The neat distinction between long- and short-term memory may be breaking down. Recent insights from neuroscience support distinctions among three general time periods of memory. Material may be actively attended in consciousness, in effect in extremely short-term memory, as just described. But two forms of what used to be considered long-term memory appear in distinctions between memory for recent and more remote events, sometimes called intermediate and long-term memory. These complementary intermediate and long-term memory systems allow both (a) rapid learning and recall of specific events, implicating the hippocampus, and (b) slow learning but rapid recognition of patterns, implicating the neocortex (medial temporal lobes) (e.g., McClelland, McNaughton, & O'Reilly, 1995; Norman & O'Reilly, 2003). These complementary learning systems reflect the hippocampus's role in recall of recent events and the higher brain's role in detecting regularities in the environment, slow to acquire and accept, but also slow to undo.

To review (see Table 4.1), associative models of memory share the assumptions that memory consists of nodes for ideas and associative links among the nodes. The associative links are posited to be labeled and strengthened by activation that spreads from node to node. The number of links to any given concept determines the number of alternative retrieval routes and hence the concepts' ease of retrieval. Long-term memory is the practically unlimited store of knowledge one has available, and short-term or working memory is the information one is actively using at any given time. Newer work distinguishes recent versus remote long-term memory.

Associative Network Models of Social Memory

Hastie's Person Memory Model

What do these cognitive models of memory say about social cognition? An example is one associative network model of social memory, PM-1 (for Person Memory; Hastie, 1988b). This model works as a computer simulation, which is an important test of its sufficiency (Ostrom, 1988). In a nutshell, PM-1 predicts extra attention to impression-*inconsistent* material (because it is surprising), resulting in extra associative linkages for those items, increasing their alternative retrieval paths and probability of recall. This is called the *inconsistency advantage.*

According to this model, the encoding process invokes a limited-capacity working memory, which allows one to form links among items; the length of time items stay in working memory depends on their relevance to the current impression judgment. A longer stay in working memory forges more links. Links form between items that are unexpected given the current impression because they stay in mind longer as people try to figure them out. (The model also posits that some links are formed stochastically; that is, randomly.) Subsequent retrieval from long-term memory initiates at a random point and randomly proceeds along pathways formed by interitem links. It terminates with repeated failures to retrieve an item not already retrieved.

Finally, the model also proposes a mechanism for impression formation, simultaneous with memory encoding and storage. The anchoring and adjustment process (described more fully in Chapter 7) essentially provides for an impression that is updated with each new piece of information, based on an equally weighted average of (a) the cumulative evaluations of the items so far and (b) the items currently staying in working memory, including the new item (N. H. Anderson, 1981; Lopes, 1982).

One of this model's strong points is its simultaneous modeling of the online impression formation process, plus memory storage and retrieval processes. For example, when people form impressions online—that is, as they receive information—their impressions result from this gradual process. However, when people do not form impressions online, they have to retrieve information to create an impression from memory. In this post hoc case, their memory for the information will correlate with their impression precisely because the impression is a memory-based construction. In the online, simultaneous impression case, memory is irrelevant to the spontaneous impression formed because different factors determine whether each piece of information is important to the impression versus memorable. People can remember trivia but discount them in the impression, for example.

Srull-Wyer Person Memory Model

Another model of person memory and judgment (Srull & Wyer, 1989) makes fundamentally similar assumptions. Basic processes create an impression from a target's behavior: (a) First, people interpret each behavior in terms of an applicable and accessible personality trait, which summarizes the behavior; this trait-behavior goes into its own unit, sometimes called a storage bin. (b) Next, they evaluate the target person as basically likeable or dislikeable. (c) Then, they interpret the person's behaviors in light of the evaluation, reviewing behaviors that are markedly inconsistent with it; and (d) when asked for a judgment, they prefer to use a trait already inferred in step (a), and simply retrieve that from its storage bin. If none of the already inferred traits are relevant, they will review the remembered behaviors to make the judgment.

The model provides a detailed analysis of known social cognitive processes. For example, early information most influences the evaluation. In other words, first impressions count. As another example, learning first about more positive attributes predisposes one toward a positive impression, a phenomenon called a primacy effect (cf. Asch, 1946; E. E. Jones & Goethals, 1972). In the Srull-Wyer model, an initial evaluation forms as soon as the information is clearly and consistently positive or negative, and subsequent behavior is interpreted in light of this initial information.

Like the Hastie model previously described, an important assumption of the Srull-Wyer model is that evaluatively inconsistent behaviors are considered thoughtfully in comparison to other behaviors. This consideration strengthens links between each inconsistent behavior and the remaining behaviors (compared to the links between each evaluatively consistent or neutral behavior and the remaining behaviors). The inconsistency advantage presumably occurs as people think about the inconsistencies, relating them to each other and to the consistent behaviors, creating associative links among them.

One can infer the point at which participants have formed their evaluative impression by observing impressions as they are being formed. That is, over blocks (clusters of stimulus behaviors), one can observe the start-up and increase of the inconsistency advantage in memory. (Essentially, one would plot the degree of inconsistency advantage in each successive block.) One study required at least five blocks of five behaviors each to show the inconsistency advantage (Srull, Lichtenstein, & Rothbart, 1985); that is, it took 25 behaviors to develop an evaluative impression strong enough to make people notice new information being inconsistent with an overall evaluative impression. This suggests that evaluatively mixed information does not quickly generate a strong evaluative impression, so it would not easily show an inconsistency advantage in memory. The inconsistency advantage may be limited to impressions with very few pieces of inconsistent information against an extraordinarily consistent information baseline.

Similarly, interfering with the formation of interitem links should eliminate the inconsistency advantage in memory; studies in which participants perform a competing online task (even rehearsing the stimulus items!) do not show the same inconsistency advantage (Srull, 1981; Srull et al., 1985). The same is true of participants without the capacity and time to form online links (Bargh & Thein, 1985; Barrett, Tugade, & Engle, 2004; Macrae, Bodenhausen, Schloerscheidt, & Milne, 1999). Finally, although participants show an inconsistency advantage within the main person memory paradigm, they may instead preferentially recall consistent items when they have time to think over their impression afterward, perhaps due to bolstering the overall evaluative direction of the impression (Wyer & Martin, 1986). In other words, over the long term, consistent material enjoys a memorial advantage.

One positive aspect of this model was its ability to summarize vast quantities of research by Srull, Wyer, and their colleagues. One disadvantage of the Srull-Wyer model was its assumption of multiple representations ("storage bins"), all pertaining to a single person. This cumbersome idea was not endorsed by other models of person memory, and it tends to make this model both counterintuitive (not as much a technical flaw as an aesthetic one) and also perhaps overly flexible, able to account for virtually any result or its opposite.

One of the prominent features of these person memory models (both the Hastie and Srull-Wyer versions) is that they predict a recall advantage for impression inconsistent behaviors. The inconsistency advantage is explained by increased attention, linkages, and retrieval routes for inconsistent material. The inconsistency advantage was a robust effect within the standard paradigm of instilling a trait impression, then presenting a series of consistent and inconsistent behaviors and asking participants to recall the behaviors (see Srull & Wyer, 1989). However, the inconsistency advantage is *not* obtained when the research paradigm departs from the standard one in any of several ways that complicate the perceiver's task: well-established expectancies (S. T. Fiske & Neuberg, 1990; Higgins & Bargh, 1987; Ruble & Stangor, 1986), multiple trait expectancies (D. L. Hamilton, Driscoll, & Worth, 1989), behaviors that are descriptively but not evaluatively inconsistent (Wyer & Gordon, 1982), traits and behaviors overheard in a conversation (Wyer, Budesheim, & Lambert, 1990), time to think about one's impression afterwards (Wyer & Martin, 1986), having to make a complex judgment (Bodenhausen & Lichtenstein, 1987; Bodenhausen & Wyer, 1985) under cognitive load or selective memory (Garcia-Marques, Hamilton, & Maddox, 2002), and under multitask conditions (Macrae et al., 1999). Also, when it does occur, the inconsistency advantage occurs for impressions of individuals who are expected to have coherent personalities and not so much for groups, which are viewed as containing less coherent "personalities" (Rothbart, Evans, & Fulero, 1979; Srull et al., 1985).

Marques-Hamilton Person Memory Model

Although the Hastie and Srull-Wyer models can account for many of these results, people probably use multiple processing strategies, depending on the circumstances, as in the dual-process modes described in Chapter 2. Indeed, a newer model suggests that people use distinct retrieval processes, depending on their task (Garcia-Marques & Hamilton, 1996). When they attempt to recall information, they use an exhaustive strategy, but when they want to remember instances to make a frequency judgment, for example, they use a heuristic retrieval strategy. The exhaustive strategy favors memory for inconsistency, whereas the heuristic strategy favors memory for consistency. Consistent with other dual-process models, this is called the twofold retrieval by associative pathways (TRAP) model.

Carlston's Associative Systems Theory

According to associative systems theory (AST), representations of other people develop through the use of four primary mental systems: (a) the visual system, (b) the verbal/semantic system, (c) the affective system, and (d) the action system (Carlston, 1994). These four modalities are relatively independent at lower levels related to immediate encoding but intertwine as representations become more abstract. Many of the mechanisms otherwise relate to other associative memory models. This view explicitly adds other modalities to the associative memory models' primary focus on cognitive modalities, most notably affect and action.

Conclusion

The most influential model of memory in social cognition has been the node–link structure proposed by associative memory models. In this view, each concept (trait, behavior, person's name) is represented as a node, with links formed by relating two items to each other. Memory retrieval proceeds along the pathways provided by the network. The recall advantage for expectancy inconsistent versus expectancy consistent information, under some circumstances, is one of the major empirical legacies of these models. Newer approaches that build on procedural memory, parallel processes, and social neuroscience go beyond these early controversies.

PROCEDURAL AND DECLARATIVE MEMORY: WHAT MEMORY DOES

The Basic Cognitive Model of Procedural and Declarative Memory

As just described, many models assume that memory includes an associative network of concepts, a long-term store of content knowledge. This *declarative memory* is sometimes contrasted with one form of automaticity described earlier, *procedural knowledge* (Squire, 1987). In Chapter 2 we explained one form of automatic processing as proceduralization—that is, the speed-up of judgments with practice. However, we did not locate procedural processes within a larger model of memory. With some additional background on memory, we can do so, building on recent memory models (e.g., J. R. Anderson et al., 2004). Respectively, they roughly cover the "what" (declarative) and the "how" (procedural) forms of memory.

Newer associative network models posit that declarative memory is activated as a joint function of its general usefulness in the past and its current relevance; together they control both probability and speed of retrieval (Anderson et al., 2004). Retrieval from declarative memory implicates the hippocampus and the temporal lobes. (Recall the taxi drivers with enlarged hippocampi for street location memory in Chapter 1.) Declarative long-term memory includes both *episodic* memory for specific events (Tulving, 1983) and *semantic* memory for facts, word meaning, and encyclopedic knowledge (Squire, 1992). Consistent with earlier ideas about short-term memory, retrieved material occupies a space-limited buffer associated with the ventrolateral prefrontal cortex (Buckner, Kelley, & Petersen, 1999; Wagner, Paré-Blagoev, Clark, & Poldrack, 2001). Related chunks of knowledge activate together, akin to short-term or working memory.

Procedural knowledge concerns skills—namely, how to do things—and is hypothesized to be represented differently from how we have been discussing it. Procedural knowledge is represented as condition-action pairs, or if-then statements, called *productions*. When an input pattern matches the "if," or condition, part of the production, the "then," or action, part immediately operates. For example, a condition might include "if the envelope is addressed to me and advertises a large cash prize." The action part of the production, for some of us, includes "then discard without opening," while for others it must include "then open, read, and respond immediately." Various common cognitive productions (such as matching, selection, and execution) make up procedural memory, which globally implicates a loop involving the basal ganglia (Anderson et al., 2004). People's current goals determine which procedures fire; the goals may be associated with the dorsolateral prefrontal cortex. The current goal may occupy a buffer that serves to track one's progress in achieving an outcome.

Procedural Models of Social Memory

As described previously, content knowledge is initially represented in the declarative associative networks long familiar to social cognition researchers. The advantages of declarative representation include easy learning, for one simply links ideas; wide availability of use, namely, in any situation that cues part of the structure; and flexibility, that is, enabling one to work in various directions among associations, depending on need (E. R. Smith, 1998). Thus declarative knowledge is general and independent of domain and is probably accessible to consciousness and verbal expression. Hence it has been amenable to the methods most commonly used by social cognition researchers.

The disadvantage of declarative knowledge is that it tends to be slower and to use up one's limited-capacity working (short-term) memory. Accordingly, as certain processes are used repeatedly, they eventually may be proceduralized to be more efficient, as noted earlier.[1]

Smith's Proceduralization

Social processes are nothing if not frequent, so it makes sense that some would be proceduralized, as we saw in the examples of automaticity. Specifically, we described the work of E. R. Smith and his colleagues, who have applied the principles of procedural memory in particular to the speed-up of social inferences with practice (E. R. Smith, 1990; E. R. Smith & DeCoster, 1998); as noted, these practice effects provide one explanation for automaticity.

In addition, Smith and his colleagues propose that procedural memory provides an alternative explanation for priming effects, discussed in light of memory models. Recall that priming demonstrates the impact of a recently or frequently activated category on the processing of category-relevant information. Priming effects are typically interpreted in terms of category accessibility, using declarative (associative network) memory. That is, models describe activation as spreading from a prime to relevant concepts along the associative network's pathways. Any linked concept can prime another, whether the priming is based on words, faces, or symbols. The process itself is general, working the same way for any content linked in the associative network.

However, studies suggest that some priming effects can instead be process specific, as a procedural account would suggest (E. R. Smith & Branscombe, 1987, 1988; E. R. Smith, 1989; cf. Higgins & Chaires, 1980). Consider the different specific processes that can prime a personality trait: For example, one might read the word and think about it, or one might generate it from an obvious behavioral instance. When a subsequent task repeats the exact same process (i.e., reading the

---

[1]Proceduralization is viewed as the second step of a two-step process of *compilation*. First, certain actions that are always executed together may be combined into a single mega-step via *composition*. What began as a sequence of steps ("if envelope is addressed to me and advertises prize, then open it," followed by "if envelope advertises a prize and has just been opened, then check eligibility") may end up as one more complex step ("if envelope is addressed to me and advertises a prize, then open and check eligibility"). The second way to compile certain processes is via *proceduralization*, as when one learns to sort one's mail more rapidly, applying general procedures to specific repeated experiences. When every envelope from a certain place fails to provide an unambiguous, unconditional prize, one quickly learns the procedure: "If envelope is addressed to me from Cash Grand Prizes Clearinghouse, then discard." For simplicity here and because this distinction is not universal, we discuss only proceduralization.

trait or generating it from behavior), a form of priming occurs; namely, a speed-up of subsequent access to the word. This speed-up depends on the specific process (reading or generating), not just on previous exposure to the concept. When the practice task uses *different* priming processes than the test task (e.g., generating at practice and reading at test), the trait concept is just as accessible as when the practice and test tasks use the *same* priming processes (e.g., generate at both or reading at both). Nevertheless, greater speed-up occurs when the same exact task procedure is repeated. Thus some priming effects occur from repeated procedures per se in addition to the category accessibility effects of declarative associative memory. This does not replace accessibility but essentially suggests that specific processes can be primed as well.

Lewicki's Implicit Memory

Other applications of procedural memory may explain the accessibility of certain attitudes (see Chapter 10), the selection of one inference or category from among many possible ones (cf. Chapter 11), and the learning of complex patterns that cannot be articulated (Lewicki, Czyzewska, & Hoffman, 1987; Musen & Squire, 1993; for a review, see Seger, 1994). The more a particular procedure is practiced, the more likely it is to be used again instead of other equally applicable procedures. In this view, such procedural effects are a form of "implicit memory," which is a term for the influence of past judgmental processes on current judgments and reactions (E. R. Smith & Branscombe, 1988; see Jacoby & Kelley, 1987, for another discussion of unconscious memory). Procedural memory ideas have not overtaken social cognition, but their considerable influence appears in work on implicit associations (see Chapters 11–12).

Conclusion

Procedural memory introduces the idea of if-then automatic procedures built up through practice to become automatic processes. Social cognition applications of procedural memory focus mainly on priming specific operations and other instances of implicit memory (see Table 4.1).

PARALLEL VERSUS SERIAL PROCESSING: COORDINATING MEMORY PROCESSES

Cutting across issues of declarative (associative) and procedural memory is the issue of parallel versus serial processing. The traditional associative network models viewed spreading activation as a *parallel* process of activating many related pathways at once, but overall processes of encoding, memory retrieval, and response are generally viewed as a *serial* sequence of steps. Social categories are often seen as activating before the activation of individuating information (as described in Chapter 2). This could occur via either serial or parallel processing. That is, serially, first one is activated, then the other. Or if both are activated in parallel, perhaps the category information is processed faster and beats out the individuating information. The serial processing idea is more prevalent in earlier information processing models, so the newer models focus more on parallel processes, as this section explains.

The Basic Cognitive Model of Parallel Processing

Parallel distributed processing (PDP) is an approach to the structure of cognition that developed as an alternative to more traditional, mostly serial models of mental structure. For reasons that remain obscure, one of us found herself describing PDP to her 80-year-old great aunt, always an astute and intellectually challenging conversationalist, who demanded a sample of "the wave of the future" in cognition research. PDP seemed a safe bet in that the great aunt could be guaranteed to know even less about it than the author did. Precariously launched on an explanation, the metaphor for PDP that came to mind was an old-fashioned time and temperature sign board composed of lightbulbs. Such signs were made of a grid of bulbs, different combinations lighting up depending on the numerals that needed to be displayed. Each lightbulb contributes to all the times and temperatures displayed by being on or off within the overall pattern. In this over-simplified and deeply flawed PDP metaphor, born of desperation, individual memory units are lightbulbs, each unit participating in many different memory patterns, as simply one feature of the whole. The same bulb could be part of the numeral "1" or "2." Moreover, the numeral "2" could appear in different positions on the board, depending on whether the time were 2:00 or 7:32.

Consider how this approach differs from associative network models of memory. In such models, each node uniquely represents a concept, and when it is sufficiently activated, the concept is retrieved. In a PDP model, each unit helps to represent many different concepts, which are retrieved when the appropriate pattern of activation occurs across all the basic units. Thus, to return to the time and temperature sign, the specific numeral "3" could occur on the right, left, or middle of the sign, as needed, depending only on the correct configuration of lightbulbs being on. Thus no single lightbulb represents "3," but instead the pattern does, and which set of bulbs do the job is arbitrary. This differs considerably from a neon sign, for example, that has one structure dedicated to lighting up for one particular number whenever it is needed. Traditional memory models would roughly resemble a series of neon letters linked to each other. (The great aunt was skeptical but intrigued.)

PDP models essentially deal with the subatomic particles of perception and cognition. PDP models assume that memory consists of elementary units (the bulbs in our metaphor) that are connected with facilitative and inhibitory links to each other. The connections represent *constraints* about what units are associated, and the *connection strengths* represent the type and magnitude of association. Only the strengths of connections are stored, so that the pattern can be re-created by activating parts of it and waiting for the connections to reverberate throughout the system until the entire pattern is activated.

The full theory of PDP is beyond the scope of this book (for an accessible introduction, see McClelland, Rumelhart, & Hinton, 1986). For the most part, it has been applied to issues of motor control (typing, reaching) and perception at the level of individual letters in a word. One interpretation of PDP models is that they aim at a different and lower level than the network models of memory described earlier. That is, a node in the network metaphor would be not a single neuron but a pattern of activation over neurons. If one considers PDP only as a lower-level elaboration of network models—that is, operating at the level of neurons—its implications for social cognition's more macro level of analysis would be limited.

Nevertheless, PDP does have potential utility for a social level of analysis. In the more traditional associative models, knowledge is represented statically. That is, knowledge does not change its form between long-term and working memory because it is essentially just more or less activated. In PDP models, however, the patterns themselves are not stored, but the strengths of connections among basic units are stored, enabling the patterns to be re-created. From a practical perspective, this allows knowledge to be implicit in the system rather than being an explicit set of stored rules.

PDP also allows imperfect stimulus patterns to be recognized because approximations can activate part of the pattern of connections, which subsequently generate the remaining aspects of the pattern. PDP models are good at considering several sources of information simultaneously. They are parallel processors, in contrast to the more traditional serial processing models.

Recent models of memory combine serial and parallel processes (e.g., J. R. Anderson et al., 2004). For example, declarative memory retrieval might simultaneously search many related memories in parallel, but the content that comes to mind might form a serial bottleneck because one can attend to only one retrieved memory at a time. Similarly, several potential productions might be activated in parallel in procedural memory, but only a single production could fire at a time, serially.

Parallel Constraint Satisfaction in Social Cognition

One possible domain of PDP application in social cognition is to stereotypes, and in particular to how they simultaneously interact with each other. For example, combining one's knowledge about traditional Amish farmers and progressive Montessori teachers, one can imagine someone who occupies both roles by considering their shared "back to basics" perspective and shared emphasis on patience. Moreover, one can imagine the person's likely response to novel issues (e.g., cell phones in the classroom). PDP models allow for such emergent properties of previous knowledge.

Kunda-Thagard Parallel Constraint Satisfaction Model

A pertinent example in social cognition is a parallel constraint satisfaction theory (Kunda & Thagard, 1996). Introduced briefly in Chapter 2 as a single-mode alternative to the dual-mode models, it views impression formation as similar to text comprehension. The perceiver needs to interpret and integrate a variety of incoming information simultaneously with accessing the relevant knowledge base, which includes representations of stereotypes and traits. The model emphasizes the simultaneity of these processes, balancing the mutual and immediate influence of inputs ranging from the more concrete (e.g., interpretation of specific behaviors) to the more abstract (e.g., application of expectations or stereotypes). All information considered at once constrains the other currently accessed information. For example, a shove coming from a friend may come across as playful, whereas a shove coming from a stranger may come across as violent. The model posits that expectancies and new information constrain each other's interpretation, especially when information is ambiguous. Chapter 11 on stereotyping revisits these issues, but at present the point is that processing can occur in parallel, with a variety of information mutually influencing each other's interpretations. The model works as a computer simulation of impression formation processes.

Van Overwalle's Connectionist Models

The connectionist model of impression formation also applies PDP principles to social cognition (Van Overwalle & Labiouse, 2004). This model goes beyond the Kunda-Thagard parallel constraint satisfaction model because it includes a learning component as well as the perception component. This model also has an initial activation phase in which external inputs (e.g., stimuli) are balanced against internal ones (e.g., expectations). After this activation phase, the connectionist model adds *consolidation* in long-term memory. Consolidation occurs when the external inputs do not precisely match the internal linkages. The model then adjusts the long-term links based on its discrepancy from the short-term input. It's a reality check, in effect. In this model, mismatched expectations should change to fit the most typical input from the environment over time.

Two principles emerge from this computer simulation model. First, *acquisition* reflects the sheer effects of more confirming information over less of it in what is often termed the *set size effect*. People are more certain the more support they have for their perceptions. The other principle is *competition* among the links, whereby the successful (accurate) ones are strengthened at the expense of the less successful (inaccurate) ones. Thus, if the system initially believes that all cats have stubs for tails because its first cat was a Manx, subsequent encounters with fully tailed cats will strengthen the tail belief at the expense of the stub belief.

The computer simulation re-creates standard impression formation effects, such as assimilation and contrast priming effects, the inconsistency advantage in certain kinds of recall, and particular patterns of primacy and recency (greater weighting of early and recent information under specific circumstances). The same connectionist model also applies to a range of social cognition topics: causal attributions (Van Overwalle, 1998), dual-process models of attitudes (Van Overwalle & Siebler, 2005), cognitive dissonance (Van Overwalle & Jordens, 2002), group biases (Van Rooy, Van Overwalle, Vanhoomissen, Labiouse, & French, 2003), and communication (Van Overwalle & Heylighen, 2006).

Kashima's Tensor-Product Model

A related model is the tensor-product model (Kashima, Woolcock, & Kashima, 2000), which uses a Hebbian learning approach instead of the competition approach used in the Van Overwalle connectionist model. A Hebbian approach describes some kinds of associative learning by changes in the strength of links between nerve cells; simultaneous activation strengthens the links, but there is no provision for inhibition of unactivated links. Also, it is not viewed as a literal representation of neural networks. Nevertheless, this model nicely describes several phenomena in forming impressions of groups.

Conclusion

PDP connectionist models have proved popular for computer simulation models of social cognition in various forms. Another connectionist model addresses basic Gestalt principles of causal reasoning, cognitive consistency, and goal-directed behavior (see Chapters 1, 6, 9, and 15; Read, Vanman, & Miller, 1997). Still others address the self-concept (Nowak, Vallacher, Tesser, & Borkowski, 2000), attitude learning (Eiser, Fazio, Stafford, & Prescott, 2003), and perceptions of outgroups (Read & Urada, 2003). This approach also goes by the name dynamical perspective (Vallacher, Read, & Nowak, 2002).

EMBODIED MEMORY: INCLUDING PHYSICAL REPRESENTATION

A Basic Cognitive Model of Perceptual Symbol Systems

PDP approaches originally developed ways to understand perceptual recognition of familiar patterns, for example, a blurred, chipped, or degraded letter. Perceptual approaches in general were not typically viewed as tenable conceptual systems, just as recording systems. However, a newer perceptual theory of knowledge aims to fill that gap (Barsalou, 1999b).

Perceptual symbols encode experience, both external and internal. This form of memory representation incorporates bottom-up perceptual processes, that is, processes that work from direct perceptual experiences and resulting associations in the brain that activate sensory motor areas. Perceptual experiences can include all the senses, plus introspection and proprioception (sense of one's own bodily position from internal feedback). Selective attention picks out features of the environment, for example, not every available stimulus but specific components. This perceptual side captures useful information about edges, colors, movement, temperature, and the like. It is *embodied* in the sense that the information includes both external stimuli (temperature) and bodily experiences (pain). It is also embodied in the sense that it prepares the perceiver for appropriate action (avoidance). In this way, it is a more sophisticated 21st century version of Gibsonian ecological perception described in Chapter 3, as in "perceiving is for doing."

In addition to the perceptual side, this form of memory representation also captures top-down expectations, after perceptual experiences. The perceptual symbol systems (PSS) record the neural activation during stimulus input, but they also reactivate later for conceptual processing. PSS can represent objects in their presence (perception) or in their absence (imagery or conception). *Imagery* differs from conception in being more conscious and specific about the sensory motor representation, as when you close your eyes and visualize your childhood home. *Conception* entails knowing about it without consciously retrieving visual (or other sensory motor) details.

The key components of PSS include the *simulator* that first registers and later re-creates a perceptual experience. Essentially, it is the pattern of brain activation created by selective attention at the perceptual stage. Related perceptual symbols organize into simulators that allow the system to represent specific entities (e.g., what you see the first time to arrive at a new home). The representation is dynamic, changing as you experience more information (walking in, living there over time). The simulator contains two kinds of structures: the underlying *frame* that integrates across experience with that category (that home, homes in general), and the *simulations* that can be created from the frame; simulations create the experience of a particular example on a particular occasion.

In this view, at one extreme cognitive processes involve bottom-up sensory motor perceptions. At the other extreme are top-down sensory motor representations that include conception and imagery. Intermediate are processes such as priming, filling gaps where information is missing, anticipating future events, and interpreting ambiguous information. These all entail complementary processes that are part perceptual and part top-down. The PSS view differs from the associative network models in a particularly important way: The perceptual symbols represent sensory modality, whereas the earlier models were *amodal* in the sense that memory represented abstract structures regardless of original type of sensory or internal input. PSS represent abstract concepts by the integrative frames across specific experiences, selecting the core features, and by incorporating both physical and introspective experiences. From the PSS perspective, working memory runs the perceptual simulations (e.g., as a buffer containing information just experienced). Long-term memory records the experience and relevant simulations. We have described this model at some length because it may prove useful to social cognition researchers in the future, as some current work suggests.

Social Cognitive Models of Embodiment

The PSS view appeals to social cognition settings because of its focus not just on archiving information but on preparation for situated action (Barsalou, 1999b). Social interaction is nothing if not situated action. The main intellectual message of social psychology is that social situations greatly influence thoughts, feelings, and behaviors. Social psychologists thus are adopting the embodied cognition viewpoint, as anticipated by Zajonc and Markus's (1984) description of the "hard interface."

Embodied cognition places the actor squarely in interpersonal context, in socially situated cognition (E. R. Smith & Semin, 2004). Embodiment plausibly underlies social information processing both in direct perception—*online cognition* during interaction—and in the absence of the considered social object—*offline cognition* (Niedenthal, Baraslou, Winkielman, Krauth-Gruber, & Ric, 2005). PSS applies to several recent findings involving effects of facial or bodily positions on social cognition. For example, when people are induced to nod their head vertically or shake their head horizontally while receiving a persuasive communication, they are, respectively, more or less likely to agree with it (Wells & Petty, 1980). When people hold a pencil horizontally in their teeth—making them contract their zygomaticus smile muscles—they find cartoons funnier than when they hold the pencil with their lips (Strack, Martin, & Stepper, 1988). People like unfamiliar Chinese ideographs better when they flex their arms, mimicking an approach motion, than when they extend their arm, making an avoidance motion (Cacioppo, Priester, & Berntson, 1993). When people adopt different postures characteristic of emotions such as sadness, they report feeling those emotions more (Duclos et al., 1989), and making a fist relates to people's conceptions of power (Schubert, 2004). All these examples suggest an effect of embodiment on emotions and evaluations.

In Chapter 3 we saw the reverse: Conceptual priming through words or visual priming through faces makes people enact relevant stereotypic behaviors (Bargh, Chen, & Burrows, 1996). But the effects of bottom-up sensory motor representation and top-down generalized concepts and images are reciprocal between embodiment and affective experience: People feel particularly understood when they imitate each other's nonverbal behavior during interaction (Chartrand & Bargh, 1999). Empathy operates partly through bodily channels (Decéty & Chaminade, 2003). The representation of an emotional experience is especially likely to occur through embodied knowledge about the emotion (Barrett, 2006).

Conclusion

Memory models often build on the idea that associative networks organize concepts in long-term memory and that the currently most activated associations represent short-term or working memory. This framework underlies most work on social memory. When researchers turn to memory in action—what it does—they distinguish declarative memory (the associative networks of what is recalled) and procedural memory (the if-then pairs that determine how recall triggers other operations). Memory models increasingly focus on simultaneous parallel procedures to coordinate memory processes, not just serially sequenced processes. And models of embodied cognition rely on sensory motor perceptual systems for both bottom-up perception and top-down conceptual representation.

SOCIAL MEMORY STRUCTURES: WHY SOCIAL MEMORY MATTERS

"I love you, Jane . . . I mean, Sally." What happens when you call someone by another person's name? People typically are annoyed at being treated as equivalent to the other person (or as less cognitively accessible than the other person). And well they should be annoyed, although we know of worse cases in which people confuse their children with the dog (A. P. Fiske et al., 1991). What happens when you forget someone's name or their confidences? Feelings are hurt, and personal tragedies can ensue. People use broad expectations and categories to organize their memory for other people. This is often functional, but it has its drawbacks. Social cognition research has long focused on this tension between the general and the particular. In this final section we discuss mental representations of social categories and specific social exemplars because these structures cut across different memory theories, and all are crucial to social life.

Social Categories

Categories describe our expectations about, for example, people, entities, or social groups. Like it or not, we all make assumptions about other people, ourselves, and the situations we encounter. Sometimes we are dramatically misled by our expectations. However, much of the time our expectations are functional, and indeed, we would be unable to operate without them. Such expectations, assumptions, and generic prior knowledge allow us some sense of prediction and control, which is essential to our well-being (Chapter 2).

Could we do without categories? Consider the seemingly objective alternative of operating within situations and with people about whom we have virtually no expectations or prior knowledge. Arriving on a new campus the first day, coming into an unfamiliar culture for the first time, or meeting a stranger whose gender, age, and role are mysterious—these all are disorienting encounters that challenge our ability to function without the normal level of prediction and control provided by expectations. Prior knowledge about the campus (a map, for instance), guides to the culture (from travel books), or an introduction to the stranger (by a mutual friend) would facilitate each encounter. Of course, our inevitable reliance on such prior knowledge is not perfectly adaptive. We may rely on the wrong assumptions, or our assumptions may be overly rigid. But on the whole, such expectations are useful.

Category-Driven Versus Data-Driven Processes

Categories represent knowledge about a concept; sometimes termed a *schema*, such an abstract representation includes the concept's attributes and the relations among them (S. T. Fiske & Linville, 1980; Macrae & Bodenhausen, 2001; Rumelhart & Ortony, 1977; S. E. Taylor & Crocker, 1981). Categorical person perception facilitates what is variously termed top-down, conceptually driven, or theory-driven processes, which simply means processes heavily influenced by one's organized prior knowledge as opposed to processes that are more bottom-up, stimulus driven, or data driven (Abelson, 1981; Bobrow & Norman, 1975; Rumelhart & Ortony, 1977). As people's theories and concepts about the world, categorical perceptions are concerned with the general case, abstract generic knowledge that holds across many particular instances. The basic message of this research has been that people simplify reality by storing knowledge at a molar, inclusive level rather than squirreling away, one-by-one, all the original individual experiences in their raw forms, which would be pure data-driven processing.

Recently, however, social and cognitive psychologists have taken a closer look at data-driven processes by focusing on their interplay with category-driven processes. Data-driven processes demonstrate ordinary people's sensitivity to the specific qualities of another individual or situation. Purely categorical theories have, in the extreme case, portrayed people as blithely glossing over important details, as stubbornly refusing to see the information in front of them, and as maintaining their schemas at any cost. In contrast, data-driven approaches show that people do indeed care about the information given (Higgins & Bargh, 1987). We consider both types of phenomena in this section, beginning with categorical processes.

As noted, our perceptions of the world reflect an interplay between what's out there and what we bring to it. We are, paradoxically, more aware of the contributions of the world out there than of our own contributions to our cognitive processes. That is, we know we are encoding information, but we underestimate the roles of selective attention, interpretation, and gap-filling. Expectations are structured knowledge that we bring to everyday perceptions, so expectations emphasize our active construction of reality. This is not to say that we are unconstrained by the stimuli themselves; contrary to Gertrude Stein, "there is a there there."

Categorical expectations emphasize the part of the perceptual interplay— our own contribution—that is mostly preconscious. We experience the world as if we have added nothing to it, so common sense tells us that we perceive an unchanged or literal copy of the environment. We experience perception as instantaneous and direct, as if our brains were simply videotaping the surroundings. Both ordinary people and some philosophers have held this commonsense view that perceptions are unfiltered and veridical (Aristotle, 1931; J. Mill, 1869). An emphasis on the importance of less-filtered experience continues in the present-day study of exemplars (covered later in this section).

In contrast, Gestalt psychology encouraged a different view of perception (Brunswik, 1956; Koffka, 1935). As we noted in Chapter 1, Gestalt psychologists argued that perception is constructive and that perceptions are mediated by the interpretive faculties of nerves and brain. What we "see" in any given stimulus depends on context; for example, the "1"s in "1952" and in "life" objectively are quite similar, but we interpret them differently because of their respective contexts. Context provides a different Gestalt, or configuration, that alters the meaning of the individual elements. Hence, the whole is more than the simple combination of its parts. The Gestalt emphasis on people's perception of configurations in context anticipates social categories and expectations as configurations-in-context actively contributed by the perceiver. This organized prior knowledge shapes what is perceived and remembered in much the same way that context-based Gestalt configurations do, but generally as more complex types of configurations involving people and situations. Gestalt stimulus configurations guided two theoretical developments that directly precede current categorical theories: Solomon Asch's (1946) configural model of forming impressions of others (Chapter 1) and Fritz Heider's (1958) theory of social configurations that produce psychological balance (Chapter 9).

Categorical Perception

The commonsense view and the classical view have been that one can precisely define the boundaries of everyday categories (E. E. Smith & Medin, 1981), just as one imagines being able to do in science or mathematics (although even there the classical assumption is questioned). On closer examination, this proves not to be possible. Building on principles first noted by Wittgenstein (1953), several principles derived in cognitive psychology (Mervis & Rosch, 1981; Rosch, 1978, 1987) and social-personality psychology (Cantor & Mischel, 1979) describe how people categorize things, situations, and other people.

One core notion is that natural categories do not have necessary and sufficient attributes. Instead, the category members fall within fuzzy boundaries, so it is not always clear which instances belong in the category. For example, Monopoly, baseball, and charades are good examples of the category games, but what about playing house, torturing ants, and betting on the Superbowl? The perception that some instances are more typical than others led to the idea that instances range from being quite typical to atypical, with a most typical or prototypical instance best representing the category. The *prototype* is the "central tendency" or average of the category members.[2]

People may never actually encounter their prototypes in real life because they are abstracted from experiences with examples. Even though none of the instances may itself be a perfect prototype, people abstract out the most typical features (Hayes-Roth & Hayes-Roth, 1977; Posner & Keele, 1968, 1970; Reed, 1972). People then decide if a new instance fits the category by assessing its similarity to the prototype.

In this view, category members are related by the criterion of family resemblance. Any given pair of category members will share some features with each other and other features with other category members. For example, Twenty Questions and baseball both include a certain number of turns (the 20 questions or the nine innings), whereas tag and Monopoly do not. On the other hand, Twenty Questions and tag are both played without specific equipment, whereas

---

[2]This central tendency could come from the arithmetic mean or mode, depending on whether the particular dimension is continuous (e.g., height) or discrete (color).

baseball and Monopoly both require specialized equipment. The more features an instance shares with other category members, the more consistently, consensually, and quickly it is identified as a category member (McCloskey & Glucksberg, 1978; Rosch, 1978; E. E. Smith, Shoben, & Rips, 1974). Thus any given feature is not necessarily present in all category members, only more or less probably so. The point is that the internal structure of categories is more fluid than the classical view would have it, and that it can be well described as a fuzzy set centering around a prototype.

Moving from within-category to between-category structure, categories are often thought to be organized hierarchically at varying levels of inclusion. That is, under the broad category "entertainment," one might include (at least) games, parties, television, books, and movies. Under each of these subcategories, one would have several more subordinate categories, such as car games, board games, outdoor games. Different levels of categorization are useful for different purposes (Rosch, Mervis, Gray, Johnson, & Boyes-Braem, 1976). For example, people propose "let's play a game" or "let's go to a movie" (intermediate level) more often than the generic "let's have some entertainment" and more often than the specific "let's play a car game." In this view, such basic-level or intermediate categories for objects are rich in the attributes people associate with them, are easily distinguished from related categories, and involve well-practiced everyday behaviors.

Categorical Person Perception

Just as we categorize different kinds of things and activities, so we also categorize different kinds of people, often according to their personalities. Suppose you see a list of another person's prototypically extraverted attributes, such as being energetic, entertaining, and friendly. Later, you may be unsure whether you also saw other prototypical attributes, such as outgoing and lively (Cantor & Mischel, 1979; Tsujimoto, 1978). Activating some of the attributes activated related ones, so it is hard to remember which you saw and which you inferred from the prototype. This fits the view that people seem to extract a trait prototype from exposure to category-consistent information. Social categories thus may be viewed as fuzzy sets (without rigid boundaries) centering on a prototype.

One implication of this view is that category-based thinking can generate false memories. People store the general prototype and fit the gist of new information to it. Hence, they may remember category-consistent information that never occurred. In one study (Macrae, Schloerscheidt, Bodenhausen, & Milne, 2002), participants saw 60 first names, half male and half female, paired equally often with the gender-typed occupations of mechanic and hairdresser; that is, half were gender consistent and half gender inconsistent. Later, they had to recognize which names they had previously seen, out of a batch of 120; if they said the name was previously seen, they also had to state its occupation. As is typical with simple materials, and as explained by several person memory models described earlier, people more easily recalled expectancy–inconsistent names (male hairdressers and female mechanics).

More interesting from the categorical perspective were the false memories. False alarms mistakenly identify distracter items on the test as being part of the original set. These false alarms were twice as likely to be expectancy consistent as expectancy inconsistent. That is, when they did falsely identify a name as familiar, they most often identified those names as having the gender-consistent occupation. What's more, these false memories were accompanied by a feeling of knowing, so when people falsely recognized a name and attributed a gender-consistent occupation, they were more likely to have a feeling of familiarity for the gender-consistent than gender-inconsistent cases. All this especially occurred when people were either distracted or elderly.

The implication is that people can experience a feeling of knowing when a memory is entirely false, and that category-based consistency underlies this phenomenon. Recall the opening example about witnessing a mugging. Do you remember the older woman, the busy intersection, the parked cars, and the traffic light? What about the mugger's sweatshirt, mentioned later? And his cap? What did he steal? Her purse, you answer. Right. What color was his cap? Where were the parked cars? Well, actually, we never mentioned either the cap or the parked cars, but in dozens of controlled experiments, people are led to experience clear and persistent false memories for events that never happened (Loftus, 2004). Lawyers can plant false memories by asking leading questions ("Did you see the parked cars?" when there weren't any). This throws into question, for example, allegedly repressed and recovered memories that may result from other people's suggestions (Loftus & Davis, 2006). Importantly, the suggestions have to fit with known categories of experience that are plausible in retrospect. Various forms of categorical processing could account for these effects.[3]

Critiques of Category and Prototype Views

Social categories have well-established effects, but the models are changing as the field progresses. First, one modification of the basic approach suggests that social categories are more often represented by ideals or extremes (Barsalou, 1985; Chaplin, John, & Goldberg, 1988). That is, the best example of a nun may in fact be the ideal nun rather than an average nun. In this view, ideals are especially likely to be used for goal-oriented categories with a particular purpose intrinsic to them, in which the best example is one that most completely fulfills the category's goal. It may also be that people have separate representations of the best category member and the average category member; if you ask "Could you suggest the best example of a local restaurant?" my interpretation of the question may lead me to recommend either the best restaurant or the most typical (not at all the same!).

A more drastic critique of prototypes rejects altogether the idea of a summary representation (ideal *or* typical), arguing that categories are represented as a collection of exemplars previously encountered. As it is rather a strong critique, we will discuss this perspective later. For now, the point is that prototypes may not be the only way that categories are stored.

Second, social categories also had been viewed as being automatically activated upon perceiving an instance. The original views held that categorization was essentially automatic and inevitable, but later views have interpreted category activation as conditionally automatic, depending on various factors including one's goals (Macrae & Bodenhausen, 2000; also see Chapter 2).

---

[3]A failure of *source-monitoring* (remembering the origin of a memory; Johnson, 2006) also contributes in another way. The idea suggested by the lawyer fits expectations about the event, and also one forgets where the idea came from. Failure of source-monitoring accounts for some forms of inadvertent plagiarism (Macrae, Bodenhausen, & Guglielmo, 1999).

Third, recall that the basic or intermediate levels of nonsocial categories apparently dominate people's everyday usage; the same may not be so true for social categories (Holyoak & Gordon, 1984). In using social categories, people's specific goals and expertise most likely determine which levels they choose to use (Cantor & Kihlstrom, 1987; Hampson, John, & Goldberg, 1986). This raises the further possibility that goals and expertise also determine people's choice of levels in nonsocial categories. In both social and nonsocial categories, however, some levels may function as default options, all else being equal.

A fourth issue is the extent to which social categories form a clear hierarchy, with higher levels subsuming lower levels. Social categories had been viewed as being hierarchically organized, with categories becoming more inclusive as they become broader (Cantor & Mischel, 1979); that is, people can list more instances and more attributes that go with broader categories (Goldberg, 1986; Hampson, Goldberg, & John, 1987). This overall approach proved initially useful but provoked several critiques.

Many social categories are not so neat, representing a fuzzy hierarchy in which class inclusions do not work strictly. For example, some data indicate that refusing to share (behavioral level) is a subset of being stingy (lower level), which is clearly one specific way of being unkind (upper level); all this would fit a hierarchy, but not all traits are structured so neatly. People report, for example, that being passive (more concrete, lower level) is not necessarily one specific way of being introverted (more abstract, upper level). Accordingly, the vertical connections between upper and lower levels are not always clear-cut (Hampson et al., 1986). Moreover, for some categories such as gender, the upper levels (male) do not provide richer associations than do the lower levels (the stereotypic businessman) (Deaux, Winton, Crowley, & Lewis, 1985), contrary to hierarchical predictions.

Perhaps the hierarchy notion needs to be discarded altogether; people may not think in hierarchies at all except when psychologists constrain them to do so. People may actually make associations in complex networks that resemble a tangled web rather than a hierarchy (Cantor & Kihlstrom, 1987). Imagine a neat hierarchy, from extravert at the top level, to politician, comedian, and bully at the intermediate level, with specific attributes (socially skilled, self-confident) at the lowest level. In a strict hierarchy, of course, some attributes are true of the superordinate level, and they are inherited by each of the lower levels. However, people's associations are not always so neat (Andersen & Klatzky, 1987). Attributes perceived to hold for the top-level category (e.g., extraverts are self-confident) do not always hold for all the intermediate-level categories (politicians are self-confident, but comedians and bullies are not). Moreover, some intermediate-level categories (bullies) are associated with other intermediate-level categories (politicians) but not with the overarching category (extravert). The overlapping nature of social categories differentiates them from object categories (Lingle, Altom, & Medin, 1984), at least as nonsocial categories have been studied so far.

To summarize, the prototype approach has introduced several ideas: namely, that social categories do not have rigid boundaries but rather operate as fuzzy sets, organized around a prototypical or average category member, against which other members are judged for typicality, so that category members are related by family resemblance rather than by necessary and sufficient rules for inclusion. However, some social categories may be organized around ideal or extreme cases rather than prototypes. The prototype approach originally proposed that social categories are arranged hierarchically, with a most useful intermediate level functioning as basic. But organization in terms of hierarchies and basic levels has been questioned, suggesting that social categories are related in more flexible and complex ways.[4]

Usage of Social Categories

Current research views social categories as conditionally activated and applied, though everyday life often meets the conditions that activate categories, as we indicated in Chapter 2. Categories can be activated, applied, and even inhibited, depending on social conditions (Macrae & Bodenhausen, 2000).

Category activation depends on attentional resources (Gilbert & Hixon, 1991). That is, under some rare circumstances, people may not notice another person's race, gender, or age. Under extreme cognitive overload, perceivers may identify the person's category, but they may not activate the associated stereotypes. If the stereotypes are indeed activated, however, cognitive load increases the odds of applying them.

People belong to multiple categories, and when one is activated, others are inhibited (Bodenhausen & Macrae, 1998). Category salience, chronic accessibility (Chapter 3), and processing goals (Chapter 2) determine which categories are activated and which are inhibited. People sometimes can inhibit category-congruent information intentionally, although this is costly to attentional resources (Macrae, Bodenhausen, Milne, & Ford, 1997). Relevant information can also be inhibited inadvertently. When people repeatedly retrieve one kind of information, related but not retrieved information is inhibited, a kind of adaptive forgetting that enables the mind to focus on what is currently relevant (MacLeod & Macrae, 2001).

Even if activated, categories may be applied in different ways, or not applied at all. We will come back to this point, but the point here is that category activation and application depend on a variety of conditions.

Exemplars

Cognitive Models of Exemplars

Just as the prototype view of categories was developed in reaction to the shortcomings of the classical view, so the exemplar view originally developed in reaction to the shortcomings of the prototype view (see E. E. Smith & Medin, 1981, for a review), and it may be best understood in that light. As a counterpoint to the prototype perspective, the exemplar approach suggests that one remembers separate instances or exemplars one has actually encountered rather than some average prototype one has abstracted from experience. One has several

[4]Besides the criticisms specific to social cognition just discussed, the prototype approach has been criticized on three basic points: (1) people know more about a concept than simply its features, for they also know which features tend to go together; for example, birds that sing tend to be small and to fly, but large birds tend not to sing or fly; (2) people also know the constraints, that there are limits on what features may be posited; for example, one does not posit how many pistons a bird has; and (3) context matters; for example, "bird" in the woods suggests a different sort than "bird" in a nursery school classroom (Lingle et al., 1984; Murphy & Medin, 1985; E. E. Smith & Medin, 1981).

exemplars for a category and, in this view, people categorize a thing by see-ing whether it resembles a lot of remembered exemplars from a single category. Although the prototype and exemplar view have subsequently been integrated by many researchers, especially those in social cognition, it is useful first to understand the pure exemplar view.

The exemplar view has several advantages. First, it most directly accounts for people's knowledge of specific examples that guide their understanding of the category. To illustrate, if asked whether restaurants typically contain equal numbers of tables for two or tables for more, one may have to consult several specific mental examples of restaurants to answer the question. Or if someone asserts that all restaurants have cashiers, one may retrieve a specific counterex-ample to refute the statement. This reliance on concrete instances suggests but, of course, does not require the idea of exemplars. (The prototype view does not dispute that people can remember some specific instances, but the instances are not the focus of the prototype view.)

More important, people know a lot about the possible variability between category members; consider the big variety of Chinese restaurants versus the sameness of a particular fast food chain. A true prototype theory cannot rep-resent information about variability; a pure prototype model would represent only the category average, not its variability. Exemplars provide a simple way to model variability across category members. It is easy to describe people's knowledge of such variation by positing exemplars, although equivalents might be possible within the prototype approach.

Another major advantage of the exemplar view, and probably the best argu-ment for it, is its ability to account for correlations of attributes within a category. For example, people know that within the category restaurant, formica tables tend to go with paying the cashier directly, and tablecloths tend to go with pay-ing through the server. They know this through their theories about inexpensive, convenience-oriented businesses as compared to other kinds (Murphy & Medin, 1985). A single summary prototype does not easily handle this knowledge. The knowledge of which attributes tend to be correlated among category members is especially important in social perception because people have implicit theories about which traits go together (e.g., based on remembering several friends who are both ambitious and hard-working) and which do not (e.g., not being able to retrieve examples of people who are both ambitious and kind; Schneider, 1973).

Finally, the exemplar view makes it easier to modify existing categories with new instances. In the exemplar approach, the new instance may be added as yet another exemplar, which will then contribute to subsequent category judgments (Lingle et al., 1984). In comparison, it is less clear how prototypes are modified, but we will return to this issue.

Social Cognitive Models of Exemplars

The social evidence for exemplars is growing. For example, although not inter-preted in terms of exemplars, one series of studies (Gilovich, 1981) showed that people's judgments are affected by irrelevant similarities to specific past examples; a new football player from the same hometown as a famous football player may be considered a good bet even though hometown is not especially diagnostic of athletic ability. People's political judgments are also shaped by advocates drawing lessons from history, even when the prior example is similar to the current one only in nondiagnostic ways. As another example, people's judgments about a member of a foreign culture are more heavily influenced by the foreigner's irrelevant similarity to a previously encountered exemplar rather than by general rules they had learned about the culture (Read, 1983, 1984, 1987). If people have causal theories (e.g., that the exemplar somehow influences the new instance), they are even more likely to use the exemplar. And in more every-day settings, people deciding which of two strangers is more approachable will choose the one most superficially similar to another stranger who was recently kind to them (or, conversely, least similar to a recently mean person), without apparently being aware of the reasons for their choice (Lewicki, 1985).

Familiarity, similarity to a previously known individual, whether consciously perceived or not, may create a sense of shared attitudes, attraction, predictability, and safety (S. T. Fiske, 1982, pp. 62–66; Genaro & Cantor, 1987; White & Shapiro, 1987). Familiarity may be a required mechanism for the operation of exemplars. When people encounter unfamiliar compound categories (e.g., male elementary school teachers), they rely on memory for specific instances, whereas when they encounter familiar compound categories (e.g., female elementary school teachers), they rely on abstract stereotypes. It is the familiarity per se that changes the judgment strategy (Groom, Sherman, Lu, Conrey, & Keijzer, 2005).

Although some of these studies were explicitly based on exemplar models from cognitive psychology and some were not, they all demonstrate the effect of single, concrete, prior experiences on subsequent judgments and behavior, and as such they provide a counterpoint to the influence of more global, abstract categories.

Some more direct discussion of the evidence for exemplars comes from work on the perceived variability of social categories. For example, people perceive increased variability in groups as their impressions become more differentiated (Linville, Salovey, & Fischer, 1986). As you learn more about a particular group of foreigners through an exchange program, you perceive them to come in more different varieties than you did beforehand (and they view citizens of your country as more variable as well). Linville, Fischer, and Salovey (1989) have explicitly argued that this effect can be best described by exemplar models. Some effects of abstract, category-level information can be explained in terms of pure exemplar models to show that the abstract representations are not necessary, although they certainly may be involved (E. R. Smith, 1988).[5] People do seem to use both abstract and exemplar information when provided; that is, they consider both their generalizations about the other nationality as well as specific citizens they have known. Moreover, when people are first given abstract information, followed by information about specific instances, they perceive less variability and make their judgments based on such prototypes more than when the order is reversed or when they are given no abstract information (Medin, Altom, & Murphy, 1984; Park & Hastie, 1987; E. R. Smith & Zarate, 1992).

Problems

Evidence for exemplars is not at all clear-cut. That is, people do understand that some groups are more variable than others, and they use this information, first, in deciding whether to generalize from an individual to the group and,

---

[5]One may also reinterpret earlier work on the retrieval of behavioral instances versus global traits as compatible with this view (e.g., Lingle, Geva, Ostrom, Lieppe, & Baumgardner, 1979; see Chapter 4).

second, in classifying new individuals. This might seem to argue for exemplars, but knowledge about variability does not seem to be based on memory for exemplars (Park & Hastie, 1987). Similarly, people often perceive minimal variability in outgroups (i.e., groups of which they are not a member), but differences in exemplar frequencies may (Linville et al., 1986, 1989; Ostrom & Sedikides, 1992) or may not (Judd & Park, 1988) be responsible. Researchers attempt to clarify the role of exemplars.

One intriguing possibility is that people may be most likely to use exemplars when they are trying to account for something out of the ordinary. Sometimes we need to know whether something that has just happened is normal or not; that is, we need an immediate check on how surprising it was (assuming we do not already have a relevant schema). For example, when involved in an accident, people think of similar accidents in their past and of the events leading up to the incident to judge how surprising or avoidable it was, and even how upset to be. An elegant and explicit model of exemplars was developed to describe just this process of people's post hoc normality judgments (Kahneman & Miller, 1986). Unlike category models, which focus on anticipation and prediction based on what seems typical or probable in the future given one's abstracted prior experience, norm theory focuses on post hoc interpretation based on an encounter with a particular stimulus in a particular context, with the aim of judging whether the stimulus was normal or surprising. Category and schema theories describe reasoning forward, norm theory describes reasoning backward. According to norm theory, people consider a particular stimulus in light of exemplars it brings to mind. These exemplars allow people to compare the instance to the sum of the previous experiences to see the degree to which the instance is normal or surprising. People compute this sum on the fly, so it is ad hoc rather than explicit prior knowledge. We return to this model in Chapter 7, but for present purposes norm theory illustrates the uses of exemplars in active judgment processes.

Prototypes or Exemplars: A Resolution

Exemplar models are not sufficient by themselves any more than prototype models were sufficient by themselves. People rely on a mixture of representations (cf. M. B. Brewer, 1988; Cantor & Kihlstrom, 1987; J. B. Cohen & Basu, 1987; Groom et al., 2005; Lingle et al., 1984; Linville et al., 1989; Messick & Mackie, 1989; E. E. Smith & Medin, 1981). People clearly do recall specific instances and use them to classify new instances, but specific instances also give rise to category generalizations that in turn facilitate classification of new instances, so people are using both (Elio & Anderson, 1981). People can rely on direct experience with exemplars or on previously provided prototypes to classify new instances, depending on the task and the information available (Medin et al., 1984).

Moreover, because use or development of abstract representations depends on the demands of the task, abstraction of a prototype is not automatic (Whittlesea, 1987). Indeed, exemplars may be more basic (and therefore more likely to be automatic) because they are used (a) when people's cognitive capacity is strained, (b) for more complex concepts, and (c) especially by younger children (Kossan, 1981; cf. Kemler Nelson, 1984).

Exemplars may be more basic building blocks for abstract generalizations such as categories, but once the category is established, exceptions require unpacking the category to return to the more concrete individual exemplar level. That is, cognitive generalizations may start with exemplars and return to them for troubleshooting. As we saw earlier, whereas familiar groups encourage abstractions, unfamiliar groups encourage exemplar usage (Groom et al., 2005). A summary-plus-exception model captures this idea in individual impression formation (Babey, Queller, & Klein, 1998). People generalize across individual instances of behavior and retain both the summary and the instances. Trait judgments rely on both the summary and the specific exceptional episodes (Klein, Cosmides, Tooby, & Chance, 2001).

Exemplars might be useful when the summary abstraction is insufficient for reasons besides exceptions to the rule. When people are motivated or simply have more information, exemplars provide elaborated processing. People apparently use both exemplars and prototypes to represent groups to which they belong, but only prototypes to represent groups to which they do not belong and about which they therefore know less (Judd & Park, 1988). People could also use exemplars to represent both their own and other groups, but they have more exemplars available for their own group (Linville et al., 1989).

Clearly, people can use either abstract category-level information, such as prototypes, or instances and memory for exemplars to make categorical judgments. Which people do so and when is the interesting question (cf. M. B. Brewer, 1988; Park & Hastie, 1987; S. J. Sherman & Corty, 1984, pp. 237–245; E. R. Smith & Zárate, 1992). When people do each doubtless depends on task demands and individual differences. For example, the capacity and the motivation to be accurate or to focus on individuals would probably encourage exemplar-based processes over prototype-based processes (S. T. Fiske & Neuberg, 1990; Kruglanski, 1990; Messick & Mackie, 1989).

When all is said and done, what ultimate use are fuzzy concepts and concrete exemplars in loose hierarchies in tangled webs? Cantor and Kihlstrom (1987) argue that this framework (a) captures the social perceiver's need to represent both the gist of a category and its variability, allowing an economical, functional core representation as well as acknowledging the variability of instances within the category, and (b) describes the multiple paths people use in responding flexibly to the fluidity of social interaction.

Summary

This chapter on mental representation focused on memory; that is, what stays in our heads. We began with associative networks that organize memory in the basic cognitive model, with the basic distinction of long-term versus short-term memory. Associative network models of social memory build on this work. In addition, procedural memory informs some models of social memory. Finally, cognitive models of parallel versus serial processing for coordinating memory processes inform ideas about parallel constraint satisfaction in social cognition.

Social memory structures matter to social cognition, as we saw in discussing the unique features of categorical person perception and uses of social categories. In response to critiques of classic category and prototype views, the exemplar view, with its own advantages and disadvantages, offers an alternative and a combined resolution.

We have focused here on general principles of mental representation that will be useful as we encounter representations of self, causality, attitudes, and stereotypes. Just as in Chapter 2 on dual-mode models, these ideas about mental representation are converging on a consensus useful to the wider field of social cognition.

PART TWO

Topics in Social Cognition

From Self to Society

CHAPTER 5

Self in Social Cognition

MENTAL REPRESENTATIONS OF THE SELF ◆ SELF-REGULATION ◆ MOTIVATION
AND SELF-REGULATION ◆ THE SELF AS A REFERENCE POINT

Understanding the self has been one of the most enthusiastically pursued goals
in psychology. William James' (1907) analysis laid the groundwork for many
enduring concerns, and sociologists Charles Cooley (1902) and George Herbert
Mead (1934) provided frameworks for understanding the self in social interaction. In the past three decades, social cognition researchers have taken up this
challenge and added fundamentally to our understanding of the self.

In this chapter, we begin with mental representations of the self; namely,
what makes up the sense of self that most people experience subjectively. We then
explore self-regulation and consider how the self guides the processing of self-
relevant information, enabling people to both understand the meaning of situations for themselves and promote their interests, goals, and values. We examine
how self-relevant goals lead people to alter or maintain their self-conceptions
and social interactions. Overarching motives that guide self-regulation include
a desire for accurate knowledge of the self, a consistent sense of self, self-
improvement, and self-enhancement, which is the tendency to seek and maintain
a favorable self-concept. Finally, we consider how knowledge of the self affects
how we interpret the behavior of other people, often without our awareness.

MENTAL REPRESENTATIONS OF THE SELF

Self-Concept

The knowledge that people have about themselves is extensive and complex.
During childhood, we are treated in particular ways by parents, teachers, and
friends, and we participate in religious, ethnic, or cultural activities that come to
be significant aspects of ourselves. In addition, we develop a sense of what our
personal characteristics are and a sense of what others around us feel we might do
or should do to fulfill our own and others' expectations. We have a private sense
of self as well as selves we present to other people. We know ourselves as active
participants in the ongoing action of the environment and as people who have
already experienced and reflected upon many events and relationships. We know
ourselves by our roles, such as student or spouse, and we have an impression of
our personal qualities and attributes. We can say quickly and with confidence
whether we are outgoing or shy, adventurous or conventional, athletic or clumsy.
The collection of beliefs we hold about ourselves is called the *self-concept*.

Mental representations of the self are complex. Sometimes we are concerned with maintaining self-esteem; at other times we want to maintain a consistent sense of self, and at other times our thoughts, emotions, and behaviors may be guided by needs to belong or to be efficacious (Vignoles, Regalia, Manzi, Golledge, & Scabini, 2006). In part as a result of this flexibility, much of our self-encoding is done in person-situation-interaction terms (Mendoza-Denton, Ayduk, Mischel, Shoda, & Testa, 2001). That is, we have different senses of ourself in particular situations. As such, different aspects of the self are engaged by different situational norms and pressures. A person may have one conception of herself in academic situations that involves the perceptions that she is bright, attentive, and interested in learning, and a different set of self-beliefs for social situations, which may include being somewhat shy but friendly and generally well-liked. In this viewpoint, self-representation in memory is similar to the representation of other constructs and involves the self in meaningful activities. Which aspect of the self influences ongoing thought and behavior depends in large part on which aspect of the self is accessed. This aspect of the self is referred to as the *working self-concept* (Markus & Kunda, 1986). Thus, for example, your working self-concept for academic situations will typically be quite different in content from the one you have for social situations.

In addition to situational variability in the self, there is variability in the self that depends on the activation of relations with significant others. In important respects, conceptions of the self include knowledge about significant others (Andersen & Chen, 2002). People who have had an influence on one's self or with whom one has been emotionally involved, including parents, siblings, close friends, and past and present partners, are linked to the self through knowledge that maintains the unique aspects of the self in relation to these significant others. A person's repertoire of relational selves can be an important source of influence on behavior in social situations. The activation of mental representations of a significant other evokes the relational self with that significant other, a process that has been referred to as transference (Andersen & Chen, 2002). You may, for example, behave like an entirely autonomous mature person until you get home for the holidays, at which point your relational selves as daughter and younger sister may be activated, leading to quite profound effects on your behavior that conflict with your usual conceptions of your self.

Typically we construe ourselves in complementary fashion vis-à-vis others (Tiedens & Jimenez, 2003). For example, we reciprocate warm (or quarrelsome) behavior, and thus assimilate on the agreeableness-quarrelsomeness dimension, whereas in terms of control, we contrast our behavior with others, deferring when a relational partner is dominant but taking charge when the partner defers. In both cases, complementary self-construal guides behavior and is more likely to do so with people we know well (Tiedens & Jimenez, 2003). Relational selves are important sources both of stability in the self-concept (in terms of stable representations of significant others) and of variability (when different relational selves are activated in different situations).

Self-Schemas

In the array of information that people hold about themselves, most people have clear conceptions of themselves on some attributes and less clear conceptions on others. Those qualities about which people are certain are termed *self-schemas;* they are cognitive-affective structures that represent the self's qualities in a given domain. People are self-schematic on dimensions that are important to them, on which they think of themselves as extreme, and on which they are certain that the opposite does not hold (Markus, 1977). Self-schemas organize and direct the processing of information relevant to that domain. Connie may feel that she is hardworking and full of integrity but may be unsure whether to describe herself as shy. Daniel may be certain that he is not shy but uncertain about whether he could call himself a hard worker. In this case, Connie is schematic for the dimensions hardworking and integrity but not for shy, whereas Daniel is schematic for the dimension shy but not for being a hard worker.

Possible and feared selves—that is, selves we would like to become or that we fear becoming, respectively—also guide how we think about ourselves and how we select situations and social roles (Markus & Nurius, 1986; Markus & Wurf, 1987). For example, the possible self of becoming a professor might lead one to seek out opportunities to supervise student research projects, whereas the feared self of being jobless might lead one to redouble efforts to publish research articles. Possible selves can change in response to input from the environment and affect consequent behavior. For example, in one study, low-income eighth-graders participated in a brief intervention that led them to believe that their possible selves might include academic success. This brief intervention increased test scores, grades, and academic initiative and decreased depression, absences, and misbehavior in school over a 2-year period; these changes were mediated by changes in the possible selves these students had incorporated into their identity (Oyserman, Bybee, & Terry, 2006). (See Figure 5.1.)

Neural Bases of Self-Views

Clearly, to function effectively in the world, people need to be able to distinguish between things that are "me" and "not me." Evidence suggests that this function is associated with activity in an area of the prefrontal cortex in the left cerebral hemisphere (Kircher et al., 2002; Turk et al., 2002). That is, the sense of self that

FIGURE 5.1. How self-schemas, ability, and possible selves interact to regulate performance

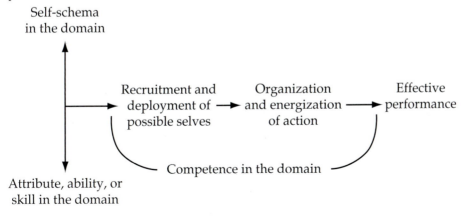

most of us experience subjectively appears to emerge from the functions of a left hemisphere "interpreter" (Gazzaniga, 2000), which integrates diverse self-relevant processing in different parts of the brain (Turk, Heatherton, Macrae, Kelley, & Gazzaniga, 2003). The representations people hold of themselves in long-term memory are similar to those held about other concepts, but they are more complex and varied and more likely to be used to interpret the meaning of situations and of other people's actions than are other accessible constructs.

Recent research has clarified the patterns of brain activity that occur when people are reflecting on their self-views and compared them with how people perceive others' views of them. For example, in one study (Ochsner et al., 2005) participants' brains were scanned while they rated adjectives as self-descriptive, descriptive of a friend, descriptive of the friend's view of them, or descriptive of a person not close to them; a perceptual task not related to people was the comparison condition. For all of the person appraisal tasks, activation of the medial prefrontal cortex (mPFC) was seen relative to the comparison perception task. This finding is consistent with manifold studies suggesting the importance of mPFC activity in social judgment generally (see Chapter 1). In addition, a larger network involving the posterior cingulate/precuneus and multiple regions of the temporal lobe was evoked for all self and other evaluations. Of interest, the neural systems involved in direct appraisals of the self were found to be very similar to those involved in appraisals of close others, and they appear to have a lot in common in terms of the neural pathways evoked relative to appraisals of people with whom one is less close (Ochsner et al., 2005).

Research like this raises the question of how much the neural representation of others is incorporated into our self-concept and how much it is distinct. Activation of the lateral PFC distinguishes self-ratings from those made of a close other. Direct appraisals of the self as compared to others lead to greater activity in the mPFC and right rostrolateral PFC. It appears that making judgments about the self also selectively activates Brodmann's area 10 (Heatherton et al., 2006). Thus, distinctive areas within the medial prefrontal cortex are activated for self as opposed to intimate others, indicating that self-knowledge is represented at least semi-independently of information about intimate others.

With respect to self-views, neuroimaging investigations indicate that self-schematic information is processed at the neural level differently from nonschematic information (Lieberman, Jarcho, & Satpute, 2004). Echoing the distinction made in Chapter 2 between controlled and automatic processing, processing non-self-schematic information (e.g., athletes processing words related to acting) leads to activation of brain regions involved in effortful and intentional processing and the retrieval of episodic memories; brain regions implicated include the lateral prefrontal cortex, hippocampus, and posterior parietal cortex. By contrast, processing self-schematic information (e.g., athletes responding to words reflecting athletics) activates brain regions involved in automatic, motivational, and affective processing, specifically the ventromedial prefrontal cortex, nucleus accumbens, and amygdala. This latter pattern suggests that as strong self-schemas within a domain develop, their neural representation moves to regions of the brain that are more affective, motivational, and automatic.

Self-Esteem

Another important concept involved in mental representations of the self is *self-esteem*, which is the evaluation we make of ourselves. People are concerned not only with what they are like but also with how they value those qualities. Self-esteem is a valuable resource because it can help people maintain well-being, set appropriate goals, savor their positive experiences, and cope successfully with difficult situations (Christensen, Wood, & Barrett, 2003; Creswell et al., 2005; Sommer & Baumeister, 2002; Wood, Heimpel, & Michela, 2003).

There is an important social component to self-esteem. People are inherently social, and their desire for self-esteem is driven, in part, by this need to connect with others and gain their approval (Leary & Baumeister, 2000). As such, a person's self-esteem may be thought of as a "sociometer"—a general indicator of how one is doing in the eyes of others.

Self-esteem may be assessed explicitly, as when people respond to questions such as "I feel that I have a number of good qualities" (see Table 5.1). It may also be assessed implicitly, for example, by assessing whether people value the letters in their name or whether they are relatively quick to link positive adjectives to the self (e.g., Koole, Dijksterhuis, & van Knippenberg, 2001). Sometimes there is a discrepancy between explicit and implicit assessments of self-esteem; when this is the case, people must devote more processing time to understanding their self-conceptions (Briñol, Petty, & Wheeler, 2006). People who have high explicit self-esteem but low implicit self-esteem are prone to behaving defensively (Jordan, Spencer, & Zanna, 2003). For example, they may put other people down as a way of maintaining their own self-esteem because their self-views are fragile and require continual reinforcement (Jordan, Spencer, & Zanna, 2005; Kernis, 2003).

The distinction between implicit and explicit self-esteem suggests that not only do people explicitly seek to feel good about themselves, but their implicit or unconscious self-evaluations also influence their judgments and behavior. People tend to prefer people, places, and things that resemble the self, a

---

TABLE 5.1. Self-Esteem Scale

Indicate whether each item is true (T) or false (F) for you.

___1. I feel that I have a number of good qualities.

___2. I feel I do not have much to be proud of.

___3. At times I think I am no good at all.

___4. I feel I am a person of worth, at least on an equal basis with others.

___5. All in all, I feel that I am a failure.

___6. On the whole, I am satisfied with myself.

If you answered "true" on items 1, 4, and 6, you scored high on self-esteem. If you answered "true" to items 2, 3, and 5, you scored low on self-esteem. The entire scale includes 10 items.

Source: Adapted from M. Rosenberg, *Society and the adolescent self-image.* Copyright © 1965 by Princeton University Press. © renewed. Used by permission of Dr. Florence Rosenberg.

tendency that has been referred to as implicit egotism (Pelham, Carvallo, & Jones, 2005). For example, women with names like Georgia, Louise, and Virginia are disproportionately likely to have lived in the states that resemble their names (Pelham, Mirenberg, & Jones, 2002). As noted, people prefer the letters in their own names to letters not contained in their names (J. T. Jones, Pelham, Mirenberg, & Hetts, 2002). Considerable evidence now suggests that unconscious self-evaluations influence not only mundane but also major daily life decisions, such as the choice of where to live (Pelham et al., 2005).

Self-esteem is important because it reflects what people believe they need to be or do to have worth as a person (Crocker & Knight, 2005). In addition to an overall sense of self-esteem, people hold specific evaluations of themselves in particular life domains that influence their global feelings of self-worth. These have been referred to as contingencies of self-worth; that is, people are selective about the domains on which they base their self-worth. For example, for one person, being a poor student may not matter much and have little bearing on self-esteem, but if one is from a family in which intellectual achievements are very important, then being a poor student may reflect back on self-esteem. In the domains of contingent self-worth, people pursue self-esteem by trying to validate their abilities and qualities, activities that may have costs to mental and physical health, as they strive to maintain a sense of self-worth in those domains (Crocker & Knight, 2005). Thus, although thinking well of oneself has important benefits, the pursuit of self-esteem can be costly.

Culture and the Self

Conceptions of the self vary depending on one's cultural background (Rhee, Uleman, Lee, & Roman, 1995; Triandis, McCusker, & Hui, 1990). Markus and Kitayama (1991) contrasted American and Japanese cultures to illustrate the substantial differences in self-conceptions that exist between Western and East Asian cultures. They argued that European Americans have a strong emphasis on individuality and how one can distinguish oneself from others by emphasizing and making use of one's unique talents. This *independent self* is "a bounded, unique, more or less integrated motivational and cognitive universe, a dynamic center of awareness, emotion, judgment, action, organized into a distinctive whole and set constrastively both against other such wholes and against a social and natural background" (Geertz, 1975, p. 48). By contrast, the *interdependent self* of many East Asian, Southern European, and Latin American cultures consists of seeing oneself as part of encompassing social relationships and adjusting one's behavior to what one perceives to be the thoughts, feelings, and actions of others in the relationship (Markus & Kitayama, 1991). From the standpoint of interdependence, the self becomes meaningful and complete largely within the context of social relationships rather than through independent, autonomous action. Items that assess these two concepts are illustrated in Table 5.2.

People from both independent and interdependent cultures possess a set of internal qualities, such as abilities or opinions. However, in independent cultures these attributes are experienced as fixed and relatively stable from situation to situation, whereas in interdependent cultures these qualities are thought to be more situation specific and unstable rather than defining characteristics of the self (Bochner, 1994; Cousins, 1989). The interdependent self is not an

TABLE 5.2. The Measurement of Independent and Interdependent Self-Construals

Indicate the extent to which you agree or disagree with each of the items below based on the following scale:

1	2	3	4	5	6	7
Strongly disagree						Strongly agree

___1. I have respect for authority figures with whom I interact.

___2. I am comfortable with being singled out for praise or rewards.

___3. My happiness depends on the happiness of those around me.

___4. Speaking up in class is not a problem for me.

___5. I should take into consideration my parents' advice when making education and career plans.

___6. My personal identity independent of others is very important to me.

If you answered "agree" on items 1, 3, and 5, you scored high in interdependence, whereas if you answered "agree" on items 2, 4, and 6, you scored high in independence. Note that the entire scale is longer than the excerpt above.

Source: T. M. Singelis, *Personality and Social Psychology Bulletin, 20* (5), pp. 580–591, copyright © 1994 by Sage Publications, Inc. Reprinted by permission of Sage Publications, Inc.

autonomous, bounded whole but changes its nature depending on the social context (Kanagawa, Cross, & Markus, 2001). In interdependent cultures, the emphasis on blending in is so fundamental that attributes that uniquely differentiate one person from another are not regarded as particularly representative of the self. For example, a child from a family in an independent cultural context might experience pressure to develop her talents fully because achieving distinctively on the basis of one's abilities is a valued cultural outcome. By contrast, a child growing up in an interdependent cultural or familial context might experience the pressure to achieve in the form of obligations to family and to the larger social group.

Although being independent is very well defined, note that interdependency may assume different forms, depending on culture and gender. For example, women are more interdependent than men but not in the same way that East Asians may be considered interdependent (Cross, Bacon, & Morris, 2000; Cross & Vick, 2001). Women's interdependence has been referred to as relational interdependence (Cross et al., 2000; Guimond, Chatard, Martinot, Crisp, & Redersdorff, 2006). For example, a European American mother may experience interdependency as an obligation to promote the goals and talents of her children so that they will be successful, and she may make many sacrifices with respect to her own personal agenda to achieve these outcomes. This is not the same as the East Asian sense of connectedness, which stems more from a sense of harmonious interdependency with the social group. These two types of interdependency are different from that experienced in many Latin cultures in which social goals, such as meeting obligations to family and friends, often take priority over personal ones. We raise this point because in the sections to follow interdependency has been studied largely as a distinction between European American and East Asian cultures. The multiple forms of interdependency have been noted but have received little attention with respect to their implications for cognitive and emotional information processing and for behavioral self-regulation.

Culture, Cognition, and Emotion

There are fundamental cultural differences in cognition: European Americans tend to extract central or distinctive elements from the context, whereas East Asians are more likely to view the world in a more holistic manner (Masuda & Nisbett, 2001). This distinction carries through in self-perception as well. People who hold an independent sense of self see themselves as distinctive and strive to maximize achievement of their personal goals. For example, in one study, personally choosing a task to perform enhanced motivation for European Americans, whereas it had a lesser effect on Asian students' intrinsic motivation; the Asian students' motivation was higher when they were told that someone close to them had chosen the task for them (Iyengar & Lepper, 1999). European Americans select tasks on which they will do well and on which they have done well in the past, whereas East Asians' choices of tasks are based less on such expectations and prior performance (Oishi & Diener, 2003). Motivational differences reliably follow from this distinction as well. Whereas European Americans tend to strive for personal achievement, East Asians strive for the achievement of group goals or see the goals they implement as representing group norms. Table 5.3 summarizes some key differences between an independent and interdependent sense of self.

These differences in goals also affect memory (Woike, Gershkovich, Piorkowski, & Polo, 1999). For example, European Americans are likely to

TABLE 5.3. Summary of Key Differences Between an Independent and an Interdependent Perception of Self

Feature Compared	Independent	Interdependent
Definition	Separate from social context	Connected with social context
Structure	Bounded, unitary, stable	Flexible, variable
Important features	Internal, private (abilities, thoughts, feelings)	External, public (statuses, roles, relationships)
Tasks	Be unique Express self Realize internal attributes Promote own goals Be direct: say what's on your mind	Belong, fit in Occupy one's proper place Engage in appropriate action Promote others' goals Be indirect: read other's mind
Role of others	*Self-evaluation:* others important for social comparison, reflected appraisal	*Self-definition:* self defined by relationships with others in specific contexts
Basis of self-esteem[a]	Ability to express self; validate internal attributes	Ability to adjust, restrain self, maintain harmony with social context

[a]Esteeming the self may be primarily a Western phenomenon, and the concept of self-esteem should perhaps be replaced by "self-satisfaction," or by a term that reflects the realization that one is fulfilling the culturally mandated task.

Source: H. R. Markus and S. Kitayama. (1991). Culture and the self: Implications for cognition, emotion, and motivation. *Psychological Review, 98,* 224–253. Copyright © 1991 by the American Psychological Association. Reprinted with permission.

reconstruct events in terms of specific actors and their personal qualities, whereas East Asians are more likely to refer to the social groups to which those actors belong (Menon, Morris, Chiu, & Hong, 1999). European Americans are more likely to ignore the context in the inferences they draw about the social environment, whereas those with interdependent self-construals process social information by paying attention to the relation of themselves or others to the social context (Kühnen, Hannover, & Schubert, 2001).

These distinctions carry over into the experience of emotion. People with an independent sense of self experience ego-focused emotions frequently, such as the experience of pride over doing well or frustration over the feeling that personal goals have been thwarted (Mesquita, 2001). In contrast, cultures with interdependent self-conceptions tend to experience other-focused emotions, such as the Japanese experience of *amae,* the sense of being lovingly cared for and dependent on another's indulgence (Markus & Kitayama, 1991).

The bases for self-esteem are influenced heavily by sense of self. People with an independent sense of self are more likely to endorse items such as, "I feel I am a person of worth" on self-esteem scales than people with an interdependent sense of self (Markus & Kitayama, 1991; Yik, Bond, & Paulhus, 1998). In addition, the importance attached to self-esteem and its implication for life satisfaction varies between independent and interdependent cultures. In a study of 31 cultures, Diener and Diener (1995) found that the relation of self-esteem to life satisfaction was lower in interdependent cultures, whereas in independent cultures individuals with high self-esteem reported high life satisfaction as well. In interdependent social contexts, approval from others for subscribing to social norms is a better predictor of life satisfaction.

Individual and collective processes in the construction of the self are abetted by the types of situations that different cultures afford their members. Situations in the United States are relatively conducive to self-enhancement (that is, regarding and promoting the self in positive terms), and thus Americans engage in self-enhancement. By contrast, Japanese situations are relatively conducive to self-criticism, and Japanese people are more likely to engage in self-criticism. For example, a U.S. student studying in Japan reported that volleyball, which is a relaxing fun sport in the United States that gives people the opportunity to demonstrate their prowess or total lack of talent amidst great cheering and booing, is much more competitive and serious in Japan, organized as a win or lose situation and thus conducive to people experiencing self-criticism or the implicit criticism of others if they play poorly (Kitayama, Markus, Matsumoto, & Norasakkunkit, 1997).

Findings such as these have led many researchers to question the fundamental nature of self-esteem, especially whether it has any transcultural implications. Yet people from interdependent cultures who score high on Western self-esteem scales exhibit behavior consistent with Western people high in self-esteem, such as self-protective responses to negative feedback. Moreover, even in interdependent cultures there are tendencies to self-enhance indirectly, for example, by overvaluing the letters in one's name (Kitayama & Karasawa, 1997).

As may be apparent, much of the research on independent versus interdependent sense of self has contrasted European Americans living in the United States with Japanese nationals. In some respects, each culture may be an extreme example on these dimensions, with European Americans being extreme on the independent sense of self and its implications for cognition and emotion, and the Japanese being extreme on the interdependent sense of self and its implications for cognition and emotion. Extreme examples tend to foster strong contrasts. As noted, the gaps in our knowledge regarding the interdependent self and its implications for cognition, emotion, and behavior also suffer both from lack of research in interdependent cultures generally and from examining primarily one type of interdependence.

SELF-REGULATION

Self-regulation refers to the ways in which people control and direct their own actions, emotions, and thoughts. It focuses especially on how people formulate goals and pursue them. Much self-regulation occurs virtually automatically without any awareness or conscious thought. We respond to cues that are salient in the environment and relevant to our enduring interests and goals, and these factors automatically guide our behavior (Lieberman et al., 2004). But at other times, we consciously and actively intervene to control our thoughts, emotions, and behaviors (Brandstätter & Frank, 2002).

Sources of Influence on Self-Regulation

There are several important sources of influence on our self-regulatory activities. One influence is the content of self-regulation; namely, what is in the working self-concept. Situational cues, social roles, values, and strongly held self-conceptions influence which aspects of the self predominate in the working self-concept (e.g., Verplanken & Holland, 2002). For example, in a classroom situation, the contextual influences on our behavior are likely to be achievement-related, but our behavior will also be influenced by the extent to which achievement concerns are an enduring part of our personal goals. The working self-concept, in turn, is modified by what goes on in the situation. For example, speaking publicly in class but giving the wrong answer may lead one person with low achievement goals to find the situation to be funny, whereas for someone who values achievement goals, the same incident may lead to embarrassment and redoubled efforts to be accurate the next time (Crocker & Knight, 2005; Ehrlinger & Dunning, 2003).

As this example also shows, sometimes the working self-concept is at odds with the stable self-concept (Arndt, Schimel, Greenberg, & Pyszczynski, 2002). Following the delivery of an incorrect answer to a question in a classroom situation, one may feel stupid and embarrassed, thereby influencing the working self-concept, but assuming that these events do not repeat themselves regularly, the impact may be only short term and not affect the enduring self-concept. If these types of events recur with regularity, however, the enduring self-concept may change as well. For example, if staying out late and going to clubs is part of your self-concept as a party person, that aspect of your self-concept is likely to change once you have children. The working self-concept is an important concept because it explains how different aspects of the self may guide social behavior under different circumstances, and, in turn, be modified by feedback from those situations, ultimately affecting the enduring self-concept.

Behavioral Approach and Avoidance

Self-regulation involves fundamental decisions about what people and situations to approach and which ones to avoid. Research suggests that people have two semi-independent motivational systems that help to regulate behavior in these situations: an appetitive system, referred to as the behavioral activation system (BAS), and an aversive system, or behavioral inhibition system (BIS). The expression of positive, or approach, motivational concerns is associated with left frontal activation, which is consistent with the research on the involvement of left frontal activation in goal pursuit (Harmon-Jones, Lueck, Fearn, & Harmon-Jones, 2006). When BAS is activated, people tend to approach other people or activities in the environment. When BIS is activated, people are more likely to avoid other people or activities (Carver & White, 1994; see Gray, 1990). Negative or withdrawal motivation is associated with activation of the right frontal region of the cortex (Harmon-Jones et al., 2006).

A number of factors influence whether BAS or BIS is a predominating force, affecting behavior at any given time. Daily experiences, for example, influence the activation of these systems. If good things are happening to you, you are more likely to be in a state of activation (BAS) than in a state of inhibition (BIS) (Gable, Reis, & Elliot, 2000). When things are not going well, behavioral inhibition (BIS) may enable you to regroup.

BIS and BAS also reflect reliable individual differences. Some people have a stronger behavioral activation system, whereas others have a stronger behavioral inhibition system (Carver & White, 1994). BAS-oriented people experience more positive events and positive affect in their lives, whereas BIS-dominated people tend to experience more negative affect (Updegraff et al., 2004). BIS and BAS are important for guiding the self's behavior.

Self-Discrepancy Theory

In a theory that relates to this distinction, Higgins (1987, 1989b) examined how self-discrepancies guide emotions and behavior directed toward solving those discrepancies. He distinguished between two types of self-guides: those that result from a shortfall between one's current self and one's ideal self, and those that result from a discrepancy between one's current self and the ought self.

People differ in whether they are primarily driven by the *ideal self* or the *ought self* (Strauman, 1996). The ideal self is who one wants to be; the ought self is who one thinks one should be, a viewpoint that is influenced heavily by one's beliefs about appropriate behavior for the self (duties and obligations) and the expectations that others have for the self. In a key study, Higgins, Klein, and Strauman (1985) had college students fill out a questionnaire regarding their self-perceptions, including how they would ideally like to be and how they felt they ought to be. At a later time, they filled out the same questionnaire from the standpoint of their mother, father, and closest friend and rated the extent to which each of the personal attributes they rated was relevant or meaningful to them. Discrepancies between the actual self and the ideal self produced dejection-related emotions and loss of self-esteem (see also Higgins, Shah, and Friedman, 1997; Moretti & Higgins, 1990). For example, failing to get into graduate school produced disappointment and sadness. Perceived discrepancies between one's

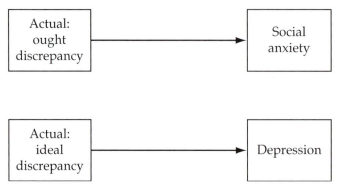

FIGURE 5.2. Emotional consequences of self-discrepancies

actual self and a friend's or parent's vision of what the self ought to be produced anxiety. For example, perceiving that one was not going to be the successful physician of one's father's dream produced anxiety but not sadness. The more important the personal attribute was to the respondent, the greater the emotion experienced (Higgins, 1999), and the more one was self-focused, the greater the emotions experienced as well (Higgins et al., 1997; Phillips & Silvia, 2005).

Discrepancies from one's ideal self facilitate efforts to achieve that ideal (a promotion orientation in service of behavioral activation), whereas efforts to meet the expectation of others represent a prevention or inhibitory focus (Förster, Higgins, & Idson, 1998). Perhaps because a prevention focus is fueled by anxiety, people are faster off the mark to meet prevention-related goals than promotion-related goals (Freitas, Liberman, Salovey, & Higgins, 2002). This general orientation toward approach (promotion goals) versus avoidance (prevention goals), to a degree, reflects stable personality traits, with extraversion the exemplar of approach and neuroticism the exemplar of avoidance (Carver, Sutton, & Scheier, 2000). (See Figure 5.2.)

People experience a greater sense of well-being when there is a fit between the goals they are pursuing and their regulatory orientation (Higgins, 2005). That is, people who are motivated to achieve their ideal selves experience well-being when they feel they are moving closer to those self standards, whereas people who are driven more by desire to avoid negative outcomes and to meet the expectations of others experience greater well-being when they believe they are upholding these social expectations (Higgins, Idson, Freitas, Spiegel, & Molden, 2003).

As noted, one of the chief sources of influence on our self-conceptions is socialization. Socialization and culture influence which of these regulatory foci predominates. Some people are raised in families in which the opinions of others represent a strong source of influence on self-conceptions. Often, this emphasis is accompanied by a parenting style marked by criticism or rejection. Others are raised in families in which they are urged to become their ideal selves, an orientation more likely to develop in a warm and supportive environment. These differences give rise to the development of different standards for the self and for evaluating the self. Cultural differences, likewise, influence what aspects of the self govern self-regulatory behavior. People who are raised with a sense of themselves as independent, autonomous individuals are likely to be motivated by discrepancies between themselves and their ideal selves (a promotion focus), whereas those who are raised with an interdependent sense of self are more attentive to the concerns or demands of others in the social environment (Lee, Aaker, & Gardner, 2000).

Different patterns of brain activation characterize a promotion versus a prevention orientation. A promotion regulatory focus tends to be associated with greater left frontal activity, whereas a prevention regulatory focus is associated with greater right frontal activity. This asymmetry is not surprising inasmuch as promotion focused goals are associated with approaching desired outcomes, whereas prevention focused goals are more associated with avoiding undesired outcomes (Amodio, Shah, Sigelman, Brazy, & Harmon-Jones, 2004). For example, in one study (Johnson et al., 2006), when people were asked to reflect on their hopes and aspirations, medial prefrontal and anterior cingulate cortex activation was predominant (relative to non-self-relevant thought), whereas when people were asked to reflect on their duties and obligations (a prevention focus), activity in the posterior cingulate cortex and precuneus showed relatively greater activity. It may be that the medial prefrontal cortex reflects agentic self-reflection and that the posterior medial cortex is associated with experiential self-reflection. Alternatively, medial prefrontal cortex activation may be associated with an inward focus, whereas posterior cingulate activation is associated with a more outward or social focus (Johnson et al., 2006).

Self-Efficacy and Personal Control

Another important set of influences on self-regulation include *self-efficacy* and a sense of personal *control*. Self-efficacy beliefs refer to the specific expectations that we hold about our abilities to accomplish specific tasks (Bandura, 2006). Whether a person undertakes an activity or strives to meet a particular goal depends heavily on whether the person believes he or she will be efficacious in performing these actions. Suppose, for example, that you are offered a prestigious teaching position in the Netherlands but are told that within three years you must be able to lecture in Dutch. Although you may desperately want to accept the position, a low sense of self-efficacy for learning Dutch might lead to a decision not to accept it.

In addition to highly specific control-related perceptions of abilities to perform particular behaviors (self-efficacy beliefs), people have a general sense of personal control or mastery that enables them to plan, cope with setbacks, and pursue self-regulatory activities. People who have a strong sense of control or personal mastery are more likely to undertake activities in service of their goals, whereas those who have a low sense of personal mastery or control may be less likely to do so.

In a study that illustrates this point, Pham, Taylor, and Seeman (2001) gave college students who were either high or low in their sense of mastery a manipulation that made salient the unpredictable aspects of college life, its predictable aspects, or neutral features of the college environment. Students in the unpredictable condition were reminded how it is sometimes difficult to get into the classes of one's choice, whereas those in the predictable condition were reminded that exam times and paper dates are always posted at the beginning of the quarter. After reading this manipulation, the students listed their thoughts and feelings about college, and their heart rate and blood pressure were assessed. Students who had been exposed to the predictable college manipulation made more references to the future and more references to personal goals in their thoughts listing. They also had lower blood pressure and heart rate compared to those who read about the neutral features of the college environment and especially the unpredictable aspects of the college environment. The students who were chronically high in personal mastery were more optimistic and future oriented than those low in personal mastery. This study shows that enduring expectations of control, as well as factors that may make control or lack of control salient in a particular situation, influence self-regulatory activity at the cognitive, motivational, and physiological levels.

Self-Focus

Self-regulation is also influenced by the direction of attention, including whether attention is directly inward toward the self or outward toward the environment (Duval & Wicklund, 1972; Silvia & Duval, 2001). When we are focused on ourselves, a state called *self-awareness* (Wicklund & Frey, 1980), we are more likely to evaluate our behavior against a standard and subsequently set an adjustment process in motion for meeting the standard. For example, upon catching your reflection in passing a store window, you may notice your poor posture and sloppy attire and resolve to fix both in the future.

As this example suggests, self-attention causes people to compare themselves to standards, such as those for intellectual performance, physical appearance, athletic prowess, and moral integrity (Macrae, Bodenhausen, & Milne, 1998). We try to conform to the standard, evaluate our behavior against it, decide that our behavior either matches the standard or does not, and continue adjusting and comparing until we meet the standard or give up. This process is called feedback, and the theory is called the *cybernetic theory of self-regulation* (Carver & Scheier, 1998). (See Figure 5.3.)

Implicit in these theoretical arguments is the idea that self-focus is often experienced as aversive and that people find ways not only to adjust their behavior or personal qualities but also to direct attention away from themselves (Flory, Räikkönen, Matthews, & Owens, 2000). For example, at the end of a bad day, people often need to keep themselves from focusing on personal issues or problems at work and so turn to such activities as drinking or television to reduce self-focus (Moskalenko & Heine, 2003).

Threats to Self-Regulation

There are reliable circumstances in which the ability to self-regulate may be compromised. One such condition is social exclusion. When a person has been excluded or rejected by a social group, he or she has more difficulty performing subsequent tasks. The person quits sooner on a frustrating task, attention is impaired, and the person show less self-control (Baumeister, DeWall, Ciarocco, & Twenge, 2005). For example, in one experiment participants who were told that no one else in their group wanted to work with them ate more cookies than participants who had not experienced rejection (Baumeister et al., 2005, Study 2). The person who has been excluded adopts a defensive state of mind that is

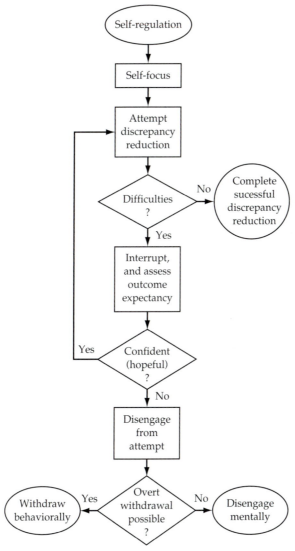

FIGURE 5.3. Cybernetic theory of self-attention and self-regulation
Source: After Carver, 1979.

characterized by lethargy, a poor sense of time, and avoidance of meaningful thought, emotions, and self-awareness (Twenge, Catanese, & Baumeister, 2003).

More generally, many circumstances involving self-regulation create self-control dilemmas in which one must choose between two preeminent goals or sacrifice short-term costs for long-term benefits. For example, one may have to have an uncomfortable and inconvenient medical procedure to rule out a potentially serious condition. Anticipated short-term costs such as these elicit self-control efforts that attempt to minimize the short-term costs (Trope & Fishbach, 2000). One may distract oneself or focus on the benefits of the short-term efforts, for example. In this way self-control helps people act according to their long-term interests by not succumbing to short-term temptations.

Do self-control dilemmas pit reason against emotion, or do some emotions support efforts at control? Research suggests that although hedonic emotions are associated with a short-term perspective, self-conscious emotions are associated with a long-term perspective and may help in resolving self-control dilemmas (Giner-Sorolla, 2001). Using evidence from patients with orbitofrontal lesions who show regulatory deficits with respect to self-control, Beer and colleagues (Beer, Heerey, Keltner, Scabini, & Knight, 2003) showed that self-conscious emotions (such as embarrassment or guilt) are important for regulating social behavior and that inappropriate self-conscious emotions (as in the patients with lesions) are associated with deficient behavioral self-regulation. Evidence such as this suggests that self-regulation depends on both rational responses to situations as well as self-conscious emotional responses.

Active self-regulation can be an effortful process, especially when one is simultaneously engaged in other activities. This load impairs activities that require active self-regulation but leaves more automatic self-regulation untouched. When a person's self-regulatory resources are depleted, complex thinking is impaired but performance of simple tasks is not (Schmeichel, Vohs, & Baumeister, 2003; see also Vohs & Schmeichel, 2003).

Neural Bases of Self-Regulation

Social cognition researchers are beginning to understand some of the neural bases of self-regulation, and as noted in Chapter 2, the dual-processing distinction is helpful for thinking about these patterns. Deliberate self-regulation implicates different brain regions than automatic self-regulation (Banfield, Wyland, Macrae, Münte, & Heatherton, 2004). The prefrontal cortex is involved in conscious self-regulation; that is, higher-order executive control of lower-order processes responsible for the planning and execution of behavior. In particular, the dorsolateral prefrontal cortex (dlPFC), which is implicated in spatial and conceptual reasoning processes more generally, has been tied to planning, processing novel information, making choices, controlling memory and working memory, and language functioning (see Banfield et al., 2004, for a review). The dlPFC is also implicated in behavioral self-regulation, specifically selecting and initiating actions (e.g., Spence & Frith, 1999). Converging evidence for this view of the dlPFC is provided by studies reporting that damage to this region can result in apathy and diminished attention as well as compromised planning, judgment, and insight (Dimitrov, Grafman, Soares, & Clark, 1999), among other consequences, suggesting poor executive functioning.

The ventromedial prefrontal cortex (vmPFC), which is connected to limbic structures that are involved in emotional processing (Pandya & Barnes, 1987), is especially implicated in how we control our behavioral and emotional output and how we interact with others (Dolan, 1999). The orbitofrontal cortex (OFC), a portion of the vmPFC, is activated in situations involving emotional processing, reward, inhibition, decision making, self-awareness, and strategic regulation (see Banfield et al., 2004, for a review). Damage to this area has been tied to striking behavior changes and a disregard for the potential future consequences of one's behavior (Bechara, Damasio, Damasio, & Anderson, 1994). Damage to the OFC leads to an inability to adjust one's behavior on the basis of whether it will be perceived as acceptable or moral by others (E. Goldberg, 2001).

The anterior cingulate cortex (ACC) interacts with the PFC in monitoring and guiding behavior. It is implicated both in the processing of cognitive information (anterior portion) and in affective and evaluative processing (see Bush, Luu, & Posner, 2000, for a review). ACC function and its connections to the motor and cognitive systems appear to be critical to the ability to translate an intention into action (Banfield et al., 2004). The ACC also plays an important role in processing conflicting information and has been conceptualized as a region that may trigger a shift from automatic to controlled processing (Botvinick et al., 2004). Thus, for example, if one is self-schematic for athletics, a sudden departure from one's usual athletic prowess should trigger ACC activity and initiation of controlled processing in the PFC to comprehend the implications for the self and actively regulate subsequent behavior (Lieberman et al., 2002).

MOTIVATION AND SELF-REGULATION

Self-regulation is governed heavily by enduring self-relevant concerns. These include the needs for an accurate sense of self, a consistent sense of self, an improving self, and a positive sense of self. In terms of the social motives listed in Chapters 1 and 2, accuracy and consistency are versions of a social understanding motive, whereas improving and maintaining a positive sense of self are two different ways to self-enhance.

Need for Accuracy

It is virtually axiomatic that to make our future outcomes predictable and controllable, we need a fairly accurate assessment of our abilities, opinions, beliefs, and emotions (Trope, 1975, 1983). Accurate self-assessments enable us to anticipate circumstances and control our future behavior (Trope & Bassok, 1982).

When a situation arises in which we need to know our ability on a task, Trope suggests that we pick tasks that will be the most informative (i.e., diagnostic) of our ability. If you want to get accurate feedback about your mathematics ability, a sample Graduate Records Examination (GRE) math section will be more diagnostic than a children's arithmetic test or your performance on a problem with which mathematicians have been grappling for decades.

Feedback from comparisons with others, what are called *social comparisons*, can also meet a need for accurate self-assessment if no objective task is available (Festinger, 1954). For example, if you are invited to a formal dance and you're not sure how a good a dancer you are, you are unlikely to go to either a children's dancing class or a ballroom competition. You might, instead, try out your dancing abilities in a setting that offers you opportunities to compare yourself to others, such as a club, to determine if you will need lessons to look good at the ball. Having an accurate sense of self is important when knowledge of our abilities is uncertain (Sorrentino & Roney, 1986).

Of interest is the fact that people are especially likely to seek accurate self-relevant information if they anticipate that the news will be good, but they also often show a desire for self-assessment even when they anticipate that the news may be bad (Brown, 1990). If you expect that your dancing ability is nonexistent, your efforts at self-assessment may confirm that belief, and it may be prudent to feign an injury on the day of the ball.

Need for Consistency

Following from the need for an accurate self-concept is the idea that we need a consistent self-concept rather than one that varies from situation to situation. We need to believe that we have intrinsic qualities and goals that will remain relatively stable over time (Swann, 1983). People often seek out situations and interpret their behavior in ways that conform to their preexisting self-conceptions, and they avoid or resist situations and feedback that are at odds with their self-conceptions. This process is called *self-verification*.

For example, suppose you have just started graduate school. During the first social event you are relatively quiet and keep to yourself. If a classmate comes up to you and says "There's no need to be shy; these people won't bite," you may feel offended. Perhaps you didn't talk much because you are learning the lay of the land or perhaps you're just under the weather, but you may think of yourself as someone who is usually fairly outgoing. At the next social event you may be more outgoing than usual as a way of convincing both yourself and others of your enduring quality as an outgoing person (Swann & Read, 1981).

People seek to confirm their positive attributes, but sometimes they seek to confirm their negative ones as well. If you've done well in your statistics class but know that math is generally not your strong point, you may resist a classmate's effort to convince you to take the more advanced stats class so you can maintain your preexisting belief about your math ability.

The need to see oneself accurately and consistently has effects on behavior. We selectively interact with people who see us as we see ourselves (e.g., Swann, Stein-Seroussi, & Giesler, 1992). For example, think how comforting it is to be able to relax in the presence of people who know both your strengths and weaknesses and love you nonetheless. Still, generally speaking, we like the people who see us positively and who value us for the same things we value in ourselves.

Most of the time people are able to maintain their views of themselves without any active or conscious effort. Maintaining a consistent sense of self is part of the process of interacting with family, friends, and coworkers in familiar settings performing familiar tasks. It is primarily when we receive discrepant feedback that we focus our attention on the threat to a consistent self-conception and either seek to expel the incorrect view or question whether we should change our self-conception (Madon et al., 2001), reflecting a shift from automatic to controlled processing (Chapter 2).

As is true for other aspects of social cognition, the desire for a consistent self varies from culture to culture. In independent cultures, people seek ways to express their distinctive personal qualities. In interdependent contexts, in which situational influences or social norms guide behavior, people may express inconsistent beliefs about themselves across different contexts (Choi & Choi, 2002). For example, European Americans may see themselves as moderately achievement oriented across many contexts, whereas East Asians may see themselves as quite achievement oriented in some contexts and less so in others. Overall, East Asians view themselves as more flexible across situations, whereas European Americans view themselves more consistently across situations (Suh, 2002).

Need for Improvement

In addition to the needs for an accurate and consistent sense of self, people are motivated by their desire to improve. Many self-regulatory activities serve this need (Kasser & Ryan, 1996). For people to use their self-regulatory activities in service of self-improvement, they need goals toward which they can strive. Such goals are provided by any of several sources. Markus's concept of possible selves, for example, incorporates the visions that people have of themselves in the future (Markus & Nurius, 1986). By developing and envisioning a possible self in the future, a person may be able to set appropriate goals, make progress toward achieving those goals, and chart how much progress he or she is making.

Self-improvement may also be served by *upward social comparisons* (Taylor & Lobel, 1989; J. V. Wood, 1989). Many people believe this is one of the main reasons having a mentor is so important. People who embody the attributes or skills we wish to obtain or possess can motivate us and also be a source of specific information that is helpful for improvement.

Self-improvement is also motivated by criticism, whether explicit from other people or implicit in the feedback of one's poor performance. The perception that one has fallen short of one's own goal or significant others' aspirations can be esteem-reducing, but it can also contribute to efforts to improve. The desire for self-improvement appears to be an especially important motivation for East Asians (Heine et al., 2001).

Not all efforts toward self-improvement are successful. Making changes and maintaining those changes successfully are difficult processes. Sometimes people perceive that they have improved when they have not (A. E. Wilson & Ross, 2001). For example, if a student goes through a study skills program to improve her skills, she is likely to come out of the experience believing that her skills have improved whether or not it is true. This occurs because people have theories about stability and change that may distort their self-assessments, not just of their current standing but of their past standing as well (Conway & Ross, 1984; Ross, 1989). By distorting one's earlier skill level as poorer than it actually was, one may assume that one's current skill level represents improvement (see also Libby, Eibach, & Gilovich, 2005). These insights also point to a large literature on self-enhancement, to which we now turn.

Self-Enhancement

In addition to the needs for accurate and consistent information about ourselves, we need to feel good about ourselves and maintain self-esteem. At least in Western cultures there appear to be cognitive and motivational benefits of having high self-esteem. People with high self-esteem have a clear sense of what their personal qualities are. They think well of themselves, set appropriate goals, use feedback in a manner that maintains their self-esteem, savor their positive experiences, and cope well with difficult situations (e.g., K. L. Sommer & Baumeister, 2002; Wood et al., 2003).

Collectively, the need for and efforts undertaken to maintain or create a positive sense of self is referred to as *self-enhancement*. Self-enhancement needs appear to be important, perhaps even preeminent, much of the time (Sedikides, 1993), at least in Western cultures. Self-enhancement needs become especially important following instances of threat, failure, or blows to self-esteem (e.g., Beauregard & Dunning, 1998; Krueger, 1998). The desire for a positive sense of self is driven at least in part by the need to connect with others and gain their approval, as was noted earlier in regard to the sociometer concept offered by Leary and Baumeister (2000). Social threats become threats to self-esteem, which in turn activate the need to regain approval and acceptance. From this vantage point, self-enhancement needs are driven socially by one's assessment of how one is viewed in the eyes of others.

One way in which people satisfy their self-enhancement needs is by holding self-perceptions that are falsely positive and somewhat exaggerated with respect to their actual abilities, talents, and social skills. Taylor and Brown (1988) have called these *positive illusions*. There are at least three types of positive illusions: People tend to see themselves more positively than is true; they believe they have more control over the events around them than is actually the case; and they are unrealistically optimistic about the future. For example, when students are asked to describe how accurately positive and negative personality adjectives describe them and others, most evaluate themselves more favorably than they evaluate others (e.g., Suls, Lemos, & Stewart, 2002). We remember positive information about ourselves, but negative information often slips conveniently from mind (Sedikides & Green, 2000). If pressed, most of us would have more difficulty reconstructing past circumstances when we failed than circumstances when we succeeded (Story, 1998). We believe we are more likely than others to engage in selfless, kind, and generous acts (Epley & Dunning, 2000). We often remember our performance as more positive than it actually was (Crary, 1966). We believe we are happier than most other people (Klar & Giladi, 1999). We believe that those who flatter us are credible and discerning (Vonk, 2002). We respond to threats by bolstering our self-perceptions in other life domains (Boney-McCoy, Gibbons, & Gerrard, 1999) and by making *downward social comparisons* to others less fortunate than ourselves (Wills, 1981). And perhaps most poignant of all, we see ourselves as less biased than we believe others to be (Ehrlinger, Gilovich, & Ross, 2005; Pronin, Lin, & Ross, 2002). In each case, people can self-enhance by seeing themselves as better than other people, or by seeing themselves as better than others see them (Kwan, John, Kenny, Bond, & Robins, 2004).

How do people successfully monitor reality and maintain accurate perceptions about themselves and the world if positive illusions are clouding their vision? Although absolute accuracy may be inflated, relative accuracy seems to be quite high. For example, if one compares a person's self-assessments on a broad array of traits with the same assessments made by a friend, the correlation between the ratings is extremely high, even though people see themselves more positively than their friends see them (Taylor, Lerner, Sherman, Sage, & McDowell, 2003a).

But there are also predictable circumstances in which assessments of the self, the world, and the future become more realistic. When people are about to get feedback from others, they are more realistic, even pessimistic, about the news they will get (K. M. Taylor & Shepperd, 1998). When people are in the process of deciding between alternative courses of action or are setting personal goals, they are more accurate and honest with themselves (S. E. Taylor & Gollwitzer, 1995). People are more modest in their self-appraisals when they believe other people will have accurate information about them, when their self-descriptions can be easily verified, when they expect to receive self-relevant feedback (Armor

& Taylor, 1998), or if their self-assessments can potentially be disconfirmed (e.g., Dunning, Meyerowitz, & Holzberg, 1989), such as expecting to perform a task that will confirm an ability or not (Armor & Sackett, 2006). Self-enhancement is more evident when the personal quality being evaluated is ambiguous rather than concrete. Thus, as accountability becomes more likely, self-perceptions become more accurate in the absolute sense. Self-enhancement is greater at the beginning of a project when it has the power to motivate a person to carry through efforts to achieve personal goals than at the end of a project when modest achievements and discrepancies from hoped for results might be dispiriting (Shepperd, Ouellette, & Fernandez, 1996).

Why are most people so apparently self-enhancing in their self-perceptions? Moreover, why do these self-enhancing perceptions persist if they do not conform to reality? Taylor and Brown (1988) argued that self-enhancing positive illusions are adaptive for mental health (S. E. Taylor et al., 2003a; S. E. Taylor, Lerner, Sherman, Sage, & McDowell, 2003b). Positive self-perceptions, unrealistic optimism about the future, and a false sense of personal control may help us to feel better about ourselves (Regan, Snyder, & Kassin, 1995), develop the motivation to pursue goals (S. E. Taylor & Gollwitzer, 1995), and persist longer in trying to achieve our goals (Armor & Taylor, 2003). Self-enhancing perceptions foster many of the tasks that are regarded as evidence of successful life adjustment: a personal sense of well-being, persistence toward goals, and the ability to engage in creative, productive work (see Brown & Dutton, 1995). Positive self-regard is thought to foster good social relationships as well (Taylor et al., 2003a). However, it appears that this finding has an upward limit. People who are notably self-enhancing in public settings can alienate others (e.g., Bonano, Field, Kovacevic, & Kaltman, 2002; Robins & Beer, 2001).

Moreover, people with high self-esteem can become mean, nasty, and self-important under conditions of threat such as when their personal attributes are challenged or their goals are threatened (Baumeister, Smart, & Boden, 1996); this is evidenced through such behaviors as increased stereotyping, disparagement of others, and downward social comparisons (e.g., Heatherton & Vohs, 2000; Vohs & Heatherton, 2004; see also Baumeister, Campbell, Krueger, & Vohs, 2003). These self-regulation failures appear to be more common among people who are defensively high in self-esteem rather than those who are more secure in their high self-esteem (Lambird & Mann, 2006).

Nonetheless, self-enhancement can often yield another unexpected benefit. When people are feeling good about themselves and are not threatened by nagging questions about their self-worth, they are often more receptive to negative information about themselves (e.g., Trope & Neter, 1994). Research suggests that people who are, by nature, more optimistic about the future also process personally relevant risk-related information less defensively than people who are less optimistic (Aspinwall & Brunhart, 1996). When people are feeling good about themselves, they are more positive about other people as well (Ybarra, 1999). Social validation—that is, being accepted for who we are—also reduces defensiveness, and after people have reflected on being liked for intrinsic aspects of themselves, they are more receptive to potentially threatening information (Schimel, Arndt, Pyszczynski, & Greenberg, 2001).

Additional evidence for benefits of a positive sense of self comes from people with chronically low self-esteem. People with low self-esteem have less clear self-conceptions, think of themselves in more unfavorable terms, often select unrealistic goals or shy away from goals altogether, tend to be pessimistic about the future, remember their past experiences more negatively, wallow in their negative moods rather than adopting mood regulation techniques to restore a positive mood, have more adverse emotional and behavioral reactions to negative feedback, are less able to generate positive feedback for themselves, make upward social comparisons that yield negative self-evaluations (Vohs & Heatherton, 2004), are more concerned about their impact on other people, and are more vulnerable to depression or rumination when they encounter setbacks or stress (Brown & Marshall, 2001; Di Paula & Campbell, 2002; Heatherton & Vohs, 2000; Josephs, Bosson, & Jacobs, 2003; Kernis, Paradise, Whitaker, Wheatman, & Goldman, 2000; Leary, Tambor, Terdal, & Downs, 1995; Setterlund & Niedenthal, 1993; Sommer & Baumeister, 2002).

Self-enhancement also appears to confer biological benefits during times of stress. We are all familiar with stress: the heart beats faster, blood pressure goes up, and we feel anxious. People who perceive themselves positively, even more positively than others perceive them, have lower cortisol levels and lower heart rate and blood pressure responses to stressful tasks in the laboratory (Creswell et al., 2005; Taylor et al., 2003b). These patterns suggest that self-enhancement can be protective against stressful circumstances that might otherwise be personally threatening and have adverse effects on health. More generally, self-esteem and an internal locus of control have been tied to a lower cortisol response to psychological stress and greater hippocampal volume in younger people and to less age-related cognitive decline, better cortisol regulation, and less global brain volume decline in older adults (Pruessner et al., 2005)

Self-Affirmation

Self-affirmation theory (Steele, 1988) addresses self-enhancement needs and maintains that people cope with threats to their self-worth by affirming unrelated aspects of themselves (e.g., Aronson, Blanton, & Cooper, 1995; Blanton, Cooper, Skurnik, & Aronson, 1997; Koole, Smeets, van Knippenberg, & Dijksterhuis, 1999; see Sherman & Cohen, 2006, for a review). Considerable research supports the idea that when people have an opportunity to affirm valued aspects of the self, they are less likely to respond defensively to threat. For example, in an experimental study, Sherman, Nelson, and Steele (2000) instructed half of a group of college student participants to reflect on a personally important value; the other half reflected on a less important personal value. The participants were then shown an AIDS education video. Those who had completed the value affirmation task viewed themselves as at increased risk for HIV and engaged in more positive health behaviors (namely, purchasing condoms and taking educational brochures) compared to those who had reflected on a relatively unimportant value. These findings suggest that a self-affirming experience reduces defensive responses to threatening health information. This is consistent with the evidence just reviewed indicating that when people feel good about themselves they are more receptive to potentially negative information. Studies show that the affirmation of personal values can attenuate perceptions of threat (Sherman & Cohen, 2002) and reduce the tendency to ruminate after failure (Koole et al., 1999).

Consistent with the findings from self-enhancement research more generally, self-affirmation may also have benefits for health. In an experimental study in which participants completed a value affirmation task or a control task, those who affirmed their values had significantly lower cortisol responses to laboratory stressors. Those who were also high in self-esteem and optimism who had affirmed their personal values reported experiencing less stress in response to the laboratory stressors. Thus, reflecting on personal values (an act of self-affirmation) can keep neuroendocrine and psychological responses to stress at low levels (Creswell et al., 2005).

An important implication of findings from self-affirmation theory is that self-enhancement is a maintenance motive. People do not strive to have the most positive self-assessment possible but rather strive to maintain an adequate level of self-regard. Indeed, once a certain level of self-esteem is reached, people may actually avoid activities that might enhance it further (Tesser, Crepaz, Collins, Cornell, & Beach, 2000; Zuckerman & O'Loughlin, 2006).

Self-Evaluation Maintenance

Tesser (1988) suggested another social mechanism whereby people facilitate and maintain their positive self-regard—namely, how they deal with the performance of people around them with whom they might compare themselves. For example, John's best friend, Mark, recently won a prestigious prize for writing a short story. Will John be pleased and eager to tell others about his friend's success, or might he instead feel envious of Mark's success and unhappy to be reminded that he is a less talented writer? Tesser's *self-evaluation maintenance theory* deals with questions like these and addresses how cognitions about the self influence feelings and behavior more generally.

Generally speaking, the behavior of people who are close to us has more impact on us, psychologically speaking, than the behavior of people who are distant. Thus, a critical situation arises when a person we are close to performs well. Whether John will be delighted for Mark or feel envy instead will depend critically on how central writing is to John's self-conception. If John is also a writer who has been trying to get his work published, then Mark's strong performance is likely to be personally threatening and lead to negative emotions and efforts to avoid Mark in the future (the comparison effect). However, if John is an attorney and does not write short stories, he may be delighted with Mark's success and take pride in Mark's award (the reflection effect). Thus the same factors—personal closeness to a target and the target's strong performance—can lead to opposite effects on one's own emotions and behavior, depending on whether another person's performance is relevant or irrelevant to one's self-definition. (See Figure 5.4.)

Terror Management Theory

Threat is an important stimulus to self-enhancement, and there is perhaps no greater threat than death (Gailliot, Schmeichel, & Baumeister, 2006). Terror management theory draws on this insight (Greenberg, Pyszczynski, & Solomon, 1986). According to the theory, people are biologically driven for self preservation, and the threat of death is managed at both the cultural level, by developing worldviews that provide meaning and purpose, and at the individual level, through self-esteem. The theory maintains that people form systems of thoughts and beliefs that endow their lives and the world in which they live with a sense of enduring meaning. These views help people to manage their mortality and the

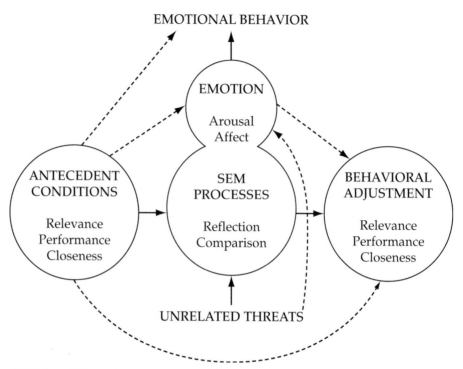

FIGURE 5.4. Schematic representation of the self-evaluation maintenance model
Source: After Tesser, 1988.

anxiety that their vulnerability produces (Greenberg, Pyszczynski, & Solomon, 1986). At the individual level, people strive to maintain a positive sense of self, which likewise reduces the anxiety associated with mortality.

The theory generates a number of specific predictions as to how cultural worldviews and self-esteem help to ward off the threat of death. One prediction is that people will suppress death-related thoughts when death is made salient, a prediction for which considerable evidence exists (Greenberg, Arndt, Schimel, Pyszczynski, & Solomon, 2001; Schmeichel & Martens, 2005). The importance of a cultural worldview for coping with the terror of mortality also predicts that when death is made salient, people will especially subscribe to and attempt to live up to culturally approved standards of behavior. Such actions help protect them from the anxiety that their vulnerability to death might otherwise create (Greenberg, Porteus, Simon, Pyszczynski, & Solomon, 1995). Thus acts of subscribing to social or cultural norms are, in essence, soothing or reassuring. Consistent with the theory, people are more likely to act on their beliefs and assert their values in the face of challenges if mortality has been made salient as compared to no threat of mortality (McGregor et al., 1998).

But the fear of death and the fact that it leads people to subscribe more fully to social norms also mean that people's evaluations of others who violate norms may be more harsh. One study, for example, found that following a manipulation that made mortality salient, people were more likely to blame severely injured innocent victims in an apparent effort to restore a sense of order to a frightening environment (Hirschberger, 2006). Likewise, activities that promote or restore self-esteem help people manage the terror of mortality by allowing them to reaffirm their intrinsic value and importance. The threat of death requires active self-regulation to alleviate disturbing thoughts about mortality (Gailliot et al., 2006).

Culture and Self-Enhancement

Both the existence of self-enhancement and the needs that it serves represent insights about the self within cultural boundaries. The characterization of self-enhancement just described and the conclusions from the empirical research better characterize Westerners, particularly people in the United States, than people in other countries, especially East Asian countries. East Asians are more self-critical than those from Western cultures, and self-serving attributions are less common in East Asian cultures (Heine & Renshaw, 2002), as we will see in Chapter 6 on causal attribution. In East Asian cultures, self-effacing biases are often more commonly documented than self-enhancing biases. In one study in which Japanese students outperformed another student, they regarded their success as situationally caused, whereas when they were outperformed by another, they were more likely to attribute that person's performance to personal qualities (Takata, 1987). These more modest self-perceptions among East Asians appear to be quite consistent (Heine, Takata, & Lehman, 2000; Oishi, Wyre, & Colcombe, 2000).

It may, however, be the case that needs met by self-enhancement in Western cultures are met in different forms in Eastern cultures. For example, enhancing the social group and one's standing with respect to the group may meet enhancement needs in interdependent cultures (Sedikides, Gaertner, & Toguchi, 2003). Kurman (2001) compared participants from collectivistic (Singapore, China) and individualistic (Israeli Jews) cultures and found that self-enhancement of traits reflecting personal agency was associated with an independent self-construal. Self-enhancement of communal traits was associated with an interdependent self-construal. These findings imply that enhancement of the self or one's social group may have some universality but assume different forms, depending on the values of the culture in which it is expressed (Sedikides et al., 2003).

Reconciling the Motives That Guide Self-Regulation

Each of the motives just described—need for accuracy, need for consistency, self-improvement, and self-enhancement—governs behavior under somewhat different circumstances. The search for accurate feedback about the self appears to be dominant under conditions of instability or ambiguity regarding one's standing on a dimension (e.g., Sorrentino & Roney, 1986; Trope, 1979). The quest for consistent information is strongest when one is certain of one's standing on the attribute but feedback or circumstances have challenged one's self-perceptions (Pelham, 1990). A consistent sense of self about which one is certain is also more characteristic of people who have a prevention focus in their lives (Leonardelli, Lakin, & Arkin, in press). When the personal self is activated, people demonstrate self-enhancement by contrasting away from undesirable targets and assimilating toward desirable ones; but when the relational self is activated, complementary behavior is seen (i.e., contrast behavior on the dominant-submission dimension and assimilation behavior on the agreeable-quarrelsome dimension) (Stapel & Van der Zee, 2006).

Self-enhancement needs appear to be preponderant, at least in Western cultures and under conditions of threat. Self-presentational needs may also trigger self-enhancing behavior (Baumeister, Tice, & Hutton, 1989). Cognitions about the self stray in the direction of consistency, whereas affective reactions to the self stray in the direction of enhancement. That is, we like to feel certain of our attributes, whether positive or negative, but we are happiest when we get positive feedback (Swann, Pelham, & Krull, 1989). People motivated primarily by a promotion focus (a concern with growth and nurturance) are more concerned with self-esteem compared to those with a predominant prevention focus (Leonardelli et al., in press).

Much self-regulatory activity in service of self-enhancement (at least in Western cultures), and potentially also self-improvement, may occur automatically without awareness. However, a search for accurate or consistent feedback is more likely to implicate controlled processing because automatic processes are likely to have been interrupted by a challenge to or ambiguity regarding one's self-perceptions. A final way in which all of these motives can be simultaneously satisfied is by the fact that the human mind is very flexible and capable of construing information in ways that may be consistent with a variety of motives. People want to believe that they are consistent and may distort the degree to which this is true (Wells & Iyengar, 2005). People want to maintain a positive sense of self and can do so by being critical of their distant past selves, thereby achieving an illusion that they have improved (A. E. Wilson & Ross, 2001).

THE SELF AS A REFERENCE POINT

The concept of self is important not only for understanding how people perceive themselves and regulate their behavior but also for providing a lens through which we interpret the qualities and behavior of other people.

Self-Referencing

Social cognition researchers have long observed that information that is learned with reference to the self has an advantage in memory over other kinds of information. Early research supported a "depth of processing" (Rogers, Kuiper, & Kirker, 1977) account of this phenomenon, which maintains that information that is made self-relevant leaves a richer, more interconnected, and more enduring memory trace. Developments in social cognitive neuroscience have made it possible to understand the neural basis of such effects in the brain (Heatherton, Macrae, & Kelley, 2004). For example, W. M. Kelley and associates (2002) asked participants to judge trait adjectives as either self-descriptive or descriptive of George Bush or to judge whether the traits were presented in uppercase letters. Semantic processing tasks typically lead to activation in the left prefrontal cortex, and this was true for all three experimental conditions. For the trials involving self-referencing, the medial prefrontal cortex (mPFC) was also implicated. Moreover, the level of activity in the mPFC was correlated with how well participants remembered the items on the memory task, suggesting that mPFC contributes to the formation of self-relevant memories (Macrae, Moran, Heatherton, Banfield, & Kelley, 2004).

These self-referencing effects have been referred to as "simulation theory." According to the theory, one way that people infer the mental states of others is to imagine their own thoughts, emotions, or behaviors in a similar setting. A particular region of the ventromedial PFC that has been previously implicated in self-referencing tasks is activated in response to ratings made of similar others, but less so if one is rating dissimilar others (Mitchell, Banaji, & Macrae, 2005).

Converging evidence for this point comes from studies of people who have damage to areas of the prefrontal cortex (Stuss & Levine, 2002); such damage has been tied to impairments in the ability to reflect on the self and to be introspective. These findings suggest that the self-reference effect in memory depends on the ability to reflect on the self and that neural activity in the mPFC may underlie self-reflection (Heatherton et al., 2004).

Social Projection

The self actively constructs the social world, to a large degree, in its own image. We use our beliefs and personal qualities to construct our assessments of others. *Social projection* refers to the fact that people estimate their own preferences, traits, problems, activities, and attitudes to be characteristic of others, or at least more characteristic of others than the evidence warrants (Mullen & Goethals, 1990). We assume that others share our characteristics, emotions, and motives (Holmes, 1978) and use the same traits to describe acquaintances as we use to describe ourselves (Shrauger & Patterson, 1974). Social projection effects can be quite powerful. They occur even when people have time to think about their assessments of others' characteristics (Krueger & Stanke, 2001), when they receive feedback about the accuracy of their assessments (Krueger & Clement, 1994), and when they are given relevant information about others (Alicke & Largo, 1995; Kenny & Acitelli, 2001).

Do we project our own attitudes, characteristics, and values onto others because we have a motivation to see our characteristics as good or because the self provides a useful set of cognitive heuristics by which people can draw inferences rapidly and confidently? Both appear to be true. Decades of research that has pitted cognitive explanations against motivational ones suggest that these two sources of influence are hard to separate. Motivational influences are likely to affect judgments by exerting effects on cognitive processing (Dunning, 1999; Gollwitzer & Moskowitz, 1996; Kunda, 1990).

The desire to see the self in positive terms contributes to social projection processes. We define social concepts that we use for judging others in self-serving ways (Dunning, Perie, & Story, 1991). We use traits central to our own self-conceptions for evaluating others (Alicke, 1985). We make self-serving social comparisons to others (Dunning & Hayes, 1996). We spontaneously judge other people by comparing them with ourselves (Mussweiler & Bodenhausen, 2002). We assume that others share our weaknesses but that our strengths are unique (false uniqueness bias) (J. D. Campbell, 1986; Mullen & Goethals, 1990; Suls & Wan, 1987). We distance ourselves from others who we believe share our weaknesses (Schimel, Pyszczynski, Greenberg, O'Mahen, & Arndt, 2000).

Nor is the target on whom we project our positive qualities randomly selected. We tend to attribute our own attitudes and qualities to attractive targets (Granberg & Brent, 1980; Marks & Miller, 1982), and we project our undesirable qualities onto unattractive or unfavorable targets (e.g., Bramel, 1963; Sherwood, 1979). Both types of projection become more likely when a person has experienced some threat to self-esteem, such as negative feedback or a poor performance. By contrast, when a person has affirmed the self or has received positive feedback, the tendencies toward social projection and defensive social projection are muted (Dunning, 2003; Kunda, 1990). For example, S. J. Sherman, Presson, and Chassin (1984) gave participants false feedback about their performance on a task and then asked the students to estimate the number of students who would perform well or poorly on the task. They posed the same question to a group of participants who had not actually performed the task or received feedback. Those who had failed estimated that a greater number of others would fail as well compared to those who had merely received information that someone else had failed. Of interest is the fact that depressed people show less social projection, suggesting a compromised ability to repair threats to the self (e.g., Agostinelli, Sherman, Presson, & Chassin, 1992; Tabachnik, Crocker, & Alloy, 1983). These converging sources of evidence underscore the fact that the tendency to use the self as a standard for inferring qualities in the social world is at least partly guided by self-enhancement needs.

The tendency for projection to guide judgments is evident in stereotyping processes as well. Threats to self-image reliably increase the likelihood that a person will apply a negative stereotype to a member of a stereotyped group. In one study (Fein & Spencer, 1997), participants were given positive or negative feedback about their performance on an intelligence test, and in an ostensibly unrelated study, they were asked to evaluate an applicant for a job based on her application materials and interview. The applicant was portrayed as either Jewish or not Jewish. Participants who had received negative feedback rated the job candidate less favorably if she was labeled as Jewish, whereas participants who had received positive feedback rated the two job candidates equally regardless of background. Research from terror management theory makes a similar point: Reminding people of their own mortality increases their need to affirm self-worth, which in turn enhances the use of stereotypes to characterize others (Greenberg et al., 1990; Schimel et al., 1999).

Stereotypes also help us to invalidate the expertise of those who view us negatively. After being criticized, for example, a person may use a negative stereotype to discredit an evaluator to minimize the self-deflating aspects of the criticism. For example, students' evaluations of their professors depend heavily on the grades they expect to receive from them (Sinclair & Kunda, 2000). When flattered by others whom they might otherwise stereotype, people instead suspend their stereotypes and judge the positive evaluator in a positive manner (Sinclair & Kunda, 1999). Thus stereotyping can serve a self-enhancement purpose.

Summary

The self is an important source of social cognition. People hold complex and varied representations of themselves, including both their current attributes and attributes that may characterize them in the future. The self-concept varies depending on the situation in which one finds oneself, leading to temporary alterations in the working self-concept, and the self-concept also includes representations about significant others. Beliefs about one's current and future qualities act as reference points for setting goals and guiding behavior directed toward those goals. Self-esteem is the valuation one makes of the self, and it includes explicit self-evaluations as well as implicit ones.

Self-conceptions and the cognitions, emotions, and goals that accompany them vary by cultural context. Whereas the independent self, characteristic of Western cultures, reflects a conception of self that is autonomous and self-serving, the interdependent self reflects a self-conception that is interconnected with the social group and influenced substantially by group standards and guidelines. These differences substantially affect the motives and processes that guide self-regulation.

Self-regulation refers to the ways in which people control and direct their actions. The working self-concept, which consists of both stable self-conceptions and representations of situational forces, enables people to negotiate situations. Self-regulation is also influenced by whether one holds a promotion or a prevention focus with respect to personal goals and whether one's attention is directed inward toward the self or outward toward the environment. Generally, self-focus functions to increase the correspondence between behavior and salient standards. Self-regulatory behavior may be either self-consciously activated or automatically pursued, and psychologists have begun to understand which brain regions are implicated in these different types of processing.

Self-regulation is guided by underlying motivational processes, and chief among these are the overarching goals of the need for accuracy, the need for a consistent sense of self, the desire to improve, and self-enhancement, which is the tendency to hold and maintain a favorable self-conception. These overarching goals, which are influenced by situational context, influence how people take in and represent information about themselves in memory, and they also influence which situations people choose to enter and which companions they choose for social interaction. Each of these motives has powerful effects on behavior under different circumstances.

Beliefs about the self influence the accessibility of constructs used for judging others. Under neutral circumstances, a person may use personal beliefs and characteristics as a basis for inferring the qualities of others. But conditions of personal threat appear to potentiate a broad array of social projection processes, ranging from assuming one's weaknesses are widely shared to stereotyping vulnerable social groups.

Attribution Processes

Why is my friend acting so distant? Why did the teacher ignore my comment in class? Every day we encounter events that require explanation. Attribution—the attempt to identify what factors give rise to what outcomes—is important for explaining events, and consequently, it is important for social cognition more generally.

WHAT IS ATTRIBUTION?

Attribution is fundamentally concerned with how people infer causal relations and the characteristics of other people in the environment. These are overlapping but also somewhat distinct processes.

Causal Attributions

Attributional processes are in large part for the purpose of inferring the causes of events. Take the hypothetical example of a fight between two friends over whether New Year's Day should be celebrated by going to a hockey game or a basketball game. On the surface of it, such a conflict should be trivial, but as many of us know, such arguments can often mean much more than meets the eye and lead to hurt feelings or even estrangement. How does one go about inferring what is going on in this situation? One might think about what one knows about each of the two friends, which provides knowledge about their respective dispositions, such as whether they are routinely quarrelsome or have an enduring need to be in control. One may think about the relationship that the two have with each other, and wonder if this is a need on the part of one or both to dominate the situation. One may think about the circumstances of the argument, note that both have had several beers, and reflect upon the fact that alcohol often fuels contentious behavior. Causal reasoning, thus, recruits knowledge of other people's qualities and knowledge of situational dynamics to infer the cause or causes of an event.

When research on causal reasoning began in the 1970s, several well-developed models outlined the often-complex reasoning that was believed to go into inferring causality, especially in ambiguous circumstances. These analyses created the impression that explicit causal reasoning is time consuming, ubiquitous, and central to other inferential processes and behavior. However, the idea that people use much of their cognitive capacity much of the time for causal reasoning is unlikely to be true. As noted in Chapters 1 and 2, cognitive capacity is costly in time and attentional resources, and we can devote our attention to only a few bits of information at any given time. By contrast, long-term memory is virtually limitless, so it is likely that we solve many causal dilemmas simply by accessing long-term memory for information about causes relating to specific people, situations, or events. That is, much of our understanding of causes is embedded in the mental representations we hold about particular life domains. We hear about the breakup of friends, John and Deborah, and we do not need to use laborious causal rules to understand why. We know why couples break up: they tire of each other, they have grown apart, they argue all the time, one betrayed the other, or there is a combination of causes. The job of causal reasoning in such a case is to discover which of a limited number of domain-specific causes applies in the particular case.

Decades of research have yielded additional insights about causal reasoning. The dual-processing distinction introduced in Chapter 2 applies to causal reasoning just as it applies to other kinds of social cognition. Much causal reasoning occurs very quickly and virtually automatically. One of the earliest insights to emerge from attribution research was the fact that people do not review a broad array of evidence in service of the best possible causal explanation for an event but rather often seize upon a single sufficient explanation that will explain the situation at hand.

Decades of research on causal reasoning has also revealed the circumstances under which we do interrupt our automatic information processing, shift to controlled processing, and focus our attention explicitly on asking and answering the question "Why did that happen?" Explicit causal reasoning is most likely to occur when something unexpected or negative happens (Kanazawa, 1992; Wong & Weiner, 1981). If we pick an elective course and it proves to be interesting, we do not stop to ask why. In passing, we may congratulate ourselves on the wise choice we made. Otherwise, because the outcome is positive and expected, there is no particular reason to look for a cause. Instead, we reserve that capacity for circumstances of apparent failure, especially unexpected ones. We lavish causal attention on the interesting elective we picked that turned out to be a crashing bore because the result was an unexpected and negative occurrence.

Another important theme in understanding causal reasoning harks back to the point made in the first chapter, namely, that social cognition is social. As is true for other kinds of problems, we do not engage in causal reasoning in a social vacuum. As will be seen, some of the guiding attribution theories implicitly represent the social perceiver as lost in thought, attempting to solve causal dilemmas alone, as if Albert Camus were characterizing the social perceiver. The world is typically not so asocial. Often, when we want to solve a causal dilemma, we simply ask another person. Hearing about an unexpected divorce among our friends, we ask someone in a position to know, "Why?" For example, Hilton and Slugoski (1986) suggested that when an outcome differs from what is expected, what they call an "abnormal condition," an explanation is sought. One person communicates to another the information that will uniquely close the gap in the listener's knowledge.

Basic Principles of Causation

Research on children's attribution processes highlights some basic principles of causation that people initially learn in their efforts to understand cause-effect relations (e.g., Kassin & Pryor, 1985). It is worth examining these principles because adults often use them when inferring causality, particularly in circumstances that are ambiguous or in settings about which they are poorly informed or have little information.

A fundamental principle of cause-effect relations is that *causes precede effects* (Kassin & Pryor, 1985). This principle appears to be well established by the time a child is 3 and is virtually never contradicted in spontaneous causal attribution. A second basic principle is that people perceive as causal those factors that have *temporal contiguity* with the effect. We are more inclined to attribute a factor as causal if it occurred immediately before an effect took place, but not if it took place some time before. People also draw on *spatial contiguity* in inferring cause-effect relations. Thus, for example, a suspect in a robbery would be dismissed from consideration if it were found that he was in another town at the time it occurred. *Perceptually salient stimuli* are more likely to be perceived as causal than stimuli that are in the visual background (S. E. Taylor & Fiske, 1975, 1978). *Causes resemble effects.* For example, people generally assume that big effects are produced by big causes, and that little effects are produced by little causes (see also Kelley & Michela, 1980). Thus the development of a malignancy might be attributed to a major stressor, such as divorce. *Representative causes* are attributed to effects (Tversky & Kahneman, 1982). Thus, for example, a patient unfamiliar with the causes of cancer may attribute a malignant lump to an injury because other kinds of lumps are caused by injuries.

These basic principles are also employed by adults, at least under some circumstances (Einhorn & Hogarth, 1986; S. E. Taylor, 1982). For example, people who lack knowledge about a particular causal domain may resort to these basic causal rules to understand causal relations in that domain; by contrast, people who are knowledgeable or sophisticated in the domain may instead consider primarily causal information that is domain relevant. For example, Taylor, Lichtman, and Wood (1984) interviewed cancer patients and found that the causal explanations generated by these cancer patients varied, depending on how knowledgeable they were about cancer. Those who were unsophisticated about cancer drew on concepts such as spatiotemporal contiguity, for example, inferring that their breast cancer had been caused by being bumped in the breast. By contrast, those who were sophisticated about the causes of cancer were more likely to attribute their cancers to cancer-related causes, such as diet or a genetic predisposition.

In situations characterized by high uncertainty or lack of knowledge, people may resort to basic principles (e.g., "What major event happened recently that might account for this disease?"). By contrast, in circumstances in which people have a lot of knowledge about a specific domain, they may access domain-specific causal knowledge to infer causality rather than employing a general causal inferential model. Thus, for example, if your washing machine stops working, the repairperson is likely to have a limited set of very well-defined causes in mind with estimates of each one's likelihood of explaining the problem.

Dispositional Attributions

As will be seen, much of our causal attributional reasoning focuses on other people, what characteristics they have, and why they exhibit the behaviors they do. This type of reasoning builds on *theory of mind*. Children develop abilities early in life to understand what is going on in another person's mind. As early as age 2, children have developed a system for reasoning about other people's goals, perceptions, and emotions. By about age 4, a system for representing the contents of people's beliefs develops (Saxe, Carey, & Kanwisher, 2004).

In adulthood, the social perceiver sometimes is interested in temporary qualities of the person that may explain an action, such as emotions, intentions, and desires, but more commonly is concerned with inferring enduring dispositions, such as beliefs, traits, and abilities (Gilbert, 1998). The process of attributing dispositional qualities to other people is remarkably quick and is often based on the faintest of cues. For example, people draw trait inferences from physical attributes such as facial appearance, gender, race, and age. Indeed, judgments can be made after a 100 millisecond exposure to a person's face (Willis & Todorov, 2006). More astonishing is the fact that these judgments correlate very well with the same judgments made in the absence of time constraints. In short, a 10th of a second is often sufficient for people to make specific trait inferences from faces, reflecting a fast, intuitive, effortless process.

But are judgments such as these consequential? The answer appears to be yes. In one study, participants saw the faces of U.S. congressional candidates and were asked to infer their competence based solely on their facial appearance. These rapid assessments of competence actually predicted the outcomes of U.S. congressional elections at a better than chance level. Moreover, those judgments were significantly related to the margin of victory, such that those senators whose faces were perceived to be especially competent won by a larger margin (Todorov, et al., 2005). Thus instead of the rational, deliberate consideration that is usually assumed to characterize most people's inferences, such as their vote for a congressional representative, rapid effortless trait inferences appear to contribute to voting choices. As this research suggests, dispositional attribution is often a rapid, virtually automatic process.

Neural Bases of Inferences About Others

Several brain regions are reliably engaged when people are drawing inferences about others. Theory of mind research has implicated a network of brain areas that includes the anterior paracingulate cortex, the posterior superior temporal sulcus (pSTS) at the temporoparietal junction (TPJ), and the temporal pole (Gallagher & Frith, 2003). As is true for many aspects of social cognition, the medial prefrontal cortex (mPFC) is activated both when processing one's own experiences and when one is inferring the mental states of others. Dorsal mPFC is implicated in a broad array of tasks that require understanding the mental state of others. The right TPJ is recruited selectively for the attribution of mental states but not for other social information about a person (Rilling, Sanfey, Aronson, Nystrom, & Cohen, 2004). (See Figure 6.1.)

Studies that have examined neural correlates of theory of mind when people are actually involved in social interaction also implicate the anterior paracingulate cortex, alternatively described as the mPFC (Gallagher, Jack, Roepstorff,

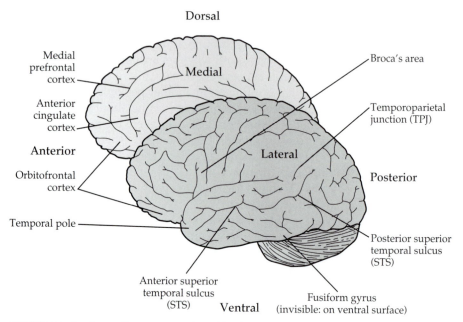

FIGURE 6.1. A schematic representation of brain regions associated with the attribution of mental states: beliefs, desires, perceptions, and/or emotions.
Source: From "Understanding other minds: Linking developmental psychology and functional neuroimaging," by R. Saxe, S. Carey, & N. Kanwisher. Reprinted, with permission, from the Annual Review of Psychology, *Volume 55, © 2004, by Annual Reviews, www.annualreviews.org*

& Frith, 2002; McCabe, Houser, Ryan, Smith, & Trouard, 2001). Activation in the anterior paracingulate cortex (or pACC) and the posterior STS can appear to be stronger when actual human partners are involved rather than hypothetical interaction partners (Rilling et al., 2004). That is, some areas that appear to be involved in reasoning about others' minds may be differentially involved during actual social interaction.

EARLY CONTRIBUTIONS TO ATTRIBUTION THEORY

The next sections address classic contributions to theory and research on attribution. In reading about this work, it will be helpful to keep these earlier points in mind: Much attributional reasoning focuses on inferring other people's dispositional qualities. Much attributional reasoning is effortless and virtually automatic. Much causal inference is domain specific, determined largely by the range of causes likely to apply in that domain and not by more abstract generic causal processes. Explicit attributional reasoning is reserved for special occasions, most notably when unexpected and negative events occur. And like all social reasoning, attributional reasoning is inherently social: When we are at a loss to explain an event, we ask someone.

Early attribution theory models deal with why and how the social perceiver uses information to arrive at explanations for events. It examines what information is gathered and how it is combined to form a judgment. Thus attribution theory is concerned with the generic principles that people employ that might be used to explain behavior and events across a wide variety of domains.

Why do people make attributions? Attribution theory and research have generally assumed either implicitly or explicitly that attributional analysis is initiated by people's needs to predict the future and to control events (Heider, 1958; Jones & Davis, 1965; Kelley, 1967). The assumption is that understanding the factors that give rise to a particular outcome can enable one to control its likelihood or at least to predict when it will happen. Following from this point is the observation that causal attribution is important for the pursuit of goals. One must know why things happen to make them happen.

Six different theoretical traditions form the backbone of early attribution theory. The first is Heider's (1958) analysis of commonsense psychology. His insights strongly influenced both E. E. Jones and Davis's (1965) analysis of correspondent inference, a theory of how people infer other people's dispositions, and Harold Kelley's (1967) ANOVA model, which is a normative model of causal inference. Other attribution approaches have been primarily concerned with self-attribution. Schachter's (1964) theory of emotional lability and Bem's (1967, 1972) self-perception theory extended attribution principles to the self-perception of emotions and attitudes, respectively. Bernard Weiner's (1979, 1985) attributional theory, pursued largely in the domains of achievement behavior and helping, articulated a dimensional structure for understanding causal inference and helped to extend attributional reasoning to expectations, emotions, and behavior.

As these diverse origins might imply, attribution theory is a set of theories that share certain fundamental principles or assumptions. The first already noted characteristic these models share is that they are generic, in other words, relatively content free. It is assumed that people infer causality in roughly the same way regardless of the particular domain in which they are attempting to draw a causal inference. Thus the rules you might follow in trying to understand why you have gotten sick should be roughly the same as the rules you would follow to understand why your houseplant is dying. A second assumption is minimal determinism: A relatively simple set of rules can be uncovered that explain how people infer causality. A third assumption made by attribution theorists is that there is a motivational point of departure. People have some reason to search for the cause or causes of another person's behavior. For the most part, the early theories also assumed that once the motivational point of departure has initiated the causal attribution process, the search for a causal explanation proceeds in a relatively cold, nonmotivational manner. As such, attribution theories tend to make the normative assumption that people are essentially rational problem solvers with a few acknowledged biases, but who tend to process information about the world much as a "naive scientist" might (Kelley, 1967).

Heider's Theory of Naive Psychology

The historical origin of attribution theory was Heider's 1958 book, *The Psychology of Interpersonal Relations*. Heider maintained that a systematic understanding of how people comprehend the social world can be enlightened by commonsense psychology: the ways in which people think about and infer meaning from what occurs around them. Early writings on person perception had emphasized the conditions under which people accurately perceive the qualities of another person. Heider's vision of the social perceiver, by contrast, was heavily influenced by the philosophy of Emmanuel Kant, and so Heider was concerned with what the perceiver contributes to the perception process. This commonsense psychology, or naive epistemology, can be inferred from the natural language that people employ for describing their experience. This is not to say that people have insight into all the reasoning processes they use, but only that commonsense psychology provides the evidentiary basis for understanding implicit attribution processes.

Heider was especially concerned with how people extract dispositional properties—that is, invariances—from the range of behaviors to which they are exposed. According to Heider, fundamental to the question of why someone behaves as he or she does is whether the locus of causality for that behavior is within the person (personal causation) or outside the person (impersonal causation), or both. Personal factors relevant to attributions consist of the *ability* to accomplish that action and *motivation* (trying). As seen in Figure 6.2, ability combines with environmental factors to influence the capacity for action; capacity, thus, is a joint function of the person's abilities (for example, talents and strengths) and the environment's facilitating or inhibiting influences (such as task difficulty or chance). Motivation is a joint function of the actor's intentions (goals and plans) and exertion (effort). For example, I may be able to complete my calculus homework and have enough time to do so, but if I decide not to do it or expend no effort, it may remain undone. Action implies that a person has both the capacity and the motivation to perform a behavior. Whether one *can* succeed is a joint function of environmental forces and ability; whether one *does* succeed is additionally determined by the motivational factors of intention and effort.

Because Heider's goal in *The Psychology of Interpersonal Relations* was broader than providing a theory of attribution, he left his theoretical statements about causality at a relatively undeveloped level. His major contribution to attribution theory was to define many of the basic issues that would later be explored more systematically in other theoretically guided ventures. In particular, he noted that the social perceiver searches for invariances in the environment; that is, factors that predictably and reliably account for both stability and change in an environment. This assumption was important for the development of Jones and Davis's correspondent inference theory and Kelley's attribution theory, as will be seen next.

FIGURE 6.2. Heider's attribution theory
Source: From "Ordinary personology," by D. T. Gilbert. Reprinted, with permission, from The handbook of social psychology, *1998, 4th edition, p. 97.*

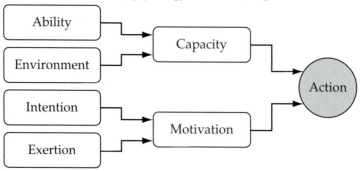

Jones and Davis's Correspondent Inference Theory

Jones and Davis's (1965) correspondent inference theory is essentially a theory of person perception. It maintains that the goal of the social perceiver is to identify intentions underlying behavior with the purpose of inferring dispositions that will be robust across situations. This theory focuses on how people go about inferring the intentions of others. We search for explanations for other people's behavior that are both stable and informative. According to the theory, the behavior of another person is most informative if it can be judged to be intentional and to have been produced by a consistent underlying intention, not one that changes from situation to situation.

Some of the cues people use for inferring others' dispositions can lead to quite rapid causal inferences. For example, the *social desirability* of an outcome is an important and valuable cue for the social perceiver. Behavior that is low in social desirability is more likely to be attributed to a person's disposition (assuming it is not accidental) than socially desirable behavior; socially desirable behavior may simply follow from social norms. As such, socially desirable behavior is uninformative about the unique qualities of a particular actor because it describes how most people would behave in the same situation.

Other conditions that help resolve the ambiguity of an action's meaning include whether the person's behavior is part of a *social role*, and whether the person's behavior meets *prior expectations*. Behavior that is constrained by a social role or that meets expectations is also not particularly informative about an actor's underlying dispositions, although it may be causally informative about why an action occurred. For example, when a firefighter puts out a fire, we do not assume that he or she is helpful; it is part of the job.

Jones and Davis hypothesized that the social perceiver uses the unique consequences of a person's behavior to infer dispositions through the *analysis of noncommon effects* (see Figure 6.3). That is, they suggested that the social perceiver asks the question, "What is this action producing that other actions would not have produced?" By comparing the consequences of an action that is actually taken with the consequences of actions that are not taken, one may infer the strength of the underlying intention by looking for distinctive consequences. For example, if I am offered two jobs that are very similar except that one has a sports center and I choose that one, then you might infer that a sports center is especially important to me. Furthermore, if many relatively negative elements (such as a lower salary or a smaller cubicle) are incorporated into the chosen alternative relative to the unchosen ones, you may infer that the distinctive elements of my choice (the sports center) are especially important to me. A disposition will be more confidently inferred when there are fewer noncommon effects between the chosen and unchosen alternatives.

As Figure 6.3 suggests, the analysis of noncommon effects can be a time-consuming and complex process. Among other complications is the fact that a person needs to infer qualities that are not present and thus go well beyond the information given to search out a causal explanation. When and whether people engage in such extensive reasoning are important potential qualifications to the analysis of noncommon effects.

The degree to which people see another person's behavior as dispositionally based increases with *hedonic relevance* (that is, whether the action obstructs

STUDENT A's CHOICE   STUDENT B's CHOICE

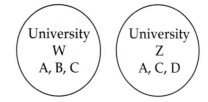

A. Prestigious school   A. Prestigious school
B. Clinical program   B. Clinical program
C. Desirable location   C. Desirable location
D. Lots of requirements   D. Lots of requirements

Result: Student chooses University X.   *Result*: Student chooses University W.

Conclusion: University X has the noncommon effect of a clinical program.   *Conclusion*: Either the student wants clinical training or he does not want to do a lot of work.

Inference: The student wants clinical training.   *Inference*: Inference unclear due to absence of noncommon effects.

FIGURE 6.3. Analysis of noncommon effects of choosing a graduate school
Source: After E. E. Jones & Davis, 1965.

or promotes the perceiver's own goals and interests) and with the perception of *personalism* (the perceiver's perception that the actor intended to benefit or harm the perceiver). As we will see, the tendency to process the information differently when it has implications for the self's goals and outcomes is a robust influence on attributional inference.

Another potential basis for inferring an actor's disposition is whether the behavior of the actor is *situationally constrained* or whether it occurs because of the actor's choice. For example, suppose you are asked to take part in a class-room debate, and the teacher assigns you the position of arguing in favor of capital punishment. Knowing that you had been assigned this side of the debate, it would be unwise of your audience to infer that your statements reflect your true beliefs. If, however, you chose to argue in favor of capital punishment, then the audience might appropriately conclude that your statements do reflect your underlying beliefs.

This prediction from correspondent inference theory—namely, that dispositional attributions are qualified by relevant situational information—was empirically supported to only a degree and ultimately gave rise to one of the most important insights empirical research revealed about causal attribution: People often ignore contextual information about circumstances that constrain an actor's behavior and instead infer an actor's disposition from his or her behavior. There is a pervasive tendency for people to assume that if an actor engages in an activity, such as arguing against capital punishment, the behavior is indicative of the person's underlying beliefs, even when there are plausible situational factors that can explain or at least influence the behavior (Jones & Harris, 1967). A large empirical literature demonstrates that Westerners underappreciate the impact of situational forces on others' behaviors even when that situational information is fairly salient (e.g., Gilbert & Malone, 1995).

To summarize, Jones and Davis developed a theory of why and how people infer others' dispositions. It was a highly influential theory that guided person perception research over the next several decades. Among the many important insights that emerged from its empirical legacy is the fact that people not only wish to infer the dispositions of others but are biased to do so and often ignore relevant qualifying information. Second, the theory and its research legacy began to focus the field on the issue of when and why people expend cognitive effort to infer causality and when they seize upon simple cues as bases of causal inference instead.

Kelley's Attribution Contributions

Kelley's attribution theory was concerned with the conditions under which people seek to validate their causal attributions. Knowledge about the world, especially the social world, is often elusive or ambiguous. Although people usually have enough information to function effectively on a social level (see Thibaut & Kelley, 1959), under some circumstances our information is inadequate. This may occur if one's beliefs receive little support from others, when problems exist that are beyond one's capabilities, when information about a situation is poor or ambiguous, when one's views have been labeled as untrue or inappropriate, or when one encounters an experience that produces low self-esteem (Kelley, 1967). Under these circumstances, people seek additional information to validate a tentative impression or to develop an explanation. In short, uncertainty prompts causal analysis. For example, if you did well academically in college and find that you are not doing as well in graduate school, that condition will prompt efforts to understand the underlying causes.

The Covariation Model

When information falls below an adequate level, we seek out information along three dimensions: distinctiveness, does the impression occur when the entity is there versus when it is not (note that an entity may be another person or a thing); consistency over time and modality, does the impression occur each time and each way the entity is there; and consensus, is the impression experienced by other people in the same way? As an example, consider a young man who goes with a young woman (entity) to a party only to find himself ignored while she flirts with several other men. He is likely to wonder why she bothered to go out with him in the first place and to be (at least) curious about why this has happened. The three dimensions along which he will test his attributions, are as follows:

> *Distinctiveness:* Does the effect occur when the entity (the young woman) is there and when it is not? (For example, is she the only woman to have behaved this way toward him, or have other women done the same thing in the past?)

Consistency Over Time/Modality: Does the effect occur each time the entity is present and regardless of the form of the interactions? (For example, has she done this to him before and at other events as well as at parties?)

Consensus: Do other people experience the same effect with respect to this entity? (For example, has she done this to other people?)

According to Kelley, one is able to make a confident entity attribution with the combination of high distinctiveness, high consistency, and high consensus information. In this case, one may conclude that this entity, the young woman, is an impossible hussy if she is the only person who treats the wretched young man this way (high distinctiveness); if she has always done this in the past, assuming he has been foolish enough to take her out before (high consistency); and if others have had similar experiences with her (high consensus).

Other combinations of information can also yield meaningful causal inferences. For example, suppose we learn that the young lady has never ignored other dates before (low consensus), she has always ignored this date in the past (high consistency), and most other women have also ignored this young man (low distinctiveness). One might be inclined to think there is something rather offensive about the young man, such as rude manners or bad breath. The combination of low distinctiveness, high consistency, and low consensus reliably produces this kind of person attribution (McArthur, 1972).

Covariation principles can also be employed to form joint attributions of causality. Suppose we learned that the young man has never been ignored by another date (high distinctiveness), the young lady has never ignored any other date (low consensus), but she has always ignored this fellow every time they have gone out together (high consistency). Under these circumstances, we would be inclined to attribute responsibility to them jointly, concluding that they are a fatal combination as well as gluttons for punishment (McArthur, 1972.) Table 6.1 shows how the covariation model can be used to reach different causal attributions.

Kelley suggested that the social perceiver collects information along one dimension while holding other dimensions constant, may do this serially for all of the dimensions, and then essentially calculates an F ratio analogous to the statistical technique of analysis of variance in which one seeks high variance in the numerator and low variance in the denominator. That is, one looks for conditions that are highly distinctive with low variance across time, modality, and persons. If my roommate is cold and distant every time I bring home a friend, that is high covariation. If she is cold and distant only sometimes when I bring home a friend, that is lower covariation.

It is important to recognize that Kelley's model is a normative model of inference; that is, it is a formal, idealized set of rules for validating attributions. Kelley did not believe that people routinely calculate F ratios in everyday life. Nonetheless, it is worth asking how well this normative model describes causal inference. Empirical evidence suggests that social perceivers depart in many ways from the model of causal inference that Kelley detailed. Some of the empirical deviations result from the fact that particular constellations of consensus, consistency, and distinctiveness information are often unavailable to people (Hewstone & Jaspers, 1987; Jaspers, Hewstone, & Fincham, 1983). People *can* use information across these dimensions systematically and in roughly the

TABLE 6.1. Using Kelley's Covariation Model to Answer the Question: Why Does Ralph (person) Trip Over Joan's (entity) Feet While Dancing?

	High distinctiveness				Low distinctiveness			
Distinctiveness	Ralph does not trip over almost any other partner's feet.				Ralph trips over lots of partners' feet.			
	High consistency		Low consistency		High consistency		Low consistency	
Consistency	In the past, Ralph has almost always tripped over Joan's feet.		In the past, Ralph has never tripped over Joan's feet.		In the past, Ralph has almost always tripped over Joan's feet.		In the past, Ralph has almost never tripped over Joan's feet.	
	High consensus	Low consensus	High consensus	Low consensus	High consensus	Low consensus	High consensus	Low consensus
Consensus	Almost everyone else who dances with Joan trips over her feet.	Hardly anyone else who dances with Joan trips over her feet.	Almost everyone else who dances with Joan trips over her feet.	Hardly anyone else who dances with Joan trips over her feet.	Almost everyone else who dances with Joan trips over her feet.	Hardly anyone else who dances with Joan trips over her feet.	Almost everyone else who dances with Joan trips over her feet.	Hardly anyone else who dances with Joan trips over her feet.
Attribution	Joan is not coordinated. She is at fault. An entity attribution should be made.	Ralph and Joan are jointly responsible. Both are necessary to produce the outcome. A person-entity attribution is warranted.	Usually Ralph is able to overcome Joan's uncoordination, but not today. A circumstance attribution is warranted.	It's a bad day. A circumstance attribution is warranted.	Ralph and Joan are jointly responsible. Either is sufficient to cause the outcome. A person-entity attribution is warranted.	Ralph is uncoordinated and is at fault. A person attribution should be made.	Ralph and Joan are both uncoordinated. Usually they overcome it. But not today. Attribution is ambiguous.	Ralph is uncoordinated. Joan is usually able to overcome it. But not today. Attribution is ambiguous.

ways Kelley outlined when the information is given to them in this form (e.g., McArthur, 1972), but they do not systematically collect information along these dimensions on their own (Fiedler, Walther, & Nickel, 1999). Often, people draw on whatever covariation information *is* available to identify the necessary and sufficient conditions for the occurrence of an effect (Hewstone & Jaspers, 1987). Echoing an important insight from Jones and Davis, research using Kelley's model has found that people exhibit a robust tendency to seek and use information about a target individual; in other words, just as Jones and Davis hypothesized, people tend to make dispositional attributions.

Research has also suggested that, in forming a causal judgment, the social perceiver uses consensus information the least; what other people think tends to be less important to our attributions than what we think other people think, in part because we assume that our personal opinions are widely shared (Olson, Ellis, & Zanna, 1983). This phenomenon is known as the *false consensus effect*. Because we regard our own behavior as typical or expected, we assume that under the same circumstances other people would react in the same way. We overestimate how typical our behavior is; overestimate the typicality of our feelings, beliefs, and opinions; and assume that a lot of other people feel the same way that we do. Therefore, when drawing causal inferences, we may not need to know whether others believe as we do; we believe that they do (Mullen & Goethals, 1990).

Neuroimaging techniques have enabled attribution researchers to locate the specific neural regions in the brain that are implicated in different types of causal attributions and have also provided some support for Kelley's model. As noted, three neural regions have been consistently implicated in inferences about others' dispositions: medial prefrontal cortex (mPFC), superior temporal sulcus (STS), and anterior temporal poles (e.g., Frith & Frith, 2001; Leslie, 1994). Using McArthur's (1972) paradigm in the scanner, Harris, Todorov, and Fiske (2005) presented participants with combinations of consensus, distinctiveness, and consistency information about an actor's behavior and examined patterns of brain activation as a function of these different information combinations (see Table 6.1). The combination of low consensus, low distinctiveness, and high consistency led to person attributions as predicated and uniquely elicited activation in the superior temporal sulcus. Low distinctiveness coupled with high consistency (regardless of consensus) evoked mPFC activation relative to the other conditions; this pattern is consistent with evidence that people often neglect consensus information in favor of distinctiveness and consistency. These results are important because they converge with results from research on theory of mind but also because they go beyond that work by identifying the neural activation patterns associated with specific types of attribution.

Occurrences Versus Actions

Causal attribution processes vary with the characteristics of the event requiring explanation. Kruglanski (1975) distinguished between *occurrences* (which are not completely voluntary) and *actions* (which are voluntary). Although occurrences can be caused by either internal (personal) or external (situational) factors, he argued that actions are always internally caused. He further maintained that actions consist of two subtypes: *endogenous acts* (acts that are committed as ends in themselves) and *exogenous acts* (acts that are committed in service of other goals). For example, if I read a paper you have written because I am interested in the topic, my action would be endogenously based, whereas if I read it because you are a student in my class, then my action is exogenously based. Kruglanski's theory predicts that exogenously attributed acts are seen as less freely chosen and yield less pleasure.

The distinction between action and occurrence is not merely an intuitively sensible one. The distinction implies that different kinds of information will be useful for interpreting the different kinds of behaviors. Zuckerman and Feldman (1984), for example, found that consensus information is sought out for occurrences to infer their cause, whereas distinctiveness information is sought out to understand the reasons underlying voluntary behavior (actions). Emotional responses are considered to be occurrences not under voluntary control. Thus, to understand why John lost his composure when he saw Bob, the perceiver determines if other people reacted to Bob the same way (consensus information). In contrast, knowing that "John hit Bob when he came into the room" (a voluntary action) leads people to find out whether John has hit other people (distinctiveness information).

Causal Schemas

Kelley's models of causal schemas were also influential on the field. Specifically, he detailed the concepts of *multiple necessary causal schemas,* which are characterized by the need for the presence of several contributing causes to produce an effect, and *multiple sufficient causal schemas,* which are characterized by conditions in which a behavior may be due to any of several present causes. Thus, to succeed on a very difficult task requires both effort and ability (multiple necessary causes), whereas to succeed on a very simple task requires only a little bit of ability or a little bit of effort (multiple sufficient causes). For example, to win a marathon, multiple causes will need to be present to produce the outcome, including ability, effort, good training, and favorable course conditions. But if I beat my 4-year-old niece at checkers, you can attribute my victory to my ability, my effort, the fact that the task is more familiar to me, or the fact that I can cheat and she will not know how to catch me. Any of the causes will do.

Kelley made other important contributions to the study of causal attribution. He articulated the *discounting principle,* which maintains that people discount the importance of one cause to the extent that there is another sufficient cause present, and its mirror image, the *augmenting principle,* which maintains that people augment the value of a cause to the extent that alternative causes are not present. On the whole, research evidence supports the discounting principle (e.g., Van Overwalle & Van Rooy, 2001); the augmenting principle, which requires people to generate information that is not present, may typically play a lesser role in attribution processes.

Kelley's attribution theory generated a substantial amount of research and continues to influence work on causal reasoning to the present day. Among his important contributions were the identification of conditions that prompt efforts to validate one's causal beliefs and the articulation of many of the dimensions and methods that people use to infer whether their attributions are valid.

We now turn our attention to two theories that concern attributions about the self. Schachter's theory addresses the attribution of one's emotional states, and Bem's theory concerns the processes whereby people infer their attitudes from their behavior.

Schachter's Theory of Emotional Lability

Schachter's theory of emotional lability, which is an attribution theory about the labeling of arousal states, initially arose from his work on social comparison processes. Schachter (1959) noticed that under conditions of stress, people sometimes choose to affiliate with others for the apparent purpose of comparing their emotional states. He reasoned that if people do so, then their emotional states must be somewhat labile and potentially subject to multiple interpretations.

To see if the interpretation of arousal is indeed malleable, Schachter and Singer (1962) conducted a now-classic experiment. One group of undergraduate participants was injected with epinephrine: half were told its true side effects (rapid breathing, flushing, increased heart rate), and half were told to expect effects that are not, in fact, produced by epinephrine (e.g., dizziness, slight headache). A control group was given no drug. Participants were then placed in a room with a confederate and were instructed to fill out some papers. After a brief time (during which the epinephrine took effect in those who had received it), the confederate began to act in either a euphoric manner (engaging in silly antics) or in an angry manner (ripping up papers and stomping around the room).

Schachter and Singer reasoned that if physiological experience is indeed subject to multiple interpretations, then those participants who found themselves in a state of arousal with no explanation for it would be searching for an explanation for their state. For these participants, the behavior of the confederate could act as a salient cue for explaining their arousal. Participants who had been informed about the side effects of epinephrine, in contrast, already had an adequate explanation for their arousal state and could remain amused or annoyed by the confederate without acquiring his mood. Participants in the control condition would have no arousal state to explain and also should not catch the mood of the confederate. Generally speaking, this is what Schachter and Singer found, although the findings are very weak. Nonetheless, Schachter and Singer's paper had enormous heuristic value in generating research about the nature of emotional states and the misattribution of arousal.

One of the most important insights provided by Schachter's work is the idea that attributions for arousal are, to a degree, malleable. This point is important because it suggests that emotional reactions induced by a threatening experience can potentially be reattributed to a neutral or less threatening source, thereby reducing anxiety or stress. A number of efforts were undertaken to address this *misattribution effect* (Valins, 1966). Researchers explored the possibility that certain disorders that are caused or exacerbated by anxiety, such as stuttering, impotence, and insomnia, might be ameliorated if people can be induced to reattribute their arousal to a neutral source instead, such as an inert pill.

Although modest empirical support was found for misattribution predictions in laboratory studies (e.g., Ross, Rodin, & Zimbardo, 1969; Storms & Nisbett, 1970), the misattribution effect was neither reliable enough nor powerful enough to produce the kind of significant clinical applications that were originally anticipated. For example, when people are in a state of high anxiety or arousal, they are often motivated to do a thorough search of what is causing this state (Maslach, 1979). Also, people are more likely to attribute arousal to a negative source, such as a feeling of unease or nervousness, than to a positive or neutral source (Marshall & Zimbardo, 1979). For misattribution effects to occur, the alternative source to which arousal might be attributed must be plausible, unambiguous, and salient; the actual cause of the arousal must not be obvious; and the person must believe that the misattribution source has more impact on his or her arousal than it actually does (Olson & Ross, 1988). Misattribution effects are limited to a rather narrow range of emotion-inducing stimuli (Parkinson, 1985), and they are typically short-lived (Nisbett & Valins, 1972).

Moreover, more recent research on emotional states suggests that arousal is not as undifferentiated as Schachter and Singer maintained and that different emotional experiences produce distinct underlying physiological and neurological signatures. Although access to these underlying biological differences in emotional states may sometimes be limited, the distinctive patterns of arousal associated with different emotions may provide people with more knowledge about their arousal states than Schachter and Singer's theory assumed. People can reattribute arousal from one stimulus to another, particularly when they underestimate how long arousal from an unrelated source lasts (Zillmann, 1978) or when the circumstances involving misattribution are short-lived and uninvolving. But when people have strong motives and multiple methods for understanding their emotional experiences, those sources of knowledge overrule misattribution.

Bem's Self-Perception Theory

In 1967 Daryl Bem offered a radical behaviorist view of how people infer the attitudes that underlie their behavior. He maintained that people often infer their own attitudes much as they infer the attitudes of others—that is, by observing their own behavior. He argued that internal cues about people's preferences and beliefs are neither as directly accessible to them nor as unambiguous as one might imagine. Consequently, we observe what we do ("I listen to a lot of jazz") and infer from that our preferences ("I must like jazz").

Research has since suggested that Bem's ideas regarding self-perception are true primarily when our preexisting attitudes or internal cues are weak but not when we have well-defined, easily accessed beliefs or strong affective preferences (Bem, 1972). Self-perception effects are also stronger for behavioral acts that are consistent with preexisting attitudes as compared to actions that are counter to our attitudinal positions (Fazio, Zanna, & Cooper, 1977).

One of the most fruitful aspects of Bem's self-perception theory concerned inferences about motivation. Bem's theory predicts that when people are attempting to understand why they perform particular tasks, they consider whether their behavior is under the control of external forces or internal desires. Behavior attributed to external factors ("I'm paid for doing this") produces an external attribution, whereas performing the same task for minimal reward leads to an assumption of intrinsic interest ("I'm not paid very much for doing this. I must really enjoy the work."). Because intrinsic interest can be made more or less salient and because external rewards may also be more or less salient, these findings suggest that intrinsic versus extrinsic motivation for performing tasks is, to a degree, flexible and depends upon focus of attention and what information is salient at the time (e.g., Lepper, Greene, & Nisbett, 1973; Sansone & Harackiewicz, 2000).

Bem's self-perception theory was important for attribution theory for several reasons. First, it was one of the first efforts to articulate how people infer the causes of their own behavior. Second, it posited a simple model of self-perception, which, although not the whole picture, is one way that people infer their own beliefs. The simplicity of Bem's model regarding the thought processes of the social perceiver foreshadows the insight that much apparently complex inferential work is, in fact, accomplished quite quickly with minimal complex cognitive computation. The implicit emphasis of the theory on the capacity limitations of the social perceiver and the use of shortcuts to solve problems quickly are important themes.

Weiner's Attribution Contributions

Weiner's attribution model derived initially from Heider's theory, but in important respects it is quite different from attribution models developed by other theorists. Whereas other models of the attribution process attempted to establish generic or content-free rules, Weiner's model was developed in the context of a specific behavior: namely, achievement behavior.

When a little-known, predominantly Hispanic high school in East Los Angeles, California, startled the testing world by achieving mathematics scores on standardized tests that greatly exceeded their past performance and that of most other schools in the nation, everyone wanted to know why. Ultimately, the dramatic rise in scores was credited to the teaching of one particularly gifted teacher, but at the time testing officials were so surprised by the outcome that they forced the students to take the exam again, feeling that cheating must have taken place. This example illustrates several important points about causal attributions in achievement situations. First, unexpected results prompt causal attribution. If the students had achieved the expected scores, no one would have found it necessary to explain the outcome.

Second, the dimensions of locus, stability, and controllability help us to understand the perceived causes of a behavior. Consider first *locus* and the potential internal causes it generates for behavior. *Aptitude* is both stable and uncontrollable, presumably because it is determined by raw intelligence. *Mood* is also uncontrollable, but it is unstable: one's mood varies from situation to situation but generally not as a function of one's own attempts to control it. *Effort* is controllable, but it may be either stable or unstable. The typical effort one puts into a task (e.g., studying 3 hours each night) is stable, but the effort exerted for a particular task (e.g., studying extra hard for a test) is unstable. When we consider external causes, *objective task difficulty* is stable and uncontrollable: the task cannot be changed. *Luck* is both unstable and uncontrollable. Some external factors are controllable, however. A teacher's belief in your inherent ability, for example, is stable and under personal control. And, finally, unusual help from another person is controllable but unstable. For example, a friend may help you study for a particular test, but she may not do so again.

To summarize Weiner's model briefly, three dimensions underlie the causal attributions that are made for the achievement outcomes of success and failure. The *stability* dimension indicates whether the cause will change and is strongly associated with subsequent expectations of success or failure. The *locus* dimension concerns whether an individual attributes performance to internal or external factors and is tied to changes in self-esteem-related emotions such as pride and shame. The *controllability* dimension relates to whether a person has control over the outcome (see Figure 6.4).

The theory also details predictions regarding expectations and emotional consequences of attributions. In the typical achievement situation, people first determine whether they succeeded or failed and feel happiness or unhappiness accordingly. They then make a causal attribution for that outcome, which leads to more specific emotional responses: for example, guilt over an effort attribution for failure or pride over an ability attribution for success. People then generate expectations of the probability of subsequent success, and these expectations are again followed by predictable emotional responses: for example, an attribution of failure to low ability produces low expectations of subsequent success as well as feelings of hopelessness. Expectations and emotional reactions jointly determine subsequent performance. Weiner's model is, thus, a dynamic one, focusing on how attributions regulate expectations, emotions, and behavior over time.

FIGURE 6.4. A causal analysis of achievement behavior
Source: After Weiner, 1979.

These insights were subsequently extended to helping behavior. According to Weiner (1980), potential helpers make inferences about the cause of another person's need. Personal control is an important variable for such inferences. We are more likely to help someone if we believe the cause of the problem is outside the person's control rather than if it is controllable. For example, students report that they would be more likely to lend their lecture notes to a classmate who needed them because of something uncontrollable, such as being absent due to a family death, than because of something controllable, such as being absent due to a hangover (Weiner, 1980). Attributions also affect our emotional responses to another person's need. We feel sympathy and concern for people who suffer through no fault of their own. We feel anger or contempt for those who are responsible for their own problems (Schmidt & Weiner, 1988).

PROCESSES UNDERLYING ATTRIBUTION

Whereas early attribution theories were concerned primarily with the logical principles that characterize attribution processes, subsequent research has focused primarily on the mental operations by which attributions are made. In other words, what actually happens in a person's head when he or she makes a dispositional inference about a new roommate or tries to understand the origins of an enduring quarrel between two friends (Gilbert, 1998)?

The cognitive revolution of the 1970s that so heavily influenced social cognition research in other domains also influenced research on attribution processes. Using an information processing framework, attribution researchers have investigated operational phases of the attribution process.

Stage Models of the Attribution Process

Much of this work began with Trope's two-stage model of attribution processes. Trope made the important point that judgments about others' dispositions are an end product of both a spontaneous identification process and a deliberate inferential process. That is, identification of the action is an automatic process that occurs virtually instantaneously, whereas, under many circumstances, it will be followed by a more controlled attributional inference stage (see Figure 6.5). At the identification stage, the actor's immediate behavior, the situation in which it occurs, and any prior information about the actor are identified in terms of disposition-relevant categories. For example, perceivers may categorize a behavior as aggressive or nonaggressive, the situation as facilitating or inhibiting aggression, and the actor as being aggressive or nonaggressive in the past. The identification of each of these informational cues may be influenced by expectancies generated by the other cues. Prior information about the actor and information about the immediate situation may influence how behavior is identified. For example, information indicating that the actor has been aggressive in the past and that the situation facilitates aggression may bias perceivers toward identifying a behavior as aggressive.

Regardless of whether they are biased or unbiased, the identifications are used as data for subsequent inferences regarding the actor's true dispositions. At the second stage, situational expectancies are subtracted from the disposition

FIGURE 6.5. Stage models of the attribution process
Source: From "Ordinary personology," by D. T Gilbert. Reprinted, with permission, from The handbook
of social psychology, *1998, 4th edition, p. 113.*

implied by the identified behavior. By the *subtractive rule,* inhibiting situational
inducements augment and facilitating situational inducements attenuate the
diagnostic value of the identified behavior regarding the corresponding disposition. For example, perceivers will see aggressive behavior as less diagnostic of
dispositional aggression when the situation facilitates aggression than when it
inhibits aggression. The diagnostic value of the immediate behavior is combined
with prior information about the actor to yield the actual judgment about the
actor's dispositions.

The two-stage model suggests that, depending on how situational, behavioral, and prior information are utilized at the identification stage, their effects
on dispositional judgment may reflect or may fail to reflect their utilization at
the inferential stage. Situational information illustrates this logic. Situational
information has opposite effects on dispositional judgment at the identification
stage and at the inferential stage. At the identification stage, situational information may lead perceivers to categorize the behavior in terms of the dispositional
category. Thus, a situation viewed as facilitating aggression augments the perception that the behavior is an aggressive one. The subsequent reliance on this
identification as evidence for the corresponding disposition may or may not offset the subtraction of the situation at the inferential stage. Thus, even though the
impact of the situation may attenuate the perception of dispositional aggression
at the inference stage, this may not totally cancel the facilitative impact of the
situation on perceptions of aggressiveness at the identification phase.

The stronger the effect of situational information on behavior identification,
the greater the likelihood that situational information will produce no effect or
additive effects rather than subtractive effects on dispositional judgments. A
series of studies by Trope and his colleagues varied one determinant of the effect
of situational information on behavior identification, namely, the ambiguity of
the behavior (Trope, 1986; Trope, Cohen, & Maoz, 1988). In one of the studies,
subjects saw ambiguous or unambiguous facial reactions to positive or negative
emotional situations and were asked either to identify what the face expressed

or to infer the target's emotional disposition (Trope, 1986). The identification and dispositional inference data supported the model. For example, the identification of unambiguous facial expressions was unaffected by situational provocation, and, as required by the subtractive rule, inferences of dispositional anger from such faces were attenuated by situational provocation. In contrast, situational provocation biased the identification of the ambiguous faces as expressing even more anger than justified by the provocation. Instead of attenuating inferences of dispositional anger, provocation only enhanced such inferences. These results suggest that ambiguity allows the situation to bias behavior identification, which, in turn, masks the subtraction of the situation at the inferential stage.

Elements of these insights have been incorporated into several subsequent stage models of the attribution process. For example, Quattrone (1982) maintained that dispositional anchoring is fundamental to stage models of the attribution process and that situational adjustment may occur only later. Similarly, Uleman and colleagues hypothesized that trait inference is a spontaneous, rapid process. For example, in one study, Winter, Uleman, and Cunniff (1985) had participants complete math problems with interposed distracter sentences that implied traits. Although the trait terms were not explicitly mentioned and subjects believed that the sentences they had heard were irrelevant to their task, when the trait terms were later provided to participants, they served as retrieval cues for the sentences. Apparently participants had spontaneously generated the trait term without being aware that they had done so. Evidence for automatic behavior identification is quite plentiful, and most researchers now concur in the belief that dispositional attribution to human action can occur very early on in the perception of human action, and that it is at least spontaneous and probably automatic (Todorov Uleman, 2002, 2003, 2004).

The process of dispositional attribution follows several stages that recently have been integrated into a synthetic model (Gilbert, 1998). This model has received empirical support at both the psychological and neural levels. Specifically, Gilbert and colleagues maintain that the attribution process consists of three stages: a categorization stage, in which the individual asks, "What is the stimulus configuration?"; a characterization stage, in which dispositional qualities are attributed to the action; and a correction phase, in which situational and other sources of information may be used to discount or augment the initial dispositional attribution (see Figure 6.5).

Gilbert and colleagues' tests of this integrative model build on the assumption that people's attentional capacities are limited and easily overwhelmed. As such, cognitive load or "busyness," which may involve the simultaneous performance of other tasks or attentional diversion to other stimuli, will diminish attentional resources for inference processes. Although cognitive load would be expected to have little effect on automatic processes, it should interfere with controlled processes and thus impair people's abilities to correct their automatic dispositional characterizations using information about the situation. Gilbert, Pelham, and Krull (1988) tested this hypothesis. Participants listened to a person read an assigned pro- or anti-abortion speech. Participants in the nonbusy condition simply listened to the speech whereas those in the busy condition listened to the speech knowing that later they would also be asked to read and write a speech. One can infer that these latter participants were cognitively busy because, as they observed the other reciting his speech, they were presumably thinking about what their own speeches would be like. The participants who were not busy made use of the situational information—namely, the fact that the actor had been assigned his essay portion—to discount the importance of the actor's attitude in producing the behavior. In contrast, the busy perceivers were unable to make use of this situational information and discount appropriately, and instead their dispositional attributions heavily relied on the target's behavior and not on the situational information at hand.

The results of this study and others like it support the idea that dispositional attribution is a relatively spontaneous and simple process, whereas the use of contextual information to qualify or discount the role of dispositional factors is a more complex process, requiring a greater commitment of cognitive resources. In an intriguing replication of this effect, Gilbert, Krull, and Pelham (1988) demonstrated that when people are self-regulating (that is, monitoring their own behavior), they act as cognitively busy subjects do. In other words, they are less able to make use of qualifying situational information than people who are not self-regulating to correct their dispositional characterizations of a target. Thus social interaction, during which people are usually both forming impressions of others and self-regulating, may usually proceed with people making dispositional attributions with relatively little qualification on the basis of situational information.

Neural Bases of Dispositional Attributions

Recent developments in brain science have provided a model of the integrative stage theory at the neural level. Lieberman and colleagues (2002) describe two networks that characterize autonomic and controlled processing respectively: (1) the X system (reflexive), which implicates the amygdala, dorsal anterior cingulate, basal ganglia, ventromedial prefrontal cortex, and lateral temporal cortex, which are regions that are implicated in automatic processing, and (2) the C system (reflective), implicating the lateral prefrontal cortex, medial prefrontal cortex, rostral anterior cingulate, posterior parietal cortex, and the medial temporal lobe regions, which are involved in controlled processing. X system processes guide thought and behavior when things are going smoothly and are implicated in the relatively automatic attribution of the causes of action to dispositional factors. The X system is biased toward features that are present in the question or hypothesis the person is trying to answer. Because favored hypothetical causes are dispositional, the result is likely to be dispositional attributions at the initial stage of processing, as the theory predicts.

The reflective system (C system) is engaged by signaling from the anterior cingulate, as may occur when a conflict arises or goals are thwarted or when more controlled processing is required to interpret the meaning of behavior. Controlled processes are involved in the more complex and qualified attributions we make that incorporate contextual or situational information. Conditions such as high accountability for one's inferences or outcome dependency would produce a switch to C system processing, or if X system processes fail to disambiguate the meaning of behavior, the C system may be brought online. When people lack motivation or attentional resources to do thorough processing, they may instead focus on a simple hypothetical cause, access the consistency of the identified action with that cause, and disregard alternatives.

ATTRIBUTIONAL BIASES

Causal attribution is marked by a number of errors and biases, and we now turn to the most common and important ones.

Fundamental Attribution Error

The most commonly documented bias in social perception, one that has accordingly been called the *fundamental attribution error* (Heider, 1958; Ross, 1977) or the *correspondence bias* (Jones & Davis, 1965), is to overattribute another person's behavior to dispositional causes. Instead of realizing that forces such as social norms or social pressure lead to particular behaviors, social perceivers often assume that another person's behavior is indicative of that person's stable qualities.

What leads to the fundamental attribution error? One factor may be that behavior engulfs the field (Heider, 1958). That is, what is dominant when one observes another person is that person's behavior; the person moves, talks, and engages in other actions that attract attention. Background factors may be less salient. Consequently, aspects of the person may come to be overrated as causally important because of a perceptual bias (S. E. Taylor & Fiske, 1975, 1978). The bias toward dispositional attributions cannot be solely an outgrowth of perceptual experience, however. For example, the fundamental attribution error is also strong when paper-and-pencil descriptions of other people's behaviors are used, settings in which behavior does not engulf the perceptual field (e.g., Winter & Uleman, 1984). Other evidence inconsistent with the perceptual explanation includes the facts that the tendency to attribute behavior to dispositions increases with age during childhood (Rholes, Jones, & Wade, 1988) and that predictions of distant future behavior are more marked by the fundamental attribution error than are predictions about current behavior (Nussbaum, Trope, & Liberman, 2003). Thus the fundamental attribution error is robust.

Nonetheless, there are qualifications to the fundamental attribution error. Some of these depend on the specific domain under investigation; that is, behaviors in different domains map onto dispositions in different ways. For example, whereas friendly behavior may map onto a disposition of friendliness in a linear fashion (the more friendly a person is, the more likely one is to infer that he is friendly by nature), other behaviors, such as moral actions, do not. Whereas a single dishonest action can clearly indicate a dishonest disposition, an honest behavior is not particularly enlightening: most people, even dishonest people, behave honestly much of the time (Reeder, 1993; Reeder & Brewer, 1979). Through experience, people learn exactly how behaviors in different domains may map onto underlying dispositions.

Certain factors reliably increase or decrease the strength of the fundamental attribution error. When a social perceiver has time to reflect on the underlying meaning of an actor's behavior, he or she is more likely to qualify dispositional inferences with reference to qualifying situational information (Weary, Reich, & Tobin, 2001). However, a state of cognitive busyness, as noted, leads people to focus on the most salient or meaningful aspects of a situation and to pay less attention to less salient contextual factors (Chun, Spiegel, & Kruglanski, 2002), leading to a stronger tendency to make dispositional attributions. Because the social world is busy, dispositional attribution is often the rule.

The tendency to make dispositional attributions for another person's behavior is increased when people are in a good mood (Forgas, 1998) but can be reduced when people are accountable to others for their judgments (e.g., Tetlock, 1985), or when they believe the other person may have ulterior motives for performing an action (Fein, Hilton, & Miller, 1990). For example, when you see a famous actor or actress endorsing a particular product, you assume that person is paid well for the endorsement and do not make a dispositional attribution. If your outcomes are at least partly dependent on the behavior of another person, you are also motivated to be more accurate and engage in more effortful processing than if your outcomes are not dependent on another person. Thus, in a situation of outcome dependency, you shift your analysis from a category-based inference to a lower-level person-based one and seek specific dispositional attributions for this particular person (Neuberg & Fiske, 1987).

We are more likely to qualify or mute dispositional attributions for the behavior of people we know well than for people we know less well. As we become more familiar with another person, we take a broader array of information into account, such as his or her personal goals or worldview, and draw less on abstract traits to build an impression of the person (Idson & Mischel, 2001). With increasing information about the person or an insufficient basis for inferring a motive, people begin to look more to the situation for an explanation for behavior (Reeder, Vonk, Ronk, Ham, & Lawrence, 2004; Wellbourne, 2001). We are also more likely to make situational inferences when we expect to have contact with the person in the future.

How significant is the fundamental attribution error? On the face of it, people appear to ignore important qualifying situational information when drawing inferences about others' dispositional characteristics. Yet there are adaptive aspects of the fundamental attribution error. When people draw dispositional attributions, they may not mean exactly the same thing by those attributions as researchers studying trait inferences think they mean. They may not, for example, assume that if behavior is attributed to a certain trait, the person will necessarily evidence behavior consistent with that underlying trait across a broad variety of situations. This is the psychologist's meaning of disposition, not the layperson's. Rather, the layperson may be seeking circumscribed accuracy (Swann, 1984), asking questions such as, "If this person were put in the same situation again, would he or she do the same thing?" A dispositional attribution leads one to generate a prediction for the person, whereas an attribution to situational factors does not. If the goal of the perceiver's attributional quest is circumscribed predictability, then making a dispositional attribution for the behavior probably results in quite accurate attributions. If asked to make a statement that opposes abortion at a later date, the person very probably would do it again, having done it once. Dispositional attributions, then, may serve the goal of circumscribed accuracy rather than global accuracy, enabling perceivers to make confident predictions to similar situations.

Cultural Limitations on the Fundamental Attribution Error

The fundamental attribution error is stronger in Western than in non-Western cultures. In East Asian countries, the roles of context and situational forces as causes of behavior are more commonly acknowledged (e.g., Miyamoto & Kitayama, 2002; Morris & Peng, 1994). Whereas Westerners correct dispositional attributions by taking account of situational information primarily when there is extra time and attention or a reason to do so, East Asians appear to correct for the effects of situational information automatically (Knowles, Morris, Chiu, & Hong, 2001; Norenzayan, Choi, & Nisbett, 2002). One reason for this difference may be the fact that East Asian cultures are more interdependent, and people in these cultures tend to adjust their behavior more to situational norms than is true of Westerners. Consequently, an East Asian social perceiver's consideration of context information may reflect the reality of the causes of behavior (e.g., Ishii, Reyes, & Kitayama, 2003; Kitayama, Duffy, Kawamura, & Larsen, 2003; Masuda & Nisbett, 2001). By contrast, Westerners are said to be independent and thus may more commonly demonstrate behavior that is indicative of their dispositions, feeling less compunction to conform to situational pressures. Thus the Western social perceiver may be somewhat more justified in making dispositional attributions.

But the differences between Western and East Asian causal attributions may reflect more fundamental differences in cognition than this characterization suggests. The theories that East Asians hold about the workings of the world are, generally speaking, more holistic and complex than those of Westerners, and so the amount of information that East Asians consider before making an attribution is greater than is true for Westerners, contributing to the more situational, contextual attributions that East Asians typically draw (Choi, Dalal, Kim-Prieto, & Park, 2003; A. P. Fiske, Kitayama, Markus, & Nisbett, 1998).

The Actor-Observer Effect

The research legacy of attribution theory has revealed robust self-relevant biases. That is, we tend to process information somewhat differently when it involves ourselves as compared with others. Recall the last time you encountered an irritable bus driver or surly clerk. You may have thought, "what a hostile person." Now think of the last time you snapped at someone. Did you infer that you were a hostile person? Almost certainly not. No doubt you were just in a bad mood or frustrated by poor service.

The actor-observer effect maintains that people explain other people's behavior as due to dispositional factors but their own behavior as due to situational factors (Jones & Nisbett, 1972). The actor-observer effect potentially qualifies the fundamental attribution when the self is involved. However, a recent meta-analysis of 172 published studies suggests that actor-observer asymmetry is not as reliable as has been assumed (Malle, 2006). It holds primarily when the actor is presented as idiosyncratic or unusual in some way, when explanations are measured using free responses rather than rating scales, and when the event to be explained is hypothetical rather than real. Actors and observers do seek to explain different types of behaviors, but not in the way that the model assumes. Actors wonder more about their unintentional and unobservable behaviors, whereas observers more often wonder about intentional and observable behaviors (Malle & Knobe, 1997). Moreover, people sometimes see themselves as if they were observers of their own actions: for example, people make more trait self-descriptions when they consider their past behavior or their likely future behavior than their present behavior. So-called actor-observer effects are reversed when attention is directed inward (Pronin & Ross, 2006).

Decades of research have also suggested that the person-situation distinction is itself problematic. Participants have trouble using it, and researchers have difficulty coding it. Consider the statement "George is a distrustful person because he was so often betrayed by others when he was a child." Such attributions reflect some of the complexity of causal reasoning, but not in any way that maps cleanly onto a person-situation distinction (Fiske & Taylor, 1991; Malle, Knobe, O'Laughlin, Pearce, & Nelson, 2000). For example, perceivers have little trouble viewing dispositions and situations as interactive and may infer, for example, that a person is a serious student during the week and a flaming party animal on the weekend (Kammrath, Mendoza-Denton, & Mischel, 2005).

Most important, the actor-observer effect is more likely to hold when an event's valence is negative rather than positive (Malle, 2006). Thus the hostile clerk example would be an instance in which actor-observer differences for explaining behavior would hold because it involves negative behavior. However, to the extent that it exists, the actor-observer effect looks more like a self-serving attributional bias than a tendency to overattribute one's own behavior to situational factors.

Self-Serving Attributional Bias

After you have soundly beaten an opponent on the tennis court, how often do you hear a gratifying statement such as "Gee, you're much better than I am, aren't you?" Usually you hear that it was a bad day, his serve was off, he's still working on his backhand, or the sun was in his eyes. On the other hand, when you have just been badly beaten, the smug look and condescending "bad luck" from the opponent are particularly grating because you know he does not believe it was bad luck. He simply thinks he is better. The tendency to take credit for success and deny responsibility for failure is known as the self-serving attributional bias (D. T. Miller & Ross, 1975).

Meta-analyses largely confirm the predictions of the self-serving bias. People do indeed take more responsibility for success than for failure (Arkin, Cooper, & Kolditz, 1980). They attribute their success largely to internal factors and their failures to external factors (Mullen & Riordan, 1988) such as task difficulty or bad luck (Whitley & Frieze, 1986). Overall, the evidence that people take credit for success is stronger than evidence that they deny responsibility for failure. People are sometimes willing to accept responsibility for failure if they can attribute it to some factor over which they have future control, such as effort. If I blame my bad tennis game on the sun being in my eyes, that will not help me to improve my game, but if I realize that I faulted on nearly every one of my first serves, I have something to work on during my next lesson.

Self-serving biases extend beyond explanations of one's own behavior to include perceptions of one's friends and the groups with which one is allied. At the group level, this bias has been termed the *group serving bias* and refers to the tendency of ingroup members to attribute positive actions committed by their own group to positive ingroup qualities, and negative actions committed by the ingroup to external causes (Brewer & Brown, 1998).

Self-serving attribution biases may be quite functional despite their apparent tendencies to play fast and loose with the facts. Attributing success to one's own efforts, particularly one's enduring characteristics, may have motivational consequences. Schaufeli (1988), for example, found that a self-serving motivational bias among unemployed workers resulted in more labor market success because those workers who made self-serving attributions for their circumstances were more optimistic about their chances of becoming reemployed and were more motivated to seek a job. Some of the reasons underlying the self-serving bias can be explained by cognitive factors, such as the fact that we expect to succeed on most tasks that we undertake. However, motivational needs to preserve one's ego and to present oneself in the best light explain the self-serving bias as well (e.g., Reiss, Rosenfeld, Melburg, & Tedeschi, 1981).

When people make self-serving attributions, several brain regions are activated. The bilateral premotor cortex and cerebellum are typically active, suggesting that general models of goal-directed action are recruited for self-serving attributions (Blackwood et al., 2003). These areas are involved in imagined action generally. The dorsal premotor cortex tends to be more active when simulating one's own intentional actions than when simulating another person's intentional actions, and thus may be especially involved in the attribution of responsibility for actions to the self. The dorsal striatum appears to be distinctively involved in the self-serving bias. This region is implicated in motivational activity more generally. Thus the attribution of one's own positive actions to internal factors and negative actions to external factors appears to be tied to areas in the brain that are implicated in reward. The self-serving bias may itself be experienced as rewarding (Blackwood et al., 2003).

The Self-Centered Bias

If two roommates were asked to estimate how much of the housework each does, each may well believe his or her own share is larger than the other believes it is. The *self-centered bias* consists of taking more than one's share of credit or responsibility for a jointly produced outcome. There are several possible reasons for this bias (Ross & Sicoly, 1979). First, it is easier to notice and recall one's own contributions than those of another person. For example, I know when I'm doing the housework, but I may be unaware when my roommate is doing his or her share. Second, there can be esteem benefits for believing one's own contributions are greater. Each person may think of the self as the kind of person who does a lot of the activity and infer greater responsibility.

Naive Realism

A bias that incorporates some of these self-relevant biases is *naive realism;* that is, the idea that other people in general, especially those who disagree with us, are more susceptible to bias than we are ourselves (Pronin et al., 2002). By attaching greater credibility to our own introspections than we attach to the introspections of others, we provide ourselves with a false informational base that supports our own beliefs. Essentially, then, naive realism is the belief that we see the world as it truly is: if others don't see it the same way, they must be biased or guided by wrong information. Among other implications, naive realism suggests that we believe that we know other people better than they know us, resulting in an illusion of asymmetrical insight (Pronin, Kruger, Savitsky, & Ross, 2001).

Naive realism is useful for thinking about the problems that warring groups and nations have in trying to understand each others' vantage points. When one's own position seems so obvious and logical, it is difficult to construe the world in a way that might have led another group to see it so differently (Robinson, Keltner, Ward, & Ross, 1995). Moreover, opposing parties often overestimate the dissimilarities of their views, seeing their own position as more liberal and the other's position as more conservative than is actually the case (Sherman, Nelson, & Ross, 2003). Should a mediator get involved in a controversy, each side expects that the mediator will see the world as they do. And to the extent that this is not the case, one may reject the mediator as biased as well. Figure 6.6 portrays naive realism as it may operate regarding conflict situations with third-party mediators.

FIGURE 6.6. Convictions of naive realism and resulting consequences and phenomena relevant to conflict and misunderstanding

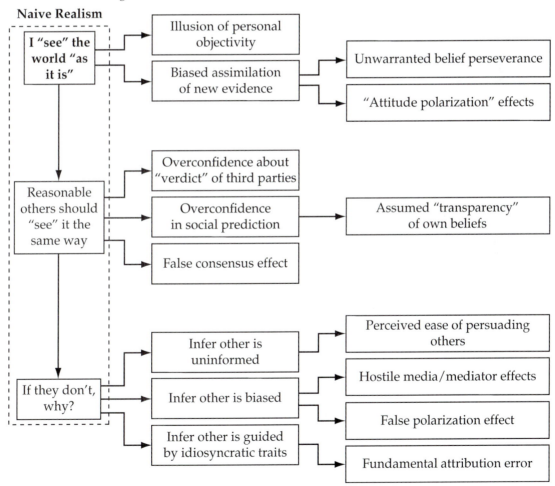

Attributions of Responsibility or Blame

Attributions of responsibility are concerned with who or what can be held accountable for an event, usually one that is negatively valenced (Shaver, 1975, 1985). Responsibility for an adverse event tends to generate an attribution if there is an identifiable source such as a particular person, a belief that the person should have been able to foresee the situation, the perception that the person's actions were not justified by the situation, and the perception that the person operated under conditions of free choice. Thus, for example, in the wake of Hurricane Katrina many people faulted President Bush for a slow and poor response to the flood victims in New Orleans because they felt he was in charge. He and other government officials should have foreseen the situation, the situation clearly necessitated action, and a range of choices could have been made that would have remedied the situation more quickly or at least not let it become so dire.

Defensive attribution, a related phenomenon, refers to the idea that people attribute more responsibility for actions that produce severe rather than mild consequences. Thus, for example, one might not attribute blame so enthusiastically to the president were the flooding minor, but the fact that the devastation was so widespread and so widely broadcast throughout the world led to more attribution of responsibility than might otherwise have been the case.

A meta-analysis of studies confirms the defensive attribution bias (Burger, 1981) and reveals that the degree to which people make defensive attributions depends on perceived similarity to the person who is seen as responsible for the adverse circumstances. When people see themselves as personally and situationally similar to a perpetrator, they attribute less responsibility to the perpetrator as the severity of the consequences increases. Presumably, the defensive attribution avoids the threatening implications for the self. When people are situationally or personally dissimilar to the perpetrator, however, they attribute more responsibility as the accident severity increases. Because most people see themselves as dissimilar to the president, the severity of the accident may account for the strong attributions of responsibility. However, among public officials who might readily imagine themselves being responsible following a major disaster, attributions of responsibility might be lower for major compared to minor outcomes; after all, they may someday be sitting in the same seat.

Summary

Attribution theory is concerned with how people infer causal relations and the dispositional characteristics of others. Some attributional inferences are formed extremely rapidly, often in milliseconds, whereas others engage more thought, as the dual-processing distinction suggests. People often draw on basic causal principles first learned in childhood, such as the notion that causes precede effects and that temporally or spatially contiguous factors produce effects.

The seminal theoretical contributions to the field of causal attribution include Heider's analysis of commonsense psychology, Jones and Davis's theory of correspondent inference, Kelley's attribution contributions, Bem's self-perception theory, and Weiner's attributional theories of achievement and helping. These theories, most notably the contributions of Jones and Davis (1965) and Kelley (1967), focus on the logical principles that characterize controlled attributional processing and detail the idealized ways in which the social perceiver might make attributions. Such theories are called norma-tive because they outline the appropriate norms or guidelines concerning how a process should proceed.

Recent theory and research on attribution processes are focused primarily on the mental operations people go through for inferring the qualities of others. Attributions of dispositions to others appear to be made spontaneously and without awareness, perhaps even automatically, when we observe or hear about another person's behavior. Using information about situational factors to qualify dispositional inferences appears to be a part of a second, less spontaneous, and more thoughtful process than involves correcting the initial disposition or inference. Unless situational information is very compelling or salient, the social perceiver may never get to the second stage of correction. In addition, if there is insufficient processing time or capacity to correct dispositional attributions, situational or context information is less likely to be incorporated into impressions.

The attribution process is also marked by certain persistent biases, most notably the tendency to make dispositional attribution for a person's behavior; the tendency to make self-serving and self-centered attributions for outcomes relevant to the self; naive realism, which stems from the perception that one's own interpretations are correct; and defensive attributions of responsibility or blame to others for serious negative outcomes.

CHAPTER 7

Heuristics and Shortcuts

Efficiency in Inference and Decision Making

WHAT ARE HEURISTICS? ◆ WHEN ARE HEURISTICS USED, AND WHEN DO THEY LEAD
TO WRONG ANSWERS? ◆ JUDGMENTS OVER TIME

The social perceiver often makes complex judgments under conditions not best suited to accuracy or thoroughness. A student must guess if a possible paper topic for a course is likely to lead to a manageable amount of literature to review, or if the literature will be too skimpy to say much or so overwhelming as to be unwieldy. A person must decide if a safe and reasonably satisfying romantic relationship should be abandoned for a new, exciting fling, the future of which is uncertain.

The rational person has been assumed by economists to make decisions by weighing pros and cons. The expected utility (EU) theory maintains that inferential behavior can be conceptualized as choices from a number of alternatives, each of which has a designated value and a probability of occurrence. According to the model, people assess the available alternatives for their likelihood and the worth of the outcomes that they promise (i.e., probability and value), calculate the utility of each outcome (the product of the value and the probability of each outcome), and choose the option that maximizes utility. Thus a person makes a decision that he or she thinks is most likely to provide the benefits that are sought.

Seemingly unlimited amounts of information could be brought to bear on life decisions, but much of it would be of uncertain value. Moreover, if thoroughly evaluated, all of these decisions could occupy the better part of the week, and nothing else would get done. For these reasons—time constraints, complexity or volume of the relevant information, and uncertainty about the quality of the evidence—it is unrealistic for the social perceiver to use exhaustive strategies for making judgments. Thus the social perceiver is, under many circumstances, a "satisficer" who makes adequate inferences and decisions rather than an "optimizer" who reaches the best possible inferences and decisions (March & Simon, 1958).

WHAT ARE HEURISTICS?

In a groundbreaking, highly influential paper, Tversky and Kahneman (1974) detailed heuristics used by people for making judgments under uncertainty. Kahneman and Tversky (1972) maintained that people often use *heuristics*, or shortcuts that reduce complex problem solving to simpler judgmental operations, to meet the pressing demands of the environment. Before turning to that important contribution, some clarifications are in order. The original Kahneman and Tversky (1972) paper described several specific heuristics commonly used to solve inferential problems. Some subsequent writing has implied that these are the primary heuristics that people use. This is an incorrect conclusion. Kahneman and Tversky's profile of selected heuristics was guided not only by the fact that these heuristics are commonly employed but by the fact that they are good examples of heuristic processes more generally.

People use manifold heuristics, some of which enjoy general use, such as mental simulation, and others that are idiosyncratic, such as a professor's heuristic for writing long and apparently thoughtful letters of recommendation in a brief period of time. People develop heuristics in their daily life for reducing complex operations to simple ones, such as reading the headlines of the newspaper on a busy day and deciding what articles to read based on that limited information. Workers employ heuristics in their jobs to reduce time-consuming activities to relatively less effortful and time-consuming ones. In short, there are many heuristics in daily life (e.g., Monin, 2003), some of which are general, such as those about which Kahneman and Tversky wrote, and many others that are more idiosyncratic.

A second common misinterpretation of the research on heuristics concerns the idea that heuristics are necessarily fallible. They are not. Heuristics are used by the social perceiver not because they generally produce incorrect and biased answers but because they typically produce correct ones. By highlighting the ways in which heuristic processing may be flawed, Kahneman and Tversky (1972) were using an illustrative strategy for impressing upon people how heuristics work. Their intention was not to lead the scientific community to the conclusion that heuristics typically produce inaccurate answers. Table 7.1 lists some of the heuristics that people use.

The Representativeness Heuristic

One heuristic, termed *representativeness,* is used to make inferences about probability (Kahneman & Tversky, 1973; Tversky & Kahneman, 1982). Essentially the social perceiver takes information about a specific instance and matches it against a general category to determine the likelihood that a match is appropriate. The representativeness heuristic can help answer questions such as these: How likely is it that person or event A is a member of category B? (e.g., Is George a football player?), or Did event A originate from process B? (e.g., Could the sequence of coin tosses H-H-T-T have occurred randomly?). Consider the following description:

> Steve is very shy and withdrawn, invariably helpful, but with little interest in people, or in the world of reality. A meek and tidy soul, he has a need for order and structure, and a passion for detail (Tversky & Kahneman, 1974, p. 1124).

Suppose you are now asked to guess Steve's occupation. Is he a farmer, a trapeze artist, a librarian, a salvage diver, or a surgeon?

TABLE 7.1. Some Heuristic Strategies for Making Judgments Under Uncertainty

Heuristic	Type of Judgment	Description	Example
Representativeness	Probability judgment	A judgment of how relevant A is to B; high relevance yields high estimates that A originates from B	Deciding that George (A) must be an engineer because he looks and acts like your stereotype of engineers (B)
Availability	Frequency or probability judgments	The estimate of how frequently or likely is a given instance or occurrence, based on how easily or quickly an association or examples come to mind	Estimating the divorce rate on the basis of how quickly one can think of examples of divorced friends
Simulation	Expectations, causal attributions, impressions, and affective experience	The ease with which a hypothetical scenario can be constructed	Getting angry because of a frustrating event on the basis of how easily one can imagine the situation occurring otherwise
Adjustment and anchoring	Estimates of position on a dimension	The process of estimating some value by starting with some initial value and then adjusting it to the new instance	Judging another person's productivity based on one's own level of productivity

With adequate information about the frequency and personal characteristics of the people in these different occupations, one could conceivably tally up the probability of a meek surgeon, a shy trapeze artist, and so on, and calculate the likelihood that Steve is in each occupation. This task would, however, take a long time, and good information on which to base the calculations would undoubtedly be lacking. In such cases, the representativeness heuristic provides a quick solution. One estimates the extent to which Steve is representative of or similar to the average person in each of the categories and makes a judgment about his occupation accordingly. In the present case, one is likely to guess that Steve is a librarian because the description of Steve is representative of attributes typically associated with librarians.

The representativeness heuristic is basically a relevancy judgment (How well do these attributes of A fit category B?) that produces a probability estimate (How probable is it that A is an instance of category B?). Using this heuristic usually produces fairly good answers—perhaps as good as those produced by a more exhaustive analysis of the information available for the task—because relevancy is usually a good criterion for making probability judgments. However, when the representativeness heuristic is used, a person may be insensitive to other factors independent of judged relevancy that affect actual probability of occurrence (Kahneman & Tversky, 1973).

One such factor is prior probability of outcomes (base rates). If Steve lives in a town with lots of chicken farmers and only a few librarians, one's judgment that he is a librarian should be tempered by this fact; it is simply more likely that he is a chicken farmer than a librarian. Nonetheless, people sometimes ignore prior probabilities and instead base their judgment solely on similarity: for example, the fact that Steve resembles a librarian.

Another factor that people often ignore in judgments of representativeness is sample size. Suppose you are at the state fair running a booth in which you try to guess the occupation of anyone who pays a quarter. Suppose 4 of your first 5 clients are librarians, and you subsequently discover that the librarians' convention is in town. How confident should you be that the next individual in line is also a librarian? Would you be more or less confident than if 12 of the first 20 individuals you saw had turned out to be librarians? Most people making this judgment feel more confident that the next individual in line is a librarian if 4 of the first 5 individuals are librarians than if 12 of the first 20 are. Their confidence is, in fact, misplaced. Sampling theory dictates that estimates derived from a large sample are more reliable than estimates derived from a small one. Thus, even though 4 out of 5 looks like better odds than 12 out of 20, the 12 out of 20 is the better indicator.

Judgments made on the basis of representativeness may also show an insensitivity to predictive value; that is, insensitivity to the relevance or quality of the information as a predictor of some outcome. For example, if the description of Steve as a meek and tidy soul had been written by Steve's kindergarten teacher after a scant few weeks of class, its relevance to Steve's career choice would be weak indeed; if written by Steve's adviser after 4 years of college, one might want to give it more weight. Nonetheless, people often behave as though information is to be trusted regardless of its source, and they may make equally strong or confident inferences regardless of the information's predictive value. This illusion of validity may be present especially when the information is a particularly good fit to the judgment. For example, if the description of Steve contained the additional sentence, "He is a bookish sort who peers intently over his reading glasses," one's confidence in Steve's status as a librarian might be vastly increased. However, upon learning that "he scuba dives in his spare time, and at one time in his life was a heavy cocaine user," we might begin to back off from a strong prediction. Whether the information is accurate and fully reliable or, alternatively, out-of-date, inaccurate, and based on hearsay may have insufficient bearing on inferences. Apparent fit or lack of fit can be the basis for its acceptance or rejection.

Finally, misconceptions about chance can also bias representativeness judgments. People have quite well-developed ideas of what chance events ought to look like. In flipping a coin several times, for example, one expects to see a sequence like H-T-H-T-T-H, not a seemingly orderly one like T-T-T-H-H-H. When asked to judge which sequence is more likely to occur, many people will erroneously pick the first one because it looks random, but the second sequence is, in fact, statistically just as likely to occur.

The representativeness heuristic is a quick, though occasionally fallible, method of estimating probability via judgments of relevancy. It is also perhaps our most basic heuristic. The act of identifying people as members of categories or the act of assigning meaning to actions is fundamental to all social inference and behavior as Chapters 2 and 3 noted. The question "What is it?" must be answered before any other cognitive task can be performed.

The Availability Heuristic

Availability is a heuristic that can be used to evaluate the likelihood of an event on the basis of how quickly instances or associations come to mind (Tversky &

Kahneman, 1973). When examples or associations are readily accessible and easily brought to mind, this fact may inflate estimates of likelihood. For example, if asked whether people seem to be changing jobs often, one might think over the number of acquaintances who have changed jobs and respond on the basis of the relative frequency of examples or ease with which examples come to mind. As is the case with the representativeness heuristic, little cognitive work need be conducted to accomplish this task. One can provide a frequency estimate on the basis of how quickly or easily instances or associations can be retrieved. If one has no trouble bringing to mind examples of people changing jobs, one will likely estimate that a lot of people are doing so, whereas if it takes a while to think of anyone who has changed jobs, one will scale down the estimate.

Under many circumstances the availability heuristic produces correct answers. After all, when examples of something can be brought to mind easily, it is usually because there are lots of them. However, biasing factors can increase or decrease the availability of some classes of phenomena or events without altering their overall number. For example, if one has recently changed jobs, one may be more likely to notice other people who have done so as well. When a class has easily retrieved instances, it will seem more numerous than will an equally frequent category that has less easily retrieved instances (Gabrielcik & Fazio, 1984). Search biases, as well as retrieval biases, can skew one's frequency estimates by biasing the number of available instances. For example, for some categories of events, it is easier to search for instances than it is for other categories. Estimating how many people are changing jobs at a job fair, would, for example, produce a higher estimate than would estimating the number of people changing jobs at an office party. The ease with which instances can be brought to mind varies dramatically between the two settings.

The ease with which one can imagine particular events is subject to certain biases. For example, when people are asked to guess the major causes of death in this country, they assume that more deaths result from dramatic events such as accidents, fires, drownings, or shootings than is actually the case. At the same time, they underestimate death from more common causes such as stroke or heart disease. Newspapers and television programs have created colorful, easily imagined instances of the former events, and hence it is easy to bring images or associations to mind, whereas a death from disease rarely makes it past the obituary page (see Slovic, Fischhoff, & Lichtenstein, 1976).

Although most researchers have assumed that ease of recall is the mechanism that explains the impact of availability on judgments, others have suggested that it may be the content of recall. If you can imagine instances easily, you will probably have more instances in mind, which may lead to the errors associated with availability. Schwarz, Bless, et al. (1991) untangled these two proposed mechanisms by manipulating volume of recall related to an instance. Some participants had to recall 12 examples of assertive (or unassertive) behaviors, which is a difficult task, whereas others had to recall 6 examples of assertive (or unassertive) behaviors, which is an easy task. Those who had the difficult task to recall 12 examples rated themselves as less assertive or unassertive, respectively (presumably because it is hard to come up with 12 examples), whereas those who had the easy task to recall 6 examples saw themselves as more assertive or unassertive, respectively. Self-assessments, thus, reflected the implications of recalled content only if recall was easy, and not if it was difficult. Ease or difficulty of recall appears to influence the impact of information on judgments via the avail-ability heuristic and not the overall content of recall. Studies have also revealed that when people believe that ease of recall is influenced by some arbitrary con-textual factor, they ignore ease of recall as a basis for their inferences (Schwarz, Bless, et al., 1991; Wänke, Schwarz, & Bless, 1995). Essentially, the phenomenal experience of ease of recall should be perceived as diagnostic for the inference, suggesting that people not only assess ease of recall but also, under some cir-cumstances, take into account factors that might artificially inflate or deflate ease of recall when basing their judgments on availability.

Ease of retrieval of instances is one way of estimating frequency via the availability heuristic, and strength of association is another. Associative bonds are strengthened by repeated examples, so the strength of an association between any two things is likely to be a fairly good indicator of the frequency of some class of events. As with ease of retrieval of instances, however, asso-ciative strength may be biased by factors irrelevant to actual numerosity. For example, if one lives in Arizona, a region of the country that attracts retirees, one may infer that there are more elderly people in the country than if one lives in a city such as Los Angeles, where widely available plastic surgery can easily obscure age.

Use of the availability heuristic increases under conditions of memory acces-sibility (MacLeod & Campbell, 1992). When particular types of events have been made accessible in memory, estimates of the future likely occurrence of simi-lar events go up. A dramatic act of terrorism, for example, will greatly inflate the perceived likelihood that similar terrorist incidents will occur. Use of the availability heuristic also increases under conditions of high memory load such as when a person is thinking about several things simultaneously. The social world is often overwhelmingly informative, and as such it usually involves high memory load conditions more than low memory load, thus facilitating the likely use of heuristics such as availability (Manis, Shedler, Jonides, & Nelson, 1993; Rothman & Hardin, 1997).

The availability heuristic has been a highly influential idea within social psychology, and it can provide an explanatory mechanism for a wide range of social phenomena, including stereotyping (D. L. Hamilton & Rose, 1980) and the perseverance of discredited beliefs (L. Ross, Lepper & Hubbard, 1975; L. Ross, Lepper, Strack, & Steinmetz, 1977; see S. E. Taylor, 1982, for a review). It has also been offered as an explanation for phenomena such as salience (S. E. Taylor & Fiske, 1978), judgments of responsibility (M. Ross & Sicoly, 1979), predictions (Carroll, 1978; Slovic et al., 1976), and causal attributions (Pryor & Kriss, 1977). However, as an explanation, the availability heuristic may well have been over-used. Many tasks do not require even the small amount of work engaged by use of the availability heuristic, and frequency judgments may well be made through other processes (Manis et al., 1993). The information we already have stored in memory, as in mental representations of well-known types of social events or people, means that answers to many of the inferences we must form are already known if we can access the correct mental representation. One implication of this assumption is that, generally, people will draw on the rep-resentativeness heuristic to identify what schema or category is appropriate for retrieving information more than they will draw on the availability heuristic for making judgments.

The Simulation Heuristic

To solve problems, people often construct hypothetical scenarios to estimate how something will come out. That is, they run events through in their mind chronologically to assess likely consequences. This inferential technique is known as the simulation heuristic (Kahneman & Tversky, 1982). Consider how you would answer the question, "What is your dad going to think when he finds out you have smashed up the car?" You may think of what you know about your father and his reactions to crises, run through these events in your mind, and generate several possibilities. The ease with which a particular ending comes to mind is used to judge what is likely to happen in real life. Your father could refuse to pay your college tuition next term or he could ignore the whole thing, but in your judgment it is easiest to imagine that he will strongly suggest that you find a job so that you can help pay for the car.

The simulation heuristic may be used for a wide variety of tasks, including prediction (How will Joan like Tom?) and causality (Is the dog or the kid to blame for the mess on the floor?). It is particularly relevant to situations of near misses. For example, consider the following scenario:

> Mr. Crane and Mr. Tees were scheduled to leave the airport on different flights, at the same time. They traveled from town in the same limousine, were caught in a traffic jam, and arrived at the airport thirty minutes after the scheduled departure time of their flights.
> Mr. Crane is told his flight left on time.
> Mr. Tees is told that his flight was delayed, and just left five minutes ago.
> Who is more upset?
> Mr. Crane or Mr. Tees? (Kahneman & Tversky, 1982, p. 203)

Virtually everyone says, "Mr. Tees." Why? Presumably, one can imagine no way that Mr. Crane could have made his plane, whereas were it not for that one long light or the slow baggage man or the illegally parked car or the error in the posted departure gate, Mr. Tees would have made it. Thus the simulation heuristic and its ability to generate "if only" conditions can be used to understand the psychology of near misses and the frustration, regret, grief, or indignation they may produce (e.g., Kruger, Wirtz, & Miller, 2005; Miller, Visser, & Staub, 2005; Seta, McElroy, & Seta, 2001).

Counterfactual Reasoning

Counterfactual reasoning of this sort—namely, the mental simulation of how events might otherwise have occurred—can have a broad range of effects on judgment. It may be used to assess causality such as by trying to identify the unique or unusual specific factor that produced a dramatic outcome (e.g., G. L. Wells & Gavanski, 1989). It influences affective responses to a particular event's outcome by providing visions of how events might have been otherwise (e.g., Seta et al., 2001), or could be, if one takes the wrong action (Kruger et al., 2005).

In particular, abnormal or exceptional events lead people to simulate alternatives that are normal and consequently dissimilar to the actual outcome (Kahneman & Miller, 1986). This contrast between the exceptional circumstance and the normal situation can intensify the emotional reaction to the unusual situation. In a role-playing situation involving compensation to victims who experienced an abnormal or normal fate, Miller and McFarland (1986) found that rewards were higher for victims in the abnormal circumstances. For example, when a man had gone shopping at a convenience store far from his house and been shot during a robbery, participants' awards of damages were higher than when he had shopped at the convenience store he normally frequented in his own neighborhood.

In counterfactual thinking, it is easier to make a downhill change (to replace an unusual event with an expected one) than it is to make an upward change (to replace a normal event with an abnormal one) (Kahneman & Miller, 1986). This leads to the prediction that it will be easier to generate a counterfactual scenario of inaction, as compared to action, rather than the reverse (Gleicher et al., 1990; Landman, 1988). For example, people find it easier to imagine that Mr. Tees could have made his plane if the construction had not been blocking his lane, whereas they are less likely to generate a scenario that Mr. Tees would have reached his plane on time if the city had built an alternate and faster route to the airport.

Imagining an alternative via counterfactual simulation can have a broad impact on expectations, causal attributions, impressions, and the affect experienced in situations. Moreover, such situations appear to be elicited by predictable circumstances (e.g., the salience of how events might otherwise have been) and to follow rules, so that probable rather than improbable elements are incorporated into the simulations.

Simulations of one's own experiences or actions are common. For example, if a person has made an error or mistake, such as leaving out in the open a lawnmower that then injured a child, simulation of how things might have been otherwise prompts regret. This is especially likely if errors associated with one's actions are inconsistent with one's personal beliefs or if errors associated with inaction are consistent with one's personal beliefs (Seta et al., 2001).

Why do people engage in counterfactual reasoning? After all, when something unexpected or negative takes place, imagining how it could have been otherwise is hardly going to change the situation. Research suggests that counterfactual thoughts about what might have been may serve any of several motives (Sanna, Chang, & Meier, 2001). In some circumstances, counterfactual thoughts may help people feel better. For example, when people have been through a stressful event, they often imagine how much worse it could have been (S. E. Taylor, Wood, & Lichtman, 1983). An automobile accident victim may focus less on the damage done to her car than on the fact that she could have been killed if the car had hit her driver's-side door. Anticipating how one will feel after taking a particular action influences behavior as well. For example, many people avoid changing answers on multiple-choice tests even though such changes may improve their scores; this may occur because they anticipate that a wrong action will generate more self-recrimination than would the inaction of leaving a wrong answer as it is (Kruger et al., 2005).

Turning to simulations of the future, imagining hypothetical future events makes those events seem more likely (S. E. Taylor, Pham, Rivkin, & Armor, 1998). Consequently, it follows that if the content of a scenario is easy to imagine, it will be perceived as more likely to occur than a scenario involving difficult-to-imagine events, a prediction that has been confirmed in several studies (e.g., C. A. Anderson & Godfrey, 1987; C. A. Anderson, Lepper, & Ross, 1980). Similarly, simply imagining oneself deciding to perform or refusing to engage in a behavior leads to corresponding changes in expectations about oneself (C. A. Anderson & Godfrey, 1987), whereas imagining someone else engaging in a behavior does not increase expectations that the self will engage in the behavior (C. A. Anderson, 1983).

Counterfactual thoughts may also serve a preparatory function for the future. If you realize that your car battery wouldn't have died if you hadn't left the inside light on, you probably won't do that again. When imagining how easily you could have avoided the problem produces negative affect, the motivation to change and improve—an emotional wake-up call—is increased (McMullen & Markman, 2000). And when there isn't anything you can do mentally to change the outcome or prepare for the future, you may embrace a counterfactual explanation that puts you in the best light ("I could have *really* bombed the test. At least I studied a little.") (Tetlock, 1998). Not surprisingly, this tendency to come up with self-enhancing counterfactual thoughts is particularly true of people with high self-esteem, especially when they are in a bad mood (Sanna, Turley-Ames, & Meier, 1999). That is, people who think well of themselves use counterfactual reasoning to repair a bad mood.

Using Mental Simulation

Simulating how events may happen provides a window on the future by helping people envision possibilities and develop plans for bringing those possibilities about (S. E. Taylor et al., 1998), but people can focus on different aspects of the future. They may envision the future as filled with bountiful possibilities, what some call "wishful thinking" or "fantasy" (Oettingen & Mayer, 2002). Or they might focus on the steps they need to take to achieve a future that is desired. Which type of mental simulation about the future helps people to achieve their goals?

If you are an avid reader of self-help books, you know that this advice-filled genre urges people to actively envision the state they hope to achieve in the future. Yet research suggests that this idea is misleading. In a study that tested this point, Pham and Taylor (1999) asked college students who were studying for an exam a few days away either to envision their satisfaction and celebration in achieving a good grade on the exam or to envision themselves studying so as to produce a good grade on the exam. That is, one group focused on the outcome to be achieved, and the other group focused on the process of achieving it. Those students who had focused on the process improved their grade compared to a control group that practiced neither mental simulation, but those students who focused on the outcome they wanted to achieve had lower scores on the exam than the control group. Clearly, if you want to use mental simulation to reach your goals, it is best not to engage in wishful thinking and fantasy but to focus your simulations clearly on what you will need to do to get there (Oettingen, Pak, & Schnetter, 2001; S. E. Taylor et al., 1998).

Simulations are more likely to increase the perceived likelihood of a potential outcome (mental addition) than to reduce the perceived likelihood of a potential consequence (mental subtraction). This asymmetry appears to occur because people give more weight to features of a particular mental simulation that serve as the subject of comparison and give more weight to factors that produce rather than inhibit a relevant outcome. So, for example, when assessing the impact of personal actions such as studying for an exam, subjects perceived more impact when the assessment was put in an additive framework ("How many more questions will you get right if you study?") as opposed to a subtractive one ("How many fewer will you get right if you do not study?"). This effect appears to be independent both of the valence of the event and whether or not a person has personal experience in the simulation domain (Dunning & Parpal, 1989).

Anchoring

When making judgments under uncertainty, people sometimes reduce ambiguity by starting with a beginning reference point, or anchor, and adjusting it to reach a final conclusion. If, for example, you are asked to guess how many people attended the latest USC-UCLA football game, and you have absolutely no idea, it is helpful to know that the previous week's game in the same stadium drew a crowd of 23,000. You may then guess 30,000, assuming that a USC-UCLA contest would draw a larger crowd. So it is with social judgments as well.

We have already discussed several phenomena that constitute instances of the anchoring heuristic. Recall the false consensus effect in attribution research. When asked to estimate how many people would perform some activity (e.g., wear a sandwich board around campus), people's estimates are substantially influenced by the decision they would make for themselves. Although we know intellectually that not everyone would behave as we do, our estimates of others' behavior are not adjusted sufficiently from the anchor that our own behavior provides. As this example suggests, a prominent anchor from which we estimate or judge others' social behavior is the self and the self's social environment (e.g., Fong & Markus, 1982; Markus & Smith, 1981). We may judge how aggressive or shy another person is as an adjusted inference from our own self-rating on these same qualities or adopt another person's perspective by adjusting from our own (Epley, Keysar, Van Boven, & Gilovich, 2004).

Judgments may also be anchored by irrelevant details of a situation that, nonetheless, suggest a beginning reference point. For example, the customary instructions given by judges to juries to consider the harshest verdict first may inadvertently function as an anchoring point (Greenberg, Williams, & O'Brien, 1986). When participants in a mock trial were induced to consider the harshest verdict first, they rendered significantly harsher verdicts than participants who were instructed to consider lenient verdicts first. Similarly, in attributing attitudes to others, you may be aware of constraints on their attitude expression (e.g., a reporter had to write a pro-war article because his editor told him to); nonetheless, with the communication itself as an anchor, you may fail to correct sufficiently for the constraints (and thus infer that the writer is indeed in favor of the war). This robust correspondence bias—failing to correct for situational constraints in the attribution of attitudes—may be understood as anchoring and insufficient adjustment effects (Quattrone, Finkel, & Andrus, 1982).

The question arises as to the mechanism underlying the anchoring effect. Research has focused on two possible explanations. One is that people hold an initial anchor value and then insufficiently adjust away from that anchor when making an inference (Epley & Gilovich, 2001). Other studies have suggested that the degree to which anchoring effects occur is determined primarily by anchor plausibility and how much knowledge a person has about the anchor and the target. The less people know about a target object, the more likely they are to assimilate a subsequent estimate to an anchor and thus adjust insufficiently (Mussweiler & Strack, 2000). According to this viewpoint, the strength of the anchoring effect depends on how applicable activated information about the anchor is (Mussweiler & Strack, 1999; Strack & Mussweiler, 1997). Essentially, then, an anchor may make knowledge salient that can be used when people need to make new judgments.

Examples of anchoring and adjustment are ubiquitous in social situations precisely because social behavior is so ambiguous and relatively free of objective yardsticks (Mussweiler, Strack, & Pfeiffer, 2000). When we can, we use ourselves as anchors (e.g., Epley et al., 2004), but when our own reference points are ambiguous, we may use the behavior and attributes of others, or we may be anchored by irrelevant details of a situation. There is no foolproof way to avoid anchoring effects, but substituting the opposite (e.g., "What would someone unlike me do?") is one strategy that may reduce their impact (Mussweiler et al., 2000).

Decision Framing Effects: Perspectives From Prospect Theory

Judgments and decisions are affected by the ways in which the initial decision or judgment question is framed; that is, how the background context of the choice is described. Kahneman and Tversky (1984; Tversky & Kahneman, 1981) suggest that people often fail to recognize that problems are similar to each other and instead are distracted by surface characteristics concerning how those problems are presented. The presentation of the problem is called the decision frame. Seemingly minor alterations in such representations can exert strong effects on decisions.

A common impactful frame is whether a decision is presented in terms of the gains it will create or the losses that might be incurred (Kahneman & Tversky, 1982). For example, research generally suggests that people become very cautious when alternatives are phrased in terms of losses, but they are far more likely to take chances when the alternatives are framed in terms of gains (e.g., Roney, Higgins, & Shah, 1995). Consider the following example:

> Imagine the United States is preparing for the outbreak of an unusual Asian disease, which is expected to kill 600 people. Two alternative programs to combat the disease have been proposed. Assume that the exact scientific estimate of the consequences of the program are as follows: If Program A is adopted, 200 people will be saved. If Program B is adopted, there is a one-third probability that 600 people will be saved, and two-thirds probability that no people would be saved. Which program would you favor?
>
> Now imagine the same situation with these two alternatives: If Program C is adopted, 400 people will die. If Program D is adopted, there is a one-third probability that no one will die, and a two-thirds probability that 600 people will die. (based on Tversky & Kahneman, 1981)

Tversky and Kahneman presented these problems to college students. When the problem was framed in terms of lives saved, 72% of the participants chose Program A. However, when the problem was phrased in terms of lives lost, 78% favored Program D, and only 22% favored Program C.

This change in focus represents a robust principle in decision making: namely, that people tend to avoid risks when they are dealing with possible gains (lives saved) but tend to seek risks when they are dealing with possible losses (lives lost). In the case of the problems phrased in terms of lives gained, people prefer to know that 200 lives would be saved for certain and avoid the option that suggests a risk that no one would be saved. In contrast, when the problem is phrased in terms of lives lost, the preference is for the option providing the possibility that no one will die. The important point, of course, is that these two problems are identical, the only difference being whether the options are phrased in terms of lives gained or lives lost.

The influence of framing is pervasive (see Levin, Schneider, & Gaeth, 1998, for a review) and is found for people with high levels of statistical sophistication as well as for statistical novices. Framing effects have been demonstrated in a wide variety of settings, including layoffs (Brockner, Wiesenfeld, & Martin, 1995), purchase of products (Levin & Gaeth, 1988), medical treatments (Levin, Schnittjer, & Thee, 1988; Rothman & Salovey, 1997), and condom use (Linville, Fischer, & Fischhoff, 1993).

Framing can interact with personal dispositions to affect choices or decisions as well. In Chapter 5 we noted that some people are promotion focused whereas others are prevention focused. Promotion focused individuals are more persuaded by appeals presented in gain than loss frames, whereas prevention focused people are more persuaded by loss frames (Lee & Aaker, 2004; Sherman, Mann, & Updegraff, 2006). For example, if a person is chronically motivated to avoid harm, an ad for a car that touts its great survival record following car crashes might be more persuasive than an ad touting its contemporary, sleek look or its powerful engine.

Prospect Theory

Building on these observations, prospect theory (Kahneman & Tversky, 1979; Tversky & Kahneman, 1981) describes the decision processes involved when people make comparisons between options. There are two important components in this theory: frame of reference and subjective value function.

Prospect theory posits that the selection of a reference point is crucial to option evaluation. A *reference point* is the internal standard with which people compare the objective value of an option so as to classify the option as something positive (i.e., better than the reference point) or as something negative (i.e., worse than the reference point). As we have seen, objectively identical options can be framed positively or negatively such that an option perceived as a gain in one frame could be perceived as a loss in another frame. A positively framed option is thought to decrease one's evoked reference point, whereas the same information framed negatively is thought to increase the evoked reference point (Abelson & Levi, 1985; Highhouse & Paese, 1996). So, for example, in the disease example described earlier, framing the alternatives in a positive way (that 200 people would be saved) would evoke a reference point comparison of zero people being saved; however, when the same problem is framed negatively (400 people will die), it leads people to adopt a reference point that presupposes that no lives are lost—that is, zero people will die. The shift in reference point between the two frames leads to a medical alternative being perceived as more attractive when it is positively framed than when it is negatively framed. That is, the positive frame leads to a sense of saving 200 lives when compared with losing everyone, whereas the negative frame leads to a sense of losing 400 lives compared against the no lives lost reference point. Frame of reference is quite impactful on judgments.

Figure 7.1 presents a typical subjective value function with a neutral reference point. The subjective value function of prospect theory is expressed as positive or negative deviations (that is, gains or losses) from a neutral point. The value function is S-shaped—concave for gains (reflecting risk aversion) and convex for losses (reflecting risk seeking)—and is steeper for losses than for gains (reflecting loss aversion). So, as the gain increases in objective value, the increase in the subjective value decreases. For example, the difference in subjective value between $10 and $20 is greater than between gains of a $110 and $120. As loss increases objectively, the drop in the subjective value decreases. So, for example, the difference in subjective value between losses of $10 and $20 is greater than that between losses of $110 and $120.

Exactly why the subjective interpretation of objectively presented information varies with gain or loss is not clear, but the effects are robust. Note that the effects of frame of reference implies that the same outcome framed positively or negatively will lead to different subjective values. Thus the same level of objective performance is perceived as better if it is positively framed than if negatively framed. It is more satisfying to know that 70% of the people you invited to a large party showed up than that 30% did not.

FIGURE 7.1. The subjective value function of prospect theory
Source: From "Prospect theory: An analysis of decision under risk," by D. Kahneman and A. Tversky, 1979, Econometrica, *47, p. 279. Copyright 1979 by The Econometric Society. Adapted with permission.*

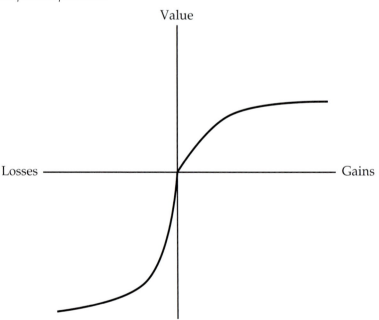

Conclusion

In this section we have seen heuristics that include representativeness, availability, simulation, plus anchoring and adjustment. In each case, heuristics are shortcuts, unified under a common mechanism: that is, when faced with difficult questions, people often substitute easier questions and answer those instead (Kahneman & Frederick, 2002). Representativeness makes a probability judgment by fitting the individual case to stereotypic resemblance, and availability does it by ease of recalling instances. Simulation forms expectations and affect based on ease of recall. Anchoring and adjustment estimates a judgment by amending an initial, base value. Each of these heuristics suggests how people construct preferences and judgments using remembered information (Weber & Johnson, 2006).

WHEN ARE HEURISTICS USED, AND WHEN DO THEY LEAD TO WRONG ANSWERS?

When Do We Use Heuristics?

Heuristics are fundamental to inference, making rapid information processing possible. However, there are times when the social perceiver becomes more thoughtful and less reliant on heuristics, and under such circumstances, better inferences may sometimes be reached. When is the social perceiver most likely to use heuristics?

People use heuristics in domains in which they have a lot of practice and have developed shortcuts that have previously served them well. They are more likely to use heuristics when they are in a good mood as opposed to when they are fearful or depressed (e.g., Bodenhausen, Kramer, & Süsser, 1994; Forgas, 1998; Ruder & Bless, 2003); however, angry people use heuristics (Tiedens, 2001). People are more likely to use heuristics to solve relatively unimportant tasks, saving online capacity for more significant judgments that must be made. People are less likely to use heuristics when the stakes are high, when they distrust the information under consideration (Schul, Mayo, & Burnstein, 2004), when they are accountable for their inferences, or when they have recently made errors or otherwise found the goodness or accuracy of their cognitions to be questionable (e.g., Tiedens & Linton, 2001).

When Do Heuristics Produce Wrong Answers?

Because heuristics are rules of thumb rather than normative models of inference, there are predictable circumstances in which the social perceiver's inferences fall short. In this section, we review what some of those conditions are. As will become evident, the heuristic processes employed by the social perceiver typically involve the use of preexisting theories or hunches to guide the consideration of information and its interpretation. In cases in which no a priori theory exists, the social perceiver may use data encountered early in the inference process to suggest a theory and from then on, use theory-guided inferential strategies. To put it simply, the social perceiver is often biased to see what he or she expects to see (Figure 7.2).

Gathering Information

Even the smallest inference or judgment begins with the process of deciding what information is relevant and sampling the information that is available. According to normative models, the social perceiver should take in all relevant information, but in fact efficiency pressures often preclude such thoroughness. This leads to a reliable shortcut in the form of gathering information in accordance with preexisting theories.

FIGURE 7.2. Social inference and its pitfalls

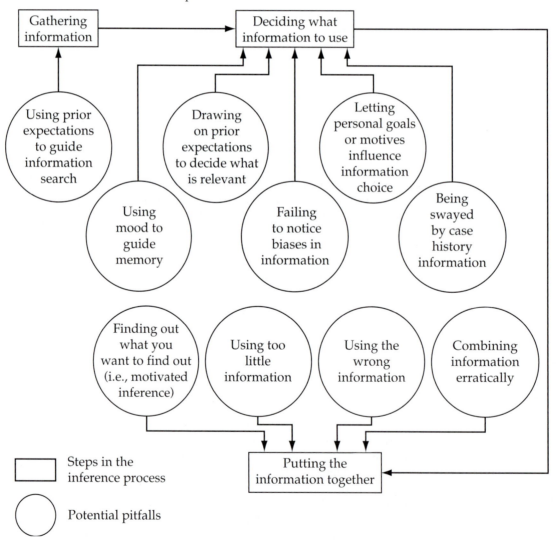

Selecting data according to preexistent expectations or theories is perfectly appropriate under many circumstances (see Nisbett & Ross, 1980). It would be a bad physician who started from scratch with each new medical case he or she encountered; letting the interpretation of symptoms be guided by the frequency of a particular illness, characteristics of the patient, knowledge of what illnesses are "going around," and the like is a superior strategy. A slightly pudgy adolescent girl with occasional fainting spells could have a brain tumor, but it is more likely that she has low blood pressure or that she is dieting and has not eaten enough food.

Nonetheless, there are many circumstances in which characterizing information on the basis of preexistent theories is unwise. Three such conditions are as follows (Nisbett & Ross, 1980). The first is if the theory itself is faulty or suspect. For example, if the physician concludes that the fainting adolescent is possessed by demons, her parents might at least want a second opinion. Second, if an individual is characterizing data on the basis of a theory but believes his or her inferences are objectively based on raw data, problems can result. The physician who sends the girl home after a cursory examination with instructions to eat a big dinner may well have ignored other less likely causes of fainting such as diabetes or epilepsy, but the physician may believe that a thorough examination was conducted. Third, theory-guided inferences create problems when the theory overrules consideration of the data altogether. The doctor who dismisses the adolescent as an overzealous dieter prior to examining her would be guilty of this error, as well as of gross negligence.

Letting theories guide sampling with respect to an inference often leads to considering too little information. If the social perceiver discovers early that the preliminary evidence that he or she has considered is consistent with the theory that is guiding the sampling of that data, then further sampling is likely to be aborted. But the perceiver may fail to appreciate the fact that the theory was used to guide consideration of data in the first place, and that these data were then used to justify greater confidence in the theory.

Sampling Information

Once the social perceiver has decided what information is relevant to an inference, a task that can be biased by preexisting theories, the data must be sampled. For example, if you want to know if the students in your class enjoy the course, you must decide whom to ask and how many people to ask. When people characterize information from samples provided to them, their accuracy in estimating frequencies, proportions, or averages is quite good so long as no prior theories or expectations are present to influence such estimates. Thus, for example, if you had students' course evaluations, you could presumably estimate their average evaluation quite easily. However, when prior theories or expectations do exist, describing data can be influenced by a priori theory or by particular characteristics of the sample (Nisbett & Ross, 1980).

When a sample is not already available, the process of sampling and drawing inferences from samples presents potential pitfalls. To begin with, sample estimates can be thrown off by extreme examples within the sample. In one study (Rothbart, Fulero, Jensen, Howard, & Birrell, 1978) participants were given information about members of two groups, including the fact that some of the members had committed crimes. For one sample, only moderate crimes were listed; in the other sample, a few examples of particularly heinous crimes were included. Although the actual frequency of committing crimes was the same in the two groups, participants appear to have employed an anchoring and adjustment heuristic and misremembered that more individuals committed crimes in the second group, presumably because the extreme examples had prompted a strong association between that group and crime.

In drawing inferences from samples, the social perceiver is often inadequately attentive to sample size. Small samples often produce poor estimates of a population's characteristics, whereas larger samples are more reliable. This principle is called the *law of large numbers*. In apparent violation, however, people will often overgeneralize from a small unrepresentative sample (Nisbett & Ross, 1980; Tversky & Kahneman, 1974). For example, on witnessing a single instance of another person's behavior, the social perceiver will often make confident predictions about that person's behavior in the future. In this context, a friend of the authors who had spent virtually all of his early years living in Manhattan revealed that, until he was 25 years old, he believed Queens was nothing more than a burial ground for the New York City area. For that entire time, his sole ventures into Queens were to Kennedy or La Guardia airports, trips that afford a view of acres and acres of cemeteries. Presumably, a better sampling of the streets of Queens would have revealed more of its riches.

People do have some intuitive appreciation of the implications of the law of large numbers, but not for all its implications (Kunda & Nisbett, 1986). The social perceiver shows a certain asymmetry in believing that one can use an aggregate to predict a single event with more confidence than one can use a single event to predict the aggregate. Thus, for example, people believe that a score on a short form of an intelligence test is better predicted by the score on the full test than a score on a full test is predicted from the score on the abbreviated test (Tversky & Kahneman, 1980). These perceptions are mistaken because predicting the aggregate (full test) from a single event (short form) is identical to predicting a single event from the aggregate. This effect seems to occur because people's intuition leads them to believe that increasing the size of the predictor sample of events increases predictability, whereas increasing the size of the predicted sample does not (Kunda & Nisbett, 1988; see also Kunda & Nisbett, 1986).

In addition to size of sample, people are sometimes insufficiently attentive to biases in samples. When gathering his or her own sample, an individual may ask a few friends or acquaintances their opinions, forgetting that a sample of one's friends is scarcely random. Usually, one picks friends or acquaintances precisely because they are similar on at least some dimensions, and hence, their opinions are likely to be at least somewhat similar to one's own.

When given information about a sample's typicality, people will sometimes fail to use it. In one study (Hamill, Wilson, & Nisbett, 1980) researchers told participants they would be viewing a videotaped interview with a prison guard who was either typical of most guards or very atypical of most guards, or about whom typicality information was not provided. Participants then saw a tape in which the guard appeared as a highly compassionate, concerned individual or as an inhumane, macho, cruel one. Participants were later asked a set of questions about the criminal justice system that included questions about prison guards. Results showed that, even though participants remembered the initial typicality information, those exposed to the interview with the humane guard were more favorable in their attitude toward prison guards than were participants who saw the interview with the inhumane guard.

Rules of sampling and characteristics of samples are not the only kinds of information that people underuse when they attempt to draw inferences. Other characteristics that bear on the relevance of data to inferences also elude the social perceiver's cognitive processing. An example is the regression effect.

Regression

Regression is a phenomenon related to prediction from probabilistic information, and it is poorly understood by most people. Regression refers to the fact that extreme events will, on average, be less extreme when reassessed at a different point in time. The message of regression is that when one must make an inference based on limited and unreliable information, one will be most accurate if one ventures a prediction that is less extreme than the information on which it is based. A restaurant that is fabulous one night will probably not be quite as good when you drag your friends there, having raved endlessly about its cuisine. Experience notwithstanding, experimental evidence, as well as common observation, consistently shows that when people are provided with extreme values of predictor information, they draw extreme inferences about subsequent behavior (Jennings, Amabile, & Ross, 1982). (See Table 7.2.)

People can sometimes "learn" inappropriate rules when they fail to appreciate regression. In a study with college students, Schaffner (1985) had undergraduates use praise and reprimand to attempt to improve the promptness of two schoolboys whose arrival times at school were, in fact, randomly determined. A strong "deterioration" in promptness following reward and "improvements" in promptness following reprimand were "found," a pattern that would be expected on the basis of regression. Nonetheless, although the participants believed their praise was effective in modifying the students' behavior, they perceived their reprimands had been more effective.

There are rare instances in which regression, or at least something very much like it, is appreciated. For example, the response of literary critics to an author's blockbusting first novel is often to hedge their bets. Praise may be glowing, but it is often couched in cautionary language that urges readers to wait for the next product; previous experience dictates that second novels are often less stellar than first ones. However, one might well ask if an appreciation of regression underlies these conservative predictions. Although in rare cases it may, more often some theory, and not random error, is credited with the poor second showing. Authors are said to "burn themselves out" on the first novel or to have "said it all," leaving no material for a second try. Others are thought to be immobilized or blocked by their first success. Although some of these points may, in fact, be true, regression alone is fully capable of accounting for the second-book effect. Yet how often has one read a review of a mediocre second novel in which the critic pointed out that the inferior second product could have been predicted by chance?

TABLE 7.2. Regression Toward the Mean: Taking the GREs Twice

TIME 1			
Given four students (A, B, C, D) of equal ability, all should score a 600 on the Graduate Record Examination:	But random factors enter in, raising or lowering their scores:	Actual scores at Time 1:	Conclusion:
A 600	−10 (slept poorly)	590	B and D look strong;
B 600	+15 (studied examples similar to test items)	615	A and C look weaker
C 600	−17 (gum chewer was a distraction)	583	
D 600	+12 (got a good seat in the test room)	612	

TIME 2			
Given same four students taking test again:	Different random factors are present, raising or lowering scores:	Actual score at Time 2:	Conclusion:
A 600	+12 (had a good breakfast)	612	A and C look stronger and
B 600	−10 (sat near the window)	590	B and D look weaker than at Time 1
C 600	−4 (had a slight cold)	596	
D 600	+5 (was "on" that day)	605	

It is difficult to determine whether people's insufficiently regressive judgments represent errors or the misapplication of a normally effective judgmental strategy. When the world is stable, people's predictions about events should show an appreciation for regression. But when the world is changing, extreme predictions generated from relevant information may be appropriate. Extreme responses can occur at random, or they can signal that there has been a change in the underlying data. Consider, as an example, a manufacturing company that has posted large losses. If those losses are seen as a random perturbation in an otherwise reasonable record, then one should predict that profits will soon regress to their mean level. However, if the large losses are seen as indicating that manufacturing is moving offshore, even more extreme predictions on the basis of the information may be justified. Thus, people may learn from their environment that extreme fluctuations often signal changing conditions, and thus their failure to be regressive may be adaptive in a changing environment. Such sensitivity to change may, however, lead them to be insufficiently regressive when random extreme values occur in stable environments.

The Dilution Effect

Suppose we tell you we have a friend, Judith, who is 35, unmarried, and has lived with the same female roommate for 5 years with whom she has just bought a house. You may conclude that she is probably a lesbian. However, if we also tell you that she is a paralegal, takes fiction writing courses in night school, drives a blue Toyota, and is very close to her brothers and sisters, you may wonder if she is a lesbian, but not immediately assume that she is. Why? The first four bits of information can be thought of as diagnostic with respect to whether Judith is a lesbian or not, because unmarried women with constant female companions are often thought to be so. However, the extra information about her job, car, and leisure activities diluted that diagnostic information with a lot of nondiagnostic information; information which would not lead you to conclude that she is a lesbian or straight, but which is simply neutral with respect to the inference. In short, we reduced her similarity to the stereotype of lesbianism by deepening her characterization and making her a person, so your confidence in drawing an extreme inference about her may thereby be lessened. When diagnostic information is diluted with nondiagnostic information, inferences are less extreme, a phenomenon known as the dilution effect (Nisbett, Zukier, & Lemley, 1981).

There are several qualifications to the dilution effect. It does not hold when prior theories about the meaning of the initial information are weak (S. T. Fiske & Neuberg, 1990; Higgins & Bargh, 1987; Ruble & Stangor, 1986). The dilution effect also appears to apply only when new nondiagnostic information is typical and not extreme (G. Zukier & Jennings, 1983–84).

In recent years psychologists have developed training techniques to reduce judgmental errors, and ironically, at least some of these efforts actually increase the dilution effect. For example, one way in which people can be induced to process social information in a more complex manner that reduces the likelihood of theory-guided inferences and overconfidence in judgments is demands for accountability: a need to justify one's judgments to others. In a study by Tetlock and Boettger (1989), participants who expected to have to justify their predictions in a judgment task diluted their predictions more in response to nondiagnostic information than did subjects who were not accountable for their inferences. Being accountable for their judgments may induce people to use a wider range of information in making those judgments, but it does not necessarily make them more discriminating judges of how useful the information is.

Base Rates Versus Case Histories

People are often required to make predictions of future events on the basis of limited data. You may need to decide, for example, whether or not to get season tickets to your local repertory theater based on the sample of plays you have seen them perform in the past. Or, in trying to match up a friend with a new companion, you may think through the likelihood of whether or not they will be a good match and will get along with each other. A normative model, termed

Bayes' theorem, dictates how tasks such as these should proceed.[1] However, even when sampling has already been done for an individual and he or she is presented with good estimates of population characteristics (such as averages, prior probabilities, or proportions), those estimates may not be appropriately brought to bear on judgment tasks.

In Chapter 6, it was pointed out that people underutilize consensus information in making causal attributions. This failure to use consensus information can be thought of as part of a larger problem: namely, the tendency of people to ignore general, broadly based information about population characteristics (base rate information) in favor of more concrete anecdotal but usually less valid and reliable information. Vibrant examples simply outweigh more reliable but abstract base rate information (Bar-Hillel, 1980; S. E. Taylor & Thompson, 1982). This reliable bias likely occurs because colorful examples are more likely to suggest theories or expectations about what is going on than is base rate information, and as noted, prior theories or expectations often bias judgmental processes even when we are unaware of them.

In one study (Hamill et al., 1980) participants read a colorful account of a woman who had been living on welfare with her numerous children for many years while maintaining a relatively affluent lifestyle. This stereotypic case of welfare abuse was set in context either by base rate statistics indicating that welfare recipients often take advantage of the system and stay on welfare a long time, or by statistics suggesting that the average welfare recipient is on the rolls only a short time, implying that the case history provided to subjects was highly atypical. Despite the available base rate information, subjects responded as if the case history were representative of welfare recipients under both conditions,

---

[1] Bayes' theorem is a normative model for making statistically optimal predictions. To illustrate, consider the following example. Suppose there are two bags of poker chips, each containing mixtures of red and blue chips. Bag A contains 10 blue and 20 red chips, and Bag B contains 20 blue and 10 red chips. The subject's task is to draw a chip three times from the bag, see what color each chip is, and put it back in the bag after he or she has seen it. The subject is further told that 80% of the time the chips will be from Bag A and that 20% of the time they will be drawn from Bag B. The subject must then use information from the chips, the general knowledge regarding the numbers of blue and red chips in each bag, and the knowledge that Bag A will be selected 80% of the time and Bag B 20% of the time to decide from which bag the three chips were drawn. Suppose the subject drew three chips, and they were blue-blue-red. Which bag would they have been drawn from? Most people would assume that it was likely that the chips came from Bag B because two-thirds of the chips in Bag B are blue. Actually, the true odds are 2 to 1 that it was Bag A.

The way in which we calculate the exact odds for this game is by using Bayes' theorem. Bayes' theorem draws on two pieces of information: The first is the prior odds that the bag is A rather than B. These odds are 4 to 1, since Bag A is chosen 80% of the time. The second piece of information is likelihood: the ratio of the probability that the sample comes from A to the probability that it comes from B.

The probability of drawing a blue is 1 out of 3 and a red is 2 of 3. Consequently, the probability of drawing blue-blue-red is $1/3 \times 1/3 \times 2/3$, which equals 2/27. If, however, the bag is B, then the probability of drawing blue-blue-red is $2/3 \times 2/3 \times 1/3$, which equals 4/27. The likelihood ratio is the probability that the sample came from A(2/27) divided by the probability that the sample came from B(4/27). This yields the odds of 1 to 2 that the sample is from Bag A rather than from Bag B. Using Bayes' theorem to combine the prior probability with the likelihood information, we multiply the prior probability (4/27) by the likelihood (1/2), which yields 2 to 1 in favor of the guess that the three chips actually came from Bag A. Most people are surprised that it is more likely that the chips came from Bag A (A. L. Glass & Holyoak, 1986). The reason for the surprise is that they ignore the base rate information that Bag A will be selected 80% of the time.

and their judgments were more influenced by it than by the more valid base rate information (Hamill et al., 1980; S. E. Taylor & Thompson, 1982).

Why are people so often swayed by colorful case history examples when better or qualifying base rate information is also available? One possibility is that people do not always see the relevance of base rate information to a particular judgment task. A certain building in Los Angeles has been occupied by four different restaurants in less than 3 years. Each has failed, and that information should give any prospective restauranteur pause for thought. Nonetheless, as each culinary venture folds, an eager new one steps in to fill the breach, only to fail again. Presumably, each idealistic entrepreneur assumes that his or her own concept is the one that will make the place work (an Irish pub, a pasta place, soup and salad). None seemingly can appreciate the base rate information that virtually screams out, "No one comes here!"

People do use base rate information when its relevance is clear. For example, people are more likely to use base rate information if it is the only information available (e.g., Hamill et al., 1980) or if its causal relevance to the judgment task is made salient (Ajzen, 1977; Hewstone, Benn, & Wilson, 1988; Tversky & Kahneman, 1980). In one study, participants were told about a late-night auto accident involving a cab that an eyewitness thought might have been blue. Participants were then informed that in that city, 85% of the cabs are green and 15% are blue. Although participants should have concluded that the culprit's cab was probably green on the basis of the base rate information, few did. Instead, most drew on the report of the eyewitness and decided the cab was probably blue. However, a second group was told that 85% of the accidents in the city are caused by blue cabs and 15% by green cabs; these participants did use the base rate information to qualify their inferences. Presumably, people see accident rate statistics as causally relevant to judgments about accidents (cf. Ajzen, 1977), whereas they do not perceive information about the prevalence of particular cabs as relevant to the judgment, although it is. Thus, when people perceive base rate information as relevant to a judgment, they use it in preference to colorful case history information.

Several theoretical explanations for the base rate fallacy have been offered. At least some so-called failures to use base rate information may be attributed to experimental procedures. Formal rules of conversation dictate that people communicate primarily information that is intended to be informative and fill a gap in a recipient's knowledge (Grice, 1975; Turnbull & Slugoski, 1988). The fact that experiments emphasize individuating case information over base rate information may lead subjects to perceive that the case history information but not the base rate information is relevant to the judgment task. Hence, the appearance of overusing case history information may simply result from conditions in which it is perceived as presented to convey meaningfulness (Schwarz, Strack et al., 1991). People can use base rate information when it is brief, is presented early in a judgment task, or is otherwise salient (Chun & Kruglanski, 2006).

Case history information is more representative of a category than base rate information is and thus more likely to invoke theories (Kahneman & Tversky, 1973). When people read case history information, they make immediate associations to larger categories and thus appear to overuse the case history information for drawing inferences. People are better able to see the diagnostic value of case history than base rate information, except under circumstances in which the diagnostic value of base rate information is highlighted (Ginossar & Trope, 1980).

To summarize, people often do not adequately incorporate base rate and other statistical information in an inference task. When other, less valid but more engaging and seemingly relevant anecdotal evidence is present, people may ignore relevant base rates (Bar-Hillel & Fischhoff, 1981; Manis, Avis, & Cardoze, 1981; Manis, Dovalina, Avis, & Cardoze, 1980). The consequences of the failure to use base rate information can be extreme, as the conjunction error illustrates.

The Conjunction Error

Comedians make their living, in part, by sketching out highly recognizable portraits of people that make us laugh. "Consider the nerd. He's an out-of-shape guy who lives in a cubicle, dresses badly, and has bad posture, right? He looks like this?" [Comedian imitates the nerd.] With each detail, the audience's laugh of recognition grows. Yet the paradox of the well-drawn portrait is that with each detail, recognizability increases but actual probability of occurrence decreases. One might well find a nerd in his cubicle and he might be out of shape, but the likelihood that he would also be round-shouldered and poorly dressed is low. The likelihood that any two or more events will co-occur (i.e., their joint probability) is the product of their probabilities of occurring alone; accordingly, their joint probability cannot exceed the probability of the least probable event. Under some circumstances, however, people make more extreme predictions for the joint occurrence of events than for a single event. This error is termed the *conjunction fallacy* (Abelson & Gross, 1987; Tversky & Kahneman, 1983).

In one study (Slovic, Fischhoff, & Lichtenstein, 1977) participants were told that an individual was gregarious and literary. When asked how likely it was that he was an engineering major, they responded that it was very unlikely. However, when asked how likely it was that he would start out as an engineering major and switch to journalism, an event with a far lower likelihood of occurrence than simply majoring in engineering, participants gave this a much higher rating. Presumably, they could readily imagine how a gregarious, literary person would decide journalism was for him and not engineering, but they could not imagine how such a person would remain an engineer.

The preference for conjunctive explanations is a robust effect. It occurs for both important and trivial actions, it occurs whether an individual has a single goal in mind for an action or multiple goals, and it occurs whether the information involved in the conjunctive explanation is plausible or implausible (Leddo, Abelson, & Gross, 1984). Efforts to train people in the statistical principles underlying the conjunctive fallacy can lower, but do not eliminate, the conjunction error (Crandall & Greenfield, 1986; Morier & Borgida, 1984).

Qualifications to the conjunction effect have been uncovered. Conjunctive explanations are more likely when participants are asked to explain an event than if they are simply asked to infer an interpretation for the event (Zuckerman, Eghrari, & Lambrecht, 1986). When actors fail to take particular actions, conjunction effects disappear; that is, people do not show a systematic preference for explanations that offer multiple explanations for inaction (Leddo et al., 1984; see also Read, 1988).

Several reasons for conjunction effects have been offered. People generally try to understand others' actions in terms of those other persons' personal goals

(Leddo et al., 1984). For example, one may visit an art gallery to relax, to get away from the office, to see the work of a particularly exciting artist, to enjoy the companionship of a friend, and to have a change of scene, all of which may occur simultaneously. Conjunctive explanations, which provide more detailed information about a particular goal or information about multiple goals, tend to be preferred because they are perceived as informative.

Conjunctive explanations may be perceived as more likely than single explanations because they co-opt alternative explanations for the behavior (Einhorn & Hogarth, 1986). Thus people are not motivated to consider alternative explanations because the conjunctive explanation appears to rule out those alternatives. Knowing that a friend treated himself to an expensive dinner because he was depressed after he and his girlfriend broke up precludes wondering whether he received a bonus at work or a gift certificate in the mail.

The representativeness heuristic, which draws on preexisting theories, is also implicated in conjunction effects (Tversky & Kahneman, 1983). As information is added to a description that rounds out a human portrait and makes the portrait seem more likely, the objective probability that the portrait is true goes down, but its resemblance to a real person goes up: it matches our general theories more closely. In short, when people are assessing the likelihood that several seemingly related events will occur in conjunction, they will often ignore the objective probability of their conjunction in favor of a theory that makes the conjoint probability of the multiple events seem true.

Integrating Information

The task of bringing information together and combining it into a judgment can be problematic when evaluated against the normative model. As in the other tasks of social inference, assimilation of information to prior knowledge or expectations is very common (Stapel & Koomen, 2000). We consider several integrative tasks here.

Assessing Covariation

Judgments of covariation—that is, how strongly two things are related—are essential to many inference tasks, both formal and informal. Much of our folk wisdom states correlations such as the adage, "Blondes have more fun." Mickey Gilley's observation, "Don't the girls all get prettier at closing time?" (Don't the boys too?), assumes a correlation between time and perceived attractiveness (Pennebaker et al., 1979). Covariation is also the basis of many formal inference tasks: Kelley's covariation model of attribution (Chapter 6) presupposes that the social perceiver is able to observe the covariation of an outcome across time, persons, and entities with at least reasonable accuracy so that an attribution can be formulated.

Given the importance of covariation to judgment tasks, the question of how well the perceiver detects covariation is a critical one. The answer seems to be not very well (see Crocker, 1981; Nisbett & Ross, 1980, for reviews) when one compares the naive perceiver's estimates with the normative statistical model for assessing covariation (see Smedslund, 1963; Ward & Jenkins, 1965, for early references). The normative model for calculating covariation consists of several specific steps, and the research evidence to date suggests that there are sources of potential bias in each step. These steps are illustrated in Figure 7.3.

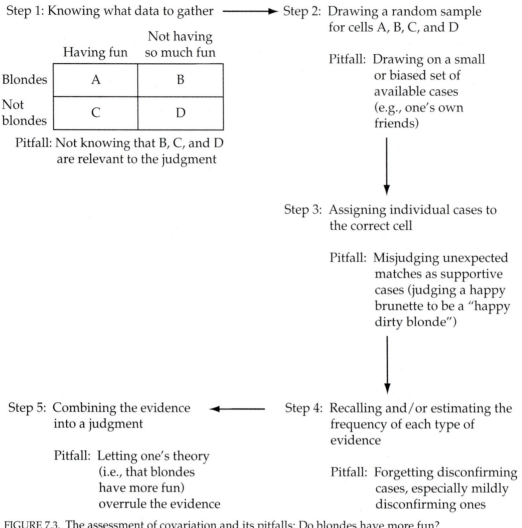

FIGURE 7.3. The assessment of covariation and its pitfalls: Do blondes have more fun?

First, the perceiver must understand what data are relevant to assess covariation. For example, to test the adage, "Blondes have more fun," one needs to know the number of blonde men and women who have fun, the number of blondes who do not, the number of brunettes and redheads who have fun, and the number of brunettes and redheads who do not. Most people do not realize that all four kinds of evidence are relevant to the covariation task; rather, they tend to concentrate primarily on the fun-loving blondes, believing that evidence supporting the adage is most relevant to its truth value. Indeed, this is a general propensity of the social perceiver that has been noted in other contexts; when testing the validity of an idea, people tend to seek instances that confirm the idea rather than instances on all sides of the issue (e.g., Arkes & Harkness, 1980). Yet, by nature, such statements as "Blondes have more fun" are comparative (All blondes or most? More fun than whom?), so all four types of information are needed.

The second step in assessing covariation is sampling cases. As has been noted, people are poor samplers. The range of acquaintances and contacts on whom they frequently draw is certainly biased, but most people seem to be unaware of this fact (Crocker, 1981). Small samples may be overused (Tversky & Kahneman, 1974), and when sample results disagree with one's own hunches, the sample results may be rejected or go unrecognized as contradictory (Arkes & Harkness, 1980; Crocker, 1981).

The third step in the covariation process is classifying instances as to type of evidence. Here again prior expectations can get in the way. Negative instances—that is, cases that contradict the proposed relationship—may be mislabeled as positive if they are ambiguous, or if not, dismissed as being due to error or faulty sampling. Positive instances that fit expectations are more quickly or easily identified and incorporated into the inference task (e.g., R. J. Harris, Teske, & Ginns, 1975; Owens, Bower, & Black, 1979). Nonoccurrences of the event are especially difficult for people to process (Allison & Messick, 1988).

In the fourth stage, the perceiver must recall the evidence and estimate the frequency of each type of evidence. Memory is certainly not infallible; it is particularly good for confirming cases, and under some circumstances, it is also good for strongly disconfirming cases. Thus, the ecstatic blonde and the deliriously happy raven-haired person may be remembered, whereas the three contented "mousy-browns" may be forgotten.

Finally, and only after the previous four steps have been completed, the social perceiver is ready to combine the evidence. How successfully is this task accomplished? In fact, the ability of the social perceiver to estimate degree of covariation once all the data have been assembled appears to be fairly good. Previous researchers have often confused errors of perceived relevance, sampling, classification, and recall of evidence as errors in computation, thereby underestimating the social perceiver's computational abilities (Crocker, 1981). This is not, however, to suggest either that the perceiver successfully computes correlation coefficients in his or her head or that estimates of covariation, however made, are usually accurate. Perceivers' estimates of covariation generally track, though appear often to underestimate, actual covariation as long as no strong prior expectation about the degree of relationship between the two variables exists (Jennings, Amabile, & Ross, 1982).

When people have a hypothesis about the relationship between variables, they tend to look for evidence that confirms that hypothesis rather than assess the evidence in a more even-handed manner (Klayman & Ha, 1987). The search for positive test cases appears to be a general strategy that cuts across many content areas and many types of inference tasks; people use it as a general problem-solving strategy (a) when they do not have available a strategy specific to the particular problem under investigation or (b) when task demands preclude the use of a more specific strategy. The positive-cases strategy may result from the tendency to test cases that are expected to have the property of interest rather than cases that do not, a heuristic that generally results in, but is not equivalent to, a confirmatory bias.

The previous discussion has implied that people usually test positive cases or engage in confirmatory biases when testing hypotheses. However, there are conditions that increase or decrease the ability to detect covariation. For example, a happy mood seems to foster top-down information processing and decrease attention to covariation information, whereas a sad mood may actually improve the detection of covariation (Braverman, 2005). There also appear to be conditions under which people use information relevant to falsification. People use information about alternative hypotheses when it is made available to them (Trope & Mackie, 1987) if it is suggested by a situational context or if it has been recently or frequently activated by other inference tasks (e.g., Ginossar & Trope, 1987).

Accuracy in the assessment of covariation is dependent in a large part on whether prior expectations and the specific information converge or diverge, with greater accuracy under conditions of convergence. From this standpoint, errors in contingency judgments may stem from a generally successful inferential strategy, which in the long run preserves accuracy by minimally altering contingency estimations from a general principle on the basis of a single and potentially aberrant encounter (Alloy & Tabachnik, 1984).

Illusory Correlation

When a relationship between two variables is expected, people often overestimate the degree of relationship that exists or impose a relationship when none actually exists. This phenomenon is termed *illusory correlation*. In an early example of the illusory correlation phenomenon, Chapman (1967) presented college student participants with lists of paired words such as lion-tiger, lion-eggs, and bacon-eggs. Participants were then asked to report how often each word was paired with each other word; in fact, all words were paired with each other an equal number of times. Nonetheless, subjects reported that words that were associated in meaning, such as bacon-eggs, had been paired more frequently than those not associated in meaning.

Sometimes illusory correlations result from structural characteristics of the evidence. Within the word list were two items that were longer than the other words in the list, specifically blossoms and notebook. Participants also inferred that these two words had more frequently been paired, apparently because they shared the distinctive quality of length. Chapman reasoned that at least two factors can produce an illusory correlation: *associative meaning*, in which two items are seen as belonging together because they "ought" to on the basis of prior expectations (e.g., bacon-eggs), and *paired distinctiveness*, in which two things are thought to go together because they share some unusual feature (e.g. blossoms-notebook). Similarly, a pseudocontingency may also be perceived if two skewed effects co-occur (Fiedler & Freytag, 2004). If a teacher has a classroom of highly aggressive children and knows that most of them watch a great deal of television, she may infer that the two phenomena are related when in fact they may have little to do with each other.

Paired distinctiveness has been examined as a basis of stereotyping (D. L. Hamilton, 1979). D. L. Hamilton and Gifford (1976) argued that paired distinctiveness can explain some negative stereotypes of minority group members. Specifically, majority group members have relatively few contacts with minority group members, and negative behaviors are also relatively infrequent. It may be that members of the majority group make an illusory correlation between the two rare events and infer that minority group members are more likely to engage in negative behaviors.

A meta-analysis suggested that the paired distinctiveness illusory correlation effect is highly consistent and moderate in size (Mullen & Johnson, 1990). Extensive research has identified the conditions under which this effect is more or less strong. The paired distinctiveness illusory correlation is stronger when the distinctive behaviors are negative and when memory load is high (Mullen & Johnson, 1990). People in a state of arousal show a stronger illusory correlation effect than unaroused participants because arousal may increase reliance on preexisting theories, and it reduces capacity for more elaborate problem solving (Kim & Baron, 1988). Illusory correlations along evaluative dimensions appear to be stronger than is true for cognitive judgments (Klauer & Meiser, 2000).

There appear to be some differences between illusory correlations formed about individuals and those formed about groups (Sanbonmatsu, Shavitt, & Gibson, 1994). Illusory correlations about individuals appear to result from online impression-based judgments, whereas those for groups seem to be memory-based (Sanbonmatsu, Sherman, & Hamilton, 1987). That is, for impressions of individuals, the bias appears to operate at encoding, not at the judgment stage (D. L. Hamilton, Dugan, & Trolier, 1985), whereas group illusory correlations may occur when attempting to recall group attributes (Sanbonmatsu et al., 1987).

The twin topics of covariation estimation and illusory correlation are important for several reasons. First, as a complex operation, the estimation of covariation represents a concatenation of many of the errors and biases in the social perceiver's intuitive strategies, such as detecting what information is relevant, sampling it correctly, and recalling it accurately. Second, because covariation is often an interim inference upon which other more complex inferences are subsequently based, the flaws that mark covariation estimation may have repercussions farther down the line in terms of the accuracy with which the social perceiver characterizes and acts on the environment. Third, errors in the estimation of covariation again highlight how the inference process is biased conservatively toward conclusions that people expect to be true and how the theories people have regarding the functioning of the social environment predominate in guiding the inference process. Finally, covariation estimation and the illusory correlations that may substitute for accurate assessment make their way into social interaction, shaping erroneous perceptions of reality as through the maintenance of stereotypes.

JUDGMENTS OVER TIME

Earlier, we described expected utility theory, which maintains that choices are guided by the probability and value of decisional options. The discounted utility (DU) model makes the additional point that the utility of any given choice diminishes as consequences are spread over time (Samuelson, 1937). Originally, this discount rate was thought to be constant over time. Decades of research, however, have clarified that departures from DU are as ubiquitous as those from EU (Frederick, Loewenstein, & O'Donoghue, 2002). Long-term choices are often determined by people's knowledge of their own preferences and how those preferences are likely to change over time. For example, given a choice between $10 today and $11 in a week, most people will choose $10 immediately. But given the choice between $10 in a year and $11 in a week and a year, most people will choose the $11 (Frederick et al., 2002).

DU also predicts that the discount rate is constant across choice types. But research reveals considerable variability in the discount rate as a function of the domain in which choices are made (Frederick et al., 2002) because there is a wide range of attitudes about the future. For example, a person may choose to exercise for health reasons but compromise that same goal by trying to manage on 3 or 4 hours' sleep a day. A person may undermine decades of careful saving with an unwise investment placed with a charlatan.

Affect-based or "hot" outcomes undergo steeper time discounting than cognition-based or "cool" outcomes (Loewenstein, 1996). Put another way, the farther in the future an event may be, the greater the weight of cognitive outcomes and the less the weight of affective outcomes. A "hot" but poorly educated dating partner may seem fantastic in the short-term, but cooler reflection on a long-term future might lead one to wonder whether that partner will be an intellectually rewarding companion and be able to pull his or her economic weight in a long-term relationship.

Small rewards are discounted more steeply than larger rewards. Ten dollars may look better today than $11 in a week, but if the corresponding figures are $1,000 and $1,100, the picture changes. In addition, abstract representative features govern decisions made for the future, whereas consideration of concrete details play a stronger role in judgments about the present.

Temporal Construal

Every day we think about and plan for future events. Temporal distance in the future not only affects the value of future outcomes, it also affects the way people mentally represent events. Imagine that you are taking a vacation in Spain 4 months from now. How are you thinking about the event? Then imagine that you are leaving for Spain tomorrow. How do your perceptions differ? In the first case, you may imagine romantic dinners very late at night, the thrill of gazing at exciting art, or the taste of unusual food. If you are leaving tomorrow, no doubt you are more concerned with where the extra set of keys is for the house sitter, whether enough dog food has been stocked in, and where the name of the hotel you're supposed to stay at in Madrid has gone.

This is the essence of temporal construal theory (Trope & Liberman, 2003): The greater the temporal distance to an event, the more likely one is to think about that event in terms of abstract features that convey the essence of the event. Thus thinking about events in the future prompts high-level construals. One thinks about future rewards in abstract form in a simple, structured, coherent manner and in terms of personal goals. Greater insight and more creative thinking may result (Förster, Friedman, & Liberman, 2004). But the closer one is to the event, the more likely one is to focus on specific, even incidental details of that same event. The lower level construals associated with more immediate outcomes tend to be specific and complex. They are often unstructured and incoherent and heavily depend on the context in which they appear. In the short-term, abstract goals are often irrelevant or set aside in favor of subordinate goals.

As temporal distance to an activity increases, the value of a high-level construal becomes more influential, and low-level construals become less influential for determining preferences. For example, the decision of whether or not to donate blood today is likely to be guided by whether one has extra time and how many other activities one has planned, whereas the decision to donate blood in 6 months is more likely to be guided by the higher level construal of whether donating to help others is a good idea. To put it another way, decisions about distant future activities are more likely to be made on the basis of how desirable they are, whereas decisions about activities in the near future are likely to be made based on how feasible they are.

Events envisioned in the future are regarded more favorably than those generated for the present. For example, the initial impetus for the trip to Spain may have been the superordinate goal of a long, romantic vacation away with one's spouse, whereas the immediate subordinate goal may be simply trying to get everything done to get to the airport on time. Given the chaos, one may wonder why one ever thought this was a good idea.

Spatial distance is related to judgments in some of the same ways that temporal distance is. For example, actions that will be performed at spatially distant locations tend to be seen as ends rather than means and tend to be described abstractly rather than concretely (Fujita, Henderson, Eng, Trope, & Liberman, 2006). In one study, when events were characterized as spatially distant, perceivers were more likely to use broad behavioral units and dispositional attributions than when events were represented as near (Henderson, Fujita, Trope, & Liberman, 2006). Distant events were seen as more likely if they were typical, and less likely if atypical compared to near events (Henderson et al., 2006). To characterize these results generally, people seem to reveal common judgmental biases when drawing inferences about distant events (see also Eyal, Liberman, Trope, & Walther, 2004). In short, temporal or spatial distance changes judgments and decisions because judgments and decisions in the distance reflect high-level rather than low-level construals.

Learning From the Past

The maxim "Those who ignore the past are condemned to relive it" implies that, were we scrupulously to turn our attention backward in time rather than forward, we would learn important lessons. Although this adage may contain an element of truth, research on hindsight questions how seriously we ought to believe it. Like the present and the future, our interpretation of the past is guided by theory. Everyone is familiar with the Monday morning quarterback who, with the advantage of retrospection, knows what could have and should have been done to win the weekend's game. He claims that the opposition's moves could have been anticipated, that the home team ought to have foreseen them, and that a particular strategy (his) clearly would have been successful.

Twenty-twenty hindsight seems to be a robust phenomenon. Work by Fischhoff and colleagues (Fischhoff, 1980, Fischhoff, Slovic, & Lichtenstein, 1977; Janoff-Bulman, Timko, & Carli, 1985) indicates that it is very difficult to ignore knowledge of an actual outcome to generate unbiased inferences about what could or should have happened. In retrospect, people exaggerate what could have been anticipated. Moreover, when people's predictions about future events are compared with postdictions about events that have already happened, results show that people distort and misremember their own predictions to conform with what really happened (Fischhoff & Beyth, 1975).

The social perceiver's ubiquitous theory-generating capacity is a major basis for reconstructing the past (cf. M. Ross, 1989). Even the most random sequence of events can be forced with enough thought into a logical causal chain. Once that causal chain of reasons is in place, it may be hard to see events as other than inevitable. Furthermore, interventions that would presumably have set some other causal sequence into effect may seem particularly compelling because they seem so logical. Chance or situational factors that may have heavily influenced what actually occurred may be overlooked. For example, in retrospect, an opponent's series of moves in a football game may appear to be part of an overall plan when in fact it capitalizes on chance events such as an injury or a fumble. Nonetheless, once labeled as a plan, it is likely to be seen as predictable ("They did the same thing in the Tennessee game."), and solutions to it may seem obvious ("We should have switched to a running game."). The preceding analysis implies that the hindsight bias is motivated more by cognitive factors related to the ability to construct causal explanations for events than by motivational factors such as the desire to appear correct in retrospect. In fact, analyses of the hindsight bias suggest that cognitive factors probably do have more of a role in the bias than motivational ones (Christensen-Szalanski & Willham, 1991).

A meta-analysis of 122 studies of the hindsight bias (Christensen-Szalanski & Willham, 1991) indicated that it is modest but reliable. It is stronger for events that happened than for events that didn't happen. The hindsight bias is reduced when people are experienced in the domain under investigation (Christensen-Szalanski & Willham, 1991). The magnitude of the bias is reduced when the outcome is hard to imagine or when alternatives are easy to imagine (Sanna & Schwarz, 2006).

What ought we to learn from the past? Rarely are the lessons of history clear because inevitably they are tinged with the advantage of hindsight. Participants in events do not know the full import of those events before they happen ("Dear Diary, The Hundred Years' War started today," Fischer, 1970, cited in Fischhoff, 1980, p. 84). Since it is hard to estimate what should have been foreseen and still harder to assess the role of environmental and chance factors in producing outcomes that have already occurred, what should actually be learned from history is often unclear.

In short, we are creatures of the present, trapped inferentially by what we already know. As in the case of other inference tasks, our methods of assessment can be driven by a priori or easily constructed theories rather than by objective data. Finally, the answers themselves, what we should be learning from the past, are indeterminate. Perhaps a better maxim than that which opened this section might be one of Fischhoff's own: "While the past entertains, enables, and expands quite readily, it enlightens only with delicate coaxing" (1980, p. 80).

Summary

Research on judgment under uncertainty has revealed the importance of heuristic strategies that people adopt for making inferences rapidly. One such heuristic is representativeness: the perceiver decides how likely it is that an object is a member of some category on the basis of whether the object's features are similar to the essential features of the category. Another heuristic is availability, which involves estimating frequency or likelihood by how quickly instances or associations can be brought to mind. The simulation heuristic uses mental rehearsal of events to determine what outcome is likely, given a set of circumstances. The anchoring heuristic enables the perceiver to use an already-existing reference point and adjust from that reference point to reach an estimate to answer some new problem. Decision framing affects inferences, especially whether a decision is framed in terms of gains or losses.

Although each of these shortcuts leads to inferences that approximate those made by normative models, each is susceptible to potential biases. Deciding what data are relevant to a judgment is often marked by prior expectations or theories, sampling is often biased, and biases in already existing samples are often ignored. Strong inferences are frequently drawn from small and unreliable samples. When good base rate information describing population characteristics is available, it is often overlooked in favor of less reliable, but seemingly more relevant case history or anecdotal information. Regression—the fact that extreme events will, on average, be less extreme when observed again—is poorly understood; instead, extreme events are frequently used to predict future extreme events. People are particularly poor at using and combining probabilistic information, often manifesting great confidence in the truth of unlikely events. When preexisting expectations or theories guide social inference, a positive test case strategy is often adopted that selectively looks for instances that test the expected inference.

There are also sources of error that affect our ability to combine information into a judgment. Covariation, the estimate of the degree of association between two events, is a concatenation of many of the previously described skills (e.g., detecting relevancy, sampling, combining information). When data are already collected and clearly summarized, instructions are clear, relevance to the statistical model is clear, and no a priori theory about degree of covariation exists, the social perceiver does fairly well at estimating covariation. However, in the absence of these factors, covariation estimates are heavily biased by prior expectations.

Temporal factors clearly guide the inference process, such as the fact that present rewards are typically valued more highly than larger, more distant rewards. In addition, abstract representative features govern decisions made for the future, whereas consideration of concrete details plays a stronger role in judgments about the present. In learning from past behavior or errors, people usually overestimate what could have been foreseen.

Accuracy and Efficiency in Social Inference

The idea that human inferential processes are typically conscious, rational, thorough, logical, and accurate was widely held early in social cognition research. This belief continues to be held to a degree in some of the behavioral sciences, despite considerable evidence that this assumption is incorrect. Why was the assumption of rationality such a cornerstone of social cognition research? One reason is that research on inference generally assumes either implicitly or explicitly that inferences are goal directed; that is, they are made to achieve some purpose. A person may need to make a decision, choose from among several options, or need to understand a situation before acting on it. If goals dominate the inference process, then clearly some ways of reaching a goal are better than others because they are more thorough and less error-prone. Accordingly, the social perceiver, it would seem, should use them.

Another reason for assuming rationality is more pragmatic. To understand the strategies used by the social perceiver, it is helpful to have a reference point for comparison. Normative models—that is, the optimal ways to use information to reach inferences—provide such reference points. Even when researchers are well aware that social inference does not correspond to normative models, the comparison of naive inference against normative models can be revealing with regard to the strategies typically used to make social inferences. Normative models for making judgments and choices are known collectively as behavioral decision theory, and it is against the principles of behavioral decision theory that social inferences have typically been compared (e.g., Einhorn & Hogarth, 1981; Hastie & Dawes, 2001).

A primary model against which human inference has been evaluated is expected utility (EU) theory, described in Chapter 7. Other normative models against which social inference is often compared include statistical knowledge, such as the computation of correlation or the law of large numbers (i.e., large samples are more reliable than small ones). We will refer to these in the sections that follow. A larger question, though, is whether normative theories provide descriptive benefit for understanding human inferential processes.

In Chapter 7 we reviewed social inference as compared against normative models, which revealed that inferential strategies often do not match the criteria dictated by normative theories. One conclusion that could be drawn from these comparisons is that our heuristics and shortcuts do not serve us very well. The evidence suggests that, like the proverbial adolescent in his first amorous forays, we may be fast, but we aren't very good. But this conclusion could be misleading.

Some departures from normative models of inference may be understood as meeting alternative goals. Rather than being motivated by accuracy, for example, the social perceiver may draw inferences that are personally motivating or rewarding, as will be seen later in this chapter and as noted in research on the self (Chapter 5). Thus, among other implications, affective considerations clearly guide social inference processes.

Another reason social inference often fails to match normative models is that the social perceiver operates not only under accuracy pressures but also under efficiency pressures, making inferences quickly in a rapidly changing environment with multiple demands. As such, many inferential tasks are solved with reference to prior expectations or theories rather than by means of an exhaustive consideration of the data at hand. Although purchasing the ingredients for a dinner party for one's employer may lead one to devote considerable thought to the purchase of each item, one's typical grocery shopping may be guided by the idea that "cheaper is better" in order to choose from an array of goods quickly. Given the need to process large amounts of information quickly, people's information processing strategies may lean toward efficiency rather than thoroughness. The criterion of efficiency is not systematically incorporated into normative models of inference, and normative models may not reflect some of the most important pressures that typically operate on the social perceiver.

An important reason inference processes often depart from normative models stems from capacity limitations on short-term memory. That is, the ability to process information online is very limited. At a minimum, the inference process is often marked by a need to use strategies that move information along quickly though not always thoroughly. The label "cognitive miser" was developed to explain the necessary stinginess with which attention and processing time are often allocated to stimuli in the real world (S. E. Taylor, 1981b). Long-term storage in memory, however, is quite cheap, a point easily illustrated by thinking over all the songs you know or the people you can identify by sight. The advantage of so much storage space is that prior information, beliefs, and inferences can be stored as knowledge structures. They are then accessible when new inferences must be drawn. Armed with limited online capacity and a large amount of stored knowledge, how do these factors affect social inference?

Long-term memory is the source of expectations and theories, and, as has been seen, social inference is heavily theory driven. Using a priori theories is likely to be an effective strategy for forming judgments and making decisions inasmuch as it represents the impact of past learning on subsequent information processing. It is efficient and effective to use our stored representations for similar situations, events, and people to interpret new and similar situations, events, and people. As such, departures from normative models of inference will tend to stray on the side of supporting already-held expectations or hypotheses and

against detecting sources of bias or error in data. A second consequence that follows from this insight is that the inference process is often conservative, avoiding new or counterintuitive beliefs.

Related to the bias in favor of prior theories and conservative inferences is a
tendency to look primarily for evidence that supports preexisting expectations
rather than to consider the full array of available evidence. As noted earlier, this
preference for cases that test the predominant expectation underlies a number
of the departures that intuitive inference demonstrates when compared against
normative models.

Overall, should we regard errors and biases in the social inference process
with alarm, bemusement, or respect? There are at least three perspectives on
this puzzle. The first position argues that the errors and biases identified in the
social inference process have considerable validity and often lead to important
errors in judgments and policy, and consequently, some efforts to improve the
inference process must be undertaken. The second perspective maintains that
errors and biases in the inference process are more apparent than real, and that
in the real world people actually perform inferential tasks quite well. Moreover,
although social perceivers are prone to certain systematic errors and biases in
their inferences, there are conditions in the real world that act as safeguards and
checks on the inference process so that some of these biases become inconsequential or self-correcting. A third, more recent, perspective argues that in some
cases rapidly formed judgments based on heuristics may be superior to those
based on more careful contemplation. We consider each perspective in turn.

ERRORS AND BIASES AS CONSEQUENTIAL: IMPROVING THE INFERENCE PROCESS

Under some circumstances, erroneous inferential strategies have severe consequences. The contribution of inferential errors to the development and maintenance of pejorative stereotypes is one striking example. Group decision making
shows marked biases in information gathering and perceptions of one's own
and another's position, indicating that severe errors can mark naturally occurring conditions of social inference (Janis, 1989). Judgmental errors have unnerv-
ing implications for fields as diverse as politics (Jervis, 1976), clinical decision
making (Turk & Salovey, 1986), and education (Simon, 1980). In short, biases in
inferential processes often matter, and accordingly, methods for the detection
and correction of biased inferences are needed.

Were one to undertake to improve the social perceiver's inferential process,
the effort would likely begin by alerting perceivers to the problem and instruct-
ing them to be attentive to inferential errors in the future. Such instructions
would presuppose that people have at least some awareness of the inferential
processes they are using and that they can draw on that awareness at will.

In a controversial paper, Nisbett and Wilson (1977b) maintained that people
have little or no access to their cognitive processes. In fact, there is a substantial
amount of anecdotal evidence from psychological studies indicating that many, if
not most, experimental participants have no idea of the forces in the experiment
influencing their behavior. Taking these observations as their point of departure,
Nisbett and Wilson conducted a series of experiments (Nisbett & Wilson, 1977a;

T. D. Wilson & Nisbett, 1978) in which they systematically manipulated factors that influenced participants' behavior and then asked the participants to report what factors led them to behave as they did. For example, in one study, billed as an investigation of consumer preferences, participants were asked to inspect four nightgowns laid out on a table and indicate which one they would choose. There is, in fact, a strong serial position effect for these kinds of tasks, such that people typically prefer the right-most item. (Why this position preference exists is not fully known.) Participants in the experiment showed this serial position effect, but when asked why they made the particular choice they had, they offered explanations that centered on qualities of the chosen garment itself. When it was suggested that serial position might have influenced their decision, participants expressed considerable skepticism.

Divergences between people's beliefs about the causes of their behavior ("I like pink, and that nightgown was pink") and the actual causes of their behaviors (the pink nightgown was the right-most choice) stem largely from the oft-noted impact of theories on judgment: We believe we do things for reasons that are known to us and are often unaware of or disbelieving about things that have influenced our behavior if they don't fit our theories.

One should not infer from the previous discussion that people are always wrong in their theories of what causes their behavior. Indeed, on many if not most occasions, people are right. If someone asks you why you are crying, and you say, "Because my boyfriend left me," you are probably correct in your analysis. The fact that a theory is correct, however, or that it correctly applies to a particular case, does not imply that its holder has special access to his or her cognitive processes (T. D. Wilson, Hull, & Johnson, 1981).

Should We Turn Inference Over to Computers?

The person's inferential shortcomings are particularly well illustrated when he or she is matched against a computer given the same information. The computer always does as well or better (Dawes, Faust, & Meehl, 1989). How can one demonstrate this fact? First, it is necessary to find a judgment task in which roughly the same kinds of information are contained in every case; second, there must be a decision rule regarding how that information is to be combined to reach a decision for each case. Such judgment tasks are relatively common. A business must replenish stock after considering demand and current inventory. Patients must be diagnosed and treated once clinical observations, symptoms, and test results are available. Students are admitted to or rejected from graduate school on the basis of test scores, grade point average, past work, and letters of recommendation.

A normatively appropriate way of completing such a task is to examine each case (e.g., student), take each of the bits of information relevant to the judgment (e.g., GPA, letters of recommendation, GRE scores), multiply each bit by its weight (e.g., count GREs twice as much as GPA and GPA half again as much as letters of recommendation), add it up for a total case score, and compare the case's score against other case scores to pick the best ones. This process employs a linear model, so-called because the total impression is an additive combination of the available information. It is a task that can be efficiently and effectively completed by a properly programmed computer. Various nonlinear combinations can also be reliably utilized to make decisions: "Weigh GPA twice as heavily as letters of recommendation, unless GPA is lower than 3.0, in which case weigh it evenly with letters." The nonlinear nature of these rules makes them no less readily programmable for a computer, and the computer is more reliable than the human decision maker.

Unfortunately, the human decision maker often has an exaggerated view of his or her ability to accomplish inferential tasks, so much so that the idea of letting it fall to a computer meets with strenuous objections. Clinical intuition, it is felt, would be sacrificed to a rigid numerical formula, and unusual instances or special cases would slip through the cracks. Anyone who has ever sat on an admissions or membership committee and seen "clinical intuition" in operation probably knows that the process is often random and inconsistent, full of blatant stereotyping, unwarranted favoritism, and irrational dislikes.

Dawes (1980) presents a particularly entertaining account of the process at several leading universities. A slang peculiar to the admissions process quickly develops. "Pinocchios" are applicants with high ratings from letter writers on all but one characteristic, such as maturity or independence; hence their profile has a long jag or nose. They are to be avoided because anyone who attracts enough attention to get that low a rating on some attribute must be really bad. "Jock essays" are essays that are too short; "geos" are students who would add geographic diversity, such as a Hawaiian applying to an east coast school. And everyone seems to be looking for the proverbial "neat small-town kid." Very often, comparisons are made to apparently similar students with whom one has already had experience. "Aha. Another Smedley. He was smart but a drudge. Not a creative bone in his body" (Abelson, 1976). Frequently, these analogies are drawn on the basis of minimal similarity, such as having a record that excels in everything except physical education.

Despite such problems, this process is loudly defended. Its advocates maintain that, generally, decision makers do use the appropriate algorithm and that departures from the model are made so as to pick up the late bloomer or the prodigal student returning to the fold. However, collectively made decisions have unique types of errors (e.g., Janis, 1972; Shaw, 1971), and trained statisticians and other experts are sometimes just as vulnerable to inferential errors as laypersons (Kahneman & Tversky, 1973; Tversky & Kahneman, 1974). Table 8.1 presents a hypothetical account of the process employed for two fictitious graduate school admissions cases given a linear decision rule, a nonlinear decision rule, and an intuitive human decision maker (see Burgess, 1941; L. R. Goldberg, 1968, 1970).

Two extensive analyses of studies have pitted the clinical judge against the computer or other mechanical aids (Meehl, 1954; J. Sawyer, 1966); both yielded the same conclusion: Computers or other mechanical aids always do as well or better than clinical judges. What does the computer do, and why does it do it so well? The computer merely does more consistently what human judges believe they do. It uses the criteria established by people, but it uses them consistently, weighs them in a reliable way, combines the information accurately, and makes a judgment.

What does the human decision maker do wrong? People usually believe they are using more cues and making more complex judgments than they actually are. One professor, upon reading this research, correlated her own rankings

TABLE 8.1. Comparison of the Linear Model, the Nonlinear Model, and a Human Decision Maker: Will Stinch and Crabble Be Admitted to Graduate School?

	Case A: Gerald Stinch	*Case B: Amanda Crabble*
	GRE: 650 Verbal, 710 Math GPA: 3.8 Letters of recommendation: Hard-working, diligent	GRE: 620 Verbal, 590 Math GPA: 2.9 Letters of recommendation A bit of a dreamer, hasn't come into her own
Linear model (as applied by computer)	Score = 2 (GREs) + 1 (GPA) + .5 (Letter of recommendation)	
Decision:	Admit Stinch.	Reject Crabble.
Nonlinear model (as applied by computer)	Score = 2 (GREs) + 1 (GPA) + .5 (Letter of recommendation), unless GPA is less than 3.0, in which case score is 3 (GREs) + .5 (GPA) + 1 (Letter of recommendation)	
Decision:	Admit Stinch.	Reject Crabble.
Human decision maker	Aha. Another Smedley. Not a creative bone in his body.	Aha. Another Woodley? She was a great theoretician—got off to a slow start, though.
Decision:	Reject Stinch.	Admit Crabble.
Probable outcome given reliable and valid admissions criteria	Stinch will do well.	Crabble will do less well.

of prospective students with several admissions criteria and found, to her embarrassment and surprise, that GRE scores were virtually the sole basis of her decisions. Not only do people not use as many cues as they think they are using, they also do not weigh those cues the way they believe they do. Although support for clinical judgment lingers, it is clear that for decisions that can be made using a constant decision rule, the computer outperforms the person. Clinical judges are, of course, important in picking out what variables need to go into the decision. However, when it comes to integrating the information to reach a decision, the person is often best left out of the process (Dawes et al., 1989).

Teaching Reasoning

Turning problems over to a computer is not always realistic. A second potential way of improving the inference process generally is through education, by teaching reasoning in a formal educational curriculum. Nisbett and his colleagues have explored the value of teaching reasoning to see if and when learning rules applicable to specific problems generalize to a wider array of problems. In one study, Fong, Krantz, and Nisbett (1986) trained participants in the law of large numbers, which maintains that information derived from large samples is more trustworthy than information derived from small samples. Some participants were given formal training in the law of large numbers, others were shown how to apply the law for several concrete example problems, a third group received both types of training, and a fourth group received no training. Results indicated that people receiving either rule-training or training by examples were more likely to reason statistically than those who received no training; the greatest amount of statistical reasoning was demonstrated by people who received training in both the abstract rule and the examples. More important, using the learning-through-examples approach (guided induction), Fong and colleagues were able to show a high degree of generalizability of the training effects: participants improved as much in domains in which they were not explicitly trained as in domains in which they were trained. People clearly possess abstract inferential rules, and they can be trained through guided induction to expand upon and improve their use of these rules in a variety of settings (see also Cheng, Holyoak, Nisbett, & Oliver, 1986).

Consistent with these conclusions, graduate training can also have a marked effect on reasoning strategies. Lehman, Lempert, and Nisbett (1988) compared graduate students in four disciplines—psychology, medicine, law, and chemistry—both initially upon entrance to graduate school and 2 years later, to see if graduate training had any impact on a variety of statistical and methodological reasoning tasks. Consistently, psychology students and, to a lesser extent, students in medicine showed improvements in their reasoning, presumably because both of these specialties involve the interpretation of probabilistic data. However, for students in chemistry, a science that deals almost exclusively with deterministic causes, no improvement was expected or found. Legal training similarly had minimal impact on changes in statistical and methodological reasoning with the exception of conditional problems, with which the law deals frequently.

The conclusion, then, is that people are capable of using abstract statistical concepts, and that they do employ them spontaneously but not always entirely correctly in relevant situations. Both formal training and training by example improve the ability to see the applicability of statistical principles to a broad range of situations and make appropriate use of them. In other circumstances, though, a computer might do a better job.

ERRORS AND BIASES IN SOCIAL INFERENCE: PERHAPS THEY DON'T MATTER?

A second perspective on errors and biases in social inference maintains that these errors may be more apparent than real. This perspective (Funder, 1987; McArthur & Baron, 1983; Swann, 1984) makes two main points. The first is that experimental research documenting errors and biases does not create the conditions under which people normally make judgments in the real world and, therefore, may make people look worse at inference tasks than they really are. According to this position, social perceivers' naive inference strategies are adapted to the ecological and interpersonal conditions under which inferences must be drawn; experimental studies that create conditions conducive to use of the normative model rarely exist in real-world judgment and decision-making situations.

Second, judgment tasks used in experimental tests are often stacked against intuitive strategies of inference (Fischhoff, 1982; Funder, 1987; Kahneman & Tversky, 1982; McArthur & Baron, 1983). For example, the tasks may be unfamiliar or unfair (e.g., being expected to calculate a correlation in one's head), or they may be misconstrued by participants. Or information may be presented in a format conducive to use of the normative model and not contain the kind of contextual detail that would facilitate the use of an effective intuitive strategy. This methodological bias in experimental evidence may lead to a more negative portrait of our inferential abilities than we deserve.

A parallel point is that normative models, as a result, may be poor standards for evaluating intuitive inferences. Conditions that make it possible to use a normative model are rarely present in the real world. Often, information is not reliable, unbiased, or complete. Even if it is, it may not be presented in a clear or usable fashion. Sometimes the information is not available, and even if it were, use of the normative model might be prohibitively time consuming.

Another problem with applying the normative model to most daily inferential situations is that normative models ignore the content and, thus, the context of a decision in favor of its formal structure. For example, deciding which of three brands of eggs to buy and deciding which of three people to marry could be treated as equivalent decisions under the normative model if the information about the three options varied from each other in the same systematic ways. Yet the intuitive processes used for the two decisions would probably vary, and rightfully so. The normative model generates inferential standards given a fixed time and environment (i.e., all other things being equal). But decisions are made and inferences are drawn in dynamic environments, so predictions made for static environments may be inappropriate for changing conditions.

There are also circumstances under which the type of judgment to be made suggests use of a different model than a normative one. Take the example of a fledgling job candidate who at lunch spills his water, sends his lamb chop flying into his neighbor's lap, and rests his elbow in the butter (Nisbett, Krantz, Jepson, & Fong, 1982). He is nervous, it is true, and his nervousness is clearly due to situational factors, not dispositional ones. Furthermore, this is a very modest sample of his behavior, and it is likely to be a very poor predictor of future behavior. Normatively, one should probably discount these incidents. But consider the alternative practical model of the person who must make the job-hiring decisions. He or she must select a candidate who can consistently perform well and perform well under pressure. Wouldn't you rather have your sales made by someone who puts his butter on his roll instead of his suit? In short, statistically normative models are only one kind of model that can be applied to social judgments. It may be the case that alternative models held by people directly involved in making those judgments generate useful criteria that inherently conflict with the standards generated by normative models.

Moreover, the task of assessing if and when a person's inferences are accurate is more complex than one might suppose. One can determine whether a judgment corresponds to some criterion (e.g., Hastie & Rasinski, 1988); whether it is shared with others (Funder, 1987); or whether it is adaptive, pragmatic, or useful (Swann, 1984). But for many social judgments, there is no criterion for determining whether or not it is actually correct because the judgments lack objective referents (Hastie & Rasinski, 1988). Moreover, as we will shortly see, inferences often serve needs other than accuracy, such as a need to protect or enhance the self or one's social group.

We do know that such factors as importance of a judgment and personal involvement in the issue lead to consideration of more information, prompt more complex judgmental strategies, and even lead to increased accuracy under some circumstances (e.g., Harkness, DeBono, & Borgida, 1985). Accountability also increases cognitive activity such that accountable judges use more complex processing strategies than unaccountable ones (Tetlock & Boettger, 1989). Beyond these observations, it is difficult to judge whether the social perceiver is more accurate in the real world than in the experimental laboratory. Moreover, there are no stringent criteria for defining what a "natural" situation is, and many real-world situations themselves may be quite unnatural with respect to the inferential strategies that social perceivers normally use (Kruglanski, 1989).

Are Inferential Errors Inconsequential or Self-Correcting?

Some of the errors produced by faulty inferential processes will not matter. For example, if one's biased impressions will not affect one's future behavior, as in forming an incorrect impression of a person one meets only once, then the error will be inconsequential. In fact, little is known about the correspondence between inferences and behavior generally; if the correspondence is low, inferential errors may matter little. Biases may also matter little if they are constant over time. For example, if one regards one's boss as gruff, it may not matter that she is gruff only when she is in the boss role if that is the only circumstance under which one interacts with her.

Inferences are not choices that, once made, commit one irrevocably to a cognitive or behavioral course. Rather, in many cases inferences may be tentative forays to be modified on the bases of the responses they evoke. Normal conversation provides a basis for reality testing one's inferences, and blatantly false conclusions with far-reaching implications are likely to be corrected. For example, if the assertion that one performs one's share of the housework meets with strenuous objections from one's spouse, that opinion is likely to be modified.

Biases may matter little when decision alternatives are of near equal value. A student choosing between Princeton and Yale may make a final decision based on one friend's experience, but stereotypes and chauvinism aside, the student will receive a trivially better education at one place over the other. Finally, our biases may have little impact on our strategies. Consider the graduate admissions process. It is the rare graduate student who turns out to be a hotshot. If one accepts five students and they have average careers and rejects five students who also have average careers, then one can find little apparent fault with one's decision-making process, even if it was actually made with flawed methods. If one of the five rejected students goes on to excel, then one might conclude that an error was made in one case and that that student should have been accepted. Still, 1 out of 10 is not a bad error rate. Obviously, this reasoning is fallacious, but it serves to underscore the fact that many of our processing errors do not yield blatantly bad results, so the processes may appear perfectly adequate.

Some intuitive strategies are relatively robust against certain errors, and in other cases one shortcoming may cancel out another (Nisbett & Ross, 1980). For example, the dilution effect (i.e., the finding that extreme predictions can be attenuated by the presence of irrelevant information) can guard against the failure to appreciate regression toward the mean.

Some sources of error will correct themselves through repeated encounters. For example, if several of one's friends have recently been divorced, one's estimate of the divorce rate may be temporarily exaggerated via the availability heuristic, but assuming that one's friends do not continue to divorce indefinitely, one's estimated divorce rate should eventually come into line with objective data.

In short, although inferential tasks in the laboratory often provide a dramatic portrayal of the human propensity for error and bias, in the real world errors and biases may matter less. People's heuristic strategies often approximate statistical and other normative models (Griffiths & Tenenbaum, 2006), and intuitive strategies may not always lead to the dramatic failures that some research highlights. There are also many circumstances in the world in which people need to be sufficiently smart but not optimally smart. Intuitive models incorporate the content of the problem to be solved. Whereas people may make quick and dirty choices and decisions for inconsequential matters, they may be more thorough and circumspect for important decisions. That is, intuitive strategies accommodate pragmatic concerns. Under certain conditions, faulty inferences will be corrected by subsequent evidence through conversation with others. In short, one answer to the question "If we're so bad at judgmental tasks, how do we do as well as we do?" is that rapid approximations of normative strategies yield a good enough way of relating to the world much of the time.

ARE RAPID JUDGMENTS SOMETIMES BETTER THAN THOUGHTFULLY CONSIDERED ONES?

Early in social cognition research, inferences based on heuristics were thought to be flawed, a position that gave way to the observation that, to meet efficiency pressures, sometimes rough approximations to the normative model may suffice for accuracy and be vastly superior for meeting efficiency needs. A more radical view is coming into acceptance at the present time: namely, at least under some circumstances, rapid heuristically based judgments may lead to superior inferences compared to deliberative conscious efforts.

The immensely popular book, *Blink,* by Malcolm Gladwell (2005), draws on compelling examples from social psychology to make the case that, for many complex decisions or choices, the brain performs a series of rapid calculations that lead to instant and often correct assessments. For example, very knowledgeable art historians evaluating a kouros reputed to have been carved in the 6th century BC rapidly concluded that the kouros was a fake, although none of them could articulate quite why.

Social psychologists have documented many other examples, such as the ability to infer a teacher's teaching ratings from students on the basis of a few seconds of videotaped observations of her teaching (Ambady & Rosenthal, 1993). The inferences from such "thin slices of behavior" make it clear that our minds are able to integrate or extract information from complex stimuli to reach apparently complex judgments in a matter of seconds. In another example, strangers observing college students' rooms judged whether the inhabitant of each room was talkative, thorough, reserved, and unselfish; their impressions correlated startlingly well with diagnostic instruments assessing conscientiousness, emotional stability, and openness to experience. All these judgments were made without the evaluators ever meeting the person involved (Gosling, Ko, Mannarelli, & Morris, 2002).

Not all instantaneous judgments are correct, of course, nor did *Blink* provide many guidelines for determining which ones might be and which ones are entirely off base. Research suggests a few conditions that may foster rapid and accurate inferences. When people have a lot of expertise in a domain and have seen lots of examples of something before, they are more likely to be able to make very rapid accurate judgments; hence, the ability of experienced curators to judge the kouros as a fake or experienced students to estimate a teacher's teaching ratings. The abilities to integrate diverse information quickly, to use several diagnostic pieces of information simultaneously, or to pick up a particularly revealing clue may be some of the sources of this expertise.

Research has also looked at this issue the other way around and shown that when people actively reason about their choices or decisions, they sometimes make worse ones. For example, if one were trying to decide whether to take a particular summer job or choose a particular major, an obvious strategy might be to evaluate each of the various aspects of the decision and analyze one's evidence for the pros and cons of each alternative. Despite the intuitive appeal of such a strategy, it actually reduces the relation between inference and behavior. Wilson and Hodges (1992) found that introspecting about the reasons one likes or dislikes some object has a disruptive effect on one's impressions and reduces the influence of those impressions on subsequent decisions. In essence, analyzing the reasons that underlie one's inferences actually causes the inferences themselves to change temporarily (Wilson, Hodges, & LaFleur, 1995; Wilson & LaFleur, 1995).

The reason this happens may be that people generally don't think a lot about their inferences; when they are induced to do so, they focus on particular aspects of the inferences, and those aspects become more salient. In doing so, they may fail to discriminate important from unimportant information or properly perceive the relevance of particular information; the result is a poorer decision quality (Tordesillas & Chaiken, 1999). Therefore, reasoning can lead to increased inconsistency in the impact that inferences have on other judgments and decisions.

In an important set of studies, Dijksterhuis and colleagues (Dijksterhuis, 2004; Dijksterhuis, Bos, Nordgren, & van Baaren, 2006) concluded that it is not always advantageous to engage in thorough, conscious deliberation before making choices. They found that simple choices, such as those made between different types of towels or oven mitts, produce better results after conscious thought, but more complex tasks, such as choosing between different houses or different cars, may be better made by unconscious thought. In four studies examining consumer choices in both the laboratory and the field, the purchases of complex products produced more satisfaction when decisions had been made in the absence of attentive deliberation; simple decisions, by contrast, appeared to benefit from deliberation.

Why might complex decisions be well served by unconscious heuristically driven processing? In a series of studies, Dijksterhuis (2004) presented participants with complex decisions in which they had to choose from various alternatives, each with several attributes. Some participants were asked to think about the decision for a few minutes; others were distracted for a few minutes and then made their decisions. Those who made the decision unconsciously (after the distraction) made the best decisions. Dijksterhuis concluded that when unconscious thought takes over, more clear, more polarized, and more integrated representations of choices are formed in memory, leading to better decisions.

Precisely because these decisions are made unconsciously, it is impossible to determine exactly what shortcuts or heuristic processes were undertaken. Nor is it clear that complex decisions would always be better made by letting the brain unconsciously sift through alternatives with multiple features. Nonetheless, Dijksterhuis's work supports an important conclusion: The idea that rational conscious deliberation always leads to better choices and should only be jettisoned in situations with efficiency pressures is clearly flawed. Under many circumstances, people have evolved heuristics and shortcuts that serve them very well in situations involving complex inference choices and decisions.

Motivated Inference

Another reason apparent errors in human inference processes may actually represent benefits, at least under some circumstances, stems from the fact that inferences serve purposes other than accuracy and efficiency. They also meet motivational needs. As we saw in Chapter 5, many of the inferences we form about our personal characteristics, the controllability and orderliness of the world, and the benign future (e.g., S. E. Taylor & Brown, 1988) reduce anxiety, meet needs for self-esteem, or generally are in service of theories about how the world works. As such, sometimes we juggle the information in the world so it will come out right.

People actively construct theories concerning why positive and negative events might befall them and enhance the perceived likelihood that positive events will happen to them (Kunda, 1987). For example, upon learning that the divorce rate for first marriages is 40%, most people predict that they will not be in that 40%, but rather will remain married to their spouse for their lifetime. They convince themselves that this is the case by highlighting their personal attributes that might be associated with a stable marriage and downplaying the significance of, or actively refuting information that might suggest, a vulnerability to divorce. Thus, for example, one might point to one's parents' 50-year marriage, the close family life that existed in one's early childhood, and the fact that one's high school relationship lasted a full 4 years as evidence for a likely stable marriage. The fact that one's husband has already been divorced once, a factor that predicts a second divorce, might be interpreted not only as not leading to divorce in one's own case but as a protective factor ("He does not want this marriage to fail like the last one, so he's working especially hard to keep our relationship strong"). The ability to draw seemingly rational relationships between our own assets and good events and to argue away associations between our own attributes and negative events helps us to maintain the correlations that we want to see in the world.

Another reason that people hold blatantly false beliefs is that such beliefs may be motivating. Each day many people make a "to do" list of the activities they hope and expect to accomplish that day. Such lists are invariably overly optimistic, and the person is left at the end of the day with many tasks undone, which are then transferred to the next day. Normatively speaking, the person's behavior should change in the direction of listing only the number of tasks he or she can reasonably be expected to complete. Yet the overly optimistic behavior persists daily despite repeated disconfirmation (Buehler, Griffin, & Ross, 1994).

It is likely that such robust inferential biases persist because they succeed in getting people to accomplish more than if their assessments of their likely accomplishments were more realistic. Such biases as unrealistic optimism and an exaggerated sense of personal control, for example, fuel the desire to reach goals that might otherwise seem out of reach and help people persist when barriers seem formidable (Armor & Taylor, 1998; Armor & Taylor, 2003; S. E. Taylor & Brown, 1988).

Certain robust inferential biases may persist not only because they fuel positive emotions and self-esteem but also because they minimize perceived risk. A friend once consulted with her accountant about what steps she should take to make her financial life more predictable and solid. His response was "Don't do anything and don't go anywhere." If we recognized objectively the risks to which we are all vulnerable, this recognition might well be incapacitating. Although people often overestimate their vulnerability to low probability risks, human inference is often marked by an underestimation of common risks (S. E. Taylor & Gollwitzer, 1995), and particularly an underestimation of cumulative risk (Knäupner, Kornik, Atkinson, Guberman, & Aydin, 2005). Some inferential biases may be protective against what might otherwise be an immobilizing appreciation of risk. Because many psychologists are involved in trying to get people to accurately recognize the risks they incur, as through faulty health behaviors, for example, it might seem counterintuitive to suggest that a potential benefit of inferential strategies is the minimization of risk. Indeed, some risks clearly need to be recognized and dealt with, for example, the necessity of using seatbelts, condoms, and health screening tests. Inferential biases that maintain or restore positive feelings may act primarily on emotions, but to the extent that they affect behavior, they may be problematic. Recall from Chapter 5, however, that when people are feeling good about themselves and their situations (i.e., they are less threatened), they are paradoxically more receptive to the behavioral implications of personal risk-related information.

A more complete consideration of the motives that social inference serves reveals that normatively incorrect inferences may nonetheless be very useful for meeting personal goals, maintaining motivation and persistence, and feeling good about oneself and one's future.

NEUROECONOMICS: BACK TO THE FUTURE?

The question of how people make and should make judgments and decisions has not only been central to social cognition research but has also been important in cognitive psychology, economics, and neuroscience. From all these contributions, a recent cross-disciplinary endeavor has emerged that has the potential to integrate these disparate lines of research. It is called neuroeconomics, and it brings together insights from the three disciplines of economics, neuroscience, and psychology (Glimcher, 2003; Glimcher & Rustichini, 2004) in ways that clarify the accuracy-efficiency tradeoff and the role of motivation in inference. Roughly, the idea is to use the expected utility (EU) model, which predominates in economics, to generate predictions about how inference *should* proceed and what brain regions may accordingly be implicated; integrate those insights with research on how inference actually *does* proceed to identify other neural subsystems that are likely to be involved (such as brain regions implicated in affective input or automatic processing); and verify these integrative predictions using insights and methodologies from neuroscience such as fMRI, to see if the brain regions expected to be implicated in inference are, in fact, activated (Sanfey, Loewenstein, McClure, & Cohen, 2006). Although neuroeconomics adopts expected utility theory as its point of departure, a fact that would seem unwise given all the research just reviewed, it qualifies those predictions with insights from the descriptive theory provided by social cognition research on judgment and decision making.

The usefulness of neuroeconomics for social cognition derives from its potential to provide a unifying theoretical perspective regarding the dynamic processes by which the brain coordinates diverse neural systems to perform the complex tasks involved in inference. From this standpoint, human behavior does not result from a single process (such as the calculation of utility) but instead results from the interaction of a number of subsystems, which may produce different dispositions toward the same information. As we have seen, inferences are often in service of goals other than maximizing utility. Thus, from the neuroeconomics perspective, human inference is characterized in terms of the interactions among different subsystems that may favor alternative processes for a given decision based on goals other than maximizing utility. These alternative goals might relate to efficiency and thus implicate brain regions involved in automatic processing, or they might implicate motivational concerns, such as the desire to feel good about the self, and thus implicate brain regions involved in reward.

The usefulness of expected utility theory stems from the fact that it provides a normative model that also generates guidelines for predicting and interpreting activity in different brain regions during social inference tasks. EU implicates reward in its value function, and a considerable amount of research has explored which regions of the brain are implicated in reward and punishment. Single-cell recordings from dopamine neurons and from neurons in the orbitocortex, striatum, and posterior cingulate cortex show relations between neural activity in these regions and reward magnitude (e.g., McClure, Daw, & Montague, 2003; Padoa-Schioppa & Assad, 2006; see Sanfey et al., 2006, for a review). The mesencephalic dopamine system may be critical to value assessment and is involved in signaling errors in reward prediction, generating learning signals, updating goal states, and updating attentional focus in working memory (Sanfey et al., 2006). The norepinephrine system is also involved in this regulatory activity, specifically in the balance between seeking to maximize utility from a particular reward and seeking new sources of potential reward.

The EU model is also helpful for identifying neural activity involved in negative utility. The anterior cingulate cortex, for example, responds to potential performance costs such as response conflict, errors, and negative feedback (Sanfey et al., 2006). Research from prospect theory (see Chapter 7) suggests that these brain regions may be more responsive to relative gains and losses than to absolute levels of reward or punishment.

In terms of probability estimation (the other component involved in utility calculations), fewer generalizations have been uncovered. Activity in the medial prefrontal cortex appears to be inversely related to the likelihood of obtaining a monetary reward (Knutson, Taylor, Kaufman, Peterson, & Glover, 2005).

Activity in the lateral intraparietal area and in regions of the frontal cortex is implicated in the computation of utility, that is, in integrating the information related to value and probability of different options (Sanfey et al., 2006). The lateral intraparietal findings are significant because this region has been implicated in motor preparation, providing a potential link between thought and behavior. Activity in the striatal reward areas also correlates with expected utility.

As noted, many decisions that people make are marked by considerable uncertainty and ambiguity due to missing, incomplete, or otherwise confusing information. When choices are marked by ambiguity, activation in the amygdala and orbitocortex is seen, and reduced activation in the striatal system (which correlates positively with expected reward) is seen. Thus there appears to be a neural circuit that responds to degree of uncertainty (Hsu, Bhatt, Adolphs, Tranel, & Camerer, 2005). This set of findings is significant because the normative model implies that computations regarding decisional alternatives are not influenced by uncertainty or ambiguity, and this research clearly indicates that they are.

How does neuroeconomics integrate predictions from social cognition research? An example of input from social cognition research comes from the vital distinction between automatic and controlled processing. Whereas automatic processes are fast and efficient, controlled processes are flexible but slow and capacity-limited (see Chapter 2). Standard economic theory clearly maps onto controlled processing better than to automatic processing. It thus implicates the lateral prefrontal cortex, medial prefrontal cortex, rostral anterior cingulate, posterior parietal cortex, and the medial temporal lobe. As noted in Chapter 2, automatic processing implicates the amygdala, dorsal anterior cingulate, basal ganglia, ventromedial prefrontal cortex, and lateral temporal cortex, among other brain regions. Thus, if there are bases for predicting whether the inferential activities involved in a particular judgment task involve automatic or controlled processing, then there is a basis for predicting in advance the brain regions in which one might expect to see activity.

Other well-documented departures from the EU model generated by social cognition research involve emotional input. When emotional content is vital to judgmental behavior, one expects to see and does see activity in the brain stem reward processing structures of the limbic system (Camerer, 2003); areas of the midbrain and cortex to which they project, including the nucleus accumbens and ventromedial frontal, orbitofrontal, and anterior cingulate cortex; and amygdala and insular cortex (Sanfey, Rilling, Aronson, Nystrom, & Cohen, 2003). Deviations from normative models that include nonlinear probability weighting or loss aversion, for example, may be explicated by exploring input from these regions.

Cunningham and colleagues (2003) examined brain systems involved in automatic versus controlled evaluative (good-bad) and nonevaluative (e.g., past-present) judgments. Negatively valenced material elicited greater activity in the amygdala than positively valenced material, regardless of whether the judgment to be made was evaluative or nonevaluative. Evaluative judgments were associated with greater medial and ventrolateral PFC activity than were nonevaluative judgments. Judgments engendering ambivalence were related to greater ventrolateral PFC activity. Automatic judgments may be especially sensitive to valence, whereas controlled processing is engaged by complex judgmental tasks. Studies such as these help to specify the predictions for neural activity that can be generated by social cognition research exploring automatic versus controlled processing and evaluation.

Input from the systems involved in the regulation of emotion may also help to explain departures from the discounted utility model. People value the present highly, and steeply discount future opportunities (see Chapter 7). Consistent with this viewpoint, choices involving immediate reward actively engage the ventral striatum as well as the medial and orbitofrontal areas, which are rich in dopaminergic innervations and are associated with the evaluation of reward. Activity in the frontal parietal region, however, correlates with deferred but superior rewards, suggesting that activity in this region may be less subject to the bias of immediacy in rewards (Sanfey et al., 2006).

Integration across these different levels of analysis adds breadth to the economic models that currently guide the study of judgment and decision making. Although complex decision making and social inference do not conform to optimal strategies, such as EU, simple mechanisms, such as heuristics, may approximate optimal strategies in ways that may make departures from normative models easy to see and interpret with reference to the psychological and neural underpinnings of those inputs (Sanfey et al., 2006). The role of emotional factors in decision making and multiple inputs from both controlled and automatic processing represent two examples of research from social cognition in which the pathways are now sufficiently well mapped as to be distinctly identifiable in the context of exploring the neural pathways known to be involved in value and predictability.

Research in neuroeconomics highlights the fact that decision making involves the interaction of multiple subsystems governed by different parameters and possibly different principles, but it also provides methodologies for understanding what these different subsystems are and by what parameters and principles they might be guided. It remains to be seen if tracking utility computations using such techniques as neuroimaging will provide insights that will generalize to complex decision tasks. But it is worth the effort, given clear predictions from normative and descriptive theory and methodologies for testing them. If evidence is exchanged among all these disciplines, the understanding of social cognition not only is likely to be improved with reference to neuroeconomics but is likely to affect the models that neuroscientists and economists explore as well.

Summary

Social cognition is typically evaluated against normative models, and these evaluations reveal that human inference is marked by several distinctive features: the use of shortcuts or heuristics to make judgments and decisions in a complex and often rapidly changing environment; the role of affective and motivational considerations in inferential processes and outcomes; and the importance of prior theories and expectations for guiding inferential search and outcomes.

How flawed is the social judgment process? Three perspectives on this issue have been voiced. The first position suggests that, at least under certain circumstances, judgmental errors and biases may produce severe distortions, and therefore it is advisable to find ways to correct the inference process. Decision-making methods that can correct for common biases or errors include the use of statistics and computers for aiding judgments. In addition, developing reasoning skills through training improves people's inferential capabilities.

A second perspective suggests that the experimental literature makes people look worse than they really are, and that intuitive inferential strategies are actually quite effective in the real world. According to this viewpoint, intuitive inferential strategies often serve us well because they take into account efficiency pressures, the specific content and context of an inferential problem, and the possibility that the environment is changing. In addition, some errors may be inconsequential for behavior, others will cancel each other out, and others may be detected through communication.

A relatively new position regarding human inference is that, at least under some circumstances, heuristically based judgments are actually better than more thoroughly considered ones. For example, experts may be able to make rapid use of vast stores of nonconscious knowledge to produce judgments that are more accurate than judgments made via conscious deliberation. For many mundane tasks as well, our minds are able to integrate or extract information from a broad array of stimuli to reach complex judgments in a matter of seconds, even milliseconds. Moreover, under at least some circumstances, conscious reflection on the beliefs that go into our inferences may actually harm the inference process.

Where is the study of social inference headed? Increasingly, insights from social cognition are being integrated with insights from economics and neuroscience, and one outcome of these interactions is the field of neuroeconomics. Neuroeconomics draws on the expected utility normative model, descriptive research from social cognition, and insights and methodologies from neuroscience to identify exactly what neurotransmitters and brain regions are implicated in particular types of inference tasks. The assumptions guiding this endeavor include the fact that, although normative models are not descriptive of human inference, inferential shortcuts may approximate normative models in ways that are useful not only for identifying what neural mechanisms may be involved in normative calculations but also in the automatic, theory-driven, and affectively based shortcuts that people often use. The potential promise of this integrative effort is that research will be able to identify the interaction of multiple subsystems governed by different parameters and different principles by testing hypotheses derived from normative and descriptive research using the methodologies of neuroscience.

Cognitive Structures of Attitudes

Suppose a high school classmate is coming to visit for the weekend, and you want to plan a little party. Your classmate happens to be gay. You wonder how your current (mostly straight) friends will react to your guest of honor if they find out. To avoid any potential awkwardness, it might be better to know your friends' attitudes before inviting them. But how best to know? With most of your friends, the topic of homosexuality may never have come up in conversation. You could ask directly, but you might not get an honest answer because some of your friends might try to conceal antigay prejudices.

Your friends' attitudes matter because they can predict behavior, but attitudes cannot be observed directly. Because an attitude must be inferred from an individual's overt response to some stimulus, it is considered a hypothetical mediating variable. That is, psychologists assume that an attitude intervenes between an observable stimulus (S) and an observable response (R), providing the necessary link. Even when S-R behaviorism dominated psychology, the attitude concept continued to be indispensable to social psychology, as noted in Chapter 1.

The core definition of this hypothetical variable, attitude, is evaluation, though definitions do vary (e.g., Ajzen, 2001; Albarracín, Johnson, & Zanna, 2005; Crano & Prislin, 2006; Eagly & Chaiken, 2005; Fiske, 2004). Attitudes categorize a stimulus along an evaluative dimension (Zanna & Rempel, 1988). As such, attitudes broadly dispose people to respond positively or negatively, as inferred from their specific cognitive, affective, and behavioral responses.

BACKGROUND

Early in the 20th century Gordon Allport (1935) declared attitudes to be "the most distinctive and indispensable concept in contemporary American social psychology" (p. 798). The field sprang from various attitude research motivated by World War II: propaganda and persuasion (Hovland, Janis, & Kelley, 1953; Hovland, Lumsdaine, & Sheffield, 1949); anti-Semitic and antidemocratic prejudice (Adorno, Frenkel-Brunswik, Levinson, & Sanford, 1950); and satisfaction and deprivation in the military (Stouffer, Suchman, DeVinney,

Star, & Williams, 1949). These early efforts leaned heavily on attitudes both as measures and as important theoretical variables. Most of the first few decades of social psychology concentrated on how to measure and define attitudes. Since then, attitudes have permeated every topic in the field. This book focuses on their cognitive correlates, and Chapter 15 considers their links to behavior.

Because attitude research dates to the beginning of social psychology, social cognition research at first seemed unnecessary to traditionalists. Social cognition's initial contribution to attitude research was a fine-grained analysis of the mediating processes (e.g., attention, memory) presumably involved in attitude formation and change. Traditional variables such as features of the communicator or the message could be examined in new ways, and this helped establish the merits of the cognitive approach. Focusing on this central area illustrated to early skeptics what was unique about social cognition approaches. Now attitudes and social cognition share the first section of the field's flagship *Journal of Personality and Social Psychology,* and attitude research fully complements social cognition perspectives by (a) revealing common processes between cognitions that are less evaluatively laden (e.g., heuristics) and those that are more so (e.g., attitudes), (b) providing theoretical breadth to some central social cognitive topics (e.g., stereotyping, prejudice), and (c) emphasizing affect (or at least evaluation) and behavior.

Although social cognition research enriches current attitude research, cognition was also present in earlier theories. Among the most influential approaches to attitudes have been the cognitive consistency theories (Abelson et al., 1968). Dominating social psychology journals in the 1960s, their fundamental assumption held that inconsistencies—among cognitions, among affects, or between cognitions and affects—cause attitude change. Cognitive dissonance theory (Festinger, 1957) and balance theory (Heider, 1958) exemplify this, as we will see. Other major theories of attitudes also reserve an important role for cognition (Fishbein, 1963; Insko & Cialdini, 1969; Kiesler, 1971; Osgood & Tannenbaum, 1955; M. J. Rosenberg, 1956, 1960). Although we can only allude to the vast literature on attitudes, the critical point is this: Cognition plays a major role in practically every attitude theory, except perhaps classically conditioned attitudes (Staats & Staats, 1958) and mere exposure effects (e.g., Zajonc, 1980b; see Chapter 14). However, until the cognitive revolution, attitude theory could not draw on advances in cognitive psychology, social cognition, and, more recently, human neuroscience.

One early attitude theory especially foreshadows modern cognitive approaches because it is expressly a sequential information processing model. Remember that Chapter 1 described early information processing models as breaking mental operations into sequential stages. McGuire's (1969, 1976, 1985) chain of cognitive responses outlines the necessary conditions, many of them cognitive, for a persuasive communication to influence behavior; the steps include exposure, attention, comprehension, yielding, retention, retrieval, decision, and behavior. Consider, as an example, political campaign literature. To be effective, not only must campaign managers expose voters to the literature, say, by distributing a leaflet under people's windshield wipers, but they also must ensure that the pamphlet grabs attention and conveys an understandable, convincing message. People have to retain their (presumably positive) new attitude, retrieve it, and decide to use it to determine the critical behavior: voting for Smedley rather than Smiley for dogcatcher. The entire sequence of carefully specified cognitive steps theoretically results in behavior. As such, the theory anticipates more recent cognitively oriented work in attitudes. Moreover, several of the stages specified by McGuire continue to be important in current work (Eagly & Chaiken, 1984).

Comparing Older and Newer Approaches to Attitudes

The newer cognitive approaches in this chapter and in Chapter 10 build on the older attitude theories in several crucial respects. Many of the critical variables are the same. Some of the methodological procedures were established long ago and continue to form the basis of research paradigms. For example, current researchers sometimes reuse old experimental designs, adding mainly a more detailed analysis of intervening processes. Another carryover from older research is that many of the current theoretical issues are variants on earlier problems. Finally, many of the older approaches were heavily cognitive, as just described.

But the older and newer approaches also differ: First are what might be called *metatheoretical* differences between the two; that is, major conceptual differences separate the overarching framework common to most consistency theories versus the overarching framework behind social cognition's approach to attitude research. Most "cognitive" consistency theories posited a strong motivational basis toward consistency; the usual metatheory behind consistency theories was a drive to reduce internal discrepancies. The consistency theories were not typically designed to be theories about the cognitive system operating on its own nonmotivational principles. A traditional consistency theory might posit that people resolve discrepancies to avoid the uncomfortable feeling of holding two conflicting beliefs. In contrast, cognitive approaches are based on current understandings of the cognitive system. For example, to deal with inconsistencies, a current cognitive approach might posit that people resolve discrepancies mainly for reasons of efficiency in memory storage.

Second, specific theoretical differences distinguish the older and newer approaches. The newer approaches explicitly draw on cognitive theories unavailable earlier. These theories potentially provide precise frameworks that detail the organization and processing of information in persuasion, which permit a more careful analysis of cognitive processes related to attitude change.

Third, many new methods for studying attitude change have evolved in directions borrowed from cognitive psychology. Attitude theories have long posited internal structures (Zajonc, 1968b), but more fine-grained analysis of cognitive organization and dynamics (typical of cognitive psychology) has become possible in attitude research with recent advances in measurement techniques. During the 1970s, information processing research on attitudes expanded in several directions based on metatheoretical, theoretical, and methodological developments.

In reviewing the directions of newer research, we will see that much of it draws on a framework for persuasion research described by Lasswell (1948) and elaborated by Hovland, Janis, and Kelley (1953): *who says what to whom in what channel with what effect.* Thus the research tends to focus on characteristics of the communicator, the message, the audience, the modality, and the lasting effects of attitude change. Although Hovland, Janis, and Kelley's program of research did not explicitly represent an information processing viewpoint, it did anticipate McGuire's chain of persuasion and other theories that emphasize internal processes such as attention and comprehension. Moreover, much of the current cognitive research is an effort to explain effects originally uncovered by the classic Hovland, Janis, and Kelley research.

This chapter first addresses some of the more strictly cognitive features of two traditional attitude theories, dissonance theory and balance theory, anticipating modern social cognition. Next, we look at three cognitive approaches that rely on people's lay theories of attitude change: the audience's attributional response to the communicator as a person, people's ideas about information exchanged in groups, and people's ideas about their own attitude change. As you will see, cognitively oriented attitude research is coming full circle to address motivational issues that originally sparked the interest of early attitude theorists.

COGNITIVE FEATURES OF TWO CONSISTENCY THEORIES

The consistency theories of attitudes proposed in the late 1950s predicted the interplay between attitudes and cognitive processes. For each case, we begin by briefly reviewing the most relevant consistency theory as background and then describe current cognitive interpretations. The sections focus on dissonance theory and selective perception, on dissonance theory and selective learning, and on balance theory and selective recall of information about others (also see Zajonc, 1968b).

Dissonance Theory and Selective Perception

Dissonance theory (Festinger, 1957) focuses on inconsistency among cognitions to describe how beliefs and behavior change attitudes. In this view, inconsistency causes a motivational state called dissonance. If you believe that smoking causes cancer (a cognition) but you smoke anyway (a conflicting cognition about behavior), you leave yourself open to cognitive dissonance. Researchers hypothesized that dissonance causes an aversive state of arousal, and subsequent work showed that to be the case (e.g., Elliott & Devine, 1994; Losch & Cacioppo, 1990; see Fazio & Cooper, 1983, for an earlier review). If you think about the inconsistency between your smoking and knowing that it causes cancer, you become uncomfortable and tense. The drive to reduce that arousal (discomfort) consequently makes you rearrange your cognitions to reduce dissonance. Although theoretically one could change one's behavior to reduce the inconsistency, most dissonance research has focused on circumstances in which the inconsistent cognitions are more likely to change. This focus on cognitive change was partly an experimental strategy to investigate cognitive processes per se. Also, behavior responds more to reality constraints (i.e., it's often public), so it is harder to change than are one's cognitions or attitudes.

Most ways to increase consistency are cognitive. Suppose that you smoke and that you have several cognitions relevant to that behavior (or pick any unhealthy habit). You may have a couple of cognitions consonant with your smoking (it tastes good; it is relaxing) and several dissonant with smoking (it causes cancer; it is expensive; it is smelly; other people dislike it). Because the number of dissonant cognitions outweigh the consonant ones, cognitive inconsistency results, and you may experience dissonance. To reduce the dissonance, you can change your cognitions in various ways: add or subtract cognitions (i.e., change your beliefs) to increase the ratio of consonant to dissonant ones (e.g., add in the idea that smoking keeps weight down and subtract the smell and the expense), or reduce the importance of dissonant conditions (e.g., I'll die of something anyway, so why worry about cancer). This by no means exhausts the possibilities (see Cooper, 1995; Petty & Wegener, 1998).

To summarize, dissonance theory posits that inconsistent cognitions cause arousal; a drive to reduce the arousal often leads to a change in one's attitude-relevant cognitions. Consequently, as we will see, people often avoid cognitions that are inconsistent with an attitude or a behavior.

Selective Perception

Consistency theorists in general (Abelson et al., 1968) posit that people seek out, notice, and interpret data to reinforce their attitudes. Dissonance theory in particular predicts that people will avoid information that increases dissonance; that is, people favor information consistent with their attitudes and behavior. For present purposes, the work on selective perception divides into selective exposure (seeking consistent information not already present), selective attention (looking at consistent information once it is there), and selective interpretation (translating ambiguous information to be consistent).

Selective exposure is a principle that deserves to be true (McGuire, 1969), but much of the initial evidence was unfortunately mixed (Brehm & Cohen, 1962; Freedman & Sears, 1965; J. Mills, 1968; Wicklund & Brehm, 1976). Intellectual honesty and fairness sometimes prompt people to seek out information that is inconsistent with their attitudes (Sears, 1965). Information's utility and novelty often override dissonance in determining exposure (Brock, Albert, & Becker, 1970). However, de facto selective exposure is clear: most of us inhabit an environment biased in favor of congenial positions (Sears, 1968; but see E. Katz, 1968). People tend to pick friends, magazines, movies, and television shows that reinforce their attitudes, which, in turn, are reinforced by those agreeing others. Also, people's contacts shape their attitudes in the first place, so people tend to agree with the information that surrounds them.

Thus initial support for selective exposure as a result of attitudes mainly pointed to de facto selective exposure. Subsequent refinement of the hypothesis suggests that various conditions that increase dissonance also increase selective exposure: having made a clear choice or public commitment (Frey, 1986); a personally important attitude (Holbrook, Berent, Krosnick, Visser, & Boninger, 2005); increasing commitment as information arrives sequentially (Jonas, Schulz-Hardt, Frey, & Thelen, 2001); limited search options, presuming supportive information is the best (Fischer, Jonas, Frey, & Schulz-Hardt, 2005); and finally, when reminded that life is short, focusing on relevant and important attitudes (Jonas, Greenberg, & Frey, 2003). Thus, under particular conditions, selective exposure to attitude-consonant information does occur. This aspect of selective perception addresses an important cognitive process—namely, information seeking—and sets up the two other aspects of selective perception: attention and interpretation.

Selective attention responds to consistency pressures. People often look longer at consistent than inconsistent evidence (Brock & Balloun, 1967; A. R. Cohen, Brehm, & Latane, 1959; Jecker, 1964). For example, one study (J. M. Olson & Zanna, 1979) divided participants into repressors (people who typically avoid threatening stimuli) and sensitizers (people who typically investigate threatening stimuli). Both groups reported their attitudes toward some paintings. The experimenter then allowed them to choose a pair to keep. The pairs all included one painting they liked and one they disliked.

After the decision, participants looked at the pair they had chosen. Dissonance theory predicts that they would focus on the positive aspects of their choice; that is, the preferred painting within the chosen pair. Only repressors behaved as predicted; their looking times at the choice-consistent painting were high compared to control subjects, and they avoided looking at the painting inconsistent with their expressed choice. Thus consistent information elicited the selective attention of repressors only. Chronic optimists, like repressors, also avoid threatening stimuli (Isaacowitz, 2005). And stress increases selective attention (Chajut & Algom, 2003), probably because of limited online resources. Selective attention, hence, operates for some of the people some of the time, and also for some stimuli some of the time; for example, people selectively attend to counterarguments that they can easily refute (Kleinhesselink & Edwards, 1975).

People also protect their attitudes by *selective interpretation* (apart from exposure and attention). People's attitudes can change their interpretations of what they see (e.g., Vidmar & Rokeach, 1974). Consider some examples: attitudes toward presidential candidates influence judged debate performance (Fazio & Williams, 1986; Holbrook et al., 2005), attitudes toward the Palestinian-Israeli conflict influence judged fairness of news coverage (Vallone, Ross, & Lepper, 1985), attitudes toward an outgroup influence attributions about the group's behavior (Pettigrew, 1979), and expectations about the introduction of the Euro influenced Germans' judgments of price increases (Traut-Mattausch, Schulz-Hardt, Greitemeyer, & Frey, 2004). Although not always based precisely on dissonance theory's predictions about selective interpretation, these examples fit it, as well as frameworks more explicitly drawn from social cognition.

Conclusion

A final word about dissonance and selective perception. Cross-cultural work suggests that cognitive dissonance operates differently in different cultural contexts. Consider an example of dissonance reduction involving retrospective perception. Typically, Europeans and European Americans justify their choices by reinterpreting their chosen alternative as clearly superior and emphasizing its virtues and downplaying its flaws while doing the reverse for nonchosen alternatives, after the fact. This process reduces the dissonance created by the virtues of the nonchosen alternatives and the pitfalls of the chosen alternative. This phenomenon, called spreading the alternatives, is well documented in these populations from early on (Brehm, 1956). However, East Asians do not necessarily justify their decisions (Heine & Lehman, 1997). In keeping with characteristics of relatively interdependent cultures, they do so only when self-relevant others are primed (Kitayama, Snibbe, Markus, & Suzuki, 2004) or when they make a choice for a friend (Hoshino-Browne et al., 2005). Thus postdecisional dissonance reduction and the effects of dissonance on selective attention and interpretation may depend on cultural context.

To summarize, dissonance theory predicts that people are motivated to avoid information that is inconsistent with their attitudes or choices. The evidence for selective exposure is mixed, but the evidence for selective attention and interpretation is stronger. From the outset people are biased at least by attention and misperception to gather data that reinforce their beliefs. This early insight from the consistency framework fits with the social cognition emphasis on analyzing the stages of information processing, so it anticipates social cognition research in this respect. Of late, this work has also profited from social cognition approaches.

Dissonance Theory and Selective Learning

Proponents of dissonance and other consistency theories also predict selective learning and memory for attitude-consistent information. This prediction was not unique to dissonance theorists; selective memory for attitude consistency was one of the first questions in attitude research (J. M. Levine & Murphy, 1943; Watson & Hartmann, 1939). Earlier and some later theories all would predict that if a couple is quarreling over whether to spend winter holidays in Vermont or in the Caribbean, the ski addict will never learn the details of bargain snorkeling tours, and the sun worshipper will never learn the details of the ski packages. Unfortunately, evidence for selective learning was "unambiguously inconclusive" (Greaves, 1972). One reviewer concluded that the published studies yielding evidence for selective learning all must be flukes because so many other studies failed to find such evidence (Greenwald, 1975). Moreover, the evidence often is flawed, and recent research suggests exactly how, based in part on insights from cognitive psychology. For example, many studies have confounded the familiarity and agreeability of arguments (Zanna & Olson, 1982). It is not surprising that the ski enthusiast would recall pro-ski arguments better than pro-sun arguments because the person has thought about the pro-ski arguments more often. Familiar arguments would be easier to recall without having to assume any dissonance-based motivation to forget the disagreeable arguments (see also Schmidt & Sherman, 1984).

Selective learning and retention of attitudinally favorable information do seem to occur under special conditions, defined in part by the contingencies of information processing. Incidental learning, rather than intentional learning, provides clearer support for selective learning effects (Malpass, 1969). That is, people are more likely to be selective when they do not know they will be tested on the material later. A travel agent who frequently has to present the details of cruises and ski packages will remember both kinds of arguments, regardless of how he or she personally feels about them. Being sufficiently motivated can overwhelm selective learning effects (Zanna & Olson, 1982).

Important attitudes specifically encourage attitude-relevant memory (Holbrook et al., 2005). In particular, strong attitudes motivate people to counterargue uncongenial messages, so they remember the message arguments (Eagly, Kulesa, Brannon, Shaw-Barnes, & Huston-Comeux, 2000); strong attitudes also motivate people to remember congenial arguments but in this case because they are pleasing. Overall, meta-analysis indicates that attitudes do not necessarily encourage attitude-consistent memory because of the effect of actively counterarguing uncongenial messages (Eagly, Chen, Chaiken, & Shaw-Barnes, 1999; Eagly, Kulesa, Chen, & Chaiken, 2001).

Other conditions that encourage selective learning depend on the kind of person one is (Zanna & Olson, 1982). People with high self-esteem are more biased in their attitudes, as are people with an internal locus of control. To return to our example, suppose one member of the couple is more self-confident and generally thinks she can influence events around her; she is precisely the one who will forget the other person's discrepant arguments. Finally, people who generally tend to repress unpleasant facts similarly tend to forget attitude-discrepant information (Zanna & Olson, 1982). The prediction of dissonance theorists and others about the selective learning of agreeable arguments does seem to be supported under the right circumstances for the right people.

Subsequent research suggests that the consistency processes may operate automatically; even people with impaired memories (amnesiacs) and people operating under cognitive load nonetheless do show dissonance-reducing attitude change (Lieberman, Ochsner, Gilbert, & Schacter, 2001). This suggests that memory's role need not be entirely explicit and conscious.

Balance Theory and Selective Recall

Adolescents fight with their parents, and their perception of these fights is shaped by the nature of their attachment to their parents (e.g., secure, ambivalent). Over time, their memory shifts to reflect their relational style even more (Feeney & Cassidy, 2003). Another consistency theory, balance theory (Heider, 1958), helps explain this. Like dissonance theory, it also inspired research on learning and retention as a function of consistency (Cottrell, Ingraham, & Monfort, 1971; Picek, Sherman, & Shiffrin, 1975; Zajonc & Burnstein, 1965). Balance theory differs from dissonance theory in that it intrinsically concerns relationships between people. According to the theory, structures in the perceiver's mind represent the perceiver (P), another person (0), and the mutual object (X). Figure 9.1 illustrates this pattern. To shift to a relatively simple example, you (P) may have an attitude toward your roommate (0) and toward his car (X), and you may perceive him as having a certain attitude toward his car. Your perceptions of the relations among you two and the old clunker may be of two sorts, either positive or negative. Liking, owning, or belonging with something is a positive relationship (+); disliking or not belonging together is a negative relationship (−).

The combination of relationships among you three may be either balanced or imbalanced. Essentially, they are balanced if you are either agreeing friends or disagreeing enemies. Suppose you like your roommate (P-0 is +), and he likes his car (0-X is +); then the three of you are a "balanced" trio if you develop an affection for the car (P-X is +).

Now consider the possibility that you like your roommate (+), he adores his car (+), and you cannot stand the car (−). Trouble awaits an imbalanced relationship such as this. Imbalanced relationships are under some pressure to change toward balance, and that is how the theory predicts attitude change. Your perception of any of the three relationships is likely to change in order to create balance. For example, people may interpret people they like (P-0 is +) as liking what they like (P-X is +, so O-X is +) and disliking what they dislike

Basic cognitive structure

Balanced structures

Imbalanced structures

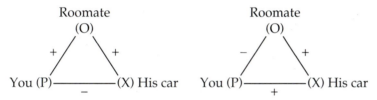

FIGURE 9.1. Balance theory triads

(P-X is −, so O-X is −). Most people interpret close friends and favored political candidates as sharing their attitudes more closely than is the case (Ottati, Fishbein, & Middlestadt, 1988), and this may even be adaptive (Levinger & Breedlove, 1966). When people become romantically involved, for example, their attitudes tend to align (Davis & Rusbult, 2001). People are uncomfortable having attitudes that disagree with liked others, and they can experience intense ambivalence as a result (Priester & Petty, 2001). In fact, priming social groups makes people's attitudes more similar to those groups, as if people are preparing to get along with them (Kawakami, Dovidio, & Dijksterhuis, 2003).

Balance theory shows how cognitive constraints shape learning and memory relevant to attitudes. The prediction that balanced relationships are easier to recall derives from consistency theories and developed through schema theories. Traditional balance research shows, for example, that people can learn and generate balanced social structures more easily than imbalanced ones (Feather, 1969; Zajonc & Burnstein, 1965). Social schema research suggests that balanced relationships are stored in memory as a single unit. People more easily remember that two friends agree or that two enemies disagree; either makes a compact chunk of memory. It is harder to recall that one of two roommates likes chocolate and the other hates it and which feels which way.

Balance researchers suggest cognitive mechanisms that explain why balanced relationships are easier to recall (Picek et al., 1975; Sentis & Burnstein,

1979). Balanced and imbalanced relationships are stored differently: People appear to store balanced relationships as a single cognitive unit, whereas imbalanced ones are stored less efficiently, in pieces. In this research, people initially learn some imbalanced triads. Subsequently, the time it takes them to retrieve a single relationship depends on the number of relationships (P-0, 0-X, X-P) the experimenter uses as a recall cue; the more pieces of the three-way imbalanced relationship that are supplied, the faster the triad of relationships can be retrieved. However, with balanced relationships, the number of pieces supplied by the experimenter does not matter; the time to retrieve the entire balanced triad is the same regardless of the number of recall cues. This implies, then, that a balanced triad is a single cognitive unit that must be retrieved all at once, but an imbalanced triad is not (Sentis & Burnstein, 1979).

In sum, people learn and recall balanced sets of information more easily than imbalanced ones. Such bits of information as agreeing friends and disagreeing enemies form a single compact cognitive unit in memory, as opposed to imbalanced combinations.

Attitudes Organize Memory

A general principle emerges from the research inspired originally by consistency theories: Attitudes serve to organize memory under many circumstances. In particular, making an attitudinal judgment improves recall of attitude-relevant evidence and creates attitude-consistent inferences. This fits with research from person perception as well (Ostrom, Lingle, Pryor, & Geva, 1980). Hence, if you judge a man's suitability as a pilot, you will remember his superior eyesight and infer that he has good spatial ability. If you judge his suitability as a comedian, on the other hand, you will recall his infectious laugh and infer that he has stage presence (Lingle et al., 1979). The effect seems to be mediated by your recalling the attitude itself, once formed, rather than retrieving and resynthesizing all the individual bits of evidence. Once you have formed an attitude about somebody as a pilot instead of a comedian, that attitude organizes subsequent judgments, including recall of the data on which the judgment was based. The attitude is easier to recall than the supporting evidence (Lingle & Ostrom, 1979; Loken, 1984).

Recent research twists this organizing role of attitudes. When people's attitudes change, they retain both the old and new attitude in memory, as the old attitude seems to go underground. Dual attitudes comprise an older, automatic attitude and the newer, explicitly accessible attitude (Wilson, Lindsey, & Schooler, 2000). Which one is expressed depends on the method of expression; the older attitude may pop out unawares when one responds automatically or under cognitive load. The coexisting attitudes can create subtle forms of ambivalence (Petty, Tormala, Briñol, & Jarvis, 2006), undermining confidence, extending consideration of pros and cons, and creating automatic neutrality under time pressure.

Conclusion

Traditional consistency theories were among the earliest frameworks to predict the effects of attitudes on selective perception, learning, and memory. This work both anticipated social cognition approaches and was ultimately much developed by them. Dissonance theory views people as motivated to avoid information inconsistent with their attitudes. Although the evidence for selective exposure is uneven, the evidence for selective attention and interpretation is clearer. Dissonance theorists and others also hypothesized the selective learning of attitudinally agreeable arguments, a prediction supported under certain circumstances for certain people for certain attitude objects. In a similar vein, balanced triads (consistent interpersonal pairs with a common attitude object) are easier to learn and remember, apparently because they form a compact unit in memory. Finally, people's attitudes more generally organize memory.

LAY THEORIES AND ATTITUDE CHANGE

So far, we have examined attitude structure and its influence on attitude change. Now we turn to people's everyday social theories about why attitudes change (and do not change). One approach examines people's ideas about the perceived social context of the communicator, as it influences the perceived validity of the message. Another examines arguments that arise when a group discusses an issue. A third approach examines people contemplating their attitudes alone and applying their own theories about attitude change to that context. All three approaches acknowledge the importance of people's own beliefs about attitude change, and they fit other cognitive approaches in emphasizing people's evaluation of the information provided.

Attributional Analyses of Communicators and Their Messages

Producers of television ads are well aware that their messages have maximum impact if delivered by a gorgeous model, a respected newscaster, or a well-known millionaire; an alternative way to increase message impact is to use a communicator blatantly similar to the ordinary person, as is done in "hidden camera" testimonials. The importance of communicator attractiveness, credibility, power, and similarity was first demonstrated by Hovland, Janis, and Kelley (1953), and these variables have generated research ever since, some to be reviewed in Chapter 10.

One of the early manifestations of social cognition research influencing attitude research came from attributional approaches to persuasion (see Eagly & Chaiken, 1984, for a review). In particular, attributional perspectives have helped attitude theorists approach the problem of communicator credibility (Eagly, Chaiken, & Wood, 1981). For example, persuasion depends in part on the recipient's analysis of why a communicator advocates a particular position. Recipients attempt to determine the validity of a persuasive message, knowing some of the communicator's dispositional and situational constraints (Figure 9.2). When you hear the president of Greenpeace speaking to the local Greenpeace chapter, you know that both his own opinion (a dispositional factor) and that of his audience (a situational factor) predispose him to advocate the environmental advantages of strict auto emission controls. If this is, in fact, the message, it is apparently less valid and less persuasive than if it were completely independent of such dispositional and situational pressures. Messages constrained by the

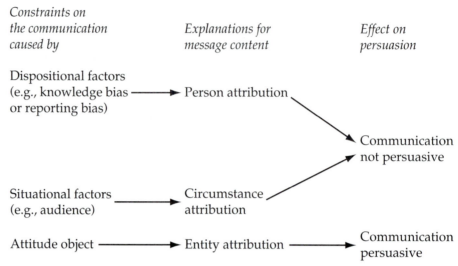

Constraints on
the communication
caused by

Explanations for
message content

Effect on
persuasion

Dispositional factors
(e.g., knowledge bias ⟶ Person attribution
or reporting bias)

Communication
not persuasive

Situational factors ⟶ Circumstance
(e.g., audience)   attribution

Attitude object ⟶ Entity attribution ⟶ Communication
persuasive

FIGURE 9.2. An attributional analysis of communicator effects in persuasion

situation or the communicator may or may not validly represent the truth, so they are not impactful. It is too easy to attribute the speaker's harangue to an (environmentalist) audience-pleasing bias or to his own biases; he can be biased either in what he is willing to say in public (reporting bias) or in what he knows (knowledge bias) (Eagly, Wood, & Chaiken, 1978). In contrast, if the president of General Motors makes the same environmentalist point to fellow industry chiefs, he is indeed believable and persuasive.

These predictions about communicator credibility derive from Kelley's (1967, 1972a) analysis of multiple sufficient causes, which states that if several plausible causes exist, the weaker ones are discounted (see Chapter 6). In this case, if both disposition (he is a crusader) and circumstances (Greenpeace audience) conspire to produce the speech, the alternative cause, the facts, need not support the speech. A careful step-by-step test of this model demonstrates that subjects' perceptions of a communicator's background (e.g., he has strong opinions) cause the predicted attributions (e.g., he is biased). Attributions that cast credibility into doubt decrease opinion change (Wood & Eagly, 1981). Thus this approach focuses on the communicator-message interaction.

Communicator attractiveness also profits from an attributional perspective. In one study, Eagly and Chaiken (1975) explored the idea that attractive communicators are not only more persuasive in general (a well-established finding) but are especially persuasive if they advocate an undesirable position. Because attractive people are expected to advocate attractive positions, an attractive person advocating an undesirable position must be doing so because the position is valid. To test this, Eagly and Chaiken presented participants with a communicator who either liked or disliked undergraduates and who made either optimistic or pessimistic statements, for example, about college graduates' employment opportunities or about the future spread of venereal disease. Attractive communicators were considerably more persuasive than unattractive communicators when advocating undesirable (pessimistic) positions (cf. Wachtler

& Counselman, 1981). Messages that are unexpected, given the communicator's dispositions and the communication setting, are more persuasive than messages that are wholly predictable on the basis of who is saying them (Eagly, Chaiken, & Wood, 1981; Goethals, 1976). An unexpected position—given the communicator's self-interest—increases perceived trustworthiness and accuracy, so it decreases message processing, resulting in heuristic agreement (Petty, Fleming, Priester, & Feinstein, 2001).

Attribution theory also explains similarity and agreement effects. Those who agree with us seem objective, responding to the facts, while those who disagree with us seem biased by their own values. Both tendencies are exaggerated by other kinds of dissimilarity between self and others (Goethals, 1976). The attributional explanation for these effects draws on Kelley's covariation model of attribution (Chapter 6) as follows: Consider two people discussing nonsmokers' rights. Their agreement means consensus, and high consensus encourages an entity attribution to the attitude object (i.e., the topic being discussed). In our example, the agreeing pair attribute their shared attitude to the justice of nonsmokers' rights. However, agreement by a dissimilar other is a particularly informative kind of consensus information (Goethals, 1976); the clearer the consensus, the more likely that the opinion is caused by the entity (the topic) in question rather than by peculiar people or situations. Consequently, if one of the pair is a smoker and the other a nonsmoker, and if they could actually agree, each would be especially persuaded that the cause was just, an entity attribution.

In contrast, low consensus, or a disagreement by another, paves the way for person or situation attributions. When the two people disagree, each thinks the other is not an objective judge of the facts but is letting emotional prejudices get in the way. Given that the situation is usually the same for both parties, the remaining cause has to be the other person's dispositions. However, the arguers are even more likely to believe each other biased (i.e., make a dispositional attribution) if one is a beleaguered smoker and the other an angry nonsmoker rather than two similar individuals. Thus a dissimilar other exaggerates the effect of disagreement as well as agreement. Intergroup cultural divides begin this way (D. T. Miller & Prentice, 1999).

People not only believe that an agreeing source is credible, they also misattribute agreeable positions to credible sources (Fragale & Heath, 2004). The heuristic implies that firm beliefs come from good sources. In general, people create a fit among a persuasive message, its source, and its validity: Familiar others are persuasive (Weisbuch, Mackie, & Garcia-Marques, 2003), reasonable messages that fit our motivational focus are persuasive (Cesario, Grant, & Higgins, 2004; Evans & Petty, 2003), and irrelevant emotions spill over to shape source trustworthiness (Dunn & Schweitzer, 2005). All this suggests fit among persuasion's elements, consistent both with attributional analyses and with balance theory.

To summarize, attribution theories of communicator-message interplay explain when people view a communication as invalid and, therefore, not persuasive—by attribution to the communicator's dispositional biases or situational pressures. Conversely, attributional analyses also explain when people view the communication as valid and persuasive—by attribution neither to the communicator nor to the situation but to the facts. When people make an entity attribution (i.e., to the attitude object), the communicator seems to present objective facts and is most persuasive. In sum, attributional analyses clarify various communicator variables interacting with message and context variables.

Group Polarization: Social Cognitive Explanations

Another cognitive analysis of attitudes examines group-level attitude change. It focuses on how people respond to the information provided by social interaction based on their theories about where they personally stand compared to other group members.

The background for group-level attitude research comes from work in the early 1960s on group decision making. Many people think that groups represent the voice of reason and compromise; decisions made by committee are supposed to be safer than decisions made by individuals. A closer look at group decisions reveals that this is not at all the case. One research area in particular focused on the comparative riskiness of group and individual decisions (Stoner, 1961; Wallach, Kogan, & Bem, 1962). Graduate students made decisions in and out of groups on items such as the following: "A college senior planning graduate work in chemistry may enter University X where, because of rigorous standards, only a fraction of the graduate students receive the PhD, or may enter University Y, which has a poorer reputation but where almost every graduate student receives the PhD." In most cases, students who discussed this case (and others like it) emerged from the group discussion favoring a riskier alternative than when they went into the discussion. Thus the group decision was riskier than the average of the individual decisions.

Quantities of research were generated by this counterintuitive result (Rajecki, 1982). Some of the explanations relied on traditional variables such as norms and values (normative influences), but one relied on a cognitive interpretation of the group interaction (an informational influence). As an example of the more traditional explanations, consider the possible influences of group norms. Researchers proposed that people in cohesive groups feel protected from the consequences of their decision; they can hide behind the group, in effect. This "diffusion of responsibility" hypothesis fell into disfavor when it was discovered that group attitudes do not change simply when a group feels cohesive; rather, some relevant discussion appears to be necessary (Pruitt & Teger, 1969).

Another traditional explanation was that people value risk more than caution. When people assemble in a group and compare their opinions, most of them discover that at least some others are taking riskier stands than they are. Because risk is valued, so the argument goes, the group gravitates toward the riskier extreme. This explanation in terms of social comparison and "risk as a value" faltered when researchers discovered that many groups shift toward a more cautious extreme after discussion (McCauley, Stitt, Woods, & Lipton, 1973). The shift toward caution also undercut the diffusion of responsibility hypothesis. Why should a group need to diffuse responsibility for more cautious decisions?

These traditional theories contrast with some possible cognitive explanations, which have support. *Persuasive arguments theory* (Burnstein & Vinokur, 1973; for a review, see Isenberg, 1986) proposed that attitudes in groups polarize toward relatively extreme (cautious or risky) alternatives when people are exposed to new information. Assume a pool of possible arguments for any given attitude.

When group members argue their positions, they encounter other people's arguments that had not yet occurred to them as individuals. Group attitude change depends on whether everyone already knows similar arguments, in which case the group members are not exposed to much new information. Change also depends on how many arguments potentially could support a given position. An attitude with many good arguments supporting it has a higher probability of those arguments coming to light than does an attitude with fewer supporting arguments.

One critical test of the persuasive arguments theory comes from a study in which students were either (1) exposed to the opinions of others and given time to think about those opinions, (2) exposed to the opinions of others and not given time to think about the opinions, or (3) not exposed to the opinions of others but given time to think about the topic (Burnstein & Vinokur, 1975). Only some students' attitudes changed: those who knew the opinions of others and who had time to generate supporting arguments for them. In other supportive studies, information is exchanged in an actual discussion (Burnstein & Sentis, 1981; Rajecki, 1982). Both the number and persuasiveness of arguments affect group polarization (Hinsz & Davis, 1984). The effect may be limited to contexts that emphasize reasonableness and considered debate (McLachlan, 1986).

Another explanation for group polarization effects relies on *social comparison theory* (see Chapter 5). In some cases, choice shift can be produced simply by information about others' positions (e.g., Teger & Pruitt, 1967). People apparently shift their opinions when they learn that, relative to the opinions of others, they themselves were not as risky as they had imagined. Such comparison processes operate most strongly when people know the risk-relevant personality traits of other people because this establishes a basis for the social comparison process (Goethals & Zanna, 1979). (For reviews of social comparison processes in group polarization, see R. Brown, 1986; Isenberg, 1986.)

A variant on the social comparison theory explanation for attitude polarization in groups comes from *social identification* and *self-categorization theories* (Turner, 1987). In Chapter 11 we explain that people categorize themselves and others into distinct social groups. As a result, people stereotype both ingroup and outgroup members and, consequently, themselves. Consistent with this theory, when people categorize others as a group and expect to join them, they perceive the group norm to be more extreme than otherwise (Mackie, 1986). Group members use the group's distinctive and consensual position to signal their identity (Postmes, Spears, Lee, & Novak, 2005). The group develops a prototype of the ideal position, which may be more extreme than the average member (McGarty, Turner, Hogg, Davidson, & Wetherell, 1992; Turner, Wetherell, & Hogg, 1989). Individuals polarize their attitudes when intergroup context is salient (Hogg, Turner, & Davidson, 1990; Turner et al., 1989). Groups polarize in the direction of the group norm especially when members are "depersonalized" (Turner, 1985) and cannot be individually identified (R. Brown, 1986; Postmes, Haslam, & Swaab, 2005; Spears, Postmes, Lea, & Wolbert, 2002, for reviews). Groups that form around a shared identity gain consensus by deduction from that identity; groups that form around relationships among independent individuals instead gain consensus by induction from members' contributions.

Group polarization effects thus depend on categorizing oneself as a member of the group making the arguments. For example, when an overheard discussion is attributed to a group one is to join, one perceives the group to have more extreme attitudes, and one's attitude shifts in conformity with those stereotypic attitudes (Mackie, 1986; Mackie & Cooper, 1984). Clearly, people use attitudes in the group categorization process (Hymes, 1986).

These cognitive theories of attitude polarization in groups provide informational bases for persuasion, either as a function of exposure to persuasive arguments, social comparison information, or prototypical ingroup opinion. These are only some of the possible explanations and only one type of attitude change in groups. Nevertheless, they illustrate the utility of cognitive approaches to understanding some aspects of groups. People's everyday ideas about the social context of their own attitudes affect their responses to information-based persuasion.

Implicit Theories About Attitude Stability and Change

People's everyday theories related to attitudes take seriously another aspect of social context—oneself. Originally, self-perception theory (D. J. Bem, 1972; see Chapter 6) posited that, when uncertain, people infer their attitudes from their own behavior. One result is that people may misrecall their own prior attitudes. After successful persuasion, people can conveniently perceive their attitudes as never having changed at all (D. J. Bem & McConnell, 1970). If a person's pre-persuasion attitudes are not salient, the person infers new attitudes from current behavior. Thus people tend to misrecall their attitudes to bring them in line with their behavior (cf. Fazio, Zanna, & Cooper, 1977; Wixon & Laird, 1976). A more recent approach elaborates perceived stability and change in one's attitudes based more explicitly on people's implicit theories of their own attitude change.

What were your attitudes toward religion 5 years ago? Fairly similar to the ones you have now? Most people assume their attitudes have been fairly stable, and in most instances they are right. However, perhaps you have undergone a conversion experience, in which case you would answer that your attitudes toward religion have changed quite a lot. Often, we stay the same, but sometimes we change. Sometimes we perceive the stability, and sometimes not. Sometimes we perceive the change, and sometimes not.

One theory (M. Ross, 1989; M. Ross & Conway, 1986) argues that people's perceptions of stability and change depend on their implicit theories of when they do and do not change. The theory posits a two-step process whereby people use their current attitudes as a starting point and then apply their theories to decide whether they would have been different in the past. Consistent with implicit theories of stability, people often do not perceive themselves to have changed when indeed they have. Subtle forms of persuasion have this impact; people perceive their initial attitudes to be similar to their current (changed) attitudes, and they claim not to have changed (D. J. Bem & McConnell, 1970; Goethals & Reckman, 1973; M. Ross & Shulman, 1973). Even when changes spontaneously emerge over time or the course of a relationship, people do not perceive their attitudes to have changed (McFarland & Ross, 1987). Moreover, because people typically assume consistency, they base their recall of past behaviors on current attitudes. The implicit theory seems to run: (a) one behaves consistently with one's attitudes, and (b) one's attitudes are stable; therefore, (c) one's current attitudes are a reliable guide to past behavior. Again, subtle persuasion can alter people's attitudes and bias their recall of prior behavior to fit their current attitude (M. Ross, McFarland, Conway, & Zanna, 1983; M. Ross, McFarland, & Fletcher, 1981). When subjects do recall past behaviors just after a changed attitude, they become more committed to the new attitude (Lydon, Zanna, & Ross, 1988; M. Ross et al., 1983). Other things being equal, we expect our attitudes to be stable and make inferences accordingly.

But other things are not always equal: people have conversions, join weight loss programs, enter therapy, get divorced, move to new places, are promoted or fired, survive wars, are victimized, grow older, and so on. People expect some events to change them, so they have implicit theories about the events' propensity to change people. Have you ever heard anyone emerge from a significant amount of therapy and perceive no change whatsoever in his or her perceptions, understanding, or feelings? People in one study skills program expected improvement, so they misperceived themselves as initially worse off than they had been and misremembered their final grades as better than they were. Both processes allowed them to see themselves as having improved, which was consistent with their theories (Conway & Ross, 1984). Such events are expected to promote change (and often do). Similarly, some attributes are expected to change (M. Ross, 1989). For example, attitudes toward social categories in general are expected to be stable across the life span, but attitudes toward one's own age group and its typical activities are expected to change with age (people do not expect attitudes toward skateboards to be stable across the life span).

Considerable evidence suggests that people's reconstruction of their own past is guided by implicit theories of stability and change. Although this evidence primarily regards perceptions of stability and change in attitudes, the theory also applies to people's construction of their own prior traits and feelings (M. Ross, 1989). According to *temporal self-appraisal theory*, people distance themselves from their negative past selves and reduce the distance to their positive past selves, especially when they have high self-esteem (M. Ross & Wilson, 2002). In general, people disparage their distant past attributes and praise their recent past selves, believing in how much they have improved (Wilson & Ross, 2001). In the attitude domain, people endorse their current attitudes and typically view them as relatively stable, at least in the recent past, enhancing their self-assurance.

Conclusion

We have seen three approaches that rely on people's own ideas about attitude change. The first examines the communicator's motives to infer the credibility of the information given. The second examines people's ideas about the information they receive in groups, both information about other people's positions relative to their own and information about the topic. The third examines people's naive theories about their own attitude change processes. All three involve people reflecting on the social circumstances of attitude change.

FUNCTIONAL DIMENSIONS OF ATTITUDES

Another approach examines the relationship of attitudes to the self in a different way. At the beginning of this chapter, we discussed cognitive features of two consistency theories of attitudes: dissonance theory and balance theory. These traditional cognitive consistency theories have a motivational basis; inconsistency is presumably aversive, prompting people to resolve the inconsistency by various means, including attitude change. Subsequent theories of attitudes have tended to focus on their cognitive dynamics such as attributional analyses, persuasive arguments theories in groups, and implicit theories of self.

Recent approaches again more actively take motivation into account, emphasizing functions that attitudes serve for people. Specifically, some of these functional approaches focus on conviction, strength, and importance, which certainly have motivational components, and others specify particular attitude functions.

Conviction, Strength, and Importance

Some attitudes centrally involve motivation, for they are held with conviction. Such attitudes tend to be stable, and people know they are stable. *Conviction* includes (Abelson, 1988) emotional commitment; attitudes that people hold with conviction are those about which they feel absolutely correct, cannot imagine ever changing their minds, are based on a moral sense of how things should be, and for which they would be willing to work. Conviction also involves ego preoccupation: often thinking about the issue, holding strong views, and being concerned. Finally, conviction implicates cognitive elaboration, which means having held the view for a while, connecting to other issues, seeing its broad implications, knowing a lot about it, and explaining it easily. Most individuals have only one or two such issues. But attitudes held with conviction are stable and carry a centrality to the self in several respects.

A related concept, attitude *strength,* illustrates some such respects (for a review, see Eagly & Chaiken, 1998). Attitude strength includes various interrelated components (Bassili & Krosnick, 2000). For example, *importance* and *certainty* both predict attempts to persuade others (Visser, Krosnick, & Simmons, 2003). Attitude strength increases until middle age and then declines, meaning that younger and older adults change their minds most easily because their attitudes are less important and certain (Visser & Krosnick, 1998).

By itself, attitude importance—a person's interest or concern about an attitude (Krosnick, 1988a)—predicts information-seeking (Visser et al., 2003). As such, it builds on attitude involvement, but involvement of a different sort than the primarily outcome-relevant kind described earlier in this chapter. Attitude importance is most similar to what has been termed *value-relevant involvement,* which generally inhibits persuasion according to a meta-analytic research review (B. T. Johnson & Eagly, 1989). Similarly, research on attitude importance argues that important attitudes are stable (Krosnick, 1989), accessible (Krosnick, 1989), and allow one to differentiate among relevant objects. For example, personally important policy attitudes (e.g., toward welfare, abortion, minorities) are accessible when one evaluates political candidates, and one can discern differences among them on that issue better than can someone for whom the attitude is not important. Consequently, important attitudes better predict preferences among presidential candidates than do unimportant attitudes (Krosnick, 1988b). Other people also appreciate the impact of attitude importance. When someone says an issue is important, observers infer that the person holds extreme attitudes (Mackie & Gastardo-Conaco, 1988).

Important attitudes also show greater consistency with each other. Thus, if one holds two important attitudes, they are unlikely to contradict each other (Judd & Krosnick, 1982). Similarly, experts for whom relevant attitudes are likely to be important also show considerable consistency among their attitudes. People who know a lot about politics, report that they are politically interested, or follow political news are especially consistent (for a review, see Judd & Krosnick, 1989). Important attitudes apparently are accessible (Bizer & Krosnick, 2001), persist over time, predict other choices, and connect to other attitudes (Judd & Krosnick, 1989).

Such attitudes are central to people's values. It would seem difficult, therefore, to change attitudes that people hold to be important. One intriguing strategy does seem to change attitudes about which people are highly certain (and therefore probably the attitudes are important ones). A communicator offers statements that are even more extreme than people's own attitudes and encourages people to endorse them. People who are certain about their attitudes recognize this apparent manipulation and resist the attempt to make them more extreme. In reaction, they change their attitude away from their own previous position. This paradoxical strategy (Swann, Pelham, & Chidester, 1988) works only with people who are certain of their attitudes. Swann and his colleagues proposed that attitudes about which one is certain are attitudes important to organizing one's experience and important to one's sense of self. Thus people attempt to self-verify (see Chapter 5) and reject the overly extreme positions by backing away from them.

Attitude Functions

Attitude functions can be divided in a few ways. Here we split them into knowledge, values, and sociality. These newer approaches explicitly incorporate motivation, reexamining traditional theories of attitudes' motivational functions (e.g., D. Katz, 1960; M. B. Smith, Bruner, & White, 1956), but with new cognitive twists.

Knowledge Functions

The most fundamental attitude function is an *object-appraisal* function, which prominently includes a cognitive knowledge function and often a utilitarian, instrumental, or goal function (Eagly & Chaiken, 1998; Greenwald, 1989; Pratkanis & Greenwald, 1989). The *knowledge* function of an attitude is fundamentally cognitive and adaptive. Attitudes help people to make sense of the world, to order and organize it. Moreover, attitudes can be *instrumental* and adaptive, helping people to avoid pain and receive rewards. The object-appraisal functions of attitudes may act as heuristics (Pratkanis, 1988), simple evaluative strategies for problem solving. For example, attitudes help define attitude-consistent information as true; liked people are assumed to have good qualities and disliked people to have bad ones. Attitudes affect a range of knowledge-related problem-solving activities: interpretation and explanation, reasoning, responses to persuasion, judgment, perceived consensus, identification of facts and errors, and prediction (see Pratkanis, 1989, for a review).

The knowledge function of attitudes may also serve schematic functions, shaping attitude-relevant memory. Attitudes can have a bipolar structure: Extreme material on either side is most easily judged and recalled (Judd & Kulik, 1980). Attitudes can also have a unipolar structure: well-elaborated supporting material on one side but little or nothing on the opposing side (see Eagly & Chaiken, 1998; Pratkanis & Greenwald, 1989, for reviews).

The motivational aspect of the knowledge function has been examined in an impressive series of studies designed to heighten people's need for cognitive clarity and structure (Jamieson & Zanna, 1989). Recall from Chapter 2 that the need for structure (Kruglanski, 1990) induces people to prematurely cease information-seeking, which leads them to rely more heavily on their already-formed schemas and attitudes. People's need for structure can be enhanced by putting them under time pressure, stress, or increased arousal. Under these conditions, people form structurally simpler attitudes, and they rely more heavily on already-formed attitudes. Similar effects (simpler attitudes under pressure) can be observed in the real-world rhetoric of political leaders (Tetlock, 1985). The knowledge functions of attitudes relate to a variety of attitude operations.

Value Functions

The *value-expressive* function of attitudes describes the importance to people of demonstrating and maintaining their long-term standards and orientations. This is similar to B. T. Johnson and Eagly's (1989) *value-relevant involvement*, which inhibits persuasion based on mere argument strength. It also relates to attitude importance and conviction, just reviewed. People seem especially committed to attitudes that serve value-expressive functions, especially when they suffer or incur costs for holding those attitudes (Lydon & Zanna, 1990).

People differ in the value-expressive functions of their attitudes. For example, low self-monitors are people who do not monitor themselves with regard to the social situation but instead rely heavily on their inner thoughts and feelings to guide their behavior (M. Snyder, 1974; see Chapter 15). Consequently, their own attitudes are more important to them than, say, the norms of the situation or the attitudes of their friends. Such people would be expected to have a stronger motivation for value expression than other people (M. Snyder & DeBono, 1985). Indeed, low self-monitors are especially likely to appeal selectively to their long-term values to justify their attitudes (Kristiansen & Zanna, 1988). Low self-monitors rely more heavily on appeals to important values (DeBono, 1987). Similarly, low self-monitors are particularly attentive to expert sources because they presumably provide reliable, value-relevant information (DeBono & Harnish, 1988).

People can have conflicting values about an attitude object, which potentially can cause problems when using an attitude to express their values. For example, Black Americans, as targets of White Americans' attitudes, elicit core values related to humanitarian and egalitarian values on one hand and to Protestant work ethic values, on the other hand (I. Katz & Hass, 1988; I. Katz, Wackenhut, & Hass, 1986). Depending on which is primed, White racial attitudes are correspondingly more positive or negative (see Dovidio & Gaertner, 1986, for related ideas).

Attitudes are likely to be more cognitively complex when they relate to core conflicting values (Tetlock, 1986). That is, assuming value expression is important, people work especially hard to reconcile important value conflicts, creating trade-offs that result in greater attitudinal and ideological complexity. Certain ideological positions, such as liberalism, entail (at least superficially) core conflicting values; this attempt to reconcile conflicting values may result in more complex reasoning styles (Tetlock, 1984, 1986), which are not merely a function of rhetorical style (Tetlock, Hannum, & Micheletti, 1984; but see Sidanius, 1988). Upward shifts in complexity on both sides generally preceded major American-Soviet agreements, and downward shifts have preceded major military-political interventions (Tetlock, 1988). Value expression can have global effects.

Social Functions

Attitudes also serve important *social-adjustive* functions for the self. Sometimes attitudes signal interpersonal priorities, sensitivity to others, and getting along with people in general. This function is similar to B. T. Johnson and Eagly's (1989) *impression-relevant involvement*, which tends to inhibit persuasion based on argument strength, presumably because that is not the most important determinant of social-adjustive attitudes. Social-adjustive attitudes are most prominent for people with a high need for affiliation, sensitivity to approval, and well-developed awareness of their self-presentation to others (Herek, 1986). For example, prejudiced or egalitarian attitudes toward homosexuals can either promote acceptance by one's immediate peer group (social-adjustive functions) or demonstrate one's core moral stands (value-expressive functions). Again, there are self-monitoring differences in that high self-monitors, being more attuned to interpersonal settings, are more likely to have socially adjustive attitudes than are low self-monitors. High self-monitors more carefully process the message of an interpersonally attractive source (DeBono & Harnish, 1988), attend more to the images projected by consumer products (DeBono & Snyder, 1989; Snyder & DeBono, 1985), and rely more heavily on consensus information (DeBono, 1987; see Snyder & DeBono, 1987, 1989, for reviews).

The central empirical issue for functional theories has always been to identify a priori the functions served by particular attitudes for particular individuals. One approach, as we have seen, is to examine individual differences (i.e., self-monitoring) in the types of attitudes individuals are likely to hold. Another intriguing approach posits that certain attitude objects are intrinsically likely to elicit attitudes serving different functions (Shavitt, 1989). That is, the social-adjustive function of high-status clothing is more readily apparent than is the social-adjustive function of one's air conditioner. Recent research supports the predominant functions of some objects, whereas others appear to elicit mixed functions brought out by different circumstances. Moreover, people show some cross-domain consistency in the functions of their attitudes, values, and even possessions (Abelson & Prentice, 1989; Prentice, 1987). The bottom line is that certain individuals, in concert with certain attitudes and certain situations, hold attitudes for different functional reasons (Snyder & DeBono, 1989).

Summary

An attitude is a hypothetical mediating variable assumed to intervene between stimulus and response. Attitudes involve at least an evaluation of the attitude object, and many definitions also include cognitions and behavioral tendencies. Social cognition's contribution to the field began with a metatheoretical approach valuing a fine-grained analysis of the cognitive processes involved in attitude formation and change. Attitude research has also borrowed specific theories and methods from social cognition research. One early theory, in particular, foreshadowed information processing approaches: McGuire's multistep chain of persuasion included various cognitive processes necessary for successful attitude change and enactment.

Two traditional cognitive consistency theories have profited from newer social cognition insights. Dissonance theory's long-standing hypothesis of selective perception to support one's attitudes includes selective exposure (seeking attitude-consistent information), selective attention (heeding attitude-consistent information), and selective interpretation (perceiving ambiguous information to be attitude-consistent). Although evidence for selective exposure entails mostly de facto rather than deliberate exposure, evidence for selective attention and interpretation fully supports the premises of dissonance theory. In addition, dissonance theory has concerned selective learning and retention of attitude-relevant information. Incidental learning of attitude-consistent information demonstrates selectivity, but intentional learning and high degrees of motivation eliminate selectivity. People with high self-esteem, an internal locus of control, or a tendency to repress unpleasant experiences all show greater selectivity effects, which is consistent with dissonance theory.

Another consistency approach, balance theory, also posits that people selectively recall information, in this case information about the attitudes of self and others. People can most readily remember that friends agree (and perhaps that enemies disagree). A balanced triad of two friends who feel the same way about particular attitude objects creates a compact cognitive unit that is easier to imagine, comprehend, and remember. An unbalanced triad is more difficult and seems to be stored in separate pieces. Attitudes in general organize memory for relevant information to the extent that people may have difficulty remembering the evidence on which their attitudes were based.

Some social cognitive approaches emphasize people's everyday theories about persuasion. For example, attributional analyses of why the communicator is delivering a particular message influence persuasion. If a communicator delivers a particular message because of the audience or other situational factors, then it is suspect. Similarly, if a communicator is dispositionally biased in terms of knowledge or reporting motives, then the message is perceived as untrustworthy. Another lay theory approach examines attitude polarization in groups as a function of persuasive arguments raised by group members, social comparison information, or group identity.

Finally, people's implicit theories about stability and change encourage people to perceive or misperceive stability and change in their own attitudes and other dispositions. People do not typically expect their attitudes to change, so they misperceive stability, even when their attitudes have been altered by subtle means. Moreover, people misrecall their prior behavior to fit their current attitudes, again in line with the general belief that attitudes are stable and behavior accordingly follows. When people's theories suggest change, however, they also (mis)perceive change following a conversion, a self-help program, therapy, and the like.

People's attitudes vary along some dimensions important to social cognition. Conviction involves several components related to the importance of one's attitudes: emotional commitment, ego preoccupation, and cognitive elaboration. A related term for conviction is value-relevant involvement, and another related concept is strength. Whatever their name, such significant attitudes are few (for most people) and resist change. Such attitudes are stable, accessible, differentiate among attitude objects, and are consistent with other attitudes. They may be open to change only by paradoxical techniques.

People's attitudes serve several functions relevant to knowledge, values, and sociality. First, people's attitudes serve a knowledge function, providing heuristics for rapid responses and schemas for organizing knowledge. As people's need for structure increases, they are more likely to rely on their ready-made attitudes or on simple attitudes quickly constructed. Attitudes can also serve a self function of value expression, allowing people to demonstrate their prized standards and orientations. The attitudes of low self-monitors are especially likely to serve value-expressive functions. When people hold core conflicting values, their relevant attitudes become more complex with the necessity of integrating them. Finally, attitudes can also serve social-adjustive self functions. They help people to fit in with other people and to demonstrate interpersonal attunement. High self-monitors, who are oriented to the social environment, are more likely to hold social-adjustive attitudes. Apart from individual differences, some attitude objects may typically elicit attitudes with particular types of functions.

The various cognitive approaches to attitudes—those elaborating traditional theories and those positing altogether new processes, those emphasizing more thoughtful or more automatic processes, and those focusing almost entirely on cognition or more actively including motivation—have various implications for intergroup stereotyping and prejudice, for affect, and for the relationship between cognition and behavior, as the next chapters indicate.

CHAPTER 10

Cognitive Processing
of Attitudes

HEURISTIC VERSUS SYSTEMATIC MODEL ◆ PERIPHERAL VERSUS CENTRAL ROUTES TO
PERSUASION: ELABORATION LIKELIHOOD MODEL ◆ MOTIVATION AND OPPORTUNITY
DETERMINE ATTITUDE PROCESSES: THE MODE MODEL ◆ IMPLICIT ASSOCIATIONS
◆ EMBODIED ATTITUDES ◆ NEURAL CORRELATES OF ATTITUDES

In the previous chapter, we examined the more explicitly cognitive aspects of several traditional attitude theories focused on attitude structure and function. Now we take up more recent attitude theories that are themselves fundamentally cognitive in orientation; they focus more on attitude processing. In this chapter we examine cognitively oriented theories that explicitly build on social cognition ideas; each one specifies different modes of attitude processing based on cognitive principles. Foreshadowed in Chapter 2, the first three focus on dual modes of attitudinal processing and, in particular, on the degree to which people's attitudes form, change, and operate in relatively thoughtful or more automatic ways. From automatic responses, we briefly touch on implicit associations. The remaining two theories examine the interplay of attitudes and our physical beings: embodied attitudes and neural aspects of attitudes.

HEURISTIC VERSUS SYSTEMATIC MODEL

Many classic theories of attitudes posit that attitudes form and change based on thoughtful consideration of issue-relevant information. For example, McGuire's (1969) chain of persuasion assumed that people process and evaluate the arguments provided, accordingly agreeing or disagreeing with the persuasive communication. Similarly, the dominant framework for studying attitudes over a period of nearly two decades, the Yale persuasive communications approach (Hovland et al., 1953), emphasized learning message content and its conscious acceptance or rejection. Moreover, one of the most comprehensive recent theories of attitudes and behavior, the theory of reasoned action (Fishbein & Ajzen, 1974), later elaborated into the theory of planned behavior (Ajzen, 1987), stated that attitudes are importantly based on people's beliefs about the attitude object (see Chapter 15). While not specifically a theory of cognitive processes, this theory does emphasize a deliberate, thoughtful process; namely, evaluating the strengths and weaknesses of one's particular beliefs, assessing their systematic implications for one's attitude, and ultimately, along with perceived norms and control, assessing their implications for one's behavior. These traditional theories essentially focus on a relatively controlled or systematic form of attitude formation and change.

The heuristic-systematic model (e.g., Chaiken, 1980; Chen & Chaiken 1999) proposes that people engage in such thoughtful processes only when they are sufficiently motivated and have the capacity to do so. When people are relatively motivated, they indeed can engage in this thoughtful effortful mode, termed *systematic processing,* which involves evaluating the pros and cons of a message's arguments. For example, systematic processing is increased by various factors that tend to increase motivation: receiving messages on topics of high personal relevance, making attitude judgments with important consequences, having sole responsibility for message evaluation, and discovering that one disagrees with the majority position (for a review, see Eagly & Chaiken, 1993). Systematic processing is characterized by sensitivity to the valence and quality of a message, issue-relevant thoughts, enhanced recall for the arguments, and relatively lasting change (e.g., Axsom, Yates, & Chaiken, 1987; Mackie, 1987; McFarland, Ross, & Conway, 1984).

In contrast to this strategy that emphasizes relatively thoughtful processing of attitude-relevant information, people often engage in a more rapid, easy, *heuristic* form of processing. According to Chaiken's theory, people learn certain persuasion heuristics or rules (in arguments, long-is-strong; in communicators, believe-beauty and trust-an-expert); these shortcuts avoid effortful processing of the actual message contents. Learned from experience, the rules are often accurate enough. Equally important, heuristic processing makes relatively few capacity demands. People apparently use the heuristic strategy when they lack room for the more systematic type of processing. When cognitive capacity is reduced, people are less likely to engage in systematic processing and more likely to engage in heuristic processing (e.g., Mackie & Worth, 1989; W. Wood, Kallgren, & Preisler, 1985).

One implication of the heuristic–systematic distinction in persuasion is that people may or may not carefully process message arguments, sometimes relying on shortcuts, sometimes engaging more comprehensive, analytic, systematic process. When they do each depends on various motives; for example, accuracy motives, defensive motives, and impression management motives all potentially influence the extent of heuristic or systematic processing (Chaiken, Liberman, & Eagly, 1989). These types of motives compare to those discussed in Chapter 2 as motives that encourage more automatic or controlled processes in general. For example, when motivated to be accepted by their partner, people use a go-along-to-get-along heuristic, expressing attitudes consistent with their partner's views (Chen, Shechter, & Chaiken, 1996).

PERIPHERAL VERSUS CENTRAL ROUTES TO PERSUASION: ELABORATION LIKELIHOOD MODEL

Another cognitively oriented model of persuasion also proposes two routes to attitude change (Petty & Cacioppo, 1981, 1986; Petty & Wegener, 1998). According to the elaboration likelihood model, the *central route* recruits active, careful thinking about (i.e., elaborating) the true merits of the message arguments and, in this sense, resembles the systematic route proposed by Chaiken's heuristic-systematic model. The *peripheral route* to persuasion includes any kind of attitude change that occurs without much thought or elaboration. As such, this route includes Chaiken's heuristic mode as well as other types of superficial attitude change. For example, mere exposure effects on evaluations (see Chapter 14) would be a peripheral (but not a heuristic) mode of persuasion.

One basic postulate of the elaboration likelihood model is that people are motivated to hold correct attitudes. With sufficient motivation and ability to process a message, people respond to argument quality. The balance of their favorable, unfavorable, and neutral thoughts then determines positive or negative attitude change by the central route, posited to be enduring. The amount and type of cognitive elaboration (issue-relevant thinking) depend on individual and situational factors. Elaboration includes making relevant associations, scrutinizing the arguments, inferring their value, and evaluating the overall message.

Methods

Elaboration is assessed in various ways (Petty & Cacioppo, 1986). One could ask people directly how much effort they invested in processing the message, but people cannot or will not always answer accurately. Two techniques have proved more successful in assessing degrees of cognitive elaboration. The first, cognitive response analysis, examines the recipient's cognitions (especially counterarguments) as the message is received (Brock, 1967); the favorability of the recipient's cognitive responses to persuasion directly relates to the degree of attitude change (Greenwald, 1968). The elaboration likelihood theory built on the earlier cognitive response technique by conceptualizing exactly how counterarguments and supporting arguments cause attitude change.

The cognitive response technique itself is a simple and elegant way to measure cognitive mediation. In general, cognitive mediation means that some stimulus causes a cognitive effect, which in turn causes an overt response. In the case of persuasive communication, cognitive mediation entails a stimulus (low or high argument quality) causing a cognitive mediator (low or high counterarguing), which in turn causes a response (attitude change). In cognitive response research, participants not only give an opinion on the topic at hand but also list their thoughts during or just after receiving the communication. The cognitive responses are scored as reactions pro and con, and thus they presumably mediate attitude change. When researchers use the cognitive response method in concert with the elaboration likelihood model, they show that attitude change often is caused by one's personal responses to a message (Figure 10.1).

Cognitive response analysis is a method, but it is not a theory. As a technique, cognitive response analysis is compatible with various attitude theories (as described in Petty, Ostrom, & Brock, 1981). Because it is a methodological technique, it does not guarantee theoretical advance by itself. The technique of cognitive response analysis has been applied to communicator, message, and audience variables (Petty, Ostrom, & Brock, 1981).

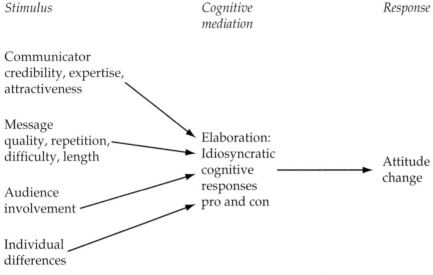

FIGURE 10.1. Cognitive response analysis

Another method for assessing elaboration involves experimental manipulation rather than measurement of cognitive elaboration as the proposed mediator. By manipulating the quality of the message itself, one can see whether participants respond differently to the strong or weak arguments. If they are sensitive to argument quality, they are presumably thinking about what they received, so they are elaborating on it and, by definition, following the central route. If they are not sensitive to argument quality, then they are not elaborating much, and they are taking the more peripheral route. Much of the elaboration likelihood research program manipulates argument quality as well as some situational variable posited to affect elaboration, and then measures both cognitive responses and attitude change.

Armed with these methods, in particular cognitive response analysis and manipulations of argument strength, the elaboration likelihood model addresses many basic processes in persuasion (Petty & Cacioppo, 1981, 1986; Petty & Wegener, 1998). It emphasizes the *extent* and the *valence* (direction) of thinking to predict attitude change, and more recently, people's *confidence* in their thoughts has emerged as an important predictor (Petty, Briñol, & Tormala, 2002). The next few sections illustrate elaboration likelihood analyses of communicator, message, and audience. As we will see, many standard attitude change effects depend on the audience's (i.e., the participant's) involvement with the persuasive message. In particular, outcome involvement, value involvement, and impression involvement all differ (Johnson & Eagly, 1989).

Communicator Effects

Who says it—the message source—heavily influences processes and outcomes of persuasion. The peripheral route often results from simple cues regarding the expertise and attractiveness of the communicator. For example, students were told that a mandatory comprehensive exam for all seniors was advocated by an expert source (Carnegie Commission on Higher Education) or by an inexpert source (a high school class). When the issue was relevant to the students—because it would be instituted at their own school the next year—the students were more sensitive to the quality of the strong or weak arguments presented, as the elaboration likelihood model would predict. Moreover, when the issue was relevant, source expertise made little difference. However, when the issue was less relevant (the exam would be instituted elsewhere or much later) and students were, therefore, less outcome involved, source expertise essentially determined their attitudes, regardless of argument quality (Petty, Cacioppo, & Goldman, 1981). Under low outcome involvement, source expertise serves as a peripheral cue to persuasion, bypassing the need to process message arguments. Similar effects obtain for attractive or famous message sources (Chaiken, 1979; Pallak, 1983; Petty, Cacioppo, & Schumann, 1983). A caution: All persuasion variables can have multiple effects. Under the right conditions, source expertise could make one pay more attention and process the message more carefully (Petty & Wegener, 1998).

Overall, communicator credibility effects typically are strongest for recipients not involved in the outcomes at stake. Uninvolved recipients are most likely to respond to superficial indications of expertise. Of course, alleged expertise is not a totally reliable reason for agreeing with someone's arguments, but it is a convenient shortcut. Much research on communicator cues may represent only those recipients operating at fairly shallow levels. In support of this, highly outcome-involved subjects express more message-oriented thoughts (Chaiken, 1980). Cognitive response analysis distinguishes between people who are responding superficially and those who are thinking hard in response to a message, so it allows one to distinguish between outcome-involved and uninvolved subjects' use of communicator cues.

Message Effects

What is said—the message—also influences persuasion, but not always in the obvious ways. The elaboration likelihood model applies to various features of the message: number of repetitions, difficulty, number of arguments, use of rhetorical questions, number of sources, and degree of distraction in its context. In each of these areas, the model has emphasized the role of recipient thought.

The research on *message repetition* is best understood as distinguishing between two different kinds of stimuli: nonlinguistic (e.g., the Coca-Cola logo) and linguistic (e.g., the persuasive message). Cognitive response analysis suggests that the differences are due to the amount and valence (direction pro or con) of thoughts generated in each case (A. Sawyer, 1981).

Researchers have long known that repeated exposures to nonlinguistic stimuli typically enhance liking in what is called the mere exposure effect (Stang, 1974; Zajonc, 1968a; for a review, see Bornstein, 1989; also see Chapter 14). Two major qualifications on the mere exposure effect are that the stimulus is initially unfamiliar and that people's initial reaction to the stimulus is neutral or positive (Grush, 1976; Harrison, 1977). When the stimulus is initially negative, the exposure effect evaporates or reverses.

In line with the peripheral route of the elaboration likelihood model, the mere exposure effect on nonlinguistic stimuli operates most clearly when recipients are essentially unthinking; that is, they cannot be generating personal responses (pro or con) to the stimulus. Hence, the more you see the Coca-Cola logo, the more you like it, assuming you do not think about it much; the logo has become as familiar as the American flag. Even animals show the effect of exposure on preference. People show the effect of repetition quite plainly under circumstances of minimal cognitive processing, or as McGuire (1969) would say, when they are behaving as lazy organisms. Accordingly, the peripheral route to persuasion best describes message repetition effects with nonlinguistic stimuli.

Nonlinguistic stimuli make a strong case for nonconscious mere exposure effects on preference. Note its stark contrast to the central route of the elaboration likelihood model as a clearly peripheral route to persuasion. Chapter 14 reviews some mere exposure research supporting nonconscious mediation (also Zajonc's separate systems view of affect and cognition; Moreland & Zajonc, 1977; W. R. Wilson, 1979). Participants who do not even recognize stimuli as familiar still show exposure effects on liking (Zajonc, 1980b). Thus the simple mere exposure effect for nonlinguistic stimuli is unconsciously mediated. People show the effect without recognizing the stimulus, without awareness, and without thought. Because message repetition effects on nonlinguistic stimuli do not appear to be mediated by conscious cognitive responses, they exemplify the peripheral route.

The second kind of stimulus in research on message repetition is linguistic; that is, the persuasive message itself. This kind of material does elicit thought, and as the elaboration likelihood model would predict, amount of thought pro and con appears to determine whether or not the linguistic mere exposure effect occurs (Petty & Cacioppo, 1981). This point is illustrated by the difference between early work on message repetition and later work using cognitive response analysis. In a study predating cognitive response analysis, W. Wilson and Miller (1968) originally found repetition effects on persuasion with prose passages; in this case the prose concerned a lawsuit for damages. Students role-played being jury members and were exposed to an attorney's arguments either one time or three times. More exposure led to more agreement. Repetition also markedly increased retention of the arguments after a week's delay. Because retention and attitude change were moderately correlated, Wilson and Miller concluded that at least some of the repetition effect was due to enhanced recall.

A decade after that effort, Cacioppo and Petty (1979) also tackled the question of what mediates message repetition effects. Armed with cognitive response analysis, they tapped participants' idiosyncratic responses to the communication immediately after hearing it. Participants retrospectively listed the thoughts they had had while listening to the communication and indicated whether each thought was pro (+), con (-), or neutral (0). In a separate measure, they were asked to recall the message's arguments. Agreement with the message was completely uncorrelated with recall, but highly correlated with both favorable thoughts (positively) and unfavorable thoughts (negatively). The number of irrelevant thoughts did not correlate with agreement. Thus cognitive responses pro and con—not recall—empirically mediated repetition effects on persuasion.

One important point is that the elaboration likelihood model supports a different sort of cognitive process model than does a model stressing recall as the mediating process. Cognitive response analysis looks at the individual's idiosyncratic reactions to the argument rather than at the person's ability simply to remember the argument as given. Cognitive response analysis successfully elucidates the processes intervening between exposure and agreement, consistent with the elaboration likelihood model's central route.

As elaboration likelihood model research on message repetition effects has continued, the exact nature of the mediating cognitive process has been specified further. People's cognitive responses to repeated messages support a two-stage model in which uncertainty reduction and tedium counterbalance each other (Berlyne, 1970; Cacioppo & Petty, 1979). In other words, the first few times your friend explains his thesis to you, repetition aids understanding and convinces you the paper is right, assuming the arguments are cogent. But after that it is a bore, and you may begin to counterargue out of sheer perversity. In the Cacioppo and Petty study, for example, agreement first increased with exposure, as participants comprehended the message and thought about it. Then agreement decreased, presumably as tedium set in. Cognitive responses pro and con followed the same pattern as did agreement—positive at first and then negative—which supports the two-factor model. Of course, this model assumes that participants follow the central route (that is, they bother to think about the message), which presupposes at least some outcome involvement; uninvolved participants do not always initially agree, then disagree (A. Sawyer, 1981).

Conceptually, message repetition effects illustrate several crucial points about the elaboration likelihood model: the importance of whether the recipient is actively thinking, and if thinking, whether those thoughts are pro or con; the possibilities for nonconscious mediation in the various peripheral routes in contrast to the conscious cognitive mediation in the central route; and the role of the elaboration likelihood model as a well-specified theory that solves old puzzles in new ways (see Crano & Prislin, 2006, and Petty & Wegener, 1998, for reviews). From an applied perspective, message repetition effects might inform advertisers who air the same television commercial several times during the late show; research suggests circumstances under which they are both right and wrong to do so.

Another type of message effect is its *difficulty*. As with repetition, the elaboration likelihood approach reveals that message difficulty effects are also influenced by outcome involvement. The number of supporting and counter-arguments people generate is a function of such involvement if the message is difficult. Consider trying to understand a difficult statistics lecture. A student who hates the course content, does not care much about the final grade, and has already given up working on the material will probably ignore the lecture and daydream. When acting as an uninvolved, lazy organism, one does not bother to absorb message content, regardless of its comprehensibility. At intermediate levels of outcome involvement, message difficulty should have maximum impact because a little added difficulty can make the critical difference between at least some processing and giving up. The majority of the statistics students presumably are at this intermediate level, and they would be sensitive to message difficulty. At high levels of outcome involvement, message difficulty again makes little difference to comprehension because people will be motivated to overcome message difficulty no matter what. (Ability helps, too, of course.) A new teaching assistant who has never heard the material before will make every effort to understand the lectures regardless of difficulty.

How, then, does message difficulty cause attitude change? An analysis that draws on cognitive response methods reveals the mediating factors to be the amount and valence of people's cognitive responses. Not surprisingly, comprehension encourages persuasion if the arguments are good (e.g., Eagly, 1974; see Eagly & Himmelfarb, 1978, for others). If you do not understand a message, you cannot easily repeat it to yourself, nor can you muster supporting arguments. People's own idiosyncratic supportive cognitive responses can strengthen the argued viewpoint, but only if people comprehend the message in the first place. The more comprehensible the message, the more the professor's audience can think positively about what he or she has said (assuming the arguments are good). Consequently, the more they comprehend the lecture's good arguments, the more they will agree with the professor (W. Wood & Eagly, 1981). In sum, message difficulty effects can be cognitively mediated (central route), as cognitive response evidence has indicated, but they need not always be (peripheral route).

Another important feature of messages is the sheer *number of arguments* that can act as a superficial cue for persuasion. Both the heuristic model (Chaiken, Liberman, & Eagly, 1989) and the elaboration likelihood model support this idea (Tormala, Petty, & Briñol, 2002). Under low personal relevance (i.e., low outcome involvement), number of arguments acts as a peripheral cue to persuasion, regardless of argument quality; under high relevance, argument quality and number of arguments together determine persuasion via the thoughtful central route (Petty & Cacioppo, 1984).

Cognitive responses explain many features of messages in addition to repetition, difficulty, and number of arguments (Petty & Cacioppo, 1981); for example, use of rhetorical questions (Petty, Rennier, & Cacioppo, 1987), multiple sources (Harkins & Petty, 1981), and environmental distractions (Petty, Wells, & Brock, 1976; for reviews, see Petty & Wegener, 1998; Petty, Wegener, & Fabrigar, 1997). In every case, the factor critical to persuasion is the amount of active cognitive elaboration, pro and con, done by the recipient. To generate favorable cognitive responses and to be maximally persuasive, a message should have good arguments, should be repeated a few times but not too many, should be comprehensible, and should be delivered in an atmosphere free of distraction. If the message has weak arguments (so could produce many counterarguments), distraction and a single exposure will inhibit those negative cognitive responses and accordingly enhance persuasion.

Overall, message effects depend on outcome involvement. Outcome involvement increases cognitive activity and subsequent attitude change for moderately repeated and comprehensible messages if the arguments are cogent. Related message effects occur for number of arguments, rhetorical questions, number of sources, and distractions.

Audience Involvement

In discussing the elaboration likelihood model, audience involvement combines with the effects of many other variables, in particular, communicator and message effects. Thus, at every step of the central persuasion process, the respondent's amount and valence of cognitive response determine the effect. Because cognitive responses demand an actively thinking recipient, audience involvement has influenced each effect so far.

However, different types of involvement have different effects. Early involvement research was operationalized in various ways, without strong agreement. For example, students might be given a message advocating a change in dormitory visitation hours at their own school versus another school (Petty & Cacioppo, 1979). Or they might be told that a change in university policy will take place in 1 year versus in 10 years (Petty, Ostrom, & Brock, 1981). The usual manipulations included some form of personal relevance and future consequence. A variant on involvement manipulated personal responsibility rather than relevance; participants were told they had sole responsibility for evaluating the message (Brickner, Harkins, & Ostrom, 1985; Petty, Harkins, & Williams, 1980).

Personal importance or relevance to one's self-concept seems to capture involvement's general conceptual meaning (Greenwald, 1981; Greenwald & Leavitt, 1984; B. T. Johnson & Eagly, 1989), but researchers have identified different types of involvement. Ego involvement (M. Sherif & Hovland, 1961), issue involvement (C A. Kiesler, Collins, & Miller, 1969), personal involvement (Apsler & Sears, 1968; C. W. Sherif, Kelly, Rodgers, Sarup, & Tittler, 1973), and vested interest (Sivacek & Crano, 1982) all imply that an issue has personal relevance or meaning, especially intrinsic importance for beliefs central to a person's identity. These terms can be contrasted with task involvement (M. Sherif & Hovland, 1961) in which the individual is concerned only with the consequences of a particular response. If a person is interested in maximizing the rewards in a given situation, that is response involvement (Zimbardo, 1960). The different types of involvement illustrate the range of factors that might make a person respond more or less thoughtfully to a persuasion attempt that is personally important (see Chaiken & Stangor, 1987, for a discussion of involvement types).

A meta-analysis of this literature (B. T. Johnson & Eagly, 1989) concluded that the involvement effects on elaboration likelihood apply most to outcome-relevant involvement, which implicates people's ability to attain desired outcomes. High involvement participants are more persuaded by strong arguments, consistent with the elaboration likelihood model, but not always less persuaded by weak arguments, despite elaboration likelihood predictions. Two other types of involvement do not obtain these effects: value-relevant involvement (implicating one's enduring principles) generally inhibits persuasion, and the same is somewhat true of impression-relevant involvement (implicating one's concern for people's opinions of self). Proponents of the elaboration likelihood model prefer to include these latter two types, involvements based on outcomes and values, in one category (Petty & Cacioppo, 1990), invoking the elaboration likelihood model postulate that (value-)involved subjects process in a biased manner because of their prior knowledge, strong attitudes, or confidence (Petty & Cacioppo, 1986; for disagreement, see B. T. Johnson & Eagly, 1990). For present purposes, the distinction at least among outcome involvement, value involvement, and impression involvement is important.

Outcome involvement has an important impact on processing messages. Regardless of specific manipulations, outcome involvement stimulates thought, which increases or decreases persuasion, depending on the cognitive responses, which in turn depend on the strength of the arguments and on the recipient's preexisting attitudes. Levels of outcome involvement lead to different types of processing, which lead to greater or lesser reliance on superficial characteristics of the communication.

One overall way to think about the effects of outcome involvement on cognitive responses and on persuasion is that less involved people seem to operate "on automatic," with little conscious thought (Chaiken, 1980; Petty & Cacioppo, 1981; see Chapter 2). Highly (outcome-)involved people operate in a relatively controlled mode, with more cognitive activity, and generate more cognitive responses that are sensitive to the message they encounter: The outcome-involved listener differentiates carefully between strong and weak arguments, and between pro and counterattitudinal arguments (Petty & Cacioppo, 1979; Petty, Cacioppo, & Goldman, 1981). Given an airtight or pro-attitudinal message, the outcome-involved recipient will not bother to counterargue, but the outcome-involved person would tend to counterargue weak or counter-attitudinal communications. Someone less outcome involved probably would generate few cognitions regardless of the message because the uninvolved person is attending only superficially. People who are outcome involved use systematic, content-based processing strategies responsive to argument quality. Less-involved people rely on peripheral strategies, such as source likeability. Outcome involvement moderates communicator and message effects (as we have seen) as well as the persistence of attitude change (Cook & Flay, 1978; Hennigan, Cook, & Gruder, 1982).

However, note that outcome-involved people do not necessarily think more objectively or accurately; they just think more, sometimes in a more biased fashion (Howard-Pitney, Borgida, & Omoto, 1986). The motivation from their involvement causes them to think harder, but their motivation also biases their interpretation of what they process (Chen, Reardon, Rea, & Moore, 1992; Liberman & Chaiken, 1992).

Other types of involvement show other effects. According to a meta-analysis (B. T. Johnson & Eagly, 1989), involvement that implicates a person's centrally held values generally inhibits persuasion. A subsequent section focusing on conviction and importance examines value involvement in more detail. Another type of involvement, impression relevance, which implicates people's self-presentational concerns, is also discussed later.

Individual Differences in Cognitive Responses and Persuasion

So far we have examined situational factors that determine the amount of thought people give to persuasive communications. Most of these situational variables interact with a recipient variable, involvement, in determining the thoughtfulness of cognitive responding, as indicated. What's more, a general dispositional factor determines the amount of cognitive responses. Table 10.1 shows some of the items on the scale. *Need for cognition* (Cacioppo & Petty, 1982; Cacioppo, Petty, & Morris, 1983) refers to people's chronic level of thoughtfulness in response to external stimuli such as persuasive messages. People high on the need for cognition generate more cognitive responses, both pro and con, to persuasive communications and are consequently likely to be more or less persuaded depending on the message. People low in need for cognition are more likely to process communications heuristically (Chaiken, 1987). The need

TABLE 10.1. Subset of the Need for Cognition Scale

1. I really enjoy a task that involves coming up with new solutions to problems.

2. I would prefer a task that is intellectual, difficult, and important to one that is somewhat important but does not require much thought.

3. Learning new ways to think doesn't excite me very much.*

4. The idea of relying on thought to make my way to the top does not appeal to me.*

5. I only think as hard as I have to.*

6. I like tasks that require little thought once I've learned them.*

7. I prefer to think about small, daily projects rather than long-term ones.*

8. I would rather do something that requires little thought than something that is sure to challenge my thinking abilities.*

9. I find little satisfaction in deliberating hard and for long hours.*

10. I don't like to have the responsibility of handling a situation that requires a lot of thinking.*

*Reverse scoring was used on this item.

Source: From J. T. Cacioppo & R. E. Petty. The need for cognition, *Journal of Personality and Social Psychology,* 1982, 42, 116–131. Copyright 1982 by the American Psychological Association. Reprinted by permission.

for cognition is an individual difference variable that specifically addresses the process (cognitive responses) presumed to mediate between external stimulus and attitude change.

Another individual difference variable, *uncertainty orientation* (Sorrentino, Bobocel, Gitta, Olso, & Hewitt, 1988; Sorrentino & Hancock, 1987; Sorrentino & Short, 1986), also affects persuasion. Certainty-oriented people stay with the familiar and the predictable, avoiding threats to their current understanding of the world, whereas uncertainty-oriented people search for meaning, attempt to make sense of their environment, and seek out novel situations. The standard elaboration likelihood effects—that personal relevance or outcome involvement leads to central processing—are predicted to hold only for uncertainty-oriented people. In contrast, certainty-oriented people apparently increase their use of heuristics under high relevance, contrary to the elaboration likelihood model. Uncertainty orientation differs from need for cognition in that need for cognition measures motivation to think, whereas uncertainty orientation measures when and what to think in the service of increasing certainty versus maintaining an open-minded approach to uncertainty.

A third individual difference variable, the *need to evaluate* (Jarvis & Petty, 1996), predicts holding more attitudes and having more pro and con thoughts in response to persuasive messages. It even predicts more pro–con thoughts in response just to considering a normal day. People high on this dimension spontaneously evaluate, forming attitudes quickly in the moment, compared to people who consult their memory for evidence (Tormala & Petty, 2001). Need to evaluate predicts consequential political effects: number of evaluative beliefs about candidates, intensity of emotional reactions toward candidates, using party identification and issues to determine candidate preferences, using the news media for gathering information, engaging in political activism, and voting or intending to vote (Bizer et al., 2004). Need to evaluate correlates moderately with the more general need for cognition, so they overlap somewhat.

Conclusion

Having spent considerable time on the elaboration likelihood model, we should note its limitations (Eagly & Chaiken, 1993; see the debate between Petty, Cacioppo, Kasmer, & Haugtvedt, 1987; Petty, Kasmer, Haugtvedt, & Cacioppo, 1987; and Stiff, 1986; Stiff & Boster, 1987). First, although it proposes that people's thoughts mediate attitude change, it does not explain why people support or counterargue what they encounter. In that sense, it leans on other theories of why people agree or disagree with communications to explain attitude change. Promising leads include, for example, when people receive a communication counter to a highly accessible attitude, they resist, intentionally or unintentionally (Zanna, 1991).

Second, it paints people as more oriented toward validating their attitudes than they may be. People are not only motivated to be accurate but also to feel secure, as the work on uncertainty orientation points out. Although Petty and Cacioppo noted that people are often only subjectively correct when they want to be rationally correct, even the attempt to be correct may not always be paramount. (One of us has a friend who defended his right to prefer a car that would make him feel foolish.) Just as elsewhere in social cognition, people are more and less motivated to be accurate, and future research will explain the when and how of accuracy motives in attitudes.

Similarly, when and how people actually are biased by prior attitudes, knowledge, value involvement, or impression-relevant involvement are still developing within this model's framework. Although the model does allow for biased information processing, its postulate that people are motivated to hold correct attitudes tended to limit its initial consideration of the conditions under which people are close-minded. One lead for studying both accuracy motivation and actual bias is people's naive theory of bias; people and situations vary in ability to identify and correct perceived biases. The flexible correction model (Wegener & Petty, 1995, 1997) assumes that overcoming bias requires more motivation and ability than failing to do so. Moreover, the direction of correction depends on one's naive theory specifying the direction of bias.

Third, persuasion variables all have multiple roles, so prediction is not simple. Some variables shift from encouraging central, "objective" processing to encouraging central but biased processing. Involvement's varying effects depend on its level (higher levels inducing more bias) or type (B. T. Johnson & Eagly, 1989). Similarly, some variables serve both as peripheral cues and as aids to central information processing (Petty & Wegener, 1998; Petty et al., 1997); number of arguments is one such variable (Petty & Cacioppo, 1986). Some of the moderating variables that determine specific effects of other variables have been identified, as this review indicates. Nevertheless, variables with multiple effects and multiple functions make it difficult to falsify the model, undermining its predictive power (Eagly & Chaiken, 1984). Future work will continue specifying the moderating variables that determine which of multiple possible effects a variable will demonstrate.

Fourth, some have questioned whether cognitive responses actually cause attitude change or are merely correlated with it (Romer, 1979). That is, if attitudes change for other reasons such as reinforcement contingencies, people may justify the change with cognitive responses pro and con, but only after the fact. In this view, cognitive responses do not cause attitude change; they merely accompany it, justify it, or serve as an alternative measure of persuasion (Eagly & Chaiken, 1984). In a related vein, some have argued that the standard manipulations of argument quality (responsiveness to which reveals the central route) also manipulate argument valence (Areni & Lutz, 1988).

Finally, as its proponents admit, the elaboration likelihood model and cognitive response analysis are not well suited to the analysis of attitude change mediated by noncognitive or nonconscious processes. For example, cognitive response analysis does not account for persuasion based on mere exposure to nonlinguistic stimuli or based on negative affect spillover from a frustratingly difficult message. And the elaboration likelihood model does not, in general, detail peripheral processes of persuasion.

In summary, despite inevitable limitations, the elaboration likelihood model and cognitive response analysis are powerful theoretical and methodological tools. Methodologically, cognitive response analysis supplies the technique of having people list their thoughts pro and con during or just after a persuasive communication. Such cognitive responses presumably mediate the effects of traditional communicator, message, and audience variables on attitude change. Theoretically, the elaboration likelihood model built on cognitive response analysis to propose that the amount and direction of people's idiosyncratic responses determine attitude change via the central or peripheral routes. The elaboration likelihood model summarizes effects of communicator, message, and audience on cognitive responses and on persuasion. In addition to these situational variables, individual differences in the need for cognition, uncertainty orientation, and need to evaluate influence how much thought people devote to persuasive communications. Overall, cognitive response analysis and the elaboration likelihood model have had a major impact on the fine-grained understanding of long-standing issues in attitude research.

MOTIVATION AND OPPORTUNITY DETERMINE ATTITUDE PROCESSES: THE MODE MODEL

So far we have examined two attitude processing models that focus on two different processes of persuasion: heuristic and systematic or peripheral and central, respectively. A third type of dual-process model examines the more automatic side in greater detail. This MODE model does not explain persuasion (i.e., how attitudes form or change); rather, it explains how attitudes, once formed, operate. It focuses on the automatic activation of attitudes.

This attitude accessibility model views an attitude as an association in memory between a given object and one's evaluation of it (Fazio, 1990; Fazio & Towles-Schwen, 1999). Associations between an attitude object and its evaluation vary in strength. The stronger the association, the more accessible one's attitude. The speed (latency) with which people can respond evaluatively to an attitude object is the most common way of measuring accessibility. For example, if people first see the priming word "cancer," they afterwards identify the stimulus word "crime" more quickly than "candy" because the first two concepts share a negative valence.

In one typical study (Fazio, Jackson, Dunton, & Williams, 1995), students saw color photographs of other students from various racial groups, which served as positive and negative primes to the extent the student was prejudiced. After seeing each photograph, they saw a (race-irrelevant) positive or negative adjective and had to say "good" or "bad," according to its obvious valence. They responded more quickly when primed with a valence-matched photograph than with a mismatch. Their prejudice facilitated evaluatively matched responses immediately following the prime. This kind of research suggests that some attitudes activate upon mere observation of the attitude object.

Several factors contribute to the accessibility of an attitude, and they include, predictably, the same factors that contribute to the accessibility of any construct, as reviewed in Chapter 3 on encoding. Recent and frequent expression of the attitude cause it to be activated more rapidly afterward (Fazio, Chen, McDonel, & Sherman, 1982; Houston & Fazio, 1989; Powell & Fazio, 1984). Moreover, reviewing one's prior attitude-congruent behavior and inferring the corresponding attitude, in a process consistent with self-perception theory (see Chapter 5), also makes attitudes more accessible (Fazio, 1987; Fazio, Herr, & Olney, 1984). Besides these situational factors that promote accessibility, individual differences also matter. Some people (namely, low self-monitors who are more attuned to their attitudes, see Chapter 15) may have chronically more accessible attitudes than others (Kardes, Sanbonmatsu, Voss, & Fazio, 1986).

Attitude accessibility has several practical implications. Accessible attitudes influence perceptions of the attitude object, facilitating attitude-consistent judgments about relevant information, such as the excellent debate performance of a favored candidate (Fazio & Williams, 1986) or the high quality of scientific evidence on one's own side of an issue (Houston & Fazio, 1989). Accessible attitudes resist contradiction (Houston & Fazio, 1989; cf. Wu & Shaffer, 1987), so they endure. In addition, accessible attitudes gloss over slight variations in the attitude object, making the attitude functionally robust for object appraisal (Fazio, Ledbetter, & Towles-Schwen, 2000). Finally, as we will see in Chapter 15, people more consistently act on their accessible attitudes.

The mere presentation of an object linked to an accessible attitude seems to trigger an automatic process whereby a strong evaluative association is activated (Fazio, 1989). For example, one set of studies primed people with a positive or negative attitude object immediately before presenting an evaluatively loaded adjective. The participants' task was to respond to the evaluative content of the adjectives (preselected to be unambiguous) by pressing a key marked "good" or "bad." Participants responded faster to the adjectives when the attitude prime and adjective stimulus were evaluatively congruent. This effect was biggest when their attitude was highly accessible (had previously elicited rapid responses) or had just been repeatedly expressed (Fazio, Sanbonmatsu, Powell, & Kardes, 1986).

Response facilitation observed in these studies may be relatively automatic. First, the sheer speed of people's responses to the adjective (less than a second) would seem to preclude controlled processing. That is, the facilitation provided by the evaluatively congruent, highly accessible attitude object in responding to the adjective was relatively instantaneous. Second, the facilitation effect evaporates when the attitude prime and adjective stimulus are separated by a full second (rather than 300 msec, as in the successful priming condition). Thus the prime's evaluative congruence facilitates responses only if the stimulus appears within a fraction of a second of the prime's initial appearance. The short duration of its effectiveness suggests automatic processing. Third, participants are instructed to focus on identifying the positive or negative valence of the adjective rather than to focus on the attitude object, which was seen as irrelevant to their main goal. Hence, the facilitation apparently occurs without intent, another feature of relatively automatic processes.

The degree to which the facilitating effect of an attitude depends on sheer accessibility (measured as speed of response to the initial attitude object) has been contested (Bargh, Chaiken, Govender, & Pratto, 1992; Bargh, Chaiken, Raymond, & Hymes, 1996; see Fazio, 2001, for a review). Instead, the effect may generalize to a variety of attitudes under a variety of circumstances. Despite such complexities, at least some attitude objects—at a minimum those with a strong association between object and evaluation—apparently automatically elicit their corresponding evaluation. This insight fits with some of the work on automatic category-based responses (Chapters 2 and 11), including schema-triggered affect (S. T. Fiske, 1982; see Chapter 13; cf. Sanbonmatsu & Fazio, 1990). Although the precise boundaries of the effect are still being identified, the work identifies a relatively automatic form of attitude processing.

IMPLICIT ASSOCIATIONS

Suppose you walk into a laboratory and the experimenter asks you to do a simple categorization task: Press the left key every time you see a word associated with older people *or* a word with unpleasant associations; press the right key every time you see a word associated with young people *or* a word with pleasant associations. You do dozens of these easy categorization pairs, and then the experimenter asks you to switch: Left key if older or pleasant; right key if younger or unpleasant. Suddenly it's harder. And suppose you learn that the order of these tasks would not have mattered (i.e., doing the second task first). (You can try this online if you search the term "implicit.") What does it mean about your attitudes toward older and younger people that the first, "congruent" task was easier?

People's simultaneous evaluative associations underlie another theory and measurement method, the Implicit Association Test (IAT; Greenwald et al., 2002; Greenwald, McGhee, & Schwartz, 1998). Consistent with ideas from balance theory, if people like themselves and link themselves with the ingroup, they will like their ingroup. The IAT posits this positive association to be strong on implicit measures that operate outside of normal explicit conscious responses. Most people show relatively automatic attitudes on the basis of common social categories such as gender, race, age, religion, nationality (Rudman, Greenwald, Mellott, & Schwartz, 1999), and even minimal, arbitrary group memberships (Ashburn-Nardo, Voils, & Monteith, 2001).

The IAT stimulated a staggering number of studies and also considerable controversy, both in short order. Although compatible techniques predated the IAT (for example, the MODE model and others; see Fazio & Olson, 2003, for a review), IAT research provocatively argued that implicit associations—split-second speed of responding to evaluatively linked items—reveal unconscious prejudice. The IAT has excellent predictive validity, correlating with reasonable criteria such as judgments, choices, behavior, and physiological responses (Poehlman, Uhlmann, Greenwald, & Banaji, 2006). What's more, the IAT works especially well in socially sensitive domains such as stereotyping and prejudice. Explicit self-reports do predict noncontroversial political and consumer choices, presumably topics where people have nothing to hide. And in cases where people are willing to report their (e.g., racial) prejudices explicitly, implicit measures correlate with those explicit admissions of prejudice (Wittenbrink, Judd, & Park, 1997). Implicit and explicit measures generally show small to medium correlations, according to meta-analysis (Hofmann, Gawronski, Gschwendner, Le, & Schmitt, 2005). Correlations increase when explicit self-reports are more spontaneous and when the measures are conceptually most similar. Overall, the IAT may have particular utility for attitudes that people hesitate to report explicitly.

The IAT's prediction of overt behavior especially matters to convincing the critics: Implicit measures best predict nonverbal behaviors, such as tone of voice (Dovidio, Kawakami, & Gaertner, 2002; Dovidio, Kawakami, Johnson, Johnson, & Howard, 1997; McConnell & Liebold, 2001), whereas explicit measures predict more overt behaviors, such as the content of speech. For example, European Americans' implicit attitudes predict early detection of threatening facial expressions in Black but not White faces (Hugenberg & Bodenhausen, 2003). The IAT also predicts financial discrimination (Rudman & Ashmore, 2007). The IAT shows traditional consistency, stability, and convergent validity of measurement (Cunningham, Preacher, & Banaji, 2001).

The core of the controversy revolves around whether to call the IAT a measure of attitudes. Arguably, if the IAT, clearly a measure of evaluative association, predicts related affect, cognition, and behavior, it is acting like an attitude. Indeed, it reliably does predict interpersonal affect, judgment, and behavior (Poehlman, Uhlmann, & Nosek, 2006). And the IAT gives people a palpable sense of the ease of certain (e.g., prejudiced) pairings over others (Ashburn-Nardo et al., 2001). At a minimum, it creates a teachable moment in seminars in which people become sensitized to the greater ease of prejudiced rather than unprejudiced associations.

In response, many have argued that the IAT merely assesses cultural beliefs (Arkes & Tetlock, 2004; Karpinski & Hilton, 2001; Kihlstrom, 2004; Olson & Fazio, 2004a; Uhlmann, Brescoll, & Paluck, 2006). However, people's attitudes do come partly from the larger culture, though they may also disagree with the culture, and the IAT should detect the difference in that case (Banaji, Nosek, & Greenwald, 2004; Lowery, Hardin, & Sinclair, 2001). This intrinsic mixing of cultural and personal associations sparked the idea of a personalized IAT, which correlates more strongly with explicit measures of attitudes and behavioral intentions (Olson & Fazio, 2004a). Instead of using generically pleasant and unpleasant words, this version uses the terms "I like" and "I don't like," paired with words associated with two contrasting societal groups, for example.

Another criticism of the IAT has been its malleability. That is, how implicit is it if people indeed can control their responses or if it changes with context? For example, race IAT results differ depending on whether people believe the IAT is assessing racism or is a nondiagnostic pilot test (Frantz, Cuddy, Burnett, Ray, & Hart, 2004). Moreover, people's IAT-assessed prejudice decreases after exposure to a variety of mitigating stimuli: positive minority and negative majority role models (Dasgupta & Greenwald, 2001), diversity training (Rudman, Ashmore, & Gary, 2001), counterstereotypic images (Blair, Ma, & Lenton, 2001; Wittenbrink, Judd, & Park, 2001b), social influence (Lowery, et al., 2001), and antiprejudice goals (Blair & Banaji, 1996).

How new is it? The IAT fits many standard social psychology findings but differs in several respects. One distinction between IAT pairings and MODE priming methods is that for the IAT people may be aware of the attitude involved, though not readily control the timing of their responses (Dasgupta, McGhee, Greenwald, & Banaji, 2000), whereas with priming people may not be aware of the prime, let alone its facilitating responses to a subsequent stimulus. Another distinction separates the IAT as a series of categorical judgments, whereas priming methods operate more readily on individual exemplars (Fazio & Olson, 2003). Implicit attitudes also generally may operate from a simple slow-learning (but durable and resistant) memory system, whereas explicit attitudes result more from a fast-learning (but flexible and context-sensitive) memory system (DeCoster, Banner, Smith, & Semin, 2006). Implicit attitudes are primarily associations, whereas explicit attitudes comprise propositions subjectively judged as true (Gawronski & Bodenhausen, 2006). And, more than many explicit attitudes, implicit attitudes may stem from early preverbal experiences, affective experiences, cultural associations, and cognitive consistency principles (Rudman, 2004; Sinclair, Dunn, & Lowery, 2005). Regardless of their special features, the impact of implicit evaluative associations is undeniable, both on individuals and on the field of attitudes.

EMBODIED ATTITUDES

The discovery of automatic or at least implicit attitudes supports other intriguing avenues for attitude research to avoid the problems of verbal self-reports, which are potentially plagued by people worrying about how they appear (social desirability). Embodied expressions of attitudes provide one route, as mentioned briefly earlier (see Chapter 4): A few decades ago, experimental participants had to make arm movements to pull or push positive and negative stimuli (e.g., "smart," "stupid"; "tasty," "putrid"); they were faster to initiate compatible movements such as pull toward positive and push away from negative (Solarz, 1960). Later results corroborated and expanded this result: Novel objects become progressively more positive or negative, respectively, with arm flexion versus extension (Cacioppo et al., 1993). This embodied valence affects novel more than familiar attitude objects (Priester, Cacioppo, & Petty, 1996). Embodied expression occurs even without a conscious goal to evaluate (Chen & Bargh, 1999), and simple exposure to novel (but valenced) stimuli speeds compatible movements (Duckworth, Bargh, Garcia, & Chaiken, 2002). Positive and negative stimuli, respectively, elicit approach (pull) and avoidance (push) responses (e.g., Neumann & Strack, 2000), and conversely, the actions themselves facilitate compatible evaluations (Centerbar & Clore, 2006).

Other kinds of body movements may also reflect and reinforce valence. As noted in Chapter 4, people who nod their heads while listening to a strong persuasive communication will agree more than people who shake their heads (Briñol & Petty, 2003). But if the message is weak, the nodders react against it, disagreeing more. In this instance of embodied cognition, the movements increase people's confidence in their own thoughts (pro or con), self-validating their attitude. Going back to the arm flexion/extension work, the movement affects only attitudes (evaluations), not other types of judgments (Cacioppo et al., 1993), and it apparently does so by associations in memory (Förster & Strack, 1997, 1998).

People's facial expressions can also affect their evaluations (Laird, 1984). In one typical paradigm, participants are induced to adopt specific facial expressions (e.g., smile, frown) without labeling them as such. For example, one experiment instructed them to contract and hold the relevant muscles one-by-one, for supposed EMG recording, until they had inadvertently assumed an emotional expression (Laird, 1974; see also Strack, Martin, & Stepper, 1988, described in Chapter 4). Other researchers have obtained similar effects (e.g., Coan, Allen, & Harmon-Jones, 2001; Cupchik & Leventhal, 1974; Duncan & Laird, 1977; Lanzetta, Cartwright-Smith, & Kleck, 1976; Rhodewalt & Comer, 1979; Zuckerman, Klorman, Larrance, & Spiegel, 1981). Embodied attitudes are here to stay.

NEURAL CORRELATES OF ATTITUDES

If attitudes are embodied, then it is easier to understand how they can also have brain signatures (see Lieberman, 2007, for a review). We are not so far from being able to read people's evaluative reactions from their patterns of brain activation. When people explicitly express their attitudes, what they say does not always correspond to what their brains suggest. Neural patterns might reflect implicit responses rather than explicit expression of attitudes. For example, immediate attitude responses differ from deliberate ones in electrocortical responses (Crites, Cacioppo, Gardner, & Berntson, 1995). As another example, people do not report attending to negative more than positive information, although the attention literature indicates they do (see Chapter 3). Similarly, the brain's evoked electrical activity (event-related brain potential) shows greater immediate impact of negative than comparably extreme positive stimuli (Ito et al., 1998). EEG recordings sensitively measure neural time sequences. People respond incredibly rapidly to human faces, as EEG data show (see Chapter 3).

Brain imaging more sensitively indexes location than EEG does. Consider implicit responses: Frequently, implicit neural responses involve amygdala activation to negative attitude objects (W. A. Cunningham et al., 2003; Hart et al., 2000; Wheeler & Fiske, 2005). For example, Whites' amygdala activation to Black faces correlates with their prejudice scores as measured by the IAT (Phelps et al., 2000; Phelps, Cannistraci, & Cunningham, 2003). The race-amygdala effects are stronger when faces appear subliminally (Cunningham,

Johnson, et al., 2004). However, implicit and explicit attitudes might seem to show contradictory neural responses. For example, African Americans show greater amygdala activity to Black faces, suggesting negativity, perhaps (Lieberman, Hariri, Jarcho, Eisenberger, & Bookheimer, 2005), but they also show more positive *explicit* attitudes toward Black faces (Nosek, Banaji, & Greenwald, 2002a).

Perhaps we need to broaden the idea of amygdala responses. The amygdala responds to emotionally significant cues that are extremely positive as well, such as photos of one's own versus someone else's child (Leibenluft, Gobbini, Harrison, & Haxby, 2004; see Zald, 2003, for a review). Hence, the amygdala responses may not indicate negative attitudes or emotions per se as much as general emotional significance, implicating vigilance. Vigilance, of course, is often needed in response to negative stimuli and sometimes in response to highly positive ones as well (such as one's own baby). Consistent with this interpretation, explicit ratings of emotional intensity correlated with amygdala response to socially relevant concepts, some negative, but also some positive, such as abortion, welfare, and happiness (Cunningham, Raye, & Johnson, 2004).

A system of areas may provide a cleaner indicator of valence than mere evaluative/emotional intensity. Part of this system may be the insula; in implicit attitudes, right insula correlates with negative valence ratings (Cunningham, Raye, & Johnson, 2004). Valence (e.g., reward and loss) relates to another likely area: the orbital frontal cortex in this attitude study and in neuroeconomics research (O'Doherty, Kringelbach, Rolls, Hornack, & Andrews, 2001). A third part of this system follows from implicit activation of attitudes that implicates the ventral medial prefrontal cortex (Knutson et al., 2005; McClure et al., 2004; Milne & Grafman, 2001).

Explicit attitudes implicate neural systems characteristic of more controlled processing, including the medial and lateral prefrontal and parietal cortex. People expressing attitudes toward topics that are not socially sensitive are more likely to express explicit attitudes that also fit their implicit attitudes, including those uncovered by neural activations. This pattern emerges toward, for example, socially relevant but not sensitive topics such as welfare (Cunningham, Raye, & Johnson, 2004); politicians and cities (Zysset, Huber, Ferstl, & von Cramon, 2002); admired and detested famous names (Cunningham et al., 2003); novel abstract graphic patterns (Jacobsen, Schubotz, Hofel, & Cramon, 2006); and representational and abstract paintings (Vartanian & Goel, 2004).

An even more obviously controlled response, regulating a socially sensitive attitude (e.g., concerning race), first involves the dorsal anterior cingulate cortex (Amodio, Harmon-Jones, et al., 2004), which is often involved in discrepancy detection (Botvinick et al., 2004). Then, perhaps in sequence, the right lateral PFC activates as people attempt to control the attitude expression (Cunningham, Johnson, et al., 2004; Cunningham, Raye, & Johnson, 2004; Richeson et al., 2003), consistent with the previous research. Activation in this right lateral PFC region apparently dampens amygdala responses (Cunningham, Johnson, et al., 2004).

Effortful control can dampen even seemingly automatic amygdala responses. Amygdala responses to emotionally negative stimuli are not inevitable, wired-in attitudes. For example, when people have to verbalize a person's racial category (Lieberman et al., 2005) or when they must infer the person's food preferences (Wheeler & Fiske, 2005), the race-amygdala effect evaporates. What's more, the amygdala effect inversely correlated with increased activity in the right ventrolateral PFC, consistent with the idea of it being involved in controlling emotional responses.

Conclusion

Perspectives on attitude processes—the heuristic-systematic model, the elaboration likelihood model, the MODE model, the IAT, embodied attitudes, and neural attitudes—integrate traditional attitude research and new insights from social cognition and social neuroscience. As such, they represent at least a "second generation" approach (S. J. Sherman, 1987). They insist that attitude formation, change, and operation are not entirely rational, in contrast to traditional approaches that presupposed recipients who necessarily learned and considered the message arguments, if persuasion was successful, and who necessarily consciously considered their attitudes when influenced by them. This older rational view failed in at least three ways First, people do not have to learn and recall a message to be persuaded by it; they may instead react to it online, resulting in an attitude based on their own responses but not on the message arguments as given. Second, people can be persuaded by more cognitively economical methods, whether persuasion heuristics or other peripheral routes. Third, people access their attitudes in relatively automatic ways, indicated by cognitive (response latency), physical (movement), and neural (activation) data.

Summary

More recent attitude theories have drawn heavily on social cognition theories and methods. Some new theories examine different types of attitude processing; some relatively thoughtful and analytic, others relatively rapid and automatic. The heuristic-systematic model posits that attitudes are often changed by cognitive shortcuts or heuristics in the form of simple persuasion rules that avert the need to process message content. Attitudes can also change by more systematic processing of the message arguments. Considerable research supports these ideas.

The elaboration likelihood model also proposes that attitudes can change by two routes, but the more automatic peripheral route includes a variety of superficial strategies, all of which share the feature of being relatively inattentive to message quality. In contrast, the central route to persuasion, typical of more motivated recipients, involves thorough consideration of the merits of the arguments given. In response to message arguments, people engage in more or less cognitive elaboration: that is, idiosyncratic responses pro or con. These, as measured by cognitive response analysis, predict attitude change via the central route. Traditional variables, such as characteristics of the communicator (credibility, expertise, and attractiveness), the message (its quality, repetition, difficulty, and length), and the audience (its outcome involvement, need for cognition, uncertainty orientation, and need to evaluate), all contribute to the degree and direction of cognitive elaboration as well as the resulting attitude change. This approach has yielded quantities of data illuminating old problems with new sophistication.

The MODE approach concentrates on the automatic activation of attitudes, based on the mere encounter with the attitude object. Attitudes activate more easily when recently or frequently activated in the past or when one has just reviewed attitude-relevant behavior. Low self-monitors, who are oriented to their attitudes, also seem to have more accessible attitudes. Easily activated attitudes more dramatically influence judgments about attitude-relevant information, resist contradiction, endure longer, and affect behavior more directly. The process seems to be relatively automatic. Clearly, some attitudes can activate immediately upon perception of the pertinent attitude object.

Implicit associations share many features of attitudes, predicting behavior. Associations between categories of an attitude object and positive or negative words show reliability and validity. Implicit associations best predict attitudes in contested or sensitive domains, whereas more traditional self-reports may best predict attitudes in more ordinary domains.

Other novel approaches to relatively spontaneous or implicit attitudes include embodied attitudes, correlated with arm flexion or extension, head nodding or shaking, and facial muscle manipulation. And neural patterns of activation implicate the amygdala in attitude intensity and other areas in valence.

CHAPTER 11

Stereotyping

Cognition and Bias

Blatant Stereotypes ◆ *Subtle Stereotypes* ◆ *Effects of Bias*

Casual forms of bias are everywhere, even at the dawn of this new century, even in enlightened institutions of higher learning, as the following examples illustrate.

- A recent college graduate, who is a South Asian woman, was driving her modest new car to work when she was pulled over by a local police officer, who asked if the car was indeed hers. After he inspected her license and registration, she asked why she had been stopped. He admitted she had not been speeding, but said, ominously, "I'll be watching you." She drove on, deeply shaken.
- Another recent college graduate, who is a Black woman, was newly arrived at graduate school. As she was squeezing past some audience members to find a seat at a colloquium, one of them mumbled "affirmative action . . ."
- A pregnant graduate student had just won a coveted fellowship. A male faculty member asked whether she could handle it.
- A White college freshman was moving into his first dorm room, which unexpectedly had no door knob. The White maintenance man, who arrived to remedy the situation, alluded to the just-finished summer program for students from underfunded public schools, saying "You just know it has to be *those people.*"

These everyday incidents cumulatively cast a chill over people's experience, and in the long run, everyday bias taxes the physical and mental well-being of targets (Major & O'Brien, 2005; Schnittker & McLeod, 2005). Eventually, bias can, in fact, kill—just more slowly and indirectly than hate crimes do.

Social cognition has much to say about ordinary bias, exemplified by everyday intergroup hassles, and the extraordinary forms of bias exemplified by hate crimes. This chapter and the next distinguish between the cognitive side of intergroup bias (namely, stereotypes) and the affective side of bias (namely, prejudice). This chapter discusses stereotypes, the next one prejudice, as linked to cognition. As you will see, although they often are correlated, distinct processes underlie each.

The most frequent intergroup distinctions in the United States at this time are gender, race, and age. Most bias research in social psychology has focused on race and gender, assuming that the processes generalize across other social categories.

This is both true and not true, as we shall see in these two chapters. Social cognition research has focused on stereotyping processes that often cut across social groups, although the contents of stereotypes and the specifics of emotional reactions do differ in accord with unique situations of biases directed toward each group.

Research on bias is abundant, even a dominant focus in the field, and much is now known (e.g., R. J. Brown & Gaertner, 2001; S. T. Fiske, 1998, 2002; Quinn, Macrae, & Bodenhausen, 2003). In accord with the basic concepts of social cognition, intergroup bias takes both automatic and controlled forms. The most significant insight in the past three decades of bias research is that everyday bias is often subtle, automatic, and unintentional, contrary to people's commonsense intuitions about it as overt bigotry. But today's subtle bias is not last century's blatant bias. In this chapter we first discuss cognitive aspects of blatant bias, which stem largely from perceived intergroup threats, both economic and value threats. Then we address subtle bias, which is automatic, ambiguous, and ambivalent; it stems from internal conflict. We close the chapter by examining the effects of bias, especially on targets.

As a preliminary note, the difference between blatant, intentional bias and subtle, perhaps unintentional bias matters quite a lot in practical terms as well as in theoretical ones. Ordinary perceivers and courts alike view intentional discrimination as far more serious and blameworthy than unintentional discrimination (S. T. Fiske, 1989; Swim, Scott, Sechrist, Campbell, & Stangor, 2003), even to the point of doubting whether people are legally responsible for unintentional discrimination and whether it can ever be avoided (Krieger & Fiske, 2006). We shall examine evidence relevant to these issues. But let's begin with the relatively rare case of extreme bigotry.

BLATANT STEREOTYPES

By some estimates, only 10% of the population in Western democracies hold extreme, blatant stereotypes. Nonetheless, they are a dangerous 10%, and they shape common knowledge about intergroup biases. Most people think that blatant bias results from realistic conflict over scarce resources, and it obviously can. Indeed, the intergroup conflict field began with this basic idea in a classic study randomly assigning summer campers to cabins and then pitting the cabins against each other for treats and privileges; conflict and bias quickly resulted (Sherif & Sherif, 1953). Other work linked economic downturns and lynching (Hovland & Sears, 1940). Realistic group conflict includes any kind of actual resource such as prestige, money, or military power (D. T. Campbell, 1965). Competition over actual resources does indeed matter both in the real world (Blake & Mouton, 1961, 1962; Bobo, 1983; Rabbie & Horowitz, 1969) and in the laboratory (Worchel, Axsom, Ferris, Samaha, & Schweitzer, 1978). Nonetheless, people have to perceive a conflict over resources, and the perceptions matter more than the reality as defined by some outside observer (Green, Glaser, & Rich, 1998; Green, Strolovitch, & Wong, 1998; Kinder & Sears, 1981; Sears & Kinder, 1985). Subjective perceptions clearly underlie conflict in the lab and in the field (R. J. Brown, Maras, Masser, Vivian, & Hewstone, 2001; Duckitt & Mphuthing, 1998; Hennessy & West, 1999; Huddy & Sears, 1995), and subjective perceptions are the stuff of social cognition.

Social Identity, Self-Categorization, and Other Identity Theories

To have intergroup conflict, people have to perceive themselves and other people as members of distinct groups. And they frequently do, although it's a subjective judgment that depends on circumstances. In this section we describe four group identity theories and some important consequences of social identities for intergroup misunderstanding.

Theories

Groups compete more than individuals do (Schopler et al., 2001), and it takes only two to tango: A pair of individuals can compete as individuals or as members of opposing groups. The perception that two people may interact as individuals or as members of their respective groups is the essential insight of *social identity theory* (SIT), which argues that interactions—even between two people—range from interpersonal to intergroup (Tajfel, 1981; Tajfel & Turner, 1979). Social identity theory claims that people seek a positive social identity to maintain their self-esteem. Social identity turns on one's membership in a distinctive group that one views positively on subjectively important dimensions (called one's ingroup), vis-à-vis a comparison group (the outgroup). In this view, even members of societally devalued groups carve out a positive social identity by emphasizing certain dimensions of their identity as their relative advantages.

Beyond the self-esteem assumption, SIT's most cognitive features specify that social identity is defined by the individual, society, and current context, so it rests on beliefs, which are cognitions. Moreover, categorization into ingroup and outgroups reduces perceived variability within the category while increasing perceived variability between categories. That is, any kind of categorization exaggerates both between-category differences (we're different from them) and within-category similarities (they're all alike, and in some important ways we are too).

Note that this theory departs from the idea of group conflict and emphasizes the mere cognitive process of categorization into groups. The original goal was to find minimal conditions for the experience of belonging in a group, and then to add progressively realistic conditions until biases emerged. To Tajfel's apparent surprise, even in experimentally created, explicitly arbitrary groups, people favored their ingroup over the outgroup when allocating limited resources (see Table 11.1). Mere categorization created bias and, with it, the research enterprise for an entire generation (for reviews, see Brewer & Brown, 1998; Hogg & Abrams, 2003).

TABLE 11.1. Tajfel Matrix

Ingroup/Outgroup Rewards, with Intergroup Differentiation Contrasting with Maximizing Joint Outcomes and Maximizing Ingroup Reward

Ingroup	7	8	9	10	11	12	13	14	15	16	17	18	19
Outgroup	1	3	5	7	9	11	13	15	17	19	21	23	25

Participant has to choose one column's pair of numbers, determining rewards to ingroup and outgroup.

As this research developed, the self-esteem hypothesis fell out of favor. The common lay assumption is that people discriminate in order to make themselves feel superior, but apparently it does not entirely work. Discriminating does elevate *state* self-esteem—a temporary affective self-assessment—but it does not alter *trait* self-esteem, one's long-term view of oneself (Oakes & Turner, 1980; Rubin & Hewstone, 1998). What's more, low self-esteem does not directly motivate discrimination, despite common sense to the contrary (Aberson, Healy, & Romero, 2000; Hewstone, Rubin, & Willis, 2002). Temporary reductions in self-esteem among people highly identified with their group might well cause discrimination in the service of social change (Turner & Reynolds, 2001), but the global self-esteem hypothesis is not supported.

Self-categorization theory (SCT) picked up the cognitive and intergroup threads of social identity theory without the self-esteem predictions (Turner, 1985). Aiming to predict actual behavior and not only perceived differences, SCT claims that social identities determine intergroup behavior; people identified with the group will actually behave more like other group members in this view. From a cognitive perspective, self-categorization theory makes the important point that the self is not fixed but depends on the salient intergroup context: One may think of oneself as a student (versus professors), a female (versus males), a White person (versus minorities), a psychology major (versus others), and so on. The operative group categorization depends on fit to the context. So-called comparative fit compares between-group differences to within-group differences in order to create what is termed a metacontrast ratio. (In statistical terms, it is equivalent to an *F* or *t*-test, putting mean differences over within-group variance.) According to SCT, the best comparison, based on actual observations, determines the relevant categorization. If you are a protestor in a demonstration confronting the police, your other category memberships matter less in that moment.

Self-categorization also depends on what is called normative fit; that is, on socially shared meaning that defines the two categories. The consensus about characteristic group differences related to the current context defines the relevant ingroup–outgroup categories. For example, students visiting a retirement home would likely self-categorize by age, whereas their visit to a rival university would instead prompt self-categorization by school. Thus self-categorization theory emphasizes psychological group membership (Turner & Reynolds, 2001).

In an entirely compatible vein, *optimal distinctiveness theory* (ODT; Brewer, 1991) argues that people balance individual autonomy and distinctiveness against belonging to the right group in order to reach a self-affirming and satisfying identity. That is, people value their group memberships, but they also value their individuality and need to strike a happy balance. This occurs across Western and non-Western cultures (Vignoles, Chryssochoou, & Breakwell, 2000) and for adolescents (Eckes, Trautner, & Behrendt, 2005) as well as undergraduates and adults (Hornsey & Jetten, 2004). People can achieve individual differentiation at the same time as ingroup belonging by maximizing the distinctiveness of their group identity.

Group distinctiveness also allays the tension of ambiguity. *Subjective uncertainty reduction theory* (Hogg & Abrams, 1993) proposes that ingroup norms reduce anxiety, especially when people are unsure in self-relevant domains. Adopting the ingroup's values and norms creates certainty, as people assimilate to the group prototype, depersonalize themselves, and shed their uncertainty. As with SIT, SCT, and ODT, this theory has essential cognitive underpinnings in normal categorization processes, but with the crucial difference that the self occupies one of the two categories.

Ingroup Favoritism

People favor the ingroup when group membership is all the information they have, as SIT's minimal group paradigm demonstrates. People favor "us" more than they explicitly disfavor "them," except that, of course, then outgroup disadvantage occurs by exclusion (Brewer, 1999; Hewstone et al., 2002; Mullen, Brown, & Smith, 1992). Indeed, ingroup favoritism exploits the *relative* advantage of ingroup over outgroup, even to the detriment of self and own group's *absolute* outcomes. For example, participants prefer to give an ingroup member 7 points and the outgroup member 1 (maximizing difference), than to give them both 13 (maximizing joint profit) or than giving the ingroup 19 and the outgroup 25 (maximizing ingroup profit) (Tajfel, Billig, Bundy, & Flament, 1971). As another example, people value their ingroup even when they are all relatively deprived together and cannot reward each other personally (Rabbie & Horwitz, 1969). Ingroup favoritism over the outgroup (intergroup differentiation) occurs especially on dimensions favoring the ingroup and increases under conflict, social breakdown, and ingroup importance; all this points to the role of ingroup favoritism as reducing subjective uncertainty when it matters most (Hogg, 1995).

People favor their ingroup because they are attracted to it, and attraction is a force that glues groups together (Hogg, 1992, 1993). Ingroup favoritism occurs automatically, as we shall see, and it increases with strong ingroup identification (Branscombe & Wann, 1994; Perreault & Bourhis, 1999) for those whose identity is under threat: embattled minorities (Mullen et al., 1992; Otten, Mummendey, & Blanz, 1996), distinctive groups (Jetten, Spears, & Manstead, 1998), and insecure high-status groups (Bettencourt, Charlton, Dorr, & Hume, 2001). The security of conforming to ingroup norms may contribute to the other cognitive feature of SIT, SCT, and related theories—namely, perceived group homogeneity.

Group Homogeneity

Categorization, as noted, reduces perceived variability within groups: "They" are all alike (Linville et al., 1989; Messick & Mackie, 1989; Mullen & Hu, 1989). Group homogeneity includes stereotyping but also dispersion (perceived spread of attributes) and similarity (Ostrom & Sedikides, 1992; Park & Judd, 1990). Outgroup homogeneity especially applies to groups that are real but unfamiliar and seen as abstractions, such as a national or ethnic group one has never encountered (Brewer & Brown, 1998; R. J. Brown, 2000; Devos, Comby, & Deschamps, 1996; Linville et al., 1989; Ostrom & Sedikides, 1992; Park, Ryan, & Judd, 1992). What's more, people think that other people especially have biases against outgroups more than they themselves do (Judd, Park, Yzerbyt, Gordijn, & Muller, 2005). Thus people expect intergroup perceptions to be biased, with each side viewing the other side as homogeneous.

Sometimes, however, "we" are all alike too. Numerical minorities view themselves as relatively homogeneous, especially on identity-relevant dimensions (Kelly, 1989; Mullen & Hu, 1989; Simon, 1992). People who especially identify with their ingroup perceive greater ingroup homogeneity (Castano &

Yzerbyt, 1998). A summary principle is that when intergroup distinctions are salient (because of threat or conflict), both ingroups and outgroups are seen as more homogeneous. And because people are especially likely to conform when ingroup identity matters most, perceived homogeneity may sometimes hold some truth.

Conclusion

What do the categorization approaches contribute to our understanding of blatant bias? They show that mere categorization is sufficient to produce overt bias. Ingroup favoritism may have automatic components, but it is largely conscious and overt, at least as measured in much of the research literature. For social cognition, the important point is that intergroup bias has important cognitive underpinnings. Moreover, threat exaggerates category-based bias, and threat itself is determined by cognitions. The next theories describe two primary bases of threat, perceived economic threat and perceived value threat.

Intergroup Ideologies

Another form of blatant bias rests on motivated social cognition. Various political ideologies correlate with perceived threats to ingroup. They all take the form of explaining society's intergroup relations as inevitable, reasonable, and legitimate: social dominance theory, right-wing authoritarianism, terror management theory, system justification theory, and theories of essentialism.

Social Dominance Theory

Groups compete for resources, and group hierarchies result. Social dominance theory (SDT) argues that group hierarchies are universal and even evolutionarily adaptive in societies beyond the hunter-gatherer stage. Some groups inevitably dominate others, and stable hierarchies regulate pointless conflict (however much the oppressed groups might wish it otherwise). Societies, groups, and individuals differ in their endorsement of social dominance (Sidanius & Pratto, 1999). With social dominance orientation comes a set of legitimizing myths, complex cognitions (beliefs and ideology) that support the status quo. Chief among those cognitions are stereotypes that keep groups in their respective places.

Individual differences in social dominance orientation (SDO) correlate with a wide range of blatant biases (e.g., Amiot & Bourhis, 2005; Pratto, Sidanius, Stallworth, & Malle, 1994; Sidanius, Pratto, & Bobo, 1996; for a recent list, see Sidanius & Pratto, 2003). Dominance interacts with intergroup contexts to reinforce the whole system in a variety of ways: High SDO predicts ingroup favoritism, not surprisingly among the powerful, but even among the powerless if they view the hierarchy as legitimate (Levin, Federico, Sidanius, & Rabinowitz, 2002). People individually high on SDO tend to choose careers that reinforce existing social dominance hierarchies (e.g., police, business, public prosecution), whereas people low on SDO tend to go into hierarchy-attenuating lines of work (social work, teaching, public defense). Once there, if the fit is good, they excel in their respective pursuits (Kemmelmeier, Danielson, & Basten, 2005; Pratto, Stallworth, Sidanius, & Siers, 1997; van Laar, Sidanius, Rabinowitz, & Sinclair, 1999).

Controversy over SDT centers on its claims of inevitability: for example, the hypothesized invariance of men's SDO scores always averaging higher than women's to account for the essential universality of men's greater political power in all developed societies. An SIT explanation argues that individual degree of gender identification causes the SDO differences (Dambrun, Duarte, & Guimond, 2004; Wilson & Liu, 2003). That is, maybe gender identification influences SDO, not the reverse: The more they identify with their gender group, the more they need to legitimate its place in the hierarchy as fixed. Similarly, instead of SDO causing inequalities, SDO scores might reflect inequalities that are salient in a given context and even a temporarily privileged position (Schmitt, Branscombe, & Kappen, 2003). Overall, a group socialization model argues that dominant (privileged) positions motivate SDO attitudes, which in turn increase prejudice (Guimond, Dambrun, Michinov, & Duarte, 2003).

SDT agrees that chronic power differences—whether based on gender, class, or race—cause different intergroup orientations between socially constructed groups (e.g., Pratto, 1999; Sidanius & Pratto, 1999). Social dominance ideologies target the most salient groups that define the sharpest power hierarchies in society at the current time. This suggests that SDO legitimates and maintains existing intergroup relations.

From a cognitive perspective on bias, SDO highlights the role of people's beliefs in a hierarchy that frequently advantages their own group's position. High SDO correlates with tough-minded views of the world as a dog-eat-dog competition (Duckitt, 2001). Its origins in unaffectionate parenting suggest a worldview in which people have to take care of themselves, and stronger groups inevitably must dominate weaker groups.

To distinguish SDO from the right-wing authoritarianism theory we discuss next, we suggest that SDO may correspond to an intergroup version of what Chapter 5 introduced as a promotion focus (Higgins, 1997). That is, high SDO would actively seek ingroup advantage in contrast to a prevention focus, which would avoid ingroup disadvantage (only sometimes the same thing). In any case, and not only as an individual difference, SDT focuses on perceived threat to resources: in other words, perceived group economic threat and promotion of the powerful ingroup's interests in a competitive world.

Right-Wing Authoritarianism

A different kind of perceived threat underlies a related dimension, namely, authoritarian beliefs. Specifically focused on perceived threat to cherished values is right-wing authoritarianism (RWA). The left-wing does not test as authoritarian per se, although both left and right can be dogmatic (Rokeach, 1960). Individuals high on RWA conform to traditional values (conventions), obey powerful leaders (authoritarian submission), sanction nonconformists (authoritarian aggression), and derogate outgroups (prejudice) (Altemeyer, 1981, 1988; Duckitt, 1993; Meloen, Van der Linden, & De Witte, 1996).

Intense ingroup identification coupled with perceived threat characterizes this belief set. If the ingroup is under threat by oppositional outsiders, then the ingroup must stick together, requiring cohesion and conformity to defend against the world's dangers. High RWA predicts bias against feminists and homosexuals, who are viewed as deviants (Haddock & Zanna, 1994; Haddock, Zanna, & Esses, 1993). High RWA correlates with various social attitudes that emphasize personal responsibility and punish deviance (in cases relating to AIDS, abortion, child abuse, drugs, homelessness, trade deficits, and higher education; Peterson,

Doty, & Winter, 1993). People high on RWA do not seek knowledge on the issues (Peterson, Duncan, & Pang, 2002) and deny the Holocaust (Yelland & Stone, 1996), perhaps because their values are unshakeable. Non-negotiable beliefs tend to predict prejudice because tolerance requires a more relativist view of variety in human groups.

If SDO corresponds to an ingroup promotion focus, as we suggest, RWA corresponds to an outgroup prevention focus. It correlates with punitive parenting, social conformity, and viewing the world as dangerous (Duckitt, 2001). The belief system represents a broad, cognitively coherent ideology. People who combine the highest levels of RWA and SDO are among the most prejudiced in society (Altemeyer, 2004) and are described as power-hungry, manipulative, amoral, dogmatic, ethnocentric, and anti-equality, positioning them as leaders of extremist fringe political groups, to society's peril.

Terror Management Theory

When people confront threats—intense uncertainty about an important negative possibility—they tend to take refuge in certainties as RWA indicates. This cognitive-motivational mix also appears when people confront their own death, which itself is certain, though the timing is not. The uncertainty in mortality salience is key (van den Bos, Poortvliet, Maas, Miedema, & van den Ham, 2005). Mortality salience makes people cling to cherished worldviews that will outlive them (a kind of vicarious immortality; Greenberg, Solomon, & Pyszczynski, 1997). People under threat of their own death validate the worldviews of their salient group identities (Halloran & Kashima, 2004). Conservatives want to conserve, and progressives want to progress, under threat (Greenberg, Simon, Pyszczynski, Solomon, & Chatel, 1992). People follow strong leaders, who reduce apparent uncertainty, under mortality salience (Landau et al., 2004).

Terror management theory (TMT) is so named because it addresses how people cope with the dread of death when it comes to mind. Most relevant to stereotyping, people seek to transcend death by identifying with their ingroups, which will outlive them (Castano & Dechesne, 2005). Under threat to self, people want to preserve the familiar, and this includes reacting against outgroups (Burris & Rempel, 2004). People respond harshly to deviant outgroups when mortality is salient (Castano, 2004; Greenberg et al., 1990; McGregor, Zanna, Holmes, & Spencer, 2001; Schimel et al., 1999), and this especially holds for people high in RWA. When the world is dangerous and threatening, conformity to bedrock values matters more. This orientation often punishes outgroups.

System Justification Theory

So far, we have seen the influences of self-protective motivations on blatant intergroup cognitions in four theories (SIT/SCT, SDT, RWA, and TMT). Another theory similarly posits ideology as soothing negative reactions (anxiety, uncertainty, discomfort), but it flies in the face of the self-protection motives implicit in the other theories. System justification theory posits that people seek to preserve and legitimate the status quo (e.g., Jost & Banaji, 1994; Jost & Hunyady, 2002). Unlike SDT, it not only argues that the advantaged do so, but provocatively argues that the disadvantaged do so as well. In this view, ego justification and even group justification give way to system justification because of its palliative effects. The idea that maintaining system stability outweighs individual and group interest receives varied support. Sometimes, at least, disadvantaged groups accept and legitimate their status, feel less entitled, favor higher status groups, and support the system despite their own best interests (e.g., Jost, Pelham, Sheldon, & Sullivan, 2003; for reviews, see Jost, Banaji, & Nosek, 2004; Jost & Hunyady, 2002). It remains to be seen under what circumstances they do this; for example, low-status groups sometimes resent or resist their status.

For high-status groups, justifying the status quo has obvious advantages. But for everyone the relationship between perceived status and perceived merit is surprisingly strong across cultures (Cuddy, Fiske, Kwan, et al., in press). Stereotyping more generally supports the status quo. For example, people view even their *own* college group as more (or less) competent when they learn that it is high- (versus low-) achieving relative to a comparison college group (Haines & Jost, 2000; Jost & Burgess, 2000). People may be motivated to view high-power groups as deserving their status to justify the system, but mainly when they personally feel they cannot change the situation (Dépret & Fiske, 1999; Pepitone, 1950; Stevens & Fiske, 2000). When one's group is devalued but boundaries are impermeable (one cannot leave), then one may under chronic or extreme circumstances internalize the inferiority (Ellemers, Spears, & Doosje, 2002).

Political conservatism, which by definition supports the status quo, fits a form of motivated social cognition—that is, a set of beliefs that correspond to various needs. (Liberalism does too, but it is to some extent the inverse of this analysis.) A meta-analysis of 88 studies (Jost, Glaser, Kruglanski, & Sulloway, 2003) found that conservative ideology correlated with death anxiety (supporting terror management theory), fear of loss (supporting social dominance theory), perceived system instability (supporting system justification theory and right-wing authoritarianism), and intolerance of ambiguity (RWA) as well as low openness to experience, intolerance for uncertainty, and need for order, structure, and closure. These last several motives support all of the theories, which jointly emphasize conservative cognitive structures that remove ambiguity in the face of threat and in the service of intergroup politics.

Entitativity and Its Heirs

The most reassuring cognitive representation of groups—the one that most removes ambiguity, uncertainty, instability, and anxiety—is one that makes the category seem objectively real. Social categories appear real, first, in being perceived entities, that is, units in the Gestalt sense (see Chapter 3). Once categorized, groups are seen to possess entitativity (D. T. Campbell, 1958), the property of being a real thing. An entitative ingroup, for example, seems coherent, feels efficacious, meets one's needs, and motivates one to identify with it (Yzerbyt, Castano, Leyens, & Paladino, 2000). Perceived entitativity tends to polarize intergroup relations (Castano, Sacchi, & Gries, 2003). It also paves the way for a variety of cognitive belief systems: essentialism, multiculturalism, and infrahumanization and dehumanization.

Essentialism

When groups are viewed as entities, they are often endowed with a second property, namely, an essence (Rothbart & Taylor, 1992; Yzerbyt, Corneille, & Estrada, 2001), which includes a foundational core often expressed as shared genes, blood, or nature. Perceived essence thus rests on interpretations of biology. People view biology as fixed (biologists, in contrast, understand its interactions with environment). People often view group categories as real biological phenomena instead of social constructions that change with history and culture.

The implications of essentialism are many. People who impute an essence to a social category also endorse stereotypes about it (Bastian & Haslam, 2006; Keller, 2005). Stereotypes help people to explain essentialized groups' characteristics as an enlightening Gestalt (Yzerbyt, Rocher, & Schadron, 1997).

Group essentialism needs to be viewed in context, of course. Both Western and East Asian cultures impute essence and entitativity to individual people more than to groups (Kashima et al., 2005) as basic person-perception principles would suggest. But when groups do seem especially essentialist (for example, in East Asia), people impute more agency to these essentialist groups; that is, they view them as capable of taking action. One of us recalls overseas news reports that would impute agency to countries ("China intends . . .") in contrast to news reports that impute agency to individuals in the government ("The President announced that he intends . . . . ": see Menon et al., 1999).

For majority members considering minorities, this kind of group agency may threaten their own position. For minority members, their ingroup's perceived essence and agency may protect their own sense of integrity. And indeed, for Dutch majority adolescents, essentialist beliefs related to resisting multiculturalism (Verkuyten & Brug, 2004). In contrast, for minority adolescents, a belief in group essence was associated with endorsing multicultural beliefs, presumably because their own embattled group identity was a source of pride.

Multiculturalism

Multicultural beliefs endorse the idea that groups differ in essential ways and that organizations should value those essential differences. Multiculturalism, in the extreme, implies biological essence, though moderate multiculturalism implies only chronic societal differences. A contrasting colorblind approach denies all differences and insists that everyone be treated identically, regardless of background. Multiculturalism fits social cognition's emphasis on the importance of categorization in intergroup perception. Indeed, students primed with a multicultural (compared to colorblind) perspective did show stronger stereotypes and more category-based judgments of individuals (Wolsko, Park, Judd, & Wittenbrink, 2000), but they also were more accurate about statistical differences between the groups. Such findings lead some to question whether perceiving group differences necessarily leads to bias, instead of recognizing and valuing multicultural differences (Park & Judd, 2005).

Infrahumanization and Dehumanization

The ultimate biological essence, of course, is being human. People ascribe human essence to their own group more than to other groups (Demoulin et al., 2004; Leyens et al., 2003). Human groups allegedly possess intelligence, language, and subtle emotions that differentiate us from animals. Focusing on the emotions, people tend to ascribe raw primary emotions (anger, happiness) to their own groups and to others, just as they do to animals. But subtle sentiments (regret, pride) are reserved for the ingroup. Subjective essentialism underlies this infrahuman (less-than-human) perception of outgroup emotions, and of course one sympathizes less with infrahumanized groups. For example, when they suffer a devastating hurricane or earthquake, their grief for lost homes and family members seems less poignant than would be our own group's reaction to comparable losses, and people accordingly help them less (Cuddy, Rock, & Norton, 2007).

People regularly minimize the humanity of others in two major ways (Haslam, 2006). First, people may treat others as animals, denying them the uniquely human attributes of culture, morality, logic, maturity, and refinement. This form of animalistic dehumanization most applies to stereotypes of outgroups based on ethnicity, immigration status, or disability. Or people may treat others as mechanistic objects, denying them typical features of human nature such as warmth, emotional responsiveness, agency, curiosity, and depth. This form of mechanistic dehumanization most applies to some medical treatment of patients and to the objectification of women (Haslam, Bain, Douge, Lee, & Bastian, 2005). Referring to the two overall types as animals and androids, one study found artists to be viewed as curious, fun-loving, and emotional (more associated with animals), whereas businesspeople were viewed as organized, hard-hearted, and shallow (more associated with automata; Loughnan & Haslam, 2007).

Intergroup contexts are not the only setting for attributing humanity; people attribute more humanity to themselves than to other individuals (Haslam et al., 2005). But intergroup dehumanization underlies some of humanity's worst mass crimes against humanity. Not only does dehumanization facilitate intergroup violence (it is easier to kill people you view as animals or machines), but ingroup violence against an outgroup also intensifies infrahumanization (Castano & Giner-Sorolla, 2006).

Conculsion Regarding Blatant Stereotypes

With dehumanization, we begin the segue into subtler forms of stereotyping. In blatant stereotyping, we have seen the beliefs that people express willingly, mostly in a conscious, controlled, intentional fashion. Most of these beliefs correlate with perceived intergroup threats. In accord with social identity theory and self-categorization theory, people identify with and protect their ingroups, contrasting those with outgroups, to the advantage of the former. Fitting social dominance theory, various societies, settings, and individuals differ in how much they endorse group hierarchies, with more intergroup dominance orientation predicting intergroup bias as a function of perceived competitive threat. Right-wing authoritarianism also reflects perceived threat but in this case to conventional values, with hostility to outgroups' conflicting values. Terror management theory describes people's tight grip on enduring ingroup values under threat of their own death, also correlating with intergroup bias. System justification theory argues that people threatened by more general system instability will legitimate the status quo positions of social groups, even (in this view) to their own group's disadvantage. Entitativity has more mixed effects. Essentialism focuses on multicultural differences, and at the extreme creates a human–nonhuman system: that is, the distinction between those of us who are truly human and those others who are less human than we are. Of all the blatant forms of bias, this one most often spills over to unspoken, indirect, unintentional forms of bias, to which we now turn.

SUBTLE STEREOTYPES

Subtle forms of stereotypes emerged in the later 20th century following dramatic changes in norms about acceptable beliefs. Unobtrusive indicators show that prejudice persists even as overt attitudes have improved (Crosby, Bromley, & Saxe, 1980; Saucier, Miller, & Doucet, 2005). Just as people no longer blow secondhand smoke in other people's faces, so people no longer express insulting stereotypes in polite company. As a result of these norm changes, along with new, sophisticated forms of measurement, researchers now can show how automatic, ambiguous, and ambivalent modern forms of stereotyping really are.

Automatic Stereotyping

A variety of cognitive associations link to people's intergroup representations. The apparent organization of these stereotypic beliefs, as well as their valence, reveals automatic processes that make stereotypes readily accessible to social cognitive processes. Chapter 12 focuses on more explicitly emotional prejudices, but the more cognitive beliefs covered here also contain valence, so they relate to prejudice as well, but along more evaluative than explicitly emotional lines. The relatively automatic cognitive processes we examine here include category confusions, aversively racist associations, indirect racial priming, implicit associations, and cognitive load. We close with a consideration of motivated control over these processes.

Category Confusions

People rapidly identify each other's gender, race, and age, using these categories to sort people. As a result, people tend to confuse other people who fall into the same category, forgetting *which* woman, *which* Latino, or *which* elderly person contributed a suggestion. In the "who-said-what" experimental paradigm, people's spontaneous memory errors more often confuse people within category than between categories (Taylor, Fiske, Etcoff, & Ruderman, 1978). A score of studies have demonstrated this confusion within categories based on gender, race, age, sexual orientation, attitudes, attractiveness, skin tone, and relationship type (e.g., Maddox & Chase, 2004; Maddox & Gray, 2002; see S. T. Fiske, 1998, pp. 371–372). Category confusions happen even when controlling for related cognitive processes such as guessing, especially when people respond rapidly (Klauer & Wegener, 1998), and concerning numerical minorities (Klauer, Wegener, & Ehrenberg, 2002). Although not to our knowledge tested subliminally (below awareness), these memory errors occur without apparent intention, effort, or control, making them relatively automatic. Moreover, these confusions encourage category-based stereotyping (Taylor et al., 1978).

Aversive Racism

Among the first to identify truly automatic forms of bias, priming experiments indicated that the us–them forms of categorization, as described by social identity theory, could kick in instantly. Whites identify positive traits (e.g., smart) faster when first primed with "Whites" than with "Blacks" (Dovidio, Evans, & Tyler, 1986; Gaertner & McLaughlin, 1983; Perdue et al., 1990). And the same pattern occurs substituting "us" versus "them" for racial labels. People's automatically positive ingroup associations recur reliably over time (Kawakami & Dovidio, 2001) and predict nonverbal behavior in interracial interactions (Dovidio, Kawakami, & Gaertner, 2002). (Overt attitudes predict overt verbal behavior.) People can control their stereotypic associations by extensive training that is specific to the particular outgroup, but it does not generalize to other outgroups (Kawakami, Dovidio, Moll, Hermsen, & Russin, 2000). Note that many of these effects emphasize the ingroup positives more than derogating the outgroup negatives.

Ingroup positivity, of course, neglects the outgroup by exclusion. In a zero-sum setting, such as hiring, even if overt biases improve, subtle biases persist, especially in ambiguous cases (Dovidio & Gaertner, 2000) and with only rare exceptions (Kawakami, Dovidio, & van Kamp, 2005). These instantaneous positive associations to the ingroup create a sense of comfort so that ingroup members just seem to fit in better.

According to a recent meta-analysis, Whites help Blacks less when they can rationalize their decision as not pertaining to race: for example, when helping would be riskier, longer, harder, effortful, or farther away (Saucier et al., 2005). Aversive racism is so-called because most people are well intentioned and reject the idea that they might have racist beliefs or intents (Gaertner & Dovidio, 1986). They express their ingroup-favoring associations only when they have apparently nonracist reasons (excuses), as when information is ambiguous. Thus one way to override such associations is to remove ambiguity. Unfortunately, life is inherently ambiguous.

A more realistic option is to capitalize on the us–them effect, but to expand the "us" to include the previous "them." For example, after the terrorist attacks of September 11, 2001, many Americans noticed improved interracial relations as national identity trumped racial identity. In a study tapping this phenomenon, being reminded that the attacks targeted all Americans served to reduce Whites' prejudices against Blacks (Dovidio et al., 2004). This approach, the common ingroup identity model (Gaertner & Dovidio, 2005), works well, apparently by increased perspective-taking and feelings of injustice (Dovidio et al., 2004), plus shared interaction and common fate (Gaertner, Sedikides, & Graetz, 1999).

Indirect Racial Attitudes

Another early entrant in cognitive approaches to stereotyping is the indirect priming technique (Fazio et al., 1986, 1995). As with aversive racism measures, the technique assesses the speed-up on people's responses given a fit in the evaluation of a prime and a stimulus (see chapter 10).

The two tasks differ, however, in the stimulus that follows the prime, and in the response required. In the aversive racism case, the ingroup or outgroup prime precedes a positive or negative race-relevant word or a meaningless string of letters. People make a lexical decision (i.e., Is this word or nonword?), which is speeded by a match between the racial prime and the valence of the stereotype-relevant word. In the indirect priming case, the initial racial prime (which could be a word or a photograph) precedes a positive or negative word *unrelated* to race, and the participant replies *good-bad* (instead of word-nonword). The aversive racism technique uses more conceptual processes because word meaning matters, whereas the indirect priming technique isolates the evaluative content because valence also matters. Conceptual versus evaluative priming does differ (Wittenbrink, Judd, & Park, 2001a). For example, conceptual processes link more to stereotyping, judgment, and impressions, whereas evaluative processes link more to affect, preferences, and social distance (Amodio & Devine, 2006). In both cases, however, the facilitation (speed-up) for some people's responses to negative, stereotypic terms following an outgroup prime provides an indirect index of racial attitudes. This cognitive facilitation places this measure alongside other measures of subtle bias.

Indirect priming measures do predict nonverbal behavior in interracial interactions, evaluations of an outgroup member's essay, emotional reactions to outgroup members, and other relevant attitudes (Fazio & Olson, 2003). Whether stereotypes and evaluations measured this way are the "real" attitude or not matters less than the observation that these upstream, relatively automatic indicators do correlate with downstream, more explicit attitudes and behaviors.

Consistent with this chapter's focus on stereotyping per se, automatically activated racial attitudes do relate to Whites' trait inferences about Blacks (e.g., Graham & Lowery, 2004). But all is not lost. Even these relatively automatic reactions can diminish, depending on the individual's motivation to avoid prejudice (Dunton & Fazio, 1997; Olson & Fazio, 2002, 2004a; Towles-Schwen & Fazio, 2003).

Implicit Association Test

Chapter 10 introduced the IAT at some length. Like the aversive racism and indirect priming measures just discussed, it has both an evaluative side and a more specific stereotype side. Here we focus on how it measures stereotypes per se, not the evaluative associations (attitudes) and not complex affective reactions (emotions). The basic IAT capitalizes on associations between ingroup (often, dominant) and positive attitude objects, as well as between outgroup (often, minority) and negative attitude objects.

Separation of implicit stereotyping and implicit evaluation in race bias comes from possibly distinct underlying neural systems for semantic versus affective memory (Amodio & Devine, 2006). White participants evaluating an African American essay writer expressed less warmth and inclination to befriend as a function of their IAT evaluative bias. In contrast, their IAT stereotyping bias (on the hackneyed images of athletic, rhythmic, unintelligent) predicted their other stereotypic ratings (lazy, dishonest, untrustworthy). In a second study, Whites' ratings of a prospective Black partner showed a similar correspondence. The evaluative IAT predicted how close they sat, reflecting the affective aspect, whereas the stereotype IAT predicted their expectancies for their partner's task performance, reflecting the more cognitive aspect (see also Neumann & Seibt, 2001).

Although mostly focused on evaluative attitudes, the implicit association test has homed in on specific stereotypes of gender-stereotyped appearance (e.g., petite), activities (e.g., football), objects (e.g., flowers), professions (e.g., mechanic), and roles (e.g., master; Blair & Banaji, 1996). Similarly, gender and strong gender identity combine with stereotyping math as male, to drive women away but men toward an implicit preference for math. As another example, women and men implicitly link their own gender to favorable trait stereotypes (Rudman, Greenwald, & McGhee, 2001).

Stereotyping and Cognitive Load

Chapter 4 on representation in memory distinguished between category activation and application, each of which depends on cognitive load (Gilbert & Hixon, 1991). To activation and application, we might add later judgment, which also depends on cognitive load. The entire set of processes is complex but efficient, with load playing different roles at each stage.

Category activation, as noted in Chapter 3 on encoding, more quickly and unintentionally emerges from faces than does individual identity (Cloutier, Mason, & Macrae, 2005; Macrae et al., 2005). That is, people notice others' general characteristics such as race or gender faster than they can name them. Although relatively automatic, category activation does vary with cognitive load, processing tasks, and context. Mere exposure to targets does not always prompt categorization (Macrae, Bodenhausen, Milne, Thorn, & Castelli, 1997). People apparently attend to cues relevant to multiple alternative categories (e.g., both gender and age), but activate only the currently most relevant category (Quinn & Macrae, 2005). Also, given multiple alternative categories, people activate the more accessible ones (Castelli, Macrae, Zogmaister, & Arcuri, 2004). Category activation also depends on context; for example, an African American shown at a family barbecue or a church cues different automatic responses than the same person on an urban street corner or with a gang (Wittenbrink, Judd, & Park, 2001b). Category activation is conditionally automatic, in the terms that Chapter 2 introduced.

Once the category is active, stereotype-consistent meanings are easier to absorb, so they require less cognitive capacity to process. Therefore, when cognitive resources are scarce, people selectively allocate attention to stereotype-inconsistent information. They especially attend to stereotype-inconsistency if they are prejudiced because they are trying to explain the inconsistency away (Sherman, Conrey, & Groom, 2004; Sherman, Lee, Bessenoff, & Frost, 1998; Sherman, Stroessner, Conrey, & Azam, 2005). At early stages of stereotype application, people prioritize a coherent impression, so they work on the inconsistencies; they then remember the inconsistent information that had required cognitive work to assimilate. However, because they have explained or assimilated it somehow, inconsistency may well not undermine their stereotypes.

At later times of application, especially under cognitive load, people rely on stored stereotypes more when making judgments (e.g., Bodenhausen & Lichtenstein, 1987; Bodenhausen & Wyer, 1985; Macrae, Hewstone, & Griffiths, 1993; van Knippenberg, Dijksterhuis, & Vermeulen, 1999). Using stereotypes frees mental capacity (Macrae, Milne, & Bodenhausen, 1994). And people with a high need for cognitive economy are especially likely to engage intergroup categorization (Stangor & Thompson, 2002). Thus, although complex, the role of cognitive load in stereotype activation, application, and judgment generally favors their efficient use and maintenance.

Stereotyping and Motivated Control

If stereotyping processes are so often automatic, how do people ever get past them? If stereotyping qualifies as conditionally automatic, then with sufficient motivation, capacity, and information, people can avert its impact. People more easily avoid relatively automatic stereotypic associations when they have enough motivation and time (Blair & Banaji, 1996; Macrae, Bodenhausen, Milne, & Ford, 1997). Practice helps diminish automatic stereotypic associations (Kawakami et al., 2000). So do perspective-taking (Galinsky & Moscowitz, 2000), guilt (Hing, Li, & Zanna, 2002), and self-focus (Dijksterhuis & van Knippenberg, 2000; Macrae, Bodenhausen, & Milne, 1998). The social influence of a minority experimenter can make a difference (Lowery et al., 2001), and affiliative motives can be key (Sinclair, Lowery, Hardin, & Colangelo, 2005). Motivation and capacity operate together to allow a more individuating focus, in addition to the easily used categorical information (for a review, see Fiske, Lin, Neuberg, 1999). Goals matter, given half a chance.

The goal of merely suppressing stereotypes, without adding alternative information, can backfire, however. If people merely try to avoid stereotypes, when they relax their guard afterward, they may experience a rebound, with redoubled stereotypic associations later (Macrae, Bodenhausen, & Milne, 1998; Macrae, Bodenhausen, Milne, & Jetten, 1994; Wegner, 1994). Motivation and capacity influence rebound effects as well (Monteith, Sherman, & Devine, 1998; N. A. Wyer, Sherman, & Stroessner, 2000). Prejudice and goals combine to predict postsuppression rebound (Monteith, Spicer, & Tooman, 1998).

Controlling one's stereotypes uses up executive control, which may explain the rebound effect. In interracial interactions, when Whites are especially concerned about appearing prejudiced, they inhibit their behavior, with good effect for their Black partners. Unfortunately for White people, they themselves do not enjoy the interaction as much (Shelton, 2003) and their executive control capacities are depleted afterward (Richeson et al., 2003; Richeson & Shelton, 2003). For Blacks trying to counteract the prejudices of a White partner, comparable damage occurs to their experience of themselves in the interaction and to their executive control afterward (Richeson, Trawalter, & Shelton, 2005; for a review, see Shelton & Richeson, 2006).

Conclusion Regarding Automatic Stereotyping

The first prong of subtle stereotyping, its automaticity, rests on basic categorization and rapid association processes. People tag other people by race, gender, age, and the like, confusing people within category and stereotyping accordingly. People's own prejudice is often aversive to them, so it tends to emerge in unintended associations that favor the ingroup. People indirectly associate positivity with the ingroup and, to a lesser extent, negativity with the outgroup. Positive and negative stereotypic associations appear in stereotype-relevant lexical decision tasks, in facilitation of valenced cues, and in rapid associations. These effects vary with cognitive load and motivation, though not simply, but mostly in the service of efficiency and stereotype maintenance.

Ambiguous Stereotyping

Modern forms of stereotyping are subtle not just because they are fast but because they are slippery. Much depends on interpretation. People deal automatically with information that is clearly stereotypic or counterstereotypic, as we have seen. But people also interpret ambiguous information to confirm their expectancies. For example, in one of the early classics, White people subliminally primed with Black stereotypic terms then interpreted ambiguous, race-unspecified behavior as more hostile (Devine, 1989). Police and probation officers subliminally primed with Black-stereotypic words then read race-unspecified vignettes about shoplifting and assault. They subsequently rated the offenders' hostility and immaturity, culpability, expected recidivism, and deserved punishment more negatively (Graham & Lowery, 2004). Stereotypic interpretations are not confined to race: People subliminally primed with rape-related terms read an ambiguous aggressive encounter between a man and a woman and then judged her more negatively afterward, especially if they endorsed beliefs in a just world, presumably because they were more likely to blame her for the ambiguous encounter (Murray, Spadafore, & McIntosh, 2005).

Nor are stereotypic interpretations of information only preconscious: People saw the same ambiguous angry-sad expression on a face that was made by hair and clothing to change gender; they then interpreted the facial expression as angry if male and sad if female, in line with gender stereotypes about emotion (Plant, Kling, & Smith, 2004). People interpret a construction worker hitting someone as punching, but a housewife as spanking (Kunda & Sherman-Williams, 1993). And this occurs even when people are not asked for their interpretations but merely later misrecognize an inference as familiar (e.g., a nun's versus a rock star's reaction to the amount of liquor served at a party; Dunning & Sherman, 1997). These interpretations occur at encoding, so they become an integral part of people's understanding of the other person.

People interpret not only the content of ambiguous information but its causal meaning. That is, when the ingroup does something good, it must be our inherent ability or goodness, but when the outgroup does the same thing, it must be due to chance or the situation. The reverse obtains for negative actions. Dubbed the ultimate attribution error (Pettigrew, 1979), the effect appears in interethnic attributions (Hewstone, 1990) and in cross-gender attributions (Deaux & Emswiller, 1974; Swim & Sanna, 1996). The effect is subtle and ambiguous because it depends on interpreting the causes underlying group behavior. This has a practical impact. For example, jurors who subscribe to a model of African Americans as agentic perpetrators are more likely to interpret an interracial dispute as their fault, whereas viewing African Americans as victims leads to viewing the Whites as guilty (Wittenbrink, Gist, & Hilton, 1997). Dispositional attributions stabilize negative outgroup stereotypes and positive ingroup ones, whereas situational attributions decrease the stability of their opposites (Sherman, Klein, Laskey, & Wyer, 1998). Some people more than others favor such fixed, entity attributions for negative stereotypes (Levy, Plaks, Hong, Chiu, & Dweck, 2001).

Subjective judgments of ambiguous information do not always favor the dominant group. Because of shifting standards, for example, a woman may be viewed as performing well (for a woman) and praised. A man would have to perform well, for a man, to receive equal praise because the standards are higher. Praise is cheap, however. When it comes to allocating scarce resources, the two genders have to compete, and then the stereotypes result in pro-male bias (Biernat & Vescio, 2002). One way to understand this complex idea of shifting standards is to contrast subjective judgments (rating people as "smart") versus apparently objective judgments (ranking the smartest people you know). These effects appear in contexts as varied as sports (Biernat & Vescio, 2002), military promotions (Biernat, Crandall, Young, Kobrynowicz, & Halpin, 1998), and hiring decisions (Biernat & Fuegen, 2001).

Stereotyping all these ways is tacit and capitalizes on the ambiguity of the information given, so the influence of the stereotype itself is ambiguous and difficult to detect. People hide their stereotypic interpretations from themselves as well as from others. For example, in evaluating job applicants, people weight their credentials differently depending on how they want the decision to come out (Norton, Vandello, & Darley, 2003). What they value in one decision may then carry over to subsequent decisions.

Stereotyping can be ambiguous too, when the situation creates ambiguity. That is, if prejudice is but one possible cause of a decision, for which nonprejudiced reasons might excuse the action, then the decision itself is ambiguous with regard to prejudice. For example, in aversive racism research, White people who score high on modern measures of subtle racism (see Table 11.2) have a variety of political opinions that all happen to disadvantage minorities. They also are less likely to help a Black person, but only when others are also present, diffusing responsibility for aid (Gaertner & Dovidio, 1986). Aggression, given nonracial excuses, works similarly; that is, White participants aggressed against Black targets less than against White targets. But if they had the excuse of being insulted by the target, they aggressed more against Blacks than Whites (Rogers & Prentice-Dunn, 1981). In a similar vein, people who have proved their moral credentials as unprejudiced subsequently feel more free to express stereotypes and prejudices (Monin & Miller, 2001).

Conclusion Regarding Ambiguous Stereotyping

What all these studies share is the ambiguity of expressing category-based cognitive biases. People interpret ambiguous information to fit their stereotypes, and this occurs both preconsciously and postconsciously. People's causal attributions for group behavior reinforce stereotypes and affect their judgments. Because of lower standards for stereotyped groups ("good for a minority"), subjective judgments may actually favor outgroups, but allocation of scarce resources (e.g., ranking) does not. People make excuses to themselves and others for stereotypic judgments, making ambiguous their use of stereotypes.

Ambivalent Stereotyping

Stereotyping can also be subtle in being ambivalent. Unlike automaticity, which became evident as more blatant controlled types of bias receded, and unlike ambiguity, which people use to excuse or disguise their stereotyping because it is aversive to them and to others, ambivalence is not new. As early as stereotypes were systematically measured, some groups elicited flat-out negative stereotypes (e.g., Turks were thought to be cruel and treacherous), and others all-out positive ones (e.g., the English were thought to be intelligent and good sports). But many others received mixed stereotypes: African Americans were allegedly lazy but musical, and Jews were allegedly industrious but mercenary (Katz & Braly, 1933). The stereotypes of Black people and Jewish people seemed inverse on competence and warmth, each high on one but low on the other (Allport, 1954). This ambivalence turns out to be a general principle of stereotype content.

When people encounter an unfamiliar group, they want to answer immediately two questions. First, in the words of sentries, "friend or foe?" This answers the group's intention for good or ill (Are they competing and exploiting, or are

TABLE 11.2. Modern Racism Scale, 2000

Denial of Continuing Racial Discrimination

1. Generations of slavery and discrimination have created conditions that make it difficult for Blacks to work their way out of the lower class. (R)
2. How much discrimination against Blacks do you feel there is in the United States today, limiting their chances to get ahead? Would you say a lot, some, just a little, or none at all?
3. Discrimination against Blacks is no longer a problem in the United States.
4. Has there been a lot of real change in the position of Black people in the past few years?

Blacks Should Work Harder

1. It's really a matter of some people not trying hard enough; if Blacks would only try hard they could be just as well off as Whites.
2. Blacks work just as hard to get ahead as most other Americans. (R)
3. Irish, Italian, Jewish, and many other minorities overcame prejudice and worked their way up. Blacks should do the same without any special favors.

Demands for Special Favors

1. Some say that the civil rights people have been trying to push too fast. Others feel that they haven't pushed fast enough. How about you? Do you think that civil rights leaders are trying to push too fast, are going too slowly, or are moving at about the right speed?
2. Black leaders have been trying to push things too fast.
3. Blacks are getting too demanding in their push for equal rights.
4. Blacks are demanding too much from the rest of the society.
5. Blacks generally do not complain as much as they should about their situation in society. (R)
6. How much of the racial tension that exists in the United States today do you think Blacks are responsible for creating? All of it, most, or not much at all?

Undeserved Outcomes

1. Over the past few years, Blacks have gotten less than they deserve. (R)
2. Over the past few years, Blacks have gotten more economically than they deserve.
3. Do Blacks get much more attention from the government than they deserve, more attention, about the right amount, less attention, or much less attention?

R indicates reverse-scored items.
Source: Sears and Henry (2003).

they harmless, even cooperative?). Competitive intent predicts stereotypes of being unsociable, cold, and untrustworthy. Second, people want to know, "able or unable?" This answers whether the group can enact their intentions (Do they have the necessary resources?). High status predicts stereotypes of perceived competence and ability (see Cuddy, Fiske, & Glick, in press, for a review).

This competence-by-warmth space describes two ambivalent combinations and two unambivalent combinations: In the United States, currently, people who are middle class, Christian, or heterosexual are seen as both warm and competent. Conversely, people who are homeless, drug-addicted, or poor (regardless of race) are stereotyped as neither warm nor competent. The ambivalent combinations reflect groups who are liked as warm but disrespected as incompetent (older people, disabled people) or groups who are disliked as not warm but respected as competent (Jews, Asians, rich people, professionals regardless of race or gender; Fiske, Xu, Cuddy, & Glick, 1999; Fiske, Cuddy, Glick, & Xu, 2002). These four combinations appear in representative U.S. samples, in Europe, and in Asia (though the warm, competent reference groups appear more modest there; Cuddy, Fiske, & Glick, 2007; Cuddy, Fiske, Kwan, et al., in press; Eckes, 2002). The four clusters also describe various subtypes within larger categories: subgroups of men and women, subgroups of gay men, distinct mental illnesses, and categories of Black people within the Black community (respectively: Clausell & Fiske, 2005; Eckes, 2002; Fiske, Moore, & Russell, 2006; Williams, 2006). These stereotypes predict specific emotional prejudices and discriminatory behaviors, as we will see later (Cuddy et al., 2007; Fiske et al., 2002).

This warmth by competence space operates in a wide range of social perception for both individual and group targets (see Fiske, Cuddy, & Glick, 2007, for a review). Related frameworks describe two similar stereotypic dimensions: competence, as self-profitable, and morality/sociability, as other-profitable (Peeters, 1983). That is, being capable requires at least an initial focus on self, whereas being warm and trustworthy requires an orientation to others. This self- and other-profitable framework applies to national groups (Phalet & Poppe, 1997) and values (Wojciszke, 1997). A third approach, enemy images theory (Alexander, Brewer, & Hermann, 1999), describes national stereotypes again in a framework that includes these competence and warmth dimensions plus power. The point here is that stereotypes have at least two dimensions, and groups can be viewed as positive on one and negative on the other, rendering the cognitions evaluatively ambivalent.

Stereotypes often evoke this tension between liking and respect. Racial ambivalence (Katz & Hass, 1988; Katz, Wackenhut, & Hass, 1986) reflects White liberals as mixing interracial reactions pro and con, viewing Black people as disadvantaged alternatively because of external obstacles such as discrimination or because of internal obstacles such as values and motivation. Ambivalent sexism (Glick & Fiske, 1996, 2001) reflects two factors: first, hostile sexism, which is resentment directed toward women who pursue nontraditional roles, gaining respect but forfeiting affection; and second, subjectively benevolent sexism directed toward women who stay within prescribed gender roles, gaining protection but forgoing respect (Glick, Diebold, Bailey-Warner, & Zhu, 1997). This pattern, again, is not new, and it holds up across cultures (Glick et al., 2000; see Glick & Fiske, 2001, for a review).

Another complementary ambivalent stereotype paints rich people as dishonest and poor people as honest (Kay & Jost, 2003). Exposing people to this stereotype increases their justification of the system. Praising winners on relevant dimensions (the rich as hard-working and intelligent) justifies the system, and praising losers on an irrelevant dimension (honest, happy) compensates the victims without undermining the system (Kay, Jost, & Young, 2005). In this view, everyone benefits from the system in at least some respects (Jost & Kay, 2005).

Conclusion Regarding Subtle Bias

Current forms of bias, shorn of blatant bias, remain automatic, ambiguous, and ambivalent. The relatively unconscious, unintentional, muddy, and mixed signals are difficult for perceivers to notice and for targets to interpret. Nevertheless, they have a chilling impact. We turn now to effects on both sides of the intergroup encounter.

EFFECTS OF BIAS

Whether blatant or subtle, stereotyping is best studied in interactions between people. Stereotyping research had emphasized Whites' perceptions of Blacks to the exclusion of Blacks' racial attitudes and how they affect interracial encounters (Hebl & Dovidio, 2005; Shelton, 2000; Vorauer, 2006). The mutual interplay of expectancies is the stuff of social interaction. Much of the work on behavior appears in Chapter 15, but here we examine stereotypic expectancies and their effects on both sides. Targets of stereotypes have multiple options for coping (Miller & Kaiser, 2001), as do perpetrators of stereotypes.

Attributional Ambiguity

Precisely because so much stereotyping is subtle, targets often may be unsure whether negative reactions are aimed at them personally as unique individuals or collectively as interchangeable members of their group. This attributional ambiguity reflects the dilemma targets face (Crocker & Major, 1989). As with all negative events, experiences of bias typically provoke appraisal of threat and subsequent coping. When intergroup interactions go badly, targets may cope by blaming prejudice instead of their own behavior, thereby protecting their self-esteem (Major, Quinton, & McCoy, 2002).

Targets are, however, reluctant to attribute negative outcomes to prejudice because of the social as well as personal costs. Socially, people who make attributions to discrimination risk being labeled as complainers, troublemakers, or worse (Kaiser & Miller, 2001b, 2003; J. K. Swim & Hyers, 1999), especially by highly prejudiced people (Czopp & Monteith, 2003). An interaction is irrevocably altered when one person raises issues of prejudice. People want to belong to their group (whether work or social), and allegations of discrimination undermine belonging; hence, people high on a need to belong are less likely to make attributions to discrimination (Carvallo & Pelham, 2006).

Personally, also, attributions to discrimination can undermine the target's sense of control. And although attributing negative outcomes to discrimination can buffer self-esteem, attributing positive outcomes to (bend-over-backwards positive) discrimination can undermine self-esteem because one cannot take credit for the success (Crocker, Voelkl, Testa, & Major, 1991). Constant attribution to discrimination damages self-esteem (Major, Testa, & Blysma, 1991). And perceiving one's personal experience as an instance of pervasive discrimination is depressing (Schmitt, Branscombe, & Postmes, 2003).

Exaggerated stigma consciousness—heightened vigilance in interacting with outgroup members—can encompass a feedback loop of negativity: Expecting prejudice leads to acting negatively, which in turn elicits the expected negative experiences (Pinel, 1999, 2002). This kind of paranoid perspective increases self-consciousness, sinister attributions, and negative perceptions of the other's attitudes (Santuzzi & Ruscher, 2002), none of them recipes for a successful interaction. Stigma consciousness, however, show substantial individual differences.

On the other hand, expectations of discrimination sometimes reflect reality, and this is the target's predicament. People and situations vary in the extent to which they resolve attributional ambiguity by playing the discrimination card, and the pattern contradicts common sense. Low-status people (women, minorities) who endorse individual effort and the Protestant ethic are less likely to make attributions to discrimination (Major, Grazmow, McCoy, Levin, Schmader, & Sidanius, 2002). On the other hand, high-status people (men, Whites) who hold the same beliefs are more likely to attribute negative outcomes to discrimination against themselves. Women and minorities actually may be less likely than men and majorities to make attributions to discrimination, perhaps because their status is less legitimated, so frustration and disappointment are familiar. Again because of cultural ideologies about entitlement and blame, heavy-weight people are less likely to make attributions to discrimination, perhaps because of the cultural ethic that people can and should control their weight (Crocker, Cornwell, & Major, 1993). Attributions to discrimination interplay with expectations about who's to blame for negative outcomes and who's entitled to good ones.

Stereotype Threat

Expectations about people's performance success and failure drive another aspect of stereotypes' effects. Group stereotypes universally include a dimension of perceived competence or incompetence, as noted earlier. Stereotypes target specific domains for specific groups: for example, women in math (Spencer, Steele, & Quinn, 1999), African Americans on standardized tests (Steele & Aronson, 1995), European Americans in sports (Stone, Lynch, Sjomeling, & Darley, 1999), men on emotional sensitivity (Koenig & Eagly, 2005; Leyens, Désert, Croizet, & Darcis, 2000), Latinos on math (Gónzales, Blanton, & Williams, 2002), older people on memory (Chasteen, Bhattacharyya, Horhota, Tam, & Hasher, 2005), previously mentally ill people on intellectual performance (Quinn, Kahng, & Crocker, 2004), and low-income people on ability testing (Croizet & Clare, 1998). In the relevant domain, if performance appears diagnostic of one's ability, then the stereotype poses a threat beyond the normal threat associated with high-level performance (e.g., Steele, 1997; for reviews, see Major & O'Brien, 2005; Steele, Spencer, & Aronson, 2002). If one fails, one suffers not only the personal humiliation of failure but also the shame of confirming stereotypes about the ingroup's intrinsic abilities. Stereotype threat occurs only if one's relevant category is salient, the domain is relevant, the test is allegedly diagnostic, and one cares about it (Steele et al., 2002).

People cope with stereotype threat sometimes by disengaging from the domain. For example, many African Americans view intelligence testing as biased and unsuited to assessing important kinds of intelligence, so self-esteem is not contingent in the long or short term on that kind of performance (Major, Spencer, Schmader, Wolfe, & Crocker, 1998). Older adults (and others) may deny the relevance of a particular form of incompetence (von Hippel, von Hippel, Conway, Preacher, Schooler, & Radvansky, 2005). This disidentification with performance explains why some group members give up on domains in which others do not expect them to excel. It is not precisely a self-fulfilling prophecy because (a) they deny or avoid the domain altogether, so they do not actually underperform but instead refuse to perform, and (b) they don't actually have to meet a prejudiced person. Stereotype threat describes the impact of ambient stereotypes, that is, stereotypes "in the air," not necessarily stereotypes in a given encounter with a prejudiced person.

People suffer from stereotype threat when they are vulnerable to salient, important negative comparisons in a diagnostic domain. Everyone can fall prey to this, with even the same group underperforming in one comparison context and overperforming in another. Asian women do better on math in a comparative context when they identify as Asians and worse in a comparative context when they identify as women (Shih, Pittinsky, & Ambady, 1999). White men underperform in a comparative context with Asians but overperform in a comparative context with White women (Aronson, Lustina, Good, Keough, Steele, & Brown, 1999). Student-athletes perform differently depending on which identity is relevant (Yopyk & Prentice, 2005).

The process of stereotype threat involves a specific context on dimensions just noted (performance stereotypes, identity salience, test diagnosticity, domain importance); such contexts are inadvertently designed to heighten vigilance and stress (Steele et al., 2002). In this setting, cognition and motivation combine to undermine performance (Wheeler & Petty, 2001). For example, arousal combines with attributions for that arousal to undermine performance (Ben-Zeev, Fein, & Inzlicht, 2005). Anxiety is subtle, measured either by physiological and nonverbal indicators or by self-reports (Bosson, Haymovitz, & Pinel, 2004; Croizet, Després, Gauzins, Huguet, Leyens, & Méot, 2004). Negative thinking and activated stereotypes may be one cognitive mechanism that interacts with motivation (Cadinu, Maass, Rosabianca, & Kiesner, 2005; Kray, Galinsky, & Thompson, 2002; Seibt & Förster, 2004; Stangor, Carr, & Kiang, 1998; Wheeler, Jarvis, & Petty, 2001). Thus trying to suppress the stereotypes does not work precisely because suppression keeps the stereotype activated (Steele et al., 2002). On the cognitive side, working memory capacity suffers (Schmader & Johns, 2003), but on the motivation side, dejection also enters in (Keller & Dauenheimer, 2003). It's a daunting mix of potential damage.

Fortunately, several antidotes do work, such as individually realizing that intelligence is not fixed but is malleable and therefore context-dependent and improvable (Aronson, Fried, & Good, 2002). Other remedies include focusing on the relative strengths of one's ingroup (Marx, Stapel, & Muller, 2005), individuating oneself (Ambady, Paik, Steele, Owen-Smith, & Mitchell, 2004), affirming a distinct valued attribute (Martens, Johns, Greenberg, & Schimel, 2006), or bifurcating one's identity (Pronin, Steele, & Ross, 2004). Learning about stereotype threat and attributing one's anxiety to stereotypes also improve performance (Johns, Schmader, & Martens, 2005).

Structural remedies include not asking for demographic information before the test, presenting the test as fair or insensitive to group differences, emphasizing the organization's commitment to diversity, blurring group boundaries, and creating identity safety (Davies, Spencer, & Steele, 2005; O'Brien & Crandall,

2003; Rosenthal & Crisp, 2006; Steele et al., 2002). Between the personal and the structural remedies, stereotypes need not threaten people's performance, but only if people know about the phenomenon.

Minority Identity and Well-Being

Stereotype threat and attributional ambiguity help explain how stereotyped targets—despite the odds—avoid being crushed. People can reinterpret or ignore the relevance of public feedback. And indeed, public regard for one's group predicts nothing about self-esteem among African Americans (Rowley, Sellers, Chavous, & Smith, 1998), nor does public regard predict one's own private regard for one's group among African Americans, although it does for Asians (Crocker, Luhtanen, Blaine, & Broadnax, 1994). Some aspects of collective self-esteem— namely, one's personal, private regard for one's group and one's own feelings of worth as a group member (living up to the group image)—do predict psychological well-being (e.g., life satisfaction, depression). Thus well-being is closely tied to private aspects of collective self-esteem (Crocker & Luhtanen, 1990).

As we saw in Chapter 5 on the self, feeling contingent on others to validate the self generally is not healthy (e.g., Crocker & Park, 2004). For example, an academic contingency for self-worth can make people depend on achievement for self-esteem, but this makes them especially vulnerable when they do fail, even occasionally, especially if they believe intelligence is fixed (not malleable; Niiya, Crocker, & Bartmess, 2004). All this can lead to further academic and even financial problems (Crocker & Luhtanen, 2003) as well as giving up on one's major (Crocker, Karpinski, Quinn, & Chase, 2003). In a completely different domain— sexual satisfaction—basing one's self-esteem on others' approval of one's gender conformity also undermines relevant experiences (Sanchez, Crocker, & Boike, 2005). Investment of self in gender ideals is generally a bad idea for men and women alike (Sanchez & Crocker, 2005). Investment of self-esteem in others' approval of one's appearance is also bad for one's health, correlating with heavier alcohol use (Luhtanen & Crocker, 2005). For heavy-weight and poor people, perhaps because the culture blames them for their conditions, self-esteem suffers (Miller & Downey, 1999; Rudman, Feinberg, & Fairchild, 2002).

In various identity domains, private regard for one's identity seems more adaptive than relying on public regard. For example, among academically at-risk African American high school students, private regard for Black people, coupled with a father's support, decreased alcohol use (Caldwell, Sellers, Bernat, & Zimmerman, 2004). Among African American college and high school students generally, private regard for Blacks, combined with centrality of one's racial identity, preserved self-esteem (Rowley et al., 1998). Private regard correlates with maternal support; together they buffer against perceived stress, diminishing anxiety and depression (Caldwell, Zimmerman, Bernat, Sellers, & Notaro, 2002).

Identity also shapes perceived discrimination. Some minority individuals are more attuned to discrimination than others. For example, Blacks for whom race is central, whose ideology is Black nationalist, and who view public regard of the ingroup as generally negative are more likely to perceive discrimination but also to be buffered from its negative mental health consequences (Sellers, Caldwell, Schmeelk-Cone, & Zimmerman, 2003; Sellers, Rowley, Chavous, Shelton, & Smith, 1997). Ethnic identity can sensitize people to discrimination

(Operario & Fiske, 2001; Sellers & Shelton, 2003; Shelton & Sellers, 2000), but the types of identity, types of discrimination, and types of outcomes matter.

On average, though, African Americans are more likely to detect subtle nonverbal indicators of prejudice than are European Americans, as indicated by accurately judging a White person's implicit and explicit prejudice (Richeson & Shelton, 2005). Monitoring an interaction for prejudice and managing it to produce positive outcomes can be depleting. The more they show ingroup favoritism (probably comparable to private regard of ingroup), the more African Americans experience loss of attentional resources *after* an interracial interaction (Richeson, Trawalter, & Shelton, 2005). That is, African Americans who prioritize their ingroup may be particularly likely to monitor interracial interactions, which is depleting. Expecting another person to be prejudiced can taint the interaction (Shelton, Richeson, & Salvatore, 2005). However, moderately prejudiced majority people who attempt to monitor their prejudice apparently can compensate: They are more engaged in the interaction. As a result, in this case a prejudiced interaction partner ironically may be preferable, at least in the short term (Shelton, Richeson, Salvatore, & Trawalter, 2005).

Perceiving discrimination is a multistep process, known as ask-answer-announce (Stangor, Swim, Secrist, DeCoster, Van Allen, & Ottenbreit, 2003). First, the idea that discrimination might be relevant has to occur to the target; one has to ask oneself the question. Contrary to dominant group intuitions, all stigmatized people do not think about discrimination at all times. Contexts and individual differences both can make the possibility of discrimination more accessible. Second, if the question is posed, one must answer, and judging a behavior as discrimination depends again on situational factors (e.g., amount and intent of harm), the role of affect, need for control, and protecting self-esteem (e.g., Sechrist, Swim, & Stangor, 2004; Swim et al., 2003). Third, even in concluding that discrimination occurred, one may or may not announce it. As noted earlier, the costs are high, and people often avoid drawing such conclusions publicly.

Lower status (often minority) group members are most likely to have concerns related to evaluations of self when their outcomes depend on the high-status person (Vorauer, 2006). They may personalize negative behaviors and experience discomfort (Vorauer & Kumhyr, 2001). Lower status group members can cope either by distancing themselves from the interaction, thereby damaging the impression they make (Kaiser & Miller, 2001a), or by overcompensating in the interaction, thereby improving the impression they make (Shelton, Richeson, & Salvatore, 2005).

Majority Concerns

Intergroup interactions have two sides, and higher status groups (usually majorities) also worry about the impression they make (Shelton & Richeson, 2006; Vorauer, 2006). Indeed, White students report wanting to have more interaction with Black peers but worry about being rejected, so they fail to initiate contact. They also attribute their Black peers' apparent lack of interest as rejection. Ironically, precisely the same process occurs for Black students regarding their White peers (Shelton & Richeson, 2005). Neither side understands the other, and this pluralistic ignorance prevents communication. When intergroup interactions do occur, low-prejudice majority people amplify their overtures to make their interest abundantly clear, whereas high-prejudice people (who are in fact less interested) tend to downplay the interest they convey (Vorauer, 2005). Dominant group members, when especially concerned about appearing prejudiced, may choke under pressure if they are low in prejudice. Conversely, if they are high in prejudice, their enhanced evaluative concerns allow them to shine—coming across as warm and friendly (Vorauer & Turpie, 2004). Ironically, minorities may prefer to interact with high-prejudice dominant group members, as noted, in the short term at least when they are motivated.

Part of what may be annoying about well-intentioned but low-prejudice people is their self-absorption. Concerns with the other person's stereotypes of self (called metastereotypes) cause majority members to focus on themselves and how they are viewed (Vorauer, Hunter, Main, & Roy, 2000; Vorauer & Kumhyr, 2001). This public self-consciousness, as noted, depletes majority group members' executive function during and after the interaction (Richeson et al., 2003; Richeson & Shelton, 2003; Richeson & Trawalter, 2005), so interracial interactions between strangers can be exhausting for everyone.

Summary

Stereotyping is the cognitive aspect of bias—most frequently based on gender, race, and age—and it comes in both blatant and subtle forms, a difference that matters in both practical and theoretical terms.

Blatant prejudice can begin with realistic intergroup conflict over tangible resources, but even under these circumstances, perceptions matter. People have to perceive conflict, and they have to perceive that they belong to separate groups in the first place. Social identity theory describes how people categorize self into an ingroup and others into outgroups, maximizing differences between them and minimizing difference within. Discriminating elevates short-term (state) self-esteem but not long-term (trait) self-esteem. Self-categorization theory jettisons the self-esteem hypothesis and focuses on comparative fit to describe behavior differences between groups and similarities within them. Normative fit incorporates groups' images. Optimal distinctiveness theory describes the balance between autonomy and belonging. Subjective uncertainty reduction theory describes the reassurance provided by group norms. The most cognitive features of these theories are ingroup favoritism (rewarding the ingroup relative to the outgroup) and perceived homogeneity (of outgroups most of the time and of ingroups under threat).

Threat enters into several theories of ideology, stereotyping, and bias. Social dominance theory describes endorsing group hierarchies under perceived economic threat to the ingroup. Right-wing authoritarianism describes endorsing status quo group boundaries under perceived threat to conventional values. Terror management theory describes adherence to cultural views that will outlast one's own lifetime, under mortality salience. System justification theory describes people's maintenance of hierarchies, even against their own self-interest, because stability may matter more. Essentialism imputes a biological basis to socially constructed groups, preserving the humanity of us and lessening the humanity of others. All these theories emphasize cognitions that resolve ambiguity, under threat, in the context of intergroup politics.

Subtle forms of stereotyping emerged as blatant forms of bias became taboo and as researchers developed more sophisticated measurement techniques based on cognitive psychology. Subtle stereotypes are automatic, ambiguous, and ambivalent. On the relatively automatic front, people unintentionally confuse other people within categories, and these confusions predict stereotyping. Aversive racism—bias abhorrent to the self—emerges in reaction time data showing instantly more favorable responses to ingroups and positive relevant terms, compared to outgroups. Aversive racism also emerges in discrimination when the prejudiced person can construct a nonracial excuse. Indirect priming also uses response times, but this technique focuses on valence matches between an outgroup and clearly positive or negative words. The implicit association test has an evaluative component (introduced in Chapter 10) and a conceptual (stereotype) component, the latter correlating with other stereotyping. All these reaction time techniques correlate especially with nonverbal and other subtle, less-monitored behaviors.

Subtle forms of stereotyping also are ambiguous in that people interpret information to fit their expectations and hide these interpretations from themselves and others. Finally, subtle stereotyping is ambivalent: Many groups are liked but disrespected or respected but disliked. All these forms of subtle stereotyping result from internal conflicts between impulses to stereotype versus personal and social sanctions against it.

Bias affects dominant and minority group members alike. Attributional ambiguity describes the predicament of understanding when feedback reflects on oneself alone and when it reflects on biases regarding one's group membership. Stereotype threat describes the double risk of performance in a domain stereotypically poor for one's group; potential failure reflects not only on oneself but also on one's group. Hence, people may disidentify with the domain or may underperform when the task is diagnostic and important and one's relevant social category is salient. As a result of stereotypic biases, minority self-esteem is often disengaged from public regard for their ingroup, focusing instead on private regard, thereby buffering the ill effects of persistent bias. Although sensitive to bias, low-power groups rarely report bias because of the social and personal costs.

Dominant group members worry about how they are evaluated by minority groups, becoming self-conscious and self-absorbed in interactions. When both majority and minority group members make the effort to overcome prejudices, the effort can deplete executive control during and after the interaction. Nevertheless, interactions can often improve.

CHAPTER 12

Prejudice

Interplay of Cognitive With Affective Biases

INTERGROUP COGNITION AND EMOTION ◆ RACIAL PREJUDICE ◆ GENDER
PREJUDICE ◆ AGE PREJUDICE ◆ SEXUAL PREJUDICE

Gut feelings drive behavior, but both interact with cognition. Affective parts of our brains evolved first and even today often respond first, as the affect and cognition chapters indicate. Intergroup relations especially illustrate the power of emotional prejudices; when people commit extreme discrimination—such as hate crimes, prisoner abuse, genocide, and terrorism—strong emotions underlie their behavior (Glaser, Dixit, & Green, 2002; Pettigrew & Meertens, 1995). Even in mundane cases, affective prejudices drive discrimination more than cognitive stereotyping does (Dovidio, Brigham, Johnson, & Gaertner, 1996; Talaska, Fiske, & Chaiken, in press; Tropp & Pettigrew, 2005a). Stereotyping is not trivial, and it occupies the majority of intergroup research. Stereotyping correlates with emotional prejudices and predicts intergroup behavior, but emotional prejudices are stronger predictors. Hence, this chapter covers the emotional prejudices that result from cognitive biases and interact with them.

Emotional prejudice goes beyond positive–negative evaluation, described in Chapters 9–10. It includes differentiated emotions such as fear, disgust, envy, pity, anxiety, and resentment, all qualitatively distinct. These specific emotions target specific groups and motivate specific behavior, so they matter in a practical way. But they also matter theoretically. Differentiated emotional prejudices not only describe the world but also predict and explain it. As we will see, several theories identify differentiated emotional prejudices and their cognitive correlates for distinct social groups (see Mackie & Smith, 2002, for a collection of theories, and Giner-Sorolla, Mackie, & Smith, 2007, for a collection of research). Note that intergroup emotion is not the traditional view of prejudice, which always focused more on attitudes. This chapter thus paves the way for the remaining chapters on the role of cognition in affect and behavior, as the book opens up to related areas, at the end.

In social cognition, the angle on such affective biases is their interplay with cognition. The first section addresses several theories of intergroup cognition and emotion; in every case, a pattern of cognitions leads to a pattern of emotions and behaviors. The other part of the chapter takes seriously the idea that distinct emotional prejudices underpin reactions to different outgroups. Four sections focus in turn on categories that have received the most research attention from social psychologists: race and ethnicity, gender, age, and sexual orientation.

INTERGROUP COGNITION AND EMOTION

Why does the annoying driver blocking your way always come from some outgroup, not your own? Affect in chance encounters, incidental affect, may be irrelevant to the group but still perhaps affect the encounter. Although one might assume that people in bad moods stereotype more, which would be a straightforward valence assumption, instead different moods have distinct effects (Bodenhausen, Mussweiler, Gabriel, & Moreno, 2001). Angry moods do make people stereotype more, in accord with common sense. However, sad moods, although negative, actually make people stereotype less because they think harder. And people often stereotype more in happy moods than in neutral ones because they cannot be bothered to think hard. Chapter 14 returns to the more general influence of moods on cognition.

Overall, groups often elicit affect as an integral function of who they (apparently) are and the situations in which they appear (Bodenhausen, 1993; Bodenhausen et al., 2001). In contrast to incidental affect, different groups trigger different affective configurations as an integral feature of the encounter, according to several theories.

Stereotype Content Model

Two fundamental dimensions describe social perception—sociability and capability (Asch, 1946; Rosenberg & Sedlak, 1972; Wojciszke, 2005; see Fiske, Cuddy, & Glick, 2007, for a review). Intergroup perception is no exception. As Chapter 11 indicated, warmth and competence form the twin dimensions that differentiate social groups. According to the stereotype content model (SCM), stereotypes along these two dimensions result from structural relations between groups (Fiske, Cuddy, Glick, & Xu, 2002; see Table 12.1). The first judgment records whether the other is on your side or not (friend or foe?). Perceived *competition* for societal resources predicts *warmth* stereotypes; cooperative insiders and allies are warm and sincere, whereas allegedly exploitative outsiders are cold and untrustworthy. The second judgment records whether the other can enact those intentions. Perceived *status* predicts *competence* stereotypes; rich people are allegedly competent, whereas poor people are allegedly incompetent.

Stereotypes thus are circumstances of immigration, history, and geography, if social structural variables predict them. The group's position in society can vary over time and conditions, and the stereotypes will follow. As noted, these dimensions appear in every culture studied (Cuddy, Fiske, Kwan, et al., in press). For example, many cultures identify a set of entrepreneurial outsiders, seen as capable but not especially warm (Jewish people and Chinese people, in their respective diasporas, have often been perceived this way). As another example, in a variety of cultures, older people are seen as incapable but warm. And in all cultures studied so far, poor people (homeless, welfare recipients, undocumented migrants, drug addicts) are seen as neither smart nor nice.

These SCM stereotypes matter because they correlate with intergroup emotions (Fiske et al., 2002) and with intergroup behavior (Cuddy, Fiske, & Glick, 2007). The BIAS map describes stereotype-based clusters of emotions that directly predict intergroup behavior. Consider the outside entrepreneurs (usually urban, and

TABLE 12.1. Stereotype Content Model: Examples

		STRUCTURAL VARIABLE: STATUS $\downarrow(+)$ *Stereotype: Competence*	
		Low	*High*
STRUCTURAL VARIABLE: COMPETITION $\downarrow(-)$ *Stereotype: Warmth*			
High	Groups	Disabled, older people	Middle-class, ingroup
	Prejudice	Pity	Pride
	Discrimination	Active help, passive harm	Active help, passive support
Low	Groups	Poor, homeless, drug addicted	Rich, Asians, Jews
	Prejudice	Disgust	Envy
	Discrimination	Active harm, passive harm	Active harm, passive support

Source: After Cuddy, Fiske, & Glick (2007); Fiske, Cuddy, Glick, & Xu (2002).

seen as rich, or at least mercenary). They elicit envy and jealousy, mixed emotions that say, "You have something we want and that we should have. We will take it if we can" (Salovey, 1991; R. Smith, 2000). Envy breeds a volatile behavioral mix: (a) grudging association, going along to get along when the social order is stable, combined with (b) active attack when the chips are down. Genocides often take this form (Staub, 1999). Again, the cognitions about social structure (competitive, high-status) underlie the stereotypes (not warm but capable), which in turn elicit the emotions (envy, resentment) and the behaviors (passive accommodation but potential active harm).

Another unstable emotional combination targets older people and those with mental or physical handicaps, all seen as incapable but warm and trust-worthy. They receive pity, a mixed emotion saying, "You are worse off than us, but as long as it's not your fault, we feel sorry." Pity motivates a confusing mix of helping and neglecting. It's demeaning to be pitied because the pitying one is on top looking down. Pity involves unequal status and undermines the target's own control (see R. Smith, 2000; Weiner, 2005). Many groups in this category are institutionalized. The typical behaviors directed toward these groups combine being helped but also abandoned, which again conveys an emotionally mixed message. As before, cognitions about social structure start this chain: perceived noncompetition and low status convey incapacity and warmth, which elicit emotions (pity, sympathy) and corresponding behaviors (active helping but social neglect).

Finally, the third kind of outgroup cluster in the SCM is the most extreme combination, less emotionally mixed but more straightforwardly awful. As noted, poor people are stereotyped as having no redeeming features (neither warm nor competent), especially if they are homeless. The same is even more true of drug addicts. These groups receive contempt and even disgust, an emotion that can also target nonsocial objects. Neuroimaging data support both the disgust reaction and the relative dehumanization of such extreme outgroups. When people look at photographs of homeless or addicted people, the normal social neural response (medial prefrontal cortex activation) simply falls below a significant baseline, and instead the insula (associated with disgust) activates (Harris & Fiske, 2006); these findings are consistent with the idea that extreme outgroups are viewed as somehow less human. Contempt and disgust both involve looking down, as does pity, but without any positive affect at all, of course. Disgust evokes avoidance, expulsion, and fear of contamination (Rozin & Fallon, 1987), and contempt also is a distancing emotion. They result in both active attack and passive neglect. According to this model then, and supported by data in which people describe societal reactions to these groups, extremely poor people are viewed as taking resources away from the rest of society (that is, competing more than cooperating) and of course as low status. The associated stereotypes comprise low perceived warmth and low perceived competence, which in turn reportedly elicit more disgust and contempt than do other groups, as well as both active and passive harm.

In contrast to the outgroup emotions of envy, pity, and disgust are the ingroup /ally/reference-group emotions of pride and admiration. Pride assimilates the other to self, and admiration places the other above the self but still assimilates (rather than envy or contempt, which contrast self and other; R. Smith, 2000). Pride and admiration motivate both passive association (go along to get along) and active helping. Being an object of pride or admiration is all good, of course, and it stems from cognitions about social structure (high-status, noncompeting) and traits (competent, warm), resulting in both active and passive facilitation.

The SCM and its behavioral extension, the BIAS map, both turn crucially on distinct intergroup emotions. These emotional prejudices ultimately result from cognitions about structural features of society: who competes with whom, and who ranks above whom. And stereotypes link the perceived social structure to the expected emotions and behaviors. In emphasizing social structures, these models fit well with the next theory, which focuses on appraisals of "good for us" versus "bad for us."

Intergroup Emotions Theory

People's sense of self extends to their group membership, as Chapters 5 and 11 indicated. Intergroup emotions theory (IET) goes one step further, to posit that people include the group in the self representation (E. Smith, 1993). The socially extended self-representation means that people respond more quickly and accurately to traits that match their self-concept *and* their ingroup concept, compared to mismatches; outgroup matches and mismatches do not show these effects (E. Smith, Coats, & Walling, 1999; E. Smith & Henry, 1996). To the extent that people treat the ingroup the way they treat the self, IET argues, their corresponding emotional reactions should also be similar.

For the self, appraisal theories of emotions describe people as evaluating stimuli initially as good-for-me versus bad-for-me, resulting in primitive positive–negative reactions. After this primary appraisal, more complex emotions result from analyzing the situation further for causes, certainty, and the like (see Chapter 13 for more detail on appraisal theories of emotions in general). In the intergroup instance, the appraisals are stereotypes, and they entail perceived responsibility, fairness, and certainty. For example, people may stereotype welfare recipients as demanding resources (tax money) from the ingroup. The intergroup appraisal would view the outgroup demands as inconsistent with ingroup motives: unfair, certain, intentional, but less powerful. The resulting emotional prejudice would be anger in the welfare case, and the associated action tendency (discrimination) would entail actively moving against the outgroup. As another example, suppose a similar appraisal (motive-inconsistent, unfair, certain, intentional) is made but the outgroup is more powerful as, for example, with some institution unfairly seizing your assets. Then one might feel intergroup fear. IET also generates predictions for intergroup disgust, contempt (dislike), and jealousy (see Table 12.2)

IET conceptualizes prejudice as a specific intergroup emotion that comes from a specific appraisal (stereotype) and creates specific emotional action tendencies (discrimination). IET focuses on intergroup particulars more than abstractions. That is, it analyzes specific intergroup experiences rather than general societal dimensions. As such, it fits an exemplar-based approach to intergroup representations (Mackie & Smith, 1998; E. Smith & DeCoster, 1998; recall Chapter 4's discussion of exemplars). In this approach, people view each other as representing multiple group memberships, as encountered in specific situations.

In one study, people categorized themselves as for or against gay marriage, then learned their attitudinal ingroup received either strong or weak support in several newspaper headlines. The study then measured anger and fear, as well as tendencies to attack or avoid the outgroup. Under these circumstances, ingroup weakness begets fear and avoidance, but ingroup strength begets anger and opposition (Mackie, Devos, & Smith, 2000). Intergroup emotions come from

TABLE 12.2. Intergroup Emotions Theory: Example Appraisal-Emotion-Action Links

	Appraisals (all motive-inconsistent)	Emotion	Action Tendency	Who
Certainty Cause Plus	Low Other or circumstance Perceiver weak	Fear	Avoid	Low status toward high status
Certainty Cause Plus	High Other or circumstance Norm violation	Disgust	Avoid	High status toward low status
Certainty Cause Plus	High Other's intent Perceiver weak Unfair	Contempt	Move against	Any
Certainty Cause Plus	High Other's intent Perceiver strong Unfair	Anger	Move against	High status toward demanding low status

Source: Adapted from Smith (1993).

people's prior intergroup experiences and intergroup ideologies. And intergroup emotions result in intergroup evaluations (Miller, Smith, & Mackie, 2004). Thus intergroup emotions mediate between cognitive appraisals and evaluations.

Intergroup emotions also trigger defensive and offensive action tendencies in specific intergroup contexts (Devos, Silver, Mackie, & Smith, 2002). The intergroup emotions are functional in regulating behavior. When behavior is blocked, they intensify, but when behavior is implemented, they discharge (Maitner, Mackie, & Smith, 2006).

Image Theory

Enemy image theory identifies national images that result from perceived international context and from perceived behavioral intentions (Alexander et al., 1999; Alexander, Brewer, & Livingston, 2005; Brewer & Alexander, 2002). The images result from, account for, and justify affective and behavioral orientations toward the other national group. The appraisal of the other nation as goal-compatible or goal-incompatible combines with its perceived status and perceived power. Out of many possible combinations, the five core, recurring images (see Table 12.3) include two in which each side views the other symmetrically—ally (goal-compatible, equal), enemy (goal-incompatible, equal)—and three asymmetrical ones: dependent (perceiver goal-independent, lower status, and lower power), imperialist (other goal-independent, higher status, and higher power), and barbarian (goal-incompatible, lower status, but higher power).

Emotions enter this theory in two respects. First, high arousal readily cues arousal-related images (e.g., barbarian), given the right eliciting conditions (Alexander et al., 1999). Second, and consistent with IET and SCM, certain relationship patterns encourage particular intergroup emotions. Allies arouse admiration and trust, encouraging cooperation. Enemies arouse anger, facilitating containment or attack. Dependents arouse disgust and contempt, facilitating exploitation or paternalism. Imperialists arouse jealousy and resentment, facilitating resistance or rebellion. And barbarians arouse fear and intimidation, facilitating defensive protection (Alexander at al., 1999; Brewer & Alexander, 2002).

TABLE 12.3. Image Theory: Examples

	Other's Status		
Goals	Equal	Lower	Higher
Symmetrically compatible	Ally		
Symmetrically incompatible	Enemy		
Other is dependent, Perceiver is independent		Dependent (Low power)	
Other is independent, Perceiver is dependent			Imperialist
Other is goal-incompatible		Barbarian (High power)	

Source: Adapted from Alexander et al. (1999).

In the closest test to date of the intergroup emotions prediction (Alexander et al., 2005), White urban high school students reported feeling more admiration (trust and respect) toward Whites and more fear and intimidation toward Blacks, consistent with their images of other Whites as allies and Blacks as enemies and barbarians. In turn, Black students reported feeling more admiration toward Black targets and more resentment (anger and disgust) toward White targets, consistent with their images of other Blacks as allies and Whites as enemies and imperialists. Overall, image theory complements the perspectives of SCM and IET, which together examine structural relations, stereotypes, emotions, and behavioral tendencies.

Biocultural Approach

A biocultural approach, like the previous theories, argues that discrete intergroup emotions result from discrete intergroup relations and predict discrete intergroup behaviors (Neuberg & Cottrell, 2002; Neuberg, Smith, & Asher, 2000). The starting point is neither social identity (as in the IET) nor social structural relations (as in the SCM and image theory), but intergroup threat viewed from a sociofunctional evolutionary perspective. The biocultural approach emphasizes human interdependence, effective group functioning, and individual adaptation to the benefits and threats of group life.

Threats to the group's integrity take various forms; they produce predictable emotions and motivations. For example, obstacles (threats to ingroup property, freedom, coordination) produce anger and efforts at removal. Contamination (threats to health or values) produces disgust and prevention. Danger produces fear and protection, and so on. Consistent with these predictions, different outgroups evoke qualitatively distinct profiles of threat and emotion (Cottrell & Neuberg, 2005), so responses differ to different ethnic groups (African Americans, Asian Americans, and Native Americans) and social groups (gay men, activist feminists, and fundamentalist Christians).

Other social-evolutionary approaches reinforce the underlying arguments. For example, they emphasize self-interest in social settings. Adaptive, self-promoting strategies include dyadic cooperation, pursuing reliable partners for social exchange; coalitional exploitation, excluding others from the ingroup and exploiting the outgroup; and avoiding potential parasites, those who carry pathogens (Kurzban & Leary, 2001). The work on evolutionary origins of stigma all balances, on one hand, adaptations for sociality, selecting appropriate partners, and on the other hand, limiting sociality to one's own advantage.

Anxiety: Integrated Threat Theory

Threats to the ingroup also are important in the integrated threat theory (ITT; Stephan & Renfro, 2002). ITT incorporates many of the variables from the previous theories, but ITT focuses on one major emotion, anxiety. ITT is a broad, generic, integrative model focused on predicting attitudes (see Table 12.4). Antecedents include intergroup relations (e.g., conflict, status inequality), individual differences (ingroup identity, contact experience), cultural dimensions (collectivism), and immediate situation (e.g., minority-majority in context).

TABLE 12.4. Integrated Threat Theory

Antecedents	Mediating Threats	Consequences
Intergroup relations	Realistic threats	Psychological reactions (cognitive and affective)
Individual differences	Symbolic threats	Behavioral reactions
Cultural dimensions		
Immediate situation		

Source: Adapted from Stephan & Renfro (2002).

Threats mediate between these antecedents and attitudes. Threats primarily differ between the realistic and symbolic. Realistic threats are perceived tangible harms to ingroup resources, especially alleged economic threats (job competition, tax costs). Symbolic threats are abstract harms to ingroup ideals (values, religion, identity, language). In addition, anxiety and negative stereotypes relate to these threats differently in the early model and the later model (Stephan & Renfro, 2002; Stephan & Stephan, 2000). Essentially, the threats are a cognitive appraisal (as in IET), and the stereotypes a cognitive response (as in the SCM); anxiety is an emotional response common to all these theories.

The main claims of this theory are several. First, it focuses on anxiety, a negative emotion in response to uncertain threats. Anxiety facilitates usage of stereotypes (Wilder, 1993). By creating arousal and self-focus, it diminishes the ability to distinguish among outgroup members. Distraction worsens the effects of anxiety, and people assimilate differences within the outgroup, increasing its perceived homogeneity as anxiety increases. ITT takes this premise to the broad context of intergroup antecedents and consequences.

Second, ITT applies to a staggering array of intergroup settings: attitudes toward immigrants (Stephan, Renfro, Esses, Stephan, & Martin, 2005; Stephan, Ybarra, & Bachman, 1999; Stephan, Ybarra, Martínez, Schwarzwald, & Tur-Kaspa, 1998), cancer and AIDS patients (Berrenberg, Finlay, Stephan, & Stephan, 2002), Blacks and Whites (Stephan et al., 2002), First Nations Canadians (Corenblum & Stephan, 2001), Mexicans and Americans (Stephan, Diaz-Loving, & Rolando, 2000), and men viewed by women (C. Stephan, Stephan, Demitrakis, Yamada, & Clason, 2000).

Third, the earlier version of ITT posed a simple causal chain: antecedents → threats (symbolic, realistic, anxiety, stereotypes) → prejudiced attitudes. Various path analyses of survey data support threat as a mediator of antecedent effects on attitudes (Corenblum & Stephan, 2001; Stephan et al., 2002; Stephan, Diaz-Loving, & Duran, 2000), and experiments further support the causal importance of threats (Stephan et al., 2005).

Finally, ITT proposes a simple-sounding intervention to overcome anxiety and perceived intergroup threats—empathy. Of course, empathy with the outgroup is easier said than felt, but empathy has improved relationships between Blacks and Whites (Finlay & Stephan, 2000). Empathy can operate cognitively (perspective-taking) or emotionally (in reaction or in parallel; Stephan & Finlay, 1999) to reduce threat and anxiety.

Guilt: Various Theories

Guilt is a useful emotion because it tells you when you have done something you wish you hadn't done, encouraging you to change your future behavior and make amends, if possible. Guilt matters as a focal intergroup emotion, at least for powerful or majority groups viewed as oppressing less powerful or minority groups. Chapter 11 noted the difficulty of suppressing stereotypes, even with motivation and the capacity to do so (e.g., Monteith, Sherman, & Devine, 1998). So guilt does not lead easily to improved intergroup responses.

Guilty feelings of compunction depend on the level of prejudice (Monteith, 1993, 1996). Low-prejudice respondents have high, internalized standards for their own interracial behavior, but when they do violate them, they feel guilty. High-prejudice respondents have lower, more externalized standards, and when they violate them, they feel angry (Zuwerink, Devine, Monteith, & Cook, 1996). Discrepancies between what you should do and what you likely would do make low-prejudice people feel guilty at all ages (Voils, Ashbrun-Nardo, & Monteith, 2002). This guilt accordingly tempers their reactions to, for example, racist jokes (Monteith & Voils, 1998). For those who do experience prejudice-related conflict, guilt links to racial ambivalence (see Chapter 11).

However, some high-prejudice people's standards do depend on a moral obligation to uphold equality of opportunity (Monteith & Walters, 1998). In either case, awareness of the discrepancy inhibits behavior, triggers guilt, and catalyzes retrospective reflection. Over time, the discrepancy-related stimuli and responses become associated with guilt, so they establish cues for control, such as behavioral inhibition and thinking ahead, which are potential control strategies (Monteith, Ashburn-Nardo, Voils, & Czopp, 2002). Guilt indeed is useful, even if not simple.

Not all standards are internal; activated social norms against prejudice can lower prejudiced responses by external incentives (Monteith, Deneen, & Tooman, 1996). Social norms and education change people by inducing guilt. For example, understanding White privilege and the prevalence of anti-Black discrimination leads to guilt, which in turn leads to favoring affirmative action as a remedy (Swim & Miller, 1999). Many Whites downplay White privilege because it undercuts their own feelings of personal merit (Lowery, Knowles, & Unzueta, 2007). Framing inequality in terms of dominant group advantage (instead of minority disadvantage) makes White people feel more guilty and more receptive to remedies such as affirmative action (Iyer, Leach, & Crosby, 2003). Conversely, people who oppose affirmative action often do so out of concern for protecting the ingroup rather than direct hostility toward the outgroup (Lowery, Unzueta, Knowles, & Goff, 2006).

However, ingroup protection cannot be the whole story in attitudes toward affirmative action. In these attitudes, racial threat to the White ingroup apparently outranks gender threat to the male ingroup. From the perspective of sheer numbers, the greater opposition to affirmative action benefiting a 13% racial minority (African Americans) makes less sense than opposition to its benefiting 50% of the population (women), if only ingroup protection were operating. So something more than ingroup protection is going on here. Perhaps people feel more guilty about female disadvantage because they feel more directly responsible.

Conclusion

Distinct social groups elicit distinct emotional responses according to several theories of intergroup emotions (the stereotype content model, intergroup emotions theory, image theory, and biocultural approach). Specific emotions, such as anxiety and guilt, although they may apply to more than one group, motivate specific responses that likewise go beyond the mere positive–negative evaluation associated with attitudes. We must, then, take seriously the idea of prejudices as emotions per se, framed in terms of their interplay with cognitions and behavior.

The constellation of prejudices differs by group, so to understand prejudice, we have to examine specific groups and beliefs about social structure. Such conclusions build on this chapter's general models of prejudice (that cluster groups along various cognitive dimensions), as well as the general models of stereotyping (reviewed in Chapter 11) and general models of attitudes (reviewed prior to that). To illustrate, we next examine a few specific prejudices. Because social psychology has focused on some groups more than others, the next sections focus on those that have generated a body of work on emotional prejudices: race, gender, age, and sexual orientation.

RACIAL PREJUDICE

American social psychologists have most often studied White racial prejudice against Blacks, probably because of Americans' particular history with regard to race. African Americans have uniquely survived the combination of two centuries' slavery, being counted as 3/5 a person; political turmoil around emancipation and reconstruction; a century's legalized segregation known as Jim Crow; the last generation's civil rights movement; ongoing racial backlash; and continuing segregation and group disadvantage. (More detailed discussion lies beyond our scope here, but see, for example, Fredrickson, 2002; Jones, 1997; Sears, 1998.)[1]

Given the importance of racial prejudice, the first social psychology studies immediately measured racial and ethnic attitudes (Bogardus, 1933; Katz & Braly, 1933; Thurstone, 1928; see Allport, 1935, for an early review). White–Black racial issues have persisted in the prejudice literature since that time, probably because racial prejudices are exceptional in several psychological respects: (a) This particular racial combination continues to carry strong emotions; (b) this type of prejudice is aversive to most of those who hold it; (c) it is not plausibly an evolved bias in itself, and ample evidence indicates social construction; and (d) racial groups remain hypersegregated, furthering the current divide in ordinary intergroup interactions. None of these features as pointedly characterizes

---

[1]Arguably, African Americans are one of the most ill-treated ethnic group in American history. This is not to diminish the importance of prejudice against Asians, Latinos, Jews, or Native Americans, which have variously resulted in internment, exclusionary immigration policies, employment discrimination, and genocide. Social psychologists in general and social cognition researchers in particular have studied these forms of ethnic prejudice less often (but for recent exceptions, see, e.g., Echebarria-Echabe & Fernández-Guede, 2006; Lin, Kwan, Cheung, & Fiske, 2005; Van Laar, Levin, Sinclair, & Sidanius, 2005).

other forms of prejudice, as we will see, but cognitive processes factor into each of them.

Racism Is Emotionally Loaded

A previous section examined White guilt regarding racism. Let us here examine the strong emotional loading of racism and how it might relate to guilt. Guilt is an other-oriented moral emotion, showing concern that one's behavior harmed another person (Tangney, Stuewig, & Mashek, 2007). Regarding racism, White guilt reflects beliefs that one's group has harmed another group, about which Whites typically have no doubt, at least as regards the past. Racial guilt may be one reason that most White students do not identify strongly with their own race (although being the majority and therefore default group surely also matters to their lack of White racial identity).

Possibly, most Whites' emotionally loaded responses would better be described as shame rather than guilt. Shame is a self-directed moral emotion, being concerned with others' evaluations (Tangney et al., 2007). Many majority members are self-concerned in interracial interactions, which fits potential shame more than guilt. In contrast, many minorities are concerned for both self and other (Shelton & Richeson, 2006; Vorauer et al., 2000; Vorauer & Kumhyr, 2001). Many Whites are potentially worried by how they are evaluated because they think Blacks expect them to be racist. Racism is emotionally loaded in part because many Whites are concerned with what Blacks think of them. Avoiding shame is part of the emotional-cognitive matrix of contemporary race relations.

What's more, as we have seen, Whites are widely acquainted with negative cultural stereotypes about Blacks, and elements of these stereotypes are emotionally threatening. American cultural stereotypes of Blacks include elements of hostility and criminality (Devine, 1989; Devine & Elliot, 1995). These cultural stereotypes put Whites on their guard, and this contributes to the emotionally loaded interaction.

But far worse, racial stereotypes and accompanying emotional prejudices create life-and-death consequences for Blacks. For example, race affects split-second shoot/not-shoot decisions paralleling those made by police officers; racial bias lowers the threshold for shooting unarmed Black men (Correll, Park, Judd, & Wittenbrink, 2002). Cultural stereotypes and emotional prejudices affect neural responses as early as 200 ms., which in turn mediate the shooter bias (Correll, Urland, & Ito, 2006). More specifically, Black faces activate crime-related associations, including the early visual detection of weapons by both students and police officers. Conversely, stereotypic associations also facilitate detection of Black faces, especially faces that are prototypically Afrocentric (Eberhardt et al., 2004). The life-and-death consequences of the interplay between cultural stereotypes and visual processing extend beyond split-second decisions, all the way to death row. Higher likelihood of being sentenced to death for the murder of a White victim disproportionately punishes Black defendants who happen to have more stereotypically Black features (controlling for a variety of features including severity of crime; Eberhardt et al., 2006). Although race–crime associations are doubtless overridden by cues to social class, gender, and age, the connection remains. Most Black families have "the conversation" with their teenage sons about what to do (and not do) in an encounter with the police. Such issues heighten the emotional tensions even in crime-irrelevant interracial interactions, in part because the cultural associations are automatic.

Automatic interracial responses often reflect emotion-laden cultural associations, even if people do not personally endorse them. From Devine's (1989) dissociation model onward (Chapter 11) and in the implicit association test (Chapters 10 and 11), we have seen that people have automatic stereotypic thoughts, which are difficult to control. Whites' efforts to be egalitarian are widely shared, so most Whites try to avoid conveying their automatic associations. Of course, people differ on their motivation to avoid prejudice, a value that dates back to childhood experiences and parental values (Towles-Schwen & Fazio, 2001). Nevertheless, salient social norms motivate Whites to inhibit prejudice, to acknowledge discrimination, and to resist hostile jokes (Crandall, Eshleman, & O'Brien, 2002). Indeed, under pressure of appearing racist, the best-intentioned people actually look even worse than the less well-intentioned people (Frantz et al., 2004; Vorauer & Turpie, 2004), and they feel worse about it (Fazio & Hilden, 2001). No wonder many Whites feel uncertain and anxious, especially in unstructured interracial interactions (Towles-Schwen & Fazio, 2003).

The speed of this emotional discomfort is breathtaking. People in general most rapidly evaluate each other's trustworthiness in less than 100 ms. (Willis & Todorov, 2006), showing amygdala and right insula responses to people perceived as untrustworthy (Winston et al., 2002). As the attitudes research notes (Chapter 10), amygdala responses reflect emotionally significant and especially negative stimuli, whereas right insula responses reflect negative stimuli, often disgust. People rapidly register each other's race, also in less than 100 ms. (Ito & Urland, 2003). Consistent with the speed of such responses, immediate neural responses fit affect-laden reactions on the basis of race (see Eberhardt, 2005, for a review).

In further support of the marked emotional loading of interracial interactions, some of the most provocative early work on the neuroscience of interracial reactions has documented amygdala responses that correlate not only with negative implicit associations (IAT) but also with indicators of vigilance and arousal, especially in Whites responding to Blacks (Cunningham, Johnson, et al., 2004; Hart et al., 2000; Lieberman et al., 2005; Phelps et al., 2000; Wheeler & Fiske, 2005). Among Whites intrinsically concerned about prejudice (high in internal but low in external motivation to control their prejudice), immediate startle-eye-blink responses (indicators of arousal) to Black faces are low, indicating less arousal and vigilance; they also show lower delayed startle-eye-blink responses, indicating less negative affect (Amodio, Harmon-Jones, & Devine, 2003). People distinguish ingroup from outgroup and evaluate accordingly, all in half a second or less (Ito, Thompson, & Cacioppo, 2004).

However, neural activity consistent with alerted control systems also occurs in Whites making unintentionally race-biased responses, especially those who can control such responses successfully (Amodio, Harmon-Jones, et al., 2004; Cunningham, Johnson, et al., 2004; Lieberman et al., 2005; Richeson et al., 2003). Thus Whites may respond immediately to Blacks as emotionally significant and perhaps negative, but they also invoke controlled processes fairly fast. In short, neural indicators implicate racial cues with immediate emotional significance.

Other physiological evidence provides converging evidence of the immediate affective loading of interracial encounters, especially for Whites. Facial muscle activity (subtle expressive movements not yet visible but tracked electro-myographically) indicates subtle racial bias (Vanman, Paul, Ito, & Miller, 1997). Whites interacting with Blacks show cardiovascular reactivity consistent with threat, especially if they have limited prior experience in cross-racial interactions (Blascovich, Mendes, Hunter, Lickel, & Kowai-Bell, 2001; Mendes, Blascovich, Lickel, & Hunter, 2002). They also perform poorly on subsequent cognitive tasks, consistent with other evidence that executive control over prejudiced responses has mental costs (Richeson & Shelton, 2003). The reverse is also true; Blacks who especially favor their ingroup also incur cognitive costs after interracial interaction (Richeson, Trawalter, & Shelton, 2005).

Given all these emotional complexities, maybe it is not surprising that people avoid interracial interactions from the first moments of attention. People's face-sensitive fusiform gyrus activates less to cross-race than same-race faces and correlates with whether one remembers them (Golby, Gabrieli, Chiao, & Eberhardt, 2001). This is, in effect, a form of perceptual avoidance. And they avoid interactions deliberately as well, thinking that the other group will reject them (Shelton & Richeson, 2005). To summarize, the emotional loading of race relations has a heavy component of shame and anxiety for Whites, with life-or-death consequences based on automatic and more deliberate reactions, as shown by cognitive, social, and neural evidence.

Much Racism Is Aversive

What is the role of deliberate control, and how is race exceptional in this regard? People are reminded of the need to watch their step when someone "plays the race card," an expression communicating that someone has upped the ante in an unpleasant and difficult way, bringing a fraught and taboo topic into an already contentious context. Whites watch themselves because being called a racist is such a potent interpersonal threat to most Whites. This is not an issue so much for the minority of blatant racists; as we saw in Chapter 11, these blatant bigots experience simple but virulent disdain and dislike, potentially deadly but fortunately relatively rare in modern egalitarian democracies. Deliberate control over their racial attitudes is not their biggest issue.

The rest of racism concerns internal and external control, and even avoidance, dubbed "aversive." Aversive racism results from a type of ambivalence including negative feelings and beliefs, coupled with paternalistic sympathy and denial of the negativity (Gaertner & Dovidio, 1986). Aversively racist Whites experience a variety of negative emotions toward Blacks—discomfort, uneasiness, and anxiety, predicting avoidance—but they experience more positive emotions toward the White ingroup, such as sympathy and admiration (Dovidio, Esses, Beach, & Gaertner, 2002). These subtle forms of discrimination also occur in Europe with regard to its new immigrants (Pettigrew & Meertens, 1995). Racism is aversive in two senses: (a) aversive racists reject its presence in themselves, and (b) it causes interracial interactions to be aversive, so they avoid them.

With regard to emotional prejudices, aversive racists theoretically show anxiety, discomfort, disgust, and fear. These emotions follow from a host of positive evaluations associated with the ingroup and negative ones associated with the outgroup (reviewed in Chapters 10 and 11; Gaertner & Dovidio, 1986). Stephan's work on anxiety (just noted) corroborates this prediction, as do nonverbal indicators of discomfort (e.g., Dovidio et al., 1997; Word, Zanna, & Cooper, 1974).

The affective-evaluative, relatively automatic component of White racial attitudes predicts their behavior, particularly voluntary interracial contact (Dovidio, Kawakami, & Gaertner, 2002; Esses & Dovidio, 2002) and nonverbal behavior (as noted in Chapters 10 and 11; Dovidio et al., 1997; Dovidio, Kawakami, & Gaertner, 2002). In contrast, the more cognitive component predicts policy preferences. For example, conservative ideology predicts stereotypes about deservingness, which in turn predicts opposing affirmative action for Blacks but not for other groups such as women (Reyna, Henry, Korfmacher, & Tucker, 2006).

Turning to the other side of aversive racism, Blacks may approach interracial encounters with potential concern about being treated in a racist manner, although individuals differ and contexts differ in the extent to which this concern is uppermost (Hyers & Swim, 1998; Operario & Fiske, 2001; Sellers & Shelton, 2003; Shelton, 2000). Any distrust stems from historic and current conditions, as well as Blacks' more common belief in the reality of discrimination compared to Whites (see Dovidio, Gaertner, Kawakami, & Hodson, 2002, for a review).

Overall, besides its emotional loading, White aversive racism and Black distrust add to the exceptional features of race-based emotional prejudice, reflecting the cognitive-affective interplay. Next, we come to perceptions of biology and race.

Racial Prejudice Is Not Plausibly Evolved

Recall that the stereotyping chapter identified perceived biological underpinnings as an issue in essentialist stereotypes. Compared to many forms of prejudice, race prejudice boasts an especially tenacious belief in biology. People greatly exaggerate the biology of racial differences. This essentialism persists despite (a) the dearth of biological evidence validating the genetics of racial groupings as currently, socially defined, and (b) the lack of evidence for an evolutionary predisposition to encode race automatically. Other social categories (gender, age) do have biological underpinnings and do fit an evolutionary explanation for rapid detection. So why are people so divided about the biology of race?

Because it seems so obvious to people, let's begin with the biological evidence for the genetics of race. The differences are surprisingly trivial. Genetic differences *within* races are about 10 times greater than genetic differences *between* races (Lewontin, 1972; Nei & Roychoudhury, 1993). Moreover, even examining differences between races, no underlying genetic patterns reliably divide people into society's racial categories (Graves, 2001; Hirschfeld, 1996; Marks, 1995). Even skin color does not identify shared genetic heritage (Parra, Amado, Lambertucci, Rocha, Antunes, & Pena, 2003). In short, genetic markers for race do not support the commonsense view of race.

We divide people into races on the basis of a configuration of cues that are socially defined. The American definitions of race originated in and justified slavery. Think about why it was socially and economically convenient for slave-era Whites to define someone with one Black parent and one White parent as Black. Different American states even defined races differently, and a person's race was sometimes the tragic basis of otherwise absurd lawsuits: A great-grandparent's hair texture could determine if a later generation's marriage was interracial and therefore illegal (Banks & Eberhardt, 1998). From the law to everyday behavior, people resist believing that racial categories are not natural (like species).

One might ask how the social construction of race and the exaggerated biology of race fit with race-related correlations to health. First, the majority of overall health disparities are due to wealth disparities (Wong, Shapiro, Boscardin, & Ettner, 2002). Race and income are correlated, of course, so effects due to the one can be mistakenly attributed to the other. Closer analysis indicates a greater influence of social class than racial classification. Independent of class, some race effects on health result from discrimination and its secondary effects on stress (Mays, Cochran, & Barnes, 2007). More specific, well-known examples of race-health correlations include sickle-cell anemia among Africans, cystic fibrosis among Europeans, and Tay-Sachs among Ashkenazi Jews. However, these diseases are extremely rare (most members of that population do not have the disease), and not everyone with the disease belongs to the population (Kittles & Weiss, 2003). Variations in disease rates correlate with biology, behavior, and environment, all of which are correlated with socially defined race. So even if socially defined race is not causal, it can be one cue to relative risks of specific diseases, along with other factors such as habits and environment. But people rely on race more readily than other causes.

The second aspect of race and biology is evolutionary. That is, common wisdom often assumes that racial prejudice is a hard-wired adaptation to alien social groups. On closer inspection, however, the differentiation of other people as racial ingroup or outgroup does not fit a plausible evolutionary explanation (Cosmides, Tooby, & Kurzban, 2003). In ancestral times, people lived in racially homogeneous groups, within local walking distances, and even encounters with enemy groups would not have crossed racial boundaries. In contrast, sex and life stage would have been important (biological) categories to detect automatically.

If not part of an evolutionary module, race detection might be the by-product of another adaptation; for example, essentialist encoding of natural kinds. Essentialist encoding of plant or animal species makes evolutionary sense, and encoding systems could easily have adapted to detect natural kinds that differ both perceptually and in their underlying shared properties. This encoding system plausibly could be recruited to respond to human physical differences socially defined as racial differences as if they were natural kinds (Cosmides et al., 2003).

Race detection might also be the by-product of sensitivity to distinct social groups and their coalitions (Kurzban & Leary, 2001; Kurzban, Tooby, & Cosmides, 2001). Hunter-gatherers lived in small bands often in conflict with other bands, so mechanisms for tracking who belongs with whom would matter. Ingroups coordinated action, so cues that predict an individual's membership in those groups would matter. Such cues might include otherwise arbitrary features such as clothing, decoration, or dialect. The mechanisms for imbuing these features with social meaning could transfer to other arbitrary features such as skin color or hair texture. The mechanism thus is adaptive and automatic, but it is applied to features that have meaning in particular historical and social contexts. Cues to religion, for example, should have parallel properties to racial cues in places with long histories of denominational conflict. Race encoding is not mandatory, but socially constructed cues to coalitions (ingroups and outgroups) may be, though they shift with context.

In contrast to the weakness of biological and evolutionary explanations for race as commonly understood, evidence for its social construction is strong. Much of it comes from facial recognition research showing that racial categorization is shaped by social context, not fixed features of faces. For example, European Americans recognize White faces more accurately than Black faces (Malpass & Kravitz, 1969), and the fusiform face area activates less to these cross-race faces (Golby et al., 2001), as noted. African Americans show this result to a lesser degree, presumably because as minorities they more often have to differentiate White faces. But contact alone does not drive this effect. Apparently, people process outgroup faces by racial category, noticing relevant cues, but do not code ingroup faces as having a race, instead noticing individuating cues (Levin, 2000). Whites' cross-race encoding deficit is not inevitable: For example, sports fans can prioritize team over race to individuate their team's members regardless of race (Cosmides et al., 2003). The importance of social context also emerges in findings that African Americans and African nationals differ in their encoding of Black and White faces.

Evidence for social construction also appears in the changing standards for judging race, and in biases that correlate with the typicality of racial features. Racial judgments operate by various routes, all socially constructed (Maddox, 2004). First, via a categorical route, a person's appearance (phenotype) determines racial category. This process can occur via a label: for example, racially ambiguous faces, morphed to be half and half, appear more "Black" or "White" depending on their label, and this especially occurs for entity theorists who believe in fixed traits (Eberhardt, Dasgupta, & Banaszynski, 2003). Categorization can also operate mainly through a single feature, such as skin tone, combined with relevant cues such as a race-related discussion (Maddox & Chase, 2004; Maddox & Gray, 2002). Categorization can operate through a configuration of race-related features (Blair, Judd, Sadler, & Jenkins, 2002; Livingston & Brewer, 2002), not just a fixed set of defining features; hence, the lack of biological markers.

Racial categorization can also operate directly from individual race-related features associated with stereotypic traits (Blair et al., 2002) or evaluations (Livingston & Brewer, 2002). For example, heavy television news viewers report more emotional discomfort after a newscast featuring a darker skinned Black perpetrator than a lighter skinned one charged with the same crime (Dixon & Maddox, 2005). Given the importance of individual features, even a person typically viewed as White might have some Afrocentric facial features, which could carry stereotypic or affective associations independent of race (Blair et al., 2002). Consistent with the idea that specific features can have major consequences, Black defendants with more Afrocentric features are more likely to land on death row than those without such features (Eberhardt et al., 2006), as noted.

These routes to racial categorization interact with conceptual information, including semantic associations to light and dark, lay theories, cultural beliefs, and personal experiences, all of which help set the social context (Maddox, 2004). For example, racially prejudiced individuals care more about accurately categorizing racially ambiguous people (Blascovich, Wyer, Swart, & Kibler, 1997). How many times have ethnically ambiguous people heard, "What are you, anyway?" (We know someone who had it made into a T-shirt.)

Despite the lack of clear biological evidence for racial differences or evolutionary accounts of racial perception and the existence of clear evidence for race as a social cognitive construction, people cling to the notion of races as natural kinds. This may diminish, over time, as more people define themselves and others as multiracial. Meanwhile, conflicts over the races' perceived biological base versus evidence to the contrary feature prominently in racial prejudice. Biology implies determinism, in many people's minds, so this is an important issue in interpersonal perception.

Segregation

So far, we have seen that racial prejudice is psychologically exceptional because of its unique emotional load, its aversive quality, its (denied) social construction, and now, because of structural features of modern society that contribute to cognitive and affective biases. American society is more racially segregated than South Africa was under the legal system of apartheid (Massey & Denton, 1993). This segregation occurs at all income levels, and though it is less for middle-class Blacks, their housing dollar goes less far as a result. Segregation is about race, not social class. And it results from skin color, not minority status. As an example of skin-color bias, Latinos who are Black are more segregated than Latinos who are White. Black Americans are more segregated and have remained segregated longer than any immigrant group, most of whom were somewhat segregated in the first generation but gradually less so over two generations. Why does this matter for social cognition of race?

Segregation is not the reported preference of African Americans, who prefer a more racially balanced neighborhood than the average European American does. Neighborhood segregation operates through rental agents and real estate agents, who steer and exclude people who do and do not fit the neighborhood. From segregation and the disproportionate poverty in the Black community comes concentrated poverty and all its ills (Massey & Denton, 1993). Schooling, employment prospects, health care availability, exposure to social disorder, and constrained social networks all follow, with crucial population-level disadvantages.

The implications for social cognition and racial prejudice are many. At a social psychological level, one of the primary effects is limited interracial contact. The consequences of this differ for minorities and majorities. In general, equal-status intergroup contact reliably reduces prejudice across a variety of group divides: sexual orientation, physical disability, race and ethnicity, mental disability, and age (Pettigrew & Tropp, 2006). The causality apparently goes from contact to prejudice reduction rather than just from low-prejudice people being more open to contact. The more the contact setting fits Allport's (1954) optimal conditions (equal status, common goals, intergroup cooperation, and authority sanction), the more effectively it reduces prejudice. In the current context emphasizing affective prejudice, contact operates primarily by increasing outgroup friendships and intergroup closeness. These dynamics decrease affective prejudice more than cognitive biases such as stereotypes or beliefs (Tropp & Pettigrew, 2005a).

The effects of contact on prejudice especially operate for exposing White Americans to Black Americans, given their respective majority–minority status (Tropp & Pettigrew, 2005b). Minority members are well aware of the intergroup situation, the respective concerns of both sides, and the possibility of prejudice.

Majority members are less likely to reflect on their own status, group identity, or problems of prejudice. Also, given relative numbers, minorities are more likely to have prior contact experience with majorities than vice versa. Hence, intergroup contact constitutes more of a novelty to majorities than minorities and perhaps is more of a shock to the emotional and cognitive systems, with more impact. Moreover, having experienced prejudice in the past, minorities are more likely to reserve judgment about whether contact conditions have truly been met (e.g., equal status). Minorities and majorities respond differently to explicit mention of group membership. Majorities feel discomfort, especially when an outgroup member brings it up, and they feel negative about the contact experience as a result (Tropp & Bianchi, 2006). For minorities, mentioning group membership does not break any taboos, but it can be interpreted positively or negatively depending on who does it and how it occurs. In particular, if it leads them to anticipate prejudice, it undermines trust and acceptance (Tropp, Stout, Boatswain, Wright, & Pettigrew, 2006). Each group's expectations about the other's prejudice depend on the salience of group membership and whether one will be viewed as typical (Tropp, 2006).

Exposure to prejudice understandably makes people feel anxious and hostile (Branscombe, Schmitt, & Harvey, 1999; Dion & Earn, 1975; Tropp, 2003). In any case, contact is a more dramatic issue in interracial prejudice than in sexism or ageism because people are more segregated by race than by gender or age. We turn to these characteristics in the next sections.

Conclusion

The interplay of cognition and prejudice regarding race shows that racial prejudice is exceptional in several respects. First, race is more emotionally loaded than other social categories, with a variety of cognitive results. Second, racial prejudice is especially aversive and therefore cognitively hidden in modern society. Third, the role of biology is particularly overestimated in commonsense theories of race when compared with the genetic and evolutionary evidence. Finally, people are more segregated by race than by other social categories so the experience of contact especially matters. All this contributes to the notable qualities of racial prejudices.

GENDER PREJUDICE

In contrast to racism, sexism has interested social psychologists only relatively recently (Deaux & LaFrance, 1998; Spence, Deaux, & Helmreich, 1985). These recent decades of gender research reflect three particular aspects of American culture (and probably most developed cultures): gender polarization, categorical divides instead of overlapping continua; androcentrism, maleness as the neutral norm; and biological essentialism, focusing on genetic predispositions more than socialization (Bem, 1993). Although all these features also occur for race, they take a different form in gender prejudices. We shall see various notable features of gender prejudice and its interplay with cognition as this section moves from (a) men's and women's unique structural relationships of heterosexual interdependence and male power in society, to (b) the resulting mixed, prescriptive stereotypes and ambivalent prejudices, to (c) biological and social bases of gender prejudice.

Intimate Interdependence and Male Status

Compared to the intense segregation of interethnic contact, men and women certainly have plenty of contact, and of the most intimate kinds. As far as we know, no one proposes to overcome sexism by increased intergroup contact. Of course, it is equal status intergroup contact that is supposed to reduce prejudice, and the genders don't often have that. One of the exceptional features of gender as an intergroup boundary is how much each ingroup needs the outgroup. More than any other societal groups, men and women have the most intimate relationships. We could not very well measure this odd ingroup–outgroup relation by the classic Bogardus (1933) social distance scale, wherein allowing the group into one's country reflects superficial acceptance, and allowing members of the group into one's family by marriage reflects intimate acceptance. Certainly both men and women would endorse all levels of social interaction. Viewed this way, men and women accept each other completely. Male–female interdependence is a wonderful fact of life.

At the same time, every culture shows male status: In society at large, men dominate women, holding more positions of power in business and government and scoring higher on development indices such as education, health, and literacy (United Nations Development Fund for Women, 2005). Even in the United States, women still earn far less than comparable men (U.S. Department of Labor, 2005), and in dual-career couples, women work a double shift—regular hours at work and longer hours at home than men do (Business and Professional Women's Foundation, 2005; Crosby, 1991; Deutsch, 1999). Female-headed households (even without children) are more likely to be in poverty than comparable male households. Women are injured and killed by men far more often than vice versa. Female fetuses are more often aborted, and female infants are more often killed at birth.[2] For social cognition, what is remarkable is the combination of intimacy and status that creates the cognitive background for gender prejudice.

Expectations for male status but heterosexual intimacy particularly clash when the typical hierarchy reverses, as when women take leadership roles in traditionally male domains. Female leaders provide a case study of gender-role tension, expressed both cognitively and affectively. Perceived incongruity between the roles expected of leaders and women suggests that (a) it will be harder for women to become leaders because they will be viewed more negatively as potential leaders, and (b) when they are leaders, the same leaderlike behavior will be evaluated more negatively in a woman compared to a man (Eagly & Karau, 2002).

A remarkable series of meta-analyses supports this role-congruity theory. Leadership is a male domain, and the roles are certainly expressed in behavior. Regarding the emergence of leaders, men more often do lead initially leaderless groups in the laboratory and in the field (Eagly & Karau, 1991), especially

---

[2]This description, if applied to any other pair of societal groups, would cause outrage. And sometimes it does, of course, both as one more example of some groups dominating others and specifically regarding women as a subordinate group. But that is not our point here.

in tasks that do not require complex social interaction. However, women more often emerge as social leaders, consistent with gender roles. When women do lead organizations, they do not differ from men on task and interpersonal orientations, contrary to stereotypes. But they do lead in a more democratic and participatory, less autocratic or directive style than men (Eagly & Johnson, 1990). Moreover, they are equally as effective as men, though less so in masculine roles and in male-dominated settings (Eagly, Karau, & Makahijani, 1995). Consistent with the effectiveness data, women receive negative evaluations when they lead in a stereotypically masculine style (especially directive or autocratic) or in a male-dominated role, and particularly from male evaluators (Eagly, Makhijani, & Klonsky, 1992). Despite these barriers, women are nearly as motivated to manage as men are (Eagly, Karau, Miner, & Johnson, 1994). In one study, both implicit and explicit gender beliefs (associating men with high authority and women with low authority), respectively, correlated with implicit and explicit prejudice against female authority (Rudman & Kiliansky, 2000). Thus people's expectations about gender reflect in part the statistical averages, but the expectations do not take account of variability around those means, nor do they acknowledge the nuances of leadership styles and the interplay of gender, behavior, and negative evaluations of role-incongruent behavior.

The incongruity between expectations about gender and job roles doubtless occurs beyond leadership. Women and men are differentially distributed into homemaker and employee roles, which guides stereotypes about men and women (Eagly & Steffan, 1984), maintaining both intimate interdependence and male status. Within employment, stereotypes of occupations fit two dimensions of gender and prestige (Glick, Wilk, & Perreault, 1995), and these images reflect the actual sex-segregation of employment (Cejka & Eagly, 1999). Women in nontraditional jobs probably face similar prejudice to that facing women leaders: difficulty entering the jobs and difficulty receiving fair evaluations. As a whole, this work engages cognitive factors, such as role expectations, stereotypes, and incongruity, with effects on attitudes (evaluations) but also on more complex affective responses.

Emotionally Mixed, Prescriptive Stereotypes and Ambivalent Prejudices

The backlash directed at men and women who do not conform to gender expectations and stereotypes suggests that people take their gender prejudices personally; these prejudices invoke uniquely personal beliefs and emotions. When women self-promote, for example, they may gain attributed competence, but they lose attributed social attractiveness (and hireability), an apparent backlash (Rudman, 1998). When either men or women succeed in gender-atypical ways, their competitors sabotage them as an excuse to repair their egos (Rudman & Fairchild, 2004). Such processes maintain cultural stereotypes as well as personal values.

Consequently, women must temper their "masculine" (agentic) side with "feminine" warmth (Rudman & Glick, 1999, 2001); Ann Hopkins learned this the hard way in a high-powered accounting firm, and social psychology explained why in her Supreme Court case (Fiske, Bersoff, Borgida, Deaux, & Heilman, 1991). Women perhaps rightly believe that behaving in too masculine a manner would forfeit heterosexual romance (Rudman & Heppen, 2003). Prescriptions for female communality arguably reinforce the status quo (Jackman, 1994; Ridgeway, 2001). Emphasis on feminine warmth results from men depending on women for sexual relations and domestic duties, which require a loving and morally pure partner (Glick & Fiske, 2001). Stereotypes describe the typical woman as sentimental, superstitious, and emotional; the warmth aspect fits the prescriptive ideal whereas the sentimental aspect is merely a descriptive stereotype (Ruble & Ruble, 1982). Female stereotypic traits carry less economic value but form an important piece of the intimate interdependence. Female gender-deviants risk their heterosexual interdependence according to these lines of research.

Conversely, stereotypically male traits carry more economic value (agency, competence) and reinforce male status because women traditionally depend on men for economic security and social prestige. Across cultures, the typical man is stereotyped as adventurous, independent, strong, and active; this descriptive stereotype also fits the prescriptive ideal (Ruble & Ruble, 1982). Prescriptive stereotypes reinforce heterosexual interdependence along with male societal dominance (Rudman & Glick, in press).

Intimate interdependence and male status together create ambivalent sexism that incorporates hostility toward women who violate gender prescriptions and benevolence toward women who uphold them (Glick & Fiske, 2001). One metaphor is the cultural carrot of benevolent sexism (BS) and the cultural stick of hostile sexism (HS). BS prescribes cherished but paternalistic stereotypes for women in traditional gender roles, liked but disrespected, whereas HS targets women who take nontraditional roles, respected but disliked. In line with these analyses of ambivalent sexism, more men than women on average do endorse hostile sexism in 19 countries (Glick et al., 2000). Men also on average endorse benevolent sexism more, although the gap is smaller, and in a few of the most sexist countries, women endorse it more. (In the worst settings, the benevolent sexism pedestal looks good, even if confining.)

All these patterns fit the idea that men have more to gain than women do from enforcing proscriptions against nontraditional roles for women (hostile sexism) because it helps to maintain their traditionally more powerful role. Conversely, women have less to lose from endorsing prescriptions for traditional roles (benevolent sexism) than they do from endorsing hostile sexism. BS has some advantages (e.g., chivalry), and women do not always view it as sexism (Kilianski & Rudman, 1998). Hostile and benevolent sexism are correlated, but they have distinct meanings. BS predicts positive (likable, moral) stereotypes of traditional women, and HS predicts negative (cold, untrustworthy) stereotypes of nontraditional women, reflecting the fundamental ambivalence.

As a cognitive belief system, ambivalent sexism has consequences. Women as well as men endorse both forms of sexism to some extent, and national averages predict UN indices of gender inequality across nations. Prejudices about men also predict gender inequality across nations (Glick et al., 2004), probably because they stereotype men as less pleasant but more powerful than women; in effect, men are stereotypically designed for dominance. Regardless of the target, gender prejudice is not a simple form of antipathy but fundamentally an ambivalent, mixed set of emotions.

Gender prejudice has interpersonal consequences beyond its link to gender inequality on a national scale (wages, education, health, as noted). For example, gender prejudice creates everyday hassles. In a diary study, college women reported one or two weekly sexist incidents (defined as stereotyping, prejudice, degrading comments, sexual objectification), and these incidents undermined their psychological well-being (Swim, Hyers, Cohen, & Ferguson, 2001). Although women mostly do not respond directly, they stew about it in private (Swim & Hyers, 1999). This preoccupation could stress physical as well as mental health.

Biological and Social Bases of Gender Prejudice

Besides social structural perceptions of heterosexual interdependence and male status and the resulting ambivalent prejudices, both biological-evolutionary and cultural explanations have been offered for the interplay of gender beliefs and feelings. In particular, sex differences in behavior and in mate preferences have attracted social-cognitive theories about why they occur and how they translate into stereotypes and prejudices. Here are some of the commonsense but provocative facts backed up by meta-analysis: Girls show more effort at self-control (inhibition and perceptual sensitivity), whereas boys are more active and intense (Else-Quest, Hyde, Goldsmith, & Van Hulle, 2006). Men are more physically aggressive than women, who are more socially aggressive (Eagly & Steffen, 1986). Men are more heroically helpful than women, who are more helpful in long-term, caring ways (Eagly & Crowley, 1986). As noted earlier, men are more likely to emerge as leaders in task-oriented groups, whereas women are more likely to emerge as social leaders (Eagly & Karau, 1991). Women more often seek older mates with higher status and good earning capacity; men more often want younger mates who are physically attractive but also good housekeepers and cooks (Buss, 1989; Buss et al., 1990). Researchers, like other people, are fond of contrasting the sexes (for a sampling, see Eagly & Wood, 1991).

Some favor explaining such gender differences in evolutionary terms. In particular, derivations from the parental investment models argue that women have always had to invest more in reproduction because of pregnancy and nursing, whereas men's required biological investment is minimal (Trivers, 1985). From this, the argument runs, men are promiscuous, and women are choosy. Men seek fertile mates to maximize their reproductive capacity, and women seek mates with resources to ensure their reproductive success (Buss, 1989; Buss & Schmitt, 1993). And women do indeed weigh social class and ambition higher than men, who weigh attractiveness higher than women do (Feingold, 1992). The evolutionary explanations are appealing in their simplicity and apparent reliance on biology, though testing them is complicated (Buss & Kenrick, 1998). Also, unlike race, one can easily argue for the ancestral conditions that would have made automatically perceiving gender to be adaptive (Cosmides et al., 2003).

Other researchers favor explaining the same differences in sociocultural terms. Social role theory also addresses gender differences in social behavior. It starts with the division of labor between men and women, which guides both gender-role expectations and sex-typed skills and beliefs, which together guide sex differences in behavior (Eagly, 1987; Eagly & Wood, 1999). Cross-cultural variation in mate preferences, for example, correlates with cultural variations in social structure; namely, gender inequality. A biosocial approach acknowledges biological differences in average size and parental investment, as well as nearly universal but culturally moderated divisions of labor. The contrast with more evolutionary theories is that the biosocial approach argues for social forces as explaining most of the variance. This approach also highlights the enormous joint contributions that men and women make to child rearing and earning (Wood & Eagly, 2002).

The most comprehensive account of cognitions and prejudices about gender will require integrative approaches that combine biological and social realities. In the end, the gender similarities are greater than the differences, and most differences are small (Hyde, 2005). For example, regarding mate preference, across 37 cultures everyone first specifies kindness, intelligence, and social skills in a prospective mate (Buss, 1989). Both biological and cultural factors matter to gender differences in behavior, and both underlie gender stereotyping and prejudice.

Conclusion

The interplay of cognition and emotional prejudices regarding gender highlights men's and women's unique structural relationships of heterosexual interdependence and male hegemony in society. The result is mixed, prescriptive stereotypes and ambivalent prejudices. All these prejudices operate in the context of biological-evolutionary and biosocial bases of gender prejudice.

AGE PREJUDICE

In this section we examine prejudice against older adults.[3] Although a host of negative adjectives stereotype older adults (see Kite & Johnson, 1988, for a meta-analysis), age stigma is mixed (Richeson & Shelton, 2006), just as gender is. If women are weak but wonderful and men are bad but bold, older adults are doddering but dear according to prevailing stereotypes. The prejudices addressed to older adults, generically, are mainly pity and sympathy (Cuddy, Norton, & Fiske, 2005). This paternalism is reserved for groups with negative outcomes that are not their fault (Fiske et al., 2002). Generically, older people are viewed in a contradictory combination of condescension and compassion. Perhaps there are cultures where older people receive respect, but older people land in the pity area across several Western and Eastern cultures (Cuddy, Fiske, Kwan, et al., in press).

Nevertheless, older people have images across the spectrum. One major difference divides the young-old (55–75 years) and the old-old (75 and up); prejudices spill over from the latter to the former (Neugarten, 1974). Like both race and gender categories, meaningful subcategories represent relatively respected, disliked, and harmless subgroups (Brewer, Dull, & Lui, 1981; Hummert, Garstka, Shaner, & Strahm, 1994, 1995). Variations in valence, vitality, and maturity run through the different images (Hummert et al., 1994; Knox, Gekoski, & Kelly, 1995), which are cued by physiognomy (Hummert, 1994) and occur relatively automatically (Hummert, Garstka, O'Brien, Greenwald, & Mellott, 2002). Like gender and race, age is among the top three most rapidly perceived features of another person (Fiske, 1998).

Ageism is unique in several respects. Like gender, age divides people within families, but like race, different age groups live in segregated circumstances. Unlike either race or gender, ageism addresses a malleable intergroup boundary

---

[3]Age prejudice includes biases against children too, but scant research has addressed this topic.

that most people hope to cross in their lifetime, but at the same time, people fear its implication of mortality.

Malleable Boundaries

Unlike gender and race, people resist their identity as older. The difference, of course, is that the gender and race are handed out at birth, whereas one acquires age gradually. As age creeps up on people, they do not necessarily internalize its negative stereotypes (for two contrasting views, see Levy & Langer, 1994; Zebrowitz, 2003). Older adults are viewed as incompetent socially, cognitively, and physically (e.g., Pasupathi, Carstensen, & Tsai, 1995; for reviews, see Nelson, 2002; Richeson & Shelton, 2006), so people are in no hurry to believe themselves "old." Indeed, although people acknowledge their chronological age, they see "old age" as a moving target that recedes as they approach its boundary (Seccombe & Ishii-Kuntz, 1991). The malleable boundary perpetually resets as people resist membership in the old-person outgroup. Older adults associate themselves with young stereotypic terms faster than with old stereotypic terms (Hummert et al., 2002).

Older people are wise to reset and resist the malleable age boundary, for a youthful identity correlates with good mental and physical health, and even several years of longevity (Hummert et al., 2002; Levy, Slade, Kunkel, & Kasl, 2002; Tuckman & Lavell, 1957). The causality of the positivity–health correlation could go either way, but priming studies suggest that the stereotype itself can damage one's health and performance. For example, even subliminal exposure to age stereotypes increases older people's cardiovascular and skin conductance reactivity to the short-term stress of math and verbal challenges (Levy, Hausdorff, Hencke, & Wei, 2000). Negative self stereotypes of aging impair older people's memory performance, self-efficacy, and even the will to live (Levy, Ashman, & Dror, 1999–2000); the ill effects are not just priming of elderly behavior per se because they do not affect younger adults, nor do positive stereotypes of aging impair older adults.

Acquired cultural beliefs shape the acquisition and damage due to age stereotypes. For example, older Chinese participants and older American deaf participants—presumably less exposed to negative age stereotypes—performed better than older, hearing Americans (Levy & Langer, 1994); comparable younger samples showed no culturally based performance differences. Within mainstream American culture, political correctness does not apply to ageism as it does to sexism and, especially, racism (Levy & Banaji, 2002), so people do not inhibit their age stereotypes as much as other kinds. Thus, when people finally enter the derogated category, they have fewer cognitive defenses to buffer the damage.

Mortality and Terror Management

Older people need buffers because aging stereotypes are uniquely related to death. Younger people may adopt negative stereotypes of older adults to distance and protect themselves (Snyder & Meine, 1994). Terror management theory (TMT; see Chapter 11) focuses on how people cope with the knowledge of their own ultimate death, so it applies well to age stereotypes and mortality salience (Greenberg, Schimel, & Mertens, 2002). Recall that TMT describes people's faith in their cultural worldviews as outlasting themselves, and thus soothing the threat posed by the certainty of their own death. One's ingroup values will endure, one hopes. Because outgroups hold different and hence challenging views, they undermine this buffer. Hence, according to TMT, people reminded of their own mortality derogate outgroups. One might expect older people to be the exception to this trend because, uniquely among outgroups, they represent precisely these comforting, familiar, traditional worldviews in most cultures. However, older people's traditional worldviews may pose a threat if those views seem outdated and obstructive. Regardless, the more fundamental threat posed by older people is their sheer existence—a reminder of one's own future decline.

TMT suggests various defenses against the mortality salience posed by older adults: physical segregation, as in institutionalization, certainly characterizes the location of old-old adults, and psychological segregation occurs through epithets and stereotypes. When these distancing attempts fail, exposure to older people may invoke the processes predicted by TMT: compensatory self-esteem-building efforts, endorsement of one's enduring worldview, derogation of outgroups, and favoring of ingroup. The mechanisms of TMT are essentially emotional prejudices, but this aspect remains to be more clearly demonstrated empirically with regard to ageism.

Conclusion

Ageism uniquely involves an outgroup with flexible boundaries that shift eventually to include the self. This cognitive shift provokes defense against its invocation of one's own eventual but certain death, toward which people may compensate with prejudice against older adults and other outgroups.

SEXUAL PREJUDICE

Prejudice against gay men and lesbians, which goes by the names heterosexism, homophobia, and sexual prejudice, differs from other prejudices in at least three primary respects. First, sexual orientation is not as visibly communicated as race, gender, and age, so its targets often control the extent to which they reveal their identity. Second, of the prejudices described so far, this one is among the most widespread. Finally, even more than sexism, heterosexism creates controversy. Not everyone agrees it is a problem. In part because of this, and because social psychological research on this topic is just beginning (Herek, 2000), our discussion of these issues will be relatively brief.

Some of the earliest studies of antigay prejudice drew on its quality of being a nonvisible, concealable identity. Early studies would tell one participant that another participant was gay and record self-report and nonverbal reactions (e.g., Farina, Allen & Saul, 1968). The reactions were uniformly negative. Consequently, much early work documented gay and lesbian people's strategies for managing their identity (Goffman, 1963). Both assumptions—that one can freely manipulate a person's apparent sexual identity and that homosexuality primarily concerns the target's stigma-management issues—raise ethical issues. (Is it really comparable to set up a straight person as gay? Is it okay to label a straight person gay or a gay person straight in a study? Is sexual prejudice really mainly about the target's stigma management or about the bias in the eye of the beholder?) More recent work avoids these ethical complexities by using surveys to document people's attitudes.

Antigay attitudes are among the most negative prejudices (Yang, 1997), and most adult Americans report them (Herek & Capitanio, 1997). Women are less prejudiced than men, and lesbians are less targeted than gay men (Herek, 2002). Uniquely among the major prejudices, sexual prejudice most centrally entails disgust, an emotion directed toward human as well as nonhuman objects (Herek & Capitanio, 1999).

Hate crimes target a fifth of lesbians and a quarter of gay men, resulting in depression, anger, anxiety, and stress, more than for comparable crime victims (Herek, Gillis, & Cogan, 1999). Sexual prejudice causes more unambiguous hate-crime violence toward gays and lesbians than the violence directed at heterosexual women and older adults. Those groups also face abuse and violence, but it is less obviously based on their social category per se. It is more likely to be intimate violence with complex causes. Like all common outgroups, gay men and lesbians also experience daily hassles with prejudice, which can undermine their mental and physical health (Swim, Pearson, & Johnston, 2006).

Summary

This chapter describes emotional prejudices and their interplay with cognitions on which they are based. Several recent theories describe specific emotions targeting particular outgroups, based on perceivers' beliefs about them. The stereotype content model predicts distinct emotional prejudices from stereotypes that themselves result from intergroup relations of status and competition. The intergroup emotions theory predicts distinct emotional prejudices from perceiver appraisals of the threat posed by each outgroup. Image theory examines structural relations between groups and posits types of outgroup images and associated emotions. The biocultural approach predicts different threats to group integrity and evolved emotional responses to preserve the group. All these theories posit intergroup behaviors stemming from outgroup emotional prejudices. Other theories focus on specific emotions of anxiety and guilt in intergroup encounters.

Taking seriously the idea that specific ingroup–outgroup prejudices reflect the unique circumstances of different groups, the chapter examines four specific kinds of prejudice. First, anti-Black racial prejudice is exceptional because it is more emotionally loaded in current society than is sexism or ageism. Racism is also more aversive to its agents than are other kinds of prejudice; people deny even to themselves that they hold these attitudes. Although people jump to biological explanations to explain racial issues, much evidence supports social cognitive construction as underlying this prejudice. Finally, Black Americans remain more segregated from the rest of society than any other outgroup, so the prospects for going beyond racial prejudices are daunting.

Gender prejudice uniquely combines high status for one group with interdependence between the two groups. The result is ambivalent prescriptive stereotypes that mix positive and negative emotions, which together maintain the status quo. Both bio-evolutionary explanations and social role theory can explain prejudices that reinforce existing arrangements.

Ageism uniquely involves a moving target, in that people both hope and fear to join the outgroup category. As such, it raises issues of mortality and emotional distancing. Finally, sexual prejudice targets a concealable stigma, but it is widespread and simultaneously controversial, evoking strong reactions on all sides. We now turn to more general theories of the affect–cognition interplay.

CHAPTER 13

From Social Cognition to Affect

DIFFERENTIATING AMONG AFFECTS, PREFERENCES, EVALUATIONS, MOODS, AND EMOTIONS
◆ *EARLY THEORIES* ◆ *PHYSIOLOGICAL THEORIES OF EMOTION*
◆ *SOCIAL COGNITIVE FOUNDATIONS OF AFFECT*

A cognitive social psychologist was once approached with the rather disconcerting opening, "You do affect, don't you?" This comment seemed odd for several reasons. For starters, the topics included in affect are beyond the capacity of any one person to presume to "do," for the literature sprawls across every domain of psychology. But even within the traditions of social psychology, if one identifies oneself as a cognitive social psychologist, affect is normally not included in what one primarily does, so the blunt question is also a bit off at least in presupposing the affect without mentioning the cognition. However, suppose the cognition is a given and that our friend is indeed a cognitive-social-psychologist-who-does-affect. This is a curious hybrid, for it results from being back-bred to achieve what originally existed as a species in the wild, natural state. In other words, cognitive social psychology is the artificial creation achieved by deliberately isolating and selecting for certain valued characteristics (e.g., a commitment to the importance of thoughts and information in social contexts). In this breeding process—some would say inbreeding—affect is one of the characteristics selected out. Hence, it is ironic that, having attained the purebred strain of cognitive social psychology, perhaps exemplified by the material in the mental representation and heuristics chapters, cognitive social psychology is reverting to its wild state to the extent that someone in the field could be approached as "doing affect."

In this chapter and the next, we do affect in several respects, although we confine ourselves to the work most linked to social cognition. As background, we cover early theories of emotion, the precursors to current cognition and emotion debates; next we discuss physiological and neuroscience theories of emotion to provide a broader context to the cognitive theories; and finally we examine social cognitive theories that describe how cognitions underlie emotions. In Chapter 14 we cover social cognitive theories that describe how affect influences cognitions and examine the premise that affect and cognition are separate, having little to do with each other. Thus this chapter concentrates on background and on social cognition as influencing affect, whereas the next concentrates on how affect influences social cognition, closing with the contrasting argument for separate systems.

Fundamental questions arise when one attempts to integrate affect and cognition. The history of research on emotion reveals long struggles over the role of cognitive processes in affect. (For reviews of cognitive and other theories of emotion, see Cacioppo & Gardner, 1999; M. S. Clark & Fiske, 1982; V. Hamilton, Bower, & Frijda, 1988; P. Shaver, 1984; Zajonc, 1998.) Two questions particularly concern us here, the influence of cognition on affect and the influence of affect on cognition. Dividing the psychology of affect and cognition in this way, of course, presupposes that the two can be usefully separated. However, the separation is not sustained, for example, by one's lived experience of affect and cognition as occurring in a simultaneous mix. For analytic convenience, this chapter and the next divide affect and cognition, examining their reciprocal influences, but it is important to note that this separation is something of a fiction.

A final word of caution: The field of affect, and likewise affect and cognition, has spawned an encyclopedic array of theories, some of which are tested by data and some of which remain untested. This inevitably creates considerably uneven scientific status for the various theories, but it also presents opportunities for the enterprising researcher. Moreover, the sheer quantity of unrelated theories challenges the capacity of any neophyte (and even the seasoned affect expert). We organize and compare theories where possible, but let the reader beware that the review of theories inevitably resembles a laundry list to the extent that the literature has generated multiple unrelated and often untested explanations.

DIFFERENTIATING AMONG AFFECTS, PREFERENCES, EVALUATIONS, ATTITUDES, MOODS, AND EMOTIONS

Affect and Company

Defining terms forces one to think hard about what is meant by affect terms used loosely in everyday language (cf. J. D. Mayer, 1986; H. A. Simon, 1982). *Affect* is a generic term for a whole range of preferences, evaluations, moods, and emotions. *Preferences* include relatively mild subjective reactions that are essentially either pleasant or unpleasant. The preferences most frequently studied by social psychologists are interpersonal evaluations: that is, simple positive and negative reactions to others, such as attraction, liking, prejudice, and so forth. Such positive and negative evaluations have obvious importance in social interaction, telling us whom to approach and whom to avoid. Such *evaluations* can also pertain to objects, and we already discussed them as attitudes.

Preferences and evaluations may be distinguished from affects that have a less specific target, that is, *moods*. One can have an evaluative reaction toward a person, but one does not typically have a mood directed toward someone. Moods affect a wide range of social cognitions and behaviors. Like preferences and evaluations, moods are primarily considered as simply positive or negative, at least as they are currently treated in the relevant literature. Preferences, evaluations, and moods are not normally fleeting experiences but typically have some duration.

Simple positive and negative reactions do not capture all the intensity and complexity of affect. Think how limited our world would be if all we could say was, "I feel good (bad) right now" or "I feel positively (negatively) toward you." More interesting and sensitive terms are needed to differentiate between being elated and contented, between being sad and angry. For instance, one person we know insists on over a dozen distinct states of being emotionally drained: tired, fatigued, sleepy, exhausted, run down, wiped out, depleted, spent, weak, limp, blank, numb, spaced out, empty. Not all of us are so subtly attuned, but most of us need more than three or four terms to describe our affective reactions. *Emotion* refers to this complex assortment of affects, beyond merely good feelings and bad, to include delight, serenity, anger, sadness, fear, and more. Emotion also can imply intense feelings with physical manifestations, including physiological arousal. Emotions can be of short or long duration, but they do not usually last over periods as long as preferences and evaluations can last.

Differentiating Positive and Negative Responses

How to characterize the rich variety of affective responses is a long-standing problem in psychology (Cacioppo & Gardner, 1999; Davitz, 1970; Ekman, 1984; Plutchik, 1980; Schlosberg, 1954; Wundt, 1897). Affects can be characterized in one of two ways that emerge consistently across analyses of the structure of emotion. The first structure emphasizes bipolar evaluation, crossed with degree of arousal. This bipolar structure best fits behavioral responses of approach (e.g., to consume) or withdrawal (e.g., from a threat; Cacioppo & Gardner, 1999). Mostly, behavioral responses are physically constrained to be largely positive or negative.

The bipolar structure sometimes appears in verbal reports and classifications of emotions. As the solid lines in Figure 13.1 indicate, two common dimensions are pleasantness/unpleasantness and high/low arousal (engagement) (e.g., Barrett & Russell, 1999; Russell, 2003). When people describe how they feel right now, or when they sort emotion words according to their similarity, these two dimensions emerge reliably. Thus one might report feeling content, happy, and pleased, but at that same moment one is unlikely also to report feeling blue, grouchy, and lonely because those terms are at the opposite ends of the same dimension. Moreover, separately, one could also report feeling aroused, astonished, and surprised, or conversely quiescent, quiet, and still. Apparently, people's commonsense theories of emotion are based on what one feels at any given point in time. In this short-run framework, the more one feels good, the less one feels bad, and this is especially true if emotions are intense (Diener & Iran-Nejad, 1986) or simple, but the degree to which one feels aroused is a separate matter. One can be happily or unhappily aroused, happily or unhappily quiescent. As noted, behavioral responses especially reflect this positive–negative bipolarity (Cacioppo & Gardner, 1999).

In contrast, suppose people are asked about their experience of emotion over time: for example, considering their life satisfaction in general, their feelings over the last year, how they feel in close relationships over time, and even their emotional reactions to presidential candidates over the course of the entire campaign (e.g., Abelson, Kinder, Peters, & Fiske, 1982; Bradburn & Caplovitz, 1965; Marcus & Mackuen, 1999; for reviews, see Cacioppo & Gardner, 1999; Diener, 1984; Watson & Tellegen, 1985). In the case of a longer time frame, people's reports of positive and negative affect are curiously independent. That is, over time, whether one has felt distressed, fearful, or hostile is unrelated to whether one has also at other times felt elated, enthusiastic, and

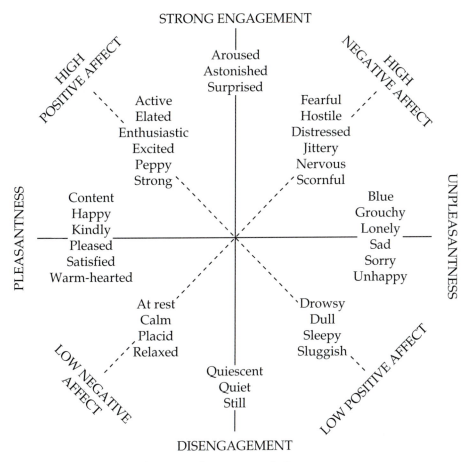

FIGURE 13.1 Two-factor solutions to the structure of affect
Source: After Watson & Tellegen, 1985.

excited (Diener & Emmons, 1984). Over time, with less intense or more complex emotions, one can observe a structure of affect that is also apparent if you rotate Figure 13.1 45°, placing "high positive affect" at the top. In some cases, one can feel much or little "pure" positive affect, and that has little bearing on whether one also feels much or little "pure" negative affect. In short, one can feel happy and sad at the same time, under some circumstances, especially looking back over a complex experience (Larsen, McGraw, & Cacioppo, 2001). This is termed a bivalent (two independent valences) structure.

What's more, the bivalent structure (separate, uncorrelated positive and negative dimensions, operating independently) goes beyond self-reported long-term experiences. The underlying psychophysiology reflects such independent positive and negative systems (Cacioppo & Berntson, 1999; we will review in the section on those theories). The debate about whether positive and negative states are uncorrelated (and thus can co-occur) continues (Green, Salovey, & Truax, 1999).

Time frame, intensity, and complexity jointly seem to determine which of two structures best captures people's emotional experiences. Intense, simple, short-term emotions show a negative correlation (i.e., inverse relation) between pleasant and unpleasant feelings, and thus a bipolar positive–negative structure. But longer term summaries of complex and perhaps less intense emotional experience show no correlation between positive and negative emotions, and thus a bivalent or bivariate, independent variables structure. In both cases, however, a two-dimensional structure captures the most consensual understanding of the structure of emotion.

Positive and negative emotions differ in how they operate. Positive emotions are relatively limited but prevalent. Recall from Chapter 3 that negative information especially captures attention, partly because it is so rare. People mostly expect and experience slightly positive outcomes, so their baseline is slightly positive; the psychological neutral point is not zero but instead slightly right of zero. This represents a positivity offset, Pollyanna effect, or positivity bias (respectively: Cacioppo & Gardner, 1999; Matlin & Stang, 1978; Sears, 1983). Negative outcomes capture more attention and resources for coping with the threat. This represents a negativity bias as one mobilizes to the challenge, minimizes it, and then restores the moderately positive equilibrium (see Cacioppo & Gardner, 1999; Fiske, 1980; Taylor, 1991).

Not only do they differ in their operating characteristics, but the two valences differ in complexity. Negative emotions, analyzed separately, seem to have a more complex dimensional structure than positive emotions analyzed separately (Averill, 1980; Ellsworth & Smith, 1988a, 1988b). Consider the differences among anger, sadness, fear, disgust, anxiety, shame, and hate. In contrast, love, serenity, pride, and joy seem more similar. Negative emotions vary in degree of human agency and situational control. For example, one feels more guilt when the human agent is self rather than another (the more responsible I feel, the more guilty), whereas the reverse is true for anger (the more responsible I feel, the less I am angry at other people; Ellsworth & Smith, 1988a). Negative emotions may also vary in degrees of certainty, attention, and anticipated effort more than positive emotions do. Positive emotions do have dimensional structure, but it tends to be simpler (Argyle & Crossland, 1987; Ellsworth & Smith, 1988b).

We have seen differences between short-term emotional responses (especially behavioral ones), which more often fit the bivalent model, and long-term emotional responses (especially self-reports), which more often fit the bipolar model. Note that people have many information sources for their emotion reports: experiential knowledge, episodic memory, situation-specific beliefs, and identity-related beliefs (Robinson & Clore, 2002a). People prioritize these information sources, preferring the most specific. People also use different processes to report current or recent emotions versus overall past patterns of emotion (Robinson & Clore, 2002b).

Basic Emotions?

The dimensional analyses of emotion are exceedingly useful, but how do we decide what is an emotion and what is not? Is pain an emotion? What about alienation, awe, challenge, or startle? No simple formula determines basic emotions, or even if basic emotions really exist (Ortony & Turner, 1990; Russell, 2003). As a consequence, theorists have focused on an alternative way to characterize the concept of emotion. Deciding what is an emotion and what is not comes much more easily if one does not require emotion to be a classical concept with necessary and sufficient defining features. According to the prototype view of categories, as described in Chapter 4, category membership is a matter of degree rather than being all or nothing. Some states are more obviously emotions (e.g., happiness, anger, sadness, love, fear, hate): They come to mind easily when people list emotions; they are likely to be labeled emotions; and they fit into the same contexts as other emotions ("He was overcome by . . . [fill in the blank]"). Moreover, the better examples of emotion share many features with other prototypic category members (heart rate increase, perspiration, obsessive concern, tears; Fehr & Russell, 1984).

Researchers have also applied prototypes to defining the meaning of particular emotions. Rigid definitions do not completely capture the characteristics of particular emotions: What exactly is love, anger, or fear? In this view, for example, people's categorization of particular emotional facial expressions, such as anger or fear, would reflect degree of fit, not an either-or decision (Russell & Bullock, 1985, 1986; Russell & Fehr, 1987; but see Ekman & O'Sullivan, 1988 vs. Russell & Fehr, 1988). However, this prototype process may operate primarily to identify emotions, whereas lay theories about emotion concepts may help explain and reason about emotions (Clore & Ortony, 1991).

Taking some nominees for core emotions (love, joy, anger, sadness, and fear), people can specify prototypical emotion episodes that might be characterized as scripts beginning with an appraisal of events that elicit emotions, which then consist of expressions, action tendencies, subjective feelings, and physiological states (P. Shaver, Schwartz, Kirson, & O'Connor, 1987). For example, prototypic joy begins with a desired outcome, an achievement, or receiving esteem and praise; then the joyous person seeks to communicate and be with others; the person has a positive outlook and feels energetic, excited, and bubbly; the person smiles and says positive, enthusiastic things. The point here is that people conceive of a prototypic experience of joy such that a good example contains all these elements and less-good examples contain fewer of them but still might be classified as joy. In-depth analyses also have concentrated on prototypes for love and commitment (Fehr, 1988) and for loneliness (Horowitz, de Sales French, & Anderson, 1982).

More generally, people have schemas for the typical physiological changes that occur during particular emotions, and these schemas are similar across cultures (Rimé, Philippot, & Cisamolo, 1990). People also have rules for guessing other people's affective reactions (Karniol, 1986). In all this work, one cannot be certain whether common individual experiences cause shared prototypes or whether the culture defines certain experiences as certain emotions, which individuals then enact as emotions. That is, the direction of causality between individual emotional prototypes and cultural expectations is not clear.

One perspective embraces the cultural determination of emotion, holding that emotions are substantially defined by culture. This social constructivist view of emotions sees emotions as transitory social roles represented cognitively in members of a shared culture. Thus emotions are identifiable roles that people assume, each with variations on a central (or prototypic) theme (e.g., Averill, 1983). In this view, emotions (a) are constituted by social rules prescribed in cultural scripts, (b) are importantly interpersonal phenomena that are interwoven with other actors as part of the larger "play" (cf. de Rivera & Grinkis, 1986),

(c) are part of a cultural story or "plot" that gives them meaning, (d) involve choice regarding one's participation as an actor, (e) require training for skilled performance, (f) require identification with the role to experience intensity, and (g) entail interpretation of the role as it fits into the larger social context (Averill, 1990c). As such, emotions entail a coherent, organized syndrome of responses (Averill, 1990b; cf. de Rivera, 1984), an entire set of characteristic responses that identify the emotion, within a certain fuzzy set of related reactions, just as prototypic features identify emotions in particular cases or emotions in general. At the psychological level, people construct their emotions from emotional meta-experience (Russell, 2003). That is, they combine features of their conscious experience of sensations, pleasantness, arousal, behavior, cognitions, and appraisal of the target of their emotions. The result is a labeled emotion, but it is fluid, and few pure instances of any given emotion (e.g., anger) occur. Some features are present; some are not, and people label emotions according to the features that accumulate and cohere.

Conclusion

To review, affect subsumes preferences, evaluations, moods, and emotions. Preferences and evaluations are simple, long-term positive or negative reactions to a target, whereas moods are simple, long-term positive or negative feelings without a specific target. Emotion refers to the richer variety of affective states, which may be intense and short-term. Various efforts to reflect the richness of emotion have used dimensional analyses, prototype models, social role approaches, and construction from meta-experience, that is, varied inputs believed relevant.

A cautionary note is important in applying the definitional points to the work reviewed in the remainder of the chapter: Many of these distinctions are not uniformly maintained by those working in the field. In fact, some of the best empirical work on affect ironically bears little relation to the best taxonomic work on affect.

EARLY THEORIES

A brief bit of historical context will frame our main task, namely, the long-standing question of the relationship between affect and cognition. Over a century ago, William James (1890/1983) proposed that the feeling of autonomic feedback (heart rate, stomach tension) and muscular feedback (posture, facial expressions) itself constitutes emotion. Conrad Lange (1885/1922) invented a similar theory at the same time as James. In this James-Lange view, the physiological patterns unique to each emotion reveal to us what we are feeling. James stated that when we see a bear in the woods, we are afraid because we tremble and run away: The physical responses cause the emotion. The James-Lange theory of emotion downplayed the role of cognition or mental activity as a sole basis for emotion. In a similar manner, Charles Darwin (1872) had proposed that the relevant muscular activity can strengthen or inhibit emotion.

Decades later, the James-Lange theory was undermined by Walter Cannon's (1927) arguments that visceral sensations are too diffuse to account for all the different emotions and that the autonomic system responds too slowly to account for the speed of emotional response. Following this critique, many psychologists assumed that physiological contributions to emotion were limited to diffuse arousal and did not include specific patterns of bodily sensation. We will come back to this point, but assuming this undifferentiated view of arousal for the moment, a basic problem still remained: if arousal is diffuse, and simply ranges from high to low, how can one account for the rich texture of emotional experience? One set of answers is physiological, and the other is cognitive.

PHYSIOLOGICAL THEORIES OF EMOTION

Physiology might still provide the richness of emotional experience, as the next four sections will explore. The first section examines emotional differentiation, most importantly through that multifaceted and highly sensitive organ, the face. Another section describes the possibility that arousal intensifies existing positive or negative feelings, in effect providing another dimension of emotion. A third possibility is that arousal is itself differentiated, contrary to the Cannon critique. A fourth section explores the possibilities that lie in new techniques to get inside the brain, such as neuroimaging. As it happens, these possibilities are not independent, but linked, as we shall see. In any case, these four sections briefly overview some noncognitive theories of emotion as background to the cognitive theories.

Facial Feedback Theory

The original facial feedback hypothesis held that emotional events directly trigger certain innate configurations of muscles, and that we become aware of feelings only upon feedback from the face (Tomkins, 1962; cf. Gellhorn, 1964). Notice how compatible this view is with the James-Lange theory, yet without having to assume that arousal is fast and differentiated, only that facial responses are. According to facial feedback theory, development and upbringing constrain the range of expressions people adopt and so also the range of emotions they can feel (Izard, 1972, 1977). Over time people build up a repertoire of emotions on the basis of the facial muscles society allows them to use in expressing their emotions. Although variants exist, the core hypothesis is that feedback from facial expressions influences emotional experience and behavior (Buck, 1980; Winton, 1986).

Unfortunately, evidence for this intriguing idea is limited to pleasant versus unpleasant experiences and, perhaps, arousal. Facial expressions reflect both pleasantness and intensity, two basic dimensions of emotion (Schlosberg, 1954). Moreover, facial expressions are related to other physiological responses in emotion. The pleasantness of a person's facial expression (as rated by observers while the person is viewing evocative photographs) can be directly related to heart rate (extreme pleasantness with acceleration, extreme unpleasantness with deceleration; Winton, Putnam, & Krauss, 1984). And the rated intensity of expression can be related to skin conductance (i.e., minute differences in amount of perspiration). Visceral responses in facial expression, heart rate, and skin conductance correlate with basic dimensions of emotions (Winton, et al., 1984) as part of an integrated configuration of physiological responses (cf. Cacioppo, Petty, & Geen, 1989; Ekman, Levenson, & Friesen, 1983; McCaul, Holmes, & Solomon, 1982; Zuckerman et al., 1981). Indeed, the face reliably reflects the pleasantness and intensity dimensions of emotion, even when overt expressions are not noticeable to observers. That is, electrodes attached to the face can detect tiny muscular (electromyographic or EMG) activity too subtle or fleeting to be seen, and this activity parallels the muscles used in overt facial expressions, reflecting two basic dimensions of emotion (Cacioppo, Petty, & Geen, 1989; Cacioppo, Petty, Losch, & Kim, 1986). For example, the lower cheek muscles that contract in a smile (zygomaticus major) and the muscles between the eyebrows that contract in a frown (corrugator supercilii) respectively index positive versus negative responses to affect-laden pictures, sounds, and words (Larsen, Norris, & Cacioppo, 2003).

There is also evidence for the fundamental idea that facial expressions exert a direct effect on reported mood, emotion, and evaluations (Laird, 1984). In one typical paradigm, participants are induced to adopt positive or negative facial expressions (e.g., smile, frown) without labeling them as such. For example, one experiment instructed them to contract and hold the relevant muscles one by one for supposed EMG recording until they had inadvertently assumed an emotional expression (Laird, 1974). Supposedly to study the physical coping strategies of people with disabilities, another experiment asked participants to hold a pen in their teeth, without using their lips, thereby simulating a smile (Strack, Martin, & Stepper, 1988). Participants then rated the funniness of cartoons, detecting more humor when they artificially maintained a smiling facial expression than when they inhibited a smile. Other researchers have obtained similar effects (e.g., Flack, 2006; Ito, Chiao, Devine, Lorig, & Cacioppo, 2006; Lanzetta et al., 1976; Rhodewalt & Corner, 1979; Zuckerman et al., 1981).

The pure form of the facial feedback hypothesis is controversial. The effect across studies appears small (Matsumoto, 1987). Moreover, some researchers do not replicate the finding that posed facial expressions change emotion (Buck, 1980; Ellsworth & Tourangeau, 1981; Tourangeau & Ellsworth, 1979; but see Hager & Ekman, 1981; Izard, 1981; Tomkins, 1981). One likely explanation for some of the contradictory findings is that telling people simply to exaggerate their spontaneous facial expressions produces changes in emotion, but rigidly posed expressions only sometimes produce changes in emotion. The conditions under which posed expressions do produce emotion are as yet unclear.

Another controversy revolves around whether or not facial feedback effects are cognitively mediated. Some researchers maintain that the effects of facial feedback on emotion are cognitively mediated, as in the self-attribution of attitudes (e.g., Laird, 1974); others argue that the effects are direct and cognitively unmediated (Gellhorn, 1964; Izard, 1972, 1977; Plutchik, 1962; Tomkins, 1962). Finally, throughout all the facial feedback research, even the most extreme precautions cannot completely silence critics who argue that subjects realize their expressions are being manipulated and so respond on the basis of experimental demand. Nevertheless, the facial feedback hypothesis—and related evidence regarding feedback from other nonverbal channels (Kellerman, Lewis, & Laird, 1989)—provides a physiological piece of the puzzle of complex differentiated emotions, probably most consistent with a constructionist account, whereby facial feedback provides mainly valence cues.

Excitation Transfer

Thus far we have seen preliminary clues to differentiating affect into discrete emotions without requiring that arousal be differentiated. That is, facial expressions provide (some among many) cues to the patterns of emotional experience, whereas arousal need only be a diffuse intensifier. It is important to know how arousal originates and how it influences emotion, and the next physiological theory we discuss focuses on arousal.

Zillmann (e.g., 1983, 1988) suggested that arousal (that is, emotional excitation of the sympathetic nervous system) has both automatic and learned origins; for example, a startle response is unconditioned but fear of airplane travel is a conditioned response. To explain both the learned and unlearned features of arousal, Zillmann (1983) maintains that emotion depends on three initially independent factors. The first two components create immediate emotional actions: (a) a dispositional component consists of learned and unlearned skeletal-motor reactions (e.g., startle responses, uncontrolled facial reactions, and involuntary emotional gestures), and (b) an excitatory component energizes the organism through learned and unlearned arousal reactions. Finally, (c) the experiential aspect involves assessment of one's initial reactions and interpretation of the situation, which can modify one's subsequent reactions.

The core of the theory, for our purposes, is that arousal is nonspecific and slow to decay, that people are inept at partitioning the sources of their arousal, and that people cognitively interpret their arousal. Hence, arousal left over from a previous setting can combine with arousal in a new situation and intensify one's emotional reaction. This idea is not without practical significance. Although plying one's date with alcohol is a traditional mode of seduction, in theory, plying the person with coffee or getting the person to yell at a basketball game could conceivably have better effects. Dancing, too, has its proponents.

Much evidence indicates that arousal from otherwise innocent sources can intensify affect toward seemingly irrelevant people and objects that come into view. A classic study by Dutton and Aron (1974) showed how excitation can transfer. They arranged for an attractive woman to interview men as they ventured across a scary suspension bridge or as they crossed a relatively sturdy wooden bridge nearby. Each man was asked to tell a story about an intentionally ambiguous picture of a young woman. As predicted, the men who crossed the scary bridge and who were presumably aroused had more sexual content in their stories than did the men who crossed the safe bridge. Moreover, they were more likely to telephone the attractive woman experimenter later than were the men from the safe bridge (for similar results, see Jacobs, Berscheid, & Walster, 1971; Stephan, Berscheid, & Walster, 1971). Thus arousal originally instigated by fear transferred to romantic or sexual attraction.[1]

Fear and romantic attraction are not the only emotions that can function in this way. When one has been angered and then is exposed to erotic stories, nude pictures, or an attractive opposite-sex confederate, reports of heightened sexual arousal often occur (e.g., Barclay, 1970; Barclay & Haber, 1965). Conversely, prior sexual arousal can increase the likelihood of aggression (e.g., Zillmann, 1971).

---

[1] Early studies of this phenomenon frequently refer to it as an analysis of heterosexual behavior, but there is no reason to think that homosexual erotic attraction would differ.

For men, a female companion's distress at a gory horror film intensifies their own enjoyment of it (Zillmann, Weaver, Mundorf, & Aust, 1986). Disgust can facilitate the enjoyment of humor (J. R. Cantor, Bryant, & Zillmann, 1974) or music (J. R. Cantor & Zillmann, 1973); the latter finding may explain the appeal of certain music videos. What is provocative about these findings is that the valence of the prior experience is irrelevant; only the arousal transfers (for dissenting views, see R. A. Baron, 1977; Branscombe, 1985).

By itself, simple physical arousal can intensify anger or sexual attraction. For example, people who have just exercised respond more aggressively or more angrily when provoked than do people not previously aroused (Zillmann, 1978; Zillmann & Bryant,1974; Zillmann, Katcher, & Milavsky, 1972). Arousal enhances romantic attraction (G. L. White, Fishbein, & Rutstein, 1981; G. L. White & Kight, 1984). Arousal even intensifies evaluations of one's alma mater (M. S. Clark, 1982), as well as one's egotistically satisfying attributions (Gollwitzer, Earle, & Stephan, 1982) and the likelihood of counterarguing a persuasive communication (Cacioppo, 1979). All these studies are consistent with the idea that excitation transfers from one source to another, intensifying subsequent affective responses. Their implications are broadened by the finding that, even if unable to take immediate action under transferred excitation, people may commit themselves to future actions (e.g., revenge) while excited, so that the effects of excitation transfer can last long after the actual arousal dissipates (Bryant & Zillmann, 1979). Arousal, thus, polarizes both positive and negative reactions (Stangor, 1990).

A question of particular interest to social cognition research is whether the effects of arousal depend on being cognitively aware of it. People respond emotionally—and perhaps also can be aroused—by an affect-laden stimulus without even being fully aware of the stimulus (Corteen & Wood, 1972; Niedenthal & Cantor, 1986; Robles et al., 1987; Spielman, Pratto, & Bargh, 1988). Excitation transfer theory argues that arousal influences emotion even when people do not consciously feel aroused but physiological measures indicate that they are indeed aroused.

Note that this differs importantly from Schachter and Singer's (1962) theory of emotion (covered in Chapter 6 and also in the next section), as well as its derivatives, which instead posit that emotion results when people label, interpret, and identify physiological arousal for which they have no immediate other explanation. The implication in Schachter's theory is that the arousal demands explanation because it has been consciously perceived. Evidence from people with spinal cord injuries indicates that the perception of arousal may not be necessary for emotional experience, as Schachter's theory assumes (Chwalisz, Diener, & Gallagher, 1988). Another important difference between the two theories is that Schachter's theory originally applied only when the initial source of arousal is ambiguous (Kenrick & Cialdini, 1977), which is not the case for the Zillmann theory. Note, however, that both theories describe roles for arousal when its current source is otherwise ambiguous.

Affective Neuroscience

So far we have seen a variety of evidence for dimensions of emotion that include positivity and negativity and intensity/arousal. As we will see, neuroscience backs up these basic features and ventures beyond to hint at greater differentiation, though the evidence here is preliminary.

Some of the earliest affective neuroscience used EEG measures to identify the timing and approximate locations of positive and negative affect responses. Midfrontal activations on the left and right, respectively, generally correspond to positive and negative emotional reactions; for the most part, these align with approach and avoidance behavioral tendencies (Coan & Allen, 2004; Davidson, 1993; Davidson & Irwin, 1999). Although first identified a couple of decades earlier than most current affective neuroscience, the simple idea of affective asymmetry is deceptive given the complexity of emotional processes. But still, the contrast between two broad motivational systems—positive (approach, reward, appetitive) and negative (avoidance, punishment, threat)—is convincing. The general neural patterns of course mask much complexity and will doubtless modify as additional data arrive. For example, anger is a negative but approach-related emotion.

More recent neuroscience uses neuroimaging, which is worse at measuring time course but better at locating specific regions, as noted earlier. Some of this related work appeared in Chapters 9 and 10, which described a role for the amygdala in emotionally intense attitudes, especially negative ones, and a possible role for the insula in negative valence.

Emotions researchers also have emphasized the importance of the amygdala in emotionally intense experiences (not just attitudes). The amygdala is implicated especially in recognizing fearful and other emotionally intense expressions as part of a larger system including the orbitofrontal cortex (Adolphs, 2002). The amygdala is reliably implicated in fear conditioning and in broader but still intense emotional experiences (Phelps, 2006). Meta-analyses agree that the amygdala is involved in fear, at least (Murphy, Nimmo-Smith, & Lawrence, 2003; Phan, Wager, Taylor, & Liberzon, 2002).

The same meta-analyses agree that the insula is involved in disgust, at a minimum. This certainly fits the idea that negative valence implicates the insula, as the attitudes work notes. Beyond the amygdala and the insula, the two meta-analyses do not agree, although hints appear: Sadness may implicate the anterior cingulate cortex, which also relates to attention and discrepancy-detection, as noted in Chapter 3.

Other basic kinds of emotions show less reliable results so far. This lack of consensus leads some to reject the relevance of neuroimaging data for detecting the essence of emotions (Barrett & Wager, 2006), but the disconnect may be partly the contrast between research focused on self-reported emotional experience versus emotion-eliciting stimuli used in most affective neuroscience research.

The message for our core focus on social cognition and affect is that the field is far from identifying differentiated "emotion areas," even if such a thing were possible. Indeed, one researcher identified this quest among the "seven sins" of affective neuroscience (Davidson, 2003). Instead, researchers should (1) recognize the intermingling of affective and cognitive neural circuits (see also Phelps, 2006); (2) acknowledge that affect involves the thinking cortex as well as the older brain's subcortical structures; (3) recognize that emotions correspond to measurable bodily responses, not just psychological constructions; (4) integrate knowledge of plausible neural circuits in the psychology of emotion; (5) realize that emotions differ with age; (6) avoid looking for emotions in discrete locations of the brain; and (7) include unconscious responses as part of emotion systems. The fast-moving work on affective neuroscience will continue to feed back to social cognition research as it develops (see also Cacioppo et al., in press).

Conclusion

Early theories of emotion set the stage for a continuing debate over the role of cognition and physiology in affective responses. James hypothesized that unique physiological patterns occur in direct response to emotional stimuli, without cognitive mediation. His view was undermined by Cannon, who argued that visceral responses are too slow and too diffuse to differentiate the many separate emotions. Facial feedback theorists argued, as James did, that the different emotions come directly from physiological sensations. But instead of relying on the arousal system, they suggested that the sensitive facial musculature provides the different patterns for various emotions. However, the evidence supports mainly a positive–negative axis. That is, the physiological evidence best differentiates partially separate positive and negative affect systems.

Taking a different tack, the arousal theorists have examined how arousal intensifies emotional responses that originate from learned or unlearned responses. Human neuroscience has identified global hemispherical asymmetries between positive (approach) and negative (avoidance) reactions, as well as brain areas recruited in emotion processing generally, but especially for intense emotions (amygdala) and negative ones (insula). All these theorists neglect cognition in emotional responses, compared to the theories covered next, but they increasingly recognize that emotions include components: conscious, unconscious, cognitive, affective, social, peripheral, subcortical, and cortical configurations. The brain is not divided up the way psychology departments are, with separate social, cognitive, affective areas. Instead they all intertwine in form and function.

Before continuing, note that an apparently erroneous presumption motivated some of the theories just covered and some of those that follow. That is, some of the search for facial origins of emotion, some of the original excitation transfer ideas, and certainly the arousal-plus-cognition theories that follow, all are based on Cannon's premise that arousal is too diffuse to account for emotional differentiation. More recent evidence has indicated that this conclusion may have been premature; distinct patterns of arousal can indeed occur for different emotions (e.g., Ax, 1953; Derryberry & Rothbart, 1988; Lacey, 1959, 1967; Lacey & Lacey, 1958, 1970; G. E. Schwartz, Davidson, & Pugash, 1976; G. E. Schwartz, Weinberger, & Singer, 1981; Tourangeau & Ellsworth, 1979; Winton et al., 1984). Note, however, that Cannon (1927) and Schachter (1964) may well have been correct in describing these patterns as not easily distinguished on an experiential level; that question is still open. Nevertheless, ironically, solving a problem that ultimately may not require solving has been partly responsible for some of the most crucial contributions to emotion theory.

SOCIAL COGNITIVE FOUNDATIONS OF AFFECT

Earlier we asked how emotions could be differentiated if physiological arousal was not; it has since become clear that a combination of physiological and neural response systems contribute to the variety of emotions. Nevertheless, physiology is by no means the whole story in emotion. In social psychology, the view of arousal as undifferentiated and inadequate to account for the variety of emotions led to a parallel effort to see how cognition could explain emotional complexity; these ideas worked essentially without reference to developing ideas about physiology.

In considering these ideas about how cognition leads to emotion, it is useful to keep in mind that many social psychologists have assumed that cognition is a major basis for affective response: for example, in studying stereotyping as an origin of prejudice (Allport, 1954), in proposing cognitive inconsistency as causing arousal that instigates attitude change (Cooper, Zanna, & Taves, 1978), in examining self-concept discrepancies as creating affect (Higgins, 1987), and more. Because of this broad treatment of affect and cognition within the traditions of social psychology, what follows is necessarily selective. Table 13.1 helps to organize four types of theory that follow.

TABLE 13.1 Theories Relating Cognitive Structure to Affect

Theories and Theorists	Cognitive Structure	Affective Impact
Interruption		
Schachter	Unexplained arousal plus cognitive interpretation	labeled emotion
Mandler	Interrupted application of schema (perceptual) or goal-directed action	positive if facilitation, easy fit; negative if blocking, hard fit
Berscheid	Interrupted interdependent goal sequence	same
Matching		
Keltner	Expectations about power relations	positive if high-power self; negative if low-power self
Fiske	Application of schema or category	associated affect[1]
Linville	Complexity of representation	moderation of affect[2]
Tesser	Elaboration of schema through thought	extremity of affect[2]
Outcomes		
Weiner	Attribution for outcome (locus, stability)	differentiated emotions
Kahneman & Miller	Comparing present outcome to norms	emotional amplification if abnormal
Managing		
Simon	Change goal priority due to environment	emotion as alerting mechanism
Oatley & Johnson-Laird	Change goal priority due to probability of success	same
Carver & Scheier	Discrepancy between current state and standard	emotion cues effort or withdrawal

Notes: [1]For attitudinal complements to schema-triggered affect, see Fazio's MODE model and Greenwald et al.'s IAT, covered in Chapter 10.
[2]To reconcile these apparently contradictory theories, see text.

Emotion as Cognition Plus Arousal: Interruption Theories

Most of us would like to think we are attracted to people because their unique personalities fit with our own unique personalities in significant, if not predestined, ways. We tend to downplay the importance of seemingly incidental factors such as proximity (living in the same courtyard), timing (being divorced long enough to be ready for a new relationship), convenience (being on the same work schedule), or irrelevant sources of arousal (meeting after an intense workout). Yet all these factors can help establish a close relationship between two people. Moreover, as Schachter's theory of emotional lability proposed (see Chapter 6), when people are aroused, they explain their arousal in different ways, depending on previous experience, socialization, and context (Schachter & Singer, 1962). Thus what one aroused person interprets as sexual attraction (Dutton & Aron, 1974) another may label love at first sight (Berscheid & Walster, 1978; Walster, 1971). Such misunderstandings have, no doubt, been the cause of much personal tragedy.

Schachter's two-component theory posits that diffuse physiological arousal catalyzes cognitive interpretation, so emotions are mediated by cognitive activity. Note how this differs from the previous views that focus more directly on unmediated physiological responses (e.g., some versions of facial feedback theory). Despite much controversy (Reisenzein, 1983), Schachter's theory has had considerable impact on social psychological thinking about emotion, as we have already seen (see Chapter 6). Moreover, recent theories take the arousal-plus-cognition viewpoint several steps further.

Mind and Arousal in Emotion

Some basic features of this theory resemble Schachter's in that physiological arousal combines with evaluative cognition to produce emotion. Visceral activation provides the intensity and particular emotional "feel" of the experience, while evaluative cognitions provide the quality of differentiated emotional experience.

George Mandler's (1975, 1990) theory, unlike Schachter's, locates a mental origin for arousal: namely, in discrepancy and interruption. In this view, most arousal follows from a perceptual or cognitive discrepancy or from the interruption or blocking of ongoing action. Disruptions by definition violate expectations, preventing either the easy application of one's schemas or the smooth continuation of one's goal-directed activity. Perceptual-cognitive interruptions include musical or visual patterns that diverge from the expected, story lines with an unexpected twist, jokes, and the like. Similarly, disruptions of goal-directed activity can interfere with complex sequences of intended activity. (Recall the last time you were working to meet a deadline and you were asked to take out the garbage.) The complexity of the interrupted activity corresponds to the amount of arousal you feel: If you drop your keys while trying to get in the door, that interrupts a relatively simple goal, so it should cause only a small amount of arousal. If you drop your keys while trying to impress the date of your dreams, that interrupts a potentially more complex goal, so it should create more arousal. As in other theories, arousal intensifies emotion.

Arousal also sets off cognitive interpretation. The interruption may be interpreted positively or negatively, depending on the type of expectation disrupted and its interpretation. With complex action sequences, you may interpret the interruption as either hindering you from your goal or unexpectedly advancing you toward it, which determines whether emotions are negative or positive. That is, if your interpretation in the key-dropping episode is that you are a hopeless, clumsy oaf, you may feel ashamed and irritated. On the other hand, if your date communicates that your nervousness is endearing, you may interpret that as unexpectedly advancing you toward your goal and feel pleased. (Admittedly, the negative emotions resulting from interruption are more intuitively compelling than the positive emotions that could result.) Whatever the cognitive interpretation, it shapes not only the quality of one's immediate affect but also one's lasting mental representation of the event.

With perceptual-cognitive schemas, the effects of interruption are more subtle than for goal-directed action sequences. The degree of interruption (and therefore arousal) more directly determines the positivity of the response, with less need for complex interpretation (Gaver & Mandler, 1987). Disconfirmations of perceptual schemas (e.g., in music, visual arts, food) range from zero (total familiarity) to extreme (total chaos and discord). On the whole, in this view (a) familiarity is pleasant but not intense; (b) a little novelty is good, for it requires slight assimilation and adds a bit of intensity to the pleasant recognition of the familiar; (c) more novelty is better if it can be reinterpreted in familiar terms, as the required adjustment adds more intensity; and (d) complete incongruity, unsuccessfully assimilated, leads to intense negative affect. One of us recently discovered how this operates, at a formal concert, as the string quartet combined the expected classical forms with jazz, causing a sizable portion of the audience to exit at intermission, presumably because the result simply did not fit their well-worn and comfortable perceptual-cognitive schemas. If asked, no doubt they would have simply reported disliking the music; Mandler does not require that interruptions and their resolutions be wholly conscious. In any case, a little novelty is a good thing (cf. Berlyne, 1970; D. W. Fiske & Maddi, 1961; Leventhal, 1984), but too much is hard to take.

Expectations, Goals, and Emotions in Close Relationships

Berscheid has presented a compelling case for the application of Mandler's theory to emotion in close relationships (Berscheid, 1982, 1983). The more intimate the relationship, the more two people's goals depend on each other (Kelley et al., 1983). The frequency, strength, diversity, and duration of dependencies on each other define the closeness of the relationship: the more intermeshed two people's daily and long-term goals, the more seriously each person can interrupt the other. Interruptions can include unexpected facilitation, causing relief, joy, and excitement, as well as unexpected hindrance, causing disappointment, frustration, and anger. Interdependent goals can range from simple behavior sequences, such as doing the laundry together, to complex behavior sequences, such as fully sharing child care or collaborating on work. The more complex the behavior sequence, the more intense the emotion when it is interrupted. The greater the interdependence, then, the greater the potential for intense negative emotion if one partner leaves, withdraws, or dies. Similarly, there is greater potential for positive emotions if one partner becomes suddenly more attuned, considerate, and helpful to the other and their shared goals. If the intermeshed sequence continues to function as usual, on the other hand, there will be no interruptions and little emotion. Hence, Berscheid notes, there is the paradox that the most intimate, involved, and interdependent relationships may show as little emotion as distant, parallel, uninvolved relationships, simply because the intimate one is running fairly smoothly. An intimate relationship is defined by the potential for—but not necessarily the experience of—emotional intensity, which results from highly interdependent goals.

The theory makes the interesting prediction that the sheer amount of emotion experienced in a relationship is negatively correlated with longevity; long-term relationships are least likely to show much emotion, either positive or negative. This prediction has been confirmed (Berscheid, Snyder, & Omoto, 1989). Consider the normal course of a long-term intimacy. At first emotions run high (both positive and negative) as two people learn all that they delightfully have in common—and all that tragically divides them. As they become better acquainted, there are simply fewer surprises (disruptions) of both the pleasant and unpleasant sort. As the novelty wears off, emotions run to fewer extremes, and either complacency or boredom may settle in. When the initial intensity fades, does that mean less potential for emotion? No. Quite the contrary. If the relationship broke up, emotional intensity would run to extremes. It is only when the long-term relationship functions smoothly that emotions seem flat and calm. The irony is that one can often only gauge the intensity of a long-term relationship when it is terminated or interrupted.

To summarize, both Mandler and Berscheid analyze emotion as resulting from interruptions. Disrupted expectations, whether in a symphony or a relationship, create arousal and cognitive interpretations. The interpretation determines the quality of affect, while the extent of the interruption and subsequent arousal determine the intensity of affect. Because expectations (schemas or goals) are cognitive structures, the models assume that cognition is a necessary antecedent for emotion.

Cognitive Structures and Affect: Matching Theory

We have seen that interruptions of cognitive structures—schemas, goals, and relationship expectations—cue affect. The theories in this section emphasize more matching world knowledge. This work examines cognitive structures such as social schemas, interpretations of outcomes that one has obtained, and the imagined outcomes that might have been or might yet be. Some of it also looks at the broad interplay between emotions and goals, but with little mention of interruption, which was integral to the previous set of theories. One final note about the theories in this section: When the term *schema* is used, it refers to knowledge about concepts (as defined in Chapter 4). In this chapter, we have already come across people's schemas for the concept of emotion in general or for particular emotions. However, the schemas in this section start with other types of content that is then linked to affect by various processes (see Table 13.1).

Expectations, Motives, and Emotions in Power Relations

One theory examines the interplay among emotions and cognitions in social relationships, specifically power asymmetries (Keltner, Gruenfeld, & Anderson, 2003). Powerful people experience a world in which they control resources

(S. T. Fiske, 1993), and hence they expect both rewards and freedom to act. Low-power people experience a world in which others control resources, so they expect fewer positive outcomes and fear some negative ones.

These cognitions (experiences and expectancies) influence the people's emotions on each side of the power equation. High power is associated with approach emotions and behaviors, and thus with positive affect, as well as left frontal activity and the release of dopamine, a reward-related neurotransmitter. Specific high-power emotions include desire, enthusiasm, and pride. In the extreme case, the configuration would be mania. Attentional focus is flexible, and information-processing is automatic. Behavior is relatively extraverted, less guarded, and more open to impulses (Kettner et al., 2003).

In contrast, low power is associated with avoidant, inhibited emotions and behaviors, and thus with negative affect, as well as right frontal activity and the release of norepinephrine and cortisol, stress-related responses in the neuro-endocrine system. Specific low-power emotions include fear, shame, guilt, and embarrassment, as well as awe and gratitude. In the extreme case, the configuration would be anxiety and depression. Attentional focus is vigilant, and information-processing is narrowly focused. Behavior is relatively more inhibited and regulated. The contrasts between low-power and high-power cognitions, emotions, and behavior are, of course, theoretical extremes; actual responses are more nuanced and subtle.

Supporting research documents predicted associations among affect, cognition, and behavior. For example, in correlational research, dormitory peers nominated high-power men, who themselves reported higher baseline moods (Keltner et al., 2003). Similarly, self-reported social potency, dominance, assertiveness, and leadership correlate with positive mood (Watson & Clark, 1997). Experimental work shows power having the predicted effects (see Keltner et al., 2003). Moreover, this theory fits with other work showing effects of social expectations (cognitions) on emotions. For example, high-status people are expected to express more anger because of its relationship to control, whereas low-status people are expected to express more guilt and sadness (Tiedens, Ellsworth, & Mesquita, 2000).

Schema-Triggered Affect

Another matching approach stems from the observation that emotions can result from the successful application of affect-laden schemas. That is, some people (e.g., one's kindergarten teacher, a feared boss, judgmental clergy, intrusive out-group members) and situations (giving a talk to a large audience, receiving a call from an old friend) inspire emotion without necessarily interrupting any goals. Originally called schema-triggered affect (S. T. Fiske, 1981, 1982), this idea was later incorporated into the broader distinction between category-based responses and attribute-based responses (e.g., S. T. Fiske & Neuberg, 1990), discussed in Chapter 2. The relevant point here is that schemas based on prior experiences can carry immediate affective tags. When a new instance fits the schema, not only does prior knowledge apply but so also may prior affect. This matching effect has been demonstrated for a variety of person schemas: old flames, politicians, campus stereotypes (such as jock, nerd, artist, and gay), college majors (such as pre-med, engineering, theater), occupations (such as doctor, hotel maid, artist, loan shark), and the potentially stigmatized (schizophrenics, paraplegics) (S. T. Fiske, 1982; S. T. Fiske et al., 1987; S. T. Fiske & Pavelchak, 1986; Neuberg & Fiske, 1987; Pavelchak, 1989). More recently, the stereotype content model (see Chapter 11) describes emotional prejudices triggered by particular outgroups (elderly cue pity, rich cue envy, poor cue contempt, ingroup cues pride).

The idea that old patterns match new people and situations, invoking feelings that are essentially holdovers from prior experience, also fits the literature on transference in psychotherapy (Singer, 1988; Westen, 1988). Affective transference occurs in close relationships when a new person resembles a previous significant other (Andersen & Chen, 2002). People paired with a new person who matches a former liked partner express more positive affect than when paired with someone who matches a former disliked partner. Yoked controls do not show this difference when paired with someone else's former liked and disliked partners, so it is the unique match that matters (Berk & Andersen, 2000). Schema-triggered affect occurs in facial expressions as well (Andersen, Reznik, & Manzella, 1996). What's more, this transference occurs subliminally (Glassman & Andersen, 1999).

Schema-triggered affect even describes people's affective reactions to consumer products that fit familiar molds (Sujan, 1985) and to loaded political issues (Sears, Huddie, & Schaffer, 1986), and it is assumed to hold for any affect-laden category. Indeed, prototypes associated with affect may be easier to learn than those that are not (J. D. Mayer & Bower, 1986).

Schema Complexity and Affective Extremity

Another set of approaches focuses on the features of the schema itself and their implications for affective responses. Linville's work (1982a, 1982b; Linville, Fischer, & Salovey, 1989; Linville & Jones, 1980; Linville, Salovey, & Fischer, 1986, noted in Chapters 4 and 11) focuses on the affective consequences of informational complexity. People tend to evaluate outgroup members (low complexity) more extremely than ingroup members (high complexity), all else being equal. More generally, the theory predicts that the greater the complexity of a schema, the more moderate the affect it typically elicits. For example, if you know a dozen dimensions that determine whether a given football team is any good, your evaluation of any random team will include a lot of pluses and minuses. I can think of only two or three dimensions offhand, so any one bit of information about a team is more likely to sway my opinion to one extreme or the other. As we saw in Chapter 5, this analysis also applies to people with simple self-concepts, who appear prone to mood swings, compared to those with more complex self-concepts (Linville, 1985). People differ considerably in their complexity about different domains of knowledge (de Vries & Walker, 1987) and in their complexity about people in general (Sommers, 1981), with similar results.

Another view of the link between knowledge structures and evaluation is that thought polarizes feelings because it leads to perceiving a tighter organization of the attributes of a given stimulus in those people who possess a schema for thinking about it (Tesser, 1978). A general preference for cognitive consistency is posited so for example the more you consider your team's chances for the league championship, the more likely you will fit all of your team's attributes into place as consistently pro or consistently con. Over time people can make an instance fit the schema, so evaluation becomes more extreme as the attributes become more organized. No amount of mere thought on my part about your team will polarize my evaluations of it, according to Tesser, because I have insufficient prior knowledge to rearrange and, according to Linville, because my opinion is already fairly extreme (being more easily swayed by random factors).

Linville's complexity-extremity hypothesis and Tesser's thought polarization hypothesis may seem to make contradictory predictions, in that Linville claims that complexity moderates evaluations but Tesser claims that thought (which one might think makes schemas more complex) polarizes evaluations. However, there are several differences in the application of their theories. First, Tesser's theory states that thought makes schemas more organized, internally consistent, and evaluatively uniform, so thought indeed makes the schema (evaluatively) simpler and, therefore, more polarized, which fits Linville's predictions. Second, the complexity-extremity hypothesis refers to initial evaluations at one point in time, whereas the thought polarization hypothesis refers to changes over time (Linville, 1982b). Third, the thought-polarization effect occurs when people make an initial public commitment to their evaluations (perhaps because they are more motivated by pressures to be consistent), whereas the complexity-extremity effect obtains in the absence of such commitment (M. G. Millar & Tesser, 1986b). Finally, the thought-polarization effect occurs when the schema's dimensions are substantially correlated (i.e., ratings on one dimension predict ratings on other dimensions) because the schema's structure is more intrinsically coherent (M. G. Millar & Tesser, 1986b). The perceived correlation depends on one's familiarity with the group (Linville, Fischer, & Yoon, 1996). Hence, these thought-polarization and extremity effects are more likely for unfamiliar outgroups.

In sum, four main theories link schemas and affect. Keltner's theory links power expectancies and emotion. Fiske's theory of schema-triggered affect posits affective tags on knowledge structures. Linville's theory of schema complexity posits extreme responses to simple schemas, and Tesser's theory posits extreme responses as schemas become simpler over time.

Obtained Outcomes and Affect

Just as schema theories emphasize prior expectations about events, so other theories focus on post hoc explanations for events (see Table 13.1). Cognitions about one's outcomes underlie many common emotional experiences.

Attributions for Attained Outcomes

Previously (Chapter 6), we described Weiner's attributional theory of achievement motivation (Weiner, 1985, 1986), which describes basic dimensions that people use to understand their successes and failures: internal or external locus, stability over time, and controllability. These dimensions, in turn, provoke basic emotions as well as expectations for future outcomes. Together the emotions and expectations guide behavior.

One can demonstrate that specific emotions follow from specific causal attributions (Benesh & Weiner, 1982; Weiner, 1982, 1985). For example, pride follows from a positive outcome that is attributed to oneself (i.e., internally) and that is seen as controllable, as when one works hard and succeeds, whereas guilt follows from a negative outcome attributed to internal and controllable factors, as when one neglects work and fails. Anger follows from a negative outcome that is attributed to another (i.e., externally) and that is viewed as controllable, as when one fails because another person does not follow up with expected help, whereas gratitude follows from a positive outcome attributed to external and controllable factors, as when one succeeds because the other person does indeed help. Finally, pity results from another person's negative outcome attributed to external factors (other people or the environment) that are seen as uncontrollable; one pities the person who does not succeed due to a string of bad luck. The locus and controllability factors determine the quality of emotions, and the stability factor tends to exaggerate them. This framework has been applied, with considerable success, to cognitions and emotions in achievement settings (see Weiner, 1985, for a review). The simple distinction between being responsible or not for one's bad outcome—that is, judged responsibility—determines anger or sympathy, which in turn determine aggression or helping, according to a meta-analysis of 64 studies (Rudolph, Roesch, Greitemeyer, & Weiner, 2004).

People implicitly understand these rules of attribution and emotion, so they use them to control the emotions of others. When providing excuses for interpersonal failures, people attribute their behavior to external, uncontrollable, and unintentional factors ("The dog ate my paper"; "My car broke down"). People do not provide the real reasons for being remiss when the real reasons are internal, controllable, and intentional ("I didn't feel like doing it") or unintentional ("I forgot"). People implicitly know which excuses provoke anger and which defuse it, and experimental manipulations of the causal dimensions of excuses show that they are right (Folkes, 1982; Weiner, Amirkhan, Folkes, & Verette, 1987). People also try to control the emotions of others when hoping to elicit their help. If the cause of one's plight is controllable, one is likely to receive only anger, but if the cause is perceived as uncontrollable, then one is likely to receive both pity and help (Meyer & Mulherin, 1980; Reisenzein, 1986; G. Schmidt & Weiner, 1988; Weiner, 1980). The general principles of the attribution-emotion-action relationships develop in the naive psychology of children as young as 5 years old (Graham & Weiner, 1986; Weiner & Handel, 1985).

This analysis extends as well to stigmatizing conditions, such as AIDS, mental illness, alcoholism, and physical disability. Physical stigmas are perceived to be stable and to have uncontrollable origins, so they elicit pity and helping, but mental and behavioral stigmas are perceived to be unstable (i.e., reversible) and to have controllable origins, so they elicit anger and neglect (Weiner, Perry, & Magnusson, 1988; cf. Brickman et al., 1982). Conflicts in people's implicit attributions about stigma doubtless cause much heartbreak; for example, depressed people sometimes view their condition as uncontrollable and expect pity while those around them often see it as controllable and feel anger (Weiner, 1987). A major issue in caring for persons who are HIV-positive or who have developed AIDS is the perception of others regarding the extent to which the person had control over contracting the disease (Weiner, 1988); sufferers' perceived responsibility is one of the factors contributing to whether or not they receive help. Empirical tests of Weiner's attribution-emotion-behavior theory, as well as its clear applicability, support its usefulness as a cognitively based perspective on emotion.

Weiner's work focuses on cognitions (attributions) about outcomes already obtained. Another theory (Ortony, Clore, & Collins, 1988) similarly emphasizes obtained outcomes, but it also addresses alternative possibilities (i.e., personal goals or social standards that could or could not be met). The next section describes two theories that focus more explicitly on imagined alternative outcomes.

Alternative Outcomes and Affect

Some psychologists studying emotion have focused on cognitions about outcomes that might have been or might yet be. This section considers two such theories, both of which concern the affective impact of people imagining alternatives to current reality.

One theory that is well developed conceptually and empirically relies on the simulation heuristic. As described in Chapter 7, the simulation heuristic describes the ease of imagining alternative outcomes and its effect on post hoc inferences of probability (e.g., Kahneman & Tversky, 1982). When one can easily imagine that things might have been otherwise, one's actual state of affairs seems like more of a fluke. In contrast, when it is more difficult to imagine how things could be other than what they are, the current situation seems inevitable. For example, when you miss meeting an old friend or catching a plane by a few moments, it seems to be a quirk of fate, but when you miss by several hours, it is harder to imagine how things could have worked out differently. The emotional implications of these post hoc inferences are clear: Is it more frustrating when one just barely misses the friend or the plane, or when one misses by a wide margin? Events that are retrospectively easier to undo mentally cause more intense emotion. When a person is killed by a freak accident, it somehow seems more tragic than when the person is killed in the normal course of a high-risk job or lifestyle.

Work on norm theory extends these and related ideas into a theory of how people decide what is normal and, by exclusion, what is surprising and therefore emotion producing (Chapter 7; Kahneman & Miller, 1986). An abnormal event is one that has easily imagined alternative outcomes; these alternatives may be either constructed or remembered alternative scenarios. In either case, if there seem to be many possible alternatives, the actual events are surprising. There is an interesting parallel between these ideas and ideas about expectancy effects. That is, an event inconsistent with one's implicit norms is perceived as unlikely in retrospect; an event inconsistent with one's expectations is perceived as unlikely in the future. While schema and expectancy theories consider people's reasoning before the fact, which might be called anticipatory thinking, this theory concerns people's reasoning after the fact, which might be called backward thinking.

Norm theory's relevance for affect lies essentially in its emotional amplification hypothesis: namely, that events elicit stronger emotion when their causes are abnormal. This is especially evident for misfortunes, as in the previous examples of just-missed planes and freak accidents, both of which are particularly upsetting. Similarly, a person who wins the lottery with a ticket bought minutes before the drawing—versus one bought weeks before—feels especially lucky and happy (D. T. Miller, Turnbull, & McFarland, 1990) and probably is especially envied as well. Abnormality influences emotional reactions to other people; one feels more sympathy for someone victimized by a chance occurrence (D. T. Miller & McFarland, 1986). Again, the more easily imagined the counterfactual scenario, the more intense the emotion one experiences. In sum, this theory examines people's emotional reactions to outcomes that might have been (Kahneman and Miller's norm theory); it focuses on the emotional impact of imagining alternatives.

Emotions as Managers of Goals

Another set of approaches posits that emotions essentially manage people's priorities (see Table 13.1). This perspective starts with the observation that many emotions occur when planned behavior is interrupted, as noted in Mandler's and Berscheid's theories, or could have been interrupted, as in Kahneman and Miller's theory. However, one can examine not only how interruptions cause emotion, as in those theories, but also the reverse: How emotions cause interruptions.

Emotions can act as controls on cognition, alerting people to important goals. In this view, emotions are alarm signals consisting of interruption and arousal, and they divert people from pursuing one goal and point them toward pursuing another goal that has meanwhile increased in importance (Simon, 1967, 1982). This view follows from the premise that people are capacity-limited information processors. That is, they can pursue basically only one goal at a time, whether it is listening to a lecture, thinking about a brilliant question to ask, planning what to have for dinner, or making eyes at the attractive person nearby. An information processor potentially could handle such multiple goals by ranking their relative importance and completing each in turn, at its leisure. Unfortunately, such an obsessive android might get run over by a truck if it were only attending to the goal of locomoting to work and not attending to the goal of staying intact. That is, survival depends on the organism being able to interrupt ongoing goals before completion if other environmental contingencies demand it. Emotions, such as fear of an onrushing moving van, can prompt attention to urgent goals. Examples of such high-priority items include environmental stimuli that warn of potential danger (e.g., producing fear), physiological stimuli that demand refueling (e.g., producing hunger or sleepiness), and internal cognitive stimuli that trigger unmet psychological needs (e.g., producing common negative emotions). In this view, the physiological arousal that accompanies emotion comes from the interruption itself. Note that the interrupting effect of emotion is to alter goals rather than to disorganize one's responses. Emotions merely indicate the changing importance of different goals.

In a related view, emotions manage goals in another way when there is a change in the evaluation of a plan's likely success; they provide transitions between plans. Goals change in priority as their perceived chance of progress changes, such that impossible or completed goals are abandoned and manageable goals are pursued. Given that people have multiple goals, emotions provide a way to coordinate among them (Oatley & Johnson-Laird, 1987). Emotions are a form of internal communication about changes in the relative priority of goals as a function of perceived likelihood of success and a way to maintain those priorities. This theory also argues that emotions perform a similar function of external communication in coordinating goals with others. Thus happiness communicates, both internally and externally, that subgoals have been achieved and one should continue with the plan. Sadness communicates the failure of a major plan, which suggests giving up or searching for an alternative. Anger communicates that an active goal has been frustrated, so one will attempt to remove the obstacle or aggress. Anxiety communicates a threat to self-preservation, initiating attention to the environment and possible escape. (For commentary on this theory, see Frijda, 1987a.)

These first two promising notions of emotions as interruptions or managers of changing priorities still await direct empirical test. However, some research supports the basic premise that intense emotions interrupt planful, ongoing cognitive activities. For example, emotionally salient material presented outside awareness quickly captures conscious attention (Nielsen & Sarason, 1981). Emotionally charged events are especially memorable (R. Brown & Kulik, 1977) and occupy much of people's daily thoughts (Klinger et al., 1980). Thus emotion may well interrupt both attention and memory.

A related concept of emotion as interruption emerges from the cybernetic theory of self-attention and a program of research testing its premises (Carver & Scheier, 1982; see Chapter 5). Recall that the theory describes self-focused people as noticing discrepancies between their current state and the achievement of some goal or standard. When people notice the discrepancy, they attempt to adjust their behavior to reduce the discrepancy. The person may succeed and move on to another goal. If the person fails, the theory states that the person will keep trying. The person may try repeatedly and fail. Thus there has to be provision in the theory for the person to give up and change goals. Otherwise, it would portray the organism as marching into a corner, without knowing when it is beaten (Scheier & Carver, 1982; Scheier, Carver, & Gibbons, 1981). An affective feedback system is posited to sense and regulate the rate at which the organism is progressing toward its goal (Carver & Scheier, 1990). Emotions interrupt ongoing behavior, causing a reassessment of one's probability of success, and one redoubles effort or withdraws accordingly. Thus emotions in general may lead to self-focused attention (Salovey & Rodin, 1985). However, feelings of pleasure indicate unexpected progress toward one's goals and that one may safely attend elsewhere (Carver, 2003).

Conclusion

To a neophyte or even to a seasoned expert, the array of cognition-affect theories is a bit overwhelming, so some retrospective orientation is useful. So far we have seen three kinds of theories relating cognitive structure to affect (see Table 13.1). Mandler and Berscheid explore the emotional impact of interrupted schemas and relationship goals. Keltner, Fiske, Linville, and Tesser each explore the affective effects of successfully matching schemas and data. The third set of theories all share an adaptive, goal-oriented perspective: Although there are important differences among them, they all address the relationship between emotions and goals. Some (Weiner; Kahneman & Miller) examine the quality and intensity of emotions that result from comparing a past or present outcome to imagined alternatives relevant to one's goals. Others (Simon; Oatley & Johnson-Laird; Carver & Scheier) examine the interruptive functions of emotions in the service of furthering one's highest priority (most important and most attainable) goals.

Both the neophyte's and the expert's difficulty in absorbing this literature is increased by the unevenness of these theories. Some are comprehensive, reviewing scores of prior studies and theories and attempting to integrate them; others are focused and attempt to account for a narrow range of affective phenomena. Some have emerged from or been subjected to extensive empirical work, whereas others remain essentially untested. Our aim here is to provide some sense of the variety of ways in which various cognitive structures (schemas, goals, attributions, perceived outcomes) have been related to affect. The interested reader is encouraged to pursue the individual theories for more detail as the presentations necessarily have been brief.

Appraisal Theories

The next set of theories also link cognition and emotion, but these focus less on information-processing details. Instead, they emphasize the interpretation of implications for oneself. When we walk into a gathering of people, most of us scan the room to see who is there (people we are glad to see, people we are not so glad to see, or people we do not know) and what has been arranged for us and the other participants (seating, food and drink, decor). In effect, we appraise the situation to see its possible significance for us. An older set of cognitively oriented emotion theories revolves around such a concept of environmental appraisal. The shared premise is that we evaluate our environment for its likely impact on us. The first to develop the term *appraisal* was Magda Arnold (e.g., 1945, 1970), and her theory holds that we immediately and automatically appraise all that we encounter as a fundamental act of perception, producing tendencies to act. An important basis for appraisal is memory of similar past experiences, along with associated affect, and an important element of our plans for action is expectation about the consequences of our actions. All of this appraisal process typically occurs quite quickly, intuitively, and innately. Although not developed with reference to recent ideas about cognition, Arnold's theory anticipates the more current approaches.

Personal Meaning

A subsequent proponent of the appraisal approach was Richard Lazarus (e.g., Lazarus, 1966; Lazarus, Averill, & Opton, 1970; Lazarus & Smith, 1988). In his view, appraisal consists of evaluating any given stimulus according to its personal significance for one's own well-being. The assignment of personal meaning is viewed as a type of cognition, but not implying that cognition is necessarily conscious, verbal, deliberate, or rational. Appraisal relates one's goals and beliefs to environmental realities.

The process begins with primary appraisals, in which people assess personal relevance (what is at stake for me). Primary appraisal determines both motivational relevance (that is, with regard to one's own goals and concerns) and motivational congruence (that is, regarding whether the stimulus facilitates or thwarts one's goals). The emotional consequences of primary appraisal are relatively primitive, being simple avoidance or approach, respectively, to potential harm or benefit.

The consequences of secondary appraisal are more specific emotions. In secondary appraisal, people consider how to cope (What can I do? What are my options?). Two primary kinds of secondary appraisal include problem-focused coping, which attempts to change the relationship between the person and the environment, or if that fails, emotion-focused coping, which attempts to adjust one's reactions through avoidant attentional strategies or changing the meaning of the threat. Examples of relevant secondary appraisal processes include attributions of past accountability (credit or blame) and expectancies about the future's perceived motivational congruence (maybe this cloud has a silver lining). The most effective secondary appraisal coping strategies depend on the degree of realistic control one has and on the stage of the threat involved (i.e., whether information-gathering is still useful, whether one can realistically alter the situation, or whether it is too late to do anything). The core point is that appraisal leads to coping (through changes in attention, meaning, and actual circumstances), which changes person–environment relationships, which in turn lead to different emotions (Folkman & Lazarus, 1988a, 1988b). Lazarus's appraisal theory has primarily informed research on stress and coping (Lazarus, 2000), especially in health psychology, but as we saw in Chapter 12, it also appears in Smith and Mackie's intergroup emotions theory.

Cognitive Appraisals

Other appraisal theories focus more explicitly on people's knowledge of their circumstances and how these cognitive appraisals lead to emotion (Ellsworth & Smith, 1988a, 1988b; C. A. Smith & Ellsworth, 1985, 1987). One difference between this approach and the previous one is that this one is more explicitly cognitive, while Lazarus focuses more specifically on personal motivational meaning (Lazarus & Smith, 1988). A core idea of the cognitive appraisal approach is that people appraise various dimensions of the situation, and these dimensions determine their specific emotional reaction. In particular, once people appraise the pleasantness of the situation, more specific emotions result from evaluating, for example, agency (i.e., responsibility or control by self, other, or circumstances; how fair the situation is), uncertainty (how sure one is; how much understanding one has), and attention (attending; thinking).

Support for this explicitly cognitive approach comes from studies in which people remember experiencing particular emotions and describe their corresponding appraisals, or vice versa, as well as studies in which they report current emotions and their corresponding appraisals (Table 13.2). Among the negative emotions, for example, self-agency goes with shame and guilt; other-agency characterizes anger, contempt, and disgust; and agency due to circumstances typifies sadness (cf. Weiner's theory, covered earlier). Thus one feels shame or guilt when one is responsible for an unpleasant situation, such as inadvertently ruining a dinner party by one's thoughtless behavior. However, one feels anger, contempt, and disgust when another is responsible in the same way. Finally, one feels sadness when circumstances are responsible, as when the weather ruins an elaborate outdoor party. Other dimensions matter as well: for example, uncertainty characterizes fear, for one feels most intense fear in unpredictable and personally uncontrollable situations (a party at which several people become drunkenly violent). And the dimension of attention and thinking is important, for low levels of attention mark boredom and disgust; high levels of attention characterize frustration. (Consider the differences in one's attention to an interminable storyteller at a party; if the person is merely boring or disgusting, one ignores the

TABLE 13.2. Locations of Emotions Along the Appraisal Components

Emotion	Pleasant[a]	Responsibility/Control[b]	Certain[c]	Attention[d]	Effort[e]	Situational-Control[f]
			Component			
Happiness	1.46		0.46			
Sadness	−0.87					1.15
Anger	−0.85	−0.94			0.53	−0.96
Boredom				−1.27	−1.19	
Challenge		0.44		0.52	1.19	
Hope	0.50		−0.46			
Fear	−0.44		−0.73		0.63	0.59
Interest	1.05			0.70		0.41
Contempt	−0.89	−0.50		0.80		−0.63
Disgust		−0.50		−0.96		
Frustration	−0.88			0.60	0.48	
Surprise	1.35	−0.94	−0.73	0.40	−0.66	0.15
Pride	1.25	0.81				−0.46
Shame	−0.73	1.31				
Guilt	−0.60	1.31				

Note. Scores are standardized and scores below 1.40 are eliminated.
[a] Pleasantness: high scores indicate increased pleasantness.
[b] Responsibility/Control: high scores indicate increased self-responsibility/control.
[c] Certainty: high scores indicate increased certainty.
[d] Attentional activity: high scores indicate increased attentional activity.
[e] Effort: high scores indicate increased anticipated effort.
[f] Situational control: high scores indicate increased situational control.
Source: C. A. Smith & Ellsworth (1985).

conversational monopolist, but if the person is frustrating your attempt to tell your own story, you will attentively listen for any chance to break in.)

Among the positive emotions, people differentiate less clearly; a situation can be unpleasant in more ways than it can be pleasant, as we noted in the taxonomies at the beginning of the chapter. Pleasant situations just make people generally happy. Nevertheless, one can distinguish some specific dimensions: Surprise is associated with uncertainty and external agency; interest fits with attention; hope correlates with perceived obstacles and anticipated effort; tranquility goes with certainty, an absence of obstacles, and a lack of effort; love is associated with importance, other-agency, and a lack of effort or obstacles.

Moreover, some preliminary evidence suggests that particular appraisals influence physiological concomitants of emotion, specifically, that anticipated effort influences heart rate and that perceived obstacles influence eyebrow frown (C. A. Smith, 1989). Based on various types of physiological and self-report measures, certain cognitive appraisal dimensions appear central to certain emotions.

This empirical and conceptual work is compatible with other theories that emphasize cognitive appraisal, but this discussion has emphasized the Ellsworth and Smith approach, given their accumulating body of empirical work on appraisal dimensions. The broader collection of cognitive appraisal theories all address a common process: namely, the person encountering and interpreting the environment. Unfortunately, the various appraisal theories provide a daunting variety when considered in detail, but they do share some common themes (for other integrations, see Frijda, 1988; Scherer, 1988). In particular, the theoretical taxonomies of appraisals for specific emotions overlap considerably in the dimensions viewed as important in distinguishing the emotions, in particular, pleasantness, agency, certainty, and attention.

These common dimensions occur in three important contributions to the nature of appraisal dimensions. Roseman's (1984) appraisal theory proposes interpretive dimensions that include motivational state (appetitive and reward/aversive and punishment), motive consistency (consistent and positive/inconsistent and negative), probability (certain/uncertain), agency (circumstances/other/self), and power (strong/weak); these structural dimensions reliably influenced emotion attributions in a series of vignettes. Note the overlap of Ellsworth and Smith's dimensions with Roseman's on pleasantness, certainty, and agency.

Another taxonomic approach creates appraisal profiles (Frijda, 1987b) of different emotions—that is, their structuring along such dimensions as valence, impact, interest, globality, uncertainty, responsibility, and relevance—all of which underlie the intuitive similarity of different affective states and the action readiness that each implies. Again, some critical dimensions overlap.

A third example is notable in that this framework compares cross-cultural consensus in people's open-ended descriptions of specific emotional experiences, their antecedents, and bodily reactions (e.g., Scherer, 1984, 1988; Scherer, Wallbott, & Summerfield, 1986; Wallbott & Scherer, 1988). Important dimensions of the stimulus evaluation check (similar to appraisal) aspect include novelty, intrinsic pleasantness, significance for goals and needs, and coping potential or degree of control; these dimensions serve both social and physiological functions.

Across these cognitive appraisal theories, some central dimensions emerge: (a) pleasantness, motive consistency, and valence; (b) agency and responsibility; (c) certainty, probability, and control; and (d) attention, interest, and novelty. Accordingly, all of these highly compatible cognitive appraisal theories offer conceptual (and sometimes empirical) support for each other, suggesting that appraisal theorists are homing in on the crucial cognitive dimensions by which people appraise situations, resulting in distinct emotions.[2]

---

[2] Still other cognitively informed theories focus on more specific kinds of appraisal: for example, perceived self-efficacy as a cause of emotion (Bandura, 1982); illness cognitions and emotional coping (e.g., for empirical work, Ward, Leventhal, & Love, 1988; for the broader perceptual-motor theory of emotions, see Leventhal, 1982, 1984); or an accessible discrepancy between one's actual self and one's "ideal" or "ought" self (Higgins, 1987; see Chapter 6). In a related vein, Epstein's (1984) cognitive-experiential self theory describes the preconscious construals of potential response options that give rise to specific emotions, with particular emphasis on fear, anger, sadness, joy, and affection in everyday life.

Affective Forecasting

A related theory suggests a final type of top-down determinant of affect. People have expectations about how they will feel (about a movie, for example), and if the actual experience fits their expectancy, their affective reactions are faster; if the experience is slightly discrepant, they may still assimilate it to the expectancy. When the experience is quite discrepant and they notice it, people have more trouble forming preferences (T. D. Wilson, Dunn, Kraft, & Lisle, 1989). This type of affective expectancy complements the previous work on affect-laden schemas and cognitive appraisals.

Taking affective expectancies further, a program of research indicates that people make wrong-headedly extreme affective forecasts of their own personal upcoming emotional weather (Wilson & Gilbert, 2005). People generally overestimate the impact of negative events, such as negative feedback, room assignments, romantic breakups, unfavorable election results, not getting hired, or not getting tenure (Dunn, Wilson, & Gilbert, 2003; Gilbert, Pinel, Wilson, Blumberg, & Wheatley, 1998; Wilson, Wheatly, Meyers, Gilbert, & Axsom, 2000). People especially fall prey when the anticipated events are emotionally intense (Gilbert, Lieberman, Morewedge, & Wilson, 2004).

Several cognitive mechanisms contribute. People fail to take account of their psychological immune systems (i.e., self-protective mechanisms), which enable them to get past the blows that life deals. And their projections focus too much on the possible negative event, failing to account for other concurrent future events that will dilute its impact. People may be misled by their tendency to recall past events that were emotion-laden but atypical (Morewedge, Gilbert, & Wilson, 2005). People also overestimate the extent to which past events affected them (Wilson, Meyers, & Gilbert, 2003). Hence, people fall prey to durability bias, expecting negative events to affect them longer than they actually do.

People apparently learn little from experience (Wilson, Meyers, & Gilbert, 2001). What's more, when people do cope well, they do not credit their psychological immune systems but more typically tend to attribute their own coping to a powerful external agency such as a higher power (Gilbert, Brown, Pinel, & Wilson, 2000).

Conclusion

This section reviewed the literature on social cognition influencing affect. Some theories focus on arousal and cognition, particularly the interruption of schemas and goals as causing arousal and affect. Other theories examine cognitive structures successfully applied to stimuli, linking affect to schemas, attributions, standards, and goals. The final theory addressed the appraisal of personal significance and its emotional consequences. People are often inaccurate in projecting their appraisals of past or future events. Clearly, various types of cognition have a wide-ranging and discernable impact on affective responses, and moreover, no one explanation covers all types of affect.

Summary

The literature on affect and cognition is moving in numerous different directions simultaneously, some focusing on physiological responses and some on the ways that cognitive structures—either interrupted or successfully applied—influence affect. Some of these theoretical efforts are supported by considerably more empirical evidence than others. Nevertheless, some central themes emerge as directing research and theory.

Affect is a generic term encompassing all kinds of evaluations, moods, and emotion. Preferences include relatively mild subjective reactions that are essentially either pleasant or unpleasant; the preferences most frequently studied by social psychologists are interpersonal evaluations. Moods typically do not have a specific target, are considered as simply positive or negative, and have some duration. Emotions are more complex and differentiated affects, often include physiological responses, and can be relatively brief. The two most common ways of distinguishing among emotions are along the two dimensions of pleasantness and arousal or along two independent dimensions of positive and negative emotions. Positive emotions, analyzed separately, have a simpler structure than negative emotions. Prototype approaches have also been applied to people's culturally shared categorization of specific emotions and to the concept of emotion in general. Emotions have also been viewed as social roles enacted according to cultural rules.

Early theories of emotion posed the question of whether physiological responses precede (James, Lange) or follow (Cannon) the experience of differentiated emotions. Following this debate, many physiological theories of emotion assumed that autonomic arousal in particular was undifferentiated and that other mechanisms must account for the complexity of emotional experience. Four theories form core contributions. Facial feedback theory posits that the complex and subtle musculature of the face provides the detailed patterns of feedback that underlie different emotions. The face does reliably express basic dimensions of emotion, particularly valence and intensity. There is also some evidence that manipulated facial expressions influence the experience of affect, although this evidence has sparked considerable debate.

Excitation transfer theory posits that autonomic arousal from emotions or exercise decays slowly, and that people often cannot distinguish the source of their arousal. Consequently, prior excitation can transfer or spill over to intensify new affective responses, even those of a different valence; considerable research supports this premise. All of these modern physiological theories de-emphasize the role of cognition in generating emotion.

In contrast, social cognition research has examined how cognition might contribute to affect. One set of approaches examines the interplay between arousal and cognition, building on Schachter's two-component theory of emotion, which states that unexplained arousal leads people to search their environment for cognitive labels for their emotions. Mandler's theory of mind and emotion extends this analysis in several respects: it explains the origins of physiological arousal in the interruption of perceptual schemas or complex goal sequences. The degree of disconfirmation of a perceptual schema determines its experienced pleasantness. The interruption of a goal sequence also prompts cognitive interpretation that determines the nature of the experienced emotion. Berscheid's theory of emotion in close relationships extends this analysis to complex goal sequences in which people are interdependent: the more intimate the relationship, the more interdependence, and the more potential for interruption and, consequently, emotion. This theory explains various phenomena in relationships, and research is beginning to provide further support.

Other social cognition theories focus more specifically on cognitive structures and their impact on affect. A variety of work has examined social schemas and affect. Keltner's theory posits that high power leads to positive expectancies and affect. Fiske's theory of schema-triggered affect posits that affective values are stored at the top level of a schema, accessible immediately upon categorization of an instance as matching the affect-laden schema; research supports this idea. Considerable research has examined Linville's analysis of how informational complexity influences affect; more complex knowledge structures often lead to more moderated affect, whereas simple ones allow more extreme affect. Over time, thought polarizes affect, in Tesser's analysis: To the extent that thought organizes the relevant schema, the schema contains correlated dimensions, and the person has made a public commitment to the initial affective response; research also supports these points.

Another set of theories examines people's emotional reactions to outcomes they or others have obtained. Weiner's theory of the dimensions of attribution proposes that different configurations of attributions—involving internal and external locus, stability over time, and controllability—result in specific emotional and behavioral responses to self and others. This perspective has garnered a considerable amount of research support.

Besides already obtained outcomes, some social cognition theories of emotion have emphasized alternative outcomes: what might have been, or what might yet be. Kahneman and Miller's norm theory describes the process of deciding how surprising an outcome was compared to the alternatives. The ease of imagining alternatives determines the amount of surprise and the intensity of emotional response; research supports these ideas. These theories of obtained outcomes and alternative outcomes, as well as the theories of interruption as a basis for arousal, all posit that interruptions cause emotion.

However, emotions also cause interruptions. Several theories describe emotions as managers of goal priorities; in these views, emotions interrupt goals to suggest changes in priorities. In Simon's view, emotions serve as alarm signals, providing arousal and interruption that alert the organism to an unmet need that has shifted its urgency while the organism has been pursuing another goal. In Oately and Johnson-Laird's related view, emotions provide transitions between plans with changes in the estimated success of the plan. Although not yet tested directly, some data are consistent with these views. A third approach, based on Carver and Scheier's cybernetic model, posits an affective feedback system that senses and regulates the rate at which the organism pursues the goal; a number of studies support these ideas.

A final set of theories examines ways in which cognition generates affect. The appraisal theories, based on work by Arnold and Lazarus, describe how people assess the environment to ascertain its significance for their concerns. The appraisal of personal meaning involves preconscious and conscious cognitive assessments of, first, personal relevance and, second, coping options; research on stress and coping is consistent with this view. Cognitive appraisal assesses particular dimensions of the current situation, determining particular emotional responses; several studies of appraisal and emotions support this theory. Other theories have identified similar dimensions of appraisal leading to emotion, in particular, pleasantness, agency, certainty, and attention.

CHAPTER 14

From Affect to Social Cognition

Economists (at least the classic kind) like to believe that people make rational choices after weighing costs and benefits. Recent work on heuristics (Chapter 7) undermines the idea that these decisions are cognitively unbiased. Recent work on emotion undermines the idea that these decisions are mainly cognitive in the first place. In this chapter, we shall see that affect influences all manner of thoughts, memories, beliefs, and choices. But we will also see that people vary in their sensitivity to affective influences. Finally, as we will describe, some researchers argue that affect and cognition should be viewed as separate systems entirely. Certainly they have some distinct ways of operating.

AFFECTIVE INFLUENCES ON COGNITION

One woman, upon discovering she had lost weight, suddenly started being nicer to her dog. Another person, when tired, says "no" to virtually anything. Still another, just because the janitor unexpectedly washed out her coffee cup, felt her whole day was made. And we all have found, when we are feeling cheerful, that the ideas come thick and fast. These and related phenomena illustrate the many influences of affect on behavior, memory, judgment, decision making, and persuasion.

Before describing this research in detail, it is helpful to provide some bits of background. First, most studies have examined the effects of mood on cognition and social behavior; intense emotions have played a lesser role in this research. Second, and relatedly, experiments examining these effects typically utilize relatively minor mood manipulations, such as finding a quarter on the ground, not major life events, such as winning a million dollars in the lottery. It does not require a life-shaking affect-laden event for emotion to influence how we behave, think, decide, and create.

Third, as noted in Chapters 3 and 5, people's perceptions and expectations have a positive bias, and people generally rate others' and their own lives as moderately positive (Parducci, 1968; Sears, 1983); information processing is biased toward positive material, a finding termed the Pollyanna effect (Matlin & Stang, 1978). People remember and judge positive material more easily (e.g., Hampson & Dawson, 1985), and they make positively biased judgments. Thus, all else being equal, most people are moderately optimistic. This means that positive and negative moods are not simple opposites of each other, for positive moods fit what people feel more often and typically prefer. This asymmetry has important consequences.

The effects of positive moods are more clear-cut than are the effects of negative moods. Across research programs, the effects of positive moods are more predictable, consistent, and interpretable than are the effects of negative moods. Several reasons probably explain the uneven effects of negative moods. Positive affect is more common than negative, as just noted, so negative affect is a bigger change from the baseline and is more interruptive and distracting. Moreover, negative moods can signal situations that threaten well-being, so again, they are more disruptive. Negative emotions, in general, are more varied than positive ones, as demonstrated by studying the structure of negative and positive affect. As a result, the effects of an angry mood and a sad mood may be less similar than the effects of a joyous mood and an excited one. In addition, negative moods are aversive, so people try to manage their negative feelings more than their positive feelings. All this results in negative moods having more variable effects than do positive moods.

Mood and Helping

Good moods lead people to help others (as shown by our friend who smothers the dog with affection just because she herself is feeling thin). An inspiring array of pleasant little experiences has been examined: success on a small task, finding a coin in a pay phone, receiving a free sample, being given a cookie or candy, viewing a series of pleasant slides, listening to soothing music, being told one is helpful, experiencing good weather, and remembering positive events from the past (for a review, see Penner, Dovidio, Piliavin, & Schroeder, 2005). Even the fragrance of roasting coffee or baking cookies can make people more likely to change a dollar or retrieve a pen for a stranger in a shopping mall (Baron, 1997). These little rays of sunshine all have the salutary effect of making the world a better place: Recipients will mail a lost letter; help someone pick up dropped papers, packages, or books; donate to or solicit for charity; volunteer their time; agree to donate blood; give more positive advice; or make a phone call for a stranger (for reviews, see Forgas, 1995; Isen, 1987; J. D. Mayer & Salovey, 1988). What's more, these effects generalize across age, social class, and ethnicity (Penner et al., 2005).

Several hypotheses have been proposed to account for these effects. In one analysis of the research, Carlson, Charlin, and Miller (1988) found strong evidence for four mechanisms, all of which bear on the principle that cheerful individuals are especially sensitive to concerns about positive reinforcement. People in a good mood will help if the situation makes salient their need for rewards and emphasizes the rewards of helping.

- Mood can alter one's *focus of attention* such that one focuses on oneself or on other people. Good moods induced by focusing on one's own good fortune promote benevolence toward others, but focusing on someone else's good fortune does not increase helping and instead may provoke envy (e.g., Rosenhan, Salovey, & Hargis, 1981).
- According to the *separate process view*, people in a positive mood will help mainly if the request emphasizes the rewards of helping rather than a guilt-inducing obligation to help (e.g., M. R. Cunningham, Steinberg, & Grey, 1980; Gueguen & DeGail 2003; Perlow & Weeks, 2002).

- A third hypothesis holds that people can be placed in a good mood by having their *social outlook* improved (e.g., Holloway, Tucker, & Hornstein, 1977). When people are cheered by an interpersonal event, they are more likely to help because they focus on human goodness or community benevolence; an improved social outlook enhances prosocial values.
- Finally, people are concerned with *mood maintenance,* so cheerful people are less likely to help if it would ruin their mood (e.g., Forest, Clark, Mills, & Isen, 1979; Isen & Simmonds, 1978). However, this does not mean that they help merely to boost or maintain their mood; people help for a variety of reasons, and cheerful people are simply sensitive to and avoidant of negative affect (Isen, 1987). Cheerful people help when they have salient concerns about rewards and when the rewards of helping are clear.[1]

In a related vein, cheerful people are more sociable: They initiate interactions, express liking, self-disclose more, give advice, aggress less, and cooperate more, and this does not seem to be due to their being generally more compliant when cheerful (e.g., M. R. Cunningham, 1988; for a review, see Isen, 1987). People even become more cooperative negotiators, using less contentious tactics and increasing joint benefits (Carnevale & Isen, 1986; Forgas, 1998). People are not only usually nicer to others, but they are also nicer to themselves when they are feeling good. They reward themselves and seek positive feedback, and this is not merely due to a loss of self-control (Isen, 1987). The beneficial effects of mood appear in a variety of good-citizen behaviors in the workplace (Brief & Weiss, 2002; Forgas & George, 2001). As the emotion-helping work progresses, it is likely to focus increasingly on specific positive emotions, such as gratitude (Bartlett & DeSteno, 2006).

What about people who are temporarily depressed? People in a bad mood are sometimes more helpful than people in a neutral mood, but only under particular conditions (for a review, see Carlson & Miller, 1987). In effect, the negative mood conditions that do encourage helping are those in which guilt rather than anger is operating. That is, according to the responsibility/objective-self-awareness view, unhappy people who perceive themselves to be the cause of a negative event (e.g., breaking an experimenter's equipment or being told they are responsible for their bad mood) are helpful, assuming prosocial norms are salient (e.g., M. Rogers, Miller, Mayer, & Dural, 1982). In contrast, according to the focus of attention explanation, grumpy people who perceive a self-focused angle on a negative event (e.g., imagining their own personal reactions to a friend dying of cancer) are less helpful to others (e.g., W. Thompson, Cowan, & Rosenhan, 1980). The attentional explanation applies to helping that is instigated by both positive and negative moods; when helping focuses attention away from one's mood, the mood is weakened, but when helping focuses attention on the

---

[1]The concomitance hypothesis holds that happy people are helpful not in order to maintain their moods but rather as a side effect of being happy; for instance, because of increased liking for others or increased optimism (Manucia, Baumann, & Cialdini, 1984). This hypothesis overlaps considerably with the social outlook hypothesis and others, so it is hard to evaluate it separately, particularly when mood maintenance concerns are also evident (Carlson, Charlin, & Miller, 1988).

conditions producing one's mood, the mood is enhanced (M. G. Millar, Millar, & Tesser, 1988).

An additional explanation for the effects of bad moods on helping is more controversial. According to a negative state-relief hypothesis, unhappy people help when it could dispel their negative mood (e.g., Cialdini, Darby, & Vincent, 1973; Schaller & Cialdini, 1988), and even children are aware of the personally salutary effects of helping (Cialdini & Kenrick, 1976; Perry, Perry, & Weiss, 1986). Clearly, people attempt to regulate their moods (Baumgardner & Arkin, 1988; J. D. Mayer & Gaschke, 1988), so some version of this hypothesis is likely to hold. However, researchers disagree about the interpretation of such results (Carlson & Miller, 1987; cf. Schroeder, Davidio, Sibicky, Mathews, & Allen, 1988).

Mood and Memory

Have you ever received a piece of good news and found yourself mentally reviewing several other past experiences of being competent, good, and lovable? Present mood has important effects on memory for past experiences. Two essential phenomena have formed the core of research on mood and memory: mood-congruent memory and mood state-dependent memory.

Mood Congruence

Under many circumstances, people more easily remember material whose valence fits their current mood state (for reviews, see Blaney, 1986; Forgas, 1995; Isen, 1987; J. D. Mayer, 1986). Dozens of studies have induced moods experimentally by having participants undergo hypnosis, experience success and failure, read mood-relevant sentences (the "Velten" procedure), listen to mood-laden music, dwell on relevant past experiences, or assume positive and negative facial expressions (Blaney, 1986). In one study, moods were cued by odors picked to be pleasant (like almond essence) and unpleasant (like coal tar; Ehrlichman & Halpern, 1988). Across a variety of settings and procedures, people recall positive material in positive moods and sometimes recall negative material in negative moods (e.g., G. H. Bower, Gilligan, & Monteiro, 1981; Isen, Shalker, Clark, & Karp, 1978; Salovey & Singer, 1988; Teasdale & Russell, 1983).

Some argue that the effect is located primarily at retrieval (Blaney, 1986; Isen, 1987), but most argue that the evidence is stronger for effects at learning (G. H. Bower, 1987; J. D. Brown & Taylor, 1986; Fiedler, Nickel, Muehlfriedel, & Unkelbach, 2001; J. D. Mayer & Salovey, 1988; Nasby & Yando, 1982; J. A. Singer & Salovey, 1988). Consistent with this perspective, people more readily perceive emotion-congruent stimuli (Neidenthal & Setterlund, 1994). Most accounts assume that mood-congruence effects are fairly automatic, but some mood-congruence effects are controlled, motivated processes (Blaney, 1986).

An integrative affect infusion model (AIM) proposes that, depending on the processing mode, affective influences may be relatively automatic, controlled, or absent altogether (Forgas, 1995). That is, under *heuristic* processing, affect informs quick judgments (if I am feeling good, I must like this); this follows the mood-as-information perspective (e.g., Schwarz & Bless, 1991). Under more *substantive* (typically controlled) processing, affect primes judgments through selective attention, encoding, retrieval, and association; this follows more traditional memory models (e.g., Bower, 1991). However, affect may have little influence in two cases: either when people have *direct access* to a prior judgment or when they engage in *motivated* processing to further a preexisting goal. In these latter cases, memory, judgment, and behavior are already channeled, so they are less open to affective biases. In the context of this section on memory, AIM describes how reactions to requests show a mood-congruent bias. In one study conducted at the library, students saw pictures or text eliciting positive moods (funny cartoons) or negative moods (car accidents); they then received polite or impolite requests for paper from another student. Negative moods made people more critical of requests and less likely to comply, but this was especially true for impolite requests, which were also more memorable, consistent with a substantive processing route (Forgas, 1998).

Most mood-congruence research finds uneven effects for negative moods, and motivated, controlled processes may account for these failures to obtain strong effects for induced negative moods. That is, people try to repair negative moods, so the manipulations do not work as well (M. S. Clark & Isen, 1982; J. A. Singer & Salovey, 1988). Alternatively, the weakness of negative mood effects may result from the store of negative material in memory being less extensive and less integrated, so negative moods may not as effectively cue congruent material (Isen, 1984, 1987). Also, if negative material is less organized, it may be intrinsically harder to learn, so it is hard to equate negative and positive stimuli. Possibly, the weakness of negative mood effects is also due to there being more differentiation among negative moods (sadness, anger, fear) than among positive moods (happiness). If mood-congruence depends on matching more than just general valence but instead the specific emotion, then negative mood states would not match as easily. Also any one of them would tend to have fewer associations than would an overall happy glow (Laird et al., 1989).

Negative mood congruence does occur reliably in one important case: namely, for people who are depressed, for whom negative events are presumably mood-congruent and, therefore, memorable (Blaney, 1986; M. H. Johnson & Magaro, 1987). For example, when depressed and nondepressed people experience a series of experimenter-controlled successes and failures, depressed people underestimate successes relative to control participants (e.g., Craighead, Hickey, & DeMonbreun, 1979). The effect appears more likely to be a retrieval bias than an encoding deficit; that is, they notice the successes but just do not recall them easily. As another example, depressed people (compared to controls) underremember positive words and phrases or overrecall negative ones (e.g., Ingram, Smith, & Brehm, 1983). These negative mood-congruence effects may only occur when people focus on the applicability of the material to themselves (e.g., Bargh & Tota, 1988), but otherwise the conditions under which they have been obtained are numerous and varied. Depressed participants may deliberately focus on negative material to rebut it, to improve themselves, or to confirm their self-image, so the effects may or may not be automatic (i.e., unintentional, unconscious, and rapid; see Chapter 2). Besides individual differences in depression, people high on neuroticism also show exaggerated negative mood effects (Rusting, 1999). Extraverts show enhanced positive mood-memory effects. Either of two processes may explain personality's interplay with mood (Rusting, 1998). Mood can moderate (interact with) personality to affect cognition jointly. Or mood can mediate the personality-processing relationship such that certain personality traits predispose people to particular moods, which then affect cognition. A variety of studies support both these processes.

Altogether, a considerable amount of evidence supports the facilitating effects of congruence between mood and the material to be remembered. However, a few isolated examples of superior mood-incongruent memory complicate the usual mood-congruency effects (Fiedler, Pampe, & Scherf, 1986; Forgas, Burnham, & Trimboli, 1988; Mackie et al., 1989; Parrott & Sabini, 1990; Rusting & DeHart, 2000). As noted, people often regulate negative moods by reframing past negative events or by retrieving positive memories to counteract the bad mood, resulting in mood-incongruency effects for negative moods. Also, when people reflect on their moods, they are more likely to recall mood-incongruent events (McFarland & Buehler, 1998).

Mood-memory research is not without its problems: Within-participant designs may encourage participants to respond to experimental demand, and some research fails to include neutral-mood control groups (M. S. Clark & Williamson, 1989; J. A. Singer & Salovey, 1988). Nevertheless, some studies apparently circumvent demand by unobtrusively manipulating facial expressions rather than more overtly self-induced mood states, and these studies also show mood-congruent memory (Laird et al., 1982, 1989). Moreover, the real-world effects are especially robust: Clinically depressed patients reliably show the mood-congruency effects, and real-life events show stronger mood-congruence effects than do experimenter-provided items (e.g., Mayer, McCormick, & Strong, 1995; see Ucros, 1989, for a meta-analysis). Overall, the findings of mood-congruence seem to outweigh the failures to find such effects.

Mood State-Dependent Memory

A separate mood-and-memory phenomenon concerns the congruence between the mood context in which material is learned and the mood context in which material is retrieved. That is, if one studies for the SAT in a sad mood, one might best recall the material if taking the test also in a sad mood. Mood-dependent memory would ignore the valence of the material itself, focusing only on the fit between the two contexts.

State-dependent memory apparently exists for drug-induced states; for example, something learned while intoxicated is easier to remember while intoxicated than while sober. (This should not be interpreted as a recommendation that people who cannot remember what they did while drunk should re-create the state merely in order to find out!) The reliability of drug-induced state-dependent memory led researchers to look for a similar phenomenon in mood states. Perhaps material learned while happy is best remembered while happy, regardless of the content of the particular material.

Although it is an effect that deserves to be true, evidence for it is quite weak (Blaney, 1986; G. H. Bower & Mayer, 1989; Isen, 1987). Studies that associate half the material with one mood (e.g., happy) and the other half with another mood (e.g., sad) have more frequently obtained effects. These within-participants designs rely on the interference between the different kind of items at the testing stage. However, systematic manipulations of interference do not reliably yield the effect (G. H. Bower & Mayer, 1989), and because all participants experience both moods, the possibility of obvious hypothesis and experimental demand is then raised (Blaney, 1986; J. D. Mayer & Salovey, 1988; J. A. Singer

& Salovey, 1988; Ucros, 1989). One might, therefore, think to examine naturally occurring rather than experimenter-induced moods to minimize demand problems. However, mood dependence does not obtain for naturally occurring moods (Hasher, Rose, Zacks, Sanft, & Doren, 1985; J. D. Mayer & Bremer, 1985; J. D. Mayer & Bower, 1985).

One remaining puzzle may be clarified. As noted at the outset, drugs more reliably produce state-dependent effects, although mood does not. One possible explanation is that the state-dependency effects of drugs operate more like arousal-dependent memory, an effect that does appear to be reliable (M. S. Clark, Milberg, & Erber, 1988; M. S. Clark, Milberg, & Ross, 1983). That is, it may not be matching the valence (e.g., happy mood at learning and testing) but matching the arousal (e.g., excited at learning and testing) that creates a specific form of mood congruence.

Network Model of Mood and Memory

One theory originally proposed to account for the various effects of mood on memory was a network model (see J. A. Singer & Salovey, 1988, for a review; see Chapter 4's description of network models of memory). The theory posits that emotion is simply a retrieval cue like any other. This means that memories or events that come to mind at the same time as a given emotion are linked to that emotion, and hence (indirectly) to other emotion-congruent memories or events. Mood-congruent memory thus has an advantage because the emotion provides an additional route to the item in memory. In this view, mood-congruent memory would be based on the retrieval advantage of similar affect attached to the mood and the inherent valence of the item to be recalled. And mood state-dependent memory would rely on similar affect associated with the item at learning and at retrieval.

However, subsequent research was disappointing in its attempts to support the facilitating effects of mood on perception of similarly toned material (G. H. Bower, 1987) and on mood state-dependent retrieval, as noted earlier. Moreover, the combined effect of conceptual and emotional relatedness in memory networks is not well supported (E. J. Johnson & Tversky, 1983). Overall, the network model of mood and memory "has not fared well: . . . a few successes and several glaring failures" (G. H. Bower, 1987, p. 454), suggesting that new frameworks are needed.

In general, mood state-dependent memory effects have been stronger when there has been more possibility of experimental demand; that is, more likelihood of the experimental participants accurately perceiving and responding to the investigators' hypotheses. Effects have been larger for (a) the earlier studies that perhaps involved less rigorous procedures and more enthusiastic experimenters, (b) studies involving longer experimental sessions, (c) studies with older and perhaps more sophisticated participants, (d) participants recruited for money rather than for course credit or on a voluntary basis, and (e) studies involving fewer participants and more intense mood inductions (Ucros, 1989). One interpretation of the overall pattern of mood and memory results is that the studies work better when the induced moods are intense (J. D. Mayer & Salovey, 1988; Ucros, 1989); results are stronger when participants are selected according to their responsiveness to the mood induction or when naturally occurring moods and real-life events are used.

Conclusions

As we have seen, the evidence for mood-congruent memory is strong, while the evidence for mood state-dependent memory is weak. Despite the distinctions conventionally drawn (as here) between mood congruence and mood dependence, the distinction is not always clear in real life (Blaney, 1986; Ucros, 1989). Positive material often is acquired when one is in a positive mood or takes its positive interpretation from a positive context, thereby confounding the mood at learning with the valence of the material to be learned. Nevertheless, the two are at least conceptually distinct, and mood-congruence effects are far more reliable than mood-dependence effects.

Mood and Judgment

Politicians who smile can put their viewers in a good mood, and this translates to positive feelings about the officeholder or seeker; those who cry, scream, or frown risk negative mood-congruent responses (for a review, see Glaser & Salovey, 1998). Legal decision making is affected by emotion as well (for examples, see Bornstein & Wiener, 2006). One of the clearest effects in the mood literature is that cheerful people like just about everything better: themselves, their health, their cars, other people, the future, and even politics and criminal defendants (for reviews, see Bodenhausen, Mussweiler, Gabriel, & Moreno, 2001; Clore, Schwarz, & Conway, 1994; Crano & Prislin, 2006; Forgas, 1995; Petty, Wegener, & Fabrigar, 1997; Schwarz & Clore, 1996; Zajonc, 1998). Consider an interpersonal example: People viewing their behavior in replayed social interactions rate themselves more positively when happy (Forgas, Bower, & Krantz, 1984). This effect provides new perspective on those imaginary replays of one's behavior after a party, the interpretation of which apparently depends on the hour and condition in which one engages in such self-assessment.

The variety of cheery mood-based benevolence effects have led to the suggestion that one has multiple personalities, depending on one's current mood (G. H. Bower, 1990; cf. Epstein, 1990b). However, there are some limits on this phenomenon; for example, cheerful people do not overvalue the criminal and the unattractive (Forgas & Moylan, 1987; G. L. White, Fishbein, & Rutstein, 1981), and high levels of personal involvement may moderate mood-congruence effects (Branscombe & Cohen, 1990).

Is the converse true? Do unhappy people dislike everything? Sometimes, but the evidence is more mixed for many of the same reasons it is mixed for studies of negative mood and memory (M. S. Clark & Williamson, 1989; J. D. Mayer & Salovey, 1988). Accordingly, studies that include neutral control groups are more informative than studies that merely contrast positive and negative moods. That is, if one only compares positive and negative moods and obtains a difference, one does not know which mood had an effect. Frequently, negative mood effects do not differ from neutral mood effects, and sometimes they are even equivalent to positive mood effects, as people attempt to repair their negative moods. Hence, to detect negative mood effects, it is especially important to have a neutral control group. Some effects have emerged from negative mood studies: For example, negative moods increase the perceived likelihood of future negative events (Johnson & Tversky, 1983). People judge other people according to negative applicable traits more when temporarily depressed than when in a neutral mood (Erber, 1991). Similarly, both temporary depression and a chronic negative outlook lead people to perceive themselves as having less social support (L. H. Cohen, Towbes, & Flocco, 1988; Vinokur, Schul, & Caplan, 1987). Other examples throughout this literature show negative mood-congruent judgments.

Some other intriguing puzzles remain in this line of work. For example, not only do positive (and sometimes negative) moods show congruence in judgments, but aroused moods show judgmental congruence effects as well (M. S. Clark, Milberg, & Erber, 1984; Stangor, 1990). That is, when people are physiologically aroused (e.g., by exercise), they make arousal-congruent judgments, viewing another's ambiguously positive facial expression as more joyous than serene and interpreting an ambiguous statement ("Just look at that sunset") as an exclamation rather than a sign of contentment.

Mood researchers are moving beyond valence and arousal to complex emotions. For example, two negative and potentially aroused emotions—anger and fear—have distinct effects on judgment (Lerner & Gonzalez, 2005; Lerner & Keltner, 2001). Fear increases the perceived risk of terrorist attacks, whereas anger decreases the perceived possibility (Fischhoff, Gonzalez, Lerner, & Small, 2005). When it comes to their own choices, fearful people are pessimistic and see increased risks; fear instills a prevention or avoidance orientation. In contrast, angry people are optimistic and minimize perceived risk, consistent with their approach orientations. Anger is experienced as relatively pleasant only when people appraise the future, not the past (Lerner & Tiedens, 2006).

When it comes to other people, angry people can be a menace, and sad people can be more careful and thoughtful. Anger facilitates automatic prejudices, whereas sadness neutralizes intergroup bias (DeSteno, Dasgupta, Bartlett, & Cajdric, 2004). Anger fits intergroup competition, so it encourages prejudice. Similarly, angry and sad communications, respectively, persuade angry and sad recipients (DeSteno, Petty, Rucker, Wegener, & Braverman, 2004). Sadness and anger differentially bias the perceived likelihood of saddening and angering events (DeSteno, Petty, Wegener, & Rucker, 2000). In general, if the moods match the message, events, or recipient, then the affect-cognition effects appear strong.

Specific emotions matter in specific types of judgments. For example, many moral judgments respond to disgust. One study induced disgust by seating some participants on an old chair with a dirty, torn cushion, at a stained, sticky desk, with a chewed pen and a dried-up leftover smoothie, next to a trash can overflowing with a greasy pizza box and used tissues. Other participants landed in newer, cleaner surroundings. All then made moral judgments, reported various emotions, and completed a scale of private body consciousness (PBC; e.g., responsive to own physical sensations of hunger, illness, mood). For people high on PBC, disgust led to more severe moral judgments (Schnall, Haidt, Clore, & Jordan, 2007). Inducing disgust by hypnosis has the same effect (Wheatley & Haidt, 2005). People differ in their sensitivity to disgust across domains, including food, vermin, bodily products, and death (Haidt, McCauley, & Rozin, 1994). And cultures differ on the role of disgust in moral judgments. For example, cleaning a toilet with the country's flag might be seen by elite American college students as a matter of arbitrary convention, but by some other Americans and by Brazilian adults as intrinsically disgusting and immoral (Haidt, Koller, & Dias, 1993). Political conservatives have a multifaceted moral agenda predicted by disgust (e.g., viewing homosexuality as immoral). Liberals have a narrower moral agenda emphasizing perceived threats to autonomy (e.g., degree of harm to others) versus, for example, threats to community or divinity (Haidt & Hersh, 2001). All these moral judgments rely on intuition, which includes sudden, conscious, emotional reactions, without awareness of having gone through prior calculations (Haidt, 2001).

Emotions in general influence a wide range of judgments more than traditional decision-making research had acknowledged. In the words of one moral judgment theorist: "moral emotions and intuitions drive moral reasoning, just as surely as a dog wags its tail" (Haidt, 2001, p. 830).

Open questions remain. Children, curiously, do not always show the same effects of positive and negative moods that adults do (Forgas, Burnham, & Trimboli, 1988; Masters & Furman, 1976; cf. Barden, Garber, Leiman, Ford, & Masters, 1985). Why this is the case is not yet clear. Is it because the arousal component of their mood overwhelms its valence? Is it because they have less-developed networks of associations? Is it because they are less wellsocialized into the culturally shared effects of moods? It remains to be seen.

Another challenge for research on mood and judgment is specifying the effects of mood-incongruent stimuli. For example, mood-incongruent stimuli may interfere with information processing, causing people to evaluate others via shortcuts such as illusory correlation (Mackie et al., 1989). Similarly, mood itself may distract people from elaborative processing (Asuncion & Lam, 1995). Certainly, some theories of emotion as an interruption (noted in Chapter 13) would suggest that affect, regardless of congruence, can be disruptive. The role of moods—congruent or incongruent—as interfering with judgments is not well understood. Moreover, it would be reasonable to expect some incidence of mood-incongruent judgment effects, with the mood creating a contrast to the judged objects, although we have not seen clear demonstrations of this.

Another avenue for future research is specifying the neuroscience of emotion in decision making. In one model (Naqvi, Shiv, & Bechara, 2006), the amygdala is recruited in the sensory experience of rewards and punishments, consistent with its role in vigilance for emotionally significant events. Internal representations of the behavioral choices that brought about the positive and negative experiences implicate the ventromedial prefrontal cortex (vmPFC). During subsequent decision making, the vmPFC and dorsolateral PFC re-create these representations. The mapping of these emotional-bodily states during decision making activates the insular cortex. For example, this area activates when participants evaluate the fairness of offers by another participant (Sanfey et al., 2003; see Chapter 8). This type of insular activation may underlie visceral reactions or "gut feelings" about choices. Mesolimbic areas are implicated in the unconscious emotional biasing of choices in decision making.

Moral decisions may be especially prone to emotional influences, as suggested by neuroimaging data (Greene, Somerville, Nystrom, Darley, & Cohen, 2001; Valdesolo & DeSteno, 2006). And some people are more emotionally reactive than others. For example, an early family environment characterized by stress (e.g., harsh parenting) can carry over to dampen the typical amygdala response to fearful and angry faces (Taylor, Eisenberger, Saxbe, Lehman, & Lieberman, 2006). What's more, typically the amygdala is regulated through activation in the rvlPFC when people label their emotions, but this regulation does not occur for adults from risky families. Thus early experiences shape neural responses to emotional stimuli, and cognitive processes (labeling) can regulate (or fail to regulate) these reactions. These hypothesized mechanisms remain to be developed, and they are eliciting active research attention that will clarify the emotion-decision interaction.

In sum, the effects of positive mood on judgments are widespread within reasonable limits imposed by the stimuli being judged. The effects of negative mood are quite mixed, for reasons that remain a mystery and that demand additional work; some possible reasons discussed in earlier sections on mood and memory also apply here. Ongoing work examines more specific emotions, as well as other mood dimensions besides valence, namely, arousal. Other topics that merit additional work include effects of moods on children's judgments, the conditions under which mood-incongruent judgments will occur, and the role of neuroscience in understanding the multiple roles of emotion in decisions.

Mood and Decision-Making Style

Mood not only influences what we remember and how positively we evaluate our world, but it also influences the manner in which we make judgments (for reviews, see Bodenhausen et al., 2001; Fiedler, 1988; Forgas, 1995; Isen, 1993). As early work indicated, elated people are expansive, inclusive, and somewhat impulsive; they make decisions quickly (Isen & Means, 1983), they work quickly at simple tasks (J. D. Mayer & Bremer, 1985), they group more varied things into the same category (Isen & Daubman, 1984), they see more unusual connections among things (Isen, Johnson, Mertz, & Robinson, 1985), they have looser and less organized associations (Fiedler, 1988), they have more associations to positive words (J. D. Mayer, Mamberg, & Volanth, 1988), they are willing to take more risks if the possible losses are small (Isen & Geva, 1987), but losses loom larger to them (Isen, Nygren, & Ashby, 1988). Altogether, it would seem that positive moods are associated with factors conducive to creativity, and people will even claim a bad mood as an excuse for failure (Baumgardner, Lake, & Arkin, 1985).

As this work has continued, happy people emerge as especially flexible decision makers (Bodenhausen et al., 2001). Probably, happy people are not so much unmotivated or unable to process carefully as they are likely to interpret their mood as information indicating that all is well (Isbell, 2004), which is consistent with the affect-as-information approach (Schwarz, Bless, & Bohner, 1991). Admittedly, they often are satisfied with a quick, heuristic judgment (including stereotypes), but when motivated, they are perfectly capable of more detailed, controlled processing. Still, their tendency toward quick decisions may lead them astray, more readily relying on misinformation (Forgas, Laham & Vargas, 2005), more easily falling prey to the fundamental attribution error (Forgas, 1998), and being vulnerable to guessing errors in recognition (Bless et al., 1996). When personally uninvolved, happy people are more likely to discriminate impulsively, but when involved, they can be thoughtful (Forgas & Fiedler, 1996).

Sad people, on the other hand, are more likely to be careful and to mull over their decisions. For example, sad people feel alerted that something is amiss, so they correct their stereotypes (Lambert, Khan, Lickel, & Fricke, 1997). As Chapter 11 showed, guilt also makes people reconsider their stereotypic judgments. But sad people in particular focus on details, neglecting the big picture (Gasper & Clore, 2002). Sad people attend to details such as being polite

(Forgas, 1999), but they can also discriminate because their thoughtful processing leaves them open to the mood-congruent processing of detailed information (Forgas & Fiedler, 1996).

Mood and Persuasion

Along with being expansive and inclusive and generally pleasant to others, cheerful people are more compliant with persuasive communications, whereas angry or uncomfortable people are generally less compliant (see McGuire, 1985; Petty, Cacioppo, & Kasmer, 1988, for reviews). The positive mood results may explain the effectiveness of free samples, soothing music, and friendly banter in marketing efforts, all of which increase positive moods and therefore, perhaps, persuasion. (But the effects of anger on noncompliance oddly do not seem to discourage the relentless programs of telephone charity appeals.)

Much of the mood and persuasion research was originally conducted under a classical conditioning paradigm, but subsequent studies have suggested some roles for cognitive processes. For example, not all persuasion is automatically enhanced by positive mood; perhaps positive mood enhances persuasion only under conditions of low involvement and low cognitive activity (Petty, Cacioppo, & Kasmer, 1988; Petty, Cacioppo, Sedikides, & Strathman, 1988; Petty, Gleicher, & Baker, 1991). Positive moods themselves can be distracting and reduce cognitive capacity, leading participants to superficial but still cognitively mediated processing of messages (Mackie & Worth, 1989; Worth & Mackie, 1987). Under conditions of moderate involvement, however, affect may enhance thought because of affect's arousing and attention-getting impact. Under conditions of high involvement, mood may serve an informative function relevant to one's possible reactions, or it may bias retrieval of relevant supporting information (Petty et al., 1988). Affect as information about the state of oneself and one's environment depends on ability and motivation to process a communication (Albarracín, 2002; Albarracín & Kumkale, 2003; Albarracín & Wyer, 2001). The effect may be curvilinear, with low levels of processing making affect unnoticed and high levels making it recognizably irrelevant. Moderate levels of affect would be noticed but not recognized as irrelevant.

As this work develops, more of it will likely focus on discrete emotions, not just general moods. Specific emotional states cue expectations for events that match that emotion. Hence, emotion-matching persuasion should be most effective (DeSteno et al., 2004). So far, though, most of the work focuses on positive or negative moods.

Mood affects attitudes through multiple processes (see Petty, Wegener, & Fabrigar, 1997). Mood can act as an incidental, peripheral cue, but mood can also bias detailed processing of an argument, or even the sheer amount of processing that occurs. Multiple roles for mood thus aptly summarize a variety of mood effects on memory, judgment, decision-making style, and persuasion.

Mood and Well-Being

Cheerful people have a variety of advantages, as we have seen. These culminate in a wide array of general life outcomes: being happy improves health, friendships, marriage, income, and performance (Lyubomirsky, King, & Diener, 2005). The evidence includes cross-sectional designs in which correlations leave open the alternative possibility that success causes happiness. But the data also include numerous studies that are longitudinal (happiness precedes success) and experimental (manipulated happiness causes success). Frequent positive affect results from genetic set points in temperament, from life circumstances, and from specific activities (Lyubomirsky, Sheldon, & Schkade, 2005). Presumably, one has the most control over one's activities, habits, and practices, so these offer the best avenues for intervention. Positive affect specifically motivates effort on one's positive and active behavioral goals (Custers & Aarts, 2005), so this cognitive-affective mechanism might well account for the salutary effects of happiness.

Conclusion

Good moods often lead people to be more helpful, more sociable, and nicer to themselves, to recall pleasant things, to judge things positively, to make faster and looser decisions, to be more compliant, and generally to achieve their life goals. Bad moods have more variable effects, leading people to be more or less helpful, to remember negative things if truly depressed, sometimes to make negative judgments, to be less often compliant, and perhaps to be less successful in general. Mood operates on cognition via a variety of more automatic and more controlled routes.

AFFECT VERSUS COGNITION

We have examined research investigating some cognitive bases of emotional responses (last chapter) and some affective (mood) influences on cognition (this chapter). In the final section of this chapter, we examine the relationship between affect and cognition more explicitly, starting with the possibility that they are largely independent.

The Separate Systems View

Despite the scientific and commonsense idea that we think about things in order to know how we feel, there is a case for affect preceding cognition rather than vice versa (Zajonc, 1980b). Indeed, some of us are constantly amazed at our own ability to make major life decisions on the basis of emotional preferences guided by no apparently relevant cognitive data. (Consider how you fell into your first serious romantic involvement or your earliest image of your career; some of us can find not one iota of rational cognitive analysis in those choices.) Affective processes may operate rather independently of cognitive processes in this view. Note that this is a controversial perspective, and it depends at a minimum on how one defines the terms *affect* and *cognition*. Before detailing the objections, it is useful to present the Zajonc argument and its evidence.

The separate systems view suggests that affective and cognitive processes proceed in parallel paths without influencing each other much, under at least some circumstances. Affective processes are argued to occur at a more basic level than cognitive processes in several respects (Zajonc, 1980b):

- Affective reactions are primary. Evaluations are made and then justified; decisions are based on preference rather than computation. (Romantic involvements are a prime example of not choosing based on a cognitive list of pros and cons.)
- Affect is basic. Evaluation is a major and universal component of virtually all perception and meaning. It is difficult to understand something without evaluating it. (Consider a lonely person scouting for a mate, unable to meet anyone in any context without evaluating the person's potential availability.)
- Affective reactions are inescapable. They are demandingly present in a way that simple knowledge is not. (Attraction is harder to ignore than the other person's career plans.)
- Affective reactions tend to be irrevocable, in contrast to cognitive judgments. One's feelings cannot be wrong, but one's beliefs can be; hence, affect is less vulnerable to persuasion than cognition. (As parents of adolescents constantly discover, other people's feelings of love and anger do not respond well to counterargument.)
- Affect implicates the self. While cognitive judgments rest on features inherent in the object, affective judgments describe one's own reactions to the object. (One's affective response to another has everything to do with one's relationship to the other, but one's knowledge of the person does not necessarily depend on one's relationship.)
- Affective judgments are difficult to verbalize. Much emotional response is communicated nonverbally; words for affective reactions always seem to fall short of the experience. (Describing the superficial features of the loved one is easy, but communicating one's actual feeling of love challenges even the poets.)
- Affective reactions may not depend on cognition. The features that people use to discriminate a stimulus may not be the same features that they use to decide whether or not they like it. (Totaling up the lover's pros and cons does not necessarily predict one's feelings.)
- Affective reactions may be separated from content knowledge. One sometimes remembers how one feels about a person but cannot remember the details of where or how the person was previously encountered. (One may feel strongly about someone without remembering all the reasons why.)

Overall, this stimulating line of argument has proved controversial, so we will examine some of the relevant evidence and then some of the objections.

Evidence From Mere Exposure Research

The last pair of arguments—that affect may not depend on cognition and may be separated from knowledge of content—underlie a research program demonstrating that people can know how they feel about an object before they can recognize it. The opening bars of a classic old song on the radio may be enough to let us know whether or not this is a golden oldie we like, but many of us cannot identify it right away or even be completely certain we have heard it before. Many studies document this phenomenon of feeling a warm familiar glow that is accompanied by a total lack of recognition. More generally, people grow to like an initially unobjectionable stimulus the more frequently it is encountered; this is called the mere exposure effect (Zajonc, 1968a; see Chapter 10).

In mere exposure studies, recall that people typically see a series of nonsense words, Chinese characters, or yearbook photographs, either many times or few times. The more often people are exposed to the stimulus, the more they favor it, and this effect replicates consistently (Kunst-Wilson & Zajonc, 1980; for a review, see Bornstein, 1989). People prefer the frequent stimuli to the less frequent stimuli, even when they can only recognize them both at levels approximating chance guessing. One study found that mere exposure to Japanese ideographs influenced affect, independent of recognition for them (Moreland & Zajonc, 1977; for debate, see Birnbaum & Mellers, 1979a, 1979b; Moreland & Zajonc, 1979). Liking for frequently heard tone sequences was found consistently, even though the tones were only recognized as familiar at approximately chance levels (W. R. Wilson, 1979). Further evidence came from a study using a dichotic listening task in which the experimenter presented the tones in one ear but focused participants' attention on a literary passage presented to the other ear. Using this task, one can virtually eliminate recognition for the tone sequences, leaving affective reactions intact (Figure 14.1). Similar results have been obtained with more engaging stimuli, such as the photographs and interests of fellow students (Moreland & Zajonc, 1982). The effects are generally strongest for meaningful words (including names), polygons, and photographs, and they do not occur reliably for paintings, drawings, and matrices (Bornstein, 1989). Moreover, the effects are stronger for subliminal than for supraliminal presentation (Bornstein & D'Agostino, 1992; Janiszewski, 1993; cf. Murphy et al., 1995).

Apparently, affective processes more than cognitive ones underlie the mere exposure effect. A dissenting view has suggested, however, that brief repeated exposure activates a simple schema, which affects judgments of familiarity and liking, but also brightness, darkness, or any other stimulus-relevant judgment (G. Mandler, Nakamura, & Van Zandt, 1987); this view rejects the idea

FIGURE 14.1. Liking as a function of suboptimal affective primes and number of exposures
Source: From Murphy et al. Additivity of nonconscious affect: combined effects of priming and exposure, *Journal of Personality and Social Psychology*, 1995, 69, 589–602. Copyright 1995 by the American Psychological Association. Reprinted by permission.

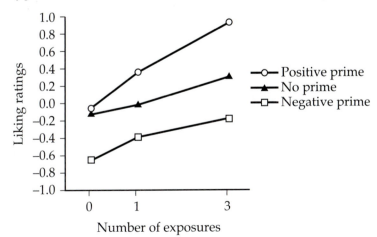

that mere exposure effects are noncognitive. Related to this idea is perceptual fluency. That is, a stimulus is more easily processed after an initial exposure, and people sometimes correctly attribute that ease of processing to indeed having seen it before (see Koriat, Goldsmith, & Pansky, 2000, for a review). But sometimes people just have a feeling of familiarity, from fluency, not being explicitly aware of having seen it before. The fluency mechanism in this case would not be strictly cognitive or affect, just the ease of encoding, which presumably increases with mere exposure. In support of this mechanism, perceptual fluency is experienced as affectively positive (Winkielman & Cacioppo, 2001). Indeed, perceptual fluency increases mere exposure effects, but only if the person does not attribute the ease of processing to prior exposure (Bornstein & D'Agostino, 1994). Clearly, mere exposure effects on liking (and perhaps on other judgments) do not depend on conscious recognition of the stimuli, itself an impressive effect.

Evidence From Person Perception, Attribution, and Attitude Research

A wide range of affective variables are independent of seemingly relevant cognitive variables. For example, evaluative impressions (one kind of affect) can be independent of memory for the details on which they were based (one kind of relevant cognition). This occurs when impressions are formed online, at the time of the initial encounter (N. H. Anderson & Hubert, 1963; Bargh & Thein, 1985; Dreben, Fiske, & Hastie, 1979; Riskey, 1979; for a review, see Hastie & Park, 1986). Thus, as you are forming an impression of someone at a party, your affective response is likely to occur independently of your later ability to remember details about the person. The exception to this apparent independence of affective responses and memory for the data on which they were based occurs when people are overloaded at the time of the encounter and do not have the motivation or the individual capacity to form an evaluative impression; in this case, their impression is memory based (Bargh & Thein, 1985). More generally, though, other social judgments and recall are often uncorrelated, as we saw in Chapter 4 (S. T. Fiske, Kenny, & Taylor, 1982; S. T. Fiske, Taylor, Etcoff, & Laufer, 1979).

Affective judgments are not necessarily based on recallable cognitions; instead they often are based on evaluations formed online. This implies that some affective reactions are better characterized as immediate responses. One must then entertain the related possibility that affective responses are also relatively direct and noncognitive. The concept of separate stores for evaluative and cognitive content (N. H. Anderson & Hubert, 1963) is one description of this process. The notion of affective reactions as a direct result of initial categorization (S. T. Fiske & Neuberg, 1990; S. T. Fiske, 1982) is another. The idea that attitude objects can directly cue the relevant attitude is also pertinent (Fazio, 1986; Fazio, Powell, & Herr, 1983). Affect may have primacy in evaluative judgments (Cervellon & Dubé, 2002; Huskinson & Haddock, 2004) although this may be most true for extreme attitudes (Giner-Sorolla, 1999, 2001). Much other relevant work demonstrates the importance of online processes in affective responses (see Chapters 2 and 3), and at least some emotional responses (startle and pupil dilation) are not preceded by identifying and judging stimuli (Schmidt-Atzert, 1988).

Objections

Quite a few theorists have responded to Zajonc's (1980b) view of emotion as a system separate from cognition. The objections have centered around the existence of nonconscious cognitive processes, the possibility of subsuming affect under other forms of cognition, the definitions of both cognition and affect, and the problems in empirically comparing the two.

Among the first to respond to Zajonc was Lazarus (1982, 1984, 1990) whose emotion theory depends on the appraisal of personal meaning, as described in Chapter 13. Lazarus argued that cognition, defined as appraisal, is necessary for emotion; appraisal interprets meaningful stimuli in terms of their significance for personal well-being. In this view, appraisal is not regarded as deliberate, rational, and conscious because it occurs from the very beginning of perceiving environmental inputs, not at the end of a long chain of serial, complete, thorough information processing. Similarly, Epstein (1983, 1984) argued that preconscious cognitions usually precede emotions, and that the Zajonc approach implicitly defines cognition as conscious, when it need not be. Thus some form of intuitive, preconscious, unintentional cognitive appraisal is seen as an integral part of all emotion. Zajonc (1984) argued that this definition of cognitive appraisal blurs the distinction between perception and cognition and that the Lazarus concept of emotion arbitrarily requires cognitive appraisal by definition. Clearly, the two viewpoints differ as to the defining features of emotion and of cognition and therefore differ as to the separation between the two.

Two other critiques of the Zajonc definitions of cognition and affect begin with the observation that cognitions can be rapid, unconscious, and automatic, just as affect is presumed to be; further, like affect, cognition can be irrational and can be tied to motor involvement (Holyoak & Gordon, 1984). In this view, the distinctions are less important than the possibility of subsuming both cognition and affect within one mental system. A related proposal specifically relies on the procedural view of memory outlined in Chapter 4; recall that this view of memory depends on highly practiced mental activities that become more rapid as they are repeated. In this view, emotion can result from unconscious pattern-matching to emotional procedures, as well as from consciously accessible nonprocedural knowledge (Branscombe, 1988). Both of these efforts subsume affect under traditionally cognitive frameworks. Others have similarly argued that affect should be treated just like all other kinds of information (N. H. Anderson, 1989).

Another possible resolution comes from recognizing two meanings of cognition (Averill, 1990a). The first, cognition$_1$, is intellective knowledge acquisition, which is the everyday (dictionary) meaning of cognition. The contrast to intellective cognition is value-laden, intuitive, or irrational thinking. The other meaning, cognition$_2$, subsumes all mental activity, as compared to behavior. This second meaning of cognition—that is, any nonbehavioral mental activity—is closer to the meaning of cognition as discussed, for example, by Lazarus in defining appraisal as a form of cognitive activity. Emotions are noncognitive in the first sense only, being nonintellective cognition—that is, being more value-laden, intuitive, and irrational. Emotions are, however, cognitive$_2$ in the sense of being generic mental processes.

The most useful point is that emotions as mental processes tend to be distinguished from intellective cognition, in typical ways:

- Emotion concerns the person's own experience as subject or origin rather than focusing on the object itself out there.
- Emotion tends to influence perceived "reality," whereas thinking to a greater extent accommodates to reality.
- Emotion views the target as important for its relationship to the person, but intellective cognition emphasizes an object's relationship to other external objects.
- Emotion involves physiological experiences, not just environmental inputs.
- Emotion regulates the intensity and style of behavior rather than the goal-directed efficiency of behavior.
- Emotion is experienced passively or as a reaction to the stimulus, but people experience themselves as the source of intellective cognition.
- Emotion commits one to action more than does the cost-benefit calculation of intellective cognition.
- Emotion norms are moral and aesthetic, whereas intellective norms are rational.
- Emotion helps define the self, rather than the world.

This is not to say that intellective cognition is necessarily rational, merely that it displays all these features less often than does emotion (cf. Epstein, 1990a).

So far, we have focused on definitional issues regarding cognition and emotion or cognition per se. Of course, the resolution to this debate also depends on how one defines emotion. For example, the original Zajonc article focused on preferences (evaluations, affective judgments, liking) rather than on moods or on full-blown emotional episodes (J. A. Russell & Woudzia, 1986). Moods and emotions, many would argue, do intrinsically depend on cognitively driven appraisal processes (e.g., see theories of Lazarus; Ellsworth & Smith, covered in Chapter 13). Preferences are relatively simple affective responses, distinguished mainly by valence, so some of the Zajonc results may pertain primarily to simple preferences and not so much to full-blown complex emotions.

Others suggest that the entire distinction is largely definitional and therefore not constructively pursued (Leventhal, 1984; Leventhal & Scherer, 1987). Instead, they suggest viewing emotion as developing from sensory-motor processes to complex cognitive-emotional patterns. Each level along this continuum entails distinct levels of memory and information processing. Each level also involves continuous appraisals (checks on the organism–environment relationship).

To all this, we would add only that there are inherent problems in comparing cognition and affect. Implicit in our discussion so far has been the idea that affect and cognition are somehow comparable. Judgments representing affect have included evaluation, preference, and differentiated emotions, while reactions representing cognition have included attention, inference, and memory. How does one decide what are the relevant cognitions and what are the comparable affective responses?

One study illustrates the complexity of this problem. In a mere exposure experiment, participants rated their recognition and liking for random polygons that had been presented at varying frequencies. Although recognition accuracy was only at chance levels, participants liked the familiar polygons better than the unfamiliar ones, confirming the standard mere exposure effect and that liking need not depend on accurate memory (Kunst-Wilson & Zajonc, 1980). But in what sense is recognition accuracy comparable to liking? The study assessed two other variables that help answer this question. Affective judgments were made more confidently and somewhat faster than recognition judgments.

Nevertheless, speed and confidence may not be the appropriate dimensions for comparing affect and cognition. The appropriate empirical tests depend on the conceptual definitions of affect and cognition, matters of some controversy, as noted earlier. For example, affect and cognition have been distinguished, respectively, as sensory versus inferential, physiological versus mental, motor versus perceptual, innate versus learned, preference versus knowledge, and liking versus discrimination. How one defines and compares affect and cognition will depend on which of these dimensions one emphasizes.

One can also question whether these are fair tests because people can be wrong about a recognition judgment but not about an affective judgment. One can also argue that recognition judgments are more complex. But the two types of judgment intrinsically differ in these ways, and one cannot make them more similar without destroying them as realistic judgments of their type. Affective judgments are by their nature subjective, simple, and direct. Trying to specify a cognitive response that is truly equivalent to a given affective response may be a losing proposition.

Trying to establish the independence of affect and cognition is also, essentially, trying to establish the null hypothesis. To the extent one argues that they are independent, one is trying to establish the absence of a relationship. This is a thankless task, as any statistics professor will insist if someone tries to prove the null hypothesis of no relationship. The more sensible task is to show on what each is based, if not entirely on each other (Zajonc, Pietromonaco, & Bargh, 1982). And because the separation is not complete, another task is to show the ways in which they do relate. The work reviewed in this and the previous chapter does just that.

Summary

In addition to considering the various influences of cognition on affect (Chapter 13), a considerable body of research has considered the influences of affect on cognition, and in particular, the influences of mood. This research finds clear effects even of small mood manipulations on a variety of cognitive processes. The effects for positive mood are more clear-cut than the effects of negative mood in general. Positive moods lead to more prosocial behavior. These robust effects may be explained by the cheerful person's sensitivity to positive reinforcement; helping in a good mood is enhanced by focus of attention on oneself, requests emphasizing the rewards of helping, an emphasis on a positive social outlook, and the opportunity to maintain one's positive mood. People in a negative mood may or may not be helpful, depending on the circumstances.

Mood reliably increases people's memory for mood-congruent material due to both automatic and controlled processes. Effects for positive moods are stronger than those for negative moods, with the exception of people who are chronically depressed, who also show strong mood-congruent memory. Another mood-memory phenomenon, mood state-dependent memory, posited that people would best recall material that was learned and retrieved in the same mood state; this hypothesis has little support.

Mood generally influences judgment in a mood-congruent direction as well. Arousal similarly creates arousal-congruent judgments. Again, the effects of positive mood are more reliable than the effects of negative moods. Moreover, the effects on adults are more reliable than the effects on children. Various explanations for the effects have been proposed but, for the most part, remain to be tested. Mood also affects people's style of decision making, with positive moods making people more expansive, inclusive, impulsive, and perhaps creative. Positive moods also make people more compliant toward attempts at persuasion, at least under low involvement.

The contrast between affect and cognition has been hotly debated, leading to a proposal that they are separate systems with affect being primary. Evidence from mere exposure and person perception research is cited in support of this perspective; people report liking frequently encountered stimuli they cannot discriminate as familiar, and people's evaluative judgments are often made online, without recall for the data on which they were based. Objections to this perspective have focused on the possibility of nonconscious cognitive processes, the role of affect within broader (cognitive) representational systems, the problems of defining both affect and cognition, and empirical tests of the differences. The most constructive course seems to be to examine the bases of each and to investigate the multiple ways in which they do relate, as reviewed here.

CHAPTER 15

Behavior and Cognition

Goal-Directed Behavior ◆ *When Are Cognitions and Behavior Related?*
◆ *Using Behavior for Impression Management* ◆ *Using Behavior*
to Test Hypotheses About Others

Most research in social cognition assumes that cognitions develop at least in part so that people will know how to behave: Thinking is for doing (Fiske, 1992). For example, if a supervisor is rude to a coworker, one tries to infer whether the supervisor is a disagreeable person, if it has been a bad day, or if the coworker has done something to deserve the treatment. Through this kind of analysis, one infers whether or not to stay out of the way of the supervisor. In this sense, cognitions give rise to behavior. Daily interactions with others also provide a constant source of information, some redundant and much new, that must be incorporated into cognitive representations. Hence, behavior also gives rise to cognitions. In this chapter, we explore the relationships between cognitions and behavior.

GOAL-DIRECTED BEHAVIOR

In Chapter 5 we introduced the concept of self-regulation, the ways in which people control and direct their behavior. Goals are clearly central to this process. How a person behaves in a situation depends upon how he or she defines it with respect to personal interests and goals. For example, two people can attend an office party with different goals in mind: One person may have the goal of impressing her boss; another may regard the same occasion as an opportunity to grab a couple of quick drinks with friends before going home. The behavior of these two people will be substantially shaped by these personal goals.

The first person will no doubt scan the room quickly to see if her boss has arrived and, upon seeing him, gravitate to that part of the room. As she laughs at her boss's jokes and attempts to find opportunities in the conversation to apprise her boss of her achievements, she may well ignore other people in the room, she may be inattentive to the fact that her glass is empty, and she may lose track of time as she pursues her goal. The other person, in contrast, may scan the room for friendly faces, join one group for a brief conversation, drift to another, replenish his drink when it is down, and leave for home when the second drink is finished. The different behaviors of these two people depend on the goals they have constructed and the strategies and plans devised for meeting those goals.

Despite the close relationship between personal goals and behavior in a given social setting, people show remarkable flexibility in their ability to adjust their perceptions of a situation in response to factors that come up. They can take active control of their thoughts and their plans, especially in response to change; they can review several alternatives for interpreting the same event; and they change their knowledge through the feedback acquired by new experiences, reworking existing beliefs, values, and goals (Showers & Cantor, 1985). For example, the woman intent on impressing her boss may shift her goal to impressing her coworkers if she learns that her boss has been called away from the office party for a meeting. Similarly, the man planning to have a couple of drinks with friends may leave the party early if he sees that none of his friends have attended. This attribute of behavioral flexibility is important and provides an antidote to some of the research on cognitive representations, which implicitly suggests that behavior is automatically enacted in response to preexisting conceptions.

As we saw in Chapters 13 and 14, affective states and emotional responses to situations also strongly influence behavior. People in a good mood behave in ways that further that mood, whereas those in a bad mood will often make efforts to improve their mood, such as by enjoying the companionship of others. More generally, people in a positive mood appear to have more flexibility and awareness of multiple ways of dealing with situations, whereas poor mood is tied to more rigid strategies of social interaction (see Showers & Cantor, 1985). In these ways, then, cognitions and affect can have powerful joint regulatory effects on behavior (Ickes, Robertson, Tooke, & Teng, 1986; Norem & Cantor, 1990; Showers & Cantor, 1985). Cognitive and affective influences on behavior are often functionally inseparable and difficult to distinguish, reciprocally influencing each other and changing in response to behavioral feedback (Norem & Cantor, 1990).

Planning and Behavior

In social situations people implicitly ask questions such as, What is going on here? Who are these people? What are they doing, and what do they want of me? What are my own goals? Do my goals conflict with theirs, and if so, how do I make a choice between them? How can I achieve the goals that I select, and how do I make a choice among the available strategies? What are the consequences for being wrong, and how can I recover from my mistakes? What consequences will my choices have on others, and what can I do about their reactions? (Cantor & Kihlstrom, 1985) The wealth of knowledge, plans, and strategies that people bring to answering these questions in social interactions is referred to as *social intelligence*. It consists of concept knowledge, such as the facts one has at hand about situations and people, and rule knowledge, which includes the ways in which we categorize people, make judgments and inferences, solve problems, and perform various actions (Cantor & Kihlstrom, 1985; cf. S. J. Read & Miller, 1989).[1]

[1]Note that Cantor and Kihlstrom's use of the term *social intelligence* includes the various knowledge, talents, plans, and strategies, as well as interpersonal skills, that people bring to social situations. Others (e.g., Allport, 1935; S. J. Read & Miller, 1989) reserve the same term only for social, expressive, and communicative skills, a more restricted use of the term.

The specific cognitions by which people self-regulate their behavior are, in large part, idiosyncratic in that individual differences in the memories that people have for themselves and for social situations and people, the concepts they hold about social situations and people, and the rules that regulate behavior in social settings differ substantially based on past experience. Crosscutting these distinctions are ways of thinking about situations, including hierarchical ones (concerned with dominance and submission), territoriality (concerned with control, competence, and achievement), and identity (concerned with self-conceptions and interpersonal affiliations). Thus, for example, the first individual at the office party may be using her concepts of hierarchy in relating to her boss and thinking in terms of the dominance/submission role requirements that govern how an individual relates to her boss. A secondary issue may be territoriality, in that the employee desirous of making a positive impression may also find it necessary to shove equally ambitious coworkers aside so she can achieve her goals. The second individual at the office party, in contrast, may be more concerned with cementing friendships through a positive social occasion and finding opportunities to express his identity in ways that are consistent with his self-conceptions.

To this point, the discussion has implied that people manage their behavior by defining the situations in which they find themselves and by developing appropriate plans and strategies for realizing whatever goals might be achieved within these situations. But it is important to remember that people actively choose and construct situations as well. Thus, for example, an employee who wishes to impress his boss need not wait around for an office party as an opportunity to do so. He may arrange a dinner party to which his boss is invited, ask the boss out for lunch, hang around in the men's room waiting for him to show up, or engage in other actions that enable him to actively create and structure situations in service of his goals (Showers & Cantor, 1985; M. Snyder, 1982). As these examples suggest, achievement of personal goals often occurs by means of conscious planning.

To understand how people choose and construct situations that meet personal goals, it is useful to divide the process into at least two stages, a motivational process and a volitional process (Gollwitzer, 1990; Heckhausen & Gollwitzer, 1987). The initial phase of motivation involves deliberation on incentives and expectations in order to choose between alternative goals and their implied courses of action. An employee at an office party may, for example, regard the party as an opportunity to impress her boss, to make an advance on a coworker, or to coordinate problem-solving efforts with a member of her office team. Each of these goals would provide different incentives and imply very different courses of action during the party.

The motivational state of mind ends when a decision is made, which is a more or less conscious choice that then leads the person into a volitional state of mind. Volition involves the consideration of when and how to act so as to implement the intended course of action. Selection among alternative goals depends on volitional strength, including how feasible, desirable, and urgent a particular goal is, and on how favorable the situation is for the realization of a goal. Recognizing that the boss is already launched in conversation and that the attractive coworker keeps looking at his watch as if he is getting ready to leave, the employee may decide to use the party as an opportunity to brainstorm with the fellow team member. After making this decision, she may be oblivious to any further actions of her boss or the attractive coworker, instead deploying her efforts to the goal she has chosen to pursue. As these observations imply, selecting a focal goal leads to goal-shielding, a process whereby the activation of the focal goal inhibits the accessibility of alternative goals. When a person's level of commitment to a focal goal is high, so is goal-related tenacity and efforts toward goal pursuit and attainment. Thus, goal-shielding has beneficial consequences for goal pursuit and attainment (Shah, Friedman, & Kruglanski, 2002). However, if alternative goals (e.g., impressing a coworker) are seen as subgoals of a larger goal (e.g., increasing one's visibility at work), goal-shielding does not occur and instead the secondary goal becomes complementary and likely to be simultaneously pursued (Fishbach, Dhar, & Zhang, 2006).

The deliberation and implementation states of mind that characterize motivation and volition, respectively, prompt quite different cognitions. When people are in a deliberative mindset, for example, they are likely to weigh alternative courses of action in a relatively even-handed manner and consider factors that both favor and oppose a particular course of action (e.g., Taylor & Gollwitzer, 1995). They are open-minded and attentive to both incidental and potentially diagnostic information (Fujita, Gollwitzer, & Oettingen, 2007). Once a course of action has been selected, however, the implementation mindset is characterized by assessments of situational contingencies that favor the selected course of action. For example, in one study participants were induced either to deliberate the merits of participating in a scavenger hunt or to imagine implementing a plan to complete the task (Armor & Taylor, 2003). Participants then participated in the scavenger hunt. Those who were in a deliberative frame of mind initially formed more pessimistic expectations about the number of objects they might find and subsequently found fewer objects relative to the participants in the implementation condition who formed overly optimistic expectations about their likely performance but actually performed well.

What accounts for persistence toward activated goals? Is it the goal itself? During implementation, the affect associated with anticipated goal attainment may be transferred to the means that must be used to achieve those goals. Thus, if you are highly invested in a particular goal, and you see particular means as essential to achieving the goal, the affect associated with the goal will likely transfer to the means, and this will further your efforts to pursue goal-related activities (e.g., Fishbach, Shah, & Kruglanski, 2004). Deliberation and implementation influence behavior as well as cognitions about forthcoming action sequences (Gollwitzer, 1990).

Sometimes goal intentions are not enough. Even though we hold goals for ourselves, our behavior fails to correspond with those goals. A number of factors may bring behavior in line with personal goals. One of these is the explicit formation of *implementation intentions*. That is, people not only formulate their goals but make explicit if-then plans, what are called implementation intentions, that specify how a goal is going to be realized. When a person makes an implementation intention explicit, the likelihood of making progress toward that goal is enhanced. For example, if you say to yourself, "I'm going to start that paper over the December holidays," the likelihood that you will do so is lower than if you say "I am going to begin the paper on December 27." Such plans can produce automatic action control because you have intentionally delegated your goal-directed thoughts to situational cues. On the morning of December 27, you may automatically begin the paper because your goal-directed activity has been switched from conscious and effortful control to automatic control by if-then situational contingencies. More than 94 studies indicate that forming implementation intentions fosters goal attainment (Gollwitzer & Sheeran, 2006).

Implementation intentions can help to create desired habits as well. Consider a graduate student who wants to make progress toward writing up research but thus far has been only somewhat successful in doing so. One possibility for making progress is to create implementation intentions that produce automatic action control. If you make writing the first task you undertake each morning and pursue it for two hours before undertaking other tasks (such as teaching, meeting with undergraduates, and going to classes), then you no longer have to rely on conscious planning to write. Writing each morning becomes automatically under the control of situational cues. Implementation intentions may, thus, be used to further important goals (Sheeran, Webb, & Gollwitzer, 2005).

Planning for achieving goals is not without pitfalls. Typically people are overly optimistic about how quickly and effortlessly they will be able to accomplish their goals. Many of us make a daily to-do list, created in a fit of unrealistic optimism at the beginning of the day, only to discover that most tasks remain undone at the end of the day. For example, we may habitually take home a briefcase full of work to do over the weekend and bring most of the work back again on Monday. Buehler, Griffin, and Ross (1994) examined this planning fallacy with respect to students attempting to complete school projects. For example, in one study students completing their senior theses were asked to estimate when the thesis would be completed and when it would be completed if the worst possible problems intervened. Only one third of the students finished their projects by their predicted completion times, and a substantial portion of the remaining students went well beyond the worst possible completion date. Nonetheless, everyone completed the project, and it is likely that without the initially overly optimistic expectations, these beneficial outcomes would not have occurred at all. Although some researchers have argued that making expectations more realistic would be useful, there is compelling evidence that overly optimistic expectations ensure that people accomplish more in a given period of time than otherwise would be the case (Armor & Taylor, 1998).

Following the pursuit of a goal, a person may evaluate whether the efforts to achieve the goal succeeded and whether the goal outcomes match the expected value of the outcomes. Such post action evaluations contribute to future goal setting and planning. In this analysis, goals are related to behavior across time, with different cognitive activities predominating and directing action at different temporal points in the motivation-action-evaluation sequence.

The Automatic Pursuit of Goals

Although the preceding analysis implies that goal-related self-regulation typically involves conscious choices and decisions, in fact, much self-regulatory activity proceeds mindlessly without awareness (Bargh, 1997; Bargh, Gollwitzer, Lee-Chai, Barndollar, & Trötschel, 2001; Dijksterhuis & Bargh, 2001). Some goals that influence behavior are chronic concerns, such as the desire to be liked, which may automatically elicit smiling and deferential behavior (Levesque & Pelletier,

2003). Indeed, a habit may be thought of, in part, as an association between a goal and an action, so that if the goal is primed, the action will occur automatically. You may have had the experience of thinking about something you needed to do at school and discovered that you are now driving in that direction even though you were headed somewhere else. Or perhaps you made late dinner plans with friends and found yourself accidentally cooking at your usual time. Many habits do indeed seem to be a result of goal-dependent automatic behavior (Aarts & Dijksterhuis, 2000; Wood, Quinn, & Kashy, 2002), including those related to seemingly complex social interactions with others (Bargh & Williams, 2006). The fact that our behavior often occurs as automatic responses to cues that are rapidly, effortlessly, and unconsciously processes is an important insight from social cognition research. It helps to explain how people go about the tasks of daily living with so little apparent thought, and it also helps us understand why we are so often creatures of our own habits.

Essentially, the years of practice we have had responding to cues in the environment have made our emotional, cognitive, and behavioral responses to many situations automatic (Aarts & Dijksterhuis, 2003). We respond to evaluative cues in the environment without needing to attend to them or think about them (Roser & Gazzaniga, 2004). For example, most of us have had so many experiences with social occasions that we are able to regulate our behavior with respect to our goals quite unconsciously, and it may take a flaw in the plan to make salient and conscious both our personal goals for a situation and the strategies designed to achieve them. Familiar situations tend to inspire mindless behavior, whereas unfamiliar situations are more likely to evoke conscious, self-regulatory efforts (Cantor & Kihlstrom, 1985). For example, the process of meeting new acquaintances in Japan may prompt an American to become intensely aware of the dynamics of social situations, inasmuch as most Westerners do not have well-developed knowledge of the norms and appropriate behaviors for many Japanese social settings.

Expertise also determines how self-consciously and how successfully people self-regulate. People who feel uncertain or confused in social settings are more likely to try to identify the prototypic actions that are successful in social situations, compared with people who are more aware of the competencies required in any given setting (Cantor, Mackie, & Lord, 1983–1984; Wicklund & Braun, 1987; see also Showers & Cantor, 1985, for a discussion of expertise). Uncertain, confused people are also more likely to characterize others through the ascription of dispositional attributions, typing them as particular sorts of people. This rigidity in perceptions may give their own behavior a certain flat, unresponsive quality compared to those who are able to maintain a more flexible or better fit between their cognitive and behavioral repertoire and the environment (Wicklund, 1986).

As noted, nonverbal behavior can also reflect social goals automatically. People often nonconsciously mimic the postures, mannerisms, and facial expressions of the people with whom they are interacting. This is easy to demonstrate on your own. Smile at a person with whom you are speaking and see if your smile isn't reciprocated. Then rest your hands on your hips and see if your partner doesn't mirror that behavior. Nonconscious mimicry is very common in social interaction, and it is an example of the fact we often use environmental cues as bases for our own behavior without awareness or intention on our part (Chartrand & Bargh, 1999).

These examples are illustrative of a profoundly important point: namely, that links between perception and action are automatic and hard-wired and are important bases not only of social understanding but also of social interaction (Knoblich & Sebanz, 2006). Mirror neurons (e.g., Rizzolatti, Fogassi, & Gallese, 2001), located in the premotor cortex, become active both when the person watches someone else perform an action and when that person performs the action. For example, people show mirror neuron activation (as well as muscle twitches) reflecting the action sequences they observe another person doing, and the activation is stronger the more expert they are in the activity (e.g., Calvo-Merino, Glaser, Grezes, Passingham, & Haggard, 2005); this activation is strongest when one observes one's own past performance. Mirror neurons appear to play a role in linking situational cues to the automatic performance of behavior in socially interactive settings.

Automatic evaluation occurs rapidly, within milliseconds (Chapter 10). For example, in one study participants were presented with word-pair sequences and asked to judge whether target adjectives were negative or positive (Fazio, Sanbonmatsu, Powell, & Kardes, 1986). The first, a prime, appeared for 200 ms, and the second, the target word, appeared 100 ms after the prime had disappeared. Despite the very rapid speed at which this task had to be accomplished, participants' ratings of the target word as positive or negative were much faster when the prime and the target had the same evaluative content (i.e., both words were negative or both were positive) than when they were incongruent.

Automatic evaluation can affect seemingly complex behavioral sequences as well. In one study participants were given word puzzles to solve that contained words suggesting either rudeness or politeness (Bargh, Chen, & Burrows, 1996). Following the puzzle task, participants were sent down the hall to a room to get credit for the experiment. However, the person who was to give the credit was involved in a lengthy personal phone conversation with a friend and did not respond to the participant. Bargh and colleagues assessed how long it took the participant to interrupt the ongoing conversation. Whereas 63% of the group primed with "rude" words interrupted, only 17% of the "polite" group did.

Research such as this attests not only to the fact that cues in the environment can automatically prime behavior but also to the fact that evaluative cues may be among the most potent cues to affect processing of subsequent information and behavior. When people have clear goals in mind, evaluation of goal-relevant information or objects becomes positive, suggesting that automatic evaluation can help to maintain goal pursuit (Ferguson & Bargh, 2004; see also Custers & Aarts, 2005). Evaluatively toned latent stimuli are easily and quickly noticed and prompt the behavioral tendency of approach or avoidance, respectively (Chen & Bargh, 1999; Wentura, Rothermund, & Bak, 2000). For example, in one study participants responded to attitude statements by either moving a lever toward them or pushing it away from them (Chen & Bargh, 1999). They were faster to respond to negatively valenced words when they pushed the lever away (avoided it) than when they pulled it toward them (approached). The reverse was true for positively valenced words (see also Neumann & Strack, 2000). Interestingly, when people are faced with temptations they want to avoid, they are quick to push away temptation-related stimuli and faster to pull toward their approach goals (Fishbach & Shah, 2006). (Also see Chapter 4.)

In similar ways, when stereotypes are unobtrusively primed, they can have an impact on subsequent behaviors (Mussweiler, 2006). For example, in one study participants were unobtrusively induced to move in the ungainly manner that is stereotypic of overweight people. Subsequently, when presented with an ambiguous target to evaluate, they attributed more overweight-stereotypic characteristics to the target than did participants in the control condition. Thus, not only do unobtrusive primes affect behavior, the feedback of one's own behavior may inadvertently influence subsequent cognitions.

Assimilation and Contrast

The research we have considered thus far suggests that automatic behavior assumes the form of assimilation of one's behavior to the cues provided by the environment. For example, when an elderly stereotype is primed, we walk more slowly, or when we are induced to walk as an overweight person, we ascribe overweight stereotypic attributes to an ambiguous target. Under some circumstances, however, seeing one thing leads to doing another: That is, there are contrast effects in automatic behavior (Dijksterhuis et al., 1998). For example, in one study, participants who had positive attitudes toward the elderly walked more slowly after being primed with the elderly stereotype, but participants who had negative attitudes toward the elderly actually walked faster (e.g., Cesario, Plaks, & Higgins, 2006). These findings both demonstrate that contrast effects may also occur in automatic behavior and that these contrast effects may be due to the cognitive processes that people go through as they are preparing for action.

Whereas traits and stereotypes tend to elicit assimilation, exemplars (that is, typical or good examples) appear to elicit judgmental contrast by evoking social comparison. For example, in one study participants were primed either with stereotypes of professors or supermodels or they were primed with exemplars of those categories (Albert Einstein and Claudia Schiffer, respectively). Being primed by the stereotypes led to behavioral assimilation; that is, participants got more answers right on a subsequent knowledge test if they had been primed with the "professor" stereotype and fewer items correct if they had been primed with the "model" stereotype (Table 15.1). However, participants primed with the exemplars demonstrated contrast effects; that is, those primed with Albert

TABLE 15.1. How Priming of Stereotypes and Exemplars Affects Behavior

	Direction of Prime	
	Intelligent	Stupid
Type of Prime	M	M
Stereotype	50	41
Exemplar	42	54

Priming of an intelligent or stupid stereotype evoked behavior consistent with that stereotype, whereas priming an exemplar associated with intelligence or not led to contrasting behavior.

Source: Adapted from "Seeing one thing and doing another: Contrast effects in automatic behavior," Dijksterhuis et al., 1998, *Journal of Personality and Social Psychology, 75,* p. 865.

Einstein did more poorly, and those primed with Claudia Schiffer did better. When presented with the specific exemplars, participants apparently engaged in social comparison, concluding "I could never do as well as Albert Einstein" or "I can certainly do better than Claudia Schiffer." When only the stereotype was primed, no social comparison was evoked, and assimilation of performance to the stereotype occurred. These data are presented in Table 15.1 (see also Dijksterhuis & van Knippenberg, 1998).

Individual Differences and Goals

Different people construe the relation of a situational cue to their own circumstances in different ways, and thus the same prime can have quite different effects on the perception and behavior of one person as opposed to another. For example, Mussweiler and Förster (2000) used a sequential priming paradigm in which participants were primed with one word and effects on behavior were observed. Men who were first primed with aggression-related words (e.g., violence) and then primed with sex-related words responded with more aggression (throwing darts at faces), but only if the target face was female; however, parallel effects did not occur for women.

Recall from Chapter 5 that some goals have a promotion focus, which involves achievement and aspiration and whose attainment brings a sense of accomplishment (e.g., getting a high grade in a course). By contrast, other goals have a prevention focus (e.g., not failing a course), which involves a sense of responsibility and whose attainment brings a sense of security. Whether one adopts a promotion or prevention focus influences behavior toward a goal. Commitment to accomplishment of goals is typically characterized by a high level of performance in an effort to reach the goal, whereas commitment to security goals is characterized by doing what is necessary (Shah, Higgins, & Friedman, 1998). Whether one adopts a promotion or a prevention focus also influences emotional responses to goals. When a promotion focus is stronger, goal attainment yields greater cheerfulness and less dejection, whereas when a prevention goal is stronger, goal attainment yields greater quiescence and less agitation (Higgins, Shah, & Friedman, 1997).

Goals can be primed by activation of representations of a significant other. Which regulatory goals are activated will be influenced by the expectations those others are perceived to have with respect to one's own personal goals. For example, suppose your father believes that achieving as much as you can in your chosen field is important, but your mother believes that not making others look bad is an important social goal. Whether your representation of your mother or father is primed could have an effect on your achievement-related behavior. If you are in a debate with a colleague and your father is salient, you might go all out to win, whereas if your mother is sitting in the front row, you might moderate your behavior so that your opponent doesn't look bad (Shah, 2003a, 2003b). Priming significant others can influence goal appraisal, the appraisal of the difficulty of the task, and reactions to one's own performance (Shah, 2003b). It can influence the perceived value of goal attainment, persistence toward the goal, and actual performance. For example, if a significant other, such as a romantic partner, has high expectations for your performance, you would be likely to believe that you can attain the goal, you will persist at the goal, and you will perform better (Shah, 2003b).

Under some circumstances, people automatically adopt and pursue a goal that is implied by someone else's behavior. Specifically, if a goal is perceived as attractive, another person's behavior directed toward that goal may act as a cue to pursuing the same goal (Aarts, Gollwitzer, & Hassin, 2004; Shah, 2003a).

Neural Underpinnings of Goal-Directed Behavior

How exactly do goals influence behavior? The cognitive control of behavior stems from the active maintenance of patterns of activity in the prefrontal cortex that represent goals and the means to achieve them (E. K. Miller & Cohen, 2001). These representations are updated regularly by experience through feedback from brain stem neuromodulatory systems. The activity in the PFC brain regions provides signals to other brain structures that guide the flow of activity along neural pathways and establish mappings between inputs of internal states and outputs needed to perform a particular task (E. K. Miller & Cohen, 2001).

Although the prefrontal cortex is not implicated for simple automatic behavior, such as reacting to a sudden sound or movement, it *is* implicated when behavior must be guided by intentions, goals, or other internal states. Thus a primary task of the prefrontal cortex appears to be representing goals and the means to achieve them for top-down regulation of activity. Increasing the personal relevance of stimuli and the intensity of approach motivation, especially, increases left frontal activation, which has been consistently tied to positive and approach motivational affect, whereas negative or withdrawal motivational affect has been associated with right frontal activation (Harmon-Jones et al., 2006).

The preceding discussion of goals assumes a degree of consistency between cognitions and behavior. Yet a striking aspect of behavior is that under some circumstances, it does not correspond to what one would expect on the basis of apparently predominant cognitions. For example, most people are horrified by the prospect of a nuclear war, and yet very few people take any action to attempt to reduce its likelihood (S. T. Fiske, 1987). We next address this issue.

WHEN ARE COGNITIONS AND BEHAVIOR RELATED?

The question, "When are cognitions and behaviors related?" is not an easy one to answer, at least not simply. First, in the social cognition arena, little research includes behavioral dependent measures, so opportunities to examine the relationship have been limited. When the cognition–behavior relationship is examined, sometimes the two parallel each other but sometimes not.

To address the cognition–behavior relationship, one may turn to related literatures in which similar problems exist. For example, those with an awareness of social psychological history should find the cognition–behavior problem all too familiar. Attitude change research of the 1950s and 1960s produced a similar situation: Researchers initially failed to examine the attitude–behavior relationship, and when it was examined, the evidence was inconsistent. Some reported relatively low relationships between cognitions and behavior (e g., Nisbett & Wilson, 1977b; Wicker, 1969), whereas others maintained that the consistency is often quite high when moderating factors are taken into account (Quattrone, 1985;

Schuman & Johnson, 1976). The literature on the correspondence between personality traits and behavior, although not cognitive in its origins, is also a useful source of hypotheses: The relationship between personality traits (which have important cognitive components) and behaviors that would theoretically be expected to follow from them sometimes proves to be weak and unreliable (Mischel, 1968).

Drawing on these literatures, the attempt to clarify when cognitions and behavior go together can take several routes: specifying which behaviors are most likely to be related to particular cognitions; improving measurement procedures so that assessments of cognitions and behaviors are more comparable; determining what features of cognitions are most likely to lead to behavioral consequences; understanding the various ways people have of conceptualizing behavior; identifying situational factors that might moderate the cognition–behavior relationship; and looking for individual differences in cognition–behavior consistency.

Which Behaviors Are Related to Cognition?

Perhaps we expect too many and too varied behaviors to be related to any given cognition. Consider the self-perception of friendliness as an example. Some people think of themselves as friendly; others do not. Considering only the people who consider themselves friendly, should we expect them to be friendly in all situations? Certainly we would expect them to be more friendly than people who consider themselves unfriendly, but there is no reason to expect that they will be friendly every minute of the day. Recall from the discussion of mental representations that prototypic persons or activities are those that are most representative of their particular category. For example, prototypic activities for friendliness might be saying hello to people on campus or welcoming new people enthusiastically. To consider oneself a friendly person, then, perhaps one need only show a high degree of consistency in these prototypic behaviors and not on behaviors less centrally related to friendliness.

In fact, research supports this contention (Mischel, 1984; Mischel & Peake, 1982). In an examination of self-rated conscientiousness, undergraduates who considered themselves conscientious (or not) were studied in a wide variety of situations that might assess conscientiousness. An independent group of raters judged each of the situations for how central or prototypic it was for conscientiousness. The investigators then calculated cross-situational consistency. Individuals who rated themselves high and low in conscientiousness did not behave differently in situations that were low in prototypicality for conscientiousness. However, when prototypic conscientiousness situations were examined, the highly conscientious individuals showed significantly greater consistency in their behavior as compared with the individuals who were low in conscientiousness (Mischel & Peake, 1982). More generally, Schutte, Kenrick, and Sadalla (1985) found that agreement among people as to which behavior a person would perform increased the more prototypical the situation was for the behavior and the more the situation constrained the behavior.

A similar argument has been made in the context of attitudes. Attitudes are often very general representations of beliefs about particular categories of people, things, or events. Whether or not an attitude predicts behavior toward any particular member of a category is influenced by the match of that instance or member to the prototype of the category. Lord, Lepper, and Mackie (1984) found that when people hold stereotypes about particular groups, they manifest that attitude in specific interactions with a particular group member primarily if that group member meets their abstracted prototype of the group.

What are the implications of these points for the cognition–behavior relationship generally? They suggest that consistency will be highest when one examines behaviors that are prototypically related to particular cognitions, but that cognition–behavior consistency will be lower when one examines behaviors that are less centrally related to the cognitions in question.

Measuring Cognitions and Behaviors

Another problem with assessing the cognition–behavior relationship concerns whether cognitions and behavior are measured at the same level of specificity. If you are asked whether you feel needy people should be helped through charity, you may well answer yes. If you are then accosted by a persistent beggar asking for a dollar, you may well decline. Although your attitudes and behavior would appear to be inconsistent, have you violated your attitudes? Not necessarily. You may, for example, feel that charity should be managed by institutions, not individuals, or that begging should be discouraged. The apparent inconsistency of your attitude and behavior is caused by the fact that your attitude was assessed very generally, but your behavior was measured in a very specific situation. When attitudes and behaviors are assessed at different levels of specificity, low correspondence may be found. How, then, can attitude and behavior assessment be made more comparable?

One solution is to measure behavior through general behavioral tendencies, employing a multiple-act criterion (e.g., Epstein, 1979; Fishbein & Ajzen, 1974). That is, instead of examining the relationship between a general attitude (i.e., toward charity in the abstract) and a single act (i.e., giving money to a specific beggar), one would measure a number of specific acts to get a general behavioral measure. For example, one might measure money given to various causes, time volunteered to help the needy, and so on. Although your general belief about charity may not predict your specific response to a particular panhandler, it should predict your charitable behavior more generally if we examine how much money, time, or effort you volunteer to each of several causes.

The multiple-act criterion may succeed in demonstrating attitude–behavior consistency because (1) multiple actions provide a better estimate of the individual's typical behavior, (2) employing multiple actions succeeds in including at least one situation that can be highly predicted by attitudes (cf. Monson, Hesley, & Chernick, 1982), or (3) multiple actions include at least two situations the individual sees as similar to each other and relevant to the attitude, thus warranting similar behavior (cf. Lord, 1982). For whichever reason, correspondence is higher when multiple-act measures of behavior are compared against global attitudes.

A debate similar to the multiple-act criterion in attitude–behavior research has emerged in the personality literature. Buss and Craik (1980, 1981) suggested that, to aid in the assessment of personality traits, the frequency of behaviors reflecting an underlying disposition should be assessed. According to their position, specific behaviors should also be identified in terms of their centrality or not to the disposition under consideration. The framework predicts that single acts on average correlate less well (than would many acts) with personality measures of the disposition in question. Moreover, responses to acts central to a disposition should correlate more highly with measures of dispositions than would responses to acts that are relatively less central to the disposition, a point consistent with the work on prototypicality previously described.

A second solution to assessing cognition–behavior correspondence is to measure cognitions more specifically. For example, if you had been asked about how you feel about giving money to beggars instead of how you feel about charity generally, high correspondence between your attitude and behavior might well have been found. Many efforts to examine the attitude–behavior relationship have adopted this approach by assessing attitudes as intentions to behave in specific ways (Ajzen & Fishbein, 1977; Fishbein & Ajzen, 1974, 1975). Fishbein and Ajzen's theory of reasoned action states that a person's behavior can be predicted directly from his or her intention, which is, in turn, a function of attitudes toward the behavior, subjective norms about what the person thinks others think he or she should do, and the relative importance of the attitudinal and normative considerations. The theory of reasoned action has been used to predict a broad array of behaviors and has been particularly productively employed in the health domain (Taylor, 2006). When intentions are stable, they predict behaviors, but when they are weak or unstable, past behavior is a better predictor of current behavior (Conner & Abraham, 2001; Sheeran, Orbell, & Trafimow, 1999).

In addition to knowing a person's attitudes, subjective norms, and behavioral intentions with respect to a given behavior, one needs to know his or her perceived behavioral control over that action (Ajzen, 1988). A test of this revision to the model found that participants not only needed to hold a behavioral intention toward a particular attitude object but also needed to feel that they were capable of performing the action contemplated. Thus feelings of perceived control or self-efficacy appear to be important in demonstrating attitude–behavior consistency, even when there is a clear behavioral intention to act upon an attitude.

Which Cognitions Predict Behavior?

One of the most frustrating aspects of the attitude–behavior relationship is that one can change cognitions that would seem to be highly related to behavior without necessarily changing those corresponding behaviors. For example, studies of beliefs about women in the workplace suggest that, increasingly, both men and women are more egalitarian concerning women and employment. However, most indicators of discrimination and harassment suggest that women still experience far more of these adverse effects than men (Kahn & Crosby, 1987). There are many reasons behavior might not match attitudes. In the previous example, Kahn and Crosby suggest that attitudes may reflect ideal or socially desirable ways of responding to a group, but behavior may be influenced by other factors, such as other attitudes (i.e., seniority should determine pay), situational factors (i.e., the characteristics of a particular woman under consideration for a particular position), individual differences in the propensity to use attitudes as guides for behavior, and the possibility of getting away with harassment and discrimination (cf. Crosby, Bromley, & Saxe, 1980). In this section, we consider further the various factors that determine which cognitions are most likely to predict behavior.

One important condition for seeing a strong relation between cognition and behavior is that the cognition be strongly held and clear. This is most evident in attitude research. Strong attitudes are typically stable: They have personal implications, and they are held about personally important issues about which a person feels extremely certain. When there are inconsistencies between attitudes and behaviors, it is often because the attitudes are weak or ambivalently held (Armitage & Conner, 2000). Attitudes that are strongly held are more likely to be accessible and, thus, influence behavior (Bizer & Krosnick, 2001; see also Posavac, Sanbonmatsu, & Fazio, 1997).

Cognitions are more likely to influence behavior when they have been rehearsed and practiced. When people hold attitudes that are highly embedded—that is, tied to other beliefs that they hold—those embedded attitudes are more strongly related to behavior than less embedded attitudes (Prislin & Oullette, 1996).

Cognitions are more likely to influence behavior if they concern a domain about which people have considerable knowledge. For example, being asked to sign a petition to protect the environment would be more likely to occur among people who not only hold pro-environmental attitudes but who know a lot about the issues involved in preserving the environment (Armitage & Conner, 2000; Kallgren & Wood, 1986).

Another factor that determines whether or not attitudes will predict behavior is the way they are formed. Attitudes formed from relevant experience predict behavior better than do attitudes based on indirect experience (Fazio & Zanna, 1981). In one study college students were asked about their attitudes regarding their university's housing shortage. Only those participants whose attitudes had been formed through relevant experience (i.e., sleeping on cots in dorm lounges for several weeks because there were no rooms) showed strong attitude–behavior relationships. Having relevant personal experience with an issue about which we form beliefs encourages people to think and talk about the issue more than if it is remote. When we have this kind of relevant experience with the attitude, it is more likely to influence behavior than if we hear about it or read about it. In addition, when people have the time and motivation to deliberate on their attitudes, they are more likely to consider the relevance of those attitudes to their behavior before deciding to act on them (Fabrigar, Petty, Smith, & Crites, 2006). Overall, attitudes that are formed through relevant experience are more specific; they are held more confidently; they are more stable; and they resist counterargument better than do attitudes not based on relevant experience (Fazio & Zanna, 1978; Zanna & Fazio, 1982). Consequently, they predict behavior.

Why are attitudes formed through relevant experience more predictive of behavior? There are several possible reasons. First, relevant experiences provide a great deal of information, so the attitudes that develop as a consequence may be better informed and more robust. Second, because behavior provided an initial basis for forming the attitude, the behavioral implications of attitudes formed through relevant experience may be more clear. Third, the links between the attitude and actual experience may make the attitude more accessible in memory, and thus it may be more likely to come to mind when one must act (Fazio & Zanna, 1981). Finally, the fact that attitudes formed through direct experience are often very specific may make specific behavioral implications clear, which may not be true for more vague general attitudes (Borgida, Swann, & Campbell, 1977).

Another factor that influences attitude–behavior consistency is vested interest. To the extent that a person's attitude involves self-interest, the person is more likely to act on it. For example, 18-year-olds are more likely to canvass against a referendum that would raise the drinking age to 21 than are 22-year-olds also against it (Sivacek & Crano, 1982). Vested interest is more likely to predict behavior for attitudes that are personally important to an individual than for attitudes that are low in personal importance (Young, Borgida, Sullivan, & Aldrich, 1987). When values relevant to the desired behavior change are made salient, behavior change is found as well (Schwartz & Inbar-Saban, 1988; see also Homer & Kahle, 1988).

Stable cognitions that are easily remembered are more likely to predict behavior than those that are less stable or nonaccessible in memory (Kraus, 1995). When people's attitudes are unstable, salient environmental cues or competing, casually held beliefs may predict behavior instead. Cognitions show an enduring relationship to behavior if they are accessed in close temporal proximity. For example, if a 20-year-old woman says she does not want to have children, this will not necessarily reflect her behavior at age 30. Attitudes that are accessible in memory affect behavior more strongly than those that are not (Kraus, 1995). A primary factor that determines whether a cognition is accessible is how frequently it is expressed. For example, if you are in a group of friends who debate U.S. foreign policy on a regular basis, those attitudes are more likely to influence your behavior. Moreover, attitudes often become more extreme when they are expressed more frequently (Downing, Judd, & Brauer, 1992). Thus, if you have multiple opportunities to express your attitudes about a war, you may come to feel strongly about it in the process. Easily accessible attitudes come to be regarded as important (Roese & Olson, 1994).

The preceding factors suggest that a strong determinant of whether an attitude will influence behavior is importance. Important attitudes are ones that reflect fundamental values, self-interest, or identification with individuals or groups that one values (Boninger, Krosnick, & Berent, 1995). Such attitudes are both resistant to persuasion and strongly predictive of behavior. Attitudes also influence behavior to the extent that they can be easily accessed by a person (e.g., Aldrich, Sullivan, & Borgida, 1989; Fazio & Williams, 1986; Kallgren & Wood, 1986; Kiesler, Nisbett, & Zanna, 1969). Sometimes we hold attitudes as general values but are not able to access them readily to influence our behavior. For example, we may believe in the need to protect the environment, but this attitude may be held at such a general level that it is not accessed for specific situations. Kallgren and Wood (1986) assessed participants' attitudes toward the preservation of the environment and also assessed the accessibility of those attitudes by how many facts the person could remember relevant to the attitude and how many past behaviors he or she could remember consistent with the attitude. Two weeks later, the participants were asked to sign and circulate a petition and to participate in a recycling project. Those participants who were able to access their prior attitudes showed substantial congruence between their attitudes and behavior, whereas those who had little access to their attitudes demonstrated little attitude–behavior consistency.

Attitude–behavior consistency also increases with the amount of information that is available about the attitude object. Using longitudinal data, A. R. Davison, Yantis, Norwood, and Montano (1985) found that more information about an attitude object produced greater congruence between attitudes and behavior, even after controlling for prior experience with the attitude and for attitude certainty.

Self-schemas also determine the attitude–behavior relationship. Those whose attitudes represent strongly held beliefs about their personal qualities are more likely to behave consistently with those attitudes than are people who hold attitudes that are not central to self-schemas (Milburn, 1987).

Overall, attitudes that matter to a person, that are based on personal experience or values, that are held with confidence, that are accessible, that have information to back them up, and that have implications for one's future show a stronger relationship to behavior than those that matter little. The implication for the cognition–behavior relationship more generally is that cognitions that emerge from personal rather than indirect experience and cognitions that have implications for one's life predict behavior better than cognitions that develop merely from mild curiosity, passing interest, or a secondhand source.

Thinking About Reasons Underlying Attitudes

Being induced to think about the reasons underlying one's attitudes reduces attitude–behavior consistency (T. D. Wilson, Dunn, Kraft, & Lisle, 1989; Wilson & Hodges, 1992). Essentially, analyzing reasons that underlie one's attitudes actually causes those attitudes to change temporarily (Wilson, Hodges, & LaFleur, 1995; Wilson & LaFleur, 1995), especially if those attitudes have little cognitive support (Maio & Olson, 1998) from other beliefs that buttress the attitude. The reason this happens may be that people do not think a lot about their attitudes, and when they are induced to do so, they may focus on particular aspects of the attitudes such that those aspects become more salient. In doing so, they may fail to discriminate important from unimportant information or properly perceive the relevance of particular information (Tordesillas & Chaiken, 1999). When trying to come up with reasons for their attitudes, people often bring to mind thoughts that are available in memory but that may not be representative of their attitude. The reasons they come up with may come from salient situational factors or from recent experiences that imply a new attitude, leading at least temporarily to attitude change.

What is the impact of assessing the reasons for one's attitudes on behavior? If behavior is measured shortly after people have expressed new attitudes, then the behavior is consistent with those new attitudes. If behavior is measured some time after attitudes have been analyzed for reasons, the behavior seems to "snap back" to the original attitude and thus is inconsistent with the attitude reported after the reasons analysis (T. D. Wilson, Kraft, & Dunn, 1989). It may also be that behavior is more under the control of affective aspects of an attitude than cognitive aspects. Because self-reports of attitudes are cognitively driven and behavior may be more affectively driven, under conditions when one has focused on the reasons underlying one's attitudes, self-reports of attitudes and behaviors may be discrepant.

As the previous analysis implies, some attitudes are more vulnerable than others to the disruption produced by focusing on reasons. Attitudes that are difficult to access, weakly held, based on very little knowledge, or affectively based are more vulnerable to reasons analysis disruption than are attitudes that are easily accessed, strongly held, based on lots of knowledge, and cognitively based (T. D. Wilson, Kraft, & Dunn, 1989; see T. D. Wilson, Dunn, et al., 1989, for a review).

What are the conditions that induce people spontaneously to come up with reasons for their attitudes? This is an important question because otherwise the effects may be experimental with rare analogues in the real world. Wilson and colleagues predicted and found that when people encounter unexpected reactions from others or have unexpected feelings about their attitude objects, they are motivated to engage in a reasons analysis (T. D. Wilson, Dunn, et al., 1989).

Affective Versus Cognitive Impacts of Attitudes

Tesser and his colleagues maintain that the type of behavior in which a person is engaged influences how focusing on affect or cognition will influence the cognition–behavior relationship (M. G. Millar & Tesser, 1986a). In its simplest form, they argued that behavior engaged in for its own sake (consummatory behavior) is driven by affect, but that behavior in service of goals (instrumental behavior) is driven by cognition. Thus they hypothesized that if one focuses on the cognitive component of an attitude, attitude–behavior congruence should increase if the behavior is instrumental. However, focusing on the emotions or affect associated with the attitude would not increase the congruence between attitude and instrumental behavior. On the other hand, focusing on the emotional component of an attitude would increase the attitude–behavior relationship if the behavior is engaged in for its own sake (consummatory), whereas focusing on the cognitive component would have no effect on the attitude–behavior relationship if the behavior is consummatory.

To test this hypothesis, Millar and Tesser (1986b) had participants solve difficult puzzles and led them to focus either on the cognitive component of the attitude (why the participant felt that way about the puzzles) or the affective aspect of the attitude (how the participant felt about the puzzles). In addition, participants were told either that they would be given a test later of their analytic ability (making their puzzle-solving activity instrumental) or that they would later have a social sensitivity test (making puzzle solving an activity undertaken in its own right, a consummatory behavior). Consistent with the predictions, participants who engaged in the puzzle activity as instrumental behavior showed consistency between evaluations of the puzzle and time spent on the puzzles only in the cognitive focus condition; those playing with the puzzles for their own sake showed high attitude–behavior congruence only in the affective focus condition.

Millar and Tesser's (1989) argument also suggested that if the affective and cognitive components of an attitude are in evaluative agreement, then focusing on either component should produce a similar evaluation regardless of the type of behavior. However, if the two are not in agreement, then focusing on the cognitive versus the affective aspects of the attitude would lead to different evaluations, depending on whether the behavior is instrumental or consummatory. Research supports this prediction as well (M. G. Millar & Tesser, 1989). Table 15.2 summarizes factors that affect the attitude–behavior relation. These factors elucidate cognition–behavior relations more generally.

Action Identification

People may label their actions in ways that affect their subsequent behavior. Specifically, actions may be identified at low levels of behavior (making idle

TABLE 15.2. Conditions That Contribute to High Attitude–Behavior Consistency

Attitude is strong.

    Unconflicted attitude

    Consistent affective and cognitive components

    Information about attitude object

    Direct personal experience with attitude object

Attitude is stable over time.

Attitude is relevant to the behavior.

Attitude is salient.

Attitude is consistent with values.

Attitude is relevant to future.

No conflicting situational pressures are present.

conversation) or at high levels in the service of some goal (trying to create a positive impression). A theory that gives psychological meaning to this phenomenon is action identification theory (Vallacher & Wegner, 1987). The theory assumes that act identities—namely, the different ways of thinking about a particular action—have systematic relations to each other in an organized cognitive representation, labeled the action identity structure. The identity structure is a hierarchical arrangement of the various identities that might be attached to a given action. Low levels identify the specifics of the action, whereas higher levels indicate a more abstract understanding of the action, indicating why it is done and what its purposes are. Putting one's feet successively in front of each other represents a very low action identity, going for a walk might represent a middle-level action identity, walking through a neighborhood to see if it is the kind of place in which one might want to live would be a high-level action identity, and planning one's future, an even higher level action identity. Together these represent some of the different levels of identification that might be applied to the same underlying action.

    The theory maintains that people have certain ideas of what they are doing or want to do and use this identification as a frame of reference for implementing that action, monitoring its occurrence, and reflecting on whether or not it is maintained. Given that a particular action can be identified either at low levels or at high levels, there is a tendency for the higher level identity to be "prepotent"; that is, to dominate the enactment and evaluation of the action. In fact, research shows that when people have only low-level understandings of what they are doing, they are predisposed to accept any higher level identity that is suggested by the context surrounding the action (e.g., Wegner, Vallacher, Kiersted, & Dizadji, 1986; Wegner, Vallacher, Macomber, Wood, & Arps, 1984). For example, in one study participants were induced to drink coffee from a strangely shaped cup, thereby focusing their attention on very low-level aspects of the action (actually getting the coffee to their mouths); other participants drank coffee from normal cups. Those drinking from the unusual cups were more receptive to a suggestion that they were seeking (or avoiding) self-stimulation, a higher level action identification than simply "drinking coffee." Moreover, they showed generalization of the self-stimulation action identification, turning up (or down) the volume of music to which they were listening (Wegner et al., 1984).

When an action cannot be maintained at a higher level, it tends to drop to a lower level of prepotency. For example, those skilled in the use of chopsticks may be able to think of consuming a Chinese meal as a delightful and tasty experience, whereas those inexperienced in the use of chopsticks may regard the experience primarily as a task of actually getting food from the plate into one's mouth. When the higher level identities of an action cannot be automatically enacted, the tendency for actions to stay identified at the higher level is lessened, and the individual moves to lower levels of action identification. More generally, actions that are successful tend to be identified and maintained at relatively high levels, whereas actions that are unsuccessful tend to be identified at lower levels (Vallacher, Wegner, & Frederick, 1987).

The level at which an action is identified depends on several factors, including the context in which the action takes place, the difficulty experienced in carrying out the action, and the person's prior experience with the action. With respect to context, situational cues will often provide a basis for a person identifying an action at a particularly high or low level. For example, the presence of one's boss at a social gathering may define one's comments about the future directions of the company as an opportunity to impress one's boss, whereas if the boss were not present, one's observations about the company's future might simply remain gratuitous observations.

With respect to action difficulty, five factors, termed maintenance indicators, determine the potential disruption of an action identity. They are the difficulty of enacting the action, familiarity with it, its complexity, the amount of time it takes to enact it, and the amount of time it takes to learn to do it well. Waiting for a bus, for example, is not difficult to enact: It is familiar to most people, it is very simple, it may take a short time, and it is not hard to learn. Consequently, the likelihood that waiting for a bus would drop to a lower level of action identification is small. However, flagging down a taxi may be somewhat more difficult to enact, being less familiar, more complex, under some circumstances take longer, and in particular cities requiring an inordinate amount of learning time. The novice cab-flagger in New York City, for example, may shift the identification of the task from flagging a cab to getting into the street with one's hand up to attract attention before other people do. Actions seen as easy to do, familiar, short in duration, and requiring little learning time tend to be maintained at their initial level compared to those that fail to meet these criteria.

Actions chunked at higher levels can often be enacted automatically. To the extent that this is true, they tend to be maintained at higher rather than lower levels. In addition, as individuals develop more experience with a particular action sequence, they will come to identify it at a higher level than if they have little experience with the action sequence (Vallacher, Wegner, & Frederick, 1987).

Whether an action is identified at a high or low level has a number of implications. As already noted, behaviors enacted at a higher level of action identification tend to be more stable than those enacted at low levels of action identification. Action identification also influences the flexibility of that action. Actions identified at a higher level, such as getting exercise, may be enacted in any of several ways, such as jogging, riding a bike, or swimming, whereas actions identified at a lower level, such as riding a bike, will show less flexibility. Actions performed at the wrong level are subject to performance impairments. Specifically, difficult tasks are performed best when identified in low-level terms, whereas easy tasks are performed best when they are identified in high-level terms. An action typically performed at a high level may be disrupted if one moves it to a lower level. For example, a broad jumper claims that, by asking one of her opponents why she places her right foot in a particular way, she can knock two feet off the opponent's jump. Conversely, when a behavior can be enacted automatically at a relatively low level of action identification, contextual effects that suggest a higher level of action identification can disrupt the performance of the behavioral sequence because the higher level of identification forces attention to the component parts in a way that is not true at the lower level of identification. For example, a person who normally meets new people quite easily without any great social discomfort may find that these behaviors become disrupted if his partner emphasizes the importance of making a good impression. Our identification of others' actions also influences our perceptions in important ways. For example, when we identify another person's actions in terms of high-level act identities, the attribution of intentionality is strong, whereas it is muted when those same actions are identified at lower levels (Kozak, Marsh, & Wegner, 2006).

Under some circumstances, action identities produce emergent action. Emergent action is defined as behavior that people find themselves doing that they did not set out to do. Given that low-level act identities tend to be subject to context effects suggesting higher level action identities, emergent action is a highly likely outcome of a low-level action identification. For example, in one study participants thought about participating in an experiment in terms of its details or more generally (Wegner et al., 1986). Those who concentrated on the details were more susceptible to suggestions from others that they were either helping the experimenter by behaving altruistically or being selfish by seeking extra course credit. These participants who initially thought of their participation at relatively low levels came to accept these action identifications, and moreover, continued the emergent action by choosing to participate in subsequent activities that were consistent with the emergent act identity. Some of the effects of action identification are presented in Table 15.3.

There are several implications of action identification theory for other topics in social cognition. Action identification may influence the attributions made for performance. For example, when people enact behaviors at relatively low levels of action identification, they are attentive to situational context effects that may change the meaning of the behavior. Consequently, if such context effects occur, they may be more likely to make situational attributions for behavior. In contrast, when an action is identified at a high level, it may be perceived as dispositionally based because it is perceived as initiated and maintained by higher level personal goals rather than situational constraints (Vallacher & Wegner, 1987).

The theory also predicts that cross-situational inconsistency in behavior need not always lead to situational attributions. If an individual has identified an action at a high level, he or she is likely to view that behavior dispositionally despite a high degree of cross-situational flexibility in enacting the goal.

TABLE 15.3. The Effects of Action Identification

	Low Level of Identification	*High level of Identification*
Example	Bike riding	Getting exercise
Flexibility	Low (There is only one way to ride a bike)	High (There are many ways to get exercise)
Stability	Low (Action identifcation subject to context effects)	High
Impact of Context	Context may move identification to higher level (e.g., bike riding becomes labeled as getting exercise)	Little impact of context on level of identification
Disruption of Behavior Sequence	Disruption less likely to occur; when it does, action identification may move to lower level	Action identification shifts to lower level
Likelihood of Emergent Action	High, because low-level behavior is responsive to context effects	Low

Source: After Vallacher & Wegner (1987).

The theory of action identification also provides a useful perspective on the apparent consistency versus malleability of the self-concept (see Chapter 5). In particular, it suggests a resolution for those theories that argue that people maintain stability in their self-concepts but high degrees of variability in their behavior. Action identification theory suggests that only behaviors enacted at high levels will be perceived as consistent with or related to self-conceptions and that large numbers of behaviors apparently inconsistent with the self-concept will not be perceived as such because they are enacted at low levels of action identification and thereby judged by the person to have few or no implications for the self-concept. In a study by Wegner et al. (1986), participants were induced to generate five one-sentence descriptions of their behavior in either relatively low-level terms or relatively high-level terms. They were then given false feedback indicating that they were either cooperative or competitive. Participants who had been led to think about their behavior at lower levels agreed with the bogus feedback more than those who had been led to conceptualize their behavior at higher levels.

Finally, action identification theory also provides a useful perspective on the identification and measurement of traits, specifically, the relatively modest success that personality researchers have had in predicting behavior from traits. Action identification theory argues that people may perform an action for any of many reasons. Some of these will be at high-level identifications, which may correspond to particular traits or other dispositional qualities, but others of them will be at very low levels, which need not be related to personality traits (Vallacher & Wegner, 1987).

Situational Factors Mediate Cognition–Behavior Consistency

Situational factors influence the cognition–behavior relationship by making particular cognitions salient as guides for behavior. Suppose you are approached by a friend who asks you to help him collect signatures on a petition that allows freshmen and sophomores to have cars on campus. What do you do? If the friend tells you he is desperate because he promised to have 100 signatures by noon and has only 60 at 10 in the morning, you might help him out of friendship. On the other hand, if a classmate walks by muttering that there are too few parking spaces for the cars already on campus, you might reconsider, not wishing to alienate your peers. Similarly, if the parking petition is billed as a question of individual rights, you might be inclined to favor it, but if you have just read a newspaper editorial decrying the recent rise in air pollution in your community, you might not help out. This example illustrates that, in trying to examine the consistency question, one must ask, "Consistent with what? Social norms? Attitudes? Which set of attitudes?" Behavior is strongly influenced by situational factors that may make salient one set of cognitions over others, and one must know which concerns are salient before one can infer degree of consistency.

Attitude–behavior consistency will be affected by which meaning of a particular attitude or behavior is made salient by situational cues. In a study that examined this point, Prislin (1987) measured participants' attitudes toward capital punishment and then asked them to make a decision in a fictitious jury case. Participants were reminded to act either in line with their attitudes (high attitude relevance) or in line with the facts (low attitude relevance). They were also told that their decision could or could not influence the decision of a real jury (high versus low behavior relevance). When external factors made neither the implications of the attitude nor the behavior especially relevant, attitude–behavior relationships were strong. However, when external factors made either the attitude or behavior relevant or both, the correlation was substantially reduced. These context effects on behavior can be very subtle and may be induced even by subliminal priming in a prior context (Herr, 1986; Neuberg, 1989).

Social norms can be strong situational determinants of behavior that overwhelm seemingly relevant attitudes (e.g., Bentler & Speckart, 1981; Fishbein & Ajzen, 1975; LaPiere, 1934; Pagel & Davidson, 1984; S. H. Schwartz & Tessler, 1972). For example, asked if you would allow Sleazy Sam into your home, you may respond with some indignation that you would not, but if he shows up at your party as a guest's date, it is unlikely that you will turn him away. Your behavior will be consistent with the norms surrounding the host or hostess role, although it will not be consistent with your attitudes about Sam. Norms are likely to be especially salient when an audience is present and when one's attention is directed outward toward the situation (rather than toward oneself); under these circumstances, behavior is likely to be strongly affected by self-presentational concerns (Cialdini, Levy, Herman, & Evenbeck, 1973).

Other situational factors favor the use of prior attitudes as a basis for behavior. For example, if situational factors focus attention inward, a person is more likely to base his or her behavior on enduring attitudes (Wicklund, 1975): Attention to the self minimizes external influences and makes one's prior attitudes more salient (see S. E. Taylor & Fiske, 1978). When people's past behaviors that suggest a particular attitude are made salient, subsequent consistency between attitudes and behavioral intentions is high.

The priming of particular constructs also affects behavior. Making extraversion salient in a particular situation, for example, will increase expressions of extraversion among most people. However, people also differ in the extent to which a primed construct may fit their own self-conception. For example, an introverted person may behave in a more extraverted way if the primed norm for a situation calls for extraverted behavior, but as the salience of the norm of extraversion declines, the person may revert more to his or her chronically accessible self-perception of introversion. A person who considers the self neither extraverted nor introverted might, instead, remain sensitive to the behavior normative for the situation, even when the salience of that norm declines (see Bargh, Lombardi, & Higgins, 1988).

Attitudinal expression is heavily influenced by context. For example, in surveys assessing attitudes toward the Republican and Democratic parties, people are typically evenhanded and fair if they are asked to comment on the two parties at the same time. In contrast, when each political party is considered in isolation, the attitudes toward the two parties diverge (Schuman & Ludwig, 1983).

The overall implications are that attention to often random situational cues can reduce attitude–behavior consistency. Research consistent with this viewpoint has demonstrated the effects of lateral orientation on attitude–behavior consistency. Specifically, research suggests that when the left hemisphere is activated in right-handed participants, attitude–behavior consistency may be low, whereas with right-induced hemispheric activation, the attitude–behavior relation may be increased (Drake & Sobrero, 1987). This may occur because attention to the self is increased with relative left hemisphere activation, whereas attention to external stimuli is enhanced during a right hemisphere pattern of activation (Drake, 1986).

Why should seemingly trivial aspects of a situation have such a clear impact on people's behavior? Situationally induced salience can put relevant attitudes or norms in the mental foreground, making them more available as guides to action (Borgida & Campbell, 1982; C. A. Kiesler, Collins, & Miller, 1969; M. Snyder, 1977). What is salient defines the situation for the individual, reducing ambiguity and inconsistency (R. Norman, 1975); it tells you what should be relevant to your behavior if you are uncertain of what to do. Finally, when global attitudes or values are made salient, responsibility for behaving consistently with one's attitude will loom large (C. A. Kiesler, 1971; S. H. Schwartz, 1978). If cognition–behavior linkages are made salient, cognitions and behaviors may typically cohere, but when situational cues are salient, behavior may be consistent with those cues.

Individual Differences Mediate Consistency

The question, "Consistent with what?" becomes even more important when we examine the role of individual differences in cognition–behavior consistency. Some people show high consistency with social norms, whereas others behave consistently with their attitudes. Some people have an overriding social goal that is manifested chronically in their behavior, whereas others show more behavioral flexibility. We now turn to these individual difference factors.

A basic question in assessing trait–behavior and attitude–behavior relations concerns the extent to which people actually think about themselves in trait terms and see behavior as highly stable across situations. J. C. Wright and Mischel (1988) predicted and found evidence that both children and adults tend to view dispositional constructs as condition–behavior contingencies rather than as invariant traits that apply across a broad array of situations. For example, adults make dispositional attributions about others' behaviors but also modify them with conditional statements ("George is outgoing except with people he doesn't know."). One implication of this point is that people may see no need to behave in accordance with their personal dispositions, inasmuch as they perceive those dispositions as only conditionally relevant to particular situations. Thus one may believe that one is a friendly person but believe that returning the greeting of a roadside vagrant is not required by the disposition "friendly."

People who are inexperienced, incompetent, or unsure of their abilities within a given performance context are more concerned with the appropriate traits and characteristics for that performance than are experienced, capable performers (Cantor, Mackie, & Lord, 1983–1984). This focus on the competencies required in a given performance context may lead to greater attempts to be congruent with situational demands, though not necessarily performance that more closely matches situational demands, which may instead depend on competence (Mischel, 1984; Wicklund, 1986; Wicklund & Braun, 1987).

Self-Monitoring

> The Vaughts liked the engineer very much, each feeling that he was his or her special sort of person. And he was. Each saw him differently.
>
> Mr. Vaught was certain he was a stout Southern lad in the old style, well-born but lusty as anyone, the sort who knows how to get along with older men. Back home he would have invited the younger man on a hunt or to his poker club, where he was certain to be a favorite. The second time Mr. Vaught saw him, he took him aside ceremoniously and invited him to Jamie's birthday party.
>
> Jamie—who, he was told, had a severe and atypical mononucleosis—saw him as a fellow technician, like himself an initiate of science, that is, of a secret, shared view of the world, a genial freemasonry which sets itself apart from ordinary folk and sees behind appearances.
>
> To Mrs. Vaught elder he was as nice as he could be. His manners were good without being too ceremonial. There was a lightness in him: He knew how to fool with her. So acute was his radar that neither Mrs. Vaught nor her husband could quite get it into their heads that he did not know everything they knew. He sounded like he did.   (*Walker Percy, The Last Gentleman, 1966*)

We all know people who blend into social situations easily. They seem to know exactly what to do or say with each person. We also know people who are themselves, regardless of what situation they are in, who rarely bend to the norms of the social setting. Such different patterns are termed high and low self-monitoring, respectively (M. Snyder, 1979). Those who act as the situation demands are monitoring themselves with respect to the situation. Those who act on their own internal demands are not monitoring themselves with respect to the situation; they are low self-monitors (M. Snyder, 1974; M. Snyder & Campbell, 1982; M. Snyder & Monson, 1975; M. Snyder & Tanke, 1976).

Self-monitoring refers to the ways in which individuals plan, act out, and regulate behavioral decisions in social situations (M. Snyder & Cantor, 1980). Behavioral choices utilize a wide range of information, including knowledge of particular social settings and knowledge of one's own abilities, resources, and stable qualities. Snyder (1974) maintained that high self-monitors are particularly sensitive to social norms, to situations, and to interpersonal cues regarding how to behave. Low self-monitors, in contrast, are less responsive to these environmental cues and instead draw on salient information from their internal selves to decide how to behave. In essence, then, when faced with a new situation, high self-monitors ask, "What is the ideal person for this situation and how can I be it?" whereas low self-monitors ask, "How can I best be me in this situation?" (M. Snyder, 1979).

Self-monitoring is assessed by a scale (M. Snyder, 1972, 1974), some items of which appear in Table 15.4. First, answer the items in the table. If you answered "false" to items 1, 3, and 5, and "true" to items 2, 4, and 6, you would tend toward the high self-monitoring side. On the other hand, if the reverse pattern characterizes your answers, you tend to be a low self-monitor.

High self-monitors are, in many ways, more socially skilled than low self-monitors (e.g., Ickes & Barnes, 1977). They can communicate a wider range of emotional states, they learn more quickly how to behave in new situations, they are more likely to initiate conversations, and they have good self-control (see M. Snyder, 1979). When asked to adopt the behavior of another type of person—for example, a reserved, withdrawn, introverted type—high self-monitors are better at it than low self-monitors (Lippa, 1976), and they also appear to be better at discerning the meaning of nonverbal behavior than low self-monitors (see M. Snyder, 1979).

When their social outcomes depend on another person, such as a potential date, high self-monitors remember more about the other person and make more

---

TABLE 15.4. Sample Items Measuring Self-Monitoring

Answer the following items true or false.

1. I find it hard to imitate the behavior of other people.	T	F
2. I would probably make a good actor.	T	F
3. In a group of people, I am rarely the center of attention.	T	F
4. I may deceive people by being friendly when I really dislike them.	T	F
5. I can only argue for ideas which I already believe.	T	F
6. I can make impromptu speeches even on topics about which I have almost no information.	T	F

Source: After M. Snyder, The self-monitoring of expressive behavior. *Journal of Personality and Social Psychology,* 1974, *30,* 526–537. Copyright 1974 by the American Psychological Association. Adapted by permission.

confident and extreme inferences about the other (Berscheid et al., 1976). To the observer, the high self-monitor appears more friendly and less anxious than the low self-monitor (Lippa, 1976).

As might be expected, high self-monitors have great interest in social information, apparently because it is useful to them. They remember information about another person with whom they will interact better than do low self-monitors (see M. Snyder, 1974). High self-monitors are particularly able to construct images of prototypic individuals in particular domains (e.g., the classic extravert or the perfect princess) than are low self-monitors and are more likely to enter a social situation when norms are clear; low self-monitors, on the other hand, are more skilled at constructing images of themselves in particular situations (e.g., how they would behave in situations calling for extravertedness), and they are more likely to enter a social situation if it fits their self-conception (M. Snyder & Gangestad, 1981).

Given differences in the styles and informational preferences of high and low self-monitors, it should not be surprising that their behavior is under the control of different standards and forces. High self-monitors describe themselves as flexible, adaptive, shrewd individuals; when asked to explain the cause of their own behavior, they are likely to point to situational factors.[2] Low self-monitors, in contrast, see themselves as more consistent and principled than highs do, and they offer dispositional explanations for their behavior (e.g., M. Snyder, 1976). Low self-monitors are more likely to show the effects of temporary mood states or fatigue on their behavior than high self-monitors, who are better able to mask these sources of internal interference (e.g., Ajzen, Timko, & White, 1982). High self-monitors also appear to be more responsive to manipulations of public self-awareness (see Chapter 5), whereas low self-monitors are more sensitive to manipulations of private self-awareness (Webb, Marsh, Schneiderman, & Davis, 1989).

These differences in self-perception are also reflected behaviorally, and as such the self-monitoring dimension helps to unravel the cognition–behavior consistency problem. Because they behave consistently with social norms that vary from situation to situation, high self-monitors show little consistency across situations. After being induced to perform a counterattitudinal behavior, high self-monitors are less likely to infer new attitudes from the counterattitudinal behavior than are low self-monitors. Low self-monitors, on the other hand, show less situational variability in their behavior, and their future behavior can be better predicted from knowledge of their relevant cognitions (M. Snyder & Swann, 1976). Their attitudes seem to be more accessible than those of high self-monitoring individuals in that their response latencies to attitudinal inquiries are faster, suggesting that low self-monitoring individuals have stronger object-evaluation associations (Kardes et al., 1986). However, there are a few situations in which high self-monitors do show attitude–behavior consistency. When the relevance of personal attitudes to behavior is made salient, they are

---

[2]Described this way, high self-monitoring individuals appear to be quite Machiavellian. However, Ickes, Reidhead, and Patterson (1986) have suggested that people high in Machiavellianism are self-oriented in their impression management efforts, whereas self-monitoring reflects an other-oriented accommodation to situations.

consistent presumably because it is socially desirable to act on one's attitudes (M. Snyder & Kendzierski, 1982; cf. M. Snyder, 1982).

High and low self-monitoring individuals differ in what is important to them in personal relationships. A study that assessed preferences for romantic and nonromantic partners found that high self-monitoring individuals were more influenced by physical attractiveness of the potential partners, whereas low self-monitors were influenced more by the personality characteristics of potential partners. High self-monitoring individuals reported that they have had a greater number of romantic partners than low self-monitoring individuals, and low self-monitoring individuals reported having dated their current partner for longer than is true for high self-monitoring individuals. In addition, high self-monitoring individuals indicated that they were willing to terminate current relationships in favor of alternative partners more than low self-monitors. Finally, low self-monitors' relationships appear to become more intimate, suggesting that they are more committed to their relationships than are high self-monitors (M. Snyder & Simpson, 1984).

To summarize, some apparent cognition–behavior discrepancies result from stable long-term differences in the goals people have for social situations. In the case of self-monitoring, the cross-situational inconsistencies of the high self-monitor express an ability and willingness to become what is necessary to be successful in a given social setting; that is, a desire to be consistent with social norms. In contrast, the high cross-situational consistency of the low self-monitor reflects a commitment to enduring principles and beliefs and a desire to act in accord with them.

USING BEHAVIOR FOR IMPRESSION MANAGEMENT

People use their behavior to create certain impressions in others' minds (Nezlek & Leary, 2002). Sometimes a person has a clear idea of the image he or she wishes to present and conscientiously goes about creating it (Kowalski & Leary, 1990). Often this is guided by the desire to convey to others that one is a successful, attractive, and likeable person. There are many reasons for wanting to create a good impression, such as increasing one's personal power, obtaining desired results like a job or a promotion, gaining approval from others, and experiencing the intrinsic satisfaction of projecting a positive image.

Making a Positive Impression

How are positive impressions created? One strategy is *behavioral matching.* If a target other person is behaving modestly, usually the impression manager will do so as well, but if the target is behaving in a self-promoting manner, so will the impression manager (e.g., Newtson & Czerlinsky, 1974). Behavioral matching is often quite automatic and beyond personal control. Earlier we noted that people automatically mimic the nonverbal behaviors of others, and this kind of behavioral matching may also contribute to a positive impression.

Conforming to situational norms also helps to create an appropriate impression. At a wedding reception, for example, it is perfectly appropriate to make a ribald toast, but it is not typically appropriate to do so at a funeral, unless one is Irish.

Ingratiation, or flattery, refers to saying positive things about the target other (Jones & Pittman, 1982). On the whole this is a successful strategy for making a positive impression, although not when one's ingratiating motive is transparently clear or when the ingratiation is too excessive or goes on for too long. Flattery is most successful if it is centered on attributes that the target person values but on which the target questions his or her standing. For example, telling a prize-winning scientist that she is smart will likely have little effect because she already knows it, but telling her that she is charming may well have an intended effect if she values but doubts her social skills.

Self-presentation is not always effective. Self-promotion—conveying positive information about one's ability to others—can be a positive impression strategy, although as we noted in Chapter 5, it can sometimes backfire; people may see one as arrogant or conceited instead.

Sometimes the impression manager does the wrong thing. You may call a current romantic partner by the name of your previous partner, or spill your soup in your lap while having lunch with a boss. One way to handle a less than stellar behavioral performance is to give excuses (Kernis & Grannemann, 1990; C. R. Snyder & Higgins, 1988). Attributing one's failure to external, uncontrollable causes (such as blaming a late arrival on a flat tire) is typically a better strategy for managing an ineffective self-presentation than causes that are internal and under your control (such as not setting the alarm clock).

Self-Handicapping

A more desperate strategy for managing failure has been called *self-handicapping* (Baumeister & Scher, 1988; Berglas & Jones, 1978). People sometimes engage in actions that provide obstacles to success so that failure can later be attributed to those obstacles. The student who stays up all night before an exam can attribute his low grade to fatigue, not to lack of ability (McCrea & Hirt, 2001). Other people are not easily persuaded by self-handicapping strategies, however (Rhodewalt, Sanbonmatsu, Tschanz, Feick, & Waller, 1995).

There are two versions of the self-handicapping strategy. One is behavioral self-handicapping by which people create genuine handicaps such as fatigue, alcohol abuse, lack of punctuality, and inattention to excuse their failures. The other strategy is self-reported handicaps by which people claim to be ill, anxious, shy, or a victim of a traumatic incident in the hopes that such states might excuse poor performance. Table 15.5 presents some strategies of self-handicapping and other forms of self-presentation, the motives they may serve, and examples of the strategies.

One of the consequences of self-handicapping is that the impression one makes is poor. Although one may avoid a low ability attribution, the price can be high: One may look lazy, anxious, drunk, or stoned instead. Moreover, a further risk of poor self-presentation is that often impression management efforts are internalized: People come to believe that they are the way they act.

TABLE 15.5. Strategies of Self-Presentation

Type of Impression Effort	Possible Motives	Representative Strategies
Creating a positive impression	Increase one's power, obtain resources; obtain approval; validate a positive self-image; be liked	Match target's behavior, convey most positive image possible; conform to norms; appreciate or flatter target; appear to be consistent
Creating an ambiguous impression	Avoid stereotyping by others; maintain behavioral freedom; maintain self-esteem; save face	Engage in inconsistent behavior; provide multiple reasons for behavior; proclaim that everyone does it (i.e., muster consensus); leave the field; avoid evaluations
Controlling a negative impression	Control one's own and others' attributions for failure; avoid low-ability attributions; avoid own or others' disappointment over future anticipated failure	Exaggerate impediments to success; exert little effort; self-handicap (i.e., engage in self-destructive behavior, such as using drugs or drinking); proclaim one's failure to be due to external and/or unstable factors; make one's attributes ambiguous

Other Strategies of Impression Management

Social anxiety, depression, shyness, and low self-esteem also influence self-presentational styles by evoking a self-protective style (Arkin, 1987; Baumeister, Tice, & Hutton, 1989; Schlenker, 1987). This style is characterized by withdrawing in social interaction, specifically, initiating fewer conversations, talking less frequently, avoiding topics that might reveal ignorance, minimizing self-disclosure, and providing self-descriptions that are modest. This interaction style centers on pleasant behaviors such as agreeing with others or smiling and avoids disagreeing with others.

Sometimes people choose to obscure others' impressions of them. Being typed as a particular sort of person can reduce a sense of personal control over one's outcomes because it implies that one is no longer free to do the opposite. Under certain circumstances, people will muddy the waters by making their attributes ambiguous. A person might engage in an inconsistent behavior or provide reasons for a behavior so that others will discount the importance of stable personality factors. For example, if you plan a party for your dorm and it is hugely successful, you might want to indicate that luck was on your side and you happened to have some free time to avoid being handed the same responsibility a few months later.

USING BEHAVIOR TO TEST HYPOTHESES
ABOUT OTHERS

We learn about other people in many ways. Sometimes we hear about them from others before meeting them, or we may have hints about them based on the situations in which we encounter them. At other times we must start from scratch, assembling an impression through information gathered from observing and talking with the person. Regardless of how an impression of another is formed, we may quickly develop hypotheses concerning what the person is like. As we are interacting with the person, how will the hypotheses influence each one's behavior? Considerable research suggests that people behave toward others in ways that tend to confirm the hypotheses they hold about those others. Perceivers often employ behavioral strategies for eliciting information about others that preferentially supports their hypotheses.

How might this process work? Suppose you learn that Ed has just returned from Tahiti, and you quickly form an image of him as a carefree adventurer who seeks exotic places. In your subsequent interactions with him, you may inquire as to other trips he has taken or hobbies he has and learn that he once sailed the Virgin Islands with friends and fed sharks at Sea World as a summer job after high school. All this may seem fairly exotic, but note that you preferentially solicited information that confirmed this image. All of us have at least a few little things about us that make us quasi-exotic, and when those bits are elicited from us in their entirety, we look much more exciting than we really are. After dating Exotic Ed for several weeks, it may emerge that his company flew him to Tahiti for the conference, his uncle is the manager of Sea World and got him the summer job, and the "friends" with whom he sailed to the Virgin Islands were his grandparents. The point is that people have a large repertoire of behaviors and experiences, and when they are preferentially sampled by selective questioning, they may fit whatever hypothesis that selective questioning is designed to assess.

To demonstrate this point, M. Snyder and Swann (1978a) told college student participants they would be interviewing another student; half were told to find out if the other was an extravert (e.g., outgoing, sociable), and half were told to find out if the other was an introvert (e.g., shy and retiring). All participants were then given a set of questions measuring introversion and extraversion, and the students were told to pick a subset of questions they would ask. Participants who were told to assess extraversion preferentially selected a disproportionate number of extraversion questions (e.g., "What would you do if you wanted to liven things up at a party?"), and those told to assess introversion picked a disproportionate number of introversion questions (e.g., "What factors make it really hard for you to open up to people?"). These questions, in turn, made the target appear particularly extraverted or introverted, respectively, because he or she was providing only the sample of behavior relevant to the questions. This confirmatory hypothesis testing bias has been demonstrated many times (e.g., Slowiaczek, Klayman, Sherman, & Skov, 1992; Snyder, Campbell, & Preston, 1982). The bias exists whether the hypothesis concerns an individual's personality traits or characteristics based on group membership such as race, sex, or sexual preference. It occurs regardless of how the hypothesis originated, how likely it is to be true, and whether incentives for accuracy are offered to the hypothesis tester (see M. Snyder & Gangestad, 1981, for a review; see also Klayman & Ha, 1987; Skov & Sherman, 1986).

Perhaps more surprising is the fact that, even when people have fairly balanced information about another person, they may selectively draw on it to support a particular hypothesis. Imagine you are at a party and someone who is clearly infatuated with your roommate inquires selectively about all his or her desirable qualities. As you respond to these questions, you may find your own impression of your roommate improving in that you have highlighted for the questioner all positive attributes and none of the negative ones.

The implications of confirmatory hypothesis testing are not confined solely to the impressions individuals form about each other in casual social settings. Another study demonstrated the potential relevance of confirmatory hypothesis testing to courtroom situations, using the example of asking witnesses leading questions (Swann, Giuliano, & Wegner, 1982). Suppose, for example, that a lawyer asks you: "Tell the jury about the last time you got into a fight." The question itself may lead people to conclude that you have a history of aggressive behavior, whether or not you do. In fact, Swann, Giuliano, and Wegner found that the conjectures embodied in such leading questions can themselves be interpreted as evidence that the respondent engages in the behavior in question. Furthermore, being put in the position of answering such a leading question forces you to provide information that further confirms the behavior. Assuming you were in at least one fight in your life, you must now tell the jury about the details of the fight. Hence, leading questions are doubly biasing; the question itself is taken as evidence for the behavior (cf. Wegner, Wenzlaff, Kerker, & Beattie, 1981), and the answer provides further such evidence.

In sum, confirmatory hypothesis testing has been demonstrated under a fairly broad range of circumstances. It is important to note, however, that methodological factors may contribute to the demonstration of the confirmatory bias. First, the to-be-tested hypothesis is often made particularly salient to participants through a description of the hypothesis in question, for example, a portrait of extraversion (see Trope & Bassok, 1982). Thus people may select questions that tend to confirm preexisting hypotheses primarily because that hypothesis is especially salient to them. Second, in some studies the list of questions given to participants tests the hypothesis (e.g., extraversion), including a heavy proportion of questions that assume that the to-be-tested hypothesis is true. Instead of questions like, "Do you like parties?" (a question to which extraverts might respond yes and introverts no), the list includes questions like, "What would you do to liven up a party?" (a question to which both introverts and extraverts would be virtually forced to give information relevant only to extraversion). When participants are allowed to create their own questions to test a hypothesis, they rarely choose such biased questions.

There seems little doubt that confirmatory hypothesis testing sometimes occurs, but how general it is remains at issue. It seems most likely to occur if people have a single clear hypothesis in mind, are relatively certain of its correctness (Swann & Giuliano, 1987), and have available only leading questions to test their hypothesis. When people actually select leading questions is still at issue. Klayman and Ha (1987) suggested that the hypothesis-confirmation bias in social interaction is a manifestation of the more general tendency to test cases that are expected to have a property of interest rather than cases that will not show the property of interest (see Chapter 7 on heuristics). As such, the tendency may be quite strong. However, it is also clear that the way the task is framed, the type of questions that are available, the degree of certainty of the perceiver about the hypothesis, and whether or not an alternative hypothesis is available will moderate the tendency to selectively confirm hypotheses (Kruglanski & Mayseless, 1988; Skov & Sherman, 1986; Trope & Mackie, 1987).

Self-Fulfilling Prophecies: When Behavior Creates Reality

As just noted, confirmatory hypothesis testing can create misperceptions of a target person in the social perceiver's mind through highlighting information that selectively favors the presentation of particular attributes. When this hypothesis-testing process also succeeds in altering the target person's behavior in the direction of the hypothesis, a self-fulfilling prophecy is said to occur. An initially false definition of a situation, then, evokes behaviors that subsequently make the false belief true (Merton, 1957).

A classic demonstration of the self-fulfilling prophecy was done in a classroom situation (Rosenthal & Jacobson, 1968). Teachers were told at the beginning of a school year that certain of their students were potential late bloomers who, with proper nurturing and guidance, could be expected to excel. In fact, there was nothing to distinguish these students from their peers: They were randomly selected. However, several months later, when the so-called late bloomers' performance was examined, not only had their schoolwork improved but their IQs had actually increased. Numerous similar investigations, many conducted in classroom settings, testify to the robustness of this "Pygmalion" effect (see Rosenthal, 1974, for a review). It holds for many different types of expectations, target persons, and situations; both positive and negative expectations can create self-fulfilling prophecies.

How do self-fulfilling prophecies come about? Rosenthal has emphasized the importance of four factors in the Pygmalion effect. First, teachers given positive expectations about students no doubt created a warmer socioemotional climate than would be expected for students about whom they had lower expectations. Feedback is also important, in that teachers gave more differentiated feedback to the "special" students than to their average students. This differentiated feedback, both positive and negative, should help the student to learn correct and incorrect responses more successfully. The input factor refers to the tendency of teachers to try to teach more and more difficult material to the students about whom they held high expectations. Finally, teachers gave the students greater opportunity for responding (output), such as the chance to answer questions in class. These four factors appear to be important in the mediation of positive expectancies. An expectation is also more likely to lead to a self-fulfilling prophecy if the expectation is held by a high-status person (e.g., an authority figure or older, male individual) than if the target is of relatively lower status (Darley & Fazio, 1980).

Perhaps the most intriguing way in which an expectation can be transmitted from perceiver to target person is through nonverbal behaviors such as eye contact, posture, smiling, nodding, and body angle. For example, a study by Word, Zanna, and Cooper (1974) demonstrated that negative expectations communicated nonverbally by an interviewer actually caused an interviewee to perform more poorly (see also M. Snyder, Tanke, & Berscheid, 1977). A substantial amount of research on self-fulfilling prophecies implies that such effects are common (see Darley & Fazio, 1980, for a review). In fact, though, several critical steps are required for the effect to occur. As Figure 15.1 indicates, the perceiver must hold an expectation about a target and behave in a manner consistent with it. The target then interprets the behavior and responds to the perceiver with actions that are subsequently interpreted by the perceiver as consistent with the original expectation (Darley & Fazio, 1980).

It would seem that checks at each step could potentially erase any self-fulfilling prophecy. However, consider the links among the various steps. If the perceiver forms a positive expectation about the target and behaves accordingly, the target is likely to assume either that the perceiver especially likes him or her and has good taste or that the perceiver is a likable person; in either case, the target is likely to reciprocate the perceiver's behavior, which will set up the self-fulfilling prophecy. Suppose now that the perceiver holds a negative expectation about the target and behaves in a cold, aloof, or even hostile manner. The target may decide that the perceiver is an unpleasant person and reciprocate the negative behaviors, thus again establishing a self-fulfilling prophecy. Alternatively, either the perceiver or the target may decide to have nothing further to do with the other, terminate the interaction, and leave the interaction. Still, the self-fulfilling prophecy will remain intact. Biases in interpretation and recall may also occur, and a target's behavior that may not confirm a perceiver's

FIGURE 15.1. Development of a self-fulfilling prophecy
Source: After Darley and Fazio, 1980.

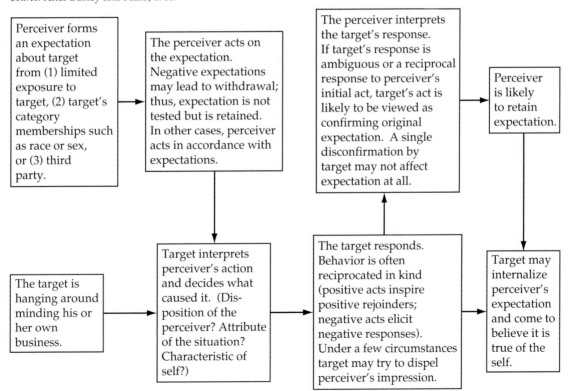

expectation may nonetheless be recalled or interpreted in a manner consistent with that expectation. Under these circumstances of cognitive distortion, the self-fulfilling prophecy will also remain intact.

Under what conditions can a self-fulfilling prophecy be undermined? There appear to be three main conditions. The goal to be accurate in the perception of a target undoes some of the behaviors usually associated with expectancy-based interactions (Neuberg, 1989). A second condition is when a perceiver "compensates" for the expectation he or she holds about a target; the third is when a target actively tries to dispel the perceiver's false expectations (self-verification).

When a perceiver holds a negative expectation about a target, such as the belief that the target is hostile or cold, the perceiver may compensate for, rather than reciprocate, the expected behavior. For example, if you expect that another person is hostile, rather than being hostile yourself (reciprocating behavior), you may decide to be extra nice (compensatory behavior), hoping that, in so doing, you may minimize the other's unpleasant behavior (see M. H. Bond, 1972; Ickes, Patterson, Rajecki, & Tanford, 1982; Shelton & Richeson, 2005; Swann & Snyder, 1980). Surprisingly though, even though the perceiver's compensatory behavior keeps the target from confirming the expectation, the expectation may nonetheless remain in the perceiver's mind (e.g., Ickes et al., 1982).

Why might this happen? As is well known from other work on theory-guided inferences and on hypothesis testing, behavior that is irrelevant to or even mildly inconsistent with prior expectations is often, nonetheless, interpreted as being consistent with prior expectations. Hence, a self-fulfilling prophecy can exist in a social perceiver's mind without it being true (see, for example, Ickes et al., 1982).

Target individuals themselves can also prevent the enactment of a self-fulfilling prophecy by refusing to be miscast into some role they feel does not fit. Each of us has no doubt had the experience of finding someone typing us in a way that does not feel correct; although one may play along temporarily, after a while one is inclined to disabuse him or her, by engaging in self-verification efforts to reaffirm one's own views of oneself. For example, if I find an acquaintance typing me as a workaholic who rarely has any fun, I will quickly do my best to counteract that impression. Such efforts may not always be successful. The target's belief about the self may be strong, but the perceiver's expectation about the target may be equally strong, thus creating a battle between the perceiver's efforts to confirm expectancies and the target's efforts to self-verify.

The conditions under which a perceiver abandons an incorrect expectation or a target comes to adopt a previously unheld self-attribute may depend on a variety of moderating conditions (Major, Cozzarelli, Testa, & McFarlin, 1988). One study found that in the battle between self-verification and expectancy confirmation effects, negative beliefs were more likely to change than positive beliefs (Major et al., 1988). Swann and Ely (1984) suggested another important condition that may moderate whether targets' self-perceptions or perceivers' behavioral expectations will win out in a social interaction; namely, certainty of one's opinions. They found that self-verification always occurred when targets were certain of their self-conceptions, and it tended to occur when both perceivers and targets were uncertain of their beliefs. Behavior confirmation—the tendency of the target to adopt behaviors related to the expectations held by the perceiver—occurred only when the perceivers were certain of their expectancies but the target was uncertain of his or her self-conception.

Research has suggested some other possibilities (Darley & Fazio, 1980): When the target believes that the perceiver's false impression is based on something the target did rather than on the perceiver's own personality or on forces in the situation, then the target may be more likely to attempt to correct the misimpression. Awareness of a perceiver's false hypothesis can also induce targets actively to overcome perceivers' expectations. Hilton and Darley (1985) found that when targets were informed that a future interaction partner had an impression of them as having a cold personality, they acted in ways designed to overcome the expectancy and were largely successful in these efforts.

Two other factors also appear to be critical in determining whether a target will attempt to dispel a perceiver's false impression. The first is how important the perceiver's impression is to the target. False impressions, especially negative ones, held by others important to the target are likely to prompt some dispelling action by the target. A second condition prompting targets to dispel a perceiver's false impression concerns how discrepant the perceiver's impression is from the target's own self-impression. Greater discrepancy prompts more efforts to undo the impression (see, for example, Baumeister & Jones, 1978). Of course, under some circumstances, the target may find the perceiver's false impression to be so desirable that the target will attempt to fit it and come to see the self as the perceiver does. This is perhaps the most extreme case of the self-fulfilling prophecy; that is, when not only the target's behavior but his or her own self-impression comes to fit the perceiver's initially false impression (Fazio, Effrein, & Falender, 1981; M. Snyder & Swann, 1978b).

Summary

How people behave in a situation depends upon how they define it and the personal goals they adopt for the situation. People show considerable flexibility in their ability to adjust their perceptions and behavioral strategies to the exigencies of a particular situation. Sometimes the self-regulation of behavior proceeds consciously and intentionally by making goals as well as the plans for achieving them explicit. People may deliberate their alternative courses of action fairly evenhandedly, but once they turn their attention to implementing their goals, cognitions often become overly optimistic. Nonetheless, these cognitions appear to be in service of goal pursuit, affecting persistence and ultimate achievement. Much goal-related self-regulation occurs automatically. However, people can change their goal achievement from conscious deliberative thinking to automatic behavior in part by forming explicit if-then implementation intentions that shift the control of action to automatic activation by situational cues.

Automatic evaluation of situational cues can occur extremely rapidly and evoke quite complex action sequences. Sometimes we assimilate our behavior to situational cues, for example, becoming more achievement oriented when others around us are doing so. At other times, contrast effects are seen: People do the opposite from behavior suggested by situational cues. The cues suggested by the salience of significant others may also activate goals and progress toward them.

The cognition–behavior relationship has been especially explored in the context of research on attitudes and behavior and the circumstances under which they cohere. Attitudes are more consistent with behaviors that are prototypic for those attitudes. Measuring attitudes and behavior at a comparable level of specificity also increases the strength of the relationship. Attitudes formed from direct experience, that are accessible, and that reflect self-interest or values predict behavior well. Focusing on the reasons underlying one's attitudes can reduce attitude–behavior consistency, although this tendency is also moderated by whether the behavior is an end in its own right or in service of another goal.

How behavior is labeled influences attitude–behavior consistency. Actions may be identified at relatively low levels, or they may be identified at higher levels. High-level behaviors tend to be seen as dispositionally based, but they also show considerable behavioral flexibility. Low-level actions, in contrast, may show stability across situations but may not be perceived as reflecting underlying dispositions. Situational factors moderate cognition–behavior consistency by making such factors as social norms or prior attitudes salient. And finally, individual differences in how people approach a situation (e.g., self-monitoring and self-consciousness) influence what attitudes will be salient and guide behavior.

People use their behavior to manage the impressions that other people form of them. Typically, a person strives to convey the most positive impression possible through such techniques as matching the target person's behaviors, flattering the target person, presenting the self positively through self-promotion efforts, or conforming to situational norms. When a poor impression is made or likely to be made, people make excuses or may self-handicap, engaging in or claiming liabilities that may account for their failure, such as fatigue, illness, or alcohol consumption.

Behavior can be used to test hypotheses about both the self and others. In such cases, people are somewhat biased to seek out information that confirms their hypotheses, within certain limits. This bias has the effect of making even conjectural or tentative hypotheses often look more true than they really are. Nonetheless, under some circumstances, testing a hypothesis about a target can lead the target to behave in ways that confirm the hypothesis; such alterations in reality are termed self-fulfilling prophecies. A self-fulfilling prophecy is most likely to occur if a high-status person holds some false positive impression toward a lower status target and behaves toward him or her with warm verbal and nonverbal behavior; under most circumstances, the target is likely to reciprocate the behavior, thus confirming the hypothesis. Negative expectations can also produce self-fulfilling prophecies, as when one individual expects another to be unpleasant, behaves unpleasantly in turn, and so elicits the very behavior from the target he or she anticipated. Potential self-fulfilling prophecies can be undermined if people feel miscast.

Overall, the close relationship between cognition and behavior is coming into view as well as some of its neural underpinnings. Top-down regulation by the prefrontal cortex and bottom-up modification of cognition via experience from the environment are becoming increasingly understood.

References

Aarts, H., Custers, R., & Wegner, D. M. (2005). On the inference of personal authorship: Enhancing experienced agency by priming effect information. *Consciousness and Cognition: An International Journal, 14,* 439–458.

Aarts, H., & Dijksterhuis, A. (2000). Habits as knowledge structures: Automaticity in goal-directed behavior. *Journal of Personality and Social Psychology, 78,* 53–63.

Aarts, H., & Dijksterhuis, A. (2003). The silence of the library: Environment, situational norm, and social behavior. *Journal of Personality and Social Psychology, 84,* 18–28.

Aarts, H., Gollwitzer, P. M., & Hassin, R. R. (2004). Goal contagion: Perceiving is for pursuing. *Journal of Personality and Social Psychology, 87,* 23–37.

Abelson, R. P. (1976). Script processing in attitude formation and decision making. In J. S. Carroll & J. W. Payne (Eds.), *Cognition and social behavior* (pp. 33–46). Hillsdale, NJ: Erlbaum.

Abelson, R. P. (1981). The psychological status of the script concept. *American Psychologist, 36,* 715–729.

Abelson, R. P. (1988). Conviction. *American Psychologist, 43,* 267–275.

Abelson, R. P., Aronson E., McGuire, W. J., Newcomb, T. M., Rosenberg, M. J., & Tannebaum, P. H. (Eds.). (1968). *Theories of cognitive consistency: A sourcebook.* Chicago: Rand McNally.

Abelson, R. P., & Gross, P. H. (1987). The strength of conjunctive explanations. *Personality and Social Psychology Bulletin, 13,* 141–155.

Abelson, R. P., Kinder, D. R., Peters, M. D., & Fiske, S. T. (1982). Affective and semantic components in political person perception. *Journal of Personality and Social Psychology, 42,* 619–630.

Abelson, R. P., & Levi, A. (1985). Decision making. In G. Lindzey & E. Aronson (Eds.), *Handbook of Social Psychology* (pp. 231–309). New York: Random House.

Abelson, R. P., & Prentice, D. A. (1989). Beliefs as possessions: A functional perspective. In A. R. Pratkanis, S. J. Breckler, & A. G. Greenwald (Eds.), *Attitude, structure and function* (pp. 361–382). Hillsdale, NJ: Erlbaum.

Aberson, C. L., Healy, M., & Romero, V. (2000). Ingroup bias and self-esteem: A meta-analysis. *Personality and Social Psychology Review, 4,* 157–173.

Ackerman, J. M., Shapiro, J. R., Neuberg, S. L., Kenrick, D. T., Becker, D. V., Griskevicius, V., Maner, J. K., & Schaller, M. (2006). They all look the same to me (unless they're angry): From out-group homogeneity to out-group heterogeneity. *Psychological Science, 17,* 836–840.

Adolphs, R. (2002). Recognizing emotion from facial expressions: Psychological and neurological mechanisms. *Behavioral and Cognitive Neuroscience Reviews, 1,* 21–62.

Adorno, T. W., Frenkel-Brunswik, E., Levinson, D. J., & Sanford, R. N. (1950). *The authoritarian personality.* New York: Harper.

A gift for vividness. (1980, October 20). *Time,* p. 68.

Agostinelli, G., Sherman, S. J., Presson, C. C., & Chassin, L. (1992). Self-perception and self-enhancement biases in estimates of population prevalence. *Personality and Social Psychology Bulletin, 18,* 631–642.

Aharon, I., Etcoff, N. L., Ariely, D., Chabris, C. F., O'Connor, E., & Breiter H. C. (2001). Beautiful faces have variable reward value: fMRI and behavioral evidence. *Neuron, 8* (32), 537–551.

Ajzen, I. (1977). Intuitive theories of events and the effects of baserate information on prediction. *Journal of Personality and Social Psychology, 35,* 303–314.

Ajzen, I. (1987). Attitudes, traits, and actions: Dispositional prediction of behavior in personality and social psychology. In L. Berkowitz (Ed.), *Advances in experimental social psychology* (Vol. 20, pp. 1–64). San Diego, CA: Academic Press.

Ajzen, I. (1988). *Attitudes, personality, and behavior.* Chicago, IL: The Dorsey Press.

Ajzen, I. (2001). Nature and operation of attitudes. *Annual Review of Psychology, 52,* 27–58.

Ajzen, I., & Fishbein, M. (1977). Attitude-behavior relations: A theoretical analysis and review of empirical research. *Psychological Bulletin, 84,* 888–918.

Ajzen, I., & Fishbein, M. (1980). *Understanding attitudes and predicting social behavior.* Englewood Cliffs, NJ: Prentice-Hall.

Ajzen, I., & Sexton, J. (1999). Depth of processing, belief congruence, and attitude-behavior correspondence. In S. Chaiken & Y. Trope (Eds.), *Dual-process theories in social psychology* (pp. 117–138). New York: Guilford Press.

Ajzen, I., Timko, C., & White, J. B. (1982). Self-monitoring and the attitude-behavior relation. *Journal of Personality and Social Psychology, 42,* 426–435.

Albarracín, D. (2002). Cognition in persuasion: An analysis of information processing in response to persuasive communications. In M. P. Zanna (Ed.), *Advances in experimental social psychology* (Vol. 34, pp. 61–130). San Francisco, CA: Academic Press.

Albarracín, D., Johnson, B. T., & Zanna, M. P. (Eds). (2005). *The handbook of attitudes.* Hillsdale, NJ: Erlbaum.

Albarracín, D., & Kumkale, G. T. (2003). Affect as information in persuasion: A model of affect identification and discounting. *Journal of Personality and Social Psychology, 84,* 453–469.

Albarracín, D., & Wyer, R. S., Jr. (2001). Elaborative and nonelaborative processing of a behavior-related communication. *Personality and Social Psychology Bulletin, 27,* 691–705.

Aldrich, J. H., Sullivan, J. L., & Borgida, E. (1989). Foreign affairs and issue voting: Do presidential candidates "waltz before a blind audience"? *American Political Science Review, 83,* 123–141.

Alexander, M. G., Brewer, M. B., & Hermann, R. K. (1999). Images and affect: A functional analysis of out-group stereotypes. *Journal of Personality and Social Psychology, 77,* 78–93.

Alexander, M. G., Brewer, M. B., & Livingston, R. W. (2005). Putting stereotype content in context: Image theory and interethnic stereotypes. *Personality and Social Psychology Bulletin, 31,* 781–794.

Alicke, M. D. (1985). Global self-evaluations as determined by the desirability and controllability of trait adjectives. *Journal of Personality and Social Psychology, 49,* 1621–1630.

Alicke, M. D., & Largo, E. (1995). The role of self in the false consensus effect. *Journal of Experimental Social Psychology, 31,* 28–47.

Allison, S. T., & Messick, D. M. (1988). The feature-positive effect, attitude strength, and degree of perceived consensus. *Personality and Social Psychology Bulletin, 14,* 231–241.

Alloy, L. B., & Tabachnik, N. (1984). Assessment of covariation by humans and animals: The joint influence of prior expectations and current situational information. *Psychological Review, 91,* 112–149.

Allport, G. W. (1935). Attitudes. In C. Murchison (Ed.), *Handbook of social psychology* (pp. 798–844). Worcester, MA: Clark University Press.

Allport, G. W. (1954). *The nature of prejudice.* Reading, MA: Addison-Wesley.

Altemeyer, B. (1981). *Right-wing authoritarianism.* Winnipeg, Canada: University of Manitoba Press.

Altemeyer, B. (1988). *Enemies of freedom: Understanding right-wing authoritarianism.* San Francisco, CA: Jossey-Bass.

Altemeyer, B. (2004). Highly dominating, highly authoritarian personalities. *Journal of Social Psychology, 144,* 421–447.

Ambady, N., Paik, S. K., Steele, J., Owen-Smith, A., & Mitchell, J. P. (2004). Deflecting negative self-relevant stereotype activation: The effects of individuation. *Journal of Experimental Social Psychology, 40,* 401–408.

Ambady, N., & Rosenthal, R. (1993). Half a minute: Predicting teacher evaluations from thin slices of nonverbal behavior and physical attractiveness. *Journal of Personality and Social Psychology, 64,* 431–441.

Amiot, C. E., & Bourhis, R. Y. (2005). Ideological beliefs as determinants of discrimination in positive and negative outcome distributions. *European Journal of Social Psychology, 35,* 581–598.

Amodio, D. M., & Devine, P. G. (2006). Implicit stereotyping vs. evaluative race bias. *Journal of Personality and Social Psychology, 91,* 652–661.

Amodio, D. M., & Frith, C. D. (2006). Meeting of minds: The medial frontal cortex and social cognition. *Nature Reviews Neuroscience, 7,* 268–277

Amodio, D. M., Harmon-Jones, E., & Devine, P. G. (2003). Individual differences in the activation and control of affective race bias as assessed by startle eyeblink response and self-report. *Journal of Personality and Social Psychology, 84,* 738–753.

Amodio, D. M., Harmon-Jones, E., Devine, P. G., Curtin, J. J., Hartley, S. L., & Covert, A. E. (2004). Neural signals for the detection of unintentional race bias. *Psychological Science, 15,* 88–93.

Amodio, D. M., Shah, J. Y, Sigelman, J., Brazy, P. C., & Harmon-Jones, E. (2004). Implicit regulatory focus associated with asymmetrical frontal cortical activity. *Journal of Experimental Social Psychology, 40,* 225–232.

Andersen, S. M., & Chen, S. (2002). The relational self: An interpersonal social-cognitive theory. *Psychological Review, 109,* 619–645.

Andersen, S. M., & Klatzky, R. L. (1987). Traits and social stereotypes: Levels of categorization in person perception. *Journal of Personality and Social Psychology, 53,* 235–246.

Andersen, S. M., Reznik, I., & Manzella, L. M. (1996). Eliciting facial affect, motivation, and expectancies in transference: Significant-other representations in social relations. *Journal of Personality and Social Psychology, 71,* 1108–1129.

Anderson, A. K., & Phelps, E. A. (2001). Lesions of the human amygdala impair enhanced perception of emotionally salient events. *Nature, 411,* 305–309.

Anderson, C. A. (1983). Abstract and concrete data in the perseverance of social theories: When weak data lead to unshakeable beliefs. *Journal of Experimental Social Psychology, 19,* 93–108.

Anderson, C. A., & Godfrey, S. S. (1987). Thoughts about actions: The effects of specificity and availability of imagined behavioral scripts on expectations about oneself and others. *Social Cognition, 5,* 238–258.

Anderson, C. A., Lepper, M. R., & Ross, L. D. (1980). Perseverance of social theories: The role of explanation in the persistence of discredited information. *Journal of Personality and Social Psychology, 39,* 1037–1049.

Anderson, J. R. (1976). *Language, memory, and thought.* Hillsdale, NJ: Erlbaum.

Anderson, J. R. (1980). *Cognitive psychology and its implications.* San Francisco, CA: Freeman.

Anderson, J. R. (1990). *Cognitive psychology and its implications* (3rd ed.). New York: Freeman.

Anderson, J. R., Bothell, D., Byrne, M. D., Douglass, S., Lebiere, C., & Qin, Y. (2004). An integrated theory of the mind. *Psychological Review, 111,* 1036–1060.

Anderson, N. H. (1981). *Foundations of information integration theory.* New York: Academic Press.

Anderson, N. H. (1989). Information integration approach to emotions and their measurement. In R. Pluchik & H. Kellerman (Eds.), *Emotion: Theory, research, and experience* (Vol. 4, pp. 133–186). New York: Academic Press.

Anderson, N. H., & Hubert, S. (1963). Effects of concomitant verbal recall on order effects in personality impression formation. *Journal of Verbal Learning and Verbal Behavior, 2,* 379–391.

Antrobus, J. S., Fein, G., Goldstein, S., & Singer, J. L. (1989). Mindwandering: Time-sharing task-irrelevant thought and imagery with experimental tasks. Unpublished manuscript.

Antrobus, J. S., Singer, J. L., Goldstein, S., & Fortgang, M. (1970). Mindwandering and cognitive structure. *Transactions of the New York Academy of Sciences, 32*, 242–252.

Apsler, R. & Sears, D. O. (1968). Warning, personal involvement, and attitude change. *Journal of Personality and Social Psychology, 9*, 162–166.

Areni, C. S., & Lutz, R. J. (1988). The role of argument quality in the elaboration likelihood model. *Advances in Consumer Research, 15*, 197–203.

Argyle, M., & Crossland, J. (1987). The dimensions of positive emotions. *British Journal of Social Psychology, 26*, 127–137.

Aristotle. (1931). On memory and recollection. In W. D. Ross (Ed.), J. I. Beare (trans.), *The works of Aristotle*. Oxford: Clarendon Press.

Arkes, H. R., & Harkness, A. R. (1980). Effect of making a diagnosis on subsequent recognition of symptoms. *Journal of Experimental Social Psychology: Human Learning and Memory, 6*, 568–575.

Arkes, H. R., & Tetlock, P. E. (2004). Attributions of implicit prejudice, or "Would Jesse Jackson 'Fail' the Implicit Association Test?" *Psychological Inquiry, 15*, 257–278.

Arkin, R. M. (1987). Shyness and self-presentation. In K. Yardley & T. Honess (Eds.), *Self and identity: Psychosocial perspectives* (pp. 187–195). London: Wiley.

Arkin, R. M., Cooper, H. M., & Kolditz, T. A. (1980). A statistical review of the literature concerning the self-serving attribution bias in interpersonal influence situations. *Journal of Personality, 48*, 435–448.

Armitage, C. J., & Conner, M. (2000). Attitudinal ambivalence: A test of three key hypotheses. *Personality and Social Psychology Bulletin, 26*, 1421–1432.

Armor, D. A., & Sackett, A. M. (2006). Accuracy, error, and bias in predictions for real versus hypothetical events. *Journal of Personality and Social Psychology, 91*, 583–600.

Armor, D. A., & Taylor, S. E. (1998). Situated optimism: Specific outcome expectancies and self-regulation. In M. P. Zanna (Ed.), *Advances in experimental social psychology* (Vol. 30, pp. 309–379). New York: Academic Press.

Armor, D. A., & Taylor, S. E. (2003). The effects of mindset on behavior: Self-regulation in deliberative and implemental frames of mind. *Personality and Social Psychology Bulletin, 29*, 86–95.

Arndt, J., Schimel, J., Greenberg, J., & Pyszczynski, T. (2002). The intrinsic self and defensiveness: Evidence that activating the intrinsic self reduces self-handicapping and conformity. *Personality and Social Psychology Bulletin, 28*, 671–683.

Arnold, M. B. (1945). Physiological differentiation of emotional states. *Psychological Review, 52*, 35–48.

Arnold, M. B. (1970). Perennial problems in the field of emotion. In M. B. Arnold (Ed.), *Feelings and emotions: The Loyola Symposium*. New York: Academic Press.

Aronson, J., Blanton, H., & Cooper, J. (1995). From dissonance to disidentification: Selectivity in the self-affirmation process. *Journal of Personality and Social Psychology, 68*, 986–996.

Aronson, J., Fried, C. B., & Good, C. (2002). Reducing the effects of stereotype threat on African American college students by shaping theories of intelligence. *Journal of Experimental Social Psychology, 38*, 113–125.

Aronson, J., Lustina, M. J., Good, C., Keough, K., Steele, C. M., & Brown, J. (1999). When White men can't do math: Necessary and sufficient factors in stereotype threat. *Journal of Experimental Social Psychology, 35*, 29–46.

Asch, S. E. (1946). Forming impressions of personality. *Journal of Abnormal and Social Psychology, 41*, 1230–1240.

Ashburn-Nardo, L., Voils, C. I., & Monteith, M. J. (2001). Implicit associations as the seeds of intergroup bias: How easily do they take root? *Journal of Personality and Social Psychology, 81*, 789–799.

Ashby, F. G., & Maddox, W. T. (2005). Human category learning. *Annual Review of Psychology, 56*, 149–178.

Aspinwall, L. G., & Brunhart, S. M. (1996). Distinguishing optimism from denial: Optimistic beliefs predict attention to health threats. *Personality and Social Psychology Bulletin, 22*, 993–1003.

Asuncion, A. G., & Lam, W. F. (1995). Affect and impression formation: Influence of mood on person memory. *Journal of Experimental Social Psychology, 31*, 437–464.

Augoustinos, M., & Walker, I. (1995). *Social cognition: An integrated introduction*. Thousand Oaks, CA: Sage.

Averill, J. R. (1980). On the paucity of positive emotions. In K. Blankstein, P. Pliner, & J. Polivy (Eds.), *Advances in the study of communication and affect, Vol. 6. Assessment and modification of emotional behavior* (pp. 7–45). New York: Plenum Press.

Averill, J. R. (1983). Studies on anger and aggression: Implications for theories of emotion. *American Psychologist, 38*, 1145–1160.

Averill, J. R. (1990a). Emotions as episodic dispositions, cognitive schemas, and transitory social roles: Steps toward an integrated theory of emotion. In D. J. Ozer, J. M. Healy Jr., & A. J. Stewart (Eds.), *Perspectives in personality (Vol. 3a): Self and emotion*. Greenwich, CT: JAI Press.

Averill, J. R. (1990b). Emotions in relation to systems of behavior. In N. L. Stein, B. Leventhal, & T. Trabasso (Eds.), *Psychological and biological approaches to emotion*. Hillsdale, NJ: Erlbaum.

Averill, J. R. (1990c). Inner feelings, works of the flesh, the beast within, diseases of the mind, driving force, and putting on a show: Six metaphors of emotion and their theoretical extensions. In D. Leary (Ed.), *Metaphors in the history of psychology*. Cambridge, MA: Cambridge University Press.

Ax, A. F. (1953). Physiological differentiation of emotional states. *Psychosomatic Medicine, 15*, 433–442.

Axsom, D., Yates, S., & Chaiken, S. (1987). Audience response as a heuristic cue in persuasion. *Journal of Personality and Social Psychology, 53*, 30–40.

Babey, S. H., Queller, S., & Klein, S. B. (1998). The role of expectancy violating behaviors in the representation of trait knowledge: A summary-plus-exception model of social memory. *Social Cognition, 16*, 287–339.

Banaji, M. R., Nosek, B. A., & Greenwald, A. G. (2004). No place for nostalgia in science: A response to Arkes and Tetlock. *Psychological Inquiry, 15*, 279–310.

Bandura, A. (1982). Self-efficacy mechanism in human agency. *American Psychologist, 37*, 122–147.

Bandura, A. (2006). Toward a psychology of human agency. *Perspectives on Psychological Science, 1*, 164–180.

Banfield, J. F., Wyland, C. L., Macrae, C. N., Münte, T. F., & Heatherton, T. F. (2004). The cognitive neuroscience of self-regulation. In R. F. Baumeister & K. D. Vohs (Eds.), *Handbook of self-regulation: Research, theory, and applications* (pp. 62–83). New York: Guilford Press.

Banks, R. R., & Eberhardt, J. L. (1998). Social psychological processes and the legal bases of racial categorization. In J. L. Eberhardt & S. T. Fiske (Eds.), *Confronting racism: The problem and the response* (pp. 54–75). Thousand Oaks, CA: Sage.

Barclay, A. M. (1970). The effect of female aggressive and sexual fantasies. *Journal of Projective Techniques and Personality Assessment, 34*, 19–26.

Barclay, A. M., & Haber, R. N. (1965). The relation of aggressive to sexual motivation. *Journal of Personality, 33*, 462–475.

Barden, R. C., Garber, J., Leiman, B., Ford, M. E., & Masters, J. C. (1985). Factors governing the effective remediation of negative affect and its cognitive and behavioral consequences. *Journal of Personality and Social Psychology, 49*, 1040–1053.

Bargh, J. A. (1984). Automatic and conscious processing of social information. In R. S. Wyer Jr. & T. K. Srull (Eds.), *Handbook of social cognition* (Vol. 3, pp. 1–44). Hillsdale, NJ: Erlbaum.

Bargh, J. A. (1988). Automatic information processing: Implications for communication and affect. In L. Donhew, H. E. Sypher, & E. T. Higgins (Eds.), *Communication, social cognition, and affect*. Hillsdale, NJ: Erlbaum.

Bargh, J. A. (1997). The automaticity of everyday life. In R. S. Wyer Jr. (Ed.), *The automaticity of everyday life* (pp. 1–62). Mahwah, NJ: Erlbaum.

Bargh, J. A. (1999). The cognitive monster: The case against the controllability of automatic stereotype effects. In S. Chaiken & Y. Trope (Eds.), *Dual-process theories in social psychology* (pp. 361–382). New York: Guilford Press.

Bargh, J. A., Bond, R. N., Lombardi, W. J., & Tota, M. E. (1986). The additive nature of chronic and temporary sources of construct accessibility. *Journal of Personality and Social Psychology, 50*, 869–879.

Bargh, J. A., Chaiken, S., Govender, R., & Pratto, F. (1992). The generality of the automatic attitude activation effect. *Journal of Personality and Social Psychology, 62,* 893–912.

Bargh, J. A., Chaiken, S., Raymond, P., & Hymes, C. (1996). The automatic evaluation effect: Unconditional automatic attitude activation with a pronunciation task. *Journal of Experimental Social Psychology, 32,* 104–128.

Bargh, J. A., Chen, M., & Burrows, L. (1996). Automaticity of social behavior: Direct effects of trait construct and stereotype activation on action. *Journal of Personality and Social Psychology, 71,* 230–244.

Bargh, J. A., Gollwitzer, P. M., Lee-Chai, A., Barndollar, K., & Trötschel, R. (2001). The automated will: Nonconscious activation and pursuit of behavioral goals. *Journal of Personality and Social Psychology, 81,* 1014–1027.

Bargh, J. A., Lombardi, W. J., & Higgins, E. T. (1988). Automaticity of chronically accessible constructs in person X situation effects on person perception: It's just a matter of time. *Journal of Personality and Social Psychology, 55,* 599–605.

Bargh, J. A., & Pietromonaco, P. (1982). Automatic information processing and social perception: The influence of trait information presented outside of conscious awareness on impression formation. *Journal of Personality and Social Psychology, 43,* 437–449.

Bargh, J. A., & Pratto, F. (1986). Individual construct accessibility and perceptual selection. *Journal of Experimental Social Psychology, 22,* 293–311.

Bargh, J. A., & Thein, R. D. (1985). Individual construct accessibility, person memory, and the recall-judgment link: The case of information overload. *Journal of Personality and Social Psychology, 49,* 1129–1146.

Bargh, J. A., & Tota, M. E. (1988). Context-dependent automatic processing in depression: Accessibility of negative constructs with regard to self but not others. *Journal of Personality and Social Psychology, 54,* 925–939.

Bargh, J. A., & Williams, E. L. (2006). The automaticity of social life. *Current Directions in Psychological Science, 15,* 1– 4.

Bar-Hillel, M. (1980). The base-rate fallacy in probability judgments. *Acta Psychologica, 44,* 211–233.

Bar-Hillel, M., & Fischhoff, B. (1981). When do base rates affect predictions? *Journal of Personality and Social Psychology, 41,* 671–680.

Baron, R. A. (1977). *Human aggression.* New York: Plenum Press.

Baron, R. A. (1997). The sweet smell of . . . helping: Effects of pleasant ambient fragrance on prosocial behavior in shopping malls. *Personality and Social Psychology Bulletin, 23,* 498–503.

Baron, R. M. (1980). Contrasting approaches to social knowing: An ecological perspective. *Personality and Social Psychology Bulletin, 6,* 590–600.

Baron, R. M. (1988). An ecological framework for establishing a dual-mode theory of social knowing. In D. Bar-Tal & A. W. Kruglanski (Eds.), *The social psychology of knowledge* (pp. 48–82). New York: Cambridge University Press.

Barrett, L. F. (2006). Solving the emotion paradox: Categorization and the experience of emotion. *Personality and Social Psychology Review, 10,* 20–46.

Barrett, L. F., & Russell, J. A. (1999). The structure of current affect: Controversies and emerging consensus. *Current Directions in Psychological Science, 8,* 10–14.

Barrett, L. F., Tugade, M. M., & Engle, R. W. (2004). Individual differences in working memory capacity and dual-process theories of the mind. *Psychological Bulletin, 130,* 553–573.

Barrett, L. F., & Wager, T. D. (2006). The structure of emotion: Evidence from neuroimaging studies. *Current Directions in Psychological Science, 15,* 79–83.

Barsalou, L. W. (1985). Ideals, central tendency, and frequency of instantiation as determinants of graded structure in categories. *Journal of Experimental Psychology: Learning, Memory, and Cognition, 11,* 629–654.

Barsalou, L. W. (1999a). Language comprehension: Archival memory or preparation for situated action? *Discourse Processes, 28,* 61–80.

Barsalou, L. W. (1999b). Perceptual symbol systems. *Behavioral and Brain Sciences, 22,* 577–660.

Bartlett, M. Y., & DeSteno, D. (2006). Gratitude and prosocial behavior: Helping when it costs you. *Psychological Science, 17,* 319–325.

Bassili, J. N., & Krosnick, J. A. (2000). Do strength-related attitude properties determine susceptibility to response effects? New evidence from response latency, attitude extremity, and aggregate indices. *Political Psychology, 21,* 107–132.

Bastian, B., & Haslam, N. (2006). Psychological essentialism and stereotype endorsement. *Journal of Experimental Social Psychology, 42,* 228–235.

Baumeister, R. F., Campbell, J. D., Krueger, J. I., & Vohs, K. D. (2003). Does high self-esteem cause better performance, interpersonal success, happiness, or healthier lifestyles? *Psychological Science in the Public Interest, 4,* 1–44.

Baumeister, R. F., DeWall, C. N., Ciarocco, N. J., & Twenge, J. M. (2005). Social exclusion impairs self-regulation. *Journal of Personality and Social Psychology, 88,* 589–604.

Baumeister, R. F., & Jones, E. E. (1978). When self-presentation is constrained by the target's knowledge. *Journal of Personality and Social Psychology, 36,* 608–618.

Baumeister, R. F., & Leary, M. R. (1995). The need to belong: Desire for interpersonal attachments as a fundamental human motivation. *Psychological Bulletin, 117,* 497–529.

Baumeister, R. F., & Scher, S. J. (1988). Self-defeating behavior patterns among normal individuals: Review and analysis of common self-destructive tendencies. *Psychological Bulletin, 104,* 3–22.

Baumeister, R. F., Smart, L., & Boden, J. M. (1996). Relation of threatened egotism to violence and aggression: The dark side of high self-esteem. *Psychological Review, 103,* 5–33.

Baumeister, R. F., Tice, D. M., & Hutton, D. G. (1989). Self-presentational motivations and personality differences in self-esteem. *Journal of Personality, 57,* 547–579.

Baumgardner, A. H., & Arkin, R. M. (1988). Affective state mediates causal attributions for success and failure. *Motivation and Emotion, 12,* 99–111.

Baumgardner, A. H., Lake, E. A., & Arkin, R. M. (1985). Claiming mood as a self-handicap: The influence of spoiled and unspoiled public identities. *Personality and Social Psychology Bulletin, 11,* 349–357.

Beauregard, K. S., & Dunning, D. (1998). Turning up the contrast: Self-enhancement motives prompt egocentric contrast effects in social judgments. *Journal of Personality and Social Psychology, 74,* 606–621.

Bechara, A., Damasio, A. R., Damasio, H., & Anderson, S. W. (1994). Insensitivity to future consequences following damage to human prefrontal cortex. *Cognition, 50,* 7–15.

Beer, J. S., Heerey, E. A., Keltner, D., Scabini, D., & Knight, R. T. (2003). The regulatory function of self-conscious emotion: Insights from patients with orbitofrontal damage. *Journal of Personality and Social Psychology, 85,* 594–604.

Bem, D. J. (1967). Self-perception: An alternative interpretation of cognitive dissonance phenomena. *Psychological Review, 74,* 183–200.

Bem, D. J. (1972). Self-perception theory. In L. Berkowitz (Ed.), *Advances in experimental social psychology* (Vol. 6, pp. 1–62). New York: Academic Press.

Bem, D. J., & McConnell, H. K. (1970). Testing the self-perception explanation of dissonance phenomena: On the salience of premanipulation attitudes. *Journal of Personality and Social Psychology, 14,* 23–31.

Bem, S. L. (1993). *The lenses of gender: Transforming the debate on sexual inequality.* New Haven: Yale University Press.

Benesh, M., & Weiner, B. (1982). On emotion and motivation: From the notebooks of Fritz Heider. *American Psychologist, 37,* 887–895.

Bentler, P. M., & Speckart, G. (1981). Attitudes cause behaviors: A structural equation analysis. *Journal of Personality and Social Psychology, 40,* 226–238.

Ben-Zeev, T., Fein, S., & Inzlicht, M. (2005). Arousal and stereotype threat. *Journal of Experimental Social Psychology, 41,* 174–181.

Berger, S. M., & Lambert, W. W. (1968). Stimulus-response theory in contemporary social psychology. In G. Lindzey & E. Aronson (Eds.), *The handbook of social psychology* (Vol. 1, 2nd ed.). Reading, MA: Addison-Wesley.

Berglas, S., & Jones, E. E. (1978). Drug choice as a self-handicapping strategy in response to noncontingent success. *Journal of Personality and Social Psychology, 36,* 405–417.

Berk, M. S., & Andersen, S. M. (2000). The impact of past relationships on interpersonal behavior: Behavioral confirmation in the social-cognitive process of transference. *Journal of Personality and Social Psychology, 79,* 546–562.

Berkowitz, L. (1974). Some determinants of impulsive aggression: Role of mediated associations with reinforcements for aggression. *Psychological Review, 81,* 165–176.

Berlyne, D. E. (1970). Novelty, complexity, and hedonic value. *Perception and Psychophysics, 8,* 279–286.

Berrenberg, J. L., Finlay, K. A., Stephan, W. G., & Stephan C. (2002). Prejudice toward people with cancer or AIDS: Applying the integrated threat model. *Journal of Applied Biobehavioral Research, 7,* 75–86.

Berry, D. S., & McArthur, L. Z. (1985). Some components and consequences of a babyface. *Journal of Personality and Social Psychology, 48,* 312–323.

Berry, D. S., & McArthur, L. Z. (1986). Perceiving character in faces: The impact of age-related craniofacial changes on social perception. *Psychological Bulletin, 100,* 3–18.

Berry, D. S., & Zebrowitz-McArthur, L. (1988). What's in a face? Facial maturity and the attribution of legal responsibility. *Personality and Social Psychology Bulletin, 14,* 23–33.

Berscheid, E. (1982). Attraction and emotion in interpersonal relationships. In M. S. Clark & S. T. Fiske (Eds.), *Affect and cognition: The 17th Annual Carnegie Symposium on Cognition* (pp. 37–54). Hillsdale, NJ: Erlbaum.

Berscheid, E. (1983). Emotion. In H. H. Kelley, E. Berscheid, A. Christensen, J. Harvey, T. Huston, G. Levinger, E. McClintock, A. Peplau, & D. Peterson (Eds.), *Close relationships* (pp. 110–168). San Francisco: Freeman.

Berscheid, E., Graziano, W. G., Monson, T. C., & Dermer, M. (1976). Outcome dependency: Attention, attribution, and attraction. *Journal of Personality and Social Psychology, 34,* 978–989.

Berscheid, E., Snyder, M., & Omoto, A. M. (1989). Issues in studying close relationships: Conceptualizing and measuring closeness. In C. Hendrick (Ed.), *Close relationships.* Newbury Park, CA: Sage.

Berscheid, E., & Walster, E. H. (1978). *Interpersonal attraction.* Reading, MA: Addison-Wesley.

Bettencourt, B. A., Charlton, K., Dorr, N. & Hume, D. L. (2001). Status differences and in-group bias: A meta-analytic examination of the effects of status stability, status legitimacy, and group permeability. *Psychological Bulletin, 127,* 520–542.

Biernat, M., & Fuegen, K. (2001). Shifting standards and the evaluation of competence: Complexity in gender-based judgment and decision making. *Journal of Social Issues, 57,* 707–724.

Biernat, M., Crandall, C. S., Young, L. V., Kobrynowicz, D., & Halpin, S. M. (1998). All that you can be: Stereotyping of self and others in a military context. *Journal of Personality and Social Psychology, 75,* 301–317.

Biernat, M., & Fuegen, K. (2001). Shifting standards and the evaluation of competence: Complexity in gender-based judgment and decision making. *Journal of Social Issues, 57,* 707–724.

Biernat, M., & Vescio, T. K. (2002). She swings, she hits, she's great, she's benched: Implications of gender-based shifting standards for judgment and behavior. *Personality and Social Psychology Bulletin, 28,* 66–77.

Birnbaum, M. H., & Mellers, B. A. (1979a). One-mediator model of exposure effects is still viable. *Journal of Personality and Social Psychology, 37,* 1090–1096.

Birnbaum, M. H., & Mellers, B. A. (1979b). Stimulus recognition may mediate exposure effects. *Journal of Personality and Social Psychology, 37,* 391–394.

Bizer, G. Y., & Krosnick, J. A. (2001). Exploring the structure of strength-related attitude features: The relation between attitude importance and attitude accessibility. *Journal of Personality and Social Psychology, 81,* 566–586.

Bizer, G. Y., Krosnick, J. A., Holbrook, A. L., Wheeler, S. C., Rucker, D. D., & Petty, R. E. (2004). The impact of personality on cognitive, behavioral, and affective political processes: The effects of need to evaluate. *Journal of Personality, 72,* 995–1027.

Blackwood, N. J., Bentall, R. P., ffytche, D. H., Simmons, A., Murray, R. M., & Howard, R. J. (2003). Self-responsibility and the self-serving bias: An fMRI investigation of causal attributions. *NeuroImage, 20,* 1076–1085.

Blair, I. V., & Banaji, M. R. (1996). Automatic and controlled processes in stereotype priming. *Journal of Personality and Social Psychology, 70,* 1142–1163.

Blair, I. V., Judd, C. M., & Chapleau, K. M. (2004). The influence of Afrocentric facial features in criminal sentencing. *Psychological Science, 15*, 674–679.

Blair, I. V., Judd, C. M., Sadler, M. S., & Jenkins, C. (2002). The role of Afrocentric features in person perception: Judging by features and categories. *Journal of Personality and Social Psychology, 83*, 5–25.

Blair, I. V., Ma, J. E., & Lenton, A. P. (2001). Imagining stereotypes away: The moderation of implicit stereotypes through mental imagery. *Journal of Personality and Social Psychology, 81*, 828–841.

Blake, R. R., & Mouton, J. S. (1961). Reactions to intergroup competition under win-lose conditions. *Management Science, 7*, 420–435.

Blake, R. R., & Mouton, J. S. (1962). The intergroup dynamics of win-loss conflict and problem-solving collaboration in union-management relations. In M. Sherif (Ed.), *International relations and leadership* (pp. 94–141). New York: Wiley.

Blaney, P. H. (1986). Affect and memory: A review. *Psychological Bulletin, 99*, 229–246.

Blanton, H., Cooper, J., Skurnik, I., & Aronson, J. (1997). When bad things happen to good feedback: Exacerbating the need for self-justification with self-affirmations. *Personality and Social Psychology Bulletin, 23*, 684–692.

Blascovich, J., Mendes, W. B., Hunter, S. B., Lickel, B. A., & Kowai-Bell, N. (2001). Perceiver threat in social interactions with stigmatized others. *Journal of Personality and Social Psychology, 80*, 253–267.

Blascovich, J., Wyer, N. A., Swart, L. A., & Kibler, J. L. (1997). Racism and racial categorization. *Journal of Personality and Social Psychology, 72*, 1364–1372.

Bless, H., Clore, G. L., Schwarz, N., Golisano, V., et al. (1996). Mood and the use of scripts: Does a happy mood really lead to mindlessness? *Journal of Personality and Social Psychology, 71*, 655–679.

Bless, H., Fiedler, K., & Strack, F. (2004). *Social cognition: How individuals construct social reality.* New York: Psychology Press.

Bobo, L. D. (1983). Whites' opposition to busing: Symbolic racism or realistic group conflict? *Journal of Personality and Social Psychology, 45*, 1196–1210.

Bobrow, D. G., & Norman, D. A. (1975). Some principles of memory schemata. In D. G. Bobrow & A. G. Collins (Eds.), *Representation and understanding: Studies in cognitive science* (pp. 131–150). New York: Academic Press.

Bochner, S. (1994). Cross-cultural differences in the self concept: A test of Hofstede's individualism/collectivisn distinction. *Journal of Cross-Cultural Psychology, 25*, 273–283.

Bodenhausen, G. V. (1993). Emotions, arousal, and stereotypic judgments: A heuristic model of affect and stereotyping. In D. M. Mackie & D. L. Hamilton (Eds.), *Affect, cognition and stereotyping* (pp. 13–37). San Diego, CA: Academic Press.

Bodenhausen, G. V., Kramer, G. P., & Süsser, K. (1994). Happiness and stereotypic thinking in social judgment. *Journal of Personality and Social Psychology, 66*, 621–632.

Bodenhausen, G. V., & Lichtenstein, M. (1987). Social stereotypes and information processing strategies: The impact of task complexity. *Journal of Personality and Social Psychology, 52*, 871–880.

Bodenhausen, G. V., & Macrae, C. N. (1998). In R. S. Wyer Jr. (Ed.), *Advances in social cognition. Vol. 11. Stereotype activation and inhibition.* Mahwah, NJ: Erlbaum.

Bodenhausen, G. V., Macrae, C. N., & Sherman, J. S. (1999). On the dialectics of discrimination: Dual processes in social stereotyping. In S. Chaiken & Y. Trope (Eds.), *Dual-process theories in social psychology* (pp. 271–290). New York: Guilford Press.

Bodenhausen, G. V., Mussweiler, T., Gabriel, S., & Moreno, K. N. (2001). In J. P. Forgas (Ed.), *Handbook of affect and social cognition* (pp. 319–342). Mahwah NJ: Erlbaum.

Bodenhausen, G. V., & Wyer, R. S., Jr. (1985). Effects of stereotypes on decision making and information-processing strategies. *Journal of Personality and Social Psychology, 48*, 267–282.

Bogardus, E. S. (1933). A social distance scale. *Sociology and Social Research, 17*, 265–271.

Bonano, G. A., Field, N. P., Kovacevic, A., & Kaltman, S. (2002). Self-enhancement as a buffer against extreme adversity: Civil war in Bosnia and traumatic loss in the United States. *Personality and Social Psychology Bulletin, 28*, 184–196.

Bond, M. H. (1972). Effect of an impression set on subsequent behavior. *Journal of Personality and Social Psychology, 24*, 301–305.

Boney-McCoy, S., Gibbons, F. X., & Gerrard, M. (1999). Self-esteem, compensatory self-enhancement, and the consideration of health risk. *Personality and Social Psychology Bulletin, 25,* 954–965.

Boninger, D. S., Krosnick, J. A., & Berent, M. K. (1995). Origins of attitude importance: Self-interest, social identification, and value relevance. *Journal of Personality and Social Psychology, 68,* 61–80.

Borgida, E., & Campbell, B. (1982). Attitude-behavior consistency: The moderating role of personal experience. *Journal of Personality and Social Psychology, 42,* 239–247.

Borgida, E., & Howard-Pitney, B. (1983). Personal involvement and the robustness of perceptual salience effects. *Journal of Personality and Social Psychology, 45,* 560–570.

Borgida, E., Swann, W. B., Jr., & Campbell, B. H. (1977, August). *Attitudes and behavior: The specificity hypothesis revisited.* Paper presented at the meeting of the American Psychological Association, San Francisco.

Boring, E. G. (1950). *A history of experimental psychology* (2nd ed). Englewood Cliffs, NJ: Prentice-Hall.

Bornstein, R. F. (1989). Exposure and affect: Overview and meta-analysis of research, 1968–1987. *Psychological Bulletin, 106,* 265–289.

Bornstein, R. F., & D'Agostino, P. R. (1992). Stimulus recognition and the mere exposure effect. *Journal of Personality and Social Psychology, 63,* 545–552.

Bornstein, R. F., & D'Agostino, P. R. (1994). The attribution and discounting of perceptual fluency: Preliminary tests of a perceptual fluency/attributional model of the mere exposure effect. *Social Cognition, 12,* 103–128.

Bornstein, B. H., & Wiener, R. L. (2006). Introduction to the special issue on emotion in legal judgment and decision making. *Law and Human Behavior, 30,* 115–118.

Bosson, J. K., Haymovitz, E. L., & Pinel, E. C. (2004). When saying and doing diverge: The effects of stereotype threat on self-reported versus non-verbal anxiety. *Journal of Experimental and Social Psychology, 40,* 247–255.

Botvinick, M. M., Cohen, J. D., & Carter, C. S. (2004). Conflict monitoring and anterior cingulate cortex: An update. *Trends in Cognitive Sciences, 8,* 539–546.

Bower, G. H. (1987). Commentary on mood and memory. *Behavior Research Therapy, 25,* 443–455.

Bower, G. H. (1990). Awareness, the unconscious, and repression: An experimental psychologist's perspective. In. J. A. Singer (Ed.), *Repression: Defense mechanism and personality style* (pp. 209–231). Chicago, IL: University of Chicago Press.

Bower, G. H. (1991). *The psychology of learning and motivation: Advances in research and theory* (Vol. 27). San Diego, CA: Academic Press.

Bower, G. H., Gilligan, S. G., & Monteiro, K. P. (1981). Selectivity of learning caused by affective states. *Journal of Experimental Psychology: General, 110,* 451–473.

Bower, G. H., & Mayer, J. D. (1989). In search of mood-dependent retrieval. *Journal of Social Behavior and Personality, 4,* 121–156.

Bradburn, N. M., & Caplovitz, D. (1965). *Reports on happiness.* Chicago: Aldine.

Bramel, D. (1963). Selection of a target for defensive projection. *Journal of Abnormal and Social Psychology, 66,* 318–324.

Brandstätter, V., & Frank, E. (2002). Effects of deliberative and implemental mindsets on persistence in goal-directed behavior. *Personality and Social Psychology Bulletin, 28,* 365–375.

Branscombe, N. R. (1985). Effects of hedonic valence and physiological arousal on emotion: A comparison of two theoretical perspectives. *Motivation and Emotion, 9,* 153–169.

Branscombe, N. R. (1988). Conscious and unconscious processing of affective and cognitive information. In K. Fiedler & J. Forgas (Eds.), *Affect, cognition, and social behavior: New evidence and integrative attempts* (pp. 3–24). Toronto, Canada: Hogrefe.

Branscombe, N. R., & Cohen, B. M. (1990). Motivation and complexity levels as determinants of heuristic use in social judgment. In J. Forgas (Ed.), *Emotion and social judgment.* Oxford: Pergamon Press.

Branscombe, N. R., Schmitt, M. T., & Harvey, R. D. (1999). Perceiving pervasive discrimination among African Americans: Implications for group identification and well-being. *Journal of Personality and Social Psychology, 77,* 135–149.

Branscombe, N. R., & Wann, D. L. (1994). Collective self-esteem consequences of outgroup derogation when a valued social identity is on trial. *European Journal of Social Psychology, 24*, 641–657.

Braverman, J. (2005). The effect of mood on detection of covariation. *Personality and Social Psychology Bulletin, 31*, 1487–1497.

Brehm, J. W. (1956). Postdecision changes in the desirability of alternatives. *Journal of Abnormal and Social Psychology, 52*, 384–389.

Brehm, J. W., & Cohen, A. R. (1962). *Explorations in cognitive dissonance.* New York: Wiley.

Brewer, M. B. (1988). A dual process model of impression formation. In T. K. Srull & R. S. Wyer Jr. (Eds.), *Advances in social cognition* (Vol. 1, pp. 1–36). Hillsdale, NJ: Erlbaum.

Brewer, M. B. (1991). The social self: On being the same and different at the same time. *Personality and Social Psychology Bulletin, 17*, 475–482.

Brewer, M. B. (1999). The psychology of prejudice: Ingroup love or outgroup hate? *Journal of Social Issues, 55*, 429–444.

Brewer, M. B., & Alexander, M. G. (2002). Intergroup emotions and images. In D. M. Mackie & E. R. Smith (Eds.), *From prejudice to intergroup emotions* (pp. 209–225). New York: Psychology Press.

Brewer, M. B., & Brown, R. J. (1998). Intergroup relations. In D. T. Gilbert, S. T. Fiske, & G. Lindzey (Eds.), *Handbook of social psychology* (4th ed., Vol. 2, pp. 554–594). New York: McGraw-Hill.

Brewer, M. B., Dull, V., & Lui, L. (1981). Perceptions of the elderly: Stereotypes as prototypes. *Journal of Personality and Social Psychology, 41*, 656–670.

Brewer, M. M., & Harasty Feinstein, A. S. (1999). Dual processes in the cognitive representation of persons and social categories. In S. Chaiken & Y. Trope (Eds.), *Dual-process theories in social psychology* (pp. 255–270). New York: Guilford Press.

Brickman, P., Rabinowitz, V. C., Karuza, J. Jr., Coates, D., Cohn, E., & Kidder, L. (1982). Models of helping and coping. *American Psychologist, 37*, 368–384.

Brickner, M. A., Harkins, S. G., & Ostrom, T. M. (1985). The effects of personal involvement: Thought provoking implications of social loafing. *Journal of Personality and Social Psychology, 51*, 763–770.

Brief, A. P., & Weiss, H. M. (2002). Organizational behavior: Affect in the workplace. *Annual Review of Psychology, 53*, 279–307.

Briñol, P., & Petty, R. E. (2003). Overt head movements and persuasion: A self-validation analysis. *Journal of Personality and Social Psychology, 84*, 1123–1139.

Briñol, P., Petty, R. E., & Wheeler, S. C. (2006). Discrepancies between explicit and implicit self-concepts: Consequences for information processing. *Journal of Personality and Social Psychology, 91*, 154–170.

Broadbent, D. (1958). *Perception and communication.* London: Pergamon Press.

Broadbent, D. (1982). Task combination and selective intake of information. *Acta Psychologica, 50*, 253–290.

Brock, T. C. (1967). Communication discrepancy and intent to persuade as determinants of counterargument production. *Journal of Experimental Social Psychology, 3*, 269–309.

Brock, T. C., Albert, S. M., & Becker, L. A. (1970). Familiarity, utility, and supportiveness as determinants of information receptivity. *Journal of Personality and Social Psychology, 14*, 292–301.

Brock, T. C., & Balloun, J. L. (1967). Behavioral receptivity to dissonant information. *Journal of Personality and Social Psychology, 6*, 413–428.

Brockner, J., Wiesenfeld, B. M., & Martin, C. L. (1995). Decision frame, procedural justice, and survivors' reactions to job layoffs. *Organizational Behavior and Human Decision Processes, 63*, 59–68.

Bronfenbrenner, U. (1977). Lewinian space and ecological substance. *Journal of Social Issues, 33*, 199–212.

Brown, J. D. (1986). Evaluations of self and others: Self-enhancement biases in social judgments. *Social Cognition, 4*, 353–376.

Brown, J. D. (1990). Evaluating one's abilities: Shortcuts and stumbling blocks on the road to self-knowledge. *Journal of Experimental Social Psychology, 26*, 149–167.

Brown, J. D., & Dutton, K. A. (1995). Truth and consequences: The costs and benefits of accurate self-knowledge. *Personality and Social Psychology Bulletin, 21,* 1288–1296.

Brown, J. D., & Marshall, M. A. (2001). Self-esteem and emotion: Some thoughts about feelings. *Personality and Social Psychology Bulletin, 27,* 575–584.

Brown, J. D., & Taylor, S. E. (1986). Affect and the processing of personal information: Evidence for mood-activated self-schemata. *Journal of Experimental Social Psychology, 22,* 436–452.

Brown, R. (1986). *Social psychology: The second edition.* New York: Free Press.

Brown, R. J. (2000). Social identity theory: Past achievements, current problems, and future challenges. *European Journal of Social Psychology, 30,* 745–778.

Brown, R. J., & Gaertner, S. L. (2001). *Blackwell handbook of social psychology: Intergroup processes.* London: Blackwell.

Brown, R., & Kulik, J. A. (1977). Flashbulb memories. *Cognition, 5,* 73–99.

Brown, R. J., Maras, P., Masser, B., Vivian, J., & Hewstone, M. (2001). Life on the ocean wave: Testing some intergroup hypotheses in a naturalistic setting. *Group Processes and Intergroup Relations, 4,* 81–97.

Bruce, V., & Young, A. (1986). Understanding face recognition. *British Journal of Psychology, 77,* 305–327.

Bruner, J. S. (1957). On perceptual readiness. *Psychological Review, 64,* 123–152.

Bruner, J. S. (1958). Social psychology and perception. In E. E. Maccoby, T. M. Newcomb, & E. L. Hartley (Eds.), *Readings in social psychology* (3rd ed.). New York: Holt, Rinehart, & Winston.

Brunswik, E. (1956). *Perception and the representative design of psychological experiments* (2nd ed.). Berkeley and Los Angeles: University of California Press.

Bryant, J., & Zillmann, D. (1979). Effect of intensification of annoyance through unrelated residual excitation on substantially delayed hostile behavior. *Journal of Experimental Social Psychology, 15,* 470–480.

Buck, R. (1980). Nonverbal behavior and the theory of emotion: The facial feedback hypothesis. *Journal of Personality and Social Psychology, 38,* 811–824.

Buckner, R. L., Kelley, W. M., & Petersen, S. E. (1999). Frontal cortex contributes to human memory formation. *Nature Neuroscience, 2,* 311–314.

Buehler, R., Griffin, D., & Ross, M. (1994). Exploring the "planning fallacy": Why people underestimate their task completion times. *Journal of Personality and Social Psychology, 67,* 366–381.

Burger, J. M. (1981). Motivational biases in the attribution of responsibility for an accident: A meta-analysis of the defensive-attribution hypothesis. *Psychological Bulletin, 90,* 496–512.

Burgess, E. W. (1941). An experiment in the standardization of the case study method. *Sociometry, 4,* 329–348.

Burnstein, E., & Schul, Y. (1982). The informational basis of social judgments: Operations in forming impressions of other persons. *Journal of Experimental Social Psychology, 18,* 217–234.

Burnstein, E., & Sentis, K. P. (1981). Attitude polarization in groups. In R. E. Petty, T. M. Ostrom, & T. C. Brock (Eds.), *Cognitive responses in persuasion* (pp. 197–216). Hillsdale, NJ: Erlbaum.

Burnstein, E., & Vinokur, A. (1973). Testing two classes of theories about group-induced shifts in individual choice. *Journal of Experimental Social Psychology, 9,* 123–137.

Burnstein, E., & Vinokur, A. (1975). What a person thinks upon learning he has chosen differently from others: Nice evidence for the persuasive-arguments explanation of choice shifts. *Journal of Experimental Social Psychology, 11,* 412–426.

Burris, C. T., & Rempel, J. K. (2004). "It's the end of the world as we know it:" Threat and the spatial-symbolic self. *Journal of Personality and Social Psychology, 86,* 19–42.

Bush, G., Luu, P., & Posner, M. (2000). Cognitive and emotional influences in anterior cingulate cortex. *Trends in Cognitive Science, 4,* 215–222.

Business and Professional Women's Foundation. (2005, July). 101 facts on the status of working women. Retrieved July 31, 2006, from http://www.bpwusa.org

Buss, D. M. (1989). Sex differences in human mate preferences: Evolutionary hypothesis tested in 37 cultures. *Behavioral and Brain Sciences, 12,* 1–49.

Buss, D. M., Abbott, M., Angleitner, A., Asherian, A., et al. (1990). International preferences in selecting mates: A study of 37 cultures. *Journal of Cross-Cultural Psychology, 21,* 5–47.

Buss, D. M., & Craik, K. H. (1980). The frequency concept of disposition: Dominance and prototypically dominant acts. *Journal of Personality, 43,* 379–392.

Buss, D. M., & Craik, K. H. (1981). The act frequency analysis of interpersonal dispositions: Aloofness, gregariousness, dominance, and submissiveness. *Journal of Personality, 49,* 175–192.

Buss, D. M., & Kenrick, D. T. (1998). Evolutionary social psychology. In D. T. Gilbert, S. T. Fiske, & G. Lindzey (Eds.), *Handbook of social psychology* (4th ed., Vol. 2, pp. 982–1026). New York: McGraw-Hill.

Buss, D. M., & Schmitt, D. P. (1993). Sexual strategies theory: An evolutionary perspective on human mating. *Psychological Review, 100,* 204–232.

Cacioppo, J. T. (1979). Effects of exogenous changes in heart rate on facilitation of thought and resistance to persuasion. *Journal of Personality and Social Psychology, 37,* 489–498.

Cacioppo, J. T., Amaral, D., Blanchard, J. J., Cameron, J. L., Carter, C. S., Crews, D. P., et al. (in press). Social neuroscience: Progress and implications for mental health. *Perspectives on Psychological Science.*

Cacioppo, J. T., & Berntson, G. G. (1992). Social psychological contributions to the decade of the brain: Doctrine of multilevel analysis. *American Psychologist, 47,* 1019–1028.

Cacioppo, J. T., & Berntson, G. G. (1999). The affect system: Architecture and operating characteristics. *Current Directions in Psychological Science, 8,* 133–137.

Cacioppo, J. T., & Gardner, W. L. (1999). Emotions. *Annual Review of Psychology, 50,* 191–214.

Cacioppo, J. T., & Petty, R. E. (1979). Effects of message repetition and position on cognitive response, recall, and persuasion. *Journal of Personality and Social Psychology, 37,* 97–109.

Cacioppo, J. T., & Petty, R. E. (1982). The need for cognition. *Journal of Personality and Social Psychology, 42,* 116–131.

Cacioppo, J. T., Petty, R. E., & Geen, T. R. (1989). Attitude structure and function: From the tripartite to the homeostasis model of attitudes. In A. R. Pratkanis, S. J. Breckler, & A. G. Greenwald (Eds.), *Attitude structure and function* (pp. 275–309). Hillsdale, NJ: Erlbaum.

Cacioppo, J. T., Petty, R. E., Losch, M. E., & Kim, H. S. (1986). Electromyographic activity over facial muscle regions can differentiate the valence and intensity of affective reactions. *Journal of Personality and Social Psychology, 50,* 260–268.

Cacioppo, J. T., Petty, R. E., & Morris, K. J. (1983). Effects of need for cognition on message evaluation, recall, and persuasion. *Journal of Personality and Social Psychology, 45,* 805–818.

Cacioppo, J. T., Priester, J. R., & Berntson, G. G. (1993). Rudimentary determinants of attitudes: II. Arm flexion and extension have differential effects on attitudes. *Journal of Personality and Social Psychology, 65,* 5–17.

Cadinu, M., Maass, A., Rosabianca, A., & Kiesner, J. (2005). Why do women underperform under stereotype threat? Evidence for the role of negative thinking. *Psychological Science, 16,* 572–578.

Caldwell, C. H., Sellers, R. M., Bernat, D. H., & Zimmerman, M. A. (2004). Racial identity, parental support, and alcohol use in a sample of academically at-risk African American high school students. *American Journal of Community Psychology, 34,* 71–82.

Caldwell, C. H., Zimmerman, M. A., Bernat, D. H., Sellers, R. M., & Notaro, P. C. (2002). Racial identity, maternal support and psychological distress among African American adolescents. *Child Development, 73,* 1322–1336.

Calvo-Merino, B., Glaser, D. E., Grezes, J., Passingham, R. E., & Haggard, P. (2005). Action observation and acquired motor skills. *Cerebral Cortex, 15,* 1243–1249.

Camerer, C. (2003). Strategizing in the brain. *Science, 300,* 1673–1675.

Campbell, D. T. (1958). Common fate, similarity, and other indices of the status of aggregates of persons as social entities. *Behavioral Science, 3,* 14–25.

Campbell, D. T. (1965). Ethnocentric and other altruistic motives. In D. Levine (Ed.), *Nebraska Symposium on Motivation* (pp. 283–311). Lincoln: University of Nebraska Press.

Campbell, J. D. (1986). Similarity and uniqueness: The effects of attribute type, relevance, and individual differences in self-esteem and depression. *Journal of Personality and Social Psychology, 50,* 281–294.

Cannon, W. B. (1927). The James-Lange theory of emotions: A critical examination and an alternative theory. *American Journal of Psychology, 39,* 106–124.

Cantor, J. R., Bryant, J., & Zillmann, D. (1974). Enhancement of humor appreciation by transferred excitation. *Journal of Personality and Social Psychology, 30,* 812–821.

Cantor, J. R., & Zillmann, D. (1973). The effect of affective state and emotional arousal on music appreciation. *Journal of General Psychology, 89,* 97–108.

Cantor, N., & Kihlstrom, J. F. (1985) Social intelligence: The cognitive basis of personality. In P. Shaver (Ed.), *Review of personality and social psychology* (Vol. 6, pp. 15–34). Beverly Hills, CA: Sage.

Cantor, N., & Kihlstrom, J. F. (1987). *Personality and social intelligence.* Englewood Cliffs, NJ: Prentice-Hall.

Cantor, N., Mackie, D. M., & Lord, C. G. (1983–1984). Choosing partners and activities: The social perceiver decides to mix it up. *Social Cognition, 2,* 256–272.

Cantor, N., & Mischel, W. (1979). Prototypes in person perception. In L. Berkowitz (Ed.), *Advances in experimental social psychology* (Vol. 12, pp. 3–52). New York: Academic Press.

Carlson, M., Charlin, V., & Miller, N. (1988). Positive mood and helping behavior: A test of six hypotheses. *Journal of Personality and Social Psychology, 55,* 211–229.

Carlson, M., & Miller, N. (1987). Explanation of the relation between negative mood and helping. *Psychological Bulletin, 102,* 91–108.

Carlston, D. E. (1994). Associated systems theory: A systematic approach to the cognitive representation of persons and events. In R. S. Wyer (Ed.), *Advances in social cognition: Associated systems theory* (Vol. 7, pp. 1–78). Hillsdale, NJ: Erlbaum.

Carlston, D. E., & Skowronski, J. J. (1994). Savings in the relearning of trait information as evidence for spontaneous inference generation. *Journal of Personality and Social Psychology, 66,* 840–856.

Carlston, D. E., Skowronski, J. J., & Sparks, C. (1995). Savings in relearning II: On the formation of behavior-based trait associations and inferences. *Journal of Personality and Social Psychology, 69,* 420–436.

Carnevale, P. J. D., & Isen, A. M. (1986). The influence of positive affect and visual access on the discovery of integrative solutions in bilateral negotiation. *Organizational Behavior and Human Decision Processes, 37,* 1–13.

Carroll, J. S. (1978). The effect of imagining an event on expectations for the event: An interpretation in terms of the availability heuristic. *Journal of Experimental Social Psychology, 14,* 88–96.

Carvallo, M., & Pelham, B. W. (2006). When fiends become friends: The need to belong and perceptions of personal and group discrimination. *Journal of Personality and Social Psychology, 90,* 94–108.

Carver, C. S. (1979). A cybernetic model of self-attention processes. *Journal of Personality and Social Psychology, 37,* 1251–1281.

Carver, C. S. (2003). Pleasure as a sign you can attend to something else: Placing positive feelings within a general model of affect. *Cognition and Emotion, 17,* 241–261.

Carver, C. S., la Voie, L., Kuhl, J., & Ganellen, R. J. (1988). Cognitive concomitants of depression: A further examination of the roles of generalization, high standards, and self-criticism. *Journal of Social and Clinical Psychology, 7,* 350–365.

Carver, C. S., & Scheier, M. F. (1982). Outcome expectancy, locus of attribution for expectancy, and self-directed attention as determinants of evaluations and performance. *Journal of Experimental Social Psychology, 18,* 184–200.

Carver, C. S., & Scheier, M. F. (1990). Origins and functions of positive and negative affect: A control-process view. *Psychological Review, 97,* 19–35.

Carver, C. S., & Scheier, M. F. (1998). *On the self-regulation of behavior.* New York: Cambridge University Press.

Carver, C. S., Sutton, S. K., & Scheier, M. F. (2000). Action, emotion, and personality: Emerging conceptual integration. *Personality and Social Psychology Bulletin, 26,* 741–751.

Carver, C. S., & White, T. L. (1994). Behavioral inhibition, behavioral activation, and affective responses to impending reward and punishment: The BIS/BAS scales. *Journal of Personality and Social Psychology, 67,* 319–333.

Castano, E. (2004). In case of death, cling to the ingroup. *European Journal of Social Psychology, 34,* 375–384.

Castano, E., & Dechesne, M. (2005). On defeating death: Group reification and social identification as immortality strategies. In W. Strobe & M. Hewstone (Eds.), *European Review of Social Psychology* (Vol. 16, pp. 221–256). New York: Psychology Press.

Castano, E., & Giner-Sorolla, R. (2006). Not quite human: Infra-humanization in response to collective responsibility for intergroup killing. *Journal of Personality and Social Psychology, 90,* 804–818.

Castano, E., Sacchi, S., & Gries, P. H. (2003). The perception of the other in international relations: Evidence for the polarizing effect of entitativity. *Political Psychology, 24,* 449–468.

Castano, E., & Yzerbyt, V. Y. (1998). The highs and lows of group homogeneity. *Behavioural Processes, 42,* 219–238.

Castelli, F., Happé F., Frith, U., & Frith, C. (2000). Movement and mind: A functional imaging study of perception and interpretation of complex intentional movement patterns. *NeuroImage, 12,* 314–325.

Castelli, L., Macrae, C. N., Zogmaister, C., & Arcuri, L. (2004). A tale of two primes: Contextual limits on stereotype activation. *Social Cognition, 22,* 233–247.

Cejka, M. A., & Eagly, A. H. (1999). Gender-stereotypic images of occupations correspond to the sex segregation of employment. *Personality and Social Psychology Bulletin, 25,* 413–423. Erratum. *Personality and Social Psychology Bulletin, 25,* 1059.

Centerbar, D. B., & Clore, G. L. (2006). Do approach-avoidance actions create attitudes? *Psychological Science, 17,* 22–29.

Cervellon, M. C., & Dubé L. (2002). Assessing the cross-cultural applicability of affective and cognitive components of attitude. *Journal of Cross Cultural Psychology, 33,* 346–357.

Cesario, J., Grant, H., & Higgins, E. T. (2004). Regulatory fit and persuasion: Transfer from "feeling right." *Journal of Personality and Social Psychology, 86,* 388–404.

Cesario, J., Plaks, J. E., & Higgins, E. T. (2006). Automatic social behavior as motivated preparation to interact. *Journal of Personality and Social Psychology, 90,* 893–910.

Chaiken, S. (1979). Communicator physical attractiveness and persuasion. *Journal of Personality and Social Psychology, 37,* 1387–1397.

Chaiken, S. (1980). Heuristic versus systematic information processing and the use of source versus message cues in persuasion. *Journal of Personality and Social Psychology, 39,* 752–766.

Chaiken, S. (1987). The heuristic model of persuasion. In M. P. Zanna, J. M. Olson, & C. P. Herman (Eds.), *Social influence: The Ontario Symposium* (Vol. 5, pp. 3–40). Hillsdale, NJ: Erlbaum.

Chaiken, S., & Eagly, A. H. (1976). Communication modality as a determinant of message persuasiveness and message comprehensibility. *Journal of Personality and Social Psychology, 34,* 605–614.

Chaiken, S., & Eagly, A. H. (1983). Communication modality as a determinant of persuasion: The role of communicator salience. *Journal of Personality and Social Psychology, 45,* 41–56.

Chaiken, S., Liberman, A., & Eagly, A. H. (1989). Heuristic and systematic information processing within and beyond the persuasion context. In J. S. Uleman & J. A. Bargh (Eds.), *Unintended thought* (pp. 212–252). New York: Guilford Press.

Chaiken, S., & Stangor, C. (1987). Attitudes and attitude change. *Annual Review of Psychology, 38,* 575–630.

Chaiken, S., & Trope, Y. (Eds.). (1999). *Dual-process theories in social psychology.* New York: Guilford Press.

Chaiken, S., & Yates, S. (1985). Affective-cognitive consistency and thought-induced attitude polarization. *Journal of Personality and Social Psychology, 49,* 1470–1481.

Chajut, E., & Algom, D. (2003). Selective attention improves under stress: Implications for theories of social cognition. *Journal of Personality and Social Psychology, 86,* 231–248.

Chang, C., & Hitchon, J. C. B. (2004). When does gender count? Further insights into gender schematic processing of female candidates' political advertisements. *Sex Roles, 51,* 197–208.

Chaplin, W. F., John, O. P., & Goldberg, L. R. (1988). Conceptions of states and traits: Dimensional attributes with ideals as prototypes. *Journal of Personality and Social Psychology, 54,* 541–557.

Chapman, L. J. (1967). Illusory correlation in observational report. *Journal of Verbal Learning and Verbal Behavior, 6,* 151–155.

Chartrand, T. L., & Bargh, J. A. (1999). The chameleon effect: The perception-behavior link and social interaction. *Journal of Personality and Social Psychology, 76,* 893–910.

Chasteen, A. L., Bhattacharyya, S., Horhota, M., Tam, R., & Hasher, L. (2005). How feelings of stereotype threat influence older adults' memory performance. *Experimental Aging Research, 31,* 235–260.

Chen, H. C., Reardon, R., Rea, C., & Moore, D. J. (1992). Forewarning of content and involvement: Consequences for persuasion and resistance to persuasion. *Journal of Experimental and Social Psychology, 28,* 523–541.

Chen, M., & Bargh, J. A. (1999). Consequences of automatic evaluation: Immediate behavioral predispositions to approach or avoid the stimulus. *Personality and Social Psychology Bulletin, 25,* 215–224.

Chen, S., & Chaiken, S. (1999). The heuristic-systematic model in its broader context. In S. Chaiken & Y. Trope (Eds.), *Dual-process theories in social psychology* (pp. 73–96). New York: Guilford Press.

Chen, S., Schechter, D., & Chaiken, S. (1996). Getting at the truth or getting along: Accuracy-versus impression-motivated heuristic and systematic processing. *Journal of Personality and Social Psychology, 71,* 262–275.

Cheng, P. W., Holyoak, K. J., Nisbett, R. E., & Oliver, L. M. (1986). Pragmatic versus syntactic approaches to training deductive reasoning. *Cognitive Psychology, 18,* 293–328.

Choi, I., & Choi, Y. (2002). Culture and self-concept flexibility. *Personality and Social Psychology Bulletin, 28,* 1508–1517.

Choi, I., Dalal, R., Kim-Prieto, C., & Park, H. (2003). Culture and judgment of causal relevance. *Journal of Personality and Social Psychology, 84,* 46–59.

Chomsky, N. (1959). Verbal behavior. [Review of Skinner's book.] *Language, 35,* 26–58.

Christensen, T. C., Wood, J. V., & Barrett, L. F. (2003). Remembering everyday experience through the prism of self-esteem. *Personality and Social Psychology Bulletin, 29,* 51–62.

Christensen-Szalanski, J. J., & Willham, C. F. (1991). The hindsight bias: A meta-analysis. *Organizational Behavior and Human Decision Processes, 48,* 147–168.

Chun, W. Y., & Kruglanski, A. W. (2006). The role of task demands and processing resources in the use of base-rate and individuating information. *Journal of Personality and Social Psychology, 91,* 205–217.

Chun, W. Y., Spiegel, S., & Kruglanski, A. W. (2002). Assimilative behavior identification can also be resource dependent: The unimodel perspective on personal-attribution phases. *Journal of Personality and Social Psychology, 83,* 542–555.

Chwalisz, K., Diener, E., & Gallagher, D. (1988). Autonomic arousal feedback and emotional experience: Evidence from the spinal cord injured. *Journal of Personality and Social Psychology, 54,* 820–828.

Cialdini, R. B., Darby, B. L., & Vincent, J. E. (1973). Transgression and altruism: A case for hedonism. *Journal of Experimental Social Psychology, 9,* 502–516.

Cialdini, R. B., & Kenrick, D. T. (1976). Altruism as hedonism: A social development perspective on the relationship of negative mood state and helping. *Journal of Personality and Social Psychology, 34,* 907–914.

Cialdini, R. B., Levy, A., Herman, C. P., & Evenbeck, S. (1973). Attitudinal politics: The strategy of moderation. *Journal of Personality and Social Psychology, 25,* 100–108.

Clark, M. S. (1982). A role for arousal in the link between feeling states, judgments, and behavior. In M. S. Clark & S. T. Fiske (Eds.), *Affect and cognition: The 17th Annual Carnegie Symposium on Cognition* (pp. 263–290). Hillsdale, NJ: Erlbaum.

Clark, M. S., & Fiske, S. T. (Eds.). (1982). *Affect and cognition: The 17th Annual Carnegie Symposium on Cognition.* Hillsdale, NJ: Erlbaum.

Clark, M. S., & Isen, A. M. (1982). Toward understanding the relationship between feeling states and social behavior. In A. Hastorf & A. Isen (Eds.), *Cognitive social psychology* (pp. 73–108). New York: Elsevier North-Holland.

Clark, M. S., Milberg, S., & Erber, R. (1984). Effects of arousal on judgments of others' emotions. *Journal of Personality and Social Psychology, 46,* 551–560.

Clark, M. S., Milberg, S., & Erber, R. (1988). Arousal-state-dependent memory: Evidence and implications for understanding social judgments and social behaviors. In K. Fiedler & J. Forgas (Eds.), *Affect, cognition, and social behavior: New evidence and integrative attempts.* Toronto, Canada: Hogrefe.

Clark, M. S., Milberg, S., & Ross, J. (1983). Arousal cues material stored in memory with a similar level of arousal: Implications for understanding the effects of mood on memory. *Journal of Verbal Learning and Verbal Behavior, 22,* 633–649.

Clark, M. S., & Williamson, G. M. (1989). Moods and social judgments. In H. L. Wagner & A. S. R. Manstead (Eds.), *Handbook of psychophysiology: Emotion and social behavior.* Chichester, England: Wiley.

Clark, N. K., & Rutter, D. R. (1985). Social categorization, visual cues, and social judgements. *European Journal of Social Psychology, 15,* 105–119.

Clausell, E., & Fiske, S. T. (2005). When do subgroup parts add up to the stereotypic whole? Mixed stereotype content for gay male subgroups explains overall ratings. *Social Cognition, 23,* 161–181.

Clore, G. L., & Ortony, A. (1991). What more is there to emotion concepts than prototypes? *Journal of Personality and Social Psychology, 60,* 48–50.

Clore, G. L., Schwarz, N., & Conway, M. (1994). Affective causes and consequences of social information processing. In R. S. Wyer Jr. & T. K. Srull (Eds.), *Handbook of social cognition. Vol. 1. Basic processes.* (2nd ed., pp. 323–417). Hillsdale, NJ: Erlbaum.

Cloutier, J., Mason, M. F., & Macrae C. N. (2005). The perceptual determinants of person construal: Reopening the social-cognition toolbox. *Journal of Personality and Social Psychology, 88,* 885–894.

Coan, J. A., & Allen, J. J. B. (2004). Frontal EEG asymmetry as a moderator and mediator of emotion. *Biological Psychology, 67,* 7–49.

Coan, J. A., Allen, J. J. B., & Harmon-Jones, E. (2001). Voluntary facial expression and hemispheric asymmetry over the frontal cortex. *Psychophysiology, 38,* 912–925.

Cohen, A. R., Brehm, J. W., & Latané, B. (1959). Choice of strategy and voluntary exposure to information under public and private conditions. *Journal of Personality, 27,* 63–73.

Cohen, C. E., & Ebbesen, E. B. (1979). Observational goals and schema activation: A theoretical framework for behavior perception. *Journal of Experimental Social Psychology, 15,* 305–329.

Cohen, J. B., & Basu, K. (1987). Alternative models of categorization: Toward a contingent processing framework. *Journal of Consumer Research, 13,* 455–472.

Cohen, L. H., Towbes, L. C., & Flocco, R. (1988). Effects of induced mood on self-reported life events and perceived and received social support. *Journal of Personality and Social Psychology, 55,* 669–674.

Collins, A. M., & Loftus, E. F. (1975). A spreading-activation theory of semantic processing. *Psychological Review, 82,* 407–428.

Collins, R. L., Taylor, S. E., Wood, J. V., & Thompson, S. C. (1988). The vividness effect: Elusive or illusory? *Journal of Experimental Social Psychology, 24,* 1–18.

Conner, M., & Abraham, C. (2001). Conscientiousness and the theory of planned behavior: Toward a more complete model of the antecedents of intentions and behavior. *Personality and Social Psychology Bulletin, 27,* 1547–1561.

Conway, M., & Ross, M. (1984). Getting what you want by revising what you had. *Journal of Personality and Social Psychology, 47,* 738–748.

Cook, T. D., & Flay, B. R. (1978). The persistence of experimentally induced attitude change. In L. Berkowitz (Ed.), *Advances in experimental social psychology* (Vol. 11, pp. 1–57). New York: Academic Press.

Cooley, C. H. (1902). *Human nature and the social order.* New York: Scribners.

Cooper, J. (1995). Cognitive dissonance theory. In A. S. R. Manstead & M. Hewstone (Eds.), *Blackwell encyclopedia of social psychology* (pp. 99–109). Oxford, UK: Blackwell.

Cooper, J., & Cooper, G. (2002). Subliminal motivation: A story revisited. *Journal of Applied Social Psychology, 32,* 2213–2227.

Cooper, J., & Fazio, R. H. (1984). A new look at dissonance theory. In L. Berkowitz (Ed.), *Advances in experimental social psychology* (Vol. 17, pp. 229–266). New York: Academic Press.

Cooper, J., Zanna, M. P., & Taves, P. A. (1978). Arousal as a necessary condition for attitude change following induced compliance. *Journal of Personality and Social Psychology, 36,* 1101–1106.

Corenblum, B., & Stephan, W. G. (2001). White fears and native apprehensions: An integrated threat theory approach to intergroup attitudes. *Canadian Journal of Behavioral Science, 33,* 251–268.

Correll, J., Park, B., Judd, C. M., & Wittenbrink, B. (2002). The police officer's dilemma: Using ethnicity to disambiguate potentially threatening individuals. *Journal of Personality and Social Psychology, 83,* 1314–1329.

Correll, J., Urland, G. R., & Ito, T. A. (2006). Event-related potentials and the decision to shoot: The role of threat perception and cognitive control. *Journal of Experimental Social Psychology, 42,* 120–128.

Corteen, R. S., & Wood, B. (1972). Automatic responses to shock-associated words in an unattended channel. *Journal of Experimental Psychology, 94,* 308–313.

Cosmides, L., Tooby, J., & Kurzban, R. (2003). Perception of race. *Trends in Cognitive Sciences, 7,* 173–179.

Cottrell, C. A., & Neuberg, S. L. (2005). Different emotional reactions to different groups: A sociofunctional threat-based approach to "prejudice." *Journal of Personality & Social Psychology, 88,* 770–789.

Cottrell, N. B., Ingraham, L. A., & Monfort, F. W. (1971). The retention of balanced and unbalanced cognitive structures. *Journal of Personality, 39,* 112–131.

Cousins, S. D. (1989). Culture and self-perception in Japan and the United States. *Journal of Personality and Social Psychology, 56,* 124–131.

Couzin, I. D., Krause, J., Franks, N. R., & Levin, S. A. (2005). Effective leadership and decision making in animal groups on the move. *Nature, 433,* 513–516.

Craighead, W. E., Hickey, K. S., & DeMonbreun, B. G. (1979). Distortion of perception and recall of neutral feedback in depression. *Cognitive Therapy and Research, 3,* 291–298.

Crandall, C. S., Eshleman, A., & O'Brien, L. T. (2002). Social norms and the expression and suppression of prejudice: The struggle for internalization. *Journal of Personality and Social Psychology, 82,* 359–378.

Crandall, C. S., & Greenfield, B. S. (1986). Understanding the conjunction fallacy: A conjunction of effects? *Social Cognition, 4,* 408–419.

Crano, W. D., & Prislin, R. (2006). Attitudes and persuasion. *Annual Review of Psychology, 57,* 345–374.

Crary, W. G. (1966). Reactions to incongruent self-experiences. *Journal of Consulting Psychology, 30,* 246–252.

Creswell, J. D., Welch, W. T., Taylor, S. E., Sherman, D. K., Gruenewald, T. L., & Mann, T. (2005). Affirmation of personal values buffers neuroendocrine and psychological stress responses. *Psychological Science, 16,* 846–851.

Crites, S. L., Cacioppo, J. T., Gardner, W. L., & Berntson, G. G. (1995). Bioelectrical echoes from evaluative categorization: II. A late positive brain potential that varies as a function of attitude registration rather than attitude report. *Journal of Personality and Social Psychology, 68,* 997–1013.

Crocker, J. (1981). Judgment of covariation by social perceivers. *Psychological Bulletin, 90,* 272–292.

Crocker, J., Cornwell, B., & Major, B. (1993). The stigma of overweight: Affective consequences of attributional ambiguity. *Journal of Personality and Social Psychology, 64,* 60–70.

Crocker, J., Karpinski, A., Quinn, D. M., & Chase S. K. (2003). When grades determine self-worth: Consequences of contingent self-worth for male and female engineering and psychology majors. *Journal of Personality and Social Psychology, 85,* 507–516.

Crocker, J., & Knight, K. M. (2005). Contingencies of self-worth. *Current Directions in Psychological Science, 14,* 200–203.

Crocker, J., & Luhtanen, R. K. (1990). Collective self-esteem and ingroup bias. *Journal of Personality and Social Psychology, 58,* 60–67.

Crocker, J., & Luhtanen, R. K. (2003). Level of self-esteem and contingencies of self-worth: Unique effects on academic, social and financial problems in college students. *Personality and Social Psychology Bulletin, 29,* 701–712.

Crocker, J., Luhtanen, R., Blaine, B., & Broadmax, S. (1994). Collective self-esteem and psychological well-being among White, Black, and Asian college students. *Personality and Social Psychology Bulletin, 20,* 503–513.

Crocker, J., & Major, B. (1989). Social stigma and self-esteem: The self-protective properties of stigma. *Psychological Review, 96,* 608–630.

Crocker, J., & McGraw, K. M. (1984). What's good for the goose is not good for the gander: Solo status as an obstacle to occupational achievement for males and females. *American Behavioral Scientist, 27,* 357–369.

Crocker, J., & Park, L. E. (2004). The costly pursuit of self-esteem. *Psychological Bulletin, 130,* 392–414.

Crocker, J., Voelkl, K., Testa, M., & Major, B. (1991). Social stigma: The affective consequences of attributional ambiguity. *Journal of Personality and Social Psychology, 60,* 218–228.

Croizet, J. C., & Claire, T. (1998). Extending the concept of stereotype threat to social class: The intellectual underperformance of students from low socioeconomic backgrounds. *Personality and Social Psychology Bulletin, 24,* 588–594.

Croizet, J. C., Després, G., Gauzins, M. E., Huguet, P., Leyens, J.-Ph., & Méot, A. (2004). Stereotype threat undermines intellectual performance by triggering a disruptive mental load. *Personality and Social Psychology Bulletin, 30,* 721–731.

Crosby, F. J. (1991). *Juggling: The unexpected advantages of balancing career and home for women and their families.* New York: Free Press.

Crosby, F. J., Bromley, S., & Saxe, L. (1980). Recent unobtrusive studies of Black and White discrimination and prejudice: A literature review. *Psychological Bulletin, 87,* 546–563.

Cross, S. E., Bacon, P. L., & Morris, M. L. (2000). The relational-interdependent self-construal and relationships. *Journal of Personality and Social Psychology, 78,* 791–808.

Cross, S. E., & Vick, N. V. (2001). The interdependent self-construal and social support: The case of persistence in engineering. *Personality and Social Psychology Bulletin, 27,* 820–832.

Csikszentmihalyi, M. (1978). Attention and the holistic approach to behavior. In K. S. Pope & J. L. Singer (Eds.), *The stream of consciousness* (pp. 335–358). New York: Plenum Press.

Csikszentmihalyi, M., & Larson, R. (1984). *Being adolescent: Conflict and growth in the teenage years.* New York: Basic Books.

Cuddy, A. J. C., Fiske, S. T., & Glick, P. (2007). The BIAS map: Behaviors from intergroup affect and stereotypes. *Journal of Personality and Social Psychology, 92,* 631–648.

Cuddy, A. J. C., Fiske, S. T., Kwan, V. S. Y., Glick, P., Demoulin, S., Leyens, J.-Ph., et al. (in press). Is the stereotype content model culture-bound? A cross-cultural comparison reveals systematic similarities and differences. *British Journal of Social Psychology.*

Cuddy, A. J. C., Norton, M. I., & Fiske, S. T. (2005) This old stereotype: The pervasiveness and persistence of the elderly stereotype. *Journal of Social Issues, 61,* 265–283.

Cuddy, A. J. C., Rock, M. S., & Norton, M. I. (2007). Aid in the aftermath of Hurricane Katrina: Inferences of secondary emotions and intergroup helping. *Group Processes and Intergroup Relations, 10,* 107–118.

Cunningham, M. R. (1988). Does happiness mean friendliness? Induced mood and heterosexual self-disclosure. *Personality and Social Psychology Bulletin, 14,* 283–297.

Cunningham, M. R., Steinberg, J., & Grey, R. (1980). Wanting to and having to help: Separate motivations for positive mood and guilt-induced helping. *Journal of Personality and Social Psychology, 38,* 181–192.

Cunningham, W. A., Johnson, M. K., Gatenby, J. C., Gore, J. C., & Banaji, M. R. (2003). Neural components of social evaluation. *Journal of Personality and Social Psychology, 85,* 639–649.

Cunningham, W. A., Johnson, M. K., Raye, C. L., Gatenby, J. C., Gore, J. C., & Banaji, M. R. (2004). Separable neural components in the processing of Black and White faces. *Psychological Science, 15,* 806–813.

Cunningham, W. A., Preacher, K. J., & Banaji, M. R. (2001). Implicit attitude measures: Consistency, stability, and convergent validity. *Psychological Science, 12,* 163–170.

Cunningham, W. A., Raye, C. L., & Johnson, M. K. (2004). Implicit and explicit evaluation: fMRI correlates of valence, emotional intensity, and control in the processing of attitudes. *Journal of Cognitive Neuroscience, 16,* 1717–1729.

Cupchik, G. C., & Leventhal, H. (1974). Consistency between expressive behavior and the evaluation of humorous stimuli: The role of sex and self-observation. *Journal of Personality and Social Psychology, 30*, 429–442.

Custers, R., & Aarts, H. (2005). Positive affect as implicit motivator: On the nonconscious operation of behavioral goals. *Journal of Personality and Social Psychology, 89*, 129–142.

Czopp, A. M., & Monteith, M. J. (2003). Confronting prejudice (literally): Reactions to confrontations of racial and gender bias. *Personality and Social Psychology Bulletin, 29*, 532–544.

Dambrun, M., Duarte, S., & Guimond, S. (2004). Why are men more likely to support group-based dominance than women? The mediating role of gender identification. *British Journal of Social Psychology, 43*, 287–297.

Darley, J. M., & Fazio, R. H. (1980). Expectancy confirmation processes arising in the social interaction sequence. *American Psychologist, 35*, 867–881.

Darwin, C. R. (1872). *The expression of emotions in man and animals*. London: John Murray.

Dasgupta, N., & Greenwald, A. G. (2001). On the malleability of automatic attitudes: Combating automatic prejudice with images of admired and disliked individuals. *Journal of Personality and Social Psychology, 81*, 800–814.

Dasgupta, N., McGhee, D. E., Greenwald, A. G., & Banaji, M. R. (2000). Automatic preference for White Americans: Eliminating the familiarity explanation. *Journal of Experimental Social Psychology, 36*, 316–328.

Davidson, R. J. (1993). Parsing affective space: Perspectives from neuropsychology and psychophysiology. *Neuropsychology, 7*, 464–475.

Davidson, R. J. (2003). Seven sins in the study of emotion: Correctives from affective neuroscience. *Brain and Cognition, 52*, 129–132.

Davidson, R. J., & Irwin, W. (1999). The functional neuroanatomy of emotion and affective style. *Trends in Cognitive Neuroscience, 3*, 11–21.

Davies, P. G., Spencer, S. J., & Steele, C. M. (2005). Clearing the air: Identity safety moderates the effects of stereotype threat on women's leadership aspirations. *Journal of Personality and Social Psychology, 88*, 276–287.

Davis, J. L., & Rusbult, C. E. (2001). Attitude alignment in close relationships. *Journal of Personality and Social Psychology, 81*, 65–84.

Davison, G. C., Feldman, P. M., & Osborn, C. E. (1984). Articulated thoughts, irrational beliefs, and fear of negative evaluation. *Cognitive Therapy and Research, 8*, 349–362.

Davison, G. C., Robins, C., & Johnson, M. K. (1983). Articulated thoughts during simulated situations: A paradigm for studying cognition in emotion and behavior. *Cognitive Therapy and Research, 7*, 17–40.

Davison, A. R., Yantis, S., Norwood, M., & Montano, D. E. (1985). Amount of information about the attitude object and attitude-behavior consistency. *Journal of Personality and Social Psychology, 49*, 1184–1198.

Davison, G. C., & Zighelboim, V. (1987). Irrational beliefs in the articulated thoughts of college students with social anxiety. *Journal of Rational-Emotive Therapy, 5*, 238–254.

Davitz, J. R. (1970). A dictionary and grammar of emotion. In M. B. Arnold (Ed.), *Feelings and emotion: The Loyola Symposium*. New York: Academic Press.

Dawes, R. M. (1980). You can't systematize human judgment: Dyslexia. In R. A. Shweder (Ed.), *New directions for methodology of social and behavioral science* (Vol. 4, pp. 67–78). San Francisco: Jossey-Bass.

Dawes, R. M, Faust, D., & Meehl, P. E. (1989). Clinical versus actuarial judgment. *Science, 243*, 1668–1674.

Deaux, K., & Emswiller, T. (1974). Explanations of successful performance on sex-linked tasks: What is skill for the male is luck for the female. *Journal of Personality and Social Psychology, 29*, 80–85.

Deaux, K., & LaFrance, M. (1998). Gender. In D. T. Gilbert, S. T. Fiske, & G. Lindzey (Eds.), *The handbook of social psychology* (4th ed., Vol. 1, pp. 788–827). New York: McGraw-Hill.

Deaux, K., & Major, B. (1977). Sex-related patterns in the unit of perception. *Personality and Social Psychology Bulletin, 3*, 297–300.

Deaux, K., Winton, W. M., Crowley, M., & Lewis, L. L. (1985). Level of categorization and content of gender stereotypes. *Social Cognition, 3*, 145–167.

DeBono, K. G. (1987). Investigating the social-adjustive and value-expressive functions of attitudes: Implications for persuasion processes. *Journal of Personality and Social Psychology, 52,* 279–287.

DeBono, K. G., & Harnish, R. J. (1988). Source expertise, source attractiveness, and the processing of persuasive information: A functional approach. *Journal of Personality and Social Psychology, 55,* 541–546.

DeBono, K. G., & Snyder, M. (1989). Understanding consumer decision-making processes: The role of form and function in product evaluation. *Journal of Applied Social Psychology, 19,* 416–424.

Decéty, J., & Chaminade, T. (2003). Neural correlates of feeling sympathy. *Neuropsychologia. Special Issue on Social Cognition, 41,* 127–138.

DeCoster, J., Banner, M. J., Smith, E. R., & Semin, G. R. (2006). On the inexplicity of the implicit: Differences in the information provided by implicit and explicit tests. *Social Cognition, 24,* 5–21.

Delle Fave, A., & Massimini, F. (2004). Parenthood and the quality of experience in daily life: A longitudinal study. *Social Indicators Research, 67,* 75–106.

Demoulin, S., Torres, R. R., Perez, A. R., Vaes, J., Paladino, M. P., Gaunt, R., Pozo, B. C., & Leyens, J.-Ph. (2004). Emotional prejudice can lead to infra-humanisation. In W. Stroebe & M. Hewstone (Eds.), *European review of social psychology* (Vol. 15, pp. 259–296). Hove, UK: Psychology Press/Taylor & Francis.

Dépret, E. F., & Fiske, S. T. (1999). Perceiving the powerful: Intriguing individuals versus threatening groups. *Journal of Experimental Social Psychology, 35,* 461–480.

de Rivera, J. (1984). The structure of emotional relationships. In P. Shaver (Ed.), *Review of personality and social psychology* (Vol. 5, pp. 116–145). Beverly Hills, CA: Sage.

de Rivera, J., & Grinkis, C. (1986). Emotions as social relationships. *Motivation and Emotion, 10,* 351–369.

Derryberry, D., & Rothbart, M. K. (1988). Arousal, affect, and attention as components of temperament. *Journal of Personality and Social Psychology, 55,* 958–966.

DeSteno, D., Dasgupta, N., Bartlett, M. Y., & Cajdric, A. (2004). Prejudice from thin air: The effect of emotion on automatic intergroup attitudes. *Psychological Science, 15,* 319–324.

DeSteno, D., Petty, R. E., Rucker, D. D., Wegener, D. T., & Braverman, J. (2004). Discrete emotions and persuasion: The role of emotion-induced expectancies. *Journal of Personality and Social Psychology, 86,* 43–56.

DeSteno, D., Petty, R. E., Wegener, D. T., & Rucker, D. D. (2000). Beyond valence in the perception of likelihood: The role of emotion specificity. *Journal of Personality and Social Psychology, 78,* 397–416.

Deutsch, F. M. (1999). *Halving it all: How equally shared parenting works.* Cambridge, MA: Harvard University Press.

Deutsch, M. A. (1968). Field theory in social psychology. In G. Lindzey & E. Aronson (Eds.), *The handbook of social psychology* (Vol. 1, 2nd ed.). Reading, MA: Addison-Wesley.

Deutsch, M. A., & Deutsch, D. (1963). Attention: Some theoretical considerations. *Psychological Review, 87,* 272–300.

Devine, P. G. (1989). Stereotypes and prejudice: Their automatic and controlled components. *Journal of Personality and Social Psychology, 56,* 5–18.

Devine, P. G., & Elliot, A. J. (1995). Are racial stereotypes really fading? The Princeton trilogy revisited. *Personality and Social Psychology Bulletin, 21,* 1139–1150.

Devine, P. G., & Monteith, M. J. (1999). Automaticity and control in stereotyping. In S. Chaiken & Y. Trope (Eds.), *Dual-process theories in social psychology* (pp. 339–360). New York: Guilford Press.

Devos, T., Comby, L., & Deschamps, J. C. (1996). Asymmetries in judgments of ingroup and outgroup variability. In W. Stroebe & M. Hewstone (Eds.), *European review of social psychology* (Vol. 7, pp. 95–104). Chichester, UK: Wiley.

Devos, T., Silver, L. A., Mackie, D. M., & Smith, E. R. (2002). Experiencing intergroup emotions. In D. M. Mackie & E. R. Smith (Eds.), *From prejudice to intergroup emotions* (pp. 111–134). New York: Psychology Press.

de Vries, B., & Walker, L. J. (1987). Conceptual/integrative complexity and attitudes toward capital punishment. *Personality and Social Psychology Bulletin, 13,* 448–457.

Dickerson, S. S., & Kemeny, M. E. (2004). Acute stressors and cortisol responses: A theoretical integration and synthesis of laboratory research. *Psychological Bulletin, 130*, 355–391.

Dickerson, S. S., Kemeny, M. E., Aziz, N., Kim, K. H., & Fahey, J. L. (2004). Immunological effects of induced shame and guilt. *Psychosomatic Medicine, 66*, 124–131.

Diener, E. (1984). Subjective well-being. *Psychological Bulletin, 95*, 542–575.

Diener, E., & Diener, M. (1995). Cross-cultural correlates of life satisfaction and self-esteem. *Journal of Personality and Social Psychology, 68*, 653–663.

Diener, E., & Emmons, R. A. (1984). The independence of positive and negative affect. *Journal of Personality and Social Psychology, 47*, 1105–1117.

Diener, E., & Iran-Nejad, A. (1986). The relationship in experience between various types of affect. *Journal of Personality and Social Psychology, 50*, 1031–1038.

Dijksterhuis, A. (2004). Think different: The merits of unconscious thought in preference development and decision making. *Journal of Personality and Social Psychology, 87*, 586–598.

Dijksterhuis, A., Aarts, H., & Smith, P. K. (2005). The power of the subliminal: On subliminal persuasion and other potential applications. In R. R. Hassan, J. Uleman, & J. A. Bargh (Eds.), *The new unconscious* (pp. 77–106). New York: Oxford University Press.

Dijksterhuis, A., & Bargh, J. A. (2001). The perception-behavior expressway: Automatic effects of social perception on social behavior. In M. P. Zanna (Ed.), *Advances in experimental and social psychology* (Vol. 33, pp. 1–40). San Diego, CA: Academic Press.

Dijksterhuis, A., Bos, M. W., Nordgren, L. F., & van Baaren, R. B. (2006). On making the right choice: The deliberation-without-attention effect. *Science, 311*, 1005–1007.

Dijksterhuis, A., Spears, R., Postmes, T., Stapel, D. A., Koomen, W., van Knippenberg, A., et al. (1998). Seeing one thing and doing another: Contrast effects in automatic behavior. *Journal of Personality and Social Psychology, 75*, 862–871.

Dijksterhuis, A., & van Knippenberg, A. (1998). The relation between perception and behavior, or how to win a game of Trivial Pursuit. *Journal of Personality and Social Psychology, 74*, 865–877.

Dijksterhuis, A., & van Knippenberg, A. (2000). Behavioral indecision: Effects of self-focus on automatic behavior. *Social Cognition, 81*, 55–74.

Dimitrov, M., Grafman, J., Soares, A. H., & Clark, K. (1999). Concept formation and concept shifting in frontal lesion and Parkinson's disease patients assessed with the California Card Sorting Test. *Neuropsychology, 13*, 135–143.

Dion, K. L., & Earn, B. M. (1975). The phenomenology of being a target of prejudice. *Journal of Personality and Social Psychology, 32*, 944–950.

Di Paula, A., & Campbell, J. D. (2002). Self-esteem and persistence in the face of failure. *Journal of Personality and Social Psychology, 83*, 711–724.

Dixon, T. L., & Maddox, K. B. (2005). Skin tone, crime news, and social reality judgments: Priming the stereotype of the dark and dangerous Black criminal. *Journal of Applied Social Psychology, 35*, 1555–1570.

Dolan, R. J. (1999). On the neurology of morals. *Nature Neuroscience, 2*, 927–929.

Dovidio, J. F., Brigham, J. C., Johnson, B. T., & Gaertner, S. L. (1996). Stereotyping, prejudice, and discrimination: Another look. In C. N. Macrae, C. Stangor, & M. Hewstone (Eds.), *Stereotypes and stereotyping*. New York: Academic Press.

Dovidio, J. F., Esses, V. M., Beach, K. R., & Gaertner, S. L. (2002). The role of affect in determining intergroup behavior: The case of willingness to engage in intergroup contact. In D. M. Mackie & E. R. Smith (Eds.), *From prejudice to intergroup emotions* (pp. 153–172). New York: Psychology Press.

Dovidio, J. F., Evans, N., & Tyler, R. B. (1986). Racial stereotypes: The contents of their cognitive representations. *Journal of Experimental Social Psychology, 22*, 22–37.

Dovidio, J. F., & Gaertner, S. L. (Eds.). (1986). *Prejudice, discrimination, and racism*. Orlando, FL: Academic Press.

Dovidio, J. F., & Gaertner, S. L. (2000). Aversive racism and selection decisions: 1989 and 1999. *Psychological Science, 11*, 315–319.

Dovidio, J. F., Gaertner, S. E., Kawakami, K., & Hodson, G. (2002). Why can't we just get along? Interpersonal biases and interracial distrust. *Cultural Diversity and Ethnic Minority Psychology, 8*, 88–102.

Dovidio, J. F., Kawakami, K., & Gaertner, S. L. (2002). Implicit and explicit prejudice and inter-racial interaction. *Journal of Personality and Social Psychology, 82*, 62–68.

Dovidio, J. F., Kawakami, K., Johnson, C., Johnson, B., & Howard, A. (1997). On the nature of prejudice: Automatic and controlled processes. *Journal of Experimental Social Psychology, 33*, 510–540.

Dovidio, J. F., ten Vergert, M., Stewart, T. L., Gaertner, S. L., Johnson, J. D., Esses, V. M., et al. (2004). Perspective and prejudice: Antecedent and mediating mechanisms. *Personality and Social Psychology Bulletin, 30*, 1537–1549.

Downing, J. W., Judd, C. M., & Brauer, M. (1992). Effects of repeated expressions on attitude extremity. *Journal of Personality and Social Psychology, 63*, 17–29.

Drake, R. A. (1986). Lateral asymmetry of impression formation. *International Journal of Neuro-science, 30*, 121–126.

Drake, R. A., & Sobrero, A. P. (1987). Lateral orientation effects upon trait-behavior and atti-tude-behavior consistency. *Journal of Social Psychology, 127*, 639–651.

Dreben, E. K., Fiske, S. T., & Hastie, R. (1979). The independence of evaluative and item in-formation: Impression and recall order effects in behavior-based impression formation. *Journal of Personality and Social Psychology, 37*, 1758–1768.

Duckitt, J. (1993). Right-wing authoritarianism among white South American students: Its measurement and correlates. *Journal of Social Psychology, 133*, 553–563.

Duckitt, J. (2001). A dual-process cognitive-motivational theory of ideology and prejudice. In M. P. Zanna (Ed.), *Advances in experimental social psychology* (Vol. 33, pp. 41–113). New York: Academic Press.

Duckitt, J., & Mphuthing, T. (1998). Group identification and intergroup attitudes: A longitudi-nal analysis in South Africa. *Journal of Personality and Social Psychology, 74*, 80–85.

Duckworth, K. L., Bargh, J. A., Garcia, M., & Chaiken, S. (2002). The automatic evaluation of novel stimuli. *Psychological Science, 13*, 513–519.

Duclos, S. E., Laird, J. D., Schneider, E., Sexter, M., Stern, L., & Van Lighten, O. (1989). Emotion-specific effects of facial expressions and postures on emotional experience. *Journal of Per-sonality and Social Psychology, 57*, 100–108.

Duncan, J. W., & Laird, J. D. (1977). Cross-modality consistencies in individual differences in self-attribution. *Journal of Personality, 45*, 191–196.

Dunn, E. W., Wilson, T. D., & Gilbert, D. T. (2003). Location, location, location: The misprediction of satisfaction in housing lotteries. *Personality and Social Psychology Bulletin, 29*, 1421–1432.

Dunn, J. R., & Schweitzer, M. R. (2005). Feeling and believing: The influence of emotion on trust. *Journal of Personality and Social Psychology, 88*, 736–748.

Dunning, D. (1999). A newer look: Motivated social cognition and the schematic representation of social concepts. *Psychological Inquiry, 10*, 1–11.

Dunning, D. (2003). The zealous self-affirmer: How and why the self lurks so pervasively be-hind social judgment. In S. J. Spencer & S. Fein (Eds.), *Motivated social perception: The On-tario Symposium* (Vol. 9, pp. 45–72). Mahwah, NJ: Erlbaum.

Dunning, D., & Hayes, A. F. (1996). Evidence for egocentric comparison in social judgment. *Journal of Personality and Social Psychology, 71*, 213–229.

Dunning, D., Meyerowitz, J. A., & Holzberg, A. D. (1989). Ambiguity and self-evaluation: The role of idiosyncratic trait definitions in self-serving assessments of ability. *Journal of Per-sonality and Social Psychology, 57*, 1082–1090.

Dunning, D., & Parpal, M. (1989). Mental addition versus subtraction in counterfactual reason-ing: On assessing the impact of personal actions and life events. *Journal of Personality and Social Psychology, 57*, 5–15.

Dunning, D., Perie, M., & Story, A. L. (1991). Self-serving prototypes of social categories. *Jour-nal of Personality and Social Psychology, 30*, 349–359.

Dunning, D., & Sherman D. A. (1997). Stereotypes and tacit inference. *Journal of Personality and Social Psychology, 73*, 459–471.

Dunton, B. C., & Fazio, R. H. (1997). An individual difference measure of motivation to control prejudiced reactions. *Personality and Social Psychology Bulletin, 23*, 316–326.

Dutton, D. G., & Aron, A. P. (1974). Some evidence for heightened sexual attraction under con-ditions of high anxiety. *Journal of Personality and Social Psychology, 30*, 510–517.

Duval, S., & Wicklund, R. A. (1972). *A theory of objective self-awareness*. New York: Academic Press.

Eagly, A. H. (1974). Comprehensibility of persuasive arguments as a determinant of opinion change. *Journal of Personality and Social Psychology, 29,* 758–773.

Eagly, A. H. (1987). *Sex differences in social behavior: A social-role interpretation*. Mahwah, NJ: Erlbaum.

Eagly, A. H., & Chaiken, S. (1975). An attribution analysis of the effect of communication characteristics on opinion change: The case of communicator attractiveness. *Journal of Personality and Social Psychology, 32,* 136–144.

Eagly, A. H., & Chaiken, S. (1984). Cognitive theories of persuasion. In L. Berkowitz (Ed.), *Advances in experimental social psychology* (Vol. 17, pp. 267–359). New York: Academic Press.

Eagly, A. H., & Chaiken, S. (1993). *The psychology of attitudes*. Orlando, FL: Harcourt Brace Jovanovich.

Eagly, A. H., & Chaiken, S. (1998). Attitude structure and function. In D. T. Gilbert, S. T. Fiske, & G. Lindzey (Eds.). *Handbook of social psychology* (4th ed., Vol. l, pp. 269–322). New York: McGraw-Hill.

Eagly, A. H., & Chaiken, S. (2005). Attitude research in the 21st century: The current state of knowledge. In D. Albarracín, B. T. Johnson, & M. P. Zanna (Eds), *The handbook of attitudes* (pp. 743–767). Mahwah, NJ: Erlbaum.

Eagly, A. H., Chaiken, S., & Wood, W. (1981). An attribution analysis of persuasion. In J. H. Harvey, W. J. Ickes, & R. F. Kidd (Eds.), *New directions in attribution research* (Vol. 3, pp. 37–62). Hillsdale, NJ: Erlbaum.

Eagly, A. H., Chen, S., Chaiken, S., & Shaw-Barnes, K. (1999). The impact of attitudes on memory: An affair to remember. *Psychological Bulletin, 125,* 64–89.

Eagly, A. H., & Crowley, M. (1986). Gender and helping behavior: A meta-analytic review of the social psychological literature. *Psychological Bulletin, 100,* 283–308.

Eagly, A. H., & Himmelfarb, S. (1978). Attitudes and opinions. *Annual Review of Psychology, 29,* 517–554.

Eagly, A. H., & Johnson, B. T. (1990). Gender and leadership style: A meta-analysis. *Psychological Bulletin, 108,* 233–256.

Eagly, A. H., & Karau, S. J. (1991). Gender and the emergence of leaders: A meta-analysis. *Journal of Personality and Social Psychology, 60,* 685–710.

Eagly, A. H., & Karau, S. J. (2002). Role congruity theory of prejudice toward female leaders. *Psychological Review, 109,* 573–598.

Eagly, A. H., Karau, S. J., & Makhijani, M. G. (1995). Gender and the effectiveness of leaders: A meta-analysis. *Psychological Bulletin, 117,* 125–145.

Eagly, A. H., Karau, S. J., Miner, J. B., & Johnson, B. T. (1994). Gender and motivation to manage in hierarchic organizations: A meta-analysis. *Leadership Quarterly, 5,* 135–159.

Eagly, A. H., Kulesa, P., Brannon, L. A., Shaw-Barnes, K., & Hutson-Comeaux, S. (2000). Why counterattitudinal messages are as memorable as proattitudinal messages: The importance of active defense against attack. *Personality and Social Psychology Bulletin, 26,* 1392–1408.

Eagly, A. H., Kulesa, P., Chen, S., & Chaiken, S. (2001). Do attitudes affect memory? Tests of the congeniality hypothesis. *Current Directions in Psychological Science, 10,* 5–9.

Eagly, A. H., Makhijani, M. G., & Klonsky, B. G. (1992). Gender and the evaluation of leaders: A meta-analysis. *Psychological Bulletin, 111,* 3–22.

Eagly, A. H., & Steffen, V. J. (1984). Gender stereotypes stem from the distribution of women and men into social roles. *Journal of Personality and Social Psychology, 46,* 735–754.

Eagly, A. H., & Steffen, V. J. (1986). Gender and aggressive behavior: A meta-analytic review of the social psychological literature. *Psychological Bulletin, 100,* 309–330.

Eagly, A. H., & Wood, W. (1991). Explaining sex differences in social behavior: A meta-analytic perspective. *Personality and Social Psychology Bulletin, 17,* 306–315.

Eagly, A. H., & Wood, W. (1999). The origins of sex differences in human behavior: Evolved dispositions versus social roles. *American Psychologist, 54,* 408–423.

Eagly, A. H., Wood, W., & Chaiken, S. (1978). Causal inferences about communicators and their effect on opinion change. *Journal of Personality and Social Psychology, 36,* 424–435.

Ebbesen, E. B. (1980). Cognitive processes in understanding ongoing behavior. In R. Hastie, T. M. Ostrom, E. B. Ebbesen, R. S. Wyer, D. L. Hamilton, & D. E. Carlston (Eds.), *Person memory: The cognitive basis of social perception* (pp. 179–226). Hillsdale, NJ: Erlbaum.

Ebbinghaus, H. (1964). *Memory: A contribution to experimental psychology.* H. A. Ruger & C. E. Bussenius (trans.). New York: Dover. (Originally published 1885)

Eberhardt, J. L. (2005). Imaging race. *American Psychologist, 60,* 181–190.

Eberhardt, J. L., Dasgupta, N., & Banaszynski, T. L. (2003). Believing is seeing: The effects of racial labels and implicit beliefs on face perception. *Personality and Social Psychology Bulletin, 29,* 360–370.

Eberhardt, J. L., Davies, P. G., Purdie-Vaughns, V. J., & Johnson, S. L. (2006). Looking deathworthy: Perceived stereotypically of Black defendants predicts capital sentencing outcomes. *Psychological Science, 17,* 383–386.

Eberhardt, J. L., Goff, P. A., Purdie, V. J., & Davies, P. G. (2004). Seeing Black: Race, crime, and visual processing. *Journal of Personality and Social Psychology, 87,* 876–893.

Echebarria-Echabe, A., & Fernandez-Guede, E. (2006). Effects of terrorism on attitudes and ideological orientation. *European Journal of Social Psychology, 36,* 259–265.

Eckes, T. (2002). Paternalistic and envious gender stereotypes: Testing predictions from the stereotype content model. *Sex Roles, 47,* 99–114.

Eckes, T., Trautner, H. M., & Behrendt, R. (2005). Gender subgroups and intergroup perception: Adolescents' views of own-gender and other-gender groups. *Journal of Social Psychology, 145,* 85–111.

Ehrlichman, H., & Halpern, J. N. (1988). Affect and memory: Effects of pleasant and unpleasant odors on retrieval of happy and unhappy memories. *Journal of Personality and Social Psychology, 55,* 769–779.

Ehrlinger, J., & Dunning, D. (2003). How chronic self-views influence (and potentially mislead) estimates of performance. *Journal of Personality and Social Psychology, 84,* 5–17.

Ehrlinger, J., Gilovich, T., & Ross, L. D. (2005). Peering into the bias blind spot: People's assessments of bias in themselves and others. *Personality and Social Psychology Bulletin, 31,* 680–692.

Einhorn, H. J., & Hogarth, R. M. (1981). Behavioral decision theory: Processes of judgment and choice. *Annual Review of Psychology, 32,* 53–88.

Einhorn, H. J., & Hogarth, R. M. (1986). Judging probable cause. *Psychological Bulletin, 99,* 3–19.

Eisen, S. V., & McArthur, L. Z. (1979). Evaluating and sentencing a defendant as a function of his salience and the observer's set. *Personality and Social Psychology Bulletin, 5,* 48–52.

Eisenberger N. I., Jarcho J. M., Lieberman, M. D., & Naliboff, B. D. (2006). An experimental study of shared sensitivity to physical pain and social rejection. *Pain, 126,* 132–138.

Eisenberger, N. I., Lieberman, M. D., & Williams, K. D. (2003). Does rejection hurt? An fMRI study of social exclusion. *Science, 302,* 290–292.

Eiser, J., Fazio, R. H., Stafford, T., & Prescott, T. J. (2003). Connectionist simulation of attitude learning: Asymmetries in the acquisition of positive and negative evaluations. *Personality and Social Psychology Bulletin, 29,* 1221–1235.

Ekman, P. (1984). Expression and the nature of emotion. In K. Scherer & P. Ekman (Eds.), *Approaches to emotion* (pp. 319–343). Hillsdale, NJ: Erlbaum.

Ekman, P., Levenson, R. W., & Friesen, W. V. (1983). Autonomic nervous system activity distinguishes among emotions. *Science, 221,* 1208–1210.

Ekman, P., & O'Sullivan, M. (1988). Comment on Russell and Fehr. *Journal of Experimental Psychology: General, 117,* 86–88.

Elio, R., & Anderson, J. R. (1981). The effects of category generalizations and instance similarity on schema abstraction. *Journal of Experimental Psychology: Human Learning and Memory, 7,* 397–417.

Elliot, A. J., & Devine, P. G. (1994). On the motivational nature of cognitive dissonance: Dissonance as psychological discomfort. *Journal of Personality and Social Psychology, 67,* 382–394.

Ellemers, N., Spears, R., & Doosje, B. (2002). Self and social identity, *Annual Review of Psychology, 53,* 161–186.

Ellsworth, P. C., & Smith, C. A. (1988a). From appraisal to emotion: Differences among unpleasant feelings. *Motivation and Emotion, 12,* 271–302.

Ellsworth, P. C., & Smith, C. A. (1988b). Shades of joy: Patterns of appraisal differentiating pleasant emotions. *Emotion and Cognition, 2,* 302–331.

Ellsworth, P. C., & Tourangeau, R. (1981). On our failure to disconfirm what nobody ever said. *Journal of Personality and Social Psychology, 40,* 363–369.

Else-Quest, N. M., Hyde, J. S., Goldsmith, H. H., & Van-Hulle, C. A. (2006). Gender differences in temperament: A meta-analysis. *Psychological Bulletin, 132,* 33–72.

Enquist, C., Newtson, D., & LaCross, K. (1979). Prior expectations and the perceptual segmentation of ongoing behavior. Unpublished manuscript, University of Virginia.

Epley, N., & Dunning, D. (2000). Feeling "holier than thou": Are self-serving assessments produced by errors in self- or social prediction? *Journal of Personality and Social Psychology, 79,* 861–875.

Epley, N., & Gilovich, T. (2001). Putting adjustment back in the anchoring and adjustment heuristic: Differential processing of self-generated and experimenter-provided anchors. *Psychological Science, 12,* 391–396.

Epley, N., Keysar, B., Van Boven, L., & Gilovich, T. (2004). Perspective taking as egocentric anchoring and adjustment. *Journal of Personality and Social Psychology, 87,* 327–339.

Epstein, S. (1979). The stability of behavior: I. On predicting most of the people much of the time. *Journal of Personality and Social Psychology, 37,* 1097–1126.

Epstein, S. (1983). The unconscious, the preconscious, and the self-concept. In J. Suls & A. Greenwald (Eds.), *Psychological perspectives on the self* (Vol. 2, pp. 220–247). Hillsdale, NJ: Erlbaum.

Epstein, S. (1984). Controversial issues in emotion theory. In P. Shaver (Ed.), *Review of personality and social psychology* (Vol. 5, pp. 64–88). Beverly Hills, CA: Sage.

Epstein, S. (1990a). Cognitive experiential self-theory. In L. Pervin (Ed.), *Handbook of personality theory and research* (pp. 165–192). New York: Guilford Press.

Epstein, S. (1990b). The self-concept, the traumatic neurosis, and the structure of personality. In D. Ozer, J. M. Healy Jr., & A. J. Stewart (Eds.), *Perspectives on personality* (Vol. 3). Greenwich, CT: JAI Press.

Erber, R. (1991). Affective and semantic priming: Effects of mood on category accessibility and inference. *Journal of Experimental Social Psychology, 27,* 480–498.

Erber, R., & Fiske, S. T. (1984). Outcome dependency and attention to inconsistent information. *Journal of Personality and Social Psychology, 47,* 709–726.

Erdley, C. A., & D'Agostino, P. R. (1988). Cognitive and affective components of automatic priming effects. *Journal of Personality and Social Psychology, 54,* 741–747.

Ericsson, K. A., & Kintsch, W. (1995). Long-term working memory. *Psychological Review, 102,* 211–245.

Ericsson, K. A., & Simon, H. A. (1980). Verbal reports as data. *Psychological Review, 87,* 215–251.

Esses, V. M., & Dovidio, J. F. (2002). The role of emotions in determining willingness to engage in intergroup contact. *Personality and Social Psychology Bulletin, 28,* 1202–1214.

Evans, L. M., & Petty, R. E. (2003). Self-guide framing and persuasion: Responsibly increasing message processing to ideal levels. *Personality and Social Psychology Bulletin, 29,* 313–324.

Eyal, T., Liberman, N., Trope, Y., & Walther, E. (2004). The pros and cons of temporally near and distant action. *Journal of Personality and Social Psychology, 86,* 781–795.

Fabrigar, L. R., Petty, R. E., Smith, S. M., & Crites, S. L., Jr. (2006). Understanding knowledge effects on attitude-behavior consistency: The role of relevance, complexity, and amount of knowledge. *Journal of Personality and Social Psychology, 90,* 556–577.

Farah, M. J. (1994). Neuropsychological inferences with an interactive brain: A critique of the "locality" assumption. *Behavioral and Brain Sciences, 22,* 287–288.

Farina, A., Allen, J. G., & Saul, B. B. (1968). The role of the stigmatized person in affecting social relationships. *Journal of Personality, 36,* 169–182.

Fazio, R. H. (1986). How do attitudes guide behavior? In R. M. Sorrentino & E. T. Higgins (Eds.), *The handbook of motivation and cognition: Foundations of social behavior* (pp. 204–243). New York: Guilford Press.

Fazio, R. H. (1987). Self-perception theory: A current perspective. In M. P. Zanna, J. M. Olson, & C. P. Herman (Eds.), *Social influence: The Ontario Symposium* (Vol. 5, pp. 129–149). Hillsdale, NJ: Erlbaum.

Fazio, R. H. (1989). On the power and functionality of attitudes: The role of attitude accessibility. In A. R. Pratkanis, S. J. Breckler, & A. G. Greenwald (Eds.), *Attitude structure and function* (pp. 153–179). Hillsdale, NJ: Erlbaum.

Fazio, R. H. (1990). Multiple processes by which attitudes guide behavior: The MODE model as an integrative framework. In M. P. Zanna (Ed.), *Advances in experimental social psychology* (Vol. 23, pp. 75–110). New York: Academic Press.

Fazio, R. H. (2001). On the automatic activation of associated evaluations: An overview. *Cognition and Emotion, 15*, 115–141.

Fazio, R. H., Chen, J., McDonel, E. C., & Sherman, S. J. (1982). Attitude accessibility, attitude-behavior consistency, and the strength of the object-evaluation association. *Journal of Experimental Social Psychology, 18*, 339–357.

Fazio, R. H., & Cooper, J. (1983). Arousal in the dissonance process. In J. T. Cacioppo & R. E. Petty (Eds.), *Social psychophysiology.* New York: Guilford Press.

Fazio, R. H., Effrein, E. A., & Falender, V. J. (1981). Self-perceptions following social interaction. *Journal of Personality and Social Psychology, 41*, 232–242.

Fazio, R. H., Herr, P. M., & Olney, T. J. (1984). Attitude accessibility following a self-perception process. *Journal of Personality and Social Psychology, 47*, 277–286.

Fazio, R. H., & Hilden, L. E. (2001). Emotional reactions to a seemingly prejudiced response: The role of automatically activated racial attitudes and motivation to control prejudiced reactions. *Personality and Social Psychology Bulletin, 27*, 538–549.

Fazio, R. H., Jackson, J. R., Dunton, B. C., & Williams, C. J. (1995). Variability in automatic activation as an unobtrusive measure of racial attitudes: A bona fide pipeline? *Journal of Personality and Social Psychology, 69*, 1013–1027.

Fazio, R. H., Ledbetter, J. E., & Towles-Schwen, T. (2000). On the costs of accessible attitudes: Detecting that the attitude object has changed. *Journal of Personality and Social Psychology, 78*, 197–210.

Fazio, R. H., & Olson, M. A. (2003). Implicit measures in social cognition research: Their meaning and use. *Annual Review of Psychology, 54*, 297–327.

Fazio, R. H., Powell, M. C., & Herr, P. M. (1983). Toward a process model of attitude-behavior relation: Accessing one's attitude upon mere observation of the attitude object. *Journal of Personality and Social Psychology, 44*, 723–735.

Fazio, R. H., Sanbonmatsu, D. M., Powell, M. C., & Kardes, F. R. (1986). On the automatic activation of attitudes. *Journal of Personality and Social Psychology, 50*, 229–238.

Fazio, R. H., & Towles-Schwen, T. (1999). The MODE model of attitude-behavior process. In S. Chaiken & Y. Trope (Eds.), *Dual-process theories in social psychology* (pp. 97–116). New York: Guilford Press.

Fazio, R. H., & Williams, C. J. (1986). Attitude accessibility as a moderator of the attitude-perception and attitude-behavior relations: An investigation of the 1984 presidential election. *Journal of Personality and Social Psychology, 51*, 505–514.

Fazio, R. H., & Zanna, M. P. (1978). Attitudinal qualities relating to the strength of the attitude-behavior relationship. *Journal of Experimental Social Psychology, 14*, 398–408.

Fazio, R. H., & Zanna, M. P. (1981). Direct experience and attitude-behavior consistency. In L. Berkowitz (Ed.), *Advances in experimental social psychology* (Vol. 14, pp. 162–203). New York: Academic Press.

Fazio, R. H., Zanna, M. P., & Cooper, J. (1977). Dissonance and self-perception: An integrative view of each theory's proper domain of application. *Journal of Experimental Social Psychology, 13*, 464–479.

Feather, N. T. (1969). Attitude and selective recall. *Journal of Personality and Social Psychology, 12*, 310–319.

Feeney, B. C., & Cassidy, J. (2003). Reconstructive memory related to adolescent-parent conflict interactions: The influence of attachment-related representations on immediate perceptions and changes in perceptions over time. *Journal of Personality and Social Psychology, 85*, 945–955.

Fehr, B. (1988). Prototype analysis of the concepts of love and commitment. *Journal of Personality and Social Psychology, 55*, 557–579.

Fehr, B., & Russell, J. A. (1984). Concept of emotion viewed from a prototype perspective. *Journal of Experimental Psychology: General, 113*, 464–486.

Fein, S., Hilton, J. L., & Miller, D. T. (1990). Suspicion of ulterior motivation and the correspondence bias. *Journal of Personality and Social Psychology, 58,* 753–764.

Fein, S., & Spencer, S. J. (1997). Prejudice as self-image maintenance: Affirming the self through derogating others. *Journal of Personality and Social Psychology, 73,* 31–44.

Feingold, A. (1992). Gender differences in mate selection preferences: A test of the parental investment model. *Psychological Bulletin, 112,* 125–139.

Ferguson, M. J., & Bargh, J. A. (2004). How social perception can automatically influence behavior. *Trends in Cognitive Science, 8,* 33–39.

Ferguson, M. J., & Bargh, J. A. (2004). Liking is for doing: The effects of goal pursuit on automatic evaluation. *Journal of Personality and Social Psychology, 87,* 557–572.

Festinger, L. (1954). A theory of social comparison processes. *Human Relations, 7,* 117–140.

Festinger, L. (1957). *A theory of cognitive dissonance.* Stanford, CA: Stanford University Press.

Fiedler, K. (1988). Emotional mood, cognitive style, and behavior regulation. In K. Fiedler & J. P. Forgas (Eds.), *Affect, cognition, and social behavior* (pp. 100–119). Toronto, Canada: Hogrefe.

Fiedler, K., & Freytag, P. (2004). Pseudocontingencies. *Journal of Personality and Social Psychology, 87,* 453–467.

Fiedler, K., Nickel, S., Muehlfriedel, T., & Unkelbach, C. (2001). Is mood congruency an effect of genuine memory or response bias? *Journal of Experimental Social Psychology, 37,* 201–214.

Fiedler, K., Pampe, H., & Scherf, U. (1986). Mood and memory for tightly organized social information. *European Journal of Social Psychology, 16,* 149–164.

Fiedler, K., Walther, E., & Nickel, S. (1999). Explaining asymmetric intergroup judgment through differential aggregation: Computer simulations and some new evidence. *European Review of Social Psychology, 10,* 1–40.

Finlay, K. A., & Stephan, W. G. (2000). Improving intergroup relations: The effects of empathy on racial attitudes. *Journal of Applied Social Psychology, 30,* 1720–1737.

Fischer, P., Jonas, E., Frey, D., & Schulz-Hardt, S. (2005). Selective exposure to information: The impact of information limits. *European Journal of Social Psychology, 35,* 469–492.

Fischhoff, B. (1980). For those condemned to study the past: Reflections on historical judgment. In R. A. Shweder (Ed.), *New directions for methodology of social and behavioral science* (Vol. 4, pp. 79–93). San Francisco: Jossey-Bass.

Fischhoff, B. (1982). Debiasing. In D. Kahneman, P. Slovic, & A. Tversky (Eds.), *Judgment under uncertainty: Heuristics and biases* (pp. 422–444). New York: Cambridge University Press.

Fischhoff, B., & Beyth, R. (1975). "I knew it would happen"—Remembered probabilities of once-future things. *Organizational Behavior and Human Performance, 13,* 1–16.

Fischhoff, B., Gonzalez, R. M., Lerner, J. S., & Small, D. A. (2005). Evolving judgments of terror risks: Foresight, hindsight, and emotion. *Journal of Experimental Psychology: Applied, 11,* 124–139.

Fischhoff, B., Slovic, P., & Lichtenstein, S. (1977). Knowing with certainty: The appropriateness of extreme confidence. *Journal of Experimental Psychology: Human Perception and Performance, 3,* 552–564.

Fishbach, A., Dhar, R., & Zhang, Y. (2006). Subgoals as substitutes or complements: The role of goal accessibility. *Journal of Personality and Social Psychology, 91,* 232–242.

Fishbach, A., & Shah, J. Y. (2006). Self-control in action: Implicit dispositions toward goals and away from temptations. *Journal of Personality and Social Psychology, 90,* 820–832.

Fishbach, A., Shah, J. Y., & Kruglanski, A. W. (2004). Emotional transfer in goal systems. *Journal of Experimental Social Psychology, 40,* 723–738.

Fishbein, M. (1963). An investigation of the relationship between beliefs about an object and the attitude toward that object. *Human Relations, 16,* 233–240.

Fishbein, M., & Ajzen, I. (1974). Attitudes toward objects as predictors of single and multiple behavioral criteria. *Psychological Review, 81,* 59–74.

Fishbein, M., & Ajzen, I. (1975). *Belief, attitude, intention, and behavior: An introduction to theory and research.* Reading, MA: Addison-Wesley.

Fiske, A. P., Haslam, N., & Fiske, S. T. (1991). Confusing one person with another: What errors reveal about the elementary forms of social relations. *Journal of Personality and Social Psychology, 60,* 656–674.

Fiske, A. P., Kitayama, S., Markus, H. R., & Nisbett, R. E. (1998). The cultural matrix of social psychology. In D. T. Gilbert, S. T. Fiske, & G. Lindzey (Eds.), *The handbook of social psychology* (4th ed., pp. 915–981). New York: McGraw-Hill.

Fiske, D. W., & Maddi, S. R. (1961). *Functions of varied experience.* Oxford, England: Dorsey.

Fiske, S. T. (1980). Attention and weight in person perception: The impact of negative and extreme behavior. *Journal of Personality and Social Psychology, 38,* 889–906.

Fiske, S. T. (1981). Social cognition and affect. In J. Harvey (Ed.), *Cognition, social behavior and the environment* (pp. 227–264). Hillsdale, NJ: Erlbaum.

Fiske, S. T. (1982). Schema-triggered affect: Applications to social perception. In M. S. Clark & S. T. Fiske (Eds.), *Affect and cognition: The 17th Annual Carnegie Symposium on Cognition* (pp. 55–78). Hillsdale, NJ: Erlbaum.

Fiske, S. T. (1988). Compare and contrast: Brewer's dual-process model and Fiske et al.'s continuum model. In T. K. Srull & R. S. Wyer (Eds.), *Advances in social cognition: A dual model of impression formation* (Vol. 1, pp. 65–76). Hillsdale, NJ: Erlbaum.

Fiske, S. T. (1989). Examining the role of intent: Toward understanding its role in stereotyping and prejudice. In J. S. Uleman & J. A. Bargh (Eds.), *Unintended thought* (pp. 253–283). New York: Guilford Press.

Fiske, S. T. (1992). Thinking is for doing: Portraits of social cognition from daguerreotype to laserphoto. *Journal of Personality and Social Psychology, 63,* 877–889.

Fiske, S. T. (1993). Social cognition and social perception. In M. R. Rosenzweig & L. W. Porter (Eds.), *Annual review of psychology* (Vol. 44, pp. 155–194). Palo Alto, CA: Annual Reviews.

Fiske, S. T. (1998). Stereotyping, prejudice, and discrimination. In D. T. Gilbert, S. T. Fiske, & G. Lindzey (Eds.), *Handbook of social psychology* (4th ed., Vol. 2, pp. 357–411). New York: McGraw-Hill.

Fiske, S. T. (2002). Five core social motives, plus or minus five. In S. J. Spencer, S. Fein, M. P. Zanna, & J. Olson (Eds.), *Motivated social perception: The Ontario Symposium* (Vol. 9, pp. 233–246). Mahwah, NJ: Erlbaum.

Fiske, S. T. (2004). *Social beings: A core motives approach to social psychology.* New York: Wiley.

Fiske, S. T. (in press). Core social motivations, a historical perspective: Views from the couch, consciousness, classroom, computers, and collectives. In W. Gardner & J. Shah (Eds.), *Handbook of motivation science.* New York: Guilford Press.

Fiske, S. T., Bersoff, D. N., Borgida, E., Deaux, K., & Heilman, M. E. (1991). Social science research on trial: The use of sex stereotyping research in *Price Waterhouse v. Hopkins. American Psychologist, 46,* 1049–1060.

Fiske, S. T., Cuddy, A. J. C., & Glick, P. (2007). Universal dimensions of social perception: Warmth and competence. *Trends in Cognitive Science, 11,* 77–83.

Fiske, S. T., Cuddy, A. J. C., Glick, P., & Xu, J. (2002). A model of (often mixed) stereotype content: Competence and warmth respectively follow from perceived status and competition. *Journal of Personality and Social Psychology, 82,* 878–902.

Fiske, S. T., Kenny, D. A., & Taylor, S. E. (1982). Structural models for the mediation of salience effects on attribution. *Journal of Experimental Social Psychology, 18,* 105–127.

Fiske, S. T., Lin, M. H., & Neuberg, S. L. (1999). The continuum model: Ten years later. In S. Chaiken & Y. Trope (Eds.), *Dual process theories in social psychology* (pp. 231–254). New York: Guilford Press.

Fiske, S. T., & Linville, P. W. (1980). What does the schema concept buy us? Symposium on social knowing. *Personality and Social Psychology Bulletin, 6,* 543–557.

Fiske, S. T., Moore, G., & Russell, A. M. (2006). *Mental illness subgroups, in the stereotype content model.* Unpublished data, Princeton University.

Fiske, S. T., & Neuberg, S. L. (1990). A continuum of impression formation, from category-based to individuating processes: Influences of information and motivation on attention and interpretation. In M. P. Zanna (Ed.), *Advances in experimental social psychology* (Vol. 23, pp. 1–74). New York: Academic Press.

Fiske, S. T., Neuberg, S. L., Beattie, A. E., & Milberg, S. J. (1987). Category-based and attribute-based reactions to others: Some informational conditions of stereotyping and individuating processes. *Journal of Experimental Social Psychology, 23,* 399–427.

Fiske, S. T., & Pavelchak, M. A. (1986). Category-based versus piecemeal-based affective responses: Developments in schema-triggered affect. In R. M. Sorrentino & E. T. Higgins (Eds.), *Handbook of motivation and cognition: Foundations of social behavior* (pp. 167–203). New York: Guilford Press.

Fiske, S. T., & Ruscher, J. B. (1989). On-line processes in category-based and individuating impressions: Some basic principles and methodological reflections. In J. N. Bassili (Ed.), *On-line cognition in person perception* (pp. 141–174). Hillsdale, NJ: Erlbaum.

Fiske, S. T., & Taylor, S. E. (1991). *Social cognition* (2nd ed.). New York: McGraw-Hill.

Fiske, S. T., Taylor, S. E., Etcoff, N. L., & Laufer, J. K. (1979). Imaging, empathy, and causal attribution. *Journal of Experimental Social Psychology, 15,* 356–377.

Fiske, S. T., Xu, J., Cuddy, A. C., & Glick, P. (1999). (Dis)respecting versus (dis)liking: Status and interdependence predict ambivalent stereotypes of competence and warmth. *Journal of Social Issues, 55,* 473–491.

Flack, W. F., Jr. (2006). Peripheral feedback effects of facial expressions, bodily postures, and vocal expressions on emotional feelings. *Cognition and Emotion, 20,* 177–195.

Flory, J. D., Räikkönen, K., Matthews, K. A., & Owens, J. F. (2000). Self-focused attention and mood during everyday social interactions. *Personality and Social Psychology Bulletin, 26,* 875–883.

Folkes, V. S. (1982). Communicating the causes of social rejection. *Journal of Experimental Social Psychology, 18,* 235–252.

Folkman, S., & Lazarus, R. S. (1988a). Coping as a mediator of emotion. *Journal of Personality and Social Psychology, 54,* 466–475.

Folkman, S., & Lazarus, R. S. (1988b). The relationship between coping and emotion: Implications for theory and research. *Social Science Medicine, 26,* 309–317.

Fong, G. T., Krantz, D. H., & Nisbett, R. E. (1986). The effects of statistical training on thinking about everyday problems. *Cognitive Psychology, 18,* 253–292.

Fong, G. T., & Markus, H. R. (1982). Self-schemas and judgments about others. *Social Cognition, 1,* 191–205.

Forest, D., Clark, M. S., Mills, J., & Isen, A. M. (1979). Helping as a function of feeling state and nature of the helping behavior. *Motivation and Emotion, 3,* 161–169.

Forgas, J. P. (1995). Mood and judgment: The affect infusion model (AIM). *Psychological Bulletin, 117,* 39–66.

Forgas, J. P. (1998). On being happy and mistaken: Mood effects on the fundamental attribution error. *Journal of Personality and Social Psychology. 75,* 318–331.

Forgas, J. P., Bower, G. H., & Krantz, S. E. (1984). The influence of mood on perceptions of social interactions. *Journal of Experimental Social Psychology, 20,* 497–513.

Forgas, J. P., Burnham, D. K., & Trimboli, C. (1988). Mood, memory, and social judgments in children. *Journal of Personality and Social Psychology, 54,* 697–703.

Forgas, J. P., & Fiedler, K. (1996). Us and them: Mood effects on intergroup discrimination. *Journal of Personality and Social Psychology, 70,* 28–40.

Forgas, J. P., & George, J. M. (2001). Affective influences on judgments and behavior in organizations: An information processing perspective. *Organizational Behavior and Human Decision Processes, 86,* 3–34.

Forgas, J. P., & Moylan, S. (1987). After the movies: Transient mood and social judgments. *Personality and Social Psychology Bulletin, 13,* 467–477.

Forgas, J. P., Laham, S., & Vargas, P. (2005). Mood effects on eyewitness memory: Affective influences on susceptibility to misinformation. *Journal of Experimental Social Psychology, 41,* 574–588.

Förster, J., Friedman, R. S., & Liberman, N. (2004). Temporal construal effects on abstract and concrete thinking: Consequences for insight and creative cognition. *Journal of Personality and Social Psychology, 87,* 177–189.

Förster, J., Higgins, T. E., & Idson, L. C. (1998). Approach and avoidance strength during goal attainment: Regulatory focus and the "goal looms larger" effect. *Journal of Personality and Social Psychology, 75,* 1115–1131.

Förster, J., & Strack, F. (1997). Motor actions in retrieval of valenced information: A motor congruence effect. *Perceptual and Motor Skills, 85,* 1419–1427.

Förster, J., & Strack, F. (1998). Motor actions in retrieval of valenced information: II. Boundary conditions for motor congruence effects. *Perceptual and Motor Skills, 86,* 1423–1426.

Fragale, A. R., & Heath, C. (2004). Evolving informational credentials: The (mis)attribution of believable facts to credible sources. *Personality and Social Psychology Bulletin, 30,* 225–236.

Frantz, C. M., Cuddy, A. J. C., Burnett, M., Ray, H., & Hart, A. J. (2004). A threat in the computer: The race implicit association test as a stereotype threat experience. *Personality and Social Psychology Bulletin, 30,* 1611–1624.

Frederick, S., Loewenstein, G., & O'Donoghue, T. (2002). Time discounting and time preference: A critical review. *Journal of Economic Literature, 40,* 351–401.

Fredrickson, G. M. (2002). *Racism: A short history.* Princeton, NJ: Princeton University Press.

Freedman, J. L., & Sears, D. O. (1965). Selective exposure. In L. Berkowitz (Ed.), *Advances in experimental social psychology* (Vol. 2, pp. 57–97). San Diego, CA: Academic Press.

Freitas, A. L., Liberman, N., Salovey, P., & Higgins, E. T. (2002). When to begin? Regulatory focus and initiating goal pursuit. *Personality and Social Psychology Bulletin, 28,* 121–130.

Frey, D. (1986). Recent research on selective exposure to information. In L. Berkowitz (Ed.), *Advances in experimental social psychology* (Vol. 19, pp. 41–80). New York: Academic Press.

Frey, F. E., & Tropp, L. R. (2006). Being seen as individuals versus as group members: Extending research on metaperception to intergroup contexts. *Personality and Social Psychology Review, 10,* 265–280.

Frijda, N. H. (1987a). Comment on Oatley and Johnson-Laird's "Towards a cognitive theory of emotions." *Cognition and Emotion, 1,* 51–58.

Frijda, N. H. (1987b). Emotion, cognitive structure, and action tendency. *Cognition and Emotion, 1,* 115–143.

Frijda, N. H. (1988). The laws of emotion. *American Psychologist, 43,* 349–358.

Frith, U., & Frith, C. (2001). The biological basis of social interaction. *Current Directions in Psychological Science, 10,* 151–155.

Fu, P. O., Kennedy, J., Tata, J., Yukl, G., Bond, M. H., et al. (2004). The impact of societal cultural values and individual social beliefs on the perceived effectiveness of managerial influence strategies: A meso approach. *Journal of International Business Studies, 35,* 284–305.

Fujita, K., Gollwitzer, P. M., & Oettingen, G. (2007). Mindsets and pre-conscious open-mindedness to incidental information. *Journal of Experimental Social Psychology, 43,* 48–61.

Fujita, K., Henderson, M. D., Eng, J., Trope, Y., & Liberman, N. (2006). Spatial distance and mental construal of social events. *Psychological Science, 17,* 278–282.

Funder, D. C. (1987). Errors and mistakes: Evaluating the accuracy of social judgment. *Psychological Bulletin, 101,* 75–90.

Gable, S. L., Reis, H. T., & Elliot, A. J. (2000). Behavioral activation and inhibition in everyday life. *Journal of Personality and Social Psychology, 78,* 1135–1149.

Gabrielcik, A., & Fazio, R. H. (1984). Priming and frequency estimation: A strict test of the availability heuristic. *Personality and Social Psychology Bulletin, 10,* 85–89.

Gaertner, S. L., & Dovidio, J. F. (1986). The aversive form of racism. In J. F. Dovidio & S. L. Gaertner (Eds.), *Prejudice, discrimination, and racism* (pp. 61–90). Orlando, FL: Academic Press.

Gaertner, S. L., & Dovidio, J. F. (2005). Understanding and addressing contemporary racism: From aversive racism to the common ingroup identity model. *Journal of Social Issues, 61,* 615–639.

Gaertner, S. L., & McLaughlin, J. P. (1983). Racial stereotypes: Associations and ascriptions of positive and negative characteristics. *Social Psychology Quarterly, 46,* 23–40.

Gaertner, S. L., Sedikides, C., & Graetz, K. (1999). In search of self-definition: Motivational primacy of the individual self, motivational primacy of the collective self, or contextual primacy? *Journal of Personality and Social Psychology, 76,* 5–18.

Gailliot, M. T., Schmeichel, B. J., & Baumeister, R. F. (2006). Self-regulatory processes defend against the threat of death: Effects of self-control depletion and trait self-control on thoughts and fears of dying. *Journal of Personality and Social Psychology, 91,* 49–62.

Galanis, C. M. B., & Jones, E. E. (1986). When stigma confronts stigma: Some conditions enhancing a victim's tolerance of other victims. *Personality and Social Psychology Bulletin, 12*, 169–177.

Galinsky, A. D., & Moskowitz, G. B. (2000). Perspective-taking: Decreasing stereotype expression, stereotype accessibility, and in-group favoritism. *Journal of Personality and Social Psychology, 78*, 708–724.

Gallagher, H. L., & Frith, C. D. (2003). Functional imaging of "theory of mind." *Trends in Cognitive Sciences, 7*, 77–83.

Gallagher, H. L., Jack, A., Roepstorff, A., & Frith, C. D. (2002). Imaging the intentional stance in a competitive game. *NeuroImage, 16*, 814–821.

Garcia-Marques, L., & Hamilton, L. (1996). Resolving the apparent discrepancy between the incongruency effect and the expectancy-based illusory correlation effect: The TRAP model. *Journal of Personality and Social Psychology, 71*, 845–860.

Garcia-Marques, L., Hamilton, L., & Maddox, K. B. (2002). Exhaustive and heuristic retrieval processes in person cognition: Further tests of the TRAP model. *Journal of Personality and Social Psychology, 82*, 193–207.

Gasper, K., & Clore, G. L. (2002). Attending to the big picture: Mood and global versus local processing of visual information. *Psychological Science, 13*, 34–40.

Gauthier, I., Skudlarski, P., Gore, J. C., & Anderson, A. W. (2000). Expertise for cars and birds recruits brain areas involved in face recognition. *Nature Neuroscience, 3*, 191–197.

Gaver, W. W., & Mandler, G. (1987). Play it again, Sam: On liking music. *Cognition and Emotion, 1*, 259–282.

Gawronski, B., & Bodenhausen, G. V. (2006). Associative and propositional processes in evaluation: An integrative review of implicit and explicit attitude change. *Psychological Bulletin, 132*, 692–731.

Gazzaniga, M. S. (2000). Cerebral specialization and interhemispheric communication: Does the corpus callosum enable the human condition? *Brain, 123*, 1293–1326.

Geertz, C. (1974). From the native's point of view: On the nature of anthropological understanding. In K. Basso & H. Selby (Eds.), *Meaning in anthropology* (pp. 221–237). Albuquerque: University of New Mexico Press.

Geertz, C. (1975). On the nature of anthropological understanding. *American Scientist, 63*, 47–53.

Gellhorn, E. (1964). Motion and emotion: The role of proprioception in the physiology and pathology of emotions. *Psychological Review, 71*, 457–472.

Genero, N., & Cantor, N. (1987). Exemplar prototypes and clinical diagnosis: Toward a cognitive economy. *Journal of Social and Clinical Psychology, 5*, 59–78.

Gernsbacher, M. A., & Kaschak, M. P. (2003). Neuroimaging studies of language production and comprehension. *Annual Review of Psychology, 54*, 91–114.

Gibson, J. J. (1966). *The senses considered as perceptual systems.* Boston: Houghton Mifflin.

Gibson, J. J. (1979). *The ecological approach to visual perception.* Boston: Houghton Mifflin.

Gilbert, D. T. (1991). How mental systems believe. *American Psychologist, 46*, 107–119.

Gilbert, D. T. (1998). Ordinary personology. In D. T. Gilbert, S. T. Fiske, & G. Lindzey (Eds.), *The handbook of social psychology* (4th ed., Vol. 2, pp. 89–150). New York: McGraw-Hill.

Gilbert, D. T. (1999). What the mind's not. In S. Chaiken & Y. Trope (Eds.), *Dual-process theories in social psychology.* New York: Guilford Press.

Gilbert, D. T., Brown, R. P., Pinel, E. C., & Wilson, T. D. (2000). The illusion of external agency. *Journal of Personality and Social Psychology, 79*, 690–700.

Gilbert, D. T., & Hixon, J. G. (1991). The trouble of thinking: Activation and application of stereotypic beliefs. *Journal of Personality and Social Psychology, 60*, 509–517.

Gilbert, D. T., Krull, D. S., & Pelham, B. W. (1988). Of thoughts unspoken: Social inference and the self-regulation of behavior. *Journal of Personality and Social Psychology, 55*, 685–694.

Gilbert, D. T., Lieberman, M. D., Morewedge, C. K., & Wilson, T. D. (2004). The peculiar longevity of things not so bad. *Psychological Science, 15*, 14–19.

Gilbert, D. T., & Malone, P. S. (1995). The correspondence bias. *Psychological Bulletin, 117*, 21–38.

Gilbert, D. T., Pelham, B. W., & Krull, D. S. (1988). On cognitive busyness: When person perceivers meet persons perceived. *Journal of Personality and Social Psychology, 54*, 733–739.

Gilbert, D. T., Pinel, E. C., Wilson, D., Blumberg, S. J., & Wheatley, T. P. (1998). Immune neglect: A source of durability bias in affective forecasting. *Journal of Personality and Social Psychology, 75,* 617–638.

Gilovich, T. (1981). Seeing the past in the present: The effect of associations to familiar events on judgments and decisions. *Journal of Personality and Social Psychology, 40,* 797–808.

Giner-Sorolla, R. (1999). Affect in attitude: Immediate and deliberative perspectives. In S. Chaiken & Y. Trope (Eds.), *Dual process theories in social psychology* (pp. 441–461). New York: Guilford Press.

Giner-Sorolla, R. (2001). Affective attitudes are not always faster: The moderating role of extremity. *Personality and Social Psychology Bulletin, 27,* 666–677.

Giner-Sorolla, R., Mackie, D. M., & Smith, E. R. (Eds.). (2007). Special issue: Intergroup emotions. *Group Processes and Intergroup Relations, 10,* 5–136.

Ginossar, Z., & Trope, Y. (1980). The effects of base rates and individuating information on judgments about another person. *Journal of Experimental Social Psychology, 16,* 228–242.

Ginossar, Z., & Trope, Y. (1987). Problem solving in judgment under uncertainty. *Journal of Personality and Social Psychology, 52,* 464–474.

Gladwell, M. (2005). *Blink: The power of thinking without thinking.* New York: Little, Brown.

Glaser, J., Dixit, J., & Green, D. P. (2002). Studying hate crime with the Internet: What makes racists advocate racial violence? *Journal of Social Issues, 58,* 177–193.

Glaser, J., & Salovey, P. (1998). Affect in electoral politics. *Personality and Social Psychology Review, 2,* 156–172.

Glass, A. L., & Holyoak, K. J. (1986). *Cognition* (2nd ed.). New York: Random House.

Glassman, N. S., & Andersen, S. M. (1999). Activating transference without consciousness: Using significant-other representations to go beyond what is subliminally given. *Journal of Personality and Social Psychology, 77,* 1146–1162.

Gleicher, F. H., Kost, K. A., Baker, S. M., Strathman, A. J., Richman, S. A., & Sherman, S. J. (1990). The role of counterfactual thinking in judgments of affect. *Personality and Social Psychology Bulletin, 16,* 284–295.

Glick, P., Diebold, J., Bailey-Werner, B., & Zhu, L. (1997). The two faces of Adam: Ambivalent sexism and polarized attitudes toward women. *Personality and Social Psychology Bulletin, 23,* 1323–1334.

Glick, P., & Fiske, S. T. (1996). The Ambivalent Sexism Inventory: Differentiating hostile and benevolent sexism. *Journal of Personality and Social Psychology, 70,* 491–512.

Glick, P., & Fiske, S. T. (2001). Ambivalent sexism. In M. P. Zanna (Ed.), *Advances in experimental social psychology* (Vol. 33, pp. 115–188). Thousand Oaks, CA: Academic Press.

Glick, P., Fiske, S. T., Mladinic, A., Saiz, J. L., Abrams, D., Masser, B., et al. (2000). Beyond prejudice as simple antipathy: Hostile and benevolent sexism across cultures. *Journal of Personality and Social Psychology, 79,* 763–775.

Glick, P., Lameriras, M., Fiske, S. T., Eckes, T., Masser, B., Volpato, C., et al. (2004). Bad but bold: Ambivalent attitudes toward men predict gender inequality in 16 nations. *Journal of Personality and Social Psychology, 86,* 713–728.

Glick, P., Wilk, K., & Perrault, M. (1995). Images of occupations: Components of gender and status in occupational stereotypes. *Sex Roles, 32,* 9–10.

Glimcher, P. D. (2003). *Decisions, uncertainty, and the brain: The science of neuroeconomics.* Cambridge, MA: MIT Press.

Glimcher, P. W., & Rustichini, A. (2004). Neuroeconomics: The consilience of brain and decision. *Science, 306,* 447–452.

Gobbini, M. I., Leibenluft, E., Santiago, N., & Haxby, J. V. (2004). Social and emotional attachment in the neural representation of faces. *NeuroImage, 22,* 1628–1635. [Erratum: *32,* 1484.]

Goethals, G. R. (1976). An attributional analysis of some social influence phenomena. In J. H. Harvey, W. J. Ickes, & R. F. Kidd (Eds.), *New directions in attribution research* (Vol. 1, pp. 291–310). Hillsdale, NJ: Erlbaum.

Goethals, G. R., & Reckman, R. F. (1973). The perception of consistency in attitudes. *Journal of Experimental Social Psychology, 9,* 491–501.

Goethals, G. R., & Zanna, M. P. (1979). The role of social comparison in choice shifts. *Journal of Personality and Social Psychology, 37,* 1469–1476.

Goffman, E. (1963). *Stigma: Notes on the management of spoiled identity*. New York: Prentice-Hall.

Golby, A. J., Gabrieli, J. D. E., Chiao, J. Y., & Eberhardt, J. L. (2001). Differential responses in the fusiform region to same-race and other-race faces. *Nature Neuroscience, 4*, 845–850.

Goldberg, E. (2001). *The executive brain: Frontal lobes and the civilized mind*. New York: Oxford University Press.

Goldberg, L. R. (1968). Simple models or simple processes? Some research on clinical judgments. *American Psychologist, 23*, 483–496.

Goldberg, L. R. (1970). Man versus model of man: A rationale, plus some evidence, for a method of improving on clinical inferences. *Psychological Bulletin, 73*, 422–432.

Goldberg, L. R. (1986). The validity of rating procedures to index the hierarchical level of categories. *Journal of Memory and Language, 25*, 323–347.

Gollwitzer, P. M. (1990). *Action phases and mindsets*. New York: Guilford Press.

Gollwitzer, P. M., Earle, W. B., & Stephan, W. G. (1982). Affect as a determinant of egotism: Residual excitation and performance attributions. *Journal of Personality and Social Psychology, 43*, 702–709.

Gollwitzer, P. M., & Moskowitz, G. B. (1996). Goal effects on action and cognition. In E. T. Higgins & A. W. Kruglanski (Eds.), *Social psychology: Handbook of basic principles* (pp. 361–399). New York: Guilford Press.

Gollwitzer, P. M., & Sheeran, P. (2006). Implementation intentions and goal achievement: A meta-analysis of effects and processes. In M.P. Zanna (Ed.), *Advances in Experimental Psychology*, (Vol. 38, pp. 69–119) San Diego, CA: Academic Press.

Gosling, S. D., Ko, S. J., Mannarelli, T., & Morris, M. E. (2002). A room with a cue: Judgments of personality based on offices and bedrooms. *Journal of Personality and Social Psychology, 82*, 379–398.

Gónzales, P. M., Blanton, H., & Williams, K. J. (2002). The effects of stereotype threat and double-minority status on the test performance of Latino women. *Personality and Social Psychology Bulletin, 28*, 659–670.

Graham, S., & Lowery, B. S. (2004) Priming unconscious racial stereotypes about adolescent offenders. *Law and Human Behavior, 28*, 483–504.

Graham, S., & Weiner, B. (1986). From an attributional theory of emotion to developmental psychology: A round-trip ticket? *Social Cognition, 4*, 152–179.

Granberg, D., & Brent, E. (1980). Perceptions of issue positions of presidential candidates. *American Scientist, 68*, 617–625.

Graves, J. (2001). *The emperor's new clothes: Biological theories of race at the millennium*. New Brunswick, NJ: Rutgers University Press.

Gray, J. A. (1990). Brain systems that mediate both emotion and cognition. *Cognition and Emotion, 4*, 269–288.

Graziano, W. G., Moore, J. S., & Collins, J. E., II. (1988). Social cognition as segmentation of the stream of behavior. *Developmental Psychology, 24*, 568–573.

Greaves, G. (1972). Conceptual system functioning and selective recall of information. *Journal of Personality and Social Psychology, 21*, 327–332.

Green, D. P., Glaser, J., & Rich, A. (1998). From lynching to gay bashing: The elusive connection between economic conditions and hate crime. *Journal of Personality and Social Psychology, 75*, 82–92.

Green, D. P., Salovey, P., & Truax, K. M. (1999). Static, dynamic, and causative bipolarity of affect. *Journal of Personality and Social Psychology, 76*, 856–867.

Green, D. P., Strolovitch, D. Z., & Wong, J. S. (1998). Defended neighborhoods, integration, and racially motivated crime. *American Journal of Sociology, 104*, 372–403.

Greenberg, J., Arndt, J., Schimel, J., Pyszczynski, T., & Solomon, S. (2001). Clarifying the function of mortality salience-induced worldview defense: Renewed suppression or reduced accessibility of death-related thoughts? *Journal of Experimental Social Psychology, 37*, 70–76.

Greenberg, J., Porteus, J., Simon, L., Pyszczynski, T., & Solomon, S. (1995). Evidence of a terror management function of cultural icons: The effects of mortality salience on the inappropriate use of cherished cultural symbols. *Personality and Social Psychology Bulletin, 21*, 1221–1228.

Greenberg, J., & Pyszczynski, T. (1985). The effects of an overheard ethnic slur on evaluations of the target: How to spread a social disease. *Journal of Experimental Social Psychology, 21,* 61–72.

Greenberg, J., Pyszczynski, T., & Solomon, S. (1986). The causes and consequences of a need for self-esteem: A terror management theory. In R. F. Baumeister (Ed.), *Public self and private self* (pp. 189–212). New York: Springer-Verlag.

Greenberg, J., Pyszczynski, T., Solomon, S., Rosenblatt, A., Veeder, M., Kirkland, S., & Lyon, D. (1990). Evidence for terror management theory II: The effects of mortality salience on reactions to those who threaten or bolster the cultural worldview. *Journal of Personality and Social Psychology, 58,* 308–318.

Greenberg, J., Schimel, J., & Meertens, A. (2002). Ageism: Denying the face of the future. In T. D. Nelson (Ed.), *Ageism: Stereotyping and prejudice against older persons* (pp. 27–48). Cambridge, MA: MIT Press.

Greenberg, J., Simon, L., Pyszczynski, T., Solomon, S., & Chatel, D. (1992). Terror management and tolerance: Does mortality salience always intensify negative reactions to others who threaten one's worldview? *Journal of Personality and Social Psychology, 63,* 212–220.

Greenberg, J., Solomon, S., & Pyszczynski, T. (1997). Terror management theory of self-esteem and cultural worldviews: Empirical assessments and conceptual refinements. In M. P. Zanna (Ed.), *Advances in experimental social psychology* (Vol. 29, pp. 61–139). San Diego, CA: Academic Press.

Greenberg, J., Williams, K. D., & O'Brien, M. K. (1986). Considering the harshest verdict first: Biasing effects on mock juror verdicts. *Personality and Social Psychology Bulletin, 12,* 41–50.

Greene, J. D., Somerville, R. B., Nystrom, L. E., Darley, J. M., & Cohen, J. D. (2001). An fMRI investigation of emotional engagement in moral judgment. *Science, 293,* 2105–2108.

Greenwald, A. G. (1968). Cognitive learning, cognitive response to persuasion and attitude change. In A. G. Greenwald, T. C. Brock, & T. M. Ostrom (Eds.), *Psychological foundations of attitudes* (pp. 147–170). New York: Academic Press.

Greenwald, A. G. (1975). Consequences of prejudice against the null hypothesis. *Psychological Bulletin, 82,* 1–20.

Greenwald, A. G. (1981). Self and memory. In G. H. Bower (Ed.), *The psychology of learning and motivation* (Vol. 15, pp. 201–236). New York: Academic Press.

Greenwald, A. G. (1989). Why attitudes are important: Defining attitude and attitude theory 20 years later. In A. R. Pratkanis, S. J. Breckler, & A. G. Greenwald (Eds.), *Attitudes structure and function* (pp. 429–440). Hillsdale, NJ: Erlbaum.

Greenwald, A. G., Banaji, M. R., Rudman, L. A., Farnham, S. D., Nosek, B. A., & Mellott, D. S. (2002). A unified theory of implicit attitudes, stereotypes, self-esteem, and self-concept. *Psychological Review, 109,* 3–25.

Greenwald, A. G., Klinger, M. R., & Liu, T. J. (1989). Unconscious processing of dichotically masked words. *Memory and Cognition, 17,* 35–47.

Greenwald, A. G., & Leavitt, C. (1984). Audience involvement in advertising: Four levels. *Journal of Consumer Research, 11,* 581–592.

Greenwald, A. G., McGhee, D. E., & Schwartz, J. L. K. (1998). Measuring individual differences in implicit cognition: The implicit association test. *Journal of Personality and Social Psychology, 74,* 1464–1480.

Grice, H. P. (1975). Logic and conversation. In P. Cole & J. L. Morgan (Eds.), *Syntax and semantics 3: Speech acts* (pp. 95–113). New York: Academic Press.

Griffiths, T. L., & Tenenbaum, J. B. (2006). Optimal predictions in everyday cognition. *Psychological Science, 17,* 767–773.

Groom, C. J., Sherman, J. W., Lu, L., Conrey, F. R., & Keijzer, S. C. (2005). Judging compound social categories: Compound familiarity and compatibility as determinants of processing mode. *Social Cognition, 23,* 291–323.

Grush, J. E. (1976). Attitude formation and mere exposure phenomena: A nonartificial explanation of empirical findings. *Journal of Personality and Social Psychology, 33,* 281–290.

Gueguen, N., & DeGail, M. (2003). The effect of smiling on helping behavior: Smiling and good Samaritan behavior. *Communication Report, 16,* 133–140.

Guimond, S., Chatard, A., Martinot, D., Crisp, R. J., & Redersdorff, S. (2006). Social comparison, self-stereotyping, and gender differences in self-construals. *Journal of Personality and Social Psychology, 90,* 221–242.

Guimond, S., Dambrun, M., Michinov, N., & Duarte, S. (2003). Does social dominance generate prejudice? Integrating individual and contextual determinants of intergroup cognitions. *Journal of Personality and Social Psychology, 84,* 697–721.

Guinote, A. (2001). The perception of group variability in a non-minority and a minority context: When adaptation leads to out-group differentiation. *British Journal of Social Psychology, 40,* 117–132.

Haddock, G., & Zanna, M. P. (1994). Preferring "housewives" to "feminists": Categorization and the favorability of attitudes toward women. *Psychology of Women Quarterly, 18,* 25–52.

Haddock, G., Zanna, M. P., & Esses, V. M. (1993). Assessing the structure of prejudicial attitudes: The case of attitudes toward homosexuals. *Journal of Personality and Social Psychology, 65,* 1105–1118.

Hager, J. C., & Ekman, P. (1981). Methodological problems in Tourangeau and Ellsworth's study of facial expression and experience of emotion. *Journal of Personality and Social Psychology, 40,* 358–362.

Haidt, J. (2001). The emotional dog and its rational tail: A social intuitionist approach to moral judgment. *Psychological Review, 108,* 814–834.

Haidt, J., & Hersh, M. A. (2001). Sexual morality: The cultures and emotions of conservatives and liberals. *Journal of Applied Social Psychology, 31,* 191–221.

Haidt, J., Koller, S. H., & Dias, M. G. (1993). Affect, culture, and morality, or is it wrong to eat your dog? *Journal of Personality and Social Psychology, 65,* 613–628.

Haidt, J., McCauley, C. & Rozin, P. (1994). Individual differences in sensitivity to disgust: A scale sampling seven domains of disgust elicitors. *Personality and Individual Differences, 16,* 701–713.

Haines, E. L., & Jost, J. T. (2000). Placating the powerless: Effects of legitimate and illegitimate explanation on affect, memory, and stereotyping. *Social Justice Research, 13,* 219–236.

Halloran, M. J., & Kashima, E. S. (2004). Social identity and worldview validation: The effects of ingroup identity primes and mortality salience on value endorsement. *Personality and Social Psychology Bulletin, 30,* 915–925.

Hamill, R., Wilson, T. D., & Nisbett, R. E. (1980). Insensitivity to sample bias: Generalizing from atypical cases. *Journal of Personality and Social Psychology, 39,* 578–589.

Hamilton, D. L. (1979). A cognitive-attributional analysis of stereotyping. In L. Berkowitz (Ed.), *Advances in experimental social psychology* (Vol. 12, pp. 53–84). New York: Academic Press.

Hamilton, D. L., Driscoll, D. M., & Worth, L. T. (1989). Cognitive organization of impressions: Effects of incongruency in complex representations. *Journal of Personality and Social Psychology, 57,* 925–939.

Hamilton, D. L., Dugan, P. M., & Trolier, T. K. (1985). The formation of stereotypic beliefs: Further evidence for distinctiveness-based illusory correlations. *Journal of Personality and Social Psychology, 48,* 5–17.

Hamilton, D. L., & Gifford, R. K. (1976). Illusory correlation in interpersonal perception: A cognitive basis of stereotypic judgments. *Journal of Experimental Social Psychology, 12,* 392–407.

Hamilton, D. L., & Rose, T. L. (1980). Illusory correlation and the maintenance of stereotypic beliefs. *Journal of Personality and Social Psychology, 39,* 832–845.

Hamilton, V., Bower, G. H., & Frijda, N. H. (Eds.). (1988). *Cognitive perspectives on emotion and motivation.* Norwood, MA: Kluwer Academic.

Hampson, S. E., & Dawson, W. J. M. (1985). Whatever happened to Pollyanna? The effects of evaluative congruence on speed of trait inference. *Personality and Social Psychology Bulletin, 11,* 106–117.

Hampson, S. E., Goldberg, L. R., & John, O. P. (1987). Category-breadth and social-desirability values for 573 personality terms. *European Journal of Personality, 1,* 241–258.

Hampson, S. E., John, O. P., & Goldberg, L. R. (1986). Category breadth and hierarchical structure in personality: Studies of asymmetries in judgments of trait implications. *Journal of Personality and Social Psychology, 51,* 37–54.

Hansen, C. H., & Hansen, R. D. (1988a). Finding the face in the crowd: An anger superiority effect. *Journal of Personality and Social Psychology, 54,* 917–924.

Hansen, C. H., & Hansen, R. D. (1988b). How rock music videos can change what is seen when boy meets girl: Priming stereotypic appraisal of social interactions. *Sex Roles, 19,* 287–316.

Harkins, S. G., & Petty, R. E. (1981). Effects of source magnification of cognitive effort on attitudes: An information-processing view. *Journal of Personality and Social Psychology, 40,* 401–413.

Harkness, A. R., DeBono, K. G., & Borgida, E. (1985). Personal involvement and strategies for making contingency judgments: A stake in the dating game makes a difference. *Journal of Personality and Social Psychology, 49,* 22–32.

Harmon-Jones, E., Lueck, L., Fearn, M., & Harmon-Jones, C. (2006). The effect of personal relevance and approach-related action expectation on relative left frontal cortical activity. *Psychological Science, 17,* 434–440.

Harris, L. T., & Fiske, S. T. (2006). Dehumanizing the lowest of the low: Neuro-imaging responses to extreme outgroups. *Psychological Science, 17,* 847–853.

Harris, L. T., Todorov, A., & Fiske, S. T. (2005). Attributions on the brain: Neuro-imaging dispositional inferences, beyond theory of mind. *NeuroImage, 28,* 763–769.

Harris, R. J., Teske, R. R., & Ginns, M. J. (1975). Memory for pragmatic implications from courtroom testimony. *Bulletin of the Psychonomic Society, 6,* 494–496.

Harrison, A. A. (1977). Mere exposure. In L. Berkowitz (Ed.), *Advances in experimental social psychology* (Vol. 10, pp. 39–83). New York: Academic Press.

Hart, A. J., Whalen, P. J., Shin, L. M., McInerney, S. C., Fischer, H., & Rauch, S. L. (2000). Differential response in the human amygdala to racial outgroup vs. ingroup face stimuli. *Neuroreport: For Rapid Communication of Neuroscience Research, 11,* 2351–2355.

Hartley, D. (1966). *Observations on man, his frame, his duty, and his expectations.* Delmar, NY: Scholastic Facsimiles. (Originally published 1749)

Harvey, J. H., Yarkin, K. L., Lightner, J. M., & Town, J. P. (1980). Unsolicited interpretation and recall of interpersonal events. *Journal of Personality and Social Psychology, 38,* 551–568.

Hasher, L., Rose, K. C., Zacks, R. T., Sanft, H., & Doren, B. (1985). Mood, recall, and selectivity effects in normal college students. *Journal of Experimental Psychology: General, 114,* 104–118.

Haslam, N. (2006). Dehumanization: An integrative review. *Personality and Social Psychology Review, 10,* 252–264.

Haslam, N., Bain, P., Douge, L., Lee, M., & Bastian, B. (2005). More human than you: Attributing humanness to self and others. *Journal of Personality and Social Psychology, 89,* 937–950.

Hastie, R. (1988a). Causes and effects of causal attribution. *Journal of Personality and Social Psychology, 46,* 44–56.

Hastie, R. (1988b). A computer simulation model of person memory. *Journal of Experimental Social Psychology, 24,* 423–447.

Hastie, R., & Carlston, D. (1980). Theoretical issues in person memory. In R. Hastie, T. M. Ostrom, E. B. Ebbesen, R. S. Wyer, D. L. Hamilton, & D. E. Carlston (Eds.), *Person memory: The cognitive basis of social perception* (pp. 1–53). Hillsdale, NJ: Erlbaum.

Hastie, R., & Dawes, R. M. (2001). *Rational choice in an uncertain world: The psychology of judgment and decision making.* San Diego, CA: Sage.

Hastie, R., & Park, B. (1986). The relationship between memory and judgment depends on whether the judgment task is memory-based or on-line. *Psychological Review, 93,* 258–268.

Hastie, R., & Rasinski, K. A. (1988). The concept of accuracy in social judgment. In D. Bar-Tal & A. W. Kruglanski (Eds.), *The social psychology of knowledge.* Cambridge, England: Cambridge University Press.

Hastorf, A. H., & Cantril, H. (1954). They saw a game: A case study. *Journal of Abnormal and Social Psychology, 49,* 129–134.

Hawkley, L. C., Burleson, M. H., Berntson, G. G., & Cacioppo, J. T. (2003). Loneliness in everyday life: Cardiovascular activity, psychosocial context, and health behaviors. *Journal of Personality and Social Psychology, 85,* 105–120.

Haxby, J. V., Gobbini, M. I., & Montgomery, K. J. (2004). Spatial and temporal distribution of face and object representations in the human brain. In M. S. Gazzaniga (Ed.), *The cognitive neurosciences* (3rd ed., pp. 889–904). Cambridge, MA: MIT Press.

Haxby, J. V., Hoffman, E. A., & Gobbini, M. I. (2000). The distributed human neural system for face perception. *Trends in Cognitive Science, 4,* 223–233.

Hayes-Roth, B., & Hayes-Roth, F. (1977). Concept learning and the recognition and classification of exemplars. *Journal of Verbal Learning and Verbal Behavior, 16,* 321–338.

Heatherton, T. F., Macrae, C. N., & Kelley, W. M. (2004). What the social brain sciences can tell us about the self. *Current Directions in Psychological Science, 13,* 190–193.

Heatherton, T. F., & Vohs, K. D. (2000). Interpersonal evaluations following threats to self: Role of self-esteem. *Journal of Personality and Social Psychology, 78,* 726–736.

Heatherton, T. F., Wyland, C. L., Macrae, C. N., Demos, K. E., Denny, B. T., & Kelley, W. M. (2006). Medial prefrontal activity differentiates self from close others. *Social Cognitive and Affective Neuroscience, 1,* 18–25.

Hebl, M. R., & Dovidio, J. F. (2005). Promoting the "social" in the examination of social stigmas. *Personality and Social Psychology Review, 9,* 156–182.

Heckhausen, H., & Gollwitzer, P. M. (1987). Thought contents and cognitive functioning in motivational versus volitional states of mind. *Motivation and Emotion, 11,* 101–120.

Heider, F. (1958). *The psychology of interpersonal relations.* New York: Wiley.

Heilman, M. E. (1980). The impact of situational factors on personnel decisions concerning women: Varying the sex composition of the applicant pool. *Organizational Behavior and Human Performance, 26,* 386–395.

Heine, S. J., & Lehman, D. R. (1997). Culture, dissonance, and self-affirmation. *Personality and Social Psychology Bulletin, 23,* 389–400.

Heine, S. J., Kitayama, S., Lehman, D. R., Takata, T., Ide, E., Leung, C., et al. (2001). Divergent consequences of success and failure in Japan and North America: An investigation of self-improving motivations and malleable selves. *Journal of Personality and Social Psychology, 81,* 599–615.

Heine, S. J., & Renshaw, K. (2002). Interjudge agreement, self-enhancement, and liking: Cross-cultural divergences. *Personality and Social Psychology Bulletin, 28,* 578–587.

Heine, S. J., Takata, T., & Lehman, D. R. (2000). Beyond self-presentation: Evidence for self-criticism among Japanese. *Personality and Social Psychology Bulletin, 26,* 71–78.

Henderson, M. D., Fujita, K., Trope, Y., & Liberman, N. (2006). Transcending the "here": The effect of spatial distance on social judgment. *Journal of Personality and Social Psychology, 91,* 845–856.

Hennessey, J., & West, M. A. (1999). Intergroup behavior in organizations: A field test of social identity theory. *Small Group Research, 30,* 361–382.

Hennigan, K. M., Cook, T. D., & Gruder, C. L. (1982). Cognitive tuning set, source credibility, and the temporal persistence of attitude change. *Journal of Personality and Social Psychology, 42,* 412–425.

Herek, G. M. (1986). The instrumentality of ideologies: Toward a neofunctional theory of attitudes. *Journal of Social Issues, 42,* 99–114.

Herek, G. M. (2000). The psychology of sexual prejudice. *Current Directions in Psychological Science, 9,* 19–22.

Herek, G. M. (2002). Gender gaps in public opinion about lesbians and gay men. *Public Opinion Quarterly, 66,* 40–66.

Herek, G. M., & Capitanio, J. P. (1997). AIDS stigma and contact with persons with AIDS: Effects of direct and vicarious contact. *Journal of Applied Social Psychology, 27,* 1–36.

Herek, G. M., & Capitanio, J. P. (1999). Sex differences in how heterosexuals think about lesbians and gay men: Evidence from survey context effects. *Journal of Sex Research, 36,* 348–360.

Herek, G. M., Gillis, J. R., & Cogan, J. C. (1999). Psychological sequelae of hate-crime victimization among lesbian, gay, and bisexual adults. *Journal of Consulting and Clinical Psychology, 67,* 945–951.

Herr, P. M. (1986). Consequences of priming: Judgment and behavior. *Journal of Personality and Social Psychology, 51,* 1106–1115.

Herr, P. M., Sherman, S. J., & Fazio, R. H. (1983). On the consequences of priming: Assimilation and contrast effects. *Journal of Experimental Social Psychology, 19,* 323–340.

Hewstone, M. (1990). The "ultimate attribution error?" A review of the literature on intergroup causal attribution. *European Journal of Social Psychology, 20,* 311–335.

Hewstone, M., Benn, W., & Wilson, A. (1988). Bias in the use of base rates: Racial prejudice in decision-making. *European Journal of Social Psychology, 18*, 161–176.

Hewstone, M., & Jaspers, J. (1987). Covariation and causal attribution: A logical model of the intuitive analysis of variance. *Journal of Personality and Social Psychology, 53*, 663–672.

Hewstone, M., Rubin, M., & Willis, H. (2002). Intergroup bias. *Annual Review of Psychology, 53*, 575–604.

Higgins, E. T. (1987). Self-discrepancy: A theory relating self and affect. *Psychological Review, 94*, 319–340.

Higgins, E. T. (1989a). Knowledge accessibility and activation: Subjectivity and suffering from unconscious sources. In J. S. Uleman & J. A. Bargh (Eds.), *Unintended thought* (pp. 75–123). New York: Guilford Press.

Higgins, E. T. (1989b). Self-discrepancy theory: What patterns of self-beliefs cause people to suffer? In L. Berkowitz (Ed.), *Advances in experimental social psychology* (pp. 93–136). San Diego: Academic Press.

Higgins, E. T. (1996). Knowledge activation: Accessibility, applicability, and salience. In E. T. Higgins & A. W. Kruglanski (Eds.), *Social psychology: Handbook of basic principles* (pp. 133–168). New York: Guilford Press.

Higgins, E. T. (1997). Beyond pleasure and pain. *American Psychologist, 52*, 1280–1300.

Higgins, E. T. (1999). Self-discrepancy: A theory relating self and affect. In R. F. Baumeister (Ed.), *Self in social psychology: Key readings in social psychology*: (pp. 150–181). Philadelphia: Psychology Press.

Higgins, E. T. (2005). Value from regulatory fit. *Current Directions in Psychological Science, 14*, 209–213.

Higgins, E. T., & Bargh, J. A. (1987). Social cognition and social perception. *Annual Review of Psychology, 38*, 369–425.

Higgins, E. T., Bargh, J. A., & Lombardi, W. J. (1985). The nature of priming effects on categorization. *Journal of Experimental Psychology: Learning, Memory, and Cognition, 11*, 59–69.

Higgins, E. T., Bond, R. N., Klein, R., & Strauman, T. J. (1986). Self-discrepancies and emotional vulnerability: How magnitude, accessibility, and type of discrepancy influence affect. *Journal of Personality and Social Psychology, 51*, 5–15.

Higgins, E. T., & Chaires, W. M. (1980). Accessibility of interrelational constructs: Implications for stimulus encoding and creativity. *Journal of Experimental Social Psychology, 16*, 348–361.

Higgins, E. T., Idson, L. C., Freitas, A. L., Spiegel, C., & Molden, D. C. (2003). Transfer of value from fit. *Journal of Personality and Social Psychology, 84*, 1140–1153.

Higgins, E. T., & King, G. A. (1981). Accessibility of social constructs: Information-processing consequences of individual and contextual variability. In N. Cantor & J. F. Kihlstrom (Eds.), *Personality, cognition, and social interaction* (pp. 69–122). Hillsdale, NJ: Erlbaum.

Higgins, E. T., King, G. A., & Mavin, G. H. (1982). Individual construct accessibility and subjective impressions and recall. *Journal of Personality and Social Psychology, 43*, 35–47.

Higgins, E. T., Klein, R., & Strauman, T. J. (1985). Self-concept discrepancy theory: A psychological model for distinguishing among different aspects of depression and anxiety. *Social Cognition, 3*, 51–76.

Higgins, E. T., Kuiper, N. A., & Olson, J. M. (1981). Social cognition: A need to get personal. In E. T. Higgins, C. P. Herman, & M. P. Zanna (Eds.), *Social cognition: The Ontario Symposium* (Vol. 1, pp. 395–420). Hillsdale, NJ: Erlbaum.

Higgins, E. T., Rholes, W. S., & Jones, C. R. (1977). Category accessibility and impression formation. *Journal of Experimental Social Psychology, 13*, 141–154.

Higgins, E. T., Shah, J. Y., & Friedman, R. S. (1997). Emotional responses to goal attainment: Strength of regulatory focus as moderator. *Journal of Personality and Social Psychology, 72*, 515–525.

Highhouse, S., & Paese, P. W. (1996). Problem domain and prospect frame: Choice under opportunity versus threat. *Personality and Social Psychology Bulletin, 22*, 124–132.

Hilton, D. J., & Slugoski, B. R. (1986). Knowledge-based causal attribution: The abnormal conditions focus model. *Psychological Review, 93*, 75–88.

Hilton, J. L., & Darley, J. M. (1985). Constructing other persons: A limit on the effect. *Journal of Experimental Social Psychology, 21,* 1–18.

Hing, L. S., Li, W., & Zanna, M. P. (2002). Inducing hypocrisy to reduce prejudicial responses among aversive racists. *Journal of Experimental Social Psychology, 38,* 71–78.

Hinsz, V. B., & Davis, J. H. (1984). Persuasive arguments theory, group polarization, and choice shifts. *Personality and Social Psychology Bulletin, 10,* 260–268.

Hirschberger, G. (2006). Terror management and attributions of blame to innocent victims: Reconciling compassionate and defensive responses. *Journal of Personality and Social Psychology, 91,* 832–844.

Hirschfeld, L. (1996). *Race in the making.* Cambridge, MA: MIT Press.

Hoffman, E. A., & Haxby, J. V. (2000). Distinct representations of eye gaze and identity in the distributed human neural system for face perception. *Nature Neuroscience, 3,* 80–84.

Hofmann, W., Gawronski, B., Gschwendner, T., Le, H., & Schmitt, M. (2005). A meta-analysis on the correlation between the implicit association test and explicit self-report measures. *Personality and Social Psychology Bulletin, 31,* 1369–1385.

Hogg, M. A. (1992). *The social psychology of group cohesiveness: From attraction to social identity.* London, UK: Harvester Wheatsheaf.

Hogg, M. A. (1993). Group cohesiveness: A critical review and some new directions. *European Review of Social Psychology, 4,* 85–111.

Hogg, M. A. (1995). Social identity theory. In A. S. R. Manstead & M. Hewstone (Eds.), *Blackwell encyclopedia of social psychology* (pp. 269–274). Oxford, UK: Blackwell.

Hogg, M. A., & Abrams, D. (1993). Towards a single-process uncertainty-reduction model of social motivation in groups. In M. A. Hogg & D. Abrams (Eds.), *Group motivation: Social psychological perspectives.* London, UK: Harvester Wheatsheaf.

Hogg, M. A., & Abrams, D. (2003). Intergroup behavior and social identity. In M. A. Hogg & J. Cooper (Eds.), *The Sage handbook of social psychology* (pp. 407–431). Thousand Oaks, CA: Sage.

Hogg, M. A., Turner, J. C., & Davidson, B. (1990). Polarized norms and social frames of reference: A test of the self-categorization theory of group polarization. *Basic and Applied Social Psychology, 11,* 77–100.

Holbrook, A. L., Berent, M. K., Krosnick, J. A., Visser, P. S., & Boninger, D. S. (2005). Attitude importance and the accumulation of attitude-relevant knowledge in memory. *Journal of Personality and Social Psychology, 88,* 749–769.

Holloway, S., Tucker, L., & Hornstein, H. A. (1977). The effects of social and nonsocial information on interpersonal behavior of males: The news makes news. *Journal of Personality and Social Psychology, 35,* 514–522.

Holmes, D. S. (1978). Projection as a defense mechanism. *Psychological Bulletin, 69,* 248–268.

Holyoak, K. J., & Gordon, P. C. (1984). Information processing and social cognition. In R. S. Wyer Jr. & T. K. Srull (Eds.), *Handbook of social cognition* (Vol. 1, pp. 39–70). Hillsdale, NJ: Erlbaum.

Holmes, D. S. (1978). Projection as a defense mechanism. *Psychological Bulletin, 69,* 248–268.

Homer, P. M., & Kahle, L. R. (1988). A structural equation test of the value-attitude-behavior hierarchy. *Journal of Personality and Social Psychology, 54,* 638–646.

Hood, B. M., Macrae, C. N., Cole-Davies, V., & Dias, M. (2003). Eye remember you: The effects of gaze direction on face recognition in children and adults. *Developmental Science, 6,* 67–71.

Hornsey, M. J., & Jetten, J. (2004). The individual within the group: Balancing the need to belong with the need to be different. *Personality and Social Psychology Review, 8,* 248–264.

Horowitz, L. M., de Sales French, R., & Anderson, C. A. (1982). The prototype of a lonely person. In L. A. Peplau & D. Perlman (Eds.), *Loneliness: A sourcebook of current theory, research and therapy* (pp. 183–205). New York: Wiley.

Horowitz, M. J. (1970). *Image formation and cognition.* New York: Appleton-Century-Crofts.

Hoshino-Browne, E., Zanna, A. S., Spencer, S. J., Zanna, M. P., Kitayama, S., & Lackenbauer, S. (2005). On the cultural guises of cognitive dissonance: The case of the Easterners and Westerners. *Journal of Personality and Social Psychology, 89,* 294–310.

House, J. S., Landis, K. R., & Umberson, D. (1988). Social relationships and health. *Science, 241,* 540–545.

Houston, D. A., & Fazio, R. H. (1989). Biased processing as a function of attitude accessibility: Making objective judgments subjectively. *Social Cognition, 7,* 51–66.

Hovland, C. I., Janis, I. L., & Kelley, H. H. (1953). *Communication and persuasion.* New Haven, CT: Yale University Press.

Hovland, C. I., Lumsdaine, A. A., & Sheffield, F. D. (1949). *Experiments in mass communication.* Princeton, NJ: Princeton University Press.

Hovland, C. I., & Sears, R. R. (1940). Minor studies of aggression: VI. Correlation of lynchings with economic indices. *Journal of Psychology, 9,* 301–310.

Howard-Pitney, B., Borgida, E., & Omoto, A. M. (1986). Personal involvement: An examination of processing differences. *Social Cognition, 4,* 39–57.

Hsu, M., Bhatt, M., Adolphs, R., Tranel, D., & Camerer, C. F. (2005). Neural systems responding to degrees of uncertainty in human decision-making. *Science, 310,* 1680–1683.

Huddy, L., & Sears, D. O. (1995). Opposition to bilingual education: Prejudice or the defense of realistic interests? *Social Psychology Quarterly, 58,* 133–145.

Hugenberg, K., & Bodenhausen, G. V. (2003). Facing prejudice: Implicit prejudice and the perception of facial threat. *Psychological Science, 14,* 640–643.

Hume, D. (1978). *A treatise on human nature being an attempt to introduce the experimental method of reasoning into moral subjects.* Fair Lawn, NJ: Oxford University Press. (Originally published 1739)

Hummert, M. L. (1994). Physiognomic cues to age and the activation of stereotypes of the elderly in interaction. *International Journal of Aging and Human Development, 39,* 5–19.

Hummert, M. L., Garstka, T. A., O'Brien, L. T., Greenwald, A. G., & Mellott, D. S. (2002). Using the implicit association test to measure age differences in implicit social cognitions. *Psychology and Aging, 17,* 482–495.

Hummert, M. L., Garstka, T. A., Shaner, J. L., & Strahm, S. (1994). Stereotypes of the elderly held by young, middle-aged, and elderly adults. *Journals of Gerontology, 49,* p240–p249.

Hummert, M. L., Garstka, T. A., Shaner, J. L., & Strahm, S. (1995). Judgments about stereotypes of the elderly: Attitudes, age associations, and typicality ratings of young, middle-aged, and elderly adults. *Research on Aging, 17,* 168–189.

Huskinson, T. L. H., & Haddock, G. (2004). Individual differences in attitude structure: Variance in the chronic reliance on affective and cognitive information. *Journal of Experimental and Social Psychology, 40,* 82–90.

Hyde, J. S. (2005). The gender similarities hypothesis. *American Psychologist, 60,* 581–592.

Hyers, L. L., & Swim, J. K. (1998). A comparison of the experiences of dominant and minority group members during an intergroup encounter. *Group Processes and Intergroup Relations, 1,* 143–163.

Hymes, R. W. (1986). Political attitudes as social categories: A new look at selective memory. *Journal of Personality and Social Psychology, 51,* 233–241.

Iacoboni, M., Lieberman, M. D., Knowlton, B. J., Molnar-Szakacs, I., Moritz, M., Throop, C. J., & Fiske, A. P. (2004). Watching social interactions produces dorsomedial prefrontal and medial parietal BOLD fMRI signal increases compared to a resting baseline. *NeuroImage, 21,* 1167–1173.

Ickes, W. J. (1984). Compositions in Black and White: Determinants of interaction in interracial dyads. *Journal of Personality and Social Psychology, 47,* 230–241.

Ickes, W. J., & Barnes, R. D. (1977). The role of sex and self-monitoring in unstructured dyadic interactions. *Journal of Personality and Social Psychology, 35,* 315–330.

Ickes, W. J., Patterson, M. L., Rajecki, D. W., & Tanford, S. (1982). Behavioral and cognitive consequences of reciprocal versus compensatory responses to preinteraction expectancies. *Social Cognition, 1,* 160–190.

Ickes, W. J., Reidhead, S., & Patterson, M. (1986). Machiavellianism and self-monitoring: As different as "me" and "you." *Social Cognition, 4,* 58–74.

Ickes, W. J., Robertson, E., Tooke, W., & Teng, G. (1986). Naturalistic social cognition: Methodology, assessment, and validation. *Journal of Personality and Social Psychology, 51,* 66–82.

Ickes, W. J., & Tooke, W. (1988). The observational method: Studying the interaction of minds and bodies. In S. W. Duck (Ed.), *Handbook of personal relationships* (pp. 79–97). New York: Wiley.

Ickes, W. J., Tooke, W., Stinson, L., Baker, V. L., & Bissonnette, V. (1988). Naturalistic social cognition: Intersubjectivity in same-sex dyads. *Journal of Nonverbal Behavior, 12,* 58–84.

Idson, L. C., & Mischel, W. (2001). The personality of familiar and significant people: The lay perceiver as a social-cognitive theorist. *Journal of Personality and Social Psychology, 80,* 585–596.

Ingram, R. E., Smith, T. W., & Brehm, S. S. (1983). Depression and information processing: Self-schemata and the encoding of self-referent information. *Journal of Personality and Social Psychology, 45,* 412–420.

Insko, C. A., & Cialdini, R. B. (1969). A test of three interpretations of attitudinal verbal reinforcement. *Journal of Personality and Social Psychology, 12,* 333–341.

Isaacowitz, D. M. (2005). The gaze of the optimist. *Personality and Social Psychology Bulletin, 31,* 407–415.

Isbell, L. M. (2004). Not all happy people are lazy or stupid: Evidence of systematic processing in happy moods. *Journal of Experimental Social Psychology, 40,* 341–349.

Isen, A. M. (1984). Toward understanding the role of affect in cognition. In R. S. Wyer Jr. & T. K. Srull (Eds.), *Handbook of social cognition* (Vol. 3, pp. 179–236). Hillsdale, NJ: Erlbaum.

Isen, A. M. (1987). Positive affect, cognitive processes, and social behavior. In L. Berkowitz (Ed.), *Advances in experimental social psychology* (Vol. 20, pp. 203–253). New York: Academic Press.

Isen, A. M. (1993). Positive affect and decision making. In M. Lewis & J. Haviland (Eds.), *Handbook of emotions* (pp. 261–277). New York: Guilford Press.

Isen, A. M., & Daubman, K. A. (1984). The influence of affect on categorization. *Journal of Personality and Social Psychology, 47,* 1206–1217.

Isen, A. M., & Geva, N. (1987). The influence of positive affect on acceptable level of risk: The person with a large canoe has a large worry. *Organizational Behavior and Human Decision Processes, 39,* 145–154.

Isen, A. M., Johnson, M. M. S., Mertz, E., & Robinson, G. F. (1985). The influence of positive affect on the unusualness of word associations. *Journal of Personality and Social Psychology, 48,* 1413–1426.

Isen, A. M., & Means, B. (1983). The influence of positive affect on decision-making strategy. *Social Cognition, 2,* 18–31.

Isen, A. M., & Noonberg, A. (1979). The effects of photographs of the handicapped on donation to charity: When a thousand words may be too much. *Journal of Applied Social Psychology, 9,* 426–431.

Isen, A. M., Nygren, T. E., & Ashby, F. G. (1988). Influence of positive affect on the subjective utility of gains and losses: It is just not worth the risk. *Journal of Personality and Social Psychology, 55,* 710–717.

Isen, A. M., Shalker, T. E., Clark, M. S., & Karp, L. (1978). Affect, accessibility of material in memory and behavior: A cognitive loop? *Journal of Personality and Social Psychology, 36,* 1–12.

Isen, A. M., & Simmonds, S. F. (1978). The effect of feeling good on a helping task that is incompatible with good mood. *Social Psychology, 41,* 346–349.

Isenberg, D. J. (1986). Group polarization: A critical review and meta-analysis. *Journal of Personality and Social Psychology, 50,* 1141–1151.

Ishii, K., Reyes, J. A., & Kitayama, S. (2003). Spontaneous attention to word content versus emotional tone: Differences among three cultures. *Psychological Science, 14,* 39–46.

Ito, T. A., Larsen, J. T., Smith, N. K., & Cacioppo, J. T. (1998). Negative information weighs more heavily on the brain: The negativity bias in evaluative categorizations. *Journal of Personality and Social Psychology, 75,* 887–900.

Ito, T. A., Chiao, K. W., Devine, P. G., Lorig, T. S., & Cacioppo, T. (2006). The influence of facial feedback on race bias. *Psychological Science, 17,* 256–261.

Ito, T. A., Thompson, E., & Cacioppo, J. T. (2004). Tracing the timecourse of social perception: The effects of racial cues on event-related brain potentials. *Personality and Social Psychology Bulletin, 30,* 1–14.

Ito, T. A., & Urland, G. R. (2003). Race and gender on the brain: Electrocortical measures of attention to the race and gender of multiple categorizable individuals. *Journal of Personality and Social Psychology, 85,* 616–626.

Iyengar, S., & Kinder, D. R. (1987). *News that matters: Television and American opinion.* Chicago: University of Chicago Press.

Iyengar, S. S., & Lepper, M. R. (1999). Rethinking the value of choice: A cultural perspective on intrinsic motivation. *Journal of Personality and Social Psychology, 76,* 349–366.

Iyer, A., Leach, C. W., & Crosby, F. J. (2003). White guilt and racial compensation: The benefits and limits of self-focus. *Personality and Social Psychology Bulletin, 29,* 117–129.

Izard, C. E. (1972). *The face of emotion.* New York: Appleton-Century-Crofts.

Izard, C. E. (1977). *Human emotions.* New York: Plenum Press.

Izard, C. E. (1981). Differential emotions theory and the facial feedback hypothesis of emotion activation: Comments on Tourangeau and Ellsworth's "The role of facial response in the experience of emotion." *Journal of Personality and Social Psychology, 40,* 350–354.

Jackman, M. R. (1994). *The velvet glove: Paternalism and conflict in gender, class, and race relations.* Berkeley, CA: University of California Press.

Jacobs, L., Berscheid, E., & Walster, E. (1971). Self-esteem and attraction. *Journal of Personality and Social Psychology, 17,* 84–91.

Jacobsen, T., Schubotz, R. I., Hofel, L., & Cramon, D. Y. (2006). Brain correlates of aesthetic judgment of beauty. *NeuroImage, 29,* 276–285. [Erratum: *32,* 486–487.]

Jacoby, L. L., & Kelley, C. M. (1987). Unconscious influences of memory for a prior event. *Personality and Social Psychology Bulletin, 13,* 314–336.

James, K. (1986). Priming and social categorizational factors: Impact on awareness of emergency situations. *Personality and Social Psychology Bulletin, 12,* 462–467.

James, W. (1907). *Pragmatism.* New York: Longmans-Green.

James, W. (1983). *The principles of psychology.* Cambridge, MA: Harvard University Press. (Originally published 1890)

Jamieson, D. W., & Zanna, M. P. (1989). Need for structure in attitude formation and expression. In A. R. Pratkanis, S. J. Breckler, & A. G. Greenwald (Eds.), *Attitude structure and function* (pp. 383–406). Hillsdale, NJ: Erlbaum.

Janis, I. L. (1972). *Victims of groupthink.* Boston: Houghton Mifflin.

Janis, I. L. (1989). *Crucial decisions: Leadership in policymaking and crisis management.* New York: Free Press.

Janiszewski, C. (1993). Preattentive mere exposure effects. *Journal of Consumer Research, 20,* 376–392.

Janoff-Bulman, R., Timko, C., & Carli, L. L. (1985). Cognitive biases in blaming the victim. *Journal of Experimental Social Psychology, 21,* 161–177.

Jarvis, W. G. G., & Petty, R. E. (1996). The need to evaluate. *Journal of Personality and Social Psychology, 70,* 172–194.

Jaspers, J. M. F., Hewstone, M., & Fincham, F. D. (1983). Attribution theory and research: The state of the art. In J. Jaspars, D. Fincham, & M. Hewstone (Eds.), *Attribution theory and research: Conceptual, developmental, and social dimensions* (pp. 3–36). London: Academic Press.

Jecker, J. D. (1964). The cognitive effects of conflict and dissonance. In L. Festinger (Ed.), *Conflict, decision, and dissonance.* Stanford, CA: Stanford University Press.

Jennings, D., Amabile, T. M., & Ross, L. D. (1982). Informal covariation assessment: Data-based vs. theory-based judgments. In A. Tversky, D. Kahneman, & P. Slovic (Eds.), *Judgment under uncertainty: Heuristics and biases* (pp. 211–230). New York: Cambridge University Press.

Jervis, R. (1976). *Perception and misperception in international politics.* Princeton, NJ: Princeton University Press.

Jetten, J., Spears, R., & Manstead, A. S. R. (1998). Defining dimensions of distinctiveness: Group variability makes a difference to differentiation. *Journal of Personality and Social Psychology, 74,* 1481–1492.

Johns, M., Schmader, T., & Martens, A. (2005). Knowing is half the battle: Teaching stereotype threat as a means of improving women's math performance. *Psychological Science, 16,* 175–179.

Johnson, B. T., & Eagly, A. H. (1989). The effects of involvement on persuasion: A meta-analysis. *Psychological Bulletin, 106,* 290–314.

Johnson, B. T., & Eagly, A. H. (1990). Involvement and persuasion: Types, traditions, and the evidence. *Psychological Bulletin, 107,* 375–384.

Johnson, E. J., & Tversky, A. (1983). Affect generalization and the perception of risk. *Journal of Personality and Social Psychology, 45,* 20–31.

Johnson, M. H., & Magaro, P. A. (1987). Effects of mood and severity on memory processes in depression and mania. *Psychological Bulletin, 101,* 28–40.

Johnson, M. K. (2006). Memory and reality. *American Psychologist, 61,* 760–771.

Johnson, M. K., Raye, C. L., Mitchell, K. J., Touryan, S. R., Greene, E. J., & Nolen-Hoeksema, S. (2006). Dissociating medial frontal and posterior cingulate activity during self-reflection. *Social Cognitive and Affective Neuroscience, 1,* 56–64.

Jolly, E. J., & Reardon, R. (1985). Cognitive differentiation, automaticity, and interruptions of automatized behaviors. *Personality and Social Psychology Bulletin, 11,* 301–314.

Jonas, E., Greenberg, J., & Frey, D. (2003). Connecting terror management and dissonance theory: Evidence that mortality salience increases the preference for supporting information after decisions. *Personality and Social Psychology Bulletin, 29,* 1181–1189.

Jonas, E., Schulz-Hardt, S., Frey, D., & Thelen, N. (2001). Confirmation bias in sequential information search after preliminary decisions: An expansion of dissonance theoretical research on selective exposure to information. *Journal of Personality and Social Psychology, 80,* 557–571.

Jones, E. E. (1990). *Interpersonal perception.* New York: Freeman.

Jones, E. E., & Davis, K. E. (1965). From acts to dispositions: The attribution process in person perception. In L. Berkowitz (Ed.), *Advances in experimental social psychology* (Vol. 2, pp. 220–266). New York: Academic Press.

Jones, E. E., & Goethals, G. R. (1972). Order effects in impression formation: Attribution context and the nature of the entity. In E. E. Jones, D. E. Kanouse, H. H. Kelley, R. E. Nisbett, S. Valins, & B. Weiner (Eds.), *Attribution: Perceiving the causes of behavior* (pp. 27–46). Morristown, NJ: General Learning Press.

Jones E. E., & Harris, V. A. (1967). The attribution of attitudes. *Journal of Experimental Social Psychology, 3,* 1–24.

Jones E. E., & McGillis, D. (1976). Correspondent inferences and the attribution cube: A comparative reappraisal. In J. H. Harvey, W. J. Ickes, & R. F. Kidd (Eds.), *New directions in attribution research* (Vol. 1, pp. 389–420). Hillsdale, NJ: Erlbaum.

Jones, E. E., & Nisbett, R. E. (1972). The actor and the observer: Divergent perceptions of the causes of behavior. In E. E. Jones, D. E. Kanouse, H. H. Kelley, R. E. Nisbett, S. Valins, & B. Weiner (Eds.), *Attribution: Perceiving the causes of behavior* (pp. 79–94). Morristown, NJ: General Learning Press.

Jones, E. E., & Pittman, T. S. (1982). Toward a general theory of strategic self-presentation. In J. Suls (Ed.), *Psychological perspectives on the self* (pp. 231–262). Hillsdale, NJ: Erlbaum.

Jones, J. T., Pelham, B. W., Mirenberg, M. C., & Hetts, J. J. (2002). Name letter preferences are not merely mere exposure: Implicit egotism as self-regulation. *Journal of Experimental Social Psychology, 38,* 170–177.

Jones, J. M. (1997). *Prejudice and racism* (2nd ed.). New York: McGraw-Hill.

Jordan, C. H., Spencer, S. J., & Zanna, M. P. (2003). "I love me . . . I love me not:" Implicit self-esteem, explicit self-esteem, and defensiveness. In S. J. Spencer, S. Fein, M. P. Zanna, & J. M. Olson (Eds.), *Motivated social perception: The Ontario symposium* (Vol. 9, pp. 117–145). Mahwah, NJ: Erlbaum.

Jordan, C. H., Spencer, S. J., & Zanna, M. P. (2005). Types of high self-esteem and prejudice: How implicit self-esteem relates to ethnic discrimination among high explicit self-esteem individuals. *Personality and Social Psychology Bulletin, 31,* 693–702.

Josephs, R. A., Bosson, J. K., & Jacobs, C. G. (2003). Self-esteem maintenance processes: Why low self-esteem may be resistant to change. *Personality and Social Psychology Bulletin, 29,* 920–933.

Jost, J. T., & Banaji, M. R. (1994). The role of stereotyping in system-justification and the production of false consciousness. *British Journal of Social Psychology, 33,* 1–27.

Jost, J. T., Banaji, M. R., & Nosek, B. A. (2004). A decade of system justification theory: Accumulated evidence of conscious and unconscious bolstering of the status quo. *Political Psychology, 25,* 881–920.

Jost, J. T., & Burgess, D. (2000). Attitudinal ambivalence and the conflict between group and system justification motives in low status groups. *Personality and Social Psychology Bulletin, 26,* 293–305.

Jost, J. T., Glaser, J., Kruglanski, A. W., & Sulloway, F. J. (2003). Political conservatism as motivated social cognition. *Psychological Bulletin, 129,* 339–375.

Jost, J. T., & Hunyady, O. (2002). The psychology of system justification and the palliative function of ideology. In W. Stroebe & M. Hewstone (Eds.), *European review of social psychology* (Vol. 13, pp. 111–153). Hove, England: Psychology Press/Taylor & Francis.

Jost, J. T., & Kay, A. C. (2005). Exposure to benevolent sexism and complementary gender stereotypes: Consequences for specific and diffuse forms of system justification. *Journal of Personality and Social Psychology, 88,* 498–509.

Jost, J. T., Pelham, B. W., Sheldon, O., & Sullivan, B. N. (2003). Social inequality and the reduction of ideological dissonance on behalf of the system: Evidence of enhanced system justification among the disadvantaged. *European Journal of Social Psychology, 33,* 13–36.

Judd, C. M., & Krosnick, J. A. (1982). Attitude centrality, organization, and measurement. *Journal of Personality and Social Psychology, 42,* 436–447.

Judd, C. M., & Krosnick, J. A. (1989). The structural bases of consistency among political attitudes: Effects of political expertise and attitude importance. In A. R. Pratkanis, S. J. Breckler, & A. G. Greenwald (Eds.), *Attitude structure and function* (pp. 99–128). Hillsdale, NJ: Erlbaum.

Judd, C. M., & Kulik, J. A. (1980). Schematic effects of social attitudes on information processing and recall. *Journal of Personality and Social Psychology, 38,* 569–578.

Judd, C. M., & Park, B. (1988). Out-group homogeneity: Judgments of variability at the individual and group levels. *Journal of Personality and Social Psychology, 54,* 778–788.

Judd, C. M., Park, B., Yzerbyt, V. Y., Gordijn, E. H., & Muller, D. (2005). Attributions of intergroup bias and outgroup homogeneity to ingroup and outgroup others. *European Journal of Social Psychology, 35,* 677–704.

Kahn, W. A., & Crosby, F. J. (1987) Discriminating between attitudes and discriminatory behaviors. In L. Larwood, B. A. Gutek, & A. H. Stromberg (Eds.), *Women and work: An annual review* (Vol. 1, pp. 215–328). Beverly Hills, CA: Sage.

Kahneman, D. (1973). *Attention and effort.* Englewood Cliffs, NJ: Prentice-Hall.

Kahneman, D. (2003). A perspective on judgment and choice. *American Psychologist, 58,* 697–720.

Kahneman, D., & Frederick, S. (2002). Representativeness revisited: Attribute substitution in intuitive judgment. In T. Gilovich, D. Griffin, & D. Kahneman (Eds.), *Heuristics and biases: The psychology of intuitive judgment* (pp. 49–81). New York: Cambridge University Press.

Kahneman, D., & Miller, D. T. (1986). Norm theory: Comparing reality to its alternatives. *Psychological Review, 93,* 136–153.

Kahneman, D., & Tversky, A. (1972). Subjective probability: A judgment of representativeness. *Cognitive Psychology, 3,* 430–454.

Kahneman, D., & Tversky, A. (1973). On the psychology of prediction. *Psychological Review, 80,* 237–251.

Kahneman, D., & Tversky, A. (1979). Prospect theory: An analysis of decision under risk. *Econometrica, 47,* 263–292.

Kahneman, D., & Tversky, A. (1982). The simulation heuristic. In D. Kahneman, P. Slovic, & A. Tversky (Eds.), *Judgment under uncertainty: Heuristics and biases* (pp. 201–208). New York: Cambridge University Press.

Kahneman, D., & Tversky, A. (1984). Choices, values, and frames. *American Psychologist, 39,* 341–350.

Kaiser, C. R., & Miller, C. T. (2001a). Reacting to impending discrimination: Compensation for prejudice and attributions to discrimination. *Personality and Social Psychology Bulletin, 27,* 1357–1367.

Kaiser, C. R., & Miller, C. T. (2001b). Stop complaining! The social costs of making attributions to discrimination. *Personality and Social Psychology Bulletin, 27,* 254–263.

Kaiser, C. R., & Miller, C. T. (2003). Derogating the victim: The interpersonal consequences of blaming events on discrimination. *Group Processes and Intergroup Relations, 6,* 227–237.

Kallgren, C. A., & Wood, W. (1986). Access to attitude-relevant information in memory as a determinant of attitude-behavior consistency. *Journal of Experimental Social Psychology, 22,* 328–338.

Kammrath, L. K., Mendoza-Denton, R., & Mischel, W. (2005). Incorporating if . . . then . . . personality signatures in person perception: Beyond the person-situation dichotomy. *Journal of Personality and Social Psychology, 88,* 605–618.

Kanagawa, C., Cross, S. E., & Markus, H. R. (2001). "Who am I?" The cultural psychology of the conceptual self. *Personality and Social Psychology Bulletin, 27,* 90–103.

Kanazawa, S. (1992). Outcome or expectancy? Antecedent of spontaneous causal attribution. *Personality and Social Psychology Bulletin, 18,* 659–668.

Kant, I. (1969 (Originally published 1781)). *Critique of pure reason.* New York: St. Martin's Press.

Kant, K. J. (1969). Influences of amygdala and medial forebrain bundle on self-stimulation in the septum. *Physiology and Behavior, 4,* 777–784.

Kanter, R. (1977). *Men and women of the corporation.* New York: Basic Books.

Kanwisher, N., McDermott, J., & Chun, M. M. (1997). The fusiform face area: A module in human extrastriate cortex specialized for face perception. *Journal of Neuroscience, 17,* 4302–4311.

Kanwisher, N., & Wojciulik, E. (2000). Visual attention: Insights from brain imaging. *Nature Reviews, 1,* 91–100.

Kardes, F. R., Sanbonmatsu, D. M., Voss, R. T., & Fazio, R. H. (1986). Self-monitoring and attitude accessibility. *Personality and Social Psychology Bulletin, 12,* 468–474.

Karniol, R. (1986). What will they think of next? Transformation rules used to predict other people's thoughts and feelings. *Journal of Personality and Social Psychology, 51,* 932–944.

Karpinski, A., & Hilton, J. L. (2001). Attitudes and the implicit associations test. *Journal of Personality and Social Psychology, 81,* 774–788.

Kashima, K., & Davison, G. C. (1989). Functional consistency in the face of topographical change in articulated thoughts. *Journal of Rational-Emotive and Cognitive-Behavior Therapy, 7,* 131–139.

Kashima, Y., Kashima, E., Chiu, C.-y., Farsides, T., Gelfand, M., Hong, Y., Kim, U., Strack, F., Werth, L., Yuki, M., & Yzerbyt, V. Y. (2005). Culture, essentialism, and agency: Are individuals universally believed to be more real entities than groups? *European Journal of Social Psychology, 35,* 147–169.

Kashima, Y., Woolcock, J., & Kashima, E. S. (2000). Group impressions as dynamic configurations: The tensor product model of group impression formation and change. *Psychological Review, 107,* 914–942.

Kasser, T., & Ryan, R. M. (1996). Further examining the American dream: Differential correlates of intrinsic and extrinsic goals. *Personality and Social Psychology Bulletin, 22,* 280–287.

Kassin, S. M., & Baron, R. M. (1985). Basic determinants of attribution and social perception. In J. Harvey & E. G. Weary (Eds.), *Attribution: Basic issues and applications* (pp. 37–64). New York: Academic Press.

Kassin, S. M., & Baron, R. M. (1986). On the basicity of social perception cues: Developmental evidence for adult processes? *Social Cognition, 4,* 180–200.

Kassin, S. M., & Pryor, J. B. (1985). The development of attribution processes. In J. Pryor & J. Day (Eds.), *The development of social cognition* (pp. 3–34). New York: Springer-Verlag.

Katz, D. (1960). The functional approach to the study of attitudes. *Public Opinion Quarterly, 24,* 163–204.

Katz, D., & Braly, K. (1933). Racial stereotypes of one hundred college students. *Journal of Abnormal and Social Psychology, 28,* 280–290.

Katz, E. (1968). On reopening the question of selectivity in exposure to mass media. In R. P. Abelson et al. (Eds.), *Theories of cognitive consistency: A sourcebook.* Chicago: Rand-McNally.

Katz, I., & Hass, R. G. (1988). Racial ambivalence and American value conflict: Correlational and priming studies of dual cognitive structures. *Journal of Personality and Social Psychology, 55,* 893–905.

Katz, I., Wackenhut, J., & Hass, R. G. (1986). Racial ambivalence, value duality, and behavior. In J. F. Dovidio & S. L. Gaertner (Eds.), *Prejudice, discrimination, and racism* (pp. 35–60). Orlando, FL: Academic Press.

Kawakami, K., & Dovidio, J. F. (2001). The reliability of implicit stereotyping. *Personality and Social Psychology Bulletin, 27,* 212–225.

Kawakami, K., Dovidio, J. F., & Dijksterhuis, A. (2003). Effect of social category priming on personal attitudes. *Psychological Science, 14,* 315–319.

Kawakami, K., Dovidio, J. F., Moll, J., Hermsen, S., & Russin, A. (2000). Just say no (to stereotyping): Effects of training in the negation of stereotypic associations on stereotype activation. *Journal of Personality and Social Psychology, 78,* 871–888.

Kawakami, K., Dovidio, J. F., & van Kamp, S. (2005). Kicking the habit: Effects of nonstereotypic association training and correction processes on hiring decisions. *Journal of Experimental Social Psychology, 41,* 68–75.

Kay, A. C., & Jost, J. T. (2003). Complementary justice: Effects of "poor but happy" and "poor but honest" stereotype exemplars on system justification and implicit activation of the justice motive. *Journal of Personality and Social Psychology, 85,* 823–837.

Kay, A. C., Jost, J. T., & Young, S. (2005). Victim derogation and victim enhancement as alternate routes to system justification. *Psychological Science, 16,* 240–246.

Keller, J. (2005). In genes we trust: The biological component of psychological essentialism and its relationship to mechanisms of motivated social cognition. *Journal of Personality and Social Psychology, 88,* 686–702.

Keller, J., & Dauenheimer, D. (2003). Stereotype threat in the classroom: Dejection mediates the disrupting threat effect on women's math performance. *Personality and Social Psychology Bulletin, 29,* 371–381.

Kellerman, J., Lewis, J., & Laird, J. D. (1989). Looking and loving: The effects of mutual gaze on feelings of romantic love. *Journal of Research in Personality, 23,* 145–161.

Kelley, H. H. (1967). Attribution theory in social psychology. In D. Levine (Ed.), *Nebraska Symposium on Motivation* (Vol. 15, pp. 192–240). Lincoln: University of Nebraska Press.

Kelley, H. H. (1972a). Attribution in social interaction. In E. E. Jones, D. E. Kanouse, H. H. Kelley, R. E. Nisbett, S. Valins, & B. Weiner (Eds.), *Attribution: Perceiving the causes of behavior* (pp. 1–26). Morristown, NJ: General Learning Press.

Kelley, H. H. (1972b). Causal schemata and the attribution process. In E. E. Jones, D. E. Kanouse, H. H. Kelley, R. E. Nisbett, S. Valins, & B. Weiner (Eds.), *Attribution: Perceiving the causes of behavior* (pp. 151–174). Morristown, NJ: General Learning Press.

Kelley, H. H., Berscheid, E., Christensen, A., Harvey, J. H., Huston, T. L., Levinger, G., et al. (1983). Analyzing close relationships. In H. H. Kelley, E. Berscheid, A. Christensen, J. H. Harvey, T. L. Huston, G. Levinger, E. McClintock, L. A. Peplau, & D. R. Peterson (Eds.), *Close relationships* (pp. 20–67). New York: Freeman.

Kelley, H. H., & Michela, J. L. (1980). Attribution theory and research. *Annual Review of Psychology, 31,* 457–501.

Kelley, W. M., Macrae, C. N., Wyland, C. L., Caglar, S., Inati, S., & Heatherton, T. F. (2002). Finding the self? An event-related fMRI study. *Journal of Cognitive Neuroscience, 14,* 785–794.

Kelly, C. (1989). Political identity and perceived intra-group homogeneity. *British Journal of Social Psychology, 28,* 239–250.

Keltner, D., Gruenfeld, D. H., & Anderson, C. (2003). Power, approach, and inhibition. *Psychological Review, 110,* 265–284.

Kemler-Nelson, D. G. (1984). The effect of intention on what concepts are acquired. *Journal of Verbal Learning and Verbal Behavior, 23,* 734–759.

Kemmelmeier, M., Danielson, C., & Basten, J. (2005). What's in a grade? Academic success and political orientation. *Personality and Social Psychology Bulletin, 31,* 1386–1399.

Kenny, D. A., & Acitelli, L. K. (2001). Accuracy and bias in the perception of the partner in a close relationship. *Journal of Personality and Social Psychology, 80,* 439–448.

Kenrick, D. T., & Cialdini, R. B. (1977). Romantic attraction: Misattribution versus reinforcement explanations. *Journal of Personality and Social Psychology, 35,* 381–391.

Kernis, M. H. (2003). Toward a conceptualization of optimal self-esteem. *Psychological Inquiry, 4,* 1–26.

Kernis, M. H., & Grannemann, B. D. (1990). Excuses in the making: A test and extension of Darley and Goethals' attributional model. *Journal of Experimental Social Psychology, 26,* 337–349.

Kernis, M. H., Paradise, A. W., Whitaker, D. J., Wheatman, S. R., & Goldman, B. N. (2000). Master of one's psychological domain? Not likely if one's self-esteem is unstable. *Personality and Social Psychology Bulletin, 26,* 1297–1305.

Kiesler, C. A. (1971). *The psychology of commitment: Experiments linking behavior to belief.* New York: Academic Press.

Kiesler, C. A., Collins, B. E., & Miller, N. (1969). *Attitude change: A critical analysis of theoretical approaches.* New York: Wiley.

Kiesler, C. A., Nisbett, R. E., & Zanna, M. P. (1969). On inferring one's beliefs from one's behavior. *Journal of Personality and Social Psychology, 11,* 321–327.

Kihlstrom, J. F. (2004). Implicit methods in social psychology. In C. Sansone, C. C. Morf, & A. T. Panter (Eds.), *The Sage handbook of methods in social psychology* (pp. 195–212). Thousand Oaks, CA: Sage.

Kilianski, S. E., & Rudman, L. A. (1998). Wanting it both ways: Do women approve of benevolent sexism? *Sex Roles, 39,* 333–352.

Kim, H-S., & Baron, R. S. (1988). Exercise and the illusory correlation: Does arousal heighten stereotypic processing? *Journal of Experimental Social Psychology, 24,* 366–380.

Kinder, D. R., & Sears, D. O. (1981). Prejudice and politics: Symbolic racism versus racial threats to the good life. *Journal of Personality and Social Psychology, 40,* 414–431.

Kircher, T. T. J., Brammer, M., Bullmore, E., Simmons, A., Bartels, M., & David, A. S. (2002). The neural correlates of intentional and incidental self processing. *Neuropsychologia, 40,* 683–692.

Kitayama, S., Duffy, S., Kawamura, T., & Larsen, J. T. (2003). Perceiving an object and its context in different cultures: A cultural look at New Look. *Psychological Science, 14,* 201–206.

Kitayama, S., & Karasawa, M. (1997). Implicit self-esteem in Japan: Name letters and birthday numbers. *Personality and Social Psychology Bulletin, 23,* 736–742.

Kitayama, S., Markus, H. R., Matsumoto, H., & Norasakkunkit, V. (1997). Individual and collective processes in the construction of the self: Self-enhancement in the United States and self-criticism in Japan. *Journal of Personality and Social Psychology, 72,* 1245–1267.

Kitayama, S., Snibbe, A. C., Markus, H. R., & Suzuki, T. (2004). Is there any "free choice"?: Self and dissonance in two cultures. *Psychological Science, 15,* 527–533.

Kite, M. E., & Johnson, B. T. (1988). Attitudes toward older and younger adults: A meta-analysis. *Psychology and Aging, 3,* 233–244.

Kittles, R. A., & Weiss, K. M. (2003). Race, ancestry, and genes: Implications for defining disease risk. *Annual Review of Geonomics and Human Genetics, 4,* 33–67.

Klar, Y., & Giladi, E. E. (1999). Are most people happier than their peers, or are they just happy? *Personality and Social Psychology Bulletin, 25,* 585–594.

Klauer, K. C., & Meiser, T. (2000). A source-monitoring analysis of illusory correlations. *Personality and Social Psychology Bulletin, 26,* 1074–1093.

Klauer, K. C., & Wegener, I. (1998). Unraveling social categorization in the "Who said what?" paradigm. *Journal of Personality and Social Psychology, 75,* 1155–1178.

Klauer, K. C., Wegener, I., & Ehrenberg, K. (2002). Perceiving minority members as individuals: The effects of relative group size in social categorization. *European Journal of Social Psychology, 32,* 223–245.

Klayman, J., & Ha, Y-W. (1987). Confirmation, disconfirmation, and information in hypothesis testing. *Psychological Review, 94,* 211–228.

Klein, M. (1967). The world of us adults and its roots in infancy. *Archivio di Psicologia, Neurologia e Psichiatria, 28,* 41–59.

Klein, S. B., Cosmides, L., Tooby, J., & Chance, S. (2001). Priming exceptions: A test of the scope hypothesis in naturalistic trait judgments. *Social Cognition, 19,* 443–468.

Kleinhesselink, R. R., & Edwards, R. E. (1975). Seeking and avoiding belief-discrepant information as a function of its perceived refutability. *Journal of Personality and Social Psychology, 31,* 787–790.

Klinger, E. (1977a). *Meaning and void: Inner experience and the incentives in people's lives.* Minneapolis: University of Minnesota Press.

Klinger, E. (1977b). The nature of fantasy and its clinical uses. *Psychotherapy: Theory, Research and Practice, 14,* 223–231.

Klinger, E. (1978). Modes of normal conscious flow. In K. S. Pope & J. L. Singer (Eds.), *The stream of consciousness: Scientific investigations into the flow of human experience*. New York: Plenum Press.

Klinger, E., Barta, S. G., & Maxeiner, M. E. (1980). Motivational correlates of thought content frequency and commitment. *Journal of Personality and Social Psychology, 39,* 1222–1237.

Knäuper, B., Kornik, R., Atkinson, K., Guberman, C., & Aydin, C. (2005). Motivation influences the underestimation of cumulative risk. *Personality and Social Psychology Bulletin, 31,* 1511–1523.

Knoblich, G., & Sebanz, N. (2006). The social nature of perception and action. *Current Directions in Psychological Science, 15,* 99–104.

Knowles, E. D., Morris, M. W., Chiu, C.-y., & Hong, Y.-y. (2001). Culture and the process of person perception: Evidence for automaticity among East Asians in correcting for situational influences on behavior. *Personality and Social Psychology Bulletin, 27,* 1344–1356.

Knox, V. J., Gekoski, W. L., & Kelly, L. E. (1995). The age group evaluation and description (AGED) Inventory: A new instrument for assessing stereotypes of and attitudes toward age groups. *International Journal of Aging and Human Development, 40,* 31–55.

Knutson, B., Taylor, J., Kaufman, M., Peterson, R., & Glover, G. (2005). Distributed neural representation of expected value. *Journal of Neuroscience, 25,* 4806–4812.

Koenig, A. M., & Eagly, A. H. (2005). Stereotype threat in men on a test of social sensitivity. *Sex Roles, 52,* 489–496.

Koffka, K. (1935). *Principles of Gestalt psychology.* New York: Harcourt, Brace, & World.

Kohler, W. (1976 (Originally published 1938)). *The place of value in a world of facts.* New York: Liveright.

Koole, S. L., Dijksterhuis, A., & van Knippenberg, A. (2001). What's in a name: Implicit self-esteem and the automatic self. *Journal of Personality and Social Psychology, 80,* 669–685.

Koole, S. L., Smeets, K., van Knippenberg, A., & Dijksterhuis, A. (1999). The cessation of rumination through self-affirmation. *Journal of Personality and Social Psychology, 77,* 111–125.

Koriat, A., Goldsmith, M., & Pansky, A. (2000). Toward a psychology of memory accuracy. *Annual Review of Psychology, 51,* 481–537.

Kossan, N. E. (1981). Developmental differences in concept acquisition strategies. *Child Development, 52,* 290–298.

Kowalski, R. M., & Leary, M. R. (1990). Strategic self-presentation and the avoidance of aversive events: Antecedents and consequences of self-enhancement and self-depreciation. *Journal of Experimental Social Psychology, 26,* 322–336.

Kozak, M. N., Marsh, A. A., & Wegner, D. M. (2006). What do I think you're doing? Action identification and mind attribution. *Journal of Personality and Social Psychology, 90,* 543–555.

Kraus, S. J. (1995). Attitudes and the prediction of behavior: A meta-analysis of the empirical literature. *Personality and Social Psychology Bulletin, 21,* 58–75.

Krauss, R. M. (1981). Impression formation, impression management, and nonverbal behaviors. In E. T. Higgins, C. P. Herman, & M. P. Zanna (Eds.), *Social cognition: The Ontario Symposium* (Vol. 1, pp. 323–341). Hillsdale, NJ: Erlbaum.

Kray, L. J., Galinsky, A. D., & Thompson, L. (2002). Reversing the gender gap in negotiations: An exploration of stereotype regeneration. *Organizational Behavior and Human Decision Processes, 87,* 386–409.

Krieger, L. H., & Fiske, S. T. (2006). Behavioral realism in employment discrimination law: Implicit bias and disparate treatment. *California Law Review, 94,* 997–1062.

Kristiansen, C. M., & Zanna, M. P. (1988). Justifying attitudes by appealing to values: A functional perspective. *British Journal of Social Psychology, 27,* 247–256.

Krosnick, J. A. (1988a). Attitude importance and attitude change. *Journal of Experimental Social Psychology, 24,* 240–255.

Krosnick, J. A. (1988b). The role of attitude importance in social evaluation: A study of policy preferences, presidential candidate evaluations, and voting behavior. *Journal of Personality and Social Psychology, 55,* 196–210.

Krosnick, J. A. (1989). Attitude importance and attitude accessibility. *Personality and Social Psychology Bulletin, 15,* 297–308.

Krueger, J. I. (1998). Enhancement bias in descriptions of self and others. *Personality and Social Psychology Bulletin, 24*, 505–516.

Krueger, J. I., & Clement, R. W. (1994). The truly false consensus effect: An ineradicable and egocentric bias in social perception. *Journal of Personality and Social Psychology, 67*, 596–610.

Krueger, J. I., & Stanke, D. (2001). The role of self-referent and other referent knowledge in perceptions of group characteristics. *Personality and Social Psychology Bulletin, 27*, 878–888.

Kruger, J. I., Wirtz, D., & Miller, D. T. (2005). Counterfactual thinking and the first instinct fallacy. *Journal of Personality and Social Psychology, 88*, 725–735.

Kruglanski, A. W. (1975). The endogenous-exogenous partition in attribution theory. *Psychological Review, 82*, 387–406.

Kruglanski, A. W. (1980). Lay epistemo-logic-process and contents: Another look at attribution theory. *Psychological Review, 87*, 70–87.

Kruglanski, A. W. (1989). The psychology of being "right": On the problem of accuracy in social perception and cognition. *Psychological Bulletin, 106*, 395–409.

Kruglanski, A. W. (1990). Motivations for judging and knowing: Implications for causal attribution. In E. T. Higgins & R. M. Sorrentino (Eds.), *Handbook of motivation and cognition: Foundations of social behavior* (Vol. 2, pp. 333–368). New York: Guilford Press.

Kruglanski, A. W., & Mayseless, O. (1988). Contextual effects in hypothesis testing: The role of competing alternatives and epistemic motivations. *Social Cognition, 6*, 1–20.

Kruglanski, A. W., Thompson, E. P., & Spiegel, S. (1999). Separate or equal? Bimodal notions of persuasion and a single-process "unimodel." In S. Chaiken & Y. Trope (Eds.), *Dual-process theories in social psychology* (pp. 293–313). New York: Guilford Press.

Kruglanski, A. W., & Webster, D. M. (1996). Motivated closing of the mind: "Seizing" and "freezing." *Psychological Review, 103*, 263–283.

Kühnen, U., Hannover, B., & Schubert, B. (2001). The semantic-procedural interface model of the self: The role of self-knowledge for context-dependent versus context-independent modes of thinking. *Journal of Personality and Social Psychology, 80*, 397–409.

Kunda, Z. (1987). Motivated inference: Self-serving generation and evaluation of causal theories. *Journal of Personality and Social Psychology, 53*, 636–647.

Kunda, Z. (1990). The case for motivated reasoning. *Psychological Bulletin, 108*, 480–498.

Kunda, Z. (1999). *Social cognition: Making sense of people.* Cambridge, MA: MIT Press.

Kunda, Z., & Nisbett, R. E. (1986). Prediction and the partial understanding of the law of large numbers. *Journal of Experimental Social Psychology, 22*, 339–354.

Kunda, Z., & Nisbett, R. E. (1988). Predicting individual evaluations from group evaluations and vice versa: Different patterns for self and other? *Personality and Social Psychology Bulletin, 14*, 326–334.

Kunda, Z., & Sherman-Williams, B. (1993). Stereotypes and the construal of individuating information. *Personality and Social Psychology Review, 9*, 2–16.

Kunda, Z., & Thagard, P. (1996). Forming impressions from stereotypes, traits, and behaviors: A parallel-constraint-satisfaction theory. *Psychological Review, 103*, 284–308.

Kunst-Wilson, W. R., & Zajonc, R. B. (1980). Affective discrimination of stimuli that cannot be recognized. *Science, 207*, 557–558.

Kurman, J. (2001). Self-enhancement: Is it restricted to individualistic cultures? *Personality and Social Psychology Bulletin, 27*, 1705–1716.

Kurzban, R., & Leary, M. R. (2001). Evolutionary origins of stigmatization: The functions of social exclusion. *Psychological Bulletin, 127*, 187–208.

Kurzban, R., Tooby, J., & Cosmides, L. (2001). Can race be erased? Coalitional computation and social categorization. *Proceedings of the National Academy of Sciences of the United States of America, 98*, 15387–15392.

Kwan, V. S. Y., John, O. P., Kenny, D. A., Bond, M. H., & Robins, R. W. (2004). Reconceptualizing individual differences in self-enhancement bias: An interpersonal approach. *Psychological Review, 111*, 94–110.

Lacey, J. I. (1959). Psychophysiological approaches to the evaluation of psychotherapeutic process and outcome. In E. A. Rubinstein & M. B. Parloff (Eds.), *Research in psychotherapy.* Washington, DC: American Psychological Association.

Lacey, J. I. (1967). Somatic response patterning and stress: Some revisions of activation theory. In M. H. Appley & R. Trumbull (Eds.), *Psychological stress: Issues in research.* New York: Appleton-Century-Crofts.

Lacey, J. I., & Lacey, B. C. (1958). The relationship of resting autonomic activity to motor impulsivity. In H. C. Solomon, S. Cobb, & W. Pennfield (Eds.), *The brain and human behavior* (Vol. 36). Baltimore: Williams & Wilkins.

Lacey, J. I., & Lacey, B. C. (1970). Some autonomic-central nervous system interrelationships. In P. Black (Ed.), *Physiological correlates of emotion.* New York: Academic Press.

Laird, J. D. (1974). Self-attribution of emotion: The effects of expressive behavior on the quality of emotional experience. *Journal of Personality and Social Psychology, 29,* 475–486.

Laird, J. D. (1984). The real role of facial response in the experience of emotion: A reply to Tourangeau and Ellsworth, and others. *Journal of Personality and Social Psychology, 47,* 909–917.

Laird, J. D., Cuniff, M., Sheehan, K., & Shulman, D., et al. (1989). Emotion specific effects of facial expressions on memory for life events. *Journal of Social Behavior and Personality, 4,* 87–98.

Laird, J. D., Wagener, J., Halal, M., & Szegda, M. (1982). Remembering what you feel: Effects of emotion on memory. *Journal of Personality and Social Psychology, 42,* 646–657.

Lambert, A J., Khan, S. R., Lickel, B. A., & Fricke, K. (1997). Mood and the correction of positive versus negative stereotypes. *Journal of Personality and Social Psychology, 72,* 1002–1016.

Lambird, K. H., & Mann, T. (2006). When do ego threats lead to self-regulation failure? Negative consequences of defensive high self-esteem. *Personality and Social Psychology Bulletin, 32,* 1177–1187.

Landau, M. J., Solomon, S., Greenberg, J., Cohen, F., Pyszczynski, T., Arndt, J., Miller, C. H., Ogilvie, D. M., & Cook, A. (2004). Deliver us from evil: The effects of mortality salience and reminders of 9/11 on support for President George W. Bush. *Personality and Social Psychology Bulletin, 30,* 1136–1150.

Landman, J. (1988). Regret and elation following action and inaction: Affective responses to positive versus negative outcomes. *Personality and Social Psychology Bulletin, 13,* 524–536.

Lange, C. G. (1922 (Originally published 1885)). *The emotions.* Baltimore: Williams & Wilkins.

Langer, E. J., Blank, A., & Chanowitz, B. (1978). The mindlessness of ostensibly thoughtful action: The role of "placebic" information in interpersonal interaction. *Journal of Personality and Social Psychology, 36,* 635–642.

Langer, E. J., Taylor, S. E., Fiske, S. T., & Chanowitz, B. (1976). Stigma, staring, and discomfort: A novel stimulus hypothesis. *Journal of Experimental Social Psychology, 12,* 451–463.

Lanzetta, J. T., Cartwright-Smith, J., & Kleck, R. E. (1976). Effects of nonverbal dissimilation on emotional experience and autonomic arousal. *Journal of Personality and Social Psychology, 33,* 354–370.

LaPiere, R. T. (1934). Attitudes versus actions. *Social Forces, 13,* 230–237.

Larsen, J. T., McGraw A. P., & Cacioppo, J. T. (2001). Can people feel happy and sad at the same time? *Journal of Personality and Social Psychology, 81,* 684–696.

Larsen, J. T., Norris, C., & Cacioppo, J. T. (2003). Effects of positive and negative affect on electromyographic activity over zygomaticus major and corrugator supercilli. *Psychophysiology, 40,* 776–785.

Lassiter, G. D. (1988). Behavior perception, affect, and memory. *Social Cognition, 6,* 150–176.

Lassiter, G. D. (2002). Illusory causation in the courtroom. *Current Directions in Psychological Science, 11,* 204–208.

Lassiter, G. D., & Stone, J. I. (1984). Affective consequences of variation in behavior perception: When liking is in the level of analysis. *Personality and Social Psychology Bulletin, 10,* 253–259.

Lassiter, G. D., Stone, J. I., & Rogers, S. L. (1988). Memorial consequences of variation in behavior perception. *Journal of Experimental Social Psychology, 24,* 222–239.

Lasswell, H. D. (1948). The structure and function of communication in society. In L. Byron (Ed.), *Communication of ideas.* New York: Harper.

Latané B., & Bourgeois, M. J. (2001). Dynamic social impact and the consolidation, clustering, correlation, and continuing diversity of culture. In M. A. Hogg & R. S. Tindale (Eds.),

Blackwell handbook of social psychology: Group processes (pp. 235–258). Malden, MA: Blackwell.

Lazarus, R. S. (1966). *Psychological stress and the coping process*. New York: McGraw-Hill.

Lazarus, R. S. (1982). Thoughts on the relations between emotion and cognition. *American Psychologist, 37,* 1019–1024.

Lazarus, R. S. (1984). On the primacy of cognition. *American Psychologist, 39,* 124–129.

Lazarus, R. S. (1990). Constructs of the mind in adaptation. In N. L. Stein, B. Leventhal, & T. Trabasso (Eds.), *Psychological and biological approaches to emotion* (pp. 3–20). Hillsdale, NJ: Erlbaum.

Lazarus, R. S. (2000). Toward better research on stress and coping. *American Psychologist, 55,* 665–673.

Lazarus, R. S., Averill, J. R., & Opton, E. M., Jr. (1970). Towards a cognitive theory of emotion. In M. B. Arnold (Ed.), *Feelings and emotion: The Loyola Symposium*. New York: Academic Press.

Lazarus, R. S., & Smith, C. A. (1988). Knowledge and appraisal in the cognition-emotion relationship. *Cognition and Emotion, 2,* 281–300.

Leary, M. R. (1990). Responses to social exclusion: Social anxiety, jealousy, loneliness, depression, and low self-esteem. *Journal of Social and Clinical Psychology, 9,* 221–229.

Leary, M. R., & Baumeister, R. F. (2000). The nature and function of self-esteem: Sociometer theory. In M. P. Zanna (Ed.), *Advances in experimental social psychology* (Vol. 32, pp. 1–62). San Diego, CA: Academic Press.

Leary, M. R., Tambor, E. S., Terdal, S. K., & Downs, D. L. (1995). Self-esteem as an interpersonal monitor: The sociometer hypothesis. *Journal of Personality and Social Psychology, 68,* 518–530.

Leddo, J., Abelson, R. P., & Gross, P. H. (1984). Conjunctive explanations: When two reasons are better than one. *Journal of Personality and Social Psychology, 47,* 933–943.

Lee, A. Y., & Aaker, J. L. (2004). Bringing the frame into focus: The influence of regulatory fit on processing fluency and persuasion. *Journal of Personality and Social Psychology, 86,* 205–218.

Lee, A. Y., Aaker, J. L., & Gardner, W. L. (2000). The pleasures and pain of distinct self-construals: The role of interdependence in regulatory focus. *Journal of Personality and Social Psychology, 78,* 1122–1134.

Lehman, D. R., Lempert, R. O., & Nisbett, R. E. (1988). The effects of graduate training on reasoning: Formal discipline and thinking about everyday-life events. *American Psychologist, 43,* 431–442.

Leibenluft, E., Gobbini, M. I., Harrison, T., & Haxby, J. V. (2004). Mothers' neural activation in response to pictures of their children and other children. *Biological Psychiatry, 56,* 225–232.

Leonardelli, G. J., Lakin, J. L., & Arkin, R. M. (in press). A regulatory focus model of self-evaluation. *Journal of Experimental Social Psychology*.

Lepper, M. R., Greene, D., & Nisbett, R. E. (1973). Undermining children's intrinsic interest with extrinsic rewards: A test of the "overjustification" hypothesis. *Journal of Personality and Social Psychology, 28,* 129–137.

Lerner, J. S., & Gonzalez, R. M. (2005). Forecasting one's future based on fleeting subjective experiences. *Personality and Social Psychology Bulletin, 31,* 454–466.

Lerner, J. S., & Keltner, D. (2001). Fear, anger, and risk. *Journal of Personality and Social Psychology, 81,* 146–159.

Lerner, J. S., & Tiedens, L. Z. (2006). Portrait of the angry decision maker: How appraisal tendencies shape anger's influence on cognition. *Journal of Behavioral Decision Making, 19,* 115–137.

Leslie, A. M. (1994). Pretending and believing: Issues in the theory of mind. *Cognition, 50,* 211–238.

Leung, K., & Bond, M. H. (2004). Social axioms: A model for social beliefs in multicultural perspective. In M. P. Zanna (Ed.), *Advances in experimental social psychology* (Vol. 35, pp. 119–197). San Diego, CA: Academic Press.

Leventhal, H. (1982). The integration of emotion and cognition: A view from the perceptual-motor theory of emotion. In M. S. Clark & S. T. Fiske (Eds.), *Affect and cognition: The 17th Annual Carnegie Symposium on Cognition* (pp. 121–156). Hillsdale, NJ: Erlbaum.

Leventhal, H. (1984). A perceptual-motor theory of emotion. In L. Berkowitz (Ed.), *Advances in experimental social psychology* (Vol. 17, pp. 118–182). Orlando, FL: Academic Press.

Leventhal, H., & Scherer, K. (1987). The relationship of emotion to cognition: A functional approach to a semantic controversy. *Cognition and Emotion, 1,* 3–28.

Levesque, C., & Pelletier, L. G. (2003). On the investigation of primed and chronic autonomous and heteronomous motivational orientations. *Personality and Social Psychology Bulletin, 29,* 1570–1584.

Levin, D. (2000). Race as a visual feature: Using visual search and perceptual discrimination tasks to understand face categories and the cross-race recognition deficit. *Journal of Experimental Psychology: General, 129,* 559–574.

Levin, I. P., & Gaeth, G. J. (1988). How consumers are affected by the framing of attribute information before and after consuming the product. *Journal of Consumer Research, 15,* 374–378.

Levin, I. P., Schneider, S. L., & Gaeth, G. J. (1998). All frames are not created equal: A typology and critical analysis of framing effects. *Organizational Behavior and Human Decision Processes, 76,* 149–188.

Levin, I. P., Schnittjer, S. K., & Thee, S. L. (1988). Information framing effects in social and personal decisions. *Journal of Experimental Social Psychology, 24,* 520–529.

Levin, S., Federico, C. M., Sidanius, J., & Rabinowitz, J. L. (2002). Social dominance orientation and intergroup bias: The legitimation of favoritism for high-status groups. *Personality and Social Psychology Bulletin, 28,* 144–157.

Levine, J. M., & Moreland, R. L. (1998). Small groups. In D. T. Gilbert, S. T. Fiske, G. Lindzey (Eds.), *The handbook of social psychology* (4th ed., Vol. 2, pp. 415–469). New York: McGraw-Hill.

Levine, J. M., & Murphy, G. (1943). The learning and forgetting of controversial material. *Journal of Abnormal and Social Psychology, 38,* 507–517.

Levinger, G., & Breedlove, J. (1966). Interpersonal attraction and agreement. *Journal of Personality and Social Psychology, 3,* 367–372.

Levy, B., Ashman, O., & Dror, I. (1999–2000). To be or not to be: The effects of aging stereotypes on the will to live. *Omega: Journal of Death and Dying, 40,* 409–420.

Levy, B. R., & Banaji, M. R. (2002). Implicit ageism. In T. D. Nelson (Ed.), *Ageism: Stereotyping and prejudice against older persons* (pp. 49–75). Cambridge, MA: MIT Press.

Levy, B. R., Hausdorf, J. M., Hencke, R., & Wei, J. Y. (2000). Reducing cardiovascular stress with positive self-stereotypes of aging. *Journals of Gerontology: Series B: Psychological Sciences and Social Issues, 55B,* 205–213.

Levy, B. R., & Langer, E. J. (1994). Aging free from negative stereotypes: Successful memory in China and among the American deaf. *Journal of Personality and Social Psychology, 66,* 989–997.

Levy, B. R., Slade, M. D., Kunkel, S. R., & Kasl, S. V. (2002). Longevity increased by positive self-perceptions of aging. *Journal of Personality and Social Psychology, 83,* 261–270.

Levy, S. R., Plaks, J. E., Hong, Y.-y, Chiu, C.-y, & Dweck, C. S. (2001). Static versus dynamic theories and the perception of groups: Different routes to different destinations. *Personality and Social Psychology Review, 5,* 156–168.

Lewicki, P. (1985). Nonconscious biasing effects of single instances on subsequent judgments. *Journal of Personality and Social Psychology, 48,* 563–574.

Lewicki, P., Czyzewska, M., & Hoffman, H. (1987). Unconscious acquisition of complex procedural knowledge. *Journal of Experimental Psychology: Learning, Memory, and Cognition, 13,* 523–530.

Lewin, K. (1951). *Field theory in social psychology.* New York: Harper.

Lewontin, R. (1972). The apportionment of human diversity. *Evolutionary Biology, 6,* 381–398.

Leyens, J.-Ph., Cortes, B., Demoulin, S., Dovidio, J. F., Fiske, S. T., Gaunt, R., et al. (2003). Emotional prejudice, essentialism, and nationalism: The 2002 Tajfel Lecture. *European Journal of Social Psychology, 33,* 703–717.

Leyens, J.-Ph., Désert, M., Croizet, J. C., & Darcis, C. (2000). Stereotype threat: Are lower status and history of stigmatization preconditions of stereotype threat? *Personality and Social Psychology Bulletin, 26,* 1189–1199.

Liberman, A., & Chaiken, S. (1992). Defensive processing of personally relevant health messages. *Personality and Social Psychology Bulletin, 18,* 669–679.

Libby, L. K., Eibach, R. P., & Gilovich, T. (2005). Here's looking at me: The effect of memory perspective on assessments of personal change. *Journal of Personality and Social Psychology, 88,* 50–62.

Lieberman, M. D. (2007). Social cognitive neuroscience: A review of core processes. *Annual Review of Psychology, 58,* 259–289.

Lieberman, M. D., Gaunt, R., Gilbert, D. T., & Trope, Y. (2002). Reflexion and reflection: A social cognitive neuroscience approach to attributional inference. In M. P. Zanna (Ed.), *Advances in experimental social psychology* (Vol. 34, pp.199–249). San Diego: Academic Press.

Lieberman, M. D., Hariri, A., Jarcho, J. M., Eisenberger, N. I., & Bookheimer, S. Y. (2005). An fMRI investigation of race-related amygdala activity in African-American and Caucasian-American individuals. *Nature Neuroscience, 8,* 720–722.

Lieberman, M. D., Jarcho, J. M., & Satpute, A. B. (2004). Evidence-based and intuition-based self-knowledge: An fMRI study. *Journal of Personality and Social Psychology, 87,* 421–435.

Lieberman, M. D., Ochsner, K. N., Gilbert, D. T., & Schacter, D. L. (2001). Do amnesiacs exhibit cognitive dissonance reduction? The role of explicit memory and attention in attitude change. *Psychological Science, 12,* 135–140.

Lin, M. H., Kwan, V. S. Y., Cheung, A., & Fiske, S. T. (2005). Stereotype content model explains prejudice for an envied outgroup: Scale of anti-Asian American stereotypes. *Personality and Social Psychology Bulletin, 31,* 34–47.

Lingle, J. H., Altom, M. W., & Medin, D. L. (1984). Of cabbages and kings: Assessing the extendibility of natural object concept models to social things. In R. S. Wyer Jr. & T. K. Srull (Eds.), *Handbook of social cognition* (Vol. 1, pp. 71–117). Hillsdale, NJ: Erlbaum.

Lingle, J. H., Geva, N., Ostrom, T. M., Leippe, M. R., & Baumgardner, M. H. (1979). Thematic effects of person judgments on impression organization. *Journal of Personality and Social Psychology, 37,* 674–687.

Lingle, J. H., & Ostrom, T. M. (1979). Retrieval selectivity in memory-based impression judgments. *Journal of Personality and Social Psychology, 37,* 180–194.

Linville, P. W. (1982a). Affective consequences of complexity regarding the self and others. In M. S. Clark & S. T. Fiske (Eds.), *Affect and cognition: The 17th Annual Carnegie Symposium on Cognition* (pp. 79–109). Hillsdale, NJ: Erlbaum.

Linville, P. W. (1982b). The complexity-extremity effect and age-based stereotyping. *Journal of Personality and Social Psychology, 42,* 193–211.

Linville, P. W. (1985). Self-complexity and affective extremity: Don't put all your eggs in one cognitive basket. *Social Cognition, 3,* 94–120.

Linville, P. W., Fischer, G. W., & Fischhoff, B. (1993). AIDS risk perceptions and decision biases. In J. B. Pryor & G. D. Reeder (Eds.), *The social psychology of HIV infection* (pp. 5–38). Hillsdale, NJ: Erlbaum.

Linville, P. W., Fischer, G. W., & Salovey, P. (1989). Perceived distributions of the characteristics of ingroup and outgroup members: Empirical evidence and a computer simulation. *Journal of Personality and Social Psychology, 57,* 165–188.

Linville, P. W., Fischer, G. W., & Yoon, C. (1996). Perceived covariation among the features of ingroup and outgroup members: The outgroup covariation effect. *Journal of Personality and Social Psychology, 70,* 421–436.

Linville, P. W., & Jones, E. E. (1980). Polarized appraisals of outgroup members. *Journal of Personality and Social Psychology, 38,* 689–703.

Linville, P. W., Salovey, P., & Fischer, G. W. (1986). Stereotyping and perceived distributions of social characteristics: An application to ingroup-outgroup perception. In J. F. Dovidio & S. L. Gaertner (Eds.), *Prejudice, discrimination, and racism* (pp. 165–208). Orlando, FL: Academic Press.

Lippa, R. (1976). Expressive control and the leakage of dispositional introversion-extraversion during role-playing teaching. *Journal of Personality, 44,* 541–559.

Liu, J., Harris, A., & Kanwisher, N. (2002). Stages of processing in face perception: An MEG study. *Nature Neuroscience, 5,* 910–916.

Livingston, R. W., & Brewer, M. B. (2002). What are we really priming? Cue-based versus category-based processing of facial stimuli. *Journal of Personality and Social Psychology, 82,* 5–18.

Locke, J. (1979 (Originally published 1690)). *Essay concerning human understanding.* New York: Oxford University Press.

Loewenstein, G. (1996). Out of control: Visceral influences on behavior. *Organizational Behavior and Human Decision Processes, 65,* 272–292.

Loftus, E. F. (2004). Memories of things unseen. *Current Directions in Psychological Science, 13,* 145–147.

Loftus, E. F., & Davis, D. (2006). Recovered memories. *Annual Review of Clinical Psychology, 2,* 469–498.

Loken, B. (1984). Attitude processing strategies. *Journal of Experimental Social Psychology, 20,* 272–296.

Lombardi, W. J., Higgins, E. T., & Bargh, J. A. (1987). The role of consciousness in priming effects on categorization: Assimilation versus contrast as a function of awareness of the priming task. *Personality and Social Psychology Bulletin, 13,* 411–429.

Lopes, L. L. (1982). *Towards a procedural theory of judgment.* (Tech. Rep. No. 17, pp. 1–49). Madison, WI: Information Processing Program, University of Wisconsin.

Lord, C. G. (1982). Predicting behavioral consistency from an individual's perception of situational similarities. *Journal of Personality and Social Psychology, 42,* 1076–1088.

Lord, C. G., Lepper, M. R., & Mackie, D. M. (1984). Attitude prototypes as determinants of attitude-behavior consistency. *Journal of Personality and Social Psychology, 46,* 1254–1266.

Lord, C. G., & Saenz, D. S. (1985). Memory deficits and memory surfeits: Differential cognitive consequences of tokenism for tokens and observers. *Journal of Personality and Social Psychology, 49,* 918–926.

Lord, C. G., Saenz, D. S., & Godfrey, D. K. (1987). Effects of perceived scrutiny on participant memory for social interactions. *Journal of Experimental Social Psychology, 23,* 498–517.

Losch, M. E., & Cacioppo, J. T. (1990). Cognitive dissonance may enhance sympathetic tonus, but attitudes are changed to reduce negative affect rather than arousal. *Journal of Experimental Social Psychology, 26,* 289–304.

Loughnan, S., & Haslam, N. (2007). Animals and androids: Implicit associations between social categories and nonhumans. *Psychological Science, 18,* 116–121.

Lowe, C. A., & Kassin, S. M. (1980). A perceptual view of attribution: Theoretical and methodological implications. *Personality and Social Psychology, 6,* 532–542.

Lowery, B. S., Hardin, C. D., & Sinclair, S. (2001). Social influence effects on automatic racial prejudice. *Journal of Personality and Social Psychology, 81,* 842–855.

Lowery, B. S., Knowles, E. D., & Unzueta, M. M. (2007). Framing inequity safely: The motivated denial of White privilege. *Personality and Social Psychology Bulletin.*

Lowery, B. S., Unzueta, M. M., Knowles, E. D., & Goff, P. A. (2006). Concern for the ingroup and opposition to affirmative action. *Journal of Personality and Social Psychology, 90,* 961–974.

Luhtanen, R. K., & Crocker, J. (2005). Alcohol use in college students: Effects of level of self-esteem, narcissism, and contingencies of self-worth. *Psychology of Addictive Behaviors, 1,* 99–103.

Lydon, J. E., & Zanna, M. P. (1990). Commitment in the face of adversity: A value-affirmation approach. *Journal of Personality and Social Psychology, 58,* 1040–1047.

Lydon, J., Zanna, M. P., & Ross, M. (1988). Bolstering attitudes by autobiographical recall: Attitude persistence and selective memory. *Personality and Social Psychology Bulletin, 14,* 78–86.

Lynn, M., Shavitt, S., & Ostrom, T. M. (1985). Effects of pictures on the organization and recall of social information. *Journal of Personality and Social Psychology, 49,* 1160–1168.

Lyubomirsky, S., King, L., & Diener, E. (2005). The benefits of frequent positive affect: Does happiness lead to success? *Psychological Bulletin, 131,* 803–855.

Lyubomirsky, S., Sheldon, K. M., & Schkade, D. (2005). Pursuing happiness: The architecture of sustainable change. *Review of General Psychology, 9,* 111–131.

Mackie, D. M. (1986). Social identification effects in group polarization. *Journal of Personality and Social Psychology, 50,* 720–728.

Mackie, D. M. (1987). Systematic and nonsystematic processing of majority and minority persuasive communications. *Journal of Personality and Social Psychology, 53,* 41–52.

Mackie, D. M., & Cooper, J. (1984). Attitude polarization: Effects of group membership. *Journal of Personality and Social Psychology, 46,* 575–585.

Mackie, D. M., Devos, T., & Smith, E. R. (2000). Intergroup emotions: Explaining offensive action tendencies in an intergroup context. *Journal of Personality and Social Psychology, 79,* 602–616.

Mackie, D. M., & Gastardo-Conaco, M. C. (1988). The impact of importance accorded an issue on attitude inferences. *Journal of Experimental Social Psychology, 24,* 543–570.

Mackie, D. M., Hamilton, D. L., Schroth, H. A., Carlisle, C. J., Gersho, B. F., Meneses, L. M., Nedler, B. F., & Reichel, L. D. (1989). The effects of induced mood on illusory correlations. *Journal of Experimental Social Psychology, 25,* 524–544.

Mackie, D. M., & Smith, E. R. (1998). Intergroup relations: Insights from a theoretically integrative approach. *Psychological Review, 105,* 499–529.

Mackie, D. M., & Smith, E. R. (Eds.). (2002). *From prejudice to intergroup emotions.* New York: Psychology Press.

Mackie, D. M., & Worth, L. T. (1989). Cognitive deficits and the mediation of positive affect in persuasion. *Journal of Personality and Social Psychology, 57,* 27–40.

MacLeod, C., & Campbell, L. (1992). Memory accessibility and probability judgment: An experimental evaluation of the availability heuristic. *Journal of Personality and Social Psychology, 63,* 890–902.

MacLeod, M. D., & Macrae, C. N. (2001). Gone but not forgotten: The transient nature of retrieval-induced forgetting. *Psychological Science, 12,* 148–152.

Macrae, C. N., & Bodenhausen, G. V. (2000). Social cognition: Thinking categorically about others. *Annual Review of Psychology, 51,* 93–120.

Macrae, C. N., & Bodenhausen, G. V. (2001). Social cognition: Categorical person perception. *British Journal of Psychology, 92,* 239–255.

Macrae, C. N., Bodenhausen, G. V., & Guglielmo, C. (1999). Contexts of cryptomnesia: May the source be with you. *Social Cognition, 17,* 273–297.

Macrae, C. N., Bodenhausen, G. V., & Milne, A. B. (1998). Saying no to unwanted thoughts: Self-focus and the regulation of mental life. *Journal of Personality and Social Psychology, 74,* 578–589.

Macrae, C. N., Bodenhausen, G. V., Milne, A. B., & Ford, R. L. (1997). On the regulation of recollection: The intentional forgetting of stereotypical memories. *Journal of Personality and Social Psychology, 72,* 709–719.

Macrae, C. N., Bodenhausen, G. V., Milne, A. B., & Jetten, J. (1994). Out of mind but back in sight: Stereotypes on the rebound. *Journal of Personality and Social Psychology, 67,* 808–817.

Macrae, C. N., Bodenhausen, G. V., Milne, A. B., Thorn, T. M. J., & Castelli, L. (1997). On the activation of social stereotypes: The moderating role of processing objectives. *Journal of Experimental Social Psychology, 33,* 471–489.

Macrae, C. N., Bodenhausen, G. V., Schloerscheidt, A. M., & Milne, A. B. (1999). Tales of the unexpected: Executive function and person perception. *Journal of Personality and Social Psychology, 76,* 200–213.

Macrae, C. N., Hewstone, M., & Griffiths, R. J. (1993). Processing load and memory for stereotype-based information. *European Journal of Social Psychology, 23,* 77–87.

Macrae, C. N., Hood, B. M., Milne, A. B., Rowe, A. C., & Mason, M. F. (2002). Are you looking at me? Eye gaze and person perception. *Psychological Science, 13,* 460–464.

Macrae, C. N., & Lewis, H. L. (2002). Do I know you? Processing orientation and face recognition. *Psychological Science, 13,* 194–196.

Macrae, C. N., Milne, A. B., & Bodenhausen, G. V. (1994). Stereotypes as energy-saving devices: A peek inside the cognitive toolbox. *Journal of Personality and Social Psychology, 66,* 37–47.

Macrae, C. N., Moran, J. M., Heatherton, T. F., Banfield, J. F., & Kelley, W. M. (2004). Medial prefrontal activity predicts memory for self. *Cerebral Cortex, 14,* 647–654.

Macrae, C. N., Quinn, K. A., Mason, M. F., & Quadflieg, S. (2005). Understanding others: The face and person construal. *Journal of Personality and Social Psychology, 89,* 686–695.

Macrae, C. N., Schloerscheidt, A. M., Bodenhausen, G. V., & Milne, A. B. (2002). Creating memory illusions: Expectancy-based processing and the generation of false memories. *Memory, 10,* 63–80.

Maddox, K. B. (2004). Perspectives on racial phenotypicality bias. *Personality and Social Psychology Review, 8*, 383–401.

Maddox, K. B., & Chase, S. G. (2004). Manipulating subcategory salience: Exploring the link between skin tone and social perception of Blacks. *European Journal of Social Psychology, 34*, 533–546.

Maddox, K. B., & Gray, S. A. (2002). Cognitive representations of Black Americans: Re-exploring the role of skin tone. *Personality and Social Psychology Bulletin, 28*, 250–259.

Madon, S., Smith, A., Jussim, L., Russel, D. W., Eccles, J., Palumbo, P., et al. (2001). Am I as you see me or do you see me as I am? Self-fulfilling prophecies and self-verification. *Personality and Social Psychology Bulletin, 27*, 1214–1224.

Maguire, E. A., Gadian, D. G., Johnsrude, I. S., Good, C. D., Ashburner, J., Frackowiak, R. S. J., & Frith, C. D. (2000). Navigation-related structural change in the hippocampi of taxi drivers. *Proceedings of the National Academy of Sciences, 97*, 4398–4403.

Maio, G. R., & Olson, J. M. (1998). Values as truisms: Evidence and implications. *Journal of Personality and Social Psychology, 74*, 294–311.

Maitner, A. T., Mackie, D. M., & Smith, E. R. (2006). Evidence for the regulatory function of intergroup emotion: Emotional consequences of implemented or impeded intergroup action tendencies. *Journal of Experimental Social Psychology, 42*, 720–728.

Major, B., Cozzarelli, C., Testa, M., & McFarlin, D. B. (1988). Self-verification versus expectancy confirmation in social interaction: The impact of self-focus. *Personality and Social Psychology Bulletin, 14*, 346–359.

Major, B., Gramzow, R. H., McCoy, S. K., Levin, S., Schmader, T., & Sidanius, J. (2002). Perceiving personal discrimination: The role of group status and legitimizing ideology. *Journal of Personality and Social Psychology, 82*, 269–282.

Major, B., & O'Brien, L. T. (2005). The social psychology of stigma. *Annual Review of Psychology, 56*, 393–421.

Major, B., Quinton, W. J., & McCoy, S. K. (2002). Antecedents and consequences of attributions to discrimination: Theoretical and empirical advances. In M. P. Zanna (Ed.), *Advances in experimental social psychology* (Vol. 34, pp. 251–330). New York: Academic Press.

Major, B., Spencer, S., Schmader, T., Wolfe, C. T., & Crocker, J. (1998). Coping with negative stereotypes about intellectual performance: The role of psychological disengagement. *Personality and Social Psychology Bulletin, 24*, 34–50.

Major, B., Testa, M., & Blysma, W. H. (1991). Responses to upward and downward social comparisons: The impact of esteem-relevance and perceived control. In J. Suls & T. A. Wills (Eds.), *Social comparison: Contemporary theory and research* (pp. 237–260). Hillsdale, NJ: Erlbaum.

Malle, B. F. (2006). The actor-observer asymmetry in attribution: A (surprising) meta-analysis. *Psychological Bulletin, 132*, 895–919.

Malle, B. F., & Knobe, J. (1997). Which behaviors do people explain? A basic actor-observer asymmetry. *Journal of Personality and Social Psychology, 72*, 288–304.

Malle, B. F., Knobe, J., O'Laughlin, M. J., Pearce, G. E., & Nelson, S. E. (2000). Conceptual structure and social functions of behavior explanations: Beyond person-situation attributions. *Journal of Personality and Social Psychology, 79*, 309–326.

Mallon, E. B., Pratt, S. C., & Franks, N. R. (2001). Individual and collective decision-making during nest site selection by an ant *Leptothorax albipennis. Behavioral Ecology and Sociobiology, 50*, 352–359.

Malpass, R. S. (1969). Effects of attitude on learning and memory: The influence of instruction-induced sets. *Journal of Experimental Social Psychology, 5*, 441–453.

Malpass, R. S., & Kravitz, J. (1969). Recognition for faces of own and other race. *Journal of Personality and Social Psychology, 13*, 330–334.

Mandler, G. (1975). *Mind and emotion.* New York: Wiley.

Mandler, G. (1990). A constructivist theory of emotion. In N. S. Stein, B. L. Leventhal, & T. Trabasso (Eds.), *Psychological and biological approaches to emotion.* Hillsdale, NJ: Erlbaum.

Mandler, G., & Nakamura, Y. (1987). Aspects of consciousness. *Personality and Social Psychology Bulletin, 13*, 299–313.

Mandler, G., Nakamura, Y., & Van Zandt, B. J. S. (1987). Nonspecific effects of exposure on stimuli that cannot be recognized. *Journal of Experimental Psychology: Learning, Memory, and Cognition, 13*, 646–648.

Maner, J. K., & Schaller, M. (2006). They all look the same to me (unless they're angry): From out-group homogeneity to out-group heterogeneity. *Psychological Science.*

Manis, M. (1977). Cognitive social psychology. *Personality and Social Psychology Bulletin, 3,* 550–566.

Manis, M., Avis, N. E., & Cardoze, S. (1981). Reply to Bar-Hillel and Fischhoff. *Journal of Personality and Social Psychology, 41,* 681–683.

Manis, M., Dovalina, I., Avis, N. E., & Cardoze, S. (1980). Base rates can affect individual predictions. *Journal of Personality and Social Psychology, 38,* 231–248.

Manis, M., Shedler, J., Jonides, J., & Nelson, T. E. (1993). Availability heuristic in judgments of set size and frequency of occurrence. *Journal of Personality and Social Psychology, 65,* 448–457.

Manucia, G. K., Baumann, D. J., & Cialdini, R. B. (1984). Mood influences on helping: Direct effects or side effects? *Journal of Personality and Social Psychology, 46,* 357–364.

Marcel, A. J. (1983a). Conscious and unconscious perception: An approach to the relations between phenomenal experience and perceptual processes. *Cognitive Psychology, 15,* 238–300.

Marcel, A. J. (1983b). Conscious and unconscious perception: Experiments on visual masking and word recognition. *Cognitive Psychology, 15,* 197–237.

March, J. G., & Simon, G. A. (1958). *Organizations.* New York: Wiley.

Marchand, M. A. G., & Vonk, R. (2005). The process of becoming suspicious of ulterior motives. *Social Cognition, 23,* 242–256.

Marcus, G. E., & Mackuen, M. B. (1999). Anxiety, enthusiasm, and the vote: The emotional underpinnings of learning and involvement during presidential campaigns. *American Political Science Review, 87,* 672–685.

Marcus, G. E., & MacKuen, M. B. (1999). Anxiety, enthusiasm, and the vote: The emotional underpinnings of learning and involvement during presidential campaigns. In J. T. Jost & J. Sidanius (Eds.), *Political psychology: Key readings* (pp. 163–176). New York: Psychology Press.

Marks, J. (1995). *Human biodiversity: Genes, races, and history.* New York: Aldine de Gruyter.

Marks, G., & Miller, N. (1982). Target attractiveness as a mediator of assumed attitude similarity. *Personality and Social Psychology Bulletin, 8,* 728–735.

Markus, H. R. (1977). Self-schemata and processing information about the self. *Journal of Personality and Social Psychology, 35,* 63–78.

Markus, H. R., & Kitayama, S. (1991). Culture and the self: Implications for cognition, emotion, and motivation. *Psychological Review, 98,* 224–253.

Markus, H. R., & Kunda, Z. (1986). Stability and malleability of the self concept. *Journal of Personality and Social Psychology, 51,* 858–866.

Markus, H. R., & Nurius, P. (1986). Possible selves. *American Psychologist, 41,* 954–969.

Markus, H. R., & Smith, J. (1981). The influence of self-schemas on the perception of others. In N. Cantor & J. F. Kihlstrom (Eds.), *Personality, cognition, and social interaction* (pp. 233–262). Hillsdale, NJ: Erlbaum.

Markus, H. R., & Wurf, E. (1987). The dynamic self-concept: A social psychological perspective. *Annual Review of Psychology, 38,* 299–337.

Marshall, G. D., & Zimbardo, P. G. (1979). Affective consequences of inadequately explained physiological arousal. *Journal of Personality and Social Psychology, 37,* 970–988.

Martens, A., Johns, M., Greenberg, J., & Schimel, J. (2006). Combating stereotype threat: The effect of self-affirmation on women's intellectual performance. *Journal of Experimental Social Psychology, 42,* 236–243.

Martin, L. L. (1986). Set/reset: Use and disuse of concepts in impression formation. *Journal of Personality and Social Psychology, 51,* 493–504.

Martin, L. L., & Tesser, A. (1989). Toward a motivational and structural theory of ruminative thought. In J. S. Uleman & J. A. Bargh (Eds.), *Unintended thought* (pp. 306–326). New York: Guilford Press.

Marx, D. M., Stapel, D. A., & Muller, D. (2005). We can do it: The interplay of construal orientation and social comparisons under threat. *Journal of Personality and Social Psychology, 88,* 432–446.

Maslach, C. (1979). Negative emotional biasing of unexplained arousal. *Journal of Personality and Social Psychology, 37*, 953–969.

Mason, M. F., Hood, B. M., & Macrae, C. N. (2004). Look into my eyes: Gaze direction and person memory. *Memory, 12*, 637–643.

Mason, M. F., & Macrae, C. N. (2004). Categorizing and individuating others: The neural substrates of person perception. *Journal of Cognitive Neuroscience, 16*, 1785–1795.

Mason, M. F., Tatkow, E. P., & Macrae, C. N. (2005). The look of love: Gaze shifts and person perception. *Psychological Science, 16*, 236–239.

Massad, C. M., Hubbard, M., & Newtson, D. (1979). Selective perception of events. *Journal of Experimental Social Psychology, 15*, 513–532.

Massey, D. S., & Denton, N. A. (1993). *American apartheid: Segregation and the making of the underclass.* Cambridge, MA: Harvard University Press.

Masters, J. C., & Furman, W. (1976). Effects of affective states on noncontingent outcome expectancies and beliefs in internal or external control. *Developmental Psychology, 12*, 481–482.

Masuda, T., & Nisbett, R. E. (2001). Attending holistically vs. analytically: Comparing the context sensitivity of Japanese and Americans. *Journal of Personality and Social Psychology, 81*, 922–934.

Matlin, M., & Stang, D. J. (1978). *The Pollyanna principle.* Cambridge, MA: Schenkman.

Matsumoto, D. (1987). The role of facial response in the experience of emotion: More methodological problems and a meta-analysis. *Journal of Personality and Social Psychology, 52*, 769–774.

Mayer, J. D. (1986). How mood influences cognition. In N. E. Sharkey (Ed.), *Advances in cognitive science* (pp. 290–314). Chichester, West Sussex: Ellis Horwood Limited.

Mayer, J. D., & Bower, G. H. (1985). Naturally occurring mood and learning: Comment on Hasher, Rose, Zacks, Sanft, and Doren. *Journal of Experimental Psychology: General, 114*, 396–403.

Mayer, J. D., & Bower, G. H. (1986). Learning and memory for personality prototypes. *Journal of Personality and Social Psychology, 51*, 473–492.

Mayer, J. D., & Bremer, D. (1985). Assessing mood with affect-sensitive tasks. *Journal of Personality Assessment, 49*, 95–99.

Mayer, J. D., & Gaschke, Y. N. (1988). The experience and meta-experience of mood. *Journal of Personality and Social Psychology, 55*, 102–111.

Mayer, J. D., Mamberg, M. H., & Volanth, A. J. (1988). Cognitive domains of the mood system. *Journal of Personality, 56*, 453–486.

Mayer, J. D., McCormick, L. J., & Strong, S. E. (1995). Mood-congruent memory and natural mood: New evidence. *Personality and Social Psychology Bulletin, 21*, 736–746.

Mayer, J. D., & Salovey, P. (1988). Personality moderates the interaction of mood and cognition. In K. Fiedler & J. Forgas (Eds.), *Affect, cognition, and social behavior* (pp. 87–99). Toronto, Canada: Hogrefe.

Mays, V. M., Cochran, S. D., & Barnes, N. W. (2007). Race, race-based discrimination, and health outcomes among African Americans. *Annual Review of Psychology, 58*, 201–225.

McArthur, L. Z. (1972). The how and what of why: Some determinants and consequences of causal attribution. *Journal of Personality and Social Psychology, 22*, 171–193.

McArthur, L. Z. (1980). Illusory causation and illusory correlation: Two epistemological accounts. *Personality and Social Psychology Bulletin, 6*, 507–519.

McArthur, L. Z. (1981). What grabs you? The role of attention in impression formation and causal attribution. In E. T. Higgins, C. P. Herman, & M. P. Zanna (Eds.), *Social cognition: The Ontario Symposium* (Vol. 1, pp. 201–246). Hillsdale, NJ: Erlbaum.

McArthur, L. Z., & Apatow, K. (1983–1984). Impressions of baby-faced adults. *Social Cognition, 2*, 315–342.

McArthur, L. Z., & Baron, R. M. (1983). Toward an ecological theory of social perception. *Psychological Review, 90*, 215–238.

McArthur, L. Z., & Berry, D. S. (1987). Cross-cultural agreement in perceptions of babyfaced adults. *Journal of Cross-Cultural Psychology, 18*, 165–192.

McArthur, L. Z., & Ginsberg, E. (1981). Causal attribution to salient stimuli: An investigation of visual fixation mediators. *Personality and Social Psychology Bulletin, 7*, 547–553.

McArthur, L. Z., & Post, D. L. (1977). Figural emphasis and person perception. *Journal of Experimental Social Psychology, 13,* 520–535.

McArthur, L. Z., & Solomon, L. K. (1978). Perceptions of an aggressive encounter as a function of the victim's salience and the perceiver's arousal. *Journal of Personality and Social Psychology, 36,* 1278–1290.

McCabe, K., Houser, D., Ryan, L., Smith, V., & Trouard, T. (2001). A functional imaging study of cooperation in two-person reciprocal exchange. *Proceedings of the National Academy of Sciences, 98,* 11832–11835.

McCaul, K. D., Holmes, D. S., & Solomon, S. (1982). Voluntary expressive changes and emotion. *Journal of Personality and Social Psychology, 42,* 145–152.

McCauley, C., Stitt, C. L., Woods, K., & Lipton, D. (1973). Group shift to caution at the race track. *Journal of Experimental Social Psychology, 9,* 80–86.

McClelland, J. L., McNaughton, B. L., & O'Reilly R. C. (1995). Why there are complementary learning systems in the hippocampus and neocortex: Insights from the successes and failures of connectionist models of learning and memory. *Psychological Review, 102,* 419–457.

McClelland, J. L., Rumelhart, D. E., & Hinton, G. E. (1986). The appeal of parallel distributed processing. In D. E. Rumelhart, J. L. McClelland, & the PDP Research Group, *Parallel distributed processing: Explorations in the microstructure of cognition* (Vol. 1, pp. 3–44). Cambridge, MA: MIT Press.

McClosky, M. E., & Glucksberg, S. (1978). Natural categories: Well-defined or fuzzy sets. *Memory and Cognition, 6,* 462–472.

McClure, S. M., Daw, N. D., & Montague, P. R. (2003). A computational substrate for incentive salience. *Trends in Neuroscience, 26,* 423–428.

McClure, S. M., Li, J., Tomlin, D., Cypert, K. S., Montague, L. M., & Montague, P. R. (2004). Neural correlates of behavioral preference for culturally familiar drinks. *Neuron, 44,* 379–387.

McConnell, A. R., & Leibold, J. M. (2001). Relations among the implicit association test, discriminatory behavior, and explicit measures of racial attitudes. *Journal of Experimental Social Psychology, 37,* 435–442.

McCrea, S. M., & Hirt, E. R. (2001). The role of ability judgments in self-handicapping. *Personality and Social Psychology Bulletin, 27,* 1378–1389.

McFarland, C., & Buehler, R. (1998). The impact of negative affect on autobiographical memory: The role of self-focused attention to moods. *Journal of Personality and Social Psychology, 75,* 1424–1440.

McFarland, C., & Ross, M. (1987). The relation between current impressions and memories of self and dating partners. *Personality and Social Psychology Bulletin, 13,* 228–238.

McFarland, C., Ross, M., & Conway, M. (1984). Self-persuasion and self-presentation as mediators of anticipatory attitude change. *Journal of Personality and Social Psychology, 46,* 529–540.

McGarty, C., Turner, J. C., Hogg, M. A., Davidson, B., & Wetherell, M. S. (1992). Group polarization as conformity to the prototypical group member. *British Journal of Social Psychology, 31,* 11–19.

McGregor, H., Lieberman, J. D., Solomon, S., Greenberg, T., Arndt, J., Simon, L., et al. (1998). Terror management and aggression: Evidence that mortality salience motivates aggression against worldview threatening others. *Journal of Personality and Social Psychology, 74,* 590–605.

McGregor, I., Zanna, M. P., Holmes, J. G., & Spencer, S. J. (2001). Compensatory conviction in the face of personal uncertainty: Going to extremes and being oneself. *Journal of Personality and Social Psychology, 80,* 472–488.

McGuire, W. J. (1969). Nature of attitudes and attitude change. In G. Lindzey & E. Aronson (Eds.), *The handbook of social psychology* (2nd ed., Vol. 3, pp. 136–314). Reading, MA: Addison-Wesley.

McGuire, W. J. (1976). Some internal psychological factors influencing consumer choice. *Journal of Consumer Research, 2,* 302–309.

McGuire, W. J. (1985). Attitudes and attitude change. In G. Lindzey & E. Aronson (Eds.), *The handbook of social psychology* (3rd ed., Vol. 2, pp. 233–346). New York: Random House.

McKenzie-Mohr, D., & Zanna, M. P. (1990). Treating women as sexual objects: Look to the (gender schematic) male who has viewed pornography. *Personality and Social Psychology Bulletin, 16,* 296–308.

McKone, E., Kanwisher, N., & Duchaine, B. C. (2007). Can generic expertise explain special processing for faces? *Trends in Cognitive Sciences, 11,* 8–15.

McLachlan, A. (1986). Polarization and discussion context. *British Journal of Social Psychology, 25,* 345–347.

McMullen, M. N., & Markman, K. D. (2000). Downward counterfactuals and motivation: The "wake-up call" and the "Pangloss" effect. *Personality and Social Psychology Bulletin, 26,* 575–584.

Mead, G. H. (1934). *Mind, self, and society.* Chicago: University of Chicago Press.

Medin, D. L., Altom, M. W., & Murphy, T. D. (1984). Given versus induced category representations: Use of prototype and exemplar information in classification. *Journal of Experimental Psychology: Learning, Memory, and Cognition, 10,* 333–352.

Meehl, P. E. (1954). *Clinical versus statistical prediction: A theoretical analysis and review of the literature.* Minneapolis: University of Minnesota Press.

Meloen, J. D., Van der Linden, G., & De Witte, H. (1996). A test of the approaches of Adorno et al., Lederer, and Altemeyer of authoritarianism in Belgian Flanders: A research note. *Political Psychology, 17,* 643–656.

Mendes, W. B., Blascovich, J., Lickel, B. A., & Hunter, S. (2002). Challenge and threat during social interaction with White and Black men. *Personality and Social Psychology Bulletin, 28,* 939–952.

Mendoza-Denton, R., Ayduk, O., Mischel, W., Shoda, Y., & Testa, A. (2001). Person X situation interactionism in self-encoding (I am . . . when . . .): Implications for affect regulation and social information. *Journal of Personality and Social Psychology, 80,* 533–544.

Menon, T., Morris, M. W., Chiu, C.-y., & Hong, Y.-y. (1999). Culture and the construal of agency: Attribution to individual versus group dispositions. *Journal of Personality and Social Psychology, 76,* 701–717.

Merton, R. K. (1957). *Social theory and social structure.* New York: Free Press.

Mervis, C. B., & Rosch, E. H. (1981). Categorization of natural objects. *Annual Review of Psychology, 32,* 89–115.

Mesquita, B. (2001). Emotions in collectivist and individualist contexts. *Journal of Personality and Social Psychology, 80,* 68–74.

Messick, D. M., & Mackie, D. M. (1989). Intergroup relations. *Annual Review of Psychology, 40,* 45–81.

Meyer, J. P., & Mulherin, A. (1980). From attribution to helping: An analysis of the mediating effects of affect and expectancy. *Journal of Personality and Social Psychology, 39,* 201–210.

Milburn, M. A. (1987). Ideological self-schemata and schematically induced attitude consistency. *Journal of Experimental Social Psychology, 23,* 383–398.

Mill, J. S. (1869). *The analysis of the phenomena of the human mind.* New York: Kelley.

Mill, J. S. (1974 (Originally published 1843)). *System of logic, ratiocinative and inductive.* Toronto, Canada: University of Toronto Press.

Millar, M. G., Millar, K. U., & Tesser, A. (1988). The effects of helping and focus of attention on mood states. *Personality and Social Psychology Bulletin, 14,* 536–543.

Millar, M. G., & Tesser, A. (1986a). Effects of attitude and cognitive focus on the attitude-behavior relation. *Journal of Personality and Social Psychology, 51,* 270–276.

Millar, M. G., & Tesser, A. (1986b). Thought-induced attitude change: The effects of schema structure and commitment. *Journal of Personality and Social Psychology, 51,* 259–269.

Millar, M. G., & Tesser, A. (1989). The effects of affective-cognitive consistency and thought on the attitude-behavior relationship. *Journal of Experimental Social Psychology, 25,* 189–202.

Millar, M. G., Tesser, A., & Millar, K. U. (1988). The effects of a threatening life event on behavior sequences and intrusive thought: A self-disruption explanation. *Cognitive Therapy and Research, 12,* 441–457.

Miller, C. T., & Downey, K. T. (1999). A meta-analysis of heavyweight and self-esteem. *Personality and Social Psychology Review, 3*, 68–84.

Miller, C. T., & Kaiser, C. R. (2001). A theoretical perspective on coping with stigma. *Journal of Social Issues, 57*, 73–92.

Miller, D. A., Smith, E. R., & Mackie, D. M. (2004). Effects of intergroup contact and political dispositions on prejudice: Role of intergroup emotions. *Group Processes and Intergroup Relations, 7*, 221–237.

Miller, D. T., & McFarland, C. (1986). Counterfactual thinking and victim compensation: A test of norm theory. *Personality and Social Psychology Bulletin, 12*, 513–519.

Miller, D. T., & Prentice, D. A. (1999). Some consequences of a belief in group essence: The category divide hypothesis. In D. A. Prentice & D. T. Miller (Eds.), *Cultural divides: Understanding and overcoming group conflict* (pp. 213–238). New York: Russell Sage Foundation.

Miller, D. T., & Ross, M. (1975). Self-serving biases in the attribution of causality: Fact or fiction? *Psychological Bulletin, 82*, 213–225.

Miller, D. T., Turnbull, W., & McFarland, C. (1990). Counterfactual thinking and social perception: Thinking about what might have been. In M. P. Zanna (Ed.), *Advances in experimental social psychology* (Vol. 23, pp. 305–331). New York: Academic Press.

Miller, D. T., Visser, P. S., & Staub, B. D. (2005). How surveillance begets perceptions of dishonesty: The case of the counterfactual sinner. *Journal of Personality and Social Psychology, 89*, 117–128.

Miller, E. K., & Cohen, J. D. (2001). An integrative theory of prefrontal cortex function. *Annual Review of Neuroscience, 24*, 167–202.

Miller, G. A. (1956). The magical number seven, plus or minus two: Some limits on our capacity for processing information. *Psychological Review, 63*, 81–97.

Mills, J. (1968). Interest in supporting and discrepant information. In R. P. Abelson, E. Aronson, W. J. McGuire, T. M. Newcomb, M. J. Rosenberg, & P. H. Tannenbaum (Eds.), *Theories of cognitive consistency: A sourcebook*. Chicago: Rand McNally.

Milne, E., & Grafman, J. (2001). Ventromedial prefrontal cortex lesions in humans eliminate implicit gender stereotyping. *Journal of Neuroscience, 21*, 1–6.

Mischel, W. (1968). *Personality and assessment*. New York: Wiley.

Mischel, W. (1984). Convergences and challenges in the search for consistency. *American Psychologist, 39*, 351–364.

Mischel, W. (1997). Was the cognitive revolution just a detour on the road to behaviorism? On the need to reconcile situational control and personal control. In R. S. Wyer Jr. (Ed.), *The automaticity of everyday life* (pp. 181–186). Mahwah, NJ: Erlbaum.

Mischel, W., & Peake, P. K. (1982). Beyond déjà vu in the search for cross-situational consistency. *Psychological Review, 89*, 730–755.

Mitchell, J. P., Banaji, M. R., & Macrae, C. N. (2005). General and specific contributions of the medial prefrontal cortex to knowledge about mental states. *NeuroImage, 28*, 757–762.

Mitchell, J. P., Heatherton, T. F., & Macrae, C. N. (2002). Distinct neural systems subserve person and object knowledge. *Proceedings of the National Academy of Sciences, 99*, 15238–15243.

Mitchell, J. P., Macrae, C. N., & Banaji, M. R. (2005). Forming impressions of people versus inanimate objects: Social-cognitive processing in the medial prefrontal cortex. *NeuroImage, 26*, 251–257.

Miyamoto, Y., & Kitayama, S. (2002). Cultural variation in correspondence bias: The critical role of attitude diagnosticity of socially constrained behavior. *Journal of Personality and Social Psychology, 83*, 1239–1248.

Monin, B. (2003). The warm glow heuristic: When liking leads to familiarity. *Journal of Personality and Social Psychology, 85*, 1035–1048.

Monin, B., & Miller, D. T. (2001). Moral credentials and the expression of prejudice. *Journal of Personality and Social Psychology, 81*, 33–43.

Monson, T. C., Hesley, J. W., & Chernick, L. (1982). Specifying when personality traits can and cannot predict behavior: An alternative to abandoning the attempt to predict single-act criteria. *Journal of Personality and Social Psychology, 43*, 385–399.

Monteith, M. J. (1993). Self-regulation of prejudiced responses: Implications for progress in prejudice-reduction efforts. *Journal of Personality and Social Psychology, 65*, 469–485.

Monteith, M. J. (1996). Contemporary forms of prejudice-related conflict: In search of a nutshell. *Personality and Social Psychology Bulletin, 22,* 461–473.

Monteith, M. J., Ashburn-Nardo, L., Voils, C. I., & Czopp, A. M. (2002). Putting the brakes on prejudice: On the development and operation of cues for control. *Journal of Personality and Social Psychology, 83,* 1029–1050.

Monteith, M. J., Deneen, N. E., & Tooman, G. D. (1996). The effect of social norm activation on the expression of opinions concerning gay men and Blacks. *Basic and Applied Social Psychology, 18,* 267–288.

Monteith, M. J., Sherman, J. W., & Devine, P. G. (1998). Suppression as a stereotype control strategy. *Personality and Social Psychology, 36,* 125–154.

Monteith, M. J., Spicer, C. V., & Tooman, G. D. (1998). Consequences of stereotype suppression: Stereotypes on and not on the rebound. *Journal of Experimental Social Psychology, 34,* 355–377.

Monteith, M. J., & Voils, C. I. (1998). Proneness to prejudiced responses: Toward understanding the authenticity of self-reported discrepancies. *Journal of Personality and Social Psychology, 75,* 901–916.

Monteith, M. J., & Walters, G. L. (1998). Egalitarianism, moral obligation, and prejudice-related personal standards. *Personality and Social Psychology Bulletin, 24,* 186–199. [Erratum: *24,* 442.]

Montepare, J. M., & Zebrowitz-McArthur, L. (1986). The influence of facial characteristics on children's age perceptions. *Journal of Experimental Child Psychology, 42,* 303–314.

Montepare, J. M., & Zebrowitz-McArthur, L. (1987). Perceptions of adults with childlike voices in two cultures. *Journal of Experimental Social Psychology, 23,* 331–349.

Montepare, J. M., & Zebrowitz-McArthur, L. (1988). Impressions of people created by age-related qualities of their gaits. *Journal of Personality and Social Psychology, 55,* 547–556.

Mor, N., & Winquist, J. (2002). Self-focused attention and negative affect: A meta-analysis. *Psychological Bulletin, 128,* 638–662.

Moreland, R. L., & Zajonc, R. B. (1977). Is stimulus recognition a necessary condition for the occurrence of exposure effects? *Journal of Personality and Social Psychology, 35,* 191–199.

Moreland, R. L., & Zajonc, R. B. (1979). Exposure effects may not depend on stimulus recognition. *Journal of Personality and Social Psychology, 37,* 1085–1089.

Moreland, R. L., & Zajonc, R. B. (1982). Exposure effects in person perception: Familiarity, similarity, and attraction. *Journal of Experimental Social Psychology, 18,* 395–415.

Moretti, M., & Higgins, E. T. (1990). Relating self-discrepancy beyond actual self-ratings. *Journal of Experimental Social Psychology, 26,* 108–123.

Morewedge, C. K., Gilbert, D. T., & Wilson, T. D. (2005). The least likely of times: How remembering the past biases forecasts of the future. *Psychological Science, 16,* 626–630.

Morier, D. M., & Borgida, E. (1984). The conjunction fallacy: A task specific phenomenon? *Personality and Social Psychology Bulletin, 10,* 243–252.

Morris, J. S., Ohman, A., & Dolan, R. J. (1998). Conscious and unconscious emotional learning in the human amygdala. *Nature, 393,* 467–470.

Morris, M. W., & Peng, K. (1994). Culture and cause: American and Chinese attributions for social and physical events. *Journal of Personality and Social Psychology, 67,* 949–971.

Moskalenko, S., & Heine, S. J. (2003). Watching your troubles away: Television viewing as a stimulus for subjective self-awareness. *Personality and Social Psychology Bulletin, 29,* 76–85.

Moskowitz, G. B. (2005). *Social cognition: Understanding self and others.* New York: Guilford Press.

Mullen, B., Brown, R. J., & Smith, C. (1992). Ingroup bias as a function of salience, relevance, and status: An integration. *European Journal of Social Psychology, 22,* 103–122.

Mullen, B., & Goethals, G. R. (1990). Social projection, actual consensus, and valence. *British Journal of Social Psychology, 29,* 279–282.

Mullen, B., & Hu, L. (1989). Perceptions of ingroup and outgroup variability: A meta-analytic integration. *Basic and Applied Social Psychology, 10,* 233–252.

Mullen, B., & Johnson, C. (1990). Distinctiveness-based illusory correlations and stereotyping: A meta-analytic integration. *British Journal of Social Psychology, 29,* 11–27.

Mullen, B., & Riordan, C. A. (1988). Self-serving attributions for performance in naturalistic settings: A meta-analytic review. *Journal of Applied Social Psychology, 18,* 3–22.

Murphy, F. C., Nimmo-Smith, I., & Lawrence, A. D. (2003). Functional neuroanatomy of emotions: A meta-analysis. *Cognitive Affective and Behavioral Neuroscience, 3,* 207–233.

Murphy, G. L., & Medin, D. L. (1985). The role of theories in conceptual coherence. *Psychological Review, 92,* 289–316.

Murphy, S. T., Monahan, J. L., & Zajonc, R. B. (1995). Additivity of nonconscious affect: Combined effects of priming and exposure. *Journal of Personality and Social Psychology, 69,* 589–602.

Murray, J. D., Spadafore, J. A., & McIntosh, W. D. (2005). Belief in a just world and social perception: Evidence for automatic activation. *Journal of Social Psychology, 145,* 35–47.

Musen, G., & Squire, L. R. (1993). Implicit learning of color-word associations using a Stroop paradigm. *Journal of Experimental Psychology: Learning, Memory, and Cognition, 19,* 789–798.

Mussweiler, T. (2003). Comparison processes in social judgment: Mechanisms and consequences. *Psychological Review, 110,* 472–489.

Mussweiler, T. (2006). Doing is for thinking! *Psychological Science, 17,* 17–21.

Mussweiler, T., & Bodenhausen, G. (2002). I know you are but what am I? Self-evaluative consequences of judging in-group and out-group members. *Journal of Personality and Social Psychology, 82,* 19–32.

Mussweiler, T., & Förster, J. (2000). The sex → aggression link: A perception-behavior dissociation. *Journal of Personality and Social Psychology, 79,* 507–520.

Mussweiler, T., & Strack, F. (1999). Hypothesis-consistent testing and semantic priming in the anchoring paradigm: A selective accessibility model. *Journal of Experimental Social Psychology, 35,* 136–164.

Mussweiler, T., & Strack, F. (2000). Numeric judgments under uncertainty: The role of knowledge in anchoring. *Journal of Experimental Social Psychology, 36,* 495–518.

Mussweiler, T., Strack, F., & Pfeiffer, T. (2000). Overcoming the inevitable anchoring effect: Considering the opposite compensates for selective accessibility. *Personality and Social Psychology Bulletin, 26,* 1142–1150.

Naqvi, N., Shiv, B., & Bechara, A. (2006). The role of emotion in decision making: A cognitive neuroscience perspective. *Current Directions in Psychological Science, 15,* 260–264.

Nasby, W., & Yando, R. (1982). Selective encoding and retrieval of affectively-valent information: Two cognitive consequences of mood. *Journal of Personality and Social Psychology, 43,* 1244–1253.

Nasi, N., Shiv, B., & Bechara, A. (2006). The role of emotion in decision making: A cognitive neuroscience perpective. *Current Directions in Psychological Science, 15,* 260–264.

Nei, M., & Roychoudhury, A. (1993). Evolutionary relationships of human populations on a global scale. *Molecular Biology Evolution, 10,* 927–943.

Neisser, U. (1967). *Cognitive psychology.* Englewood Cliffs, NJ: Prentice-Hall.

Neisser, U. (1976). *Cognition and reality.* San Francisco: Freeman.

Neisser, U. (1980). On "social knowing." *Personality and Social Psychology Bulletin, 6,* 601–605.

Nelson, T. D. (Ed.). (2002). *Ageism: Stereotyping and prejudice against older persons.* Cambridge, MA: MIT Press.

Nesdale, A. R., Dharmalingam, S., & Kerr, G. K. (1987). Effect of subgroup ratio on stereotyping. *European Journal of Social Psychology, 17,* 353–356.

Neuberg, S. L. (1988). Behavioral implications of information presented outside of conscious awareness: The effect of subliminal presentation of trait information on behavior in the prisoner's dilemma game. *Social Cognition, 6,* 207–230.

Neuberg, S. L. (1989). The goal of forming accurate impressions during social interactions: Attenuating the impact of negative expectancies. *Journal of Personality and Social Psychology, 56,* 374–386.

Neuberg, S. L., & Cottrell, C. A. (2002). Intergroup emotions: A biocultural approach. In D. M. Mackie & E. R. Smith (Eds.), *From prejudice to intergroup emotions: Differentiated reactions to social groups* (pp. 265–283). New York: Psychology Press.

Neuberg, S. L., & Fiske, S. T. (1987). Motivational influences on impression formation: Outcome dependency, accuracy-driven attention, and individuating processes. *Journal of Personality and Social Psychology, 53,* 431–444.

Neuberg, S. L., & Newsom, J. T. (1993). Personal need for structure: Individual differences in the desire for simpler structure. *Journal of Personality and Social Psychology, 65,* 113–131.

Neuberg, S. L., Smith, D. M., & Asher, T. (2000). Why people stigmatize: Toward a biocultural framework. In T. F. Heatherton, R. E. Kleck, & M. R. Hebl (Eds.), *The social psychology of stigma* (pp. 31–61). New York: Guilford Press.

Neugarten, B. (1974, September). Age groups in American society and the rise of the young-old. *Annals of the American Academy of Political and Social Science,* 187–198.

Neumann, R., & Strack, F. (2000). Approach and avoidance: The influence of proprioceptive and exteroceptive cues on encoding of affective information. *Journal of Personality and Social Psychology, 79,* 39–48.

Neumann, R., & Seibt, B. (2001). The structure of prejudice: Associative strength as a determinant of stereotype endorsement. *European Journal of Social Psychology, 31,* 609–620.

Newman, L. S., & Uleman, J. S. (1990). Assimilation and contrast effects in spontaneous trait inference. *Personality and Social Psychology Bulletin, 16,* 224–240.

Newell, A., & Simon, H. A. (1972). *Human problem solving.* Englewood Cliffs, NJ: Prentice-Hall.

Newtson, D. (1973). Attribution and the unit of perception of ongoing behavior. *Journal of Personality and Social Psychology, 28,* 28–38.

Newtson, D. (1976). Foundations of attribution: The perception of ongoing behavior. In J. H. Harvey, W. J. Ickes, & R. F. Kidd (Eds.), *New directions in attribution research* (Vol. 1, pp. 223–248). Hillsdale, NJ: Erlbaum.

Newtson, D. (1980). An interactionist perspective on social knowing. *Personality and Social Psychology Bulletin, 6,* 520–531.

Newtson, D., & Czerlinsky, T. (1974). Adjustment of attitude communications for contrasts by extreme audiences. *Journal of Personality and Social Psychology, 30,* 829–837.

Newtson, D., & Enquist, G. (1976). The perceptual organization of ongoing behavior. *Journal of Experimental Social Psychology, 12,* 436–450.

Newtson, D., Enquist, G., & Bois, J. (1977). The objective basis of behavior units. *Journal of Personality and Social Psychology, 35,* 847–862.

Newtson, D., Hairfield, J., Bloomingdale, J., & Cutino, S. (1987). The structure of action and interaction. *Social Cognition, 5,* 191–237.

Nezlek, J. B., & Leary, M. R. (2002). Individual differences in self-presentational motives in daily social interaction. *Personality and Social Psychology Bulletin, 28,* 211–223.

Niedenthal, P. M., Barsalou, L. W., Winkielman, P., Krauth-Gruber, S., & Ric, F. (2005). Embodiment in attitudes, social perception, and emotion. *Personality and Social Psychology Review, 9,* 184–211.

Niedenthal, P. M., & Cantor, N. (1986). Affective responses as guides to category-based inferences. *Motivation and Emotion, 10,* 217–232.

Niedenthal, P. M., & Setterlund, M. B. (1994). Emotion congruence in perception. *Personality and Social Psychology Bulletin, 20,* 401–411.

Nielson, S. L., & Sarason, S. G. (1981). Emotion, personality, and selective attention. *Journal of Personality and Social Psychology, 41,* 945–960.

Niiya, Y., Crocker, J., & Bartmess, E. N. (2004). From vulnerability to resilience: Learning orientations buffer contingent self-esteem from failure. *Psychological Science, 15,* 801–805.

Nilsson, I., & Ekehammar, B. (1987). Person-positivity bias in political perception? *European Journal of Social Psychology, 17,* 247–252.

Nisbett, R. E., Krantz, D. H., Jepson, C., & Fong, G. T. (1982). Improving inductive inference. In D. Kahneman, P. Slovic, & A. Tversky (Eds.), *Judgment under uncertainty: Heuristics and biases* (pp. 445–462). New York: Cambridge University Press.

Nisbett, R. E., Peng, K., Choi, I., & Norenzayan, A. (2001). Culture and systems of thought: Holistic versus analytic cognition. *Psychological Review, 108,* 291–310.

Nisbett, R. E., & Ross, L. D. (1980). *Human inference: Strategies and shortcomings of social judgment.* Englewood Cliffs, NJ: Prentice-Hall.

Nisbett, R. E., & Valins, S. (1972). Perceiving the causes of one's own behavior. In E. E. Jones, E. E. Kanouse, H. H. Kelley, R. E. Nisbett, S. Valins, & B. Weiner (Eds.), *Attribution: Perceiving the causes of behavior* (pp. 63–78). Morristown, NJ: General Learning Press.

Nisbett, R. E., & Wilson, T. D. (1977a). The halo effect: Evidence for unconscious alteration of judgments. *Journal of Personality and Social Psychology, 35,* 250–256.

Nisbett, R. E., & Wilson, T. D. (1977b). Telling more than we can know: Verbal reports on mental processes. *Psychological Review, 84,* 231–259.

Nisbett, R. E., Zukier, H., & Lemley, R. E. (1981). The dilution effect: Non-diagnostic information weakens the implications of diagnostic information. *Cognitive Psychology, 13,* 248–277.

Norem, J. K., & Cantor, N. (1990). Capturing the "flavor" of behavior: Cognition, affect, and interpretation. In B. S. Moore & A. M. Isen (Eds.), *Affect and social behavior: Studies in emotion and social interaction* (pp. 39–63). New York: Cambridge University Press.

Norenzayan, A., Choi, I., & Nisbett, R. E. (2002). Cultural similarities and differences in social inference: Evidence from behavioral predictions and lay theories of behavior. *Personality and Social Psychology Bulletin, 28,* 109–120.

Norman, D. A. (1976). *Memory and attention: An introduction to human information processing.* New York: Plenum Press.

Norman, D. A., & Shallice, T. (1986). Attention to action: Willed and automatic control of behavior. In R. J. Davidson, G. E. Schwartz, & D. Shapiro (Eds.), *Consciousness and self regulation: Advances in research and theory* (Vol. 4, pp. 1–18). New York: Plenum Press.

Norman, K. A., & O'Reilly, R. C. (2003). Modeling hippocampal and neocortical contributions to recognition memory: A complementary-learning systems approach. *Psychological Review, 110,* 611–646.

Norman, R. (1975). Affective-cognitive consistency, attitudes, conformity, and behavior. *Journal of Personality and Social Psychology, 32,* 83–91.

Norton, M. I., Vandello, J. A., & Darley, J. M. (2004). Casuistry and social category bias. *Journal of Personality and Social Psychology, 87,* 817–831.

Nosek, B. A., Banaji, M., & Greenwald, A. G. (2002a). Harvesting implicit group attitudes and beliefs from a demonstration web site. *Group Dynamics: Theory, Research, and Practice, 6,* 101–115.

Nosek, B. A., Banaji, M. R., & Greenwald, A. G. (2002b). Math = male, me = female, therefore math = me. *Journal of Personality and Social Psychology, 83,* 44–59.

Nowak, A., Vallacher, R. R., Tesser, A., & Borkowski, W. (2000). Society of self: The emergence of collective properties in self-structure. *Psychological Review, 107,* 39–61.

Nussbaum, S., Trope, Y., & Liberman, N. (2003). Creeping dispositionism: The temporal dynamics of behavior prediction. *Journal of Personality and Social Psychology, 84,* 485–497.

Oakes, P. J., & Turner, J. C. (1980). Social categorization and intergroup behaviour: Does minimal intergroup discrimination make social identity more positive? *European Journal of Social Psychology, 10,* 295–301.

Oakes, P. J., & Turner, J. C. (1986). Authors' rejoinder to Jahoda and Tetlock. *British Journal of Social Psychology, 25,* 257–258.

Oatley, K., & Johnson-Laird, P. N. (1987). Towards a cognitive theory of emotions. *Cognition and Emotion, 1,* 29–50.

O'Brien, L. T., & Crandall, C. S. (2003). Stereotype threat and arousal: Effects on women's math performance. *Personality and Social Psychology Bulletin, 29,* 782–789.

Ochsner, K. N., Beer, J. S., Robertson, E. R., Cooper, J. C., Gabrieli, J. D. E., Kihlstrom, J. F., et al. (2005). The neural correlates of direct and reflected self-knowledge. *NeuroImage, 28,* 797–814.

O'Doherty, J., Kringelbach, M. L., Rolls, E. T., Hornak, J., & Andrews, C. (2001). Abstract reward and punishment representations in the human orbitofrontal cortex. *Nature Neuroscience, 4,* 95–102.

Oettingen, G., & Mayer, D. (2002). The motivating function of thinking about the future: Expectations versus fantasies. *Journal of Personality and Social Psychology, 83,* 1198–1212.

Oettingen, G., Pak, H.-j., & Schnetter, K. (2001). Self-regulation of goal setting: Turning free fantasies about the future into binding goals. *Journal of Personality and Social Psychology, 80,* 736–753.

Oishi, S., & Diener, E. (2003). Culture and well-being: The cycle of action, evaluation, and decision. *Personality and Social Psychology Bulletin, 29,* 939–949.

Oishi, S., Diener, E., Napa Scollon, C., & Biswas-Diener, R. (2004). Cross-situational consistency of affective experiences across cultures. *Journal of Personality and Social Psychology, 86,* 460–472.

Oishi, S., Wyer, R. S., Jr. & Colcombe, S. (2000). Cultural variation in the use of current life satisfaction to predict the future. *Journal of Personality and Social Psychology, 78,* 434–445.

Olson, J. M., Ellis, R. J., & Zanna, M. P. (1983). Validating objective versus subjective judgments: Interest in social comparison and consistency information. *Personality and Social Psychology Bulletin, 54,* 758–767.

Olson, J. M., & Ross, M. (1988). False feedback about placebo effectiveness: Consequences for the misattribution of speech anxiety. *Journal of Experimental Social Psychology, 24,* 275–291.

Olson, J. M., & Zanna, M. P. (1979). A new look at selective exposure. *Journal of Experimental Social Psychology, 15,* 1–15.

Olson, M. A., & Fazio, R. H. (2002). Implicit acquisition and manifestation of classically conditioned attitudes. *Social Cognition, 20,* 89–104.

Olson, M. A., & Fazio, R. H. (2004a). Reducing the influence of extrapersonal associations on the implicit association test: Personalizing the IAT. *Journal of Personality and Social Psychology, 86,* 653–667.

Olson, M. A., & Fazio, R. H. (2004b). Trait inferences as a function of automatically activated racial attitudes and motivation to control prejudiced reactions. *Basic and Applied Social Psychology, 26,* 1–11.

Operario, D., & Fiske, S. T. (2001). Ethnic identity moderates perceptions of prejudice: Judgments of personal versus group discrimination and subtle versus blatant bias. *Personality and Social Psychology Bulletin, 27,* 550–561.

Ortony, A., Clore, G. L., & Collins, A. (1988). *The cognitive structure of emotion.* Cambridge: Cambridge University Press.

Ortony, A., & Turner, T. J. (1990). What's basic about basic emotions? *Psychological Review, 97,* 315–331.

Osgood, C. E., & Tannenbaum, P. H. (1955). The principle of congruity in the prediction of attitude change. *Psychological Review, 62,* 42–55.

Ostrom, T. M. (1977). Between-theory and within-theory conflict in explaining context effects in impression formation. *Journal of Experimental Social Psychology, 13,* 492–503.

Ostrom, T. M. (1984). The sovereignty of social cognition. In R. S. Wyer Jr. & T. K. Srull (Eds.), *Handbook of social cognition* (Vol. 1, pp. 1–38). Hillsdale, NJ: Erlbaum.

Ostrom, T. M. (1988). Computer simulation: The third symbol system. *Journal of Experimental Social Psychology, 24,* 381–392.

Ostrom, T. M., Lingle, J. H., Pryor, J. B., & Geva, N. (1980). Cognitive organization of person impressions. In R. Hastie, T. M. Ostrom, E. B. Ebbesen, R. S. Wyer Jr., D. Hamilton, & D. E. Carlston (Eds.), *Person memory: The cognitive basis of social perception* (pp. 55–88). Hillsdale, NJ: Erlbaum.

Ostrom, T. M., & Sedikides, C. (1992). Out-group homogeneity effect in natural and minimal groups. *Psychological Bulletin, 112,* 536–552.

Ottati, V., Fishbein, M., & Middlestadt, S. E. (1988). Determinants of voters' beliefs about the candidates' stands on the issues: The role of evaluative bias heuristics and the candidates' expressed message. *Journal of Personality and Social Psychology, 55,* 517–529.

Otten, S., Mummendey, A., & Blanz, M. (1996). Intergroup discrimination in positive and negative outcome allocations: Impact of stimulus valence, relative group status, and relative group size. *Personality and Social Psychology Bulletin, 22,* 568–581.

Owens, J., Bower, G. H., & Black, J. B. (1979). The "soap-opera" effect in story recall. *Memory and Cognition, 7,* 185–191.

Oyserman, D., Bybee, D., & Terry, K. (2006). Possible selves and academic outcomes: How and when possible selves impel action. *Journal of Personality and Social Psychology, 91,* 188–204.

Padoa-Schioppa, C., & Assad, J. A. (2006). Neurons in the orbitofrontal cortex encode economic value. *Nature, 441,* 223–226.

Pagel, M. D., & Davidson, A. R. (1984). A comparison of three social-psychological models of attitude and behavioral plan: Prediction of contraceptive behavior. *Journal of Personality and Social Psychology, 47,* 517–533.

Pallak, S. R. (1983). Salience of a communicator's physical attractiveness and persuasion: A heuristic versus systematic processing interpretation. *Social Cognition, 2*, 158–170.

Pandya, D. N., & Barnes, C. L. (1987). Architecture and connections of the frontal lobe. In E. Perecman (Ed.), *The frontal lobes revisited* (pp. 41–72). New York: IRBN Press.

Parducci, A. (1968). The relativism of absolute judgments. *Scientific American, 219*, 84–90.

Park, B., & Hastie, R. (1987). Perception of variability in category development: Instance - versus abstraction-based stereotypes. *Journal of Personality and Social Psychology, 53*, 621–635.

Park, B., & Judd, C. M. (1990). Measures and models of perceived group variability. *Journal of Personality and Social Psychology, 59*, 173–191.

Park, B., & Judd, C. M. (2005). Rethinking the link between categorization and prejudice within the social cognition perspective. *Personality and Social Psychology Review, 9*, 108–130.

Park, B., Ryan, C. S., & Judd, C. M. (1992). Role of meaningful subgroups in explaining differences in perceived variability. *Journal of Personality and Social Psychology, 5*, 73–91.

Parkinson, B. (1985). Emotional effects of false autonomic feedback. *Psychological Bulletin, 98*, 471–494.

Parra, F. C., Amado, R. C., Lambertucci, J. R., Rocha, J., Antunes, C. M., & Pena, S. D. (2003). Color and genomic ancestry in Brazilians. *Proceedings of the National Academy of Sciences, 100*, 177–182.

Parrott, W. G., & Sabini, J. (1990). Mood and memory under natural conditions: Evidence for mood incongruent recall. *Journal of Personality and Social Psychology, 59*, 321–336.

Pasupathi, M., Carstensen, L. L., & Tsai, J. L. (1995). Ageism in interpersonal settings. In B. Lott & D. Maluso (Eds.), *The social psychology of interpersonal discrimination*. New York: Guilford Press.

Pavelchak, M. A. (1989). Piecemeal and category-based evaluation: An idiographic analysis. *Journal of Personality and Social Psychology, 56*, 354–363.

Peeters, G. (1983). Relational and informational patterns in social cognition. In W. Doise & S. Moscovici (Eds.), *Current issues in European social psychology* (pp. 201–237). Cambridge, England: Cambridge University Press.

Pelham, B. W. (1990). On confidence and consequence: The certainty and importance of self-knowledge. *Journal of Personality and Social Psychology, 60*, 518–530.

Pelham, B. W., Carvallo, M., & Jones, J. T. (2005). Implicit egotism. *Current Directions in Psychological Science, 14*, 106–110.

Pelham, B. W., Mirenberg, M. C., & Jones, J. K. (2002). Why Susie sells seashells by the seashore: Implicit egotism and major life decisions. *Journal of Personality and Social Psychology, 82*, 469–487.

Pennebaker, J. W., Dyer, M. A., Caulkins, R. S., Litkowitz, D. L., Ackreman, P. L., Anderson, D. B., & McGraw, K. M. (1979). Don't the girls get prettier at closing time: A country and western application to psychology. *Personality and Social Psychology Bulletin, 5*, 122–125.

Penner, L. A., Dovidio, J. F., Piliavin, J. A., & Schroeder, D. A. (2005). Prosocial behavior: Multilevel perspectives. *Annual Review of Psychology, 56*, 365–392.

Pepitone, A. (1950). Motivational effects in social perception. *Human Relations, 3*, 57–76.

Percy, W. (1966). *The last gentleman.* New York: Picador USA.

Perdue, C. W., Dovidio, J. F., Gurtman, M. B., & Tyler, R. B. (1990). Us and them: Social categorization and the process of intergroup bias. *Journal of Personality and Social Psychology, 59*, 475–486.

Perlow, L., & Weeks, J. (2002). Who's helping whom? Layers of culture and workplace behavior. *Journal of Organizational Behavior, 23*, 345–361.

Perreault, S., & Bourhis, R. Y. (1999). Ethnocentrism, social identification, and discrimination. *Personality and Social Psychology Bulletin, 25*, 92–103.

Perry, L. C., Perry, D. G., & Weiss, R. J. (1986). Age differences in children's beliefs about whether altruism makes the actor feel good. *Social Cognition, 4*, 263–269.

Peterson, B. E., Doty, R. M., & Winter, D. G. (1993). Authoritarianism and attitudes toward contemporary social issues. *Personality and Social Psychology Bulletin, 19*, 174–184.

Peterson, B. E., Duncan, L. E., & Pang, J. S. (2002). Authoritarianism and political impoverishment: Deficits in knowledge and civic disinterest. *Political Psychology, 23*, 97–112.

Peterson, B. E., & Miller, J. A. (2004). Quality of college students' experiences during cooperative learning. *Social Psychology of Education, 7*, 161–183.

Pettigrew, T. F. (1979). The ultimate attribution error: Extending Allport's cognitive analysis of prejudice. *Personality and Social Psychology Bulletin, 5*, 461–476.

Pettigrew, T. F., & Meertens, R. W. (1995). Subtle and blatant prejudice in Western Europe. *European Journal of Social Psychology, 25*, 57–75.

Pettigrew, T. F., & Tropp, L. R. (2006). A meta-analytic test of intergroup contact theory. *Journal of Personality and Social Psychology, 90*, 751–783.

Petty, R. E., Briñol, P., & Tormala, Z. L. (2002). Thought confidence as a determinant of persuasion: The self-validation hypothesis. *Journal of Personality and Social Psychology, 82*, 722–741.

Petty, R. E., & Cacioppo, J. T. (1979). Issue involvement can increase or decrease persuasion by enhancing message-relevant cognitive responses. *Journal of Personality and Social Psychology, 37*, 1915–1926.

Petty, R. E., & Cacioppo, J. T. (1981). *Attitudes and persuasion: Classic and contemporary approaches.* Dubuque, IA: W. C. Brown.

Petty, R. E., & Cacioppo, J. T. (1984). The effects of involvement on responses to argument quantity and quality: Central and peripheral routes to persuasion. *Journal of Personality and Social Psychology, 46*, 69–81.

Petty, R. E., & Cacioppo, J. T. (1986). The elaboration likelihood model of persuasion. In L. Berkowitz (Ed.), *Advances in experimental social psychology* (Vol. 19, pp. 123–205). New York: Academic Press.

Petty, R. E., & Cacioppo, J. T. (1990). Involvement and persuasion: Tradition versus integration. *Psychological Bulletin, 107*, 367–374.

Petty, R. E., Cacioppo, J. T., & Goldman, R. (1981). Personal involvement as a determinant of argument-based persuasion. *Journal of Personality and Social Psychology, 41*, 847–855.

Petty, R. E., Cacioppo, J. T., & Kasmer, J. A. (1988). The role of affect in the elaboration likelihood model of persuasion. In L. Donohew, H. E. Sypher, & E. T. Higgins (Eds.), *Communication, social cognition, and affect* (pp. 117–146). Hillsdale, NJ: Erlbaum.

Petty, R. E., Cacioppo, J. T., Kasmer, J. A., & Haugtvedt, C. P. (1987). A reply to Stiff and Boster. *Communication Monographs, 54*, 257–263.

Petty, R. E., Cacioppo, J. T., & Schumann, D. (1983). Central and peripheral routes to advertising effectiveness: The moderating role of involvement. *Journal of Consumer Research, 10*, 134–148.

Petty, R. E., Cacioppo, J. T., Sedikides, C., & Strathman, A. J. (1988). Affect and persuasion: A contemporary perspective. *American Behavioral Scientist, 31*, 355–371.

Petty, R. E., Fleming, M. A., Priester, J. R., & Feinstein, A. H. (2001). Individual versus group interest violation: Surprise as a determinant of argument scrutiny and persuasion. *Social Cognition, 19*, 418–442.

Petty, R. E., Gleicher, F., & Baker, S. M. (1991). Multiple roles for affect in persuasion. In J. Forgas (Ed.), *Emotion and social judgment.* London: Pergamon Press.

Petty, R. E., Harkins, S. G., & Williams, K. D. (1980). The effects of group diffusion of cognitive effort on attitudes: An information-processing view. *Journal of Personality and Social Psychology, 38*, 81–92.

Petty, R. E., Kasmer, J., Haugtvedt, C. P., & Cacioppo, J. T. (1987). Source and message factors in persuasion: A reply to Stiff's critique of the elaboration of the likelihood model. *Communication Monographs, 54*, 233–263.

Petty, R. E., Ostrom, T. M., & Brock, T. C. (Eds.). (1981). *Cognitive responses in persuasive communications: A text in attitude change.* Hillsdale, NJ: Erlbaum.

Petty, R. E., Rennier, G. A., & Cacioppo, J. T. (1987). Assertion versus interrogation format in opinion surveys: Questions enhance thoughtful responding. *Public Opinion Quarterly, 51*, 481–494.

Petty, R. E., Tormala, Z. L., Brinol, P., & Jarvis, W. B. G. (2006). Implicit ambivalence from attitude change: An exploration of the PAST model. *Journal of Personality and Social Psychology, 90*, 21–41.

Petty, R. E., & Wegener, D. T. (1998). Attitude change: Multiple roles for persuasion variables. In D. T. Gilbert, S. T. Fiske, & G. Lindzey (Eds.), *Handbook of social psychology* (4th ed., Vol. 1, pp. 323–390). New York: McGraw-Hill.

Petty, R. E., & Wegener, D. T. (1999). The elaboration likelihood model: Current status and controversies. In S. Chaiken & Y. Trope (Eds.), *Dual-process theories in social psychology* (pp. 37–72). New York: Guilford Press.

Petty, R. E., Wegener, D. T., & Fabrigar, L. R. (1997). Attitudes and attitude change. *Annual Review of Psychology, 48*, 609–647.

Petty, R. E., Wells, G. L., & Brock, T. C. (1976). Distraction can enhance or reduce yielding to propaganda: Thought disruption versus effort justification. *Journal of Personality and Social Psychology, 34*, 874–884.

Phalet, K., & Poppe, E. (1997). Competence and morality dimensions of national and ethnic stereotypes: A study in six Eastern-European countries. *European Journal of Social Psychology, 27*, 703–723.

Pham, L. B., & Taylor, S. E. (1999). From thought to action: Effects of process versus outcome-based mental simulations on performance. *Personality and Social Psychology Bulletin, 25*, 250–260.

Pham, L. B., Taylor, S. E., & Seeman, T. E. (2001). Effects of environmental predictability and personal mastery on self-regulatory and physiological processes. *Personality and Social Psychology Bulletin, 27*, 611–620.

Pham, M. T., Meyvis, T., & Zhou, N. (2001). Beyond the obvious: Chronic vividness of imagery and the use of information in decision making. *Organizational Behavior and Human Decision Processes, 84*, 226–253.

Phan, K. L., Wager, T., Taylor, S. F., & Liberzon, I. (2002). Functional neuroanatomy of emotion: A meta-analysis of emotion activation studies in PET and fMRI. *NeuroImage, 16*, 331–348.

Phelps, E. A. (2005). The interaction of emotion and cognition: The relation between the human amygdala and cognitive awareness. In R. R. Hassan, J. Uleman, & J. A. Bargh (Eds.), *The power of the subliminal: On subliminal persuasion and other potential applications* (pp. 61–76). New York: Oxford University Press.

Phelps, E. A. (2006). Emotion and cognition: Insights from studies of the human amygdala. *Annual Review of Psychology, 57*, 27–53.

Phelps, E. A., Cannistraci, C. J., & Cunningham, W. A. (2003). Intact performance on an indirect measure of face bias following amygdala damage. *Neuropsychologia, 41*, 203–208.

Phelps, E. A., O'Connor, K. J., Cunningham, W. A., Funayama, E. S., Gatenby, J. C., Gore, J. C., & Banaji, M. R. (2000). Performance on indirect measures of race evaluation predicts amygdala activation. *Journal of Cognitive Neuroscience, 12*, 729–738.

Phillips, A. G., & Silvia, P. J. (2005). Self-awareness and the emotional consequences of self-discrepancies. *Personality and Social Psychology Bulletin, 31*, 703–713.

Picek, J. S., Sherman, S. J., & Shiffrin, R. M. (1975). Cognitive organization and coding of social structures. *Journal of Personality and Social Psychology, 31*, 758–768.

Pinel, E. C. (1999). Stigma consciousness: The psychological legacy of social stereotypes. *Journal of Personality and Social Psychology, 76*, 114–128.

Pinel, E. C. (2002). Stigma consciousness in intergroup contexts: The power of conviction. *Journal of Experimental Social Psychology, 38*, 178–185.

Pittman, T. S. (1998). Motivation. In D. T. Gilbert, S. T. Fiske, & G. Lindzey, (Eds.), *Handbook of social psychology* (4th ed., Vol. 1, pp. 549–590). New York: McGraw-Hill.

Plant, E. A., Kling, K. C., & Smith, G. L. (2004). The influence of gender and social role on the interpretation of facial expressions. *Sex Roles, 51*, 187–196.

Plutchik, R. (1962). *The emotions: Facts, theories and a new model.* New York: Random House.

Plutchik, R. (1980). *Emotion: A psychoevolutionary synthesis.* New York: Harper & Row.

Posavac, S. S., Sanbonmatsu, D. M., & Fazio, R. H. (1997). Considering the best choice: Effects of the salience and accessibility of alternatives on attitude-decision consistency. *Journal of Personality and Social Psychology, 72*, 253–261.

Poehlman, T. A., Uhlmann, E., Greenwald, A. G., & Banaji, M. R. (2006). *Understanding and using the Implicit Association Test: III. Meta-analysis of predictive validity.* Unpublished manuscript, Yale University.

Poehlman, T. A., Uhlmann, E., & Nosek, B. A. (2006). *Automatic associations: Personal attitudes or cultural knowledge?* Unpublished manuscript, Yale University.

Posner, M. I. (1982). Cumulative development of attentional theory. *American Psychologist, 37,* 168–179.

Posner, M. I., & Keele, S. W. (1968). On the genesis of abstract ideas. *Journal of Experimental Psychology, 77,* 353–363.

Posner, M. I., & Keele, S. W. (1970). Retention of abstract ideas. *Journal of Experimental Psychology, 83,* 304–308.

Posner, M. I., & Rothbart, M. K. (1989). Intentional chapters on unintended thoughts. In J. S. Uleman & J. A. Bargh (Eds.), *Unintended thought* (pp. 450–470). New York: Guilford Press.

Postmes, T., Haslam, S. A., & Swaab, R. I. (2005). Social influence in small groups: An interactive model of social identity formation. *European Review of Social Psychology, 16,* 1–42.

Postmes, T., Spears, R., Lee, A. T., & Novak, R. J. (2005). Individuality and social influence in groups: Inductive and deductive routes to group identity. *Journal of Personality and Social Psychology, 89,* 747–763.

Powell, M. C., & Fazio, R. H. (1984). Attitude accessibility as a function of repeated attitudinal expression. *Personality and Social Psychology Bulletin, 10,* 139–148.

Pratkanis, A. R. (1988). The attitude heuristic and selective fact identification. *British Journal of Social Psychology, 27,* 257–263.

Pratkanis, A. R. (1989). The cognitive representation of attitudes. In A. R. Pratkanis, S. J. Breckler, & A. G. Greenwald (Eds.), *Attitude structure and function* (pp. 71–98). Hillsdale, NJ: Erlbaum.

Pratkanis, A. R., & Greenwald, A. G. (1989). A sociocognitive model of attitude structure and function. In L. Berkowitz (Ed.), *Advances in experimental social psychology* (Vol. 22, pp. 245–285). New York: Academic Press.

Pratto, F. (1999). The puzzle of continuing group inequality: Piecing together psychological, social, and cultural forces in social dominance theory. In M. P. Zanna (Ed.), *Advances in experimental social psychology* (Vol. 1, pp. 191–263). San Diego, CA: Academic Press.

Pratto, F., & John, O. P. (1991). Automatic vigilance: The attention-grabbing power of negative social information. *Journal of Personality and Social Psychology, 61,* 380–391.

Pratto, F., Sidanius, J., Stallworth, L. M., & Malle, B. F. (1994). Social dominance orientation: A personality variable predicting social and political attitudes. *Journal of Personality and Social Psychology, 67,* 741–763.

Pratto, F., Stallworth, L. M., Sidanius, J., & Siers, B. (1997). The gender gap in occupational role attainment: A social dominance approach. *Journal of Personality and Social Psychology, 72,* 37–53.

Prentice, D. A. (1987). Psychological correspondence of possessions, attitudes, and values. *Journal of Personality and Social Psychology, 53,* 993–1003.

Priester, J. R., Cacioppo, J. T., & Petty, R. E. (1996). The influence of motor processes on attitudes toward novel versus familiar semantic stimuli. *Personality and Social Psychology Bulletin, 22,* 442–447.

Priester, J. R., & Petty, R. E. (2001). Extending the bases of subjective attitudinal ambivalence: Interpersonal and intrapersonal antecedents of evaluative tension. *Journal of Personality and Social Psychology, 80,* 19–34.

Prislin, R. (1987). Attitude-behaviour relationship: Attitude relevance and behaviour relevance. *European Journal of Social Psychology, 17,* 483–485.

Prislin, R., & Ouellette, J. (1996). When it is embedded, it is potent: Effects of general attitude embeddedness on formation of specific attitudes and behavioral intentions. *Personality and Social Psychology Bulletin, 22,* 845–861.

Pronin, E., Gilovich, T., & Ross, L. D. (2004). Objectivity in the eye of the beholder: Divergent perceptions of self versus others. *Psychological Review, 111,* 781–799.

Pronin, E., Kruger, J., Savitsky, K., & Ross, L. D. (2001). You don't know me, but I know you: The illusion of asymmetric insight. *Journal of Personality and Social Psychology, 81,* 639–656.

Pronin, E., Lin, D. Y., & Ross, L. D. (2002). The bias blind spot: Perceptions of bias in self versus others. *Personality and Social Psychology Bulletin, 28,* 369–381.

Pronin, E., & Ross, L. D. (2006). Temporal differences in trait self-ascription: When the self is seen as an other. *Journal of Personality and Social Psychology, 90,* 197–209.

Pronin, E., Steele, C. M., & Ross, L. D. (2004). Identity bifurcation in response to stereotype threat: Women and mathematics. *Journal of Experimental Social Psychology, 40,* 152–168.

Pronin, E., Wegner, D. M., McCarthy, K., & Rodriguez, S. (2006). Everyday magical powers: The role of apparent mental causation in the overestimation of personal influence. *Journal of Personality and Social Psychology, 91,* 218–231.

Pruessner, J. C., Baldwin, M. W., Dedovic, K., Renwick, R., Mahani, N. K., Lord, C., Meaney, M., & Lupien, S. (2005). Self-esteem, locus of control, hippocampal volume, and cortisol regulation in young and old adulthood. *NeuroImage, 28,* 815–826.

Pruitt, D. G., & Teger, A. I. (1969). The risky shift in group betting. *Journal of Experimental Social Psychology, 5,* 115–126.

Pryor, J. B., & Kriss, N. (1977). The cognitive dynamics of salience in the attribution process. *Journal of Personality and Social Psychology, 35,* 49–55.

Quadflieg, S., Mason, M. F., & Macrae, C. N. (2004). The owl and the pussycat: Gaze cues and visuospatial orienting. *Psychonomic Bulletin and Review, 22,* 826–831.

Quattrone, G. A. (1982). Overattribution and unit formation: When behavior engulfs the person. *Journal of Personality and Social Psychology, 42,* 593–607.

Quattrone, G. A. (1985). On the congruity between internal states and action. *Psychological Bulletin, 98,* 3–40.

Quattrone, G. A., Finkel, S. E., & Andrus, D. C. (1982). *Anchors away! On overcoming the anchoring bias across a number of domains.* Unpublished manuscript, Stanford University.

Quinn, D. M., Kahng, S. K., & Crocker, J. (2004). Discreditable: Stigma effects of revealing a mental illness history on test performance. *Personality and Social Psychology Bulletin, 30,* 803–815.

Quinn, K. A., & Macrae, C. N. (2005). Categorizing others: The dynamics of person construal. *Journal of Personality and Social Psychology, 88,* 467–479.

Quinn, K. A., Macrae, C. N., & Bodenhausen, G. (2003). Stereotyping and impression formation: How categorical thinking shapes person perception. In M. A. Hogg & J. Cooper (Eds.), *The Sage handbook of social psychology* (pp. 87–109). Thousand Oaks, CA: Sage.

Rabbie, J., & Horowitz, M. (1969). Arousal of ingroup-outgroup bias by a chance win or loss. *Journal of Personality and Social Psychology, 13,* 269–277.

Raghubir, P., & Valenzuela, A. (2006). Center of inattention: Position biases in decision-making. *Organizational Behavior and Human Decision Processes, 99,* 66–80.

Rajecki, D. W. (1982). *Attitudes: Themes and advances.* Sunderland, MA: Sinauer.

Read, S. (1983). Once is enough: Causal reasoning from a single instance. *Journal of Personality and Social Psychology, 45,* 323–334.

Read, S. (1984). Analogical reasoning in social judgment: The importance of causal theories. *Journal of Personality and Social Psychology, 46,* 14–25.

Read, S. (1987). Similarity and causality in the use of social analogies. *Journal of Experimental Social Psychology, 23,* 189–207.

Read, S. J. (1988). Conjunctive explanations: The effect of a comparison between a chosen and a nonchosen alternative. *Journal of Experimental Social Psychology, 24,* 146–162.

Read, S. J., & Miller, L. C. (1989). Inter-personalism: Toward a goal-based theory of persons in relationships. In L. Pervin (Ed.), *Goal concepts in personality and social psychology* (pp. 413–472). Hillsdale, NJ: Erlbaum.

Read, S. J., & Urada, D. I. (2003). A neural network simulation of the outgroup homogeneity effect. *Personality and Social Psychology Review, 7,* 146–159.

Read, S. J., Vanman, E. J., & Miller, L. C. (1997). Connectionism, parallel constraint satisfaction processes, and Gestalt principles: (Re) introducing cognitive dynamics to social psychology. *Personality and Social Psychology Review, 1,* 26–53.

Reber, R., Schwarz, N., & Winkielman, P. (2004). Processing fluency and aesthetic pleasure: Is beauty in the perceiver's processing experience? *Personality and Social Psychology Review, 8,* 364–382.

Reed, G. M., Kemeny, M. E., Taylor, S. E., & Visscher, B. R. (1999). Negative HIV-specific expectancies and AIDS-related bereavement as predictors of symptom onset in asymptomatic HIV-positive gay men. *Health Psychology, 18,* 354–363.

Reed, S. K. (1972). Pattern recognition and categorization. *Cognitive Psychology, 3,* 382–407.

Reeder, G. D. (1993). Trait-behavior relations and dispositional inference. *Personality and Social Psychology Bulletin, 19*, 586–593.

Reeder, G. D., & Brewer, M. B. (1979). A schematic model of dispositional attribution in interpersonal perception. *Psychological Review, 86*, 61–79.

Reeder, G. D., Vonk, R., Ronk, M. J., Ham, J., & Lawrence, M. (2004). Dispositional attribution: Multiple inferences about motive-related traits. *Journal of Personality and Social Psychology, 86*, 530–544.

Regan, P. C., Snyder, M., & Kassin, S. M. (1995). Unrealistic optimism: Self-enhancement or person positivity? *Personality and Social Psychology Bulletin, 21*, 1073–1082.

Reisenzein, R. (1983). The Schachter theory of emotion: Two decades later. *Psychological Bulletin, 94*, 239–264.

Reisenzein, R. (1986). A structural equation analysis of Weiner's attribution-affect model of helping behavior. *Journal of Personality and Social Psychology, 50*, 1123–1133.

Reiss, M., Rosenfeld, P., Melburg, V., & Tedeschi, J. T. (1981). Self-serving attributions: Biased private perceptions and distorted public descriptions. *Journal of Personality and Social Psychology, 41*, 224–251.

Reyes, R. M., Thompson, W. C., & Bower, G. H. (1980). Judgmental biases resulting from differing availabilities of arguments. *Journal of Personality and Social Psychology, 39*, 2–12.

Reyna, C., Henry, P. J., Korfmacher, W., & Tucker, A. (2006). Examining the principles in principled conservatism: The role of responsibility stereotypes as cues for deservingness in racial policy decisions. *Journal of Personality and Social Psychology, 90*, 109–128.

Rhee, E., Uleman, J. S., Lee, H. K., & Roman, R. J. (1995). Spontaneous self-descriptions and ethnic identities in individualistic and collectivist cultures. *Journal of Personality and Social Psychology, 69*, 142–152.

Rhodewalt, F., & Comer, R. (1979). Induced-compliance attitude change: Once more with feeling. *Journal of Experimental Social Psychology, 15*, 35–47.

Rhodewalt, F., Sanbonmatsu, D. M., Tschanz, B., Feick, D. L., & Waller, A. (1995). Self-handicapping and interpersonal trade-offs: The effects of claimed self-handicaps on observers' performance evaluations and feedback. *Personality and Social Psychology Bulletin, 21*, 1042–1050.

Rholes, W. S., Jones, M., & Wade, C. (1988). Children's understanding of personal dispositions and its relationship to behavior. *Journal of Experimental Child Psychology, 45*, 1–17.

Rholes, W. S., & Pryor, J. B. (1982). Cognitive accessibility and causal attributions. *Personality and Social Psychology Bulletin, 8*, 719–727.

Richeson, J. A., Baird, A. A., Gordon, H. L., Heatherton, T. F., Wyland, C. L., Trawalter, S., & Shelton, J. N. (2003). An fMRI investigation of the impact of interracial contact on executive function. *Nature Neuroscience, 6*, 1323–1328.

Richeson, J. A., & Shelton, J. N. (2003). When prejudice does not pay: Effects of interracial contact on executive function. *Psychological Science, 14*, 287–290.

Richeson, J. A., & Shelton, J. N. (2005). Brief report: Thin slices of racial bias. *Journal of Nonverbal Behavior, 29*, 75–86.

Richeson, J. A., & Shelton, J. N. (2006). A social psychological perspective on the stigmatization of older adults. In L. L. Carstensen & C. R. Hartel (Eds.), *When I'm 64* (pp. 174–208). Washington, DC: National Research Council Committee on Aging Frontiers in Social Psychology, Personality, and Adult Developmental Psychology. The National Academies Press.

Richeson, J. A., & Trawalter, S. (2005). Why do interracial interactions impair executive function? A resource depletion account. *Journal of Personality and Social Psychology, 88*, 934–947.

Richeson, J. A., Trawalter, S., & Shelton, J. N. (2005). African Americans' implicit racial attitudes and the depletion of executive function after interracial internactions. *Social Cognition, 23*, 336–352.

Ridgeway, C. L. (2001). The emergence of status beliefs: From structural inequality to legitimizing ideology. In J. T. Jost & B. Major (Eds.), *The psychology of legitimacy* (pp. 257–277). New York: Cambridge University Press.

Rilling, J. K., Sanfey, A. G., Aronson, J. A., Nystrom, L. E., & Cohen, J. D. (2004). The neural correlates of theory of mind within interpersonal interactions. *NeuroImage, 22*, 1694–1703.

Rimé, B., Philippot, P., & Cisamolo, D. (1990). Social schemata of peripheral changes in emotion. *Journal of Personality and Social Psychology, 59,* 38–49.

Riskey, D. R. (1979). Verbal memory processes in impression formation. *Journal of Experimental Psychology: Human Learning and Memory, 5,* 271–281.

Rizzolatti, G., Fogassi, L., & Gallese, V. (2001). Neurophysiological mechanisms underlying the understanding and imitation of action. *Nature Reviews Neuroscience, 2,* 661–670.

Robins, R. W., & Beer, J. S. (2001). Positive illusions about the self: Short-term benefits and long-term costs. *Journal of Personality and Social Psychology, 80,* 340–352.

Robinson, R. J., Keltner, D., Ward, A., & Ross, L. D. (1995). Actual versus assumed differences in construal: "Naïve realism" in intergroup perception and conflict. *Journal of Personality and Social Psychology, 68,* 404–417.

Robinson, R. J., & McArthur, L. Z. (1982). The impact of salient vocal qualities on causal attributions for a speaker's behavior. *Journal of Personality and Social Psychology, 43,* 236–247.

Robinson, M. D., & Clore, G. L. (2002a). Belief and feeling: Evidence for an accessibility model of emotional self-report. *Psychological Bulletin, 128,* 934–960.

Robinson, M. D., & Clore, G. L. (2002b). Episodic and semantic knowledge in emotional self-report: Evidence for two judgment processes. *Journal of Personality and Social Psychology, 83,* 198–215.

Robles, R., Smith, R., Carver, C. S., & Wellens, A. R. (1987). Influence of subliminal visual images on the experience of anxiety. *Personality and Social Psychology Bulletin, 13,* 399–410.

Rodin, M. J. (1987). Who is memorable to whom: A study of cognitive disregard. *Social Cognition, 5,* 144–165.

Roese, N. J., & Olson, J. M. (1994). Attitude importance as a function of repeated attitude expression. *Journal of Experimental Social Psychology, 30,* 39–51.

Rogers, M., Miller, N., Mayer, F. S., & Duval, S. (1982). Personal responsibility and salience of the request for help: Determinants of the relation between negative affect and helping behavior. *Journal of Personality and Social Psychology, 43,* 956–970.

Rogers, R. W., & Prentice-Dunn, S. (1981). Deindividuation and anger-mediated interracial aggression: Unmasking regressive racism. *Journal of Personality and Social Psychology, 41,* 63–73.

Rogers, T. B., Kuiper, N. A., & Kirker, W. S. (1977). Self-reference and the encoding of personal information. *Journal of Personality and Social Psychology, 35,* 677–688.

Rokeach, M. (1960). *The open and closed mind.* New York: Basic Books.

Romer, D. (1979). Distraction, counterarguing, and the internalization of attitude change. *European Journal of Social Psychology, 9,* 1–17.

Roney, C. J. R., Higgins, E. T., & Shah, J. Y. (1995). Goals and framing: How outcome focus influences motivation and emotion. *Personality and Social Psychology Bulletin, 21,* 1151–1160.

Rosch, E. H. (1978). Principles of categorization. In E. Rosch & B. B. Lloyd (Eds.), *Cognition and categorization.* Hillsdale, NJ: Erlbaum.

Rosch, E. H. (1987). Wittgenstein and categorization research in cognitive psychology. In M. Chapman & M. Dixon (Eds.), *Meaning and the growth of understanding: Wittgenstein's significance for developmental psychology.* Berlin: Springer-Verlag.

Rosch, E. H., Mervis, C. B., Gray, W., Johnson, D., & Boyes-Braem, P. (1976). Basic objects in natural categories. *Cognitive Psychology, 8,* 382–439.

Roseman, I. J. (1984). Cognitive determinants of emotion: A structural theory. In P. Shaver (Ed.), *Review of personality and social psychology* (Vol. 5, pp. 11–36). Beverly Hills, CA: Sage.

Rosenberg, M. J. (1956). Cognitive structure and attitudinal affect. *Journal of Abnormal and Social Psychology, 53,* 367–372.

Rosenberg, M. J. (1960). An analysis of affective-cognitive consistency. In C. I. Hovland & M. J. Rosenberg (Eds.), *Attitude organization and change.* New Haven, CT: Yale University Press.

Rosenberg, S., & Sedlak, A. (1972). Structural representations of implicit personality theory. In L. Berkowitz (Ed.), *Advances in experimental social psychology* (Vol. 6, pp. 235–297). New York: Academic Press.

Rosenhan, D. L., Salovey, P., & Hargis, K. (1981). The joys of helping: Focus of attention mediates the impact of positive affect on altruism. *Journal of Personality and Social Psychology, 40*, 899–905.

Rosenthal, H. E., & Crisp, R. J. (2006). Reducing stereotype threat by blurring intergroup boundaries. *Personality and Social Psychology Bulletin, 32*, 501–511.

Rosenthal, R. (1974). *On the social psychology of the self-fulfilling prophecy: Further evidence for Pygmalion effects and their mediating mechanisms.* New York: MSS Modular Publications (Module 53).

Rosenthal, R., & Jacobson, L. F. (1968). *Pygmalion in the classroom.* New York: Holt, Rinehart, & Winston.

Roser, M., & Gazzaniga, M. S. (2004). Automatic brains—Interpretive minds. *Current Directions in Psychological Science, 13*, 56–59.

Ross, L. D. (1977). The intuitive psychologist and his shortcomings: Distortions in the attribution process. In L. Berkowitz (Ed.), *Advances in experimental social psychology* (Vol. 10, pp. 174–221). New York: Academic Press.

Ross, L. D., Lepper, M. R., & Hubbard, M. (1975). Perseverance in self-perception and social perception: Biased attribution processes in the debriefing paradigm. *Journal of Personality and Social Psychology, 32*, 880–892.

Ross, L. D., Lepper, M. R., Strack, F., & Steinmetz, J. (1977). Social explanation and social expectation: Effects of real and hypothetical explanations on subjective likelihood. *Journal of Personality and Social Psychology, 35*, 817–829.

Ross, L. D., Rodin, J., & Zimbardo, P. G. (1969). Toward an attribution therapy: The reduction of fear through induced cognitive-emotional misattribution. *Journal of Personality and Social Psychology, 12*, 279–288.

Ross, M. (1989). The relation of implicit theories to the construction of personal histories. *Psychological Review, 96*, 341–357.

Ross, M., & Conway, M. (1986). Remembering one's own past: The construction of personal histories. In R. M. Sorrentino & E. T. Higgins (Eds.), *Handbook of motivation and cognition: Foundations of social behavior* (pp. 122–144). New York: Guilford Press.

Ross, M., McFarland, C., & Fletcher, G. J. O. (1981). The effect of attitude on the recall of personal histories. *Journal of Personality and Social Psychology, 10*, 627–634.

Ross, M., McFarland, C., Conway, M., & Zanna, M. P. (1983). Reciprocal relation between attitudes and behavior recall: Committing people to newly formed attitudes. *Journal of Personality and Social Psychology, 45*, 257–267.

Ross, M., & Shulman, R. F. (1973). Increasing the salience of initial attitudes: Dissonance vs. self-perception theory. *Journal of Personality and Social Psychology, 28*, 138–144.

Ross, M., & Sicoly, F. (1979). Egocentric biases in availability and attribution. *Journal of Personality and Social Psychology, 37*, 322–337.

Ross, M., & Wilson, A. E. (2002). It feels like yesterday: Self-esteem, valence of personal past experiences, and judgments of subjective distance. *Journal of Personality and Social Psychology, 82*, 792–803.

Rothbart, M., Evans, M., & Fulero, S. (1979). Recall for confirming events: Memory processes and the maintenance of social stereotypes. *Journal of Experimental Social Psychology, 15*, 343–355.

Rothbart, M., Fulero, S., Jensen, C., Howard, J., & Birrell, B. (1978). From individual to group impressions: Availability heuristics in stereotype formation. *Journal of Experimental Social Psychology, 14*, 237–255.

Rothbart, M., & Park, B. (1986). On the confirmability and disconfirmability of trait concepts. *Journal of Personality and Social Psychology, 50*, 131–142.

Rothbart, M., & Taylor, M. (1992). Category labels and social reality: Do we view social categories as natural kinds? In G. Semin & K. Fiedler (Eds.), *Language, interaction and social cognition* (pp. 11–36). London: Sage.

Rothman, A. J., & Hardin, C. D. (1997). Differential use of the availability heuristic in social judgment. *Personality and Social Psychology Bulletin, 23*, 123–128.

Rothman, A. J., & Salovey, P. (1997). Shaping perceptions to motivate healthy behavior: The role of message framing. *Psychological Bulletin, 121*, 3–19.

Rowley, S. J., Sellers, R. M., Chavous, T. M., & Smith, M. A. (1998). The relationship between racial identity and self-esteem in African American college and high school students. *Journal of Personality and Social Psychology, 74*, 715–724.

Rozin, P., & Fallon, A. E. (1987). A perspective on disgust. *Psychological Review, 94*, 23–41.

Rubin, M., & Hewstone, M. (1998). Social identity theory's self-esteem hypothesis: A review and some suggestions for clarification. *Personality and Social Psychology Review, 2*, 40–62.

Ruble, D. N., & Ruble, T. L. (1982). Sex stereotypes. In A. G. Miller (Ed.), *In the eye of the beholder: Contemporary issues in stereotyping* (pp. 188–252). New York: Praeger.

Ruble, D. N., & Stangor, C. (1986). Stalking the elusive schema: Insights from developmental and social-psychological analyses of gender schemas. *Social Cognition, 4*, 227–261.

Ruder, M., & Bless, H. (2003). Mood and the reliance on the ease of retrieval heuristic. *Journal of Personality and Social Psychology, 85*, 20–32.

Rudman, L. A. (1998). Self-promotion as a risk factor for women: The costs and benefits of counterstereotypical impression management. *Journal of Personality and Social Psychology, 74*, 629–645.

Rudman, L. A. (2004). Sources of implicit attitudes. *Current Directions in Psychological Science, 13*, 79–82.

Rudman, L. A., & Ashmore, R. D. (2007). Discrimination and the IAT. *Group Processes and Intergroup Relations, 10*, 359–372.

Rudman, L. A., Ashmore, R. D., & Gary, M. L. (2001). "Unlearning" automatic biases: The malleability of implicit prejudice and stereotypes. *Journal of Personality and Social Psychology, 81*, 856–868.

Rudman, L. A., & Fairchild, K. (2004). Reactions to counterstereotypic behavior: The role of backlash in cultural stereotype maintenance. *Journal of Personality and Social Psychology, 87*, 157–176.

Rudman, L. A., Feinberg, J., & Fairchild, K. (2002). Minority members' implicit attitudes: Automatic ingroup bias as a function of group status. *Social Cognition, 20*, 294–320.

Rudman, L. A., & Glick, P. (1999). Feminized management and backlash toward agentic women: The hidden costs to women of a kinder, gentler image of middle managers. *Journal of Personality and Social Psychology, 77*, 1004–1010.

Rudman, L. A., & Glick, P. (2001). Prescriptive gender stereotypes and backlash toward agentic women. *Journal of Social Issues, 57*, 743–762.

Rudman, L. A., & Glick, P. (in press). *Sexism: How power and love shape gender relations.* New York: Guilford Press.

Rudman, L. A., & Goodwin, S. A. (2004). Gender differences in automatic in-group bias: Why do women like women more than men like men? *Journal of Personality and Social Psychology, 87*, 494–509.

Rudman, L. A., Greenwald, A .G., Mellott, D. S., & Schwartz, J. L. K. (1999). Measuring the automatic components of prejudice: Flexibility and generality of the implicit association test. *Social Cognition, 17*, 437–465.

Rudman, L. A., Greenwald, A. G., & McGhee, D. E. (2001). Implicit self-concept and evaluative implicit gender stereotypes: Self and ingroup share desirable traits. *Personality and Social Psychology Bulletin, 27*, 1164–1178.

Rudman, L. A., & Heppen, J. B. (2003). Implicit romantic fantasies and women's interest in personal power: A glass slipper effect? *Personality and Social Psychology Bulletin, 29*, 1357–1370.

Rudman, L. A., & Kilianski, S. E. (2000). Implicit and explicit attitudes toward female authority. *Personality and Social Psychology Bulletin, 26*, 1315–1328.

Rudolph, U., Roesch, S. C., Greitemeyer, T., & Weiner, B. (2004). A meta-analytic review of help giving and aggression from an attributional perspective: Contributions to a general theory of motivation. *Cognition and Emotion, 18*, 815–848.

Rule, B. G., Taylor, B. R., & Dobbs, A. R. (1987). Priming effects of heat on aggressive thoughts. *Social Cognition, 5*, 131–143.

Rumelhart, D. E., Lindsay, P. H., & Norman, D. A. (1972). A process model for long-term memory. In E. Tulving & W. Donaldson (Eds.), *Organization of memory.* New York: Academic Press.

Rumelhart, D. E., & Ortony, A. (1977). The representation of knowledge in memory. In R. C. Anderson, R. J. Spiro, & W. E. Montague (Eds.), *Schooling and the acquisition of knowledge* (pp. 99–136). Hillsdale, NJ: Erlbaum.

Ruscher, J. B., & Fiske, S. T. (1990). Interpersonal competition can cause individuating impression formation. *Journal of Personality and Social Psychology, 58,* 832–842.

Russell, J. A. (2003). Core affect and the psychological construction of emotion. *Psychological Review, 110,* 145–172.

Russell, J. A., & Bullock, M. (1985). Multidimensional scaling of emotional facial expressions: Similarity from preschoolers to adults. *Journal of Personality and Social Psychology, 48,* 1290–1298.

Russell, J. A., & Bullock, M. (1986). Fuzzy concepts and the perception of emotion in facial expressions. *Social Cognition, 4,* 309–341.

Russell, J. A., & Fehr, B. (1987). Relativity in the perception of emotion in facial expressions. *Journal of Experimental Psychology: General, 116,* 223–237.

Russell, J. A., & Fehr, B. (1988). Reply to Ekman & O'Sullivan. *Journal of Experimental Psychology: General, 117,* 89–90.

Russell, J. A., & Woudzia, L. (1986). Affective judgments, common sense, and Zajonc's thesis of independence. *Motivation and Emotion, 10,* 169–183.

Rusting, C. L. (1998). Personality, mood, and cognitive processing of emotional information: Three conceptual frameworks. *Psychological Bulletin, 124,* 165–196.

Rusting, C. L. (1999). Interactive effects of personality and mood on emotion-congruent memory and judgment. *Journal of Personality and Social Psychology, 77,* 1073–1086.

Rusting, C. L., & DeHart, T. (2000). Retrieving positive memories to regulate negative mood: Consequences for mood congruent memory. *Journal of Personality and Social Psychology, 78,* 737–752.

Rusting, C. L., & Larsen, R. J. (1998). Diurnal patterns of unpleasant mood: Associations with neuroticism, depression, and anxiety. *Journal of Personality, 66,* 85–103.

Saenz, D. S., & Lord, C. G. (1989). Reversing roles: A cognitive strategy for undoing memory deficits associated with token status. *Journal of Personality and Social Psychology, 56,* 698–708.

Salovey, P. (1991). Social comparison processes in envy and jealousy. In J. Suls & T. A. Wills (Eds.), *Social comparison theory: Contemporary theory and research* (pp. 261–285). Hillsdale, NJ: Erlbaum.

Salovey, P., & Rodin, J. (1985). Cognitions about the self: Connecting feeling states and social behavior. In P. Shaver (Ed.), *Review of personality and social psychology* (Vol. 6, pp. 143–166). Beverly Hills, CA: Sage.

Salovey, P., & Singer, J. A. (1988). Mood congruency effects in recall of childhood versus recent memories. *Journal of Social Behavior and Personality, 3,* 1–22.

Samuelson, P. A. (1937). A note on measurement of utility. *Review of Economic Studies, 4,* 155–161.

Sanbonmatsu, D. M., & Fazio, R. H. (1990). The role of attitudes in memory-based decision making. *Journal of Personality and Social Psychology, 59,* 614–622.

Sanbonmatsu, D. M., Shavitt, S., & Gibson, B. D. (1994). Salience, set size, and illusory correlation: Making moderate assumptions about extreme targets. *Journal of Personality and Social Psychology, 66,* 1020–1033.

Sanbonmatsu, D. M., Sherman, S. J., & Hamilton, D. L. (1987). Illusory correlation in the perception of individuals and groups. *Social Cognition, 5,* 1–25.

Sanchez, D. T., & Crocker, J. (2005). How investment in gender ideals affects well-being: The role of external contingencies of self-worth. *Psychology of Women Quarterly, 29,* 63–77.

Sanchez, D. T., Crocker, J., & Boike, K. R. (2005). Doing gender in the bedroom: Investing in gender norms and the sexual experience. *Personality and Social Psychology Bulletin, 31,* 1445–1455.

Sanders, J. D., McClure, K. A., & Zárate, M. A. (2004). Cerebral hemisphere asymmetries in social perception: Perceiving and responding to the individual and the group. *Social Cognition, 22,* 279–291.

Sanfey, A. G., Loewenstein, G., McClure, S. M., & Cohen, J. D. (2006). Neuroeconomics: Cross-currents in research on decision-making. *Trends in Cognitive Sciences, 10,* 108–116.

Sanfey, A. G., Rilling, J. K., Aronson, J. A., Nystrom, L. E., & Cohen, J. D. (2003). The neural basis of economic decision-making in the ultimatum game. *Science, 300,* 1755–1758.

Sanna, L. J., Chang, E. C., & Meier, S. (2001). Counterfactual thinking and self-motives. *Personality and Social Psychology Bulletin, 27,* 1023–1034.

Sanna, L. J. & Schwarz, N. (2006). Metacognitive experiences and human judgment. *Current Directions in Psychological Science, 15,* 172–176.

Sanna, L. J., Turley-Ames, K. J., & Meier, S. (1999). Mood, self-esteem, and simulated alternatives: Thought-provoking affective influences on counterfactual direction. *Journal of Personality and Social Psychology, 76,* 543–558.

Sansone, C., & Harackiewicz, J. M. (2000). *Intrinsic and extrinsic motivation: The search for optimal motivation and performance.* San Diego, CA: Academic Press.

Santuzzi, A. M., & Ruscher, J. B. (2002). Stigma salience and paranoid social cognition: Understanding variability in metaperceptions among individuals with recently-acquired stigma. *Social Cognition, 20,* 171–197.

Saucier, D. A., Miller, C. T., & Doucet, N. (2005). Differences in helping Whites and Blacks: A meta-analysis. *Personality and Social Psychology Review, 9,* 2–16.

Savitsky, K., Gilovich, T., Berger, G., & Medvec, V. H. (2003). Is our absence as conspicuous as we think? Overestimating the salience and impact of one's absence from a group. *Journal of Experimental Social Psychology, 39,* 386–392.

Sawyer, A. (1981). Repetition, cognitive responses, and persuasion. In R. E. Petty, T. M. Ostrom, & T. C. Brock (Eds.), *Cognitive responses in persuasion* (pp. 237-262). Hillsdale, NJ: Erlbaum.

Sawyer, J. (1966). Measurement and prediction, clinical and statistical. *Psychological Bulletin, 66,* 178–200.

Saxe, R., Carey, S., & Kanwisher, N. (2004). Understanding other minds: Linking developmental psychology and functional neuroimaging. *Annual Review of Psychology, 55,* 87–124.

Schachter, S. (1959). *The psychology of affiliation.* Stanford, CA: Stanford University Press.

Schachter, S. (1964). The interaction of cognitive and physiological determinants of emotional state. In L. Berkowitz (Ed.), *Advances in experimental social psychology* (Vol. 1, pp. 49–82). New York: Academic Press.

Schachter, S., & Singer, J. A. (1962). Cognitive, social, and physiological determinants of emotional state. *Psychological Review, 69,* 379–399.

Schaffner, P. E. (1985). Specious learning about reward and punishment. *Journal of Personality and Social Psychology, 48,* 1377–1386.

Schaller, M., & Cialdini, R. B. (1988). The economics of empathic helping: Support for a mood management motive. *Journal of Experimental Social Psychology, 24,* 163–181.

Schank, R. C., & Abelson, R. P. (1977). *Scripts, plans, goals, and understanding: An inquiry into human knowledge structures.* Hillsdale, NJ: Erlbaum.

Schaufeli, W. B. (1988). Perceiving the causes of unemployment: An evaluation of the causal dimensions scale in a real-life situation. *Journal of Personality and Social Psychology, 54,* 347–356.

Scheier, M. F., & Carver, C. S. (1982). Cognition, affect, and self-regulation. In M. S. Clark & S. T. Fiske (Eds.), *Affect and cognition: The 17th Annual Carnegie Symposium on Cognition* (pp. 157–184). Hillsdale, NJ: Erlbaum.

Scheier, M. F., Carver, C. S., & Gibbons, F. X. (1981). Self-focused attention and reactions to fear. *Journal of Research in Personality, 15,* 1–15.

Scherer, K. R. (1984). Emotion as a multicomponent process: A model and some cross-cultural data. In P. Shaver (Ed.), *Review of personality and social psychology* (Vol. 5, pp. 37–63).

Scherer, K. R. (1988). Criteria for emotion-antecedent appraisal: A review. In V. Hamilton, G. H. Bower, & N. H. Frijda (Eds.), *Cognitive perspectives on emotion and motivation* (pp. 89–112). New York: Kluwer Academic.

Scherer, K. R., Wallbott, H. G., & Summerfield, A. B. (Eds.). (1986). *Experiencing emotion: A cross-cultural study.* Cambridge, MA: Cambridge University Press.

Schimel, J., Arndt, J., Pyszczynski, T., & Greenberg, J. (2001). Being accepted for who we are: Evidence that social validation of the intrinsic self reduces general defensiveness. *Journal of Personality and Social Psychology, 80,* 35–52.

Schimel, J., Pyszczynski, T., Greenberg, J., O'Mahen, H., & Arndt, J. (2000). Running from the shadow: Psychological distancing from others to deny characteristics people fear in themselves. *Journal of Personality and Social Psychology, 78*, 446–462.

Schimel, J., Simon, L., Greenberg, J., Pyszczynski, T., Solomon, S., Waxmonsky, J., & Arndt, J. (1999). Stereotypes and terror management: Evidence that mortality salience enhances stereotypic thinking and preferences. *Journal of Personality and Social Psychology, 77*, 905–926.

Schlenker, B. R. (1987). Threats to identity: Self-identification and social stress. In C. R. Snyder & C. E. Ford (Eds.), *Coping with negative life events: Clinical and social psychological perspectives* (pp. 273–321). New York: Plenum Press.

Schlosberg, H. (1954). Three dimensions of emotion. *Psychological Review, 61*, 81–88.

Schmader, T., & Johns, M. (2003). Converging evidence that stereotype threat reduces working memory capacity. *Journal of Personality and Social Psychology, 85*, 440–452.

Schmeichel, B. J., & Martens, A. (2005). Self-affirmation and mortality salience: Affirming values reduces worldview defense and death-thought accessibility. *Personality and Social Psychology Bulletin, 31*, 658–667.

Schmeichel, B. J., Vohs, K. D., & Baumeister, R. F. (2003). Intellectual performance and ego depletion: Role of the self in logical reasoning and other information processing. *Journal of Personality and Social Psychology, 85*, 33–46.

Schmidt, D. F., & Sherman, R. C. (1984). Memory for persuasive messages: A test of a schema-copy-plus-tag model. *Journal of Personality and Social Psychology, 47*, 17–25.

Schmidt, G., & Weiner, B. (1988). An attribution-affect-action theory of behavior: Replications of judgments of help-giving. *Personality and Social Psychology Bulletin, 14*, 610–621.

Schmidt-Atzert, L. (1988). Affect and cognition: On the chronological order of stimulus evaluation and emotion. In K. Fiedler, & J. P. Forgas (Eds.), *Affect, cognition, and social behavior* (pp. 153–164). Toronto, Canada: Hogrefe.

Schmitt, M. T., Branscombe, N. R., & Kappen, D. M. (2003). Attitudes toward group-based inequality: Social dominance or social identity? *British Journal of Social Psychology, 42*, 161–186.

Schmitt, M. T., Branscombe, N. R., & Postmes, T. (2003). Women's emotional responses to the pervasiveness of gender discrimination. *European Journal of Social Psychology, 33*, 297–312.

Schnall, S., Haidt, J., Clore, G., & Jordan, A. (2007). *Irrelevant disgust makes moral judgment more severe, for those who listen to their bodies.* Unpublished manuscript.

Schneider, D. J. (1973). Implicit personality theory: A review. *Psychological Bulletin, 79*, 294–309.

Schneider, D. J., Hastorf, A. H., & Ellsworth, P. C. (1979). *Person perception.* Reading, MA: Addison-Wesley.

Schnittker, J., & McLeod, J. D. (2005). The social psychology of health disparities. *Annual Review of Sociology, 31*, 75–103.

Schooler, J. W., & Engstler-Schooler, T. Y. (1990). Verbal overshadowing of visual memories: Some things are better left unsaid. *Cognitive Psychology, 22*, 36–71.

Schopler, J., Insko, C. A., Wieselquist, J., Pemberton, M., Witcher, B., Kozar, R., Roddenberry, C., & Wildschut, T. (2001). When groups are more competitive than individuals: The domain of the discontinuity effect. *Journal of Personality and Social Psychology, 80*, 632–644.

Schroeder, D. A., Dovidio, J. F., Sibicky, M. E., Matthews, L. L., & Allen, J. L. (1988). Empathy and helping behavior: Egoism or altruism? *Journal of Experimental Social Psychology, 24*, 333–353.

Schubert, T. W. (2004). The power in your hand: Gender differences in bodily feedback from making a fist. *Personality and Social Psychology Bulletin, 30*, 757–769.

Schul, Y., Mayo, R., & Burnstein, E. (2004). Encoding under trust and distrust: The spontaneous activation of incongruent cognitions. *Journal of Personality and Social Psychology, 86*, 668–679.

Schuman, H., & Johnson, M. P. (1976). Attitudes and behavior. *Annual Review of Sociology, 2*, 161–207.

Schuman, H., & Ludwig, J. (1983). The norm of even-handedness in surveys as in life. *American Sociological Review, 48*, 112–120.

Schutte, N. S., Kenrick, D. T., & Sadalla, E. K. (1985). The search for predictable settings: Situational prototypes, constraint, and behavioral variation. *Journal of Personality and Social Psychology, 49,* 121–128.

Schwartz, G. E., Davidson, R. J., & Pugash, E. (1976). Voluntary control of patterns of EEG parietal asymmetry: Cognitive concomitants. *Psychophysiology, 13,* 498–504.

Schwartz, G. E., Weinberger, D. A., & Singer, J. A. (1981). Cardiovascular differentiation of happiness, sadness, anger, and fear following imagery and exercise. *Psychosomatic Medicine, 43,* 343–364.

Schwartz, S. H. (1978). Temporal instability as a moderator of the attitude-behavior relationship. *Journal of Personality and Social Psychology, 36,* 715–724.

Schwartz, S. H., & Inbar-Saban, N. (1988). Value self-confrontation as a method to aid in weight loss. *Journal of Personality and Social Psychology, 54,* 396–404.

Schwartz, S. H., & Tessler, R. C. (1972). A test of a model for reducing measured attitude-behavior discrepancies. *Journal of Personality and Social Psychology, 24,* 225–236.

Schwarz, N., & Bless, H. (1991). Happy and mindless, but sad and smart? The impact of affective states on analytic reasoning. In J. P. Forgas (Ed.), *Emotion and social judgments* (pp. 55–71). Elmsford, NY: Pergamon Press.

Schwarz, N., Bless, H., & Bohner, G. (1991). Mood and persuasion: Affective states influence the processing of persuasive communications. In M. P. Zanna (Ed.), *Advances in experimental social psychology* (Vol. 24, pp. 161–199). New York: Academic Press.

Schwarz, N., Bless, H., Strack, F., Klumpp, G., Rittenauer-Schatka, H., & Simons, A. (1991). Ease of retrieval as information: Another look at the availability heuristic. *Journal of Personality and Social Psychology, 61,* 195–202.

Schwarz, N., & Clore, G. L. (1996). Feelings and phenomenal experiences. In E. T. Higgins & A. W. Kruglanski (Eds.), *Social psychology: Handbook of basic principles* (pp. 433–465). New York: Guilford Press.

Schwarz, N., Strack, F., Hilton, D. J., & Naderer, G. (1991). Base-rates, representativeness, and the logic of conversation. *Social Cognition, 9,* 67–84.

Sears, D. O. (1965). Biased indoctrination and selectivity of exposure to new information. *Sociometry, 28,* 363–376.

Sears, D. O. (1968). The paradox of de facto selective exposure. In R. P. Abelson et al. (Eds.), *Theories of cognitive consistency: A sourcebook.* Chicago: Rand McNally.

Sears, D. O. (1983). The person-positivity bias. *Journal of Personality and Social Psychology, 44,* 233–240.

Sears, D. O. (1998). Racism and politics in the United States. In J. L. Eberhardt, & S. T. Fiske (Eds.), *Confronting racism: The problem and the response* (pp. 76–100). Thousand Oaks, CA: Sage.

Sears, D. O., & Henry, P. J. (2003). The origins of symbolic racism. *Journal of Personality and Social Psychology, 85,* 259–275.

Sears, D. O., Huddie, L., & Schaffer, L. G. (1986). A schematic variant of symbolic politics theory, as applied to racial and gender equality. In R. R. Lau & D. O. Sears (Eds.), *Political cognition* (pp. 159–202). Hillsdale, NJ: Erlbaum.

Sears, D. O., & Kinder, D. R. (1985). Whites' opposition to busing: On conceptualizing and operationalizing group conflict. *Journal of Personality and Social Psychology, 48,* 1148–1161.

Sears, D. O., & Whitney, R. E. (1973). Political persuasion. In I. de S. Pool, W. Schramm, F. W. Frey, N. Maccoby, & E. B. Parker (Eds.), *Handbook of communication.* Chicago: Rand McNally.

Seccombe, K., & Ishii-Kuntz, M. (1991). Perceptions of problems associated with aging: Comparisons among four older age cohorts. *Gerontologist, 31,* 527–533.

Sechrist, G. B., Swim, J. K., & Stangor, C. (2004). When do the stigmatized make attributions to discrimination occurring to the self and others? The roles of self-presentation and need for control. *Journal of Personality and Social Psychology, 87,* 111–122.

Sedikides, C. (1993). Assessment, enhancement, and verification determinants of the self-evaluation process. *Journal of Personality and Social Psychology, 65,* 317–338.

Sedikides, C., Gaertner, L., & Toguchi, Y. (2003). Pancultural self-enhancement. *Journal of Personality and Social Psychology, 84,* 60–79.

Sedikides, C., & Green, J. D. (2000). On the self-protective nature of inconsistency-negativity management: Using the person memory paradigm to examine self-referent memory. *Journal of Personality and Social Psychology, 79*, 906–922.

Seger, C. A. (1994). Implicit learning. *Psychological Bulletin, 115,* 163–196.

Segerstrom, S. C., Taylor, S. E., Kemeny, M. E., & Fahey, J. L. (1998). Optimism is associated with mood, coping and immune change in response to stress. *Journal of Personality and Social Psychology, 74,* 1646–1655.

Seibt, B., & Förster, J. (2004). Stereotype threat and performance: How self-stereotypes influence processing by inducing regulatory foci. *Journal of Personality and Social Psychology, 87,* 38–56.

Sekaquaptewa, D., & Thompson, M. (2003). Solo status, stereotype threat, and performance expectancies: Their effects on women's performance. *Journal of Experimental Social Psychology, 39,* 68–74.

Sellers, R. M., Caldwell, C. H., Schmeelk-Cone, K. H., & Zimmerman, M. A. (2003). Racial identity, racial discrimination, perceived stress, and psychological distress among African American young adults. *Journal of Health and Social Behavior, 44,* 302–317.

Sellers, R. M., Rowley, S. A. J., Chavous, T. M., Shelton, J. N., & Smith, M. A. (1997). Multidimensional inventory of Black identity: A preliminary investigation of reliability and construct validity. *Journal of Personality and Social Psychology, 73,* 805–815.

Sellers, R. M., & Shelton, J. N. (2003). The role of racial identity in perceived racial discrimination. *Journal of Personality and Social Psychology, 84,* 1079–1092.

Sentis, K. P., & Burnstein, E. (1979). Remembering schema consistent information: Effects of a balance schema on recognition memory. *Journal of Personality and Social Psychology, 37,* 2200–2211.

Seta, J. J., McElroy, T., & Seta, C. E. (2001). To do or not to do: Desirability and consistency mediate judgments of regret. *Journal of Personality and Social Psychology, 80,* 861–870.

Setterlund, M. B., & Niedenthal, P. M. (1993). "Who am I? Why am I here?" Self-esteem, self-clarity, and prototype matching. *Journal of Personality and Social Psychology, 65,* 769–780.

Shah, J. Y. (2003a). Automatic for the people: How representations of significant others implicitly affect goal pursuit. *Journal of Personality and Social Psychology, 84,* 661–681.

Shah, J. Y. (2003b). The motivational looking glass: How significant others implicitly affect goal appraisals. *Journal of Personality and Social Psychology, 85,* 424–439.

Shah, J. Y., Friedman, R., & Kruglanski, A. W. (2002). Forgetting all else: On the antecedents and consequences of goal shielding. *Journal of Personality and Social Psychology, 83,* 1261–1280.

Shah, J. Y., Higgins, E. T., & Friedman, R. S. (1998). Performance incentives and means: How regulatory focus influences goal attainment. *Journal of Personality and Social Psychology, 74,* 285–293.

Shallice, T. (1972). Dual functions of consciousness. *Psychological Review, 79,* 383–393.

Shallice, T. (1978). The dominant action system: An information-processing approach to consciousness. In K. S. Pope & J. L. Singer (Eds.), *The stream of consciousness: Scientific investigations into the flow of human experience.* New York: Plenum Press.

Shapiro, D., & Crider, A. (1969). Psychophysiological approaches in social psychology. In. G. Lindzey & E. Aronson (Eds.), *The handbook of social psychology* (Vol. 3, pp. 1–49). Reading, MA: Addison-Wesley.

Shaver, K. G. (1975). *An introduction to attribution processes.* Cambridge: Winthrop.

Shaver, K. G. (1985). *The attribution of blame: Causality, responsibility, and blameworthiness.* New York: Springer-Verlag.

Shaver, P. (Ed.). (1984). *Review of personality and social psychology: Emotions, relationships, and health* (Vol. 5). Beverly Hills, CA: Sage.

Shaver, P., Schwartz, J., Kirson, D., & O'Connor, C. (1987). Emotion knowledge: Further exploration of a prototype approach. *Journal of Personality and Social Psychology, 52,* 1061–1086.

Shavitt, S. (1989). Operationalizing functional theories of attitude. In A. R. Pratkanis, S. J. Breckler, & A. G. Greenwald (Eds.), *Attitude structure and function* (pp. 311–338). Hillsdale, NJ: Erlbaum.

Shaw, M. E. (1971). *Group dynamics.* New York: McGraw-Hill.

Shedler, J., & Manis, M. (1986). Can the availability heuristic explain vividness effects? *Journal of Personality and Social Psychology, 51,* 26–36.

Sheeran, P., Orbell, S., & Trafimow, D. (1999). Does the temporal stability of behavioral intentions moderate intention-behavior and past behavior-future behavior relations? *Personality and Social Psychology Bulletin, 25,* 721–730.

Sheeran, P., Webb, T. L., & Gollwitzer, P. M. (2005). The interplay between goal intentions and implementation intentions. *Personality and Social Psychology Bulletin, 31,* 87–98.

Sherman, J. W., Klein, S. B., Laskey, A., & Wyer, N. A. (1998). Intergroup bias in group judgment processes: The role of behavioral memories. *Journal of Experimental Social Psychology, 34,* 51–65.

Shelton, J. N. (2000). A reconceptualization of how we study issues of racial prejudice. *Personality and Social Psychology Review, 4,* 374–390.

Shelton, J. N. (2003). Interpersonal concerns in social encounters between majority and minority group members. *Group Processes & Intergroup Relations, 6,* 171–185.

Shelton, J. N., & Richeson, J. A. (2005). Intergroup contact and pluralistic ignorance. *Journal of Personality and Social Psychology, 88,* 91–107.

Shelton, J. N., & Richeson, J. A. (2006). Interracial interactions: A relational approach. In M. P. Zanna (Ed.), *Advances in experimental social psychology* (pp. 121–181). New York: Academic Press.

Shelton, J. N., Richeson, J. A., & Salvatore, J. (2005). Expecting to be the target of prejudice: Implications for interethnic interactions. *Personality and Social Psychology Bulletin, 31,* 1189–1202.

Shelton, J. N., Richeson, J. A., Salvatore, J., & Trawalter, S. (2005). Ironic effects of racial bias during interracial interactions. *Psychological Science, 16,* 397–402.

Shelton, J. N., & Sellers, R. M. (2000). Situational stability and variability in African American racial identity. *Journal of Black Psychology, 26,* 27–50.

Shepperd, J. A., Ouellette, J. A., & Fernandez, J. K. (1996). Abandoning unrealistic optimism: Performance estimates and the temporal proximity of self-relevant feedback. *Journal of Personality and Social Psychology, 70,* 844–855.

Sherer, M., & Rogers, R. W. (1984). The role of vivid information in fear appeals and attitude change. *Journal of Research in Personality, 18,* 321–334.

Sherif, C. W., Kelly, M., Rodgers, H. L., Sarup, G., & Tittler, B. (1973). Personal involvement, social judgment, and action. *Journal of Personality and Social Psychology, 27,* 311–327.

Sherif, M., & Hovland, C. I. (1961). *Social judgment: Assimilation and contrast effects in communication and attitude change.* New Haven, CT: Yale University Press.

Sherif, M., & Sherif, M. (1953). *Groups in harmony and tension: An integration of studies on intergroup relations.* Oxford, England: Harper & Brothers.

Sherman, D. K., & Cohen, G. L. (2002). Accepting threatening information: Self-affirmation and the reduction of defensive biases. *Current Directions in Psychological Science, 11,* 119–123.

Sherman, D. K., & Cohen, G. L. (2006). The psychology of self-defense: Self-affirmation theory. In M. P. Zanna (Ed.), *Advances in experimental social psychology* (Vol. 38, pp. 183–242). San Diego, CA: Academic Press.

Sherman, D. K., Mann, T., & Updegraff, J. A. (2006). Approach/avoidance orientation, message framing, and health behavior: Understanding the congruency effect. *Motivation and Emotion, 30,* 165–169.

Sherman, D. K., Nelson, L. D., & Ross, L. D. (2003). Naive realism and affirmative action: Adversaries are more similar than they think. *Basic and Applied Social Psychology, 25,* 275–289.

Sherman, D. K., Nelson, L. D., & Steele, C. M. (2000). Do messages about health risks threaten the self? Increasing the acceptance of threatening health messages via self-affirmation. *Personality and Social Psychology Bulletin, 26,* 1046–1058.

Sherman, J. W., Conrey, F. R., & Groom, C. J. (2004). Encoding flexibility revisited: Evidence for enhanced encoding of stereotype-inconsistent information under cognitive load. *Social Cognition, 22,* 214–232.

Sherman, J. W., Klein, S. B., Laskey, A., & Wyer, N. A. (1998). Intergroup bias in group judgment processes: The role of behavioral memories. *Journal of Experimental Social Psychology, 34,* 51–65.

Sherman, J. W., Lee, A. Y., Bessenhoff, G. R., & Frost, L. A. (1998). Stereotype efficiency reconsidered: Encoding flexibility under cognitive load. *Journal of Personality and Social Psychology, 75,* 589–606.

Sherman, J. W., Stroessner, S. J., Conrey, F. R., & Azam, O. A. (2005). Prejudice and stereotype maintenance processes: Attention, attribution and individuation. *Journal of Personality and Social Psychology, 89,* 607–622.

Sherman, R. C., & Titus, W. (1982). Convariation information and cognitive processing: Effects of causal implications on memory. *Journal of Personality and Social Psychology, 42,* 989–1000.

Sherman, S. J. (1987). Cognitive processes in the formation, change, and expression of attitudes. In M. P. Zanna, J. M. Olson, & C. P. Herman (Eds.), *Social influence: The Ontario Symposium* (Vol. 5, pp. 75–106). Hillsdale, NJ: Erlbaum.

Sherman, S. J., & Corty, E. (1984). Cognitive heuristics. In R. S. Wyer Jr. & T. K. Srull (Eds.), *Handbook of social cognition* (Vol. 1, pp. 189–286). Hillsdale, NJ: Erlbaum.

Sherman, S. J., Mackie, D. M., & Driscoll, D. M. (1988). Priming and the differential use of dimensions in evaluation. *Personality and Social Psychology Bulletin, 16,* 405–418.

Sherman, S. J., Presson, C. C., & Chassin, L. (1984). Mechanisms underlying the false consensus effect: The special role of threats to the self. *Personality and Social Psychology Bulletin, 10,* 127–138.

Sherwood, G. G. (1979). Classical and attributive projection: Some new evidence. *Journal of Abnormal Psychology, 88,* 635–640.

Shih, M., Pittinsky, T. L., & Ambady, N. (1999). Stereotype susceptibility: Identity salience and shifts in quantitative performance. *Psychological Science, 10,* 80–83.

Showers, C., & Cantor, N. (1985). Social cognition: A look at motivated strategies. *Annual Review of Psychology, 36,* 275–305.

Shrauger, S. J., & Patterson, M. B. (1974). Self-evaluation and the selection of dimensions for evaluating others. *Journal of Personality, 42,* 569–585.

Sidanius, J. (1988). Political sophistication and political deviance: A structural equation examination of context theory. *Journal of Personality and Social Psychology, 55,* 37–51.

Sidanius, J., & Pratto, F. (1999). *Social dominance: An intergroup theory of social hierarchy and oppression.* New York: Cambridge University Press.

Sidanius, J., & Pratto, F. (2003). Social dominance theory and the dynamics of inequality: A reply to Schmitt, Branscombe, & Keppen and Wilson & Liu. *British Journal of Social Psychology, 42,* 207–213.

Sidanius, J., Pratto, F., & Bobo, L. (1994). Social dominance orientation and the political psychology of gender: A case of invariance? *Journal of Personality and Social Psychology, 70,* 476–490.

Sidanius, J., Pratto, F., & Bobo, L. (1996). Racism, conservatism, affirmative action, and intellectual sophistication: A matter of principled conservatism or group dominance? *Journal of Personality and Social Psychology, 70,* 476–490.

Silvia, P. J., & Duval, T. S. (2001). Objective self-awareness theory: Recent progress and enduring problems. *Personality and Social Psychology Review, 5,* 230–241.

Simon, B. (1992). The perception of ingroup and outgroup homogeneity: Reintroducing the intergroup context. In W. Stroebe & M. Hewstone (Eds.), *European review of social psychology* (Vol. 3, pp. 1–30). Oxford, England: Wiley.

Simon, H. A. (1967). Motivational and emotional controls of cognition. *Psychological Review, 74,* 29–39.

Simon, H. A. (1980). Problem solving and education. In D. T. Tuma & F. Reif (Eds.), *Problem solving and education: Issues in teaching and research.* Hillsdale, NJ: Erlbaum.

Simon, H. A. (1982). Comments. In M. S. Clark & S. T. Fiske (Eds.), *Affect and cognition: The 17th Annual Carnegie Symposium on Cognition* (pp. 333–342). Hillsdale, NJ: Erlbaum.

Simpson, J. A., Oriña, M. M., & Ickes, W. J. (2003). When accuracy hurts, and when it helps: A test of the empathic accuracy model in marital interactions. *Journal of Personality and Social Psychology, 85,* 881–893.

Sinclair, S., Dunn, E., & Lowery, B. S. (2005). The relationship between parental racial attitudes and children's implicit prejudice. *Journal of Experimental Social Psychology, 41,* 283–289.

Sinclair, S., Lowery, B. S., Hardin, C. D., & Colangelo, A. (2005). Social tuning of automatic racial attitudes: The role of affiliative motivation. *Journal of Personality and Social Psychology, 89,* 583–592.

Sinclair, L., & Kunda, Z. (1999). Reactions to a Black professional: Motivated inhibition and activation of conflicting stereotypes. *Journal of Personality and Social Psychology, 77,* 885–904.

Sinclair, L., & Kunda, Z. (2000). Motivated stereotyping of women: She's fine if she praised me but incompetent if she criticized me. *Personality and Social Psychology Bulletin, 24,* 1139–1152.

Sinclair, R. C., Mark, M. M., & Shotland, R. L. (1987). Construct accessibility and generalizability across response categories. *Personality and Social Psychology Bulletin, 13,* 239–252.

Singer, J. L. (1966). *Daydreaming.* New York: Random House.

Singer, J. L. (1978). Experimental studies of daydreaming and the stream of thought. In K. S. Pope & J. L. Singer (Eds.), *The stream of consciousness: Scientific investigations into the flow of human experience.* New York: Plenum Press.

Singer, J. L. (1984). The private personality. *Personality and Social Psychology Bulletin, 10,* 7–30.

Singer, J. L. (1988). Reinterpreting the transference. In D. C. Turk & P. Salovey (Eds.), *Reasoning, inference, and judgment in clinical psychology* (pp. 182–205). New York: Free Press.

Singer, J. L., & Salovey, P. (1988). Mood and memory: Evaluating the network theory of affect. *Clinical Psychology Review, 8,* 211–251.

Sivacek, J., & Crano, W. D. (1982). Vested interest as a moderator of attitude-behavior consistency. *Journal of Personality and Social Psychology, 43,* 210–221.

Skinner, B. F. (1957). *Verbal behavior.* New York: Appleton-Century-Crofts.

Skinner, B. F. (1963). Operant behavior. *American Psychologist, 18,* 503–515.

Skov, R. B., & Sherman, S. J. (1986). Information-gathering processes: Diagnosticity, hypothesis-confirmatory strategies, and perceived hypothesis confirmation. *Journal of Experimental Social Psychology, 22,* 93–121.

Skowronski, J. J., & Carlston, D. E. (1989). Negativity and extremity biases in impression formation: A review of explanations. *Psychological Bulletin, 105,* 131–142.

Slovic, P., Fischhoff, B., & Lichtenstein, S. (1976). Cognitive processes and societal risk taking. In J. S. Carroll & J. W. Payne (Eds.), *Cognition and social behavior* (pp. 165–184). Hillsdale, NJ: Erlbaum.

Slovic, P., Fischhoff, B., & Lichtenstein, S. (1977). Behavioral decision theory. *Annual Review of Psychology, 28,* 1–39.

Slowiaczek, L. M., Klayman, J., Sherman, S. J., & Skov, R. B. (1992). Information selection and use in hypothesis testing: What is a good question, what is a good answer? *Memory and Cognition, 20,* 392–405.

Small, D. A., & Lowenstein, G. (2005). The devil you know: The effects of identifiability on punishment. *Journal of Behavioral Decision Making, 18,* 311–318.

Smedslund, J. (1963). The concept of correlation in adults. *Scandinavian Journal of Psychology, 4,* 165–173.

Smith, C. A. (1989). Dimensions of appraisal and physiological response in emotion. *Journal of Personality and Social Psychology, 56,* 339–353.

Smith, C. A., & Ellsworth, P. C. (1985). Patterns of cognitive appraisal in emotion. *Journal of Personality and Social Psychology, 48,* 813–838.

Smith, C. A., & Ellsworth, P. C. (1987). Patterns of appraisal and emotion related to taking an exam. *Journal of Personality and Social Psychology, 52,* 475–488.

Smith, E. E., & Medin, D. L. (1981). *Categories and concepts.* Cambridge, MA: Harvard University Press.

Smith, E. E., Shoben, E. J., & Rips, L. J. (1974). Structure and process in semantic memory: A featural model for semantic decisions. *Psychological Review, 81,* 214–241.

Smith, E. R. (1984). Model of social inference processes. *Psychological Review, 91,* 392–413.

Smith, E. R. (1988). Category accessibility effects in simulated exemplar-based memory. *Journal of Experimental Social Psychology, 24,* 448–463.

Smith, E. R. (1989). Procedural efficiency and on-line social judgments. In J. Bassili (Ed.), *On-line cognition in person perception* (pp. 19–38). Hillsdale, NJ: Erlbaum.

Smith, E. R. (1990). Content and process specificity in the effects of prior experiences. In T. K. Srull & R. S. Wyer Jr. (Eds.), *Advances in social cognition* (Vol. 3, pp. 1–59). Hillsdale, NJ: Erlbaum.

Smith, E. R. (1993). Social identity and social emotions: Toward new conceptualizations of prejudice. In D. M. Mackie & D. L. Hamilton (Eds.), *Affect, cognition, and stereotyping: Interactive processes in group perception* (pp. 297–315). San Diego, CA: Academic Press.

Smith, E. R. (1998). Mental representation and memory. In D. T. Gilbert, S. T. Fiske, & G. Lindzey (Eds.), *The handbook of social psychology* (4th ed., Vol. 1, pp. 391–445). New York: McGraw-Hill.

Smith, E. R., & Branscombe, N. R. (1987). Procedurally mediated social inferences: The case of category accessibility effects. *Journal of Experimental Social Psychology, 23,* 361–382.

Smith, E. R., & Branscombe, N. R. (1988). Category accessibility as implicit memory. *Journal of Experimental Social Psychology, 24,* 490–504.

Smith, E. R., Branscombe, N. R., & Bormann, C. (1988). Generality of the effects of practice on social judgment tasks. *Journal of Personality and Social Psychology, 54,* 385–395.

Smith, E. R., Coats, S., & Walling, D. (1999). Overlapping mental representations of self, ingroup, and partner: Further response time evidence and a connectionist model. *Personality and Social Psychology Bulletin, 25,* 873–882.

Smith, E. R., & DeCoster, J. (1998). Knowledge acquisition, accessibility, and use in person perception and stereotyping: Simulation with a recurrent connectionist network. *Journal of Personality and Social Psychology, 74,* 21–35.

Smith, E. R., & DeCoster, J. (2000). Dual-process models in social and cognitive psychology: Conceptual integration and links to underlying memory systems. *Personality and Social Psychology Review, 4,* 108–131.

Smith, E. R., & Henry, S. (1996). An in-group becomes part of the self: Response time evidence. *Personality and Social Psychology Bulletin, 22,* 635–642.

Smith, E. R., & Lerner, M. (1986). Development of automatism of social judgments. *Journal of Personality and Social Psychology, 50,* 246–259.

Smith, E. R., & Miller, F. D. (1979). Salience and the cognitive mediation of attribution. *Journal of Personality and Social Psychology, 37,* 2240–2252.

Smith, E. R., & Semin, G. R. (2004). Socially situated cognition: Cognition in its social context. In M. P. Zanna (Ed.), *Advances in experimental social psychology* (Vol. 36, pp. 53–116). San Diego, CA: Elsevier Academic Press.

Smith, E. R., & Zárate, M. A. (1992). Exemplar-based model of social judgment. *Psychological Review, 99,* 3–21.

Smith, M. B., Bruner, J. S., & White, R. W. (1956). *Opinions and personality.* Oxford, England: Wiley.

Smith, R. H. (2000). Assimilative and contrastive emotional reactions to upward and downward social comparisons. In J. Suls & L. Wheeler (Eds.) *Handbook of social comparison: Theory and research* (pp. 173–200). Dordrecht, NL: Kluwer.

Smith, S. M., & Shaffer, D. R. (2000). Vividness can undermine or enhance message processing: The moderating role of vividness congruency. *Personality and Social Psychology Bulletin, 26,* 769–779.

Smith, V. L., & Ellsworth, P. C. (1987). The social psychology of eyewitness accuracy: Leading questions and communicator expertise. *Journal of Applied Psychology, 72,* 294–300.

Snyder, C. R., & Higgins, R. L. (1988). Excuses: Their effective role in the negotiation of reality. *Psychological Bulletin, 104,* 23–35.

Snyder, M. (1974). The self-monitoring of expressive behavior. *Journal of Personality and Social Psychology, 30,* 526–537.

Snyder, M. (1976). Attribution and behavior: Social perception and social causation. In J. H. Harvey, W. J. Ickes, & R. F. Kidd (Eds.), *New directions in attribution research* (Vol. 1, pp. 53–72). Hillsdale, NJ: Erlbaum.

Snyder, M. (1977). Impression management. In S. Wrightsman (Ed.), *Social psychology in the seventies.* New York: Wiley.

Snyder, M. (1979). Self-monitoring processes. In L. Berkowitz (Ed.), *Advances in experimental social psychology* (Vol. 12, pp. 86–131). New York: Academic Press.

Snyder, M. (1982). When believing means doing: Creating links between attitudes and behavior. In M. P. Zanna, E. T. Higgins, & C. P. Herman (Eds.), *Consistency in social behavior: The Ontario Symposium* (Vol. 2, pp. 105–130). Hillsdale, NJ: Erlbaum.

Snyder, M., & Campbell, B. H. (1982). Self-monitoring: The self in action. In J. Suls (Ed.), *Psychological perspectives on the self* (Vol. 1, pp. 185–208). Hillsdale, NJ: Erlbaum.

Snyder, M., Campbell, B. H., & Preston, E. (1982). Testing hypotheses about human nature: Assessing the accuracy of social stereotypes. *Social Cognition, 1,* 256–272.

Snyder, M., & Cantor, N. (1980). Thinking about ourselves and others: Self-monitoring and social knowledge. *Journal of Personality and Social Psychology, 39,* 222–234.

Snyder, M., & DeBono, K. G. (1985). Appeals to image and claims about quality: Understanding the psychology of advertising. *Journal of Personality and Social Psychology, 49,* 586–597.

Snyder, M., & DeBono, K. G. (1987). A functional approach to attitudes and persuasion. In M. P. Zanna, J. M. Olson, & C. P. Herman (Eds.), *Social influence: The Ontario Symposium* (Vol. 5, pp. 107–125). Hillsdale, NJ: Erlbaum.

Snyder, M., & DeBono, K. G. (1989). Understanding the functions of attitudes: Lessons from personality and social behavior. In A. R. Pratkanis, S. J. Breckler, & A. G. Greenwald (Eds.), *Attitude structure and function* (pp. 339–360). Hillsdale, NJ: Erlbaum.

Snyder, M., & Gangestad, S. (1981). Hypothesis-testing processes. In J. H. Harvey, W. Ickes, & R. F. Kidd (Eds.), *New directions in attribution research* (Vol. 3, pp. 171–198). Hillsdale, NJ: Erlbaum.

Snyder, M., & Kendzierski, D. (1982). Acting on one's attitudes: Procedures for linking attitude and behavior. *Journal of Experimental Social Psychology, 18,* 165–183.

Snyder, M., & Miene, P. K. (1994). Stereotyping of the elderly: A functional approach. *British Journal of Social Psychology, 33,* 63–82.

Snyder, M., & Monson, T. C. (1975). Persons, situations, and the control of social behavior. *Journal of Personality and Social Psychology, 32,* 637–644.

Snyder, M., & Simpson, J. A. (1984). Self-monitoring and dating relationships. *Journal of Personality and Social Psychology, 47,* 1281–1291.

Snyder, M., & Swann, W. B., Jr. (1976). When actions reflect attitudes: The politics of impression management. *Journal of Personality and Social Psychology, 34,* 1034–1042.

Snyder, M., & Swann, W. B., Jr. (1978a). Hypothesis-testing processes in social interaction. *Journal of Personality and Social Psychology, 36,* 1202–1212.

Snyder, M., & Swann, W. B., Jr. (1978b). Behavioral confirmation in social interaction: From social perception to social reality. *Journal of Experimental Social Psychology, 14,* 148–162.

Snyder, M., & Tanke, E. D. (1976). Behavior and attitude: Some people are more consistent than others. *Journal of Personality, 44,* 501–517.

Snyder, M., Tanke, E. D., & Berscheid, E. (1977). Social perception and interpersonal behavior: On the self-fulfilling nature of social stereotypes. *Journal of Personality and Social Psychology, 35,* 656–666.

Solarz, A. K. (1960). Latency of instrumental responses as a function of compatibility with the meaning of eliciting verbal signs. *Journal of Experimental Psychology, 59,* 239–245.

Sommer, K. L., & Baumeister, R. F. (2002). Self-evaluation, persistence, and performance following implicit rejection: The role of trait self-esteem. *Personality and Social Psychology Bulletin, 28,* 926–938.

Sommers, S. (1981). Emotionality reconsidered: The role of cognition in emotional responsiveness. *Journal of Personality and Social Psychology, 41,* 553–561.

Sorrentino, R. M., Bobocel, D. R., Gitta, M. Z., Olson, J. M., & Hewitt, E. L. (1988). Uncertainty orientation and persuasion: Individual differences in the effects of personal relevance on social judgments. *Journal of Personality and Social Psychology, 55,* 357–371.

Sorrentino, R. M., & Hancock, R. D. (1987). The role of information and affective value for social influence: A case for the study of individual differences. In M. P. Zanna, J. M. Olson, & C. P. Herman (Eds.), *Social influence: The Ontario Symposium* (Vol. 5, pp. 244–268). Hillsdale, NJ: Erlbaum.

Sorrentino, R. M., & Roney, C. J. R. (1986). Uncertainty orientation, achievement-related motivation, and task diagnosticity as determinants of task performance. *Social Cognition, 4,* 420–436.

Sorrentino, R. M., & Short, J. C. (1986). Uncertainty orientation, motivation, and cognition. In R. M. Sorrentino & E. T. Higgins (Eds.), *Handbook of motivation and cognition: Foundations of social behavior* (pp. 379–403). New York: Guilford Press.

Spangler, E., Gordon, M. A., & Pipkin, R. M. (1978). Token women: An empirical test of the Kanter hypothesis. *American Journal of Sociology, 84,* 160–170.

Spears, R., Postmes, T., Lea, M., & Wolbert, A. (2002). When are net effects gross products? The power of influence and the influence of power in computer-mediated communication. *Journal of Social Issues, 58,* 91–107.

Spence, J. T., Deaux, K., & Helmreich, R. L. (1985). Sex roles in contemporary American society. In G. Lindzey & E. Aronson (Eds.), *The handbook of social psychology* (3rd ed., Vol. 2, pp. 149–178). New York: Random House.

Spence, S. A., & Frith, C. D. (1999). Towards a functional anatomy of volition. *Journal of Consciousness Studies, 6,* 11–28.

Spencer, S. J., Fein, S., Wolfe, C. T., Fong, C., & Dunn, M. A. (1998). Automatic activation of stereotypes: The role of self-image threat. *Personality and Social Psychology Bulletin, 24,* 1139–1152.

Spencer, S. J., Steele, C. M., & Quinn, D. M. (1999). Stereotype threat and women's math performance. *Journal of Experimental Social Psychology, 35,* 4–28.

Spielman, L. A., Pratto, F., & Bargh, J. A. (1988). Are one's moods, attitudes, evaluations, and emotions out of control? *American Behavioral Scientist, 31,* 296–311.

Squire, L. R. (1987). *Memory and brain.* New York: Oxford University Press.

Squire, L. R. (1992). Memory and the hippocampus: A synthesis from findings with rats, monkeys, and humans. *Psychological Review, 99,* 195–231.

Srull, T. K. (1981). Person memory: Some tests of associative storage and retrieval models. *Journal of Experimental Psychology: Human Learning and Memory, 7,* 440–462.

Srull, T. K., Lichenstein, M., & Rothbart, M. (1985). Associative storage and retrieval processes in person memory. *Journal of Experimental Psychology: Learning, Memory, and Cognition, 11,* 316–345.

Srull, T. K., & Wyer, R. S., Jr. (1979). The role of category accessibility in the interpretation of information about persons: Some determinants and implications. *Journal of Personality and Social Psychology, 37,* 1660–1672.

Srull, T. K., & Wyer, R. S., Jr. (1980). Category accessibility and social perception: Some implications for the study of person memory and interpersonal judgments. *Journal of Personality and Social Psychology, 38,* 841–856.

Srull, T. K., & Wyer, R. S., Jr. (1986). The role of chronic and temporary goals in social information processing. In R. M. Sorrentino & E. T. Higgins (Eds.), *Handbook of motivation and cognition: Foundations of social behavior* (pp. 503–549). New York: Guilford Press.

Srull, T. K., & Wyer, R. S., Jr. (1989). Person memory and judgment. *Psychological Review, 96,* 58–83.

Staats, A. W., & Staats, C. K. (1958). Attitudes established by classical conditioning. *Journal of Abnormal and Social Psychology, 57,* 37–40.

Stang, D. J. (1974). Methodological factors in mere exposure research. *Psychological Bulletin, 81,* 1014–1025.

Stangor, C. (1988). Stereotype accessibility and information processing. *Personality and Social Psychology Bulletin, 14,* 694–708.

Stangor, C. (1990). Arousal, accessibility of trait constructs, and person perception. *Journal of Experimental Social Psychology, 26,* 305–321.

Stangor, C., Carr, C., & Kiang, L. (1998). Activating stereotypes undermines task performance expectations. *Journal of Personality and Social Psychology, 75,* 1191–1197.

Stangor, C., Swim, J. K., Sechrist, G. B., DeCoster, J., Van Allen, K., & Ottenbreit, A. (2003). In W. Stroebe & M. Hewstone (Eds.), *European review of social psychology* (Vol. 14, pp. 277–311). Hove, England: Psychology Press/Taylor & Francis.

Stangor, C., & Thompson, E. P. (2002). Needs for cognitive economy and self-enhancement as unique predictors of intergroup attitudes. *European Journal of Social Psychology, 32,* 563–575.

Stapel, D. A., & Koomen, W. (2000). How far do we go beyond the information given? The impact of knowledge activation in interpretation and inference. *Journal of Personality and Social Psychology, 78,* 19–37.

Stapel, D. A., & Koomen, W. (2006). The flexible unconscious: Investigating the judgmental impact of varieties of unaware perception. *Journal of Experimental Social Psychology, 42,* 112–119.

Stapel, D. A., & Marx, D. M. (2006). Hardly thinking about others: On cognitive busyness and target similarity in social comparison effects. *Journal of Experimental Social Psychology, 42,* 397–405.

Stapel, D. A., & Van der Zee, K. I. (2006). The self salience model of other-to-self effects: Integrating principles of self-enhancement, complementarity, and imitation. *Journal of Personality and Social Psychology, 90,* 258–271.

Staub, E. (1999). The roots of evil: Social conditions, culture, personality, and basic human needs. *Personality and Social Psychology Review, 3,* 179–192.

Steele, C. M. (1988). The psychology of self-affirmation: Sustaining the integrity of the self. In L. Berkowitz (Ed.), *Advances in experimental psychology* (Vol. 21). New York: Academic Press.

Steele, C. M. (1997). A threat in the air: How stereotypes shape intellectual identity and performance. *American Psychologist, 52,* 613–629.

Steele, C. M., & Aronson, J. (1995). Stereotype threat and the intellectual test performance of African Americans. *Journal of Personality and Social Psychology, 69,* 797–811.

Steele, C. M., Spencer, S. J., & Aronson, J. (2002). Contending with group image: The psychology of stereotype and social identity threat. In M. P. Zanna (Eds.), *Advances in experimental social psychology* (Vol. 34, pp. 379–440). San Diego, CA: Academic Press.

Stephan, C. W., Stephan, W. G., Demitrakis, K. M., Yamada, A. M., & Clason, D. L. (2000). Women's attitudes toward men: An integrated threat theory approach. *Psychology of Women Quarterly, 24,* 63–73.

Stephan, W. G., Berscheid, E., & Walster, E. (1971). Sexual arousal and heterosexual perception. *Journal of Personality and Social Psychology, 20,* 93–101.

Stephan, W. G., Boniecki, K. A., Ybarra, O., Bettencourt, A., Ervin, K. S., Jackson, L. A., et al. (2002). The role of threats in the racial attitudes of Blacks and Whites. *Personality and Social Psychology Bulletin, 28,* 1242–1254.

Stephan, W. G., Diaz-Loving, R., & Duran, A. (2000). Integrated threat theory and intercultural attitudes: Mexico and the United States. *Journal of Cross Cultural Psychology, 31,* 240–249.

Stephan, W. G., & Finlay, K. A. (1999). The role of empathy in improving intergroup relations. *Journal of Social Issues, 55,* 729–743.

Stephan, W. G., & Renfro, C. L. (2002). The role of threat in intergroup relations. In D. M. Mackie & E. R. Smith (Eds.), *From prejudice to intergroup emotions* (pp. 1191–1207). New York: Psychology Press.

Stephan, W. G., & Stephan, C. W. (2000). An integrated threat theory of prejudice. In S. Oskamp (Ed.), *Reducing prejudice and discrimination* (pp. 23–45). Mahwah, NJ: Erlbaum.

Stephan, W. G., Renfro, C. L., Esses, V. M., Stephan, C. W., & Martin, T. (2005). The effects of feeling threatened on attitudes toward immigrants. *International Journal of Intercultural Relations, 29,* 1–19.

Stephan, W. G., Ybarra, O., & Bachman, G. (1999). Prejudice toward immigrants. *Journal of Applied Social Psychology, 29,* 2221–2237.

Stephan, W. G., Ybarra, O., Martinez, C. M., Schwarzwald, J., & Tur-Kaspa, M. (1998). Prejudice toward immigrants to Spain and Israel: An integrated threat theory analysis. *Journal of Cross Cultural Psychology, 29,* 559–576.

Stevens, L. E., & Fiske, S. T. (2000). Motivated impressions of a powerholder: Accuracy under task dependency and misperception under evaluation dependency. *Personality and Social Psychology Bulletin, 26,* 907–922.

Stiff, J. B. (1986). Cognitive processing of persuasive message cues: A meta-analytic review of the effects of supporting information on attitudes. *Communication Monographs, 53,* 75–89.

Stiff, J. B., & Boster, F. J. (1987). Cognitive processing: Additional thoughts and a reply to Petty, Kasmer, Haugtvedt, and Cacioppo. *Communication Monographs, 54,* 250–256.

Stone, J., Lynch, C. I., Sjomeling, M., & Darley, J. M. (1999). Stereotype threat effects on Black and White athletic performance. *Journal of Personality and Social Psychology, 77,* 1213–1227.

Stoner, J. A. F. (1961). *A comparison of individual and group decisions involving risk.* Unpublished master's thesis, School of Industrial Management, MIT.

Storms, M. D., & Nisbett, R. E. (1970). Insomnia and the attribution process. *Journal of Personality and Social Psychology, 16,* 319–328.

Story, A. L. (1998). Self-esteem and memory for favorable and unfavorable personality feedback. *Personality and Social Psychology Bulletin, 24,* 51–64.

Stouffer, S. A., Suchman, E. A., DeVinney, L. C., Star, S. A., & Williams, R. M., Jr. (1949). *The American soldier: Vol. 1. Adjustment during army life.* Princeton, NJ: Princeton University

Strack, F., Erber, R., & Wicklund, R. A. (1982). Effects of salience and time pressure on ratings of social causality. *Journal of Experimental Social Psychology, 18,* 581–594.

Strack, F., Martin, L. L., & Schwarz, N. (1988). Priming and communication: Social determinants of information use in judgments of life satisfaction. *European Journal of Social Psychology, 18,* 429–442.

Strack, F., Martin, L. L., & Stepper, S. (1988). Inhibiting and facilitating conditions of the human smile: A nonobtrusive test of the facial feedback hypothesis. *Journal of Personality and Social Psychology, 54,* 768–777.

Strack, F., & Mussweiler, T. (1997). Explaining the enigmatic anchoring effect: Mechanisms of selective accessibility. *Journal of Personality and Social Psychology, 73,* 437–446.

Strauman, T. J. (1996). Stability within the self: A longitudinal study of the structural implications of self-discrepancy theory. *Journal of Personality and Social Psychology, 71,* 1142–1153.

Strauman, T. J., & Higgins, E. T. (1987). Automatic activation of self-discrepancies and emotional syndromes: When cognitive structures influence affect. *Journal of Personality and Social Psychology, 53,* 1004–1014.

Strenta, A. C., & Kleck, R. E. (1984). Physical disability and the perception of social interaction: It's not what you look at but how you look at it. *Personality and Social Psychology Bulletin, 10,* 279–288.

Stuss, D. T., & Levine, B. (2002). Adult clinical neuropsychology: Lessons from studies of the frontal lobes. *Annual Review of Psychology, 53,* 401–433.

Suh, E. (2002). Culture, identity consistency, and subjective well-being. *Journal of Personality and Social Psychology, 83,* 1378–1391.

Sujan, M. (1985). Consumer knowledge: Effects on evaluation strategies mediating consumer judgments. *Journal of Consumer Research, 12,* 1–16.

Suls, J. M., Lemos, K., & Stewart, H. L. (2002). Self-esteem, construal, and comparisons with the self, friends, and peers. *Journal of Personality and Social Psychology, 82,* 252–261.

Suls, J. M., & Wan, C. K. (1987). In search of the false-uniqueness phenomenon: Fear and estimates of social consensus. *Journal of Personality and Social Psychology, 52,* 211–217.

Swann, W. B., Jr. (1983). Self-verification: Bringing social reality into harmony with the self. In J. M. Suls & A. G. Greenwald (Eds.), *Social psychology perspectives* (Vol. 2, pp. 33–66). Hillsdale, NJ: Erlbaum.

Swann, W. B., Jr. (1984). Quest for accuracy in person perception: A matter of pragmatics. *Psychological Review, 91,* 457–477.

Swann, W. B., Jr., & Ely, R. M. (1984). The battle of wills: Self-verification versus behavioral confirmation. *Journal of Personality and Social Psychology, 46,* 1287–1302.

Swann, W. B., Jr., & Giuliano, T. (1987). Confirmatory search strategies in social interaction: How, when, why, and with what consequences. *Journal of Consulting and Clinical Psychology, 5,* 511–524.

Swann, W. B. Jr., Giuliano, T., & Wegner, D. M. (1982). Where leading questions can lead: The power of conjecture in social interaction. *Journal of Personality and Social Psychology, 42,* 1025–1035.

Swann, W. B., Jr., Hixon, J. G., Stein-Seroussi, A., & Gilbert, D. T. (1990). The fleeting gleam of praise: Conitive processes underlying behavioral reactions to self-relevant feedback. *Journal of Personality and Social Psychology, 59,* 17–26.

Swann, W. B., Jr., Pelham, B. W., & Chidester, T. R. (1988). Change through paradox: Using self-verification to alter beliefs. *Journal of Personality and Social Psychology, 54,* 268–273.

Swann, W. B., Jr., Pelham, B. W., & Krull, D. S. (1989). Agreeable fancy or disagreeable truth? Reconciling self-enhancement and self-verification. *Journal of Personality and Social Psychology, 57*, 782–791.

Swann, W. B., Jr., & Read, S. J. (1981). Self-verification processes: How we sustain our self-conceptions. *Journal of Experimental Social Psychology, 17*, 351–370.

Swann, W. B., Jr., & Snyder, M. (1980). On translating beliefs into action: Theories of ability and their application in an instructional setting. *Journal of Personality and Social Psychology, 38*, 879–888.

Swann, W. B., Jr., Stein-Seroussi, A., & Giesler, R. B. (1992). Why people self-verify. *Journal of Personality and Social Psychology, 62*, 392–401.

Swim, J. K., & Hyers, L. L. (1999). Excuse me—What did you say?!: Women's public and private responses to sexist remarks. *Journal of Experimental Social Psychology, 79*, 238–250.

Swim, J. K., Hyers, L. L., Cohen, L. L., & Ferguson, M. J. (2001). Everyday sexism: Evidence for its incidence, nature, and psychological impact from three daily diary studies. *Journal of Experimental Social Psychology, 35*, 68–88.

Swim, J. K., & Miller, D. L. (1999). White guilt: Its antecedents and consequences for attitudes toward affirmative action. *Personality and Social Psychology Bulletin, 25*, 500–514.

Swim, J. K., Pearson, N. B., & Johnston, K. E. (2006). Daily encounters with heterosexism: A week in the life of lesbian, gay, and bisexual individuals. *Journal of Homosexuality.*

Swim, J. K., Scott, E. D., Sechrist, G. B., Campbell, B., & Stangor, C. (2003). The role of intent and harm in judgments of prejudice and discrimination. *Journal of Personality and Social Psychology, 84*, 944–959.

Swim, J. K., & Sanna, L. J. (1996). He's skilled, she's lucky: A meta-analysis of observer's attributions of women's and men's successes and failures. *Personality and Social Psychology Bulletin, 22*, 507–519.

Tabachnik, N., Crocker, J., & Alloy, L. B. (1983). Depression, social comparison, and the false consensus effect. *Journal of Personality and Social Psychology, 45*, 688–699.

Taguiri, R., & Petrullo, L. (Eds.).(1958). *Person perception and interpersonal behavior.* Palo Alto, CA: Stanford University Press.

Tajfel, H. (1981). *Human groups and social categories: Studies in social psychology.* Cambridge, MA: Cambridge University Press.

Tajfel, H., Billig, M., Bundy, R. P., & Flament, C. (1971). Social categorization and intergroup behaviour. *European Journal of Social Psychology, 1*, 149–177.

Tajfel, H., & Turner, J. C. (1979). An integrative theory of intergroup conflict. In W. G. Austin & S. Worchel (Eds.), *The social psychology of intergroup relations.* Monterey, CA: Brooks/Cole.

Takata, T. (1987). Self-deprecative tendencies in self-evaluation through social comparison. *Japanese Journal of Experimental Social Psychology, 27*, 27–36.

Talaska, C. A., Fiske, S. T., & Chaiken, S. (in press). Legitimating racial discrimination: A meta-analysis of the racial attitude-behavior literature shows that emotions, not beliefs, best predict discrimination. *Social Justice Research.*

Tanaka, J. W., & Farah, M. J. (1993). Parts and wholes in face recognition. *Quarterly Journal of Experimental Psychology: Human Experimental Psychology, 42*, 225–245.

Tangney, J. P., Stuewig, J., & Mashek, D. (2007). Moral emotions and moral behavior. *Annual Review of Psychology, 58*, 345–372.

Taylor, K. M., & Shepperd, J. A. (1998). Bracing for the worst: Severity, testing, and feedback timing as moderators of the optimistic bias. *Personality and Social Psychology Bulletin, 24*, 915–926.

Taylor, S. E. (1975). On inferring one's own attitudes from one's behavior: Some delimiting conditions. *Journal of Personality and Social Psychology, 31*, 126–131.

Taylor, S. E. (1981a). A categorization approach to stereotyping. In D. L. Hamilton (Ed.), *Cognitive processes in stereotyping and intergroup behavior* (pp. 88–114). Hillsdale, NJ: Erlbaum.

Taylor, S. E. (1981b). The interface of cognitive and social psychology. In J. Harvey (Ed.), *Cognition, social behavior, and the environment* (pp. 189–211). Hillsdale, NJ: Erlbaum.

Taylor, S. E. (1982). The availability bias in social psychology. In D. Kahneman & A. Tversky (Eds.). *Judgment under uncertainty: Heuristics and biases.* New York: Cambridge University Press.

Taylor, S. E. (1991). Asymmetrical effects of positive and negative events: The mobilization-minimization hypothesis. *Psychological Bulletin, 110,* 67–85.

Taylor, S. E. (1998). The social being in social psychology. In D. T. Gilbert, S. T. Fiske, & G. Lindzey (Eds.), *The handbook of social psychology* (4th ed., Vol. 1, pp. 58–95). New York: McGraw-Hill.

Taylor, S. E. (2006a). *Health psychology* (6th ed.). New York: McGraw-Hill.

Taylor, S. E. (2006b). Tend and befriend: Biobehavioral bases of affiliation under stress. *Current Directions in Psychological Science, 15,* 273–277.

Taylor, S. E., & Brown, J. (1988). Illusion and well-being: A social psychological perspective on mental health. *Psychological Bulletin, 103,* 193–210.

Taylor, S. E., & Crocker, J. (1981). Schematic bases of social information processing. In E. T. Higgins, C. P. Herman, & M. P. Zanna (Eds.), *Social cognition: The Ontario Symposium* (Vol. 1, pp. 89–134). Hillsdale, NJ: Erlbaum.

Taylor, S. E., Crocker, J., Fiske, S. T., Sprinzen, M., & Winkler, J. D. (1979). The generalizability of salience effects. *Journal of Personality and Social Psychology, 37,* 357–368.

Taylor, S. E., Eisenberger, N. I., Saxbe, D., Lehman, B. J., & Lieberman, M. D. (2006). Neural responses to emotional stimuli are associated with childhood family stress. *Biological Psychiatry, 60,* 296–301.

Taylor, S. E., & Fiske, S. T. (1975). Point-of-view and perceptions of causality. *Journal of Personality and Social Psychology, 32,* 439–445.

Taylor, S. E., & Fiske, S. T. (1978). Salience, attention, and attribution: Top of the head phenomena. In L. Berkowitz (Ed.), *Advances in experimental social psychology* (Vol. 11, pp. 249–288). New York: Academic Press.

Taylor, S. E., & Fiske, S. T. (1981). Getting inside the head: Methodologies for process analysis in attribution and social cognition. In J. H. Harvey, W. Ickes, & R. F. Kidd (Eds.), *New directions in attribution research* (Vol. 3, pp. 459–524). Hillsdale, NJ: Erlbaum.

Taylor, S. E., Fiske, S. T., Close, M., Anderson, C., & Ruderman, A. J. (1977). *Solo status as a psychological variable: The power of being distinctive.* Unpublished manuscript, Harvard University.

Taylor, S. E., Fiske, S. T., Etcoff, N. L., & Ruderman, A. J. (1978). Categorical and contextual bases of person memory and stereotyping. *Journal of Personality and Social Psychology, 36,* 778–793.

Taylor, S. E., & Gollwitzer, P. M. (1995). The effects of mindset on positive illusions. *Journal of Personality and Social Psychology, 69,* 213–226.

Taylor, S. E., Kemeny, M. E., Reed, G. M., Bower, J. E., & Gruenewald, T. L. (2000). Psychological resources, positive illusions, and health. *American Psychologist, 55,* 99–109.

Taylor, S. E., Lerner, J. S., Sherman, D. K., Sage, R. M., & McDowell, N. K. (2003a). Are self-enhancing cognitions associated with healthy or unhealthy biological profiles? *Journal of Personality and Social Psychology, 85,* 605–615.

Taylor, S. E., Lerner, J. S., Sherman, D. K., Sage, R. M., & McDowell, N. K. (2003b). Portrait of the self-enhancer: Well-adjusted and well-liked or maladjusted and friendless? *Journal of Personality and Social Psychology, 84,* 165–176.

Taylor, S. E., Lichtman, R. R., & Wood, J. V. (1984). Attributions, beliefs about control, and adjustment to breast cancer. *Journal of Personality and Social Psychology, 46,* 489–502.

Taylor, S. E., & Lobel, M. (1989). Social comparison activity under threat: Downward evaluation and upward contacts. *Psychological Review, 96,* 569–575.

Taylor, S. E., Pham, L. B., Rivkin, I., & Armor, D. A. (1998). Harnessing the imagination: Mental simulation and self-regulation of behavior. *American Psychologist, 53,* 429–439.

Taylor, S. E., & Thompson, S. C. (1982). Stalking the elusive "vividness" effect. *Psychological Review, 89,* 155–181.

Taylor, S. E., & Wood, J. V. (1983). The vividness effect: Making a mountain out of a molehill? In R. P. Bagozzi & A. M. Tybout (Eds.), *Advances in consumer research.* Ann Arbor: Association for Consumer Research.

Taylor, S. E., Wood, J. V., & Lichtman, R. R. (1983). It could be worse: Selective evaluation as a response to victimization. *Journal of Social Issues, 39,* 19–40.

Teasdale, J. D., & Russell, M. L. (1983). Differential effects of induced mood on the recall of positive, negative and neutral words. *British Journal of Clinical Psychology, 22,* 163–171.

Teger, A. I., & Pruitt, D. G. (1967). Comparison of group risk taking. *Journal of Experimental Social Psychology, 3,* 189–205.

Tesser, A. (1978). Self-generated attitude change. In L. Berkowitz (Ed.), *Advances in experimental social psychology* (Vol. 11, pp. 289–338). New York: Academic Press.

Tesser, A. (1988). Toward a self-evaluation maintenance model of social behavior. In L. Berkowitz (Ed.), *Advances in experimental social psychology* (Vol. 21, pp. 181–227). New York: Academic Press.

Tesser, A., Crepaz, N., Collins, S. R., Cornell, D., & Beach, J. C. (2000). Confluence of self-esteem regulation mechanisms: On integrating the self-zoo. *Personality and Social Psychology Bulletin, 57,* 442–456.

Tetlock, P. E. (1984). Cognitive style and political belief systems in the British House of Commons. *Journal of Personality and Social Psychology, 46,* 365–375.

Tetlock, P. E. (1985). Accountability: A social check on the fundamental attribution error. *Social Psychology Quarterly, 48,* 227–236.

Tetlock, P. E. (1986). Is self-categorization theory the solution to the level-of-analysis problem? *British Journal of Social Psychology, 25,* 255–256.

Tetlock, P. E. (1988). Monitoring the integrative complexity of American and Soviet policy rhetoric: What can be learned? *Journal of Social Issues, 44,* 101–132.

Tetlock, P. E. (1990). Some thoughts on fourth generational models of social cognition. *Psychological Inquiry, 1,* 212–214.

Tetlock, P. E. (1992). The impact of accountability on judgment and choice. In M. P. Zanna (Ed.), *Advances in experimental social psychology* (Vol. 23, pp. 331–376). New York: Academic Press.

Tetlock, P. E. (1998). Close-call counterfactuals and belief-system defenses: I was not almost wrong but I was almost right. *Journal of Personality and Social Psychology, 75,* 639–652.

Tetlock, P. E., & Boettger, R. (1989). Accountability: A social magnifier of the dilution effect. *Journal of Personality and Social Psychology, 57,* 388–398.

Tetlock, P. E., Hannum, K. A., & Micheletti, P. M. (1984). Stability and change in the complexity of senatorial debate: Testing the cognitive versus rhetorical style hypotheses. *Journal of Personality and Social Psychology, 46,* 979–990.

Thibaut, J. W., & Kelley, H. H. (1959). *The social psychology of groups.* New York: Wiley.

Thompson, W., Cowan, C., & Rosenhan, D. L. (1980). Focus of attention mediates the impact of negative affect on altruism. *Journal of Personality and Social Psychology, 38,* 291–300.

Thorndike, E. L. (1940). *Human nature and the social order.* New York: Macmillan.

Thurstone, L. L. (1928). An experimental study of nationality preferences. *Journal of General Psychology, 1,* 405–425.

Tiedens, L. Z. (2001). The effect of anger on the hostile inferences of aggressive and nonaggressive people: Specific emotions, cognitive processing, and chronic accessibility. *Motivation and Emotion, 25,* 233–251.

Tiedens, L. Z., Ellsworth, P. C., & Mesquita, B. (2000). Stereotypes about sentiments and status: Emotional expectations for high- and low-status group members. *Personality and Social Psychology Bulletin, 26,* 560–574.

Tiedens, L. Z., & Jimenez, M. C. (2003). Assimilation for affiliation and contrast for control: Complementary self-construals. *Journal of Personality and Social Pscyhology, 85,* 1049–1061.

Tiedens, L. Z., & Linton, S. (2001). Judgment under emotional certainty and uncertainty: The effects of specific emotions on information processing. *Journal of Personality and Social Psychology, 81,* 973–988.

Todorov, A., Gobbini, M. I., Evans, K. K, & Haxby, J. V. (2007). Spontaneous retrieval of affective person knowledge in face perception. *Neuropsychologia, 445,* 163–173.

Todorov, A., Mandisodza, A. N., Goren, A., & Hall, C. (2005). Inferences of competence from faces predict election outcomes. *Science, 308,* 1623–1626.

Todorov, A., & Uleman, J. S. (2002). Spontaneous trait inferences are bound to actors' faces: Evidence from a false recognition paradigm. *Journal of Personality and Social Psychology, 83,* 1051–1065.

Todorov, A., & Uleman, J. S. (2003). The efficiency of binding spontaneous trait inferences to actors' faces. *Journal of Experimental Social Psychology, 39,* 549–562.

Todorov, A., & Uleman, J. S. (2004). The person reference process in spontaneous trait inferences. *Journal of Personality and Social Psychology, 87,* 482–493.

Tomkins, S. S. (1962). *Affect, imagery, and consciousness* (Vol. 1). New York: Springer.

Tomkins, S. S. (1981). The role of facial response in the experience of emotion: A reply to Tourangeau and Ellsworth. *Journal of Personality and Social Psychology, 40,* 355–357.

Tordesillas, R. S., & Chaiken, S. (1999). Thinking too much or too little? The effects of introspection on the decision-making process. *Personality and Social Psychology Bulletin, 25,* 623–629.

Tormala, Z. L., & Petty, R. E. (2001). On-line versus memory-based processing: The role of "need to evaluate" in person perception. *Personality and Social Psychology Bulletin, 27,* 1599–1612.

Tormala, Z. L., Petty, R. E., & Brinol, P. (2002). Ease of retrieval effects in persuasion: A self-validation analysis. *Personality and Social Psychology Bulletin, 28,* 1700–1712.

Tourangeau, R., & Ellsworth, P. C. (1979). The role of facial response in the experience of emotion. *Journal of Personality and Social Psychology, 37,* 1519–1531.

Tourangeau, R., Rasinski, K. A., Bradburn, N. M., & D'Andrade, R. (1989). Belief accessibility and context effects in attitude measurement. *Journal of Experimental Social Psychology, 25,* 401–421.

Towles-Schwen, T., & Fazio, R. H. (2001). On the origins of racial attitudes: Correlates of childhood experiences. *Personality and Social Psychology Bulletin, 27,* 162–175.

Towles-Schwen, T., & Fazio, R. H. (2003). Choosing social situations: The relation between automatically activated racial attitudes and anticipated comfort interacting with African Americans. *Personality and Social Psychology Bulletin, 29,* 170–182.

Traut-Mattausch, E., Schulz-Hardt, S., Greitemeyer, T., & Frey, D. (2004). Expectancy confirmation in spite of disconfirming evidence: The case of price increases due to the introduction of the Euro. *European Journal of Social Psychology, 34,* 739–760.

Triandis, H. C., McCusker, C., & Hui, C. (1990). Multimethod probes of individualism and collectivism. *Journal of Personality and Social Psychology, 59,* 1006–1020.

Trivers, R. L. (1985). *Social evolution.* Menlo Park, CA: Benjamin/Cummings.

Trope, Y. (1975). Seeking information about one's own ability as a determinant of choice among tasks. *Journal of Personality and Social Psychology, 32,* 1004–1013.

Trope, Y. (1979). Uncertainty-reducing properties of achievement tasks. *Journal of Personality and Social Psychology, 37,* 1505–1518.

Trope, Y. (1983). Self-assessment in achievement behavior. In J. M. Suls & A. G. Carver (Eds.), *Psychological perspectives on the self* (Vol. 2, pp. 93–122). Hillsdale, NJ: Erlbaum.

Trope, Y. (1986). Identification and inferential processes in dispositional attribution. *Psychological Review, 93,* 239–257.

Trope, Y., & Bassok, M. (1982). Confirmatory and diagnosing strategies in social information gathering. *Journal of Personality and Social Psychology, 43,* 22–34.

Trope, Y., Cohen, O., & Maoz, Y. (1988). The perceptual and inferential effects of situational inducements on dispositional attributions. *Journal of Personality and Social Psychology, 55,* 165–177.

Trope, Y., & Fishbach, A. (2000). Counteractive self-control in overcoming temptation. *Journal of Personality and Social Psychology, 79,* 493–506.

Trope, Y., & Gaunt, R. (1999). A dual-process model of overconfident attributional inferences. In S. Chaiken & Y. Trope (Eds.), *Dual-process theories in social psychology* (pp. 161–178). New York: Guilford Press.

Trope, Y., & Liberman, N. (2003). Temporal construal. *Psychological Review, 110,* 403–421.

Trope, Y., & Mackie, D. M. (1987). Sensitivity to alternatives in social hypothesis-testing. *Journal of Experimental Social Psychology, 23,* 445–459.

Trope, Y., & Neter, E. (1994). Reconciling competing motives in self-evaluation: The role of self-control in feedback setting. *Journal of Personality and Social Psychology, 66,* 646–657.

Tropp, L. R. (2003). The psychological impact of prejudice: Implications for intergroup contact. *Group Processes and Intergroup Relations, 6,* 131–149.

Tropp, L. R. (2006). Stigma and intergroup contact among members of minority and majority status groups. In S. Levin & C. van Laar (Eds.), *Stigma and group inequality: Social psychological perspectives* (pp. 171–191). Mahwah, NJ: Erlbaum.

Tropp, L. R., & Bianchi, R. A. (2006). Valuing diversity and interest in intergroup contact. *Journal of Social Issues, 62*, 533–551.

Tropp, L. R., & Pettigrew, T. F. (2005a). Differential relationships between intergroup contact and affective and cognitive dimensions of prejudice. *Personality and Social Psychology Bulletin, 31*, 1145–1158. [Erratum: *31*, 1456.]

Tropp, L. R., & Pettigrew, T. F. (2005b). Relationships between intergroup contact and prejudice among minority and majority status groups. *Psychological Science, 16*, 951–957.

Tropp, L. R., Stout, A. M., Boatswain, C., Wright, S. C., & Pettigrew, T. F. (2006). Trust and acceptance in response to references to group membership: Minority and majority perspectives on cross-group interactions. *Journal of Applied Social Psychology, 36*, 769–794.

Trzebinski, J. (1985). Action-oriented representations of implicit personality theories. *Journal of Personality and Social Psychology, 48*, 1266–1278.

Trzebinski, J., & Richards, K. (1986). The role of goal categories in person impression. *Journal of Experimental Social Psychology, 22*, 216–227.

Tsujimoto, R. N. (1978). Memory bias toward normative and novel trait prototypes. *Journal of Personality and Social Psychology, 36*, 1391–1401.

Tuckman, J., & Lavell, M. (1957). Self classification as old or not old. *Geriatrics, 12*, 666–671.

Tulving, E. (1983). *Elements of episodic memory.* New York: Oxford University Press.

Tulving, E. (2002). Episodic memory: From mind to brain. *Annual Review of Psychology, 53*, 1–25.

Tulving, E., & Pearlstone, Z. (1966). Availability versus accessibility of information in memory for words. *Journal of Verbal Learning and Verbal Behavior, 5*, 381–391.

Turk, D. C., & Salovey, P. (1986). Clinical information processing: Bias innoculation. In R. E. Ingram (Ed.), *Information processing approaches to clinical psychology* (pp. 305–323). New York: Academic Press.

Turk, D. J., Heatherton, T. F., Kelley, W. M., Funnell, M. G., Gazzaniga, M. S., & Macrae, C. N. (2002). Mike or me? Self-recognition in a split-brain patient. *Nature Neuroscience, 5*, 841–842.

Turk, D. J., Heatherton, T. F., Macrae, C. N., Kelley, W. M., & Gazzaniga, M. S. (2003). Out of contact, out of mind: The distributed nature of the self. *Annals of New York Academy of Sciences, 1001*, 65–78.

Turnbull, W., & Slugoski, B. R. (1988). Conversational and linguistic processes in causal attribution. In D. J. Hilton (Ed.), *Contemporary science and natural explanation: Commonsense conceptions of causality* (pp. 66–93). Brighton, England: Harvester Press.

Turner, J. C. (1985). Social categorization and the self-concept: A social cognitive theory of group behavior. In E. J. Lawler (Ed.), *Advances in group processes* (Vol. 2, pp. 77–121). Greenwich, CT: JAI Press.

Turner, J. C. (1987). *Rediscovering the social group: A self-categorization theory.* New York: Basil Blackwell.

Turner, J. C. (1991). *Social influence.* Pacific Grove, CA: Brooks/Cole.

Turner, J. C., & Reynolds, K. J. (2001). The social identity perspective in intergroup relations: Theories, themes, and controversies. In R. Brown & S. L. Gaertner (Eds.), *Blackwell handbook of social psychology: Intergroup processes* (pp. 133–152). London: Blackwell.

Turner, J. C., Wetherell, M. S., & Hogg, M. A. (1989). Referent informational influence and group polarization. *British Journal of Social Psychology, 28*, 135–147.

Tversky, A., & Kahneman, D. (1973). Availability: A heuristic for judging frequency and probability. *Cognitive Psychology, 5*, 207–232.

Tversky, A., & Kahneman, D. (1974). Judgment under uncertainty: Heuristics and biases. *Science, 185*, 1124–1131.

Tversky, A., & Kahneman, D. (1980). Causal schemata in judgments under uncertainty. In M. Fishbein (Ed.), *Progress in social psychology* (pp. 49–72). Hillsdale, NJ: Erlbaum.

Tversky, A., & Kahneman, D. (1981). The framing of decisions and the psychology of choice. *Science, 211*, 453–458.

Tversky, A., & Kahneman, D. (1982). Judgments of and by representativeness. In D. Kahneman, P. Slovic, & A. Tversky (Eds.), *Judgment under uncertainty: Heuristics and biases* (pp. 84–100). New York: Cambridge University Press.

Tversky, A., & Kahneman, D. (1983). Extensional versus intuitive reasoning: The conjunction fallacy in probability judgment. *Psychological Review, 90,* 293–315.

Twenge, J. M., Catanese, K. R., & Baumeister, R. F. (2003). Social exclusion and the deconstructed state: Time perception, meaninglessness, lethargy, lack of emotion, and self-awareness. *Journal of Personality and Social Psychology, 85,* 409–423.

Ucros, C. G. (1989). Mood state-dependent memory: A meta-analysis. *Cognition and Emotion, 3,* 139–169.

Uhlmann, E. L., Brescoll, V. L., & Paluck, E. L. (2006). Are members of low status groups perceived as bad, or badly off? Egalitarian negative associations and automatic prejudice. *Journal of Experimental Social Psychology, 42,* 491–499.

Uleman, J. S. (1989). A framework for thinking intentionally about unintended thoughts. In J. S. Uleman & J. A. Bargh (Eds.), *Unintended thought* (pp. 425–449). New York: Guilford Press.

Uleman, J. S. (1999). Spontaneous versus intentional inferences in impression formation. In S. Chaiken & Y. Trope (Eds.), *Dual-process theories in social psychology* (pp. 141–160). New York: Guilford Press.

United Nations Development Fund for Women. (2005). Overview: Women, work, and poverty. *Progress of World's Women 2005.* Retrieved August 2, 2006, from http://www.unifem.org/attachments/products/PoWW2005_overview_eng.pdf.

United States Department of Labor. (2005, May). Women in the labor force, A databook. Retrieved July 28, 2006, from http://www.bls.gov/cps/wlf-databook2005.htm.

Updegraff, J. A., Gable, S. L., & Taylor, S. E. (2004). What makes experiences satisfying? The interaction of approach-avoidance motivations and emotions in well-being. *Journal of Personality and Social Psychology, 86,* 496–504.

Valdesolo, P., & DeSteno, D. (2006). Manipulations of emotional context shape moral judgment. *Psychological Science, 17,* 476–477.

Valins, S. (1966). Cognitive effects of false heart-rate feedback. *Journal of Personality and Social Psychology, 4,* 400–408.

Vallacher, R. R., Read, S. J., & Nowak, A. (2002). The dynamical perspective in personality and social psychology. *Personality and Social Psychology Review, 6,* 264–273.

Vallacher, R. R., & Wegner, D. M. (1987). What do people think they're doing? Action identification and human behavior. *Psychological Review, 94,* 3–15.

Vallacher, R. R., Wegner, D. M., & Frederick, J. (1987). The presentation of self through action identification. *Social Cognition, 5,* 301–322.

Vallone, R. P., Ross, L. D., & Lepper, M. R. (1985). The hostile media phenomenon: Biased perception and perceptions of media bias in coverage of the Beirut massacre. *Journal of Personality and Social Psychology, 49,* 577–585.

van den Bos, K., Poortvliet, P. M., Maas, M., Miedema, J., & van den Ham, E. J. (2005). An enquiry concerning the principles of cultural norms and values: The impact of uncertainty and mortality salience on reactions to violations and bolstering of cultural worldviews. *Journal of Experimental Social Psychology, 41,* 91–113.

van Knippenberg, A., Dijksterhuis, A., & Vermeulen, D. (1999). Judgment and memory of a criminal act: The effects of stereotypes and cognitive load. *European Journal of Social Psychology, 29,* 191–201.

van Laar, C., Levin, S., Sinclair, S., & Sidanius, J. (2005). The effect of university roommate contact on ethnic attitudes and behavior. *Journal of Experimental Social Psychology, 41,* 329–345.

van Laar, C., Sidanius, J., Rabinowitz, J. L., & Sinclair, S. (1999). The three Rs of academic achievement: Reading, 'riting, and racism. *Personality and Social Psychology Bulletin, 25,* 139–151.

Vanman, E. J., Paul, B. Y., Ito, T. A., & Miller, N. (1997). The modern face of prejudice and structural features that moderate the effect of cooperation on affect. *Journal of Personality and Social Psychology, 73,* 941–959.

Van Overwalle, F. (1998). Causal explanation as constraint satisfaction: A critique and a feed-forward connectionist alternative. *Journal of Personality and Social Psychology, 74,* 312–328.

Van Overwalle, F., & Heylighen, F. (2006). Talking nets: A multiagent connectionist approach to communication and trust between individuals. *Psychological Review, 113,* 606–627.

Van Overwalle, F., & Jordens, K. (2002). An adaptive connectionist model of cognitive dissonance. *Personality and Social Psychology Review, 6,* 204–231.

Van Overalle, F., & Labiouse, C. (2004). A recurrent connectionist model of person impression formation. *Personality and Social Psychology Review, 8,* 28–61.

Van Overwalle, F., & Siebler, F. (2005). A connectionist model of attitude formation and change. *Personality and Social Psychology Review, 9,* 231–274.

Van Overwalle, F., & Van Rooy, D. (2001). How one cause discounts or augments another: A connectionist account of causal competition. *Personality and Social Psychology Bulletin, 27,* 1613–1626.

Van Rooy, D., Van Overwalle, F., Vanhoomissen, T., Labiouse, C., & French, R. (2003). A recurrent connectionist model of group biases. *Psychological Review, 110,* 536–563.

Vartanian, O., & Goel, V. (2004). Neuroanatomical correlates of aesthetic preference for paintings. *Neuroreport, 15,* 893–897.

Verdoux, H., Husky, M., Tournier, M., Sorbara, F., & Swendsen, J. D. (2003). Social environments and daily life occurrence of psychotic symptoms: An experience sampling test in a nonclinical population. *Social Psychiatry and Psychiatric Epidemiology, 38,* 654–661.

Verkuyten, M., & Brug, P. (2004). Multiculturalism and group status: The role of ethnic identification, group essentialism and Protestant ethnic. *European Journal of Social Psychology, 34,* 647–661.

Verplanken, B., & Holland, R. W. (2002). Motivated decision making: Effects of activation and self-centrality of values on choices and behavior. *Journal of Personality and Social Psychology, 82,* 434–447.

Vidmar, N., & Rokeach, M. (1974). Archie Bunker's bigotry: A study in selective perception and exposure. *Journal of Communications, 24,* 36–47.

Vignoles, V. L., Chryssochoou, X., & Breakwell, G. M. (2000). The distinctiveness principle: Identity, meaning, and the bounds of cultural relativity. *Personality and Social Psychology Review, 4,* 337–354.

Vignoles, V. L., Regalia, C., Manzi, C., Golledge, J., & Scabini, E. (2006). Beyond self-esteem: Influence of multiple motives on identity construction. *Journal of Personality and Social Psychology, 90,* 308–333.

Vinokur, A., & Ajzen, I. (1982). Relative importance of prior and immediate events: A causal primacy effect. *Journal of Personality and Social Psychology, 42,* 820–829.

Vinokur, A., Schul, Y., & Caplan, R. D. (1987). Determinants of perceived social support: Interpersonal transactions, personal outlook, and transient affective states. *Journal of Personality and Social Psychology, 53,* 1137–1145.

Visser, P. S., & Krosnick, J. A. (1998). Development of attitude strength over the life cycle: Surge and decline. *Journal of Personality and Social Psychology, 75,* 1389–1410.

Visser, P. S., Krosnick, J. A., & Simmons, J. P. (2003). Distinguishing the cognitive and behavioral consequences of attitude and certainty: A new approach to testing the common-factor hypothesis. *Journal of Experimental Social Psychology, 39,* 118–141.

Vohs, K. D., Baumeister, R. F., & Ciarocco, N. J. (2005). Self-regulation and self-presentation: Regulatory resource depletion impairs impression management and effortful self-presentation depletes regulatory resources. *Journal of Personality and Social Psychology, 88,* 632–657.

Vohs, K. D., & Heatherton, T. F. (2004). Ego threat elicits different social comparison processes among high and low self-esteem people: Implications for interpersonal perceptions. *Social Cognition, 22,* 168–191.

Vohs, K. D., & Schmeichel, B. J. (2003). Self-regulation and the extended now: Controlling the self alters the subjective experience of time. *Journal of Personality and Social Psychology, 85,* 217–230.

Voils, C. I., Ashburn-Nardo, L., & Monteith, M. J. (2002). Evidence of prejudice-related conflict and associated affect beyond the college setting. *Group Processes and Intergroup Relations, 5,* 19–33.

von Hippel, W., von Hippel, C., Conway, L., Preacher, K. J., Schooler, J. W., & Radvansky, G. A. (2005). Coping with stereotype threat: Denial as an impression management strategy. *Journal of Personality and Social Psychology, 89,* 22–35.

Vonk, R. (2002). Self-serving interpretations of flattery: Why ingratiation works. *Journal of Personality and Social Psychology, 82,* 515–526.

Vorauer, J. D. (2005). Miscommunications surrounding efforts to reach out across group boundaries. *Personality and Social Psychology Bulletin, 31,* 1653–1664.

Vorauer, J. D. (2006). An information search model of evaluative concerns in intergroup interaction. *Psychological Review, 113,* 862–886.

Vorauer, J. D., Hunter, A. J., Main, K. J., & Roy, S. A. (2000). Meta-stereotype activation: Evidence from indirect measures for specific evaluative concerns experienced by members of dominant groups in intergroup interaction. *Journal of Personality and Social Psychology, 78,* 690–707.

Vorauer, J. D., & Kumhyr, S. M. (2001). Is this about you or me? Self- versus other-directed judgments and feelings in response to intergroup interaction. *Personality and Social Psychology Bulletin, 27,* 706–719.

Vorauer, J. D., & Turpie, C. A. (2004). Disruptive effects of vigilance on dominant group members' treatment of outgroup members choking versus shining under pressure. *Journal of Personality and Social Psychology, 87,* 384–399.

Wachtler, J., & Counselman, E. (1981). When increasing liking for a communicator decreases opinion change: An attributional analysis of attractiveness. *Journal of Experimental Social Psychology, 17,* 386–395.

Wagner, A. D., Paré-Blagoev, E. J., Clark, J., & Poldrack, R. A. (2001). Recovering meaning: Left prefrontal cortex guides controlled semantic retrieval. *Neuron, 31,* 329–338.

Wallach, M. A., Kogan, N., & Bem, D. J. (1962). Group influence on individual risk taking. *Journal of Abnormal and Social Psychology, 65,* 75–86.

Wallbott, H. G., & Scherer, K. R. (1988). Emotion and economic development: Data and speculations concerning the relationship between economic factors and emotional experience. *European Journal of Social Psychology, 18,* 267–273.

Walster, E. (1971). Passionate love. In B. I. Murstein (Ed.), *Theories of attraction and love.* New York: Springer.

Wänke, M., Schwarz, N., & Bless, H. (1995). The availability heuristic revisited: Experienced ease of retrieval in mundane frequency estimates. *Acta Psychologica, 89,* 83–90.

Ward, W. D., & Jenkins, H. M. (1965). The display of information and the judgment of contingency. *Canadian Journal of Psychology, 19,* 231–241.

Ward, S. E., Leventhal, H., & Love, R. (1988). Repression revisited: Tactics used in coping with a severe health threat. *Personality and Social Psychology Bulletin, 14,* 735–746.

Watson, D., & Clark, L. A. (1997). Measurement and mismeasurement of mood: Recurrent and emergent issues. *Journal of Personality and Assessment, 68,* 267–296.

Watson, D., & Tellegen, A. (1985). Toward a consensual structure of mood. *Psychological Bulletin, 98,* 219–235.

Watson, J. (1930). *Behaviorism.* New York: Norton.

Watson, W. S., & Hartmann, G. W. (1939). The frigidity of a basic attitudinal frame. *Journal of Abnormal and Social Psychology, 34,* 314–335.

Weary, G., Reich, D. A., & Tobin, S. J. (2001). The role of contextual constraints and chronic expectancies on behavior categorizations and dispositional inferences. *Personality and Social Psychology Bulletin, 27,* 62–75.

Weary, G., Swanson, H., Harvey, J. H., & Yarkin, K. L. (1980). A molar approach to social knowing. *Personality and Social Psychology Bulletin, 6,* 574–581.

Webb, W. M., Marsh, K. L., Schneiderman, W., & Davis, B. (1989). Interaction between self-monitoring and manipulated states of awareness. *Journal of Personality and Social Psychology, 56,* 70–80.

Weber, E. U., & Johnson, E. J. (2006). Constructing preferences from memories. In S. Lichtenstein & P. Slovic (Eds.), *The construction of preferences* (pp. 397–410). New York: Cambridge University Press.

Wegener, D. T., & Petty, R. E. (1995). Flexible correction processes in social judgment: The role of naive theories in corrections for perceived bias. *Journal of Personality and Social Psychology, 68,* 36–51.

Wegener, D. T., & Petty, R. E. (1997). The flexible correction model: The role of naive theories of bias in bias corrections. In M. P. Zanna (Ed.), *Advances in experimental social psychology* (pp. 141–208). San Diego, CA: Academic Press.

Wegner, D. M. (1994). Ironic processes of mental control. *Psychological Review, 101*, 34–52.

Wegner, D. M. (2003). The mind's best trick: How we experience conscious will. *Trends in Cognitive Sciences, 7*, 65–69.

Wegner, D. M., & Bargh, J. A. (1998). Control and automaticity in social life. In D. T. Gilbert, S. T. Fiske, & G. Lindzey (Eds.), *The handbook of social psychology* (4th ed., Vol. 2, pp. 446–496). New York: McGraw-Hill.

Wegner, D. M., Schneider, D. J., Carter, S. R., & White, T. L. (1987). Paradoxical effects of thought suppression. *Journal of Personality and Social Psychology, 53*, 5–13.

Wegner, D. M., Vallacher, R. R., Kiersted, G. W., & Dizadji, D. (1986). Action identification in the emergence of social behavior. *Social Cognition, 4*, 18–38.

Wegner, D. M., Vallacher, R. R., Macomber, G., Wood, R., & Arps, K. (1984). The emergence of action. *Journal of Personality and Social Psychology, 46*, 269–279.

Wegner, D. M., Wenzlaff, R., Kerker, R. M., & Beattie, A. E. (1981). Incrimination through innuendo: Can media questions become public answers? *Journal of Personality and Social Psychology, 40*, 822–832.

Wegner, D. M., & Wheatley, T. P. (1999). Apparent mental causation: Sources of the experience of will. *American Psychologist, 54*, 480–492.

Weiner, B. (1979). A theory of motivation for some classroom experiences. *Journal of Educational Psychology, 71*, 3–25.

Weiner, B. (1980). A cognitive (attribution)-emotion-action model of motivated behavior: An analysis of judgment of help-giving. *Journal of Personality and Social Psychology, 39*, 186–200.

Weiner, B. (1982). The emotional consequences of causal attributions. In M. S. Clark & S. T. Fiske (Eds.), *Affect and cognition: The 17th Annual Carnegie Symposium on Cognition* (pp. 185–210). Hillsdale, NJ: Erlbaum.

Weiner, B. (1985). An attributional theory of achievement motivation and emotion. *Psychological Review, 92*, 548–573.

Weiner, B. (1986). *An attributional theory of motivation and emotion.* New York: Springer-Verlag.

Weiner, B. (1987). The social psychology of emotion: Applications of a naive psychology. *Journal of Social and Clinical Psychology, 5*, 405–419.

Weiner, B. (1988). An attributional analysis of changing reactions to persons with AIDS. In R. A. Berk (Ed.), *The social impact of AIDS in the U.S.* (pp. 163–132). Cambridge: Abt Books.

Weiner, B. (2005). Motivation from an attributional perspective and the social psychology of perceived competence. In A. J. Elliot & C. S. Dweck (Eds.), *Handbook of competence and motivation* (pp. 73–84). New York: Guilford Press.

Weiner, B., Amirkhan, J., Folkes, V. S., & Verette, J. A. (1987). An attributional analysis of excuse giving: Studies of a naive theory of emotion. *Journal of Personality and Social Psychology, 52*, 316–324.

Weiner, B., & Handel, S. (1985). Anticipated emotional consequences of causal communications and reported communication strategy. *Developmental Psychology, 21*, 102–107.

Weiner, B., Perry, R. P., & Magnusson, J. (1988). An attributional analysis of reactions to stigmas. *Journal of Personality and Social Psychology, 55*, 738–748.

Weisbuch, M., Mackie, D. M., & Garcia-Marques, T. (2003). Prior source exposure and persuasion: Further evidence for misattributional processes. *Personality and Social Psychology Bulletin, 29*, 691–700.

Wellbourne, J. L. (2001). Changes in impression complexity over time and across situations. *Personality and Social Psychology Bulletin, 27*, 1071–1085.

Wells, G. L., & Gavanski, I. (1989). Mental simulation of causality. *Journal of Personality and Social Psychology, 56*, 161–169.

Wells, R. E., & Iyengar, S. S. (2005). Positive illusions of preference consistency: When remaining eluded by one's preferences yields greater subjective well-being and decision outcomes. *Organizational Behavior and Human Decision Processes, 98*, 66–87.

Wells, G. L., & Petty, R. E. (1980). The effects of overt head movements on persuasion: Compatibility and incompatibility of responses. *Basic and Applied Social Psychology, 1*, 219–230.

Wentura, D., Rothermund, K., & Bak, P. (2000). Automatic vigilance: The attention-grabbing power of approach- and avoidance-related social information. *Journal of Personality and Social Psychology, 78,* 1024–1037.

Wenzlaff, R. M., & Wegner, D. M. (2000). Thought suppression. *Annual Review of Psychology, 51,* 59–91.

Wenzlaff, R. M., Wegner, D. M., & Roper, D. W. (1988). Depression and mental control: The resurgence of unwanted negative thoughts. *Journal of Personality and Social Psychology, 55,* 882–892.

Westen, D. (1988). Transference and information processing. *Clinical Psychology Review, 8,* 161–179.

Whalen, P. J., Rauch, S. L., Etcoff, N. L., McInerney, S. C., Lee, M. B., & Jenike, M. A. (1998). Masked presentations of emotional facial expressions modulate amygdala activity without explicit knowledge. *Journal of Neuroscience, 18,* 411–418.

Wheatley, T., & Haidt, J. (2005). Hypnotic disgust makes moral judgments more severe. *Psychological Science, 16,* 780–784.

Wheeler, M. E., & Fiske, S. T. (2005). Controlling racial prejudice: Social cognitive goals affect amygdala and stereotype activation. *Psychological Science, 16,* 56–63.

Wheeler, S. C., Jarvis, W. B. G., & Petty, R. E. (2001). Think unto others: The self-destructive impact of negative racial stereotypes. *Journal of Experimental Social Psychology, 37,* 173–180.

Wheeler, S. C., & Petty, R. E. (2001). The effects of stereotype activation on behavior: A review of possible mechanisms. *Psychological Bulletin, 127,* 797–826.

White, G. L., Fishbein, S., & Rutstein, J. (1981). Passionate love and misattribution of arousal. *Journal of Personality and Social Psychology, 41,* 56–62.

White, G. L., & Kight, T. D. (1984). Misattribution of arousal and attraction: Effects of salience of explanations for arousal. *Journal of Experimental Social Psychology, 20,* 55–64.

White, G. L., & Shapiro, D. (1987). Don't I know you? Antecedents and social consequences of perceived familiarity. *Journal of Experimental Social Psychology, 23,* 75–92.

Whitley, B. E., Jr., & Frieze, I. H. (1986). Measuring causal attributions for success and failure: A meta-analysis of the effects of question-working style. *Basic and Applied Social Psychology, 7,* 35–51.

Whittlesea, B. W. A. (1987). Preservation of specific experiences in the representation of general knowledge. *Journal of Experimental Psychology: Learning, Memory, and Cognition, 13,* 3–17.

Wickelgren, W. A. (1981). Human learning and memory. *Annual review of psychology, 32,* 21–52.

Wicker, A. W. (1969). Attitudes vs. actions: The relationship of verbal and overt behavioral responses to attitude objects. *Journal of Social Issues, 41,* 41–78.

Wicklund, R. A. (1975). Objective self-awareness. In L. Berkowitz (Ed.), *Advances in experimental social psychology* (Vol. 8, pp. 233–275). New York: Academic Press.

Wicklund, R. A. (1986). Orientation to the environment versus preoccupation with human potential. In R. M. Sorrentino & E. T. Higgins (Eds.), *Handbook of motivation and cognition: Foundations of social behavior* (pp. 64–95). New York: Guilford Press.

Wicklund, R. A., & Braun, O. L. (1987). Incompetence and the concern with human categories. *Journal of Personality and Social Psychology, 53,* 373–382.

Wicklund, R. A., & Brehm, J. W. (1976). *Perspectives on cognitive dissonance.* Hillsdale, NJ: Erlbaum.

Wicklund, R. A., & Frey, D. (1980). Self-awareness theory: When the self makes a difference. In D. M. Wegner & R. R. Vallacher (Eds.), *The self in social psychology* (pp. 31–54). New York: Oxford University Press.

Wilder, D. A. (1978a). Effect of predictability on units of perception and attribution. *Personality and Social Psychology Bulletin, 9,* 281–284.

Wilder, D. A. (1978b). Perceiving persons as a group: Effects on attributions of causality and beliefs. *Social Psychology, 1,* 13–23.

Wilder, D. A. (1986). Social categorization: Implications for creation and reduction of intergroup bias. In L. Berkowitz (Ed.), *Advances in Experimental Social Psychology,* (Vol. 19, pp. 291–355). San Diego, CA: Academic Press.

Wilder, D. A. (1993). The role of anxiety in facilitating stereotypic judgments of outgroup behavior. In D. M. Mackie & D. L. Hamilton (Eds.), *Affect, cognition, and stereotyping: Interactive processes in group perception* (pp. 87–109). San Diego, CA: Academic Press.

Williams, K. D., Cheung, C. K. T., & Choi, W. (2000). Cyberostracism: Effects of being ignored over the Internet. *Journal of Personality and Social Psychology, 79,* 748–762.

Williams, L. N. (2006). *Applying the stereotype content model to intra-racial subgroups: Black people's perceptions about Black people in America.* Unpublished senior thesis, Princeton University.

Willis, J., & Todorov, A. (2006). First impressions: Making up your mind after 100 ms exposure to a face. *Psychological Science, 17,* 592–598.

Wills, T. A. (1981). Downward comparison principles in social psychology. *Psychological Bulletin, 90,* 245–271.

Wilson, A. E., & Ross, M. (2001). From chump to champ: People's appraisals of their earlier and present selves. *Journal of Personality and Social Psychology, 80,* 572–584.

Wilson, M. S., & Liu, J. H. (2003). Social dominance orientation and gender: The moderating role of gender identity. *British Journal of Social Psychology, 42,* 187–198.

Wilson, T. D., Dunn, D. S., Kraft, D., & Lisle, D. J. (1989). Introspection, attitude change, and attitude-behavior consistency: The disruptive effects of explaining why we feel the way we do. In L. Berkowitz (Ed.), *Advances in experimental social psychology* (Vol. 22, pp. 287–344). New York: Academic Press.

Wilson, T. D., & Gilbert, D. T. (2005). Affective forecasting: Knowing what to want. *Current Directions in Psychological Science, 14,* 131–134.

Wilson, T. D., & Hodges, S. D. (1992). Attitudes as temporary constructions. In L. L. Martin & A. Tesser (Eds.), *The construction of social judgments* (pp. 37–65). Hillsdale, NJ: Erlbaum.

Wilson, T. D., Hodges, S. D., & LaFleur, S. J. (1995). Effects of introspecting about reasons: Inferring attitudes from accessible thoughts. *Journal of Personality and Social Psychology, 69,* 16–28.

Wilson, T. D., Hull, J. G., & Johnson, J. (1981). Awareness and self-perception: Verbal reports on internal states. *Journal of Personality and Social Psychology, 40,* 53–70.

Wilson, T. D., Kraft, D., & Dunn, D. S. (1989). The disruptive effects of explaining attitudes: The moderating effect of knowledge about the attitude object. *Journal of Experimental Social Psychology, 25,* 379–400.

Wilson, T. D., & LaFleur, S. J. (1995). Knowing what you'll do: Effects of analyzing reasons on self-prediction. *Journal of Personality and Social Psychology, 68,* 21–35.

Wilson, T. D., Lindsey, S., & Schooler, T. Y. (2000). A model of dual attitudes. *Psychological Review, 107,* 101–126.

Wilson, T. D., Meyers, J., & Gilbert, D. T. (2001). Lessons from the past: Do people learn from experience that emotional reactions are short-lived? *Personality and Social Psychology Bulletin, 27,* 1648–1661.

Wilson, T. D., Meyers, J., & Gilbert, D. T. (2003). "How happy was I, anyway?": A retrospective impact bias. *Social Cognition, 21,* 421–446.

Wilson, T. D., & Nisbett, R. E. (1978). The accuracy of verbal reports about the effects of stimuli on evaluations and behavior. *Social Psychology, 41,* 118–131.

Wilson, T. D., Wheatley, T., Meyers, J. M., Gilbert, D. T., & Axsom, D. (2000). Focalism: A source of durability bias in affective forecasting. *Journal of Personality and Social Psychology, 78,* 821–836.

Wilson, W. R. (1979). Feeling more than we can know: Exposure effects without learning. *Journal of Personality and Social Psychology, 37,* 811–821.

Wilson, W. R., & Miller, H. (1968). Repetition, order of presentation, and timing of arguments and measures as determinants of opinion change. *Journal of Personality and Social Psychology, 9,* 184–188.

Winkielman, P., & Cacioppo, J. T. (2001). Mind at ease puts a smile on the face: Psychophysiological evidence that processing facilitation elicits positive affect. *Journal of Personality and Social Psychology, 81,* 989–1000.

Winston, J. S., Strange, B. A., O'Doherty, J., & Dolan, R. J. (2002). Automatic and intentional brain responses during evaluation of trustworthiness of faces. *Nature Neuroscience, 5,* 277–283.

Winter, L., & Uleman, J. S. (1984). When are social judgments made? Evidence for the spontaneousness of trait inferences. *Journal of Personality and Social Psychology, 47,* 237–252.

Winter, L., Uleman, J. S., & Cunniff, C. (1985). How automatic are social judgments? *Journal of Personality and Social Psychology, 49,* 904–917.

Winton, W. M. (1986). The role of facial response in self-reports of emotion: A critique of Laird. *Journal of Personality and Social Psychology, 37,* 1519–1531.

Winton, W. M., Putnam, L. E., & Krauss, R. M. (1984). Facial and autonomic manifestations of the dimensional structure of emotion. *Journal of Experimental Social Psychology, 20,* 195–216.

Wittenbrink, B., Gist, P. L., & Hilton, J. L. (1997). Structural properties of stereotypic knowledge and their influences on the construal of social situations. *Journal of Personality and Social Psychology, 72,* 526–543.

Wittenbrink, B., Judd, C. M., & Park, B. (1997). Evidence for racial prejudice at the implicit level and its relationship with questionnaire measures. *Journal of Personality and Social Psychology, 72,* 262–274.

Wittenbrink, B., Judd, C. M., & Park, B. (2001a). Evaluative versus conceptual judgments in automatic stereotyping and prejudice. *Journal of Experimental Social Psychology, 37,* 244–252.

Wittenbrink, B., Judd, C. M., & Park, B. (2001b). Spontaneous prejudice in context: Variability in automatically activated attitudes. *Journal of Personality and Social Psychology, 81,* 815–827.

Wittgenstein, L. (1953). *Philosophical investigations.* New York: Macmillan.

Wixon, D. R., & Laird, J. D. (1976). Awareness and attitude change in the forced-compliance paradigm: The importance of when. *Journal of Personality and Social Psychology, 34,* 376–384.

Woike, B., Gershkovich, I., Piorkowski, R., & Polo, M. (1999). The role of motives in the content and structure of autobiographical memory. *Journal of Personality and Social Psychology, 76,* 600–612.

Wojciszke, B. (1997). Parallels between competence- versus morality-related traits and individualistic versus collectivistic values. *European Journal of Social Psychology, 27,* 245–256.

Wojciszke, B. (2005). Affective concomitants of information on morality and competence. *European Psychologist, 10,* 60–70.

Wolman, C., & Frank, H. (1975). The solo woman in a professional peer group. *American Journal of Orthopsychiatry, 45,* 164–171.

Wolsko, C., Park, B., Judd, C. M., & Wittenbrink, B. (2000). Framing interethnic ideology: Effects of multicultural and color-blind perspectives on judgments of groups and individuals. *Journal of Personality and Social Psychology, 78,* 635–654.

Wong, M. D., Shapiro, M. F. , Boscardin, W. J., & Ettner, S. L. (2002). Contribution of major diseases to disparities in mortality. *New England Journal of Medicine, 347,* 1585–1592.

Wong, P. T. P., & Weiner, B. (1981). When people ask "why" questions, and the heuristics of attributional search. *Journal of Personality and Social Psychology, 40,* 650–663.

Wood, J. V. (1989). Theory and research concerning social comparisons of personal attributes. *Psychological Bulletin, 106,* 231–248.

Wood, J. V., Heimpel, S. A., & Michela, J. L. (2003). Savoring versus dampening: Self-esteem differences in regulating positive affect. *Journal of Personality and Social Psychology, 85,* 566–580.

Wood, W. (2000). Attitude change: Persuasion and social influence. *Annual Review of Psychology, 51,* 539–570.

Wood, W., & Eagly, A. H. (1981). Stages in the analysis of persuasive messages: The role of causal attributions and message comprehension. *Journal of Personality and Social Psychology, 40,* 246–259.

Wood, W., & Eagly, A. H. (2002). A cross-cultural analysis of the behavior of women and men: Implications for the origins of sex differences. *Psychological Bulletin, 128,* 699–727.

Wood, W., Kallgren, C. A., & Preisler, R. M. (1985). Access to attitude-relevant information in memory as a determinant of persuasion: The role of message attributes. *Journal of Experimental Social Psychology, 21*, 73–85.

Wood, W., Quinn, J., & Kashy, D. (2002). Habits in everyday life: Thought, emotion, and action. *Journal of Personality and Social Psychology, 83*, 1281–1297.

Worchel, S., Axsom, D., Ferris, S., Samaha, C., & Schweitzer, S. (1978). Determinants of the effect of intergroup cooperation on intergroup attraction. *Journal of Conflict Resolution, 22*, 429–439.

Word, C. O., Zanna, M. P., & Cooper, J. (1974). The nonverbal mediation of self-fulfilling prophecies in interracial interaction. *Journal of Experimental Social Psychology, 10*, 109–120.

Worth, L. T., & Mackie, D. M. (1987). The cognitive mediation of positive affect in persuasion. *Social Cognition, 5*, 76–94.

Wright, J. C., & Mischel, W. (1988). Conditional hedges and the intuitive psychology of traits. *Journal of Personality and Social Psychology, 55*, 454–469.

Wright, P., & Rip, P. D. (1981). Retrospective reports on the causes of decisions. *Journal of Personality and Social Psychology, 40*, 601–614.

Wu, C., & Shaffer, D. R. (1987). Susceptibility to persuasion appears as a function of source credibility and prior experience with the attitude object. *Journal of Personality and Social Psychology, 52*, 677–688.

Wundt, W. (1897). *Outlines of psychology.* New York: Stechert. (Translated 1907).

Wyer, N. A., Sherman, J. W., & Stroessner, S. J. (1998). The spontaneous suppression of racial stereotypes. *Social Cognition, 16*, 340–352.

Wyer, N. A., Sherman, J. W., & Stroessner, S. J. (2000). The roles of motivation and ability in controlling the consequences of stereotype suppression. *Personality and Social Psychology Bulletin, 26*, 13–25.

Wyer, R. S., Jr., Budesheim, T. L., & Lambert, A. J. (1990). Cognitive representation of conversations about persons. *Journal of Personality and Social Psychology, 58*, 218–238.

Wyer, R. S., Jr., & Gordon, S. E. (1982). The recall of information about persons and groups. *Journal of Experimental Social Psychology, 18*, 128–164.

Wyer, R. S., Jr., & Martin, L. L. (1986). Person memory: The role of traits, group stereotypes, and specific behaviors in the cognitive representation of persons. *Journal of Personality and Social Psychology, 50*, 661–675.

Wyer, R. S., Jr., & Srull, T. K. (1986). Human cognition in its social context. *Psychological Review, 93*, 322–359.

Wyland, C. L., Kelley, W. M., Macrae, C. N., Gordon, H. L., & Heatherton, T. F. (2003). Neural correlates of thought suppression. *Neuropsychologia, 41*, 1863–1867.

Yang, A. S. (1997). The polls—trends: Attitudes toward homosexuality. *Public Opinion Quarterly, 61*, 477–507.

Ybarra, O. (1999). Misanthropic person memory when the need to self-enhance is absent. *Personality and Social Psychology Bulletin, 25*, 261–269.

Yelland, L. M., & Stone, W. F. (1996). Belief in the Holocaust: Effects of personality and propaganda. *Political Psychology, 17*, 551–562.

Yik, M. S. M., Bond, M. H., & Paulhus, D. L. (1998). Do Chinese self-enhance or self-efface? It's a matter of domain. *Personality and Social Psychology Bulletin, 24*, 399–406.

Yopyk, D. J. A., & Prentice, D. A. (2005). Am I an athlete or a student? Identity salience and stereotype threat in student-athletes. *Basic and Applied Social Psychology, 27*, 329–336.

Young, J., Borgida, E., Sullivan, J. L., & Aldrich, J. (1987). Personal agendas and the relationship between self-interest and voting behavior. *Social Psychology Quarterly, 50*, 64–71.

Yzerbyt, V. Y., Castano, E., Leyens, J.-Ph., & Paladino, M. P. (2000). The primacy of the ingroup: The interplay of entitativity and identification. In W. Stroebe & M. Hewstone (Eds.), *European review of social psychology* (Vol. 11, pp. 257–295). New York: Wiley.

Yzerbyt, V. Y., Corneille, O., & Estrada, C. (2001). The interplay of subjective essentialism and entitativity in the formation of stereotypes. *Personality and Social Psychology Review, 5*, 141–155.

Yzerbyt, V. Y., Rocher, S., & Schadron, G. (1997). Stereotypes as explanations: A subjective essentialistic view of group perception. In R. Spears, P. J. Oakes, N. Ellemers, & S. A. Haslam (Eds.), *The social psychology of stereotyping and group life.* Malden, MA: Blackwell.

Zajonc, R. B. (1968a). Attitudinal effects of mere exposure. *Journal of Personality and Social Psychology, 9* (2, pt. 2), 1–27.

Zajonc, R. B. (1968b). Cognitive theories in social psychology. In G. Lindzey & E. Aronson (Eds.), *The handbook of social psychology* (2nd ed., Vol. 1, pp. 320–411). Reading, MA: Addison-Wesley.

Zajonc, R. B. (1980a). Cognition and social cognition: A historical perspective. In L. Festinger (Ed.), *Retrospections on social psychology* (pp. 180–204). New York: Oxford University Press.

Zajonc, R. B. (1980b). Feeling and thinking: Preferences need no inferences. *American Psychologist, 35,* 151–175.

Zajonc, R. B. (1984). On the primacy of affect. *American Psychologist, 39,* 117–123.

Zajonc, R. B. (1998). Emotions. In D. T. Gilbert, S. T. Fiske, & G. Lindzey (Eds), *Handbook of social psychology* (4th ed., Vol. 1, pp. 591–634). New York: McGraw-Hill.

Zajonc, R. B., & Burnstein, E. (1965). The learning of balanced and unbalanced social structures. *Journal of Personality, 33,* 153–163.

Zajonc, R. B., & Markus, H. R. (1984). Affect and cognition: The hard interface. In C. E. Izard, J. Kagan, & R. B. Zajonc (Eds.), *Emotions, cognition, and behavior.* Cambridge: Cambridge University Press.

Zajonc, R. B., Pietromonaco, P., & Bargh, J. (1982). Independence and interaction of affect and cognition. In M. S. Clark & S. T. Fiske (Eds.), *Affect and cognition: The 17th Annual Carnegie Symposium on Cognition* (pp. 211–228). Hillsdale, NJ: Erlbaum.

Zak, P. J., Kurzban, R., & Matzner, W. T. (2005). Oxytocin is associated with human trustworthiness. *Hormones and Behavior, 48,* 522–527.

Zald, D. H. (2003). The human amygdala and the emotional evaluation of sensory stimuli. *Brain Research Reviews, 41,* 88–123.

Zanna, M. P. (1991). Message receptivity: A new look at the old problem of open- vs. close-mindedness. In A. Mitchell (Ed.), *Advertising exposure: Memory and choice.* Hillsdale, NJ: Erlbaum.

Zanna, M. P., & Fazio, R. H. (1982). The attitude-behavior relation: Moving toward a third generation of research. In M. P. Zanna, E. T. Higgins, & C. P. Herman (Eds.), *Consistency in social behavior: The Ontario Symposium* (Vol. 2, pp. 283–302). Hillsdale, NJ: Erlbaum.

Zanna, M. P., & Olson, J. M. (1982). Individual differences in attitudinal relations. In M. P. Zanna, E. T. Higgins, & C. P. Herman (Eds.), *Consistency in social behavior: The Ontario Symposium* (Vol. 2, pp. 75–104). Hillsdale, NJ: Erlbaum.

Zanna, M. P., & Rempel, J. K. (1988). Attitudes: A new look at an old concept. In D. Bar-Tal & A. W. Kruglanski (Eds.), *The social psychology of knowledge* (pp. 315–334). Cambridge: Cambridge University Press.

Zárate, M. A., Sanders, J. D., & Garza, A. A. (2000). Neurological dissociations of social perceptual processes. *Social Cognition, 2000,* 223–251.

Zárate, M. A., & Smith, E. R. (1990). Person categorization and stereotyping. *Social Cognition, 8,* 161–185.

Zebrowitz, L. A. (1990). *Social perception.* Pacific-Grove, CA: Brooks-Cole.

Zebrowitz, L. A. (2003). Aging stereotypes—Internalization or inoculation? A commentary. *Journals of Gerontology: Series B: Psychological Sciences and Social Sciences, 58,* 214–215.

Zeigarnik, B. (1927). Das Bahalten erfedigter und unerledigter Handlungen. *Psychologoie Forshung, 9,* 1–85. [Translated and condensed as "On finished and unfinished tasks" in W. D. Ellis (Ed.), *A source book of gestalt psychology.* New York: Harcourt, Brace, & World, 1938.]

Zillmann, D. (1971). Excitation transfer in communication-mediated aggressive behavior. *Journal of Experimental Social Psychology, 7,* 419–434.

Zillmann, D. (1978). Attribution and misattribution of excitatory reactions. In J. H. Harvey, W. Ickes, & R. F. Kidd (Eds.), *New directions in attribution research* (Vol. 2, pp. 335–368). New York: Wiley.

Zillmann, D. (1983). Transfer of excitation in emotional behavior. In J. T. Cacioppo & R. E. Petty (Eds.), *Social psychophysiology.* New York: Guilford Press.

Zillmann, D. (1988). Cognition-excitation interdependencies in aggressive behavior. *Aggressive Behavior, 14,* 51–64.

Zillmann, D., & Bryant, J. (1974). Effect of residual excitation on the emotional response to provocation and delayed aggressive behavior. *Journal of Personality and Social Psychology, 30,* 782–791.

Zillmann, D., Katcher, A. H., & Milavsky, B. (1972). Excitation transfer from physical exercise to subsequent aggressive behavior. *Journal of Experimental Social Psychology, 8,* 247–259.

Zillmann, D., & Mundorf, N. (1987). Image effects in the appreciation of video rock. *Communication Research, 14,* 316–334.

Zillmann, D., Weaver, J. B., Mundorf, N., & Aust, C. F. (1986). Effects of an opposite-gender companion's affect to horror on distress, delight, and attraction. *Journal of Personality and Social Psychology, 51,* 586–594.

Zimbardo, P. G. (1960). Involvement and communication discrepancy as determinants of opinion conformity. *Journal of Abnormal and Social Psychology, 60,* 86–94.

Zuckerman, M., Eghrari, H., & Lambrecht, M. R. (1986). Attributions as inferences and explanations: Conjunction effects. *Journal of Personality and Social Psychology, 51,* 1144–1153.

Zuckerman, M., & Feldman, L. S. (1984). Actions and occurrences in attribution theory. *Journal of Personality and Social Psychology, 46,* 541–550.

Zuckerman, M., Klorman, R., Larrance, D. T., & Spiegel, N. H. (1981). Facial, autonomic, and subjective components of emotion: The facial feedback hypothesis versus the externalizer-internalizer distinction. *Journal of Personality and Social Psychology, 41,* 929–944.

Zuckerman, M., & O'Loughlin, R. E. (2006). Self-enhancement by social comparison: A prospective analysis. *Personality and Social Psychology Bulletin, 32,* 751–760.

Zukier, H., & Jennings, D. L. (1983–1984). Nondiagnosticity and typicality effects in prediction. *Social Cognition, 3,* 187–198.

Zuwerink, J. R., Devine, P. G., Monteith, M. J., & Cook, D. A. (1996). Prejudice toward Blacks: With and without compunction? *Basic and Applied Social Psychology, 18,* 131–150. [Erratum: 1996 (4).]

Zysset, S., Huber, O., Ferstl, E., & von Cramon, D. Y. (2002). The anterior frontomedian cortex and evaluative judgment: An fMRI study. *NeuroImage, 15,* 983–991.

Cited Author Index

Subject Index

Page numbers in *italics* indicate tables or figures.